DERIVATIVES
The Key Principles

DERIVATIVES

The Key Principles

THIRD EDITION

John-Peter Castagnino

OXFORD
UNIVERSITY PRESS

OXFORD
UNIVERSITY PRESS

Great Clarendon Street, Oxford OX2 6DP

Oxford University Press is a department of the University of Oxford.
It furthers the University's objective of excellence in research, scholarship,
and education by publishing worldwide in

Oxford New York

Auckland Cape Town Dar es Salaam Hong Kong Karachi
Kuala Lumpur Madrid Melbourne Mexico City Nairobi
New Delhi Shanghai Taipei Toronto

With offices in

Argentina Austria Brazil Chile Czech Republic France Greece
Guatemala Hungary Italy Japan Poland Portugal Singapore
South Korea Switzerland Thailand Turkey Ukraine Vietnam

Oxford is a registered trade mark of Oxford University Press
in the UK and in certain other countries

Published in the United States
by Oxford University Press Inc., New York

© Oxford University Press, 2009

The moral rights of the author have been asserted
Database right Oxford University Press (maker)

Crown copyright material is reproduced under Class Licence
Number C01P0000148 with the permission of OPSI
and the Queen's Printer for Scotland

First published 2009

All rights reserved. No part of this publication may be reproduced,
stored in a retrieval system, or transmitted, in any form or by any means,
without the prior permission in writing of Oxford University Press,
or as expressly permitted by law, or under terms agreed with the appropriate
reprographics rights organization. Enquiries concerning reproduction
outside the scope of the above should be sent to the Rights Department,
Oxford University Press, at the address above

You must not circulate this book in any other binding or cover
and you must impose the same condition on any acquirer

British Library Cataloguing in Publication Data
Data available

Library of Congress Cataloging in Publication Data
Data available

Typeset by Cepha Imaging Private Ltd, Bangalore, India
Printed in Great Britain
on acid-free paper by
CPI Antony Rowe, Chippenham

ISBN 978-0-19-955636-6

1 3 5 7 9 10 8 6 4 2

PREFACE

Derivatives: The Key Principles, now in its third edition (this is the first edition of the book published by Oxford University Press), is intended to serve as a practical guide to derivatives, developing an explanation of the different derivative products, the uses to which they are put, and where and how these products are traded. Despite their increasing prominence, derivatives have been an established part of finance and commerce more generally for a surprisingly long time (for example, option strategies were known as a matter of intuition to merchants several millennia ago), and therefore some historical context is also provided, both of derivative techniques and certain institutions at work in the markets.

This third edition, expanding on the second edition in respect of the products discussed, explains more recent innovations, such as the dynamic constant proportion portfolio insurance (CPPI) structures that are increasingly offered as a way of creating derivative investment exposures to underlying assets, and the use of derivative contracts as neat asset-financing tools. The book also charts the first steps being taken in emissions trading, and sets out some background to power trading, both of which promise to become ever more important in a world constrained by increasing demand for energy and decreasing resources, against the backdrop of the urgent need to limit environmental damage. These are developments which have gained considerable momentum since the publication of the second edition, and it is appropriate that they are now discussed in this third edition.

The book also explains how the derivative markets are regulated, mainly from the perspective of English law and the increasing volume of legislation flowing from the European Union. Since the second edition of the book was published in 2004, the offer of derivatives to retail investors has ignited considerable debate as to the most appropriate and fair way of selling sophisticated products to consumers who are neither professional nor expert in the field of finance. The conclusion, that the overall objective of the regulatory standards that are being applied must be to secure the fair treatment of consumers and to empower them to make their own properly informed investment decisions, is surely correct. At the same time, the standard of conduct that is expected of financial institutions has been confirmed in the recent decision of the House of Lords in *JP Morgan Chase Bank v Springwell Navigation Corporation*,[1] which is the latest of a direct line of authority

---

[1] [2008] EWHC 1186 (Comm).

that can be traced to the mid-1990s: there is no general duty to advise a customer as to the derivative product being sold, but if the customer is found to have relied on an erroneous statement that is made, then liability for making that erroneous statement can arise. Of course, the key element of the analysis is the extent of the experience and expertise of the customer, and the circumstances of the relationship, and the analysis is therefore consonant with the regulatory imperative to secure the fair treatment of investors through the recognition of the disparate levels of experience and expertise demonstrated in the customer base. This third edition considers the development of these regulatory and legal trends. The documents published by ISDA[2] are familiar to practitioners in the over-the-counter derivative market, and the book includes a survey of the principal materials in use, and expanding on the second edition, this third edition provides a workmanlike discussion of each of these important documents. This third edition also introduces, in an updated chapter, the important topics of the accounting and tax treatments of derivatives.

The topics to which the book refers are extremely broad, and have often individually been the subject of a substantial body of academic and practical discussion, and therefore the book only introduces the principal issues and serves to indicate the direction in which further reading might be undertaken.[3] In particular, the book cannot and does not list an exhaustive taxonomy of every type of derivative, and for that numerous trade journals and magazines are an invaluable resource,[4] but instead the book lays a firm conceptual foundation of a complex, diverse, and technical subject, and in doing so, it develops a more focused tone than that achieved by the second edition.[5]

My overall objective in writing the book has been to bridge the divide between the finance or accounting professional, who often regards a derivative as a cash flow, and the legal or regulatory professional, whose perspective is that a derivative is a contract. Of course, both viewpoints are entirely right, and the book illustrates that derivatives can only be meaningfully considered from both viewpoints.

The theme which resonates through the book is risk, both the risk to which derivatives are designed to give an exposure (whether price risk or market risk, or credit risk) and the risk to which any dealing in or selling of derivatives gives rise. The book explains how these risks are identified, quantified, controlled, and

---

[2] International Swaps and Derivatives Association, Inc. See Chapter 7.
[3] See the Bibliography.
[4] See 'Derivatives Week' magazine published by Institutional Investor Ltd., *FOW* magazine published by Euromoney Institutional Investor PLC *Journal of Derivatives & Hedge Funds* magazine published by Palgrave Macmillan Journals, and *Risk* magazine published by Incisive Media Limited.
[5] This third edition does not include the two appendices in the second edition which introduce debt securities—instead, see Fuller, *The Law and Practice of International Capital Markets* (Lexis Nexis Butterworths, 2007)—and which report the controversy of Long-Term Capital Management, which happened almost ten years ago.

ultimately exploited for reward. In particular, the techniques for managing risk that are prescribed by the voluminous regulations requiring the maintenance of adequate financial resources illustrate the advances that have been made in this area. The credit crisis which emerged in the summer of 2007, and which is continuing as this edition of the book is going to print, will undoubtedly prompt close scrutiny of both these regulations and the systems and processes that have been developed to ensure that they have been complied with. At the very least, attention will be paid to whether or not these regulations, as currently framed, have been correctly followed. The book should assist any professional involved in the derivative markets by providing a succinct overview of the different disciplines, and how these disciplines complement each other. All too often, derivatives are regarded as the cause of the gyrations and controversies, including the failure of institutions, which periodically contort the financial markets. The main tenet underlying the book is that derivatives exist merely as a piece of technology, and it is the manner in which they are used which determines whether their potential is realized for inflicting loss and damage or, more benignly, for making considerable profits. It may be flippant to draw from the world of fiction, but some truth is found in the words of the Macau gunsmith Lazar: 'Mr Bond, bullets do not kill. It is the finger that pulls the trigger'.[6]

It is emphasized that any opinion expressed in the book is my own, and not that of any other person or organization, and I wish to record my gratitude to various friends and colleagues who have offered advice and assistance during the preparation of this third edition. I have made every effort to report correctly the state of English law and regulation as at 30 June 2008, and responsibility for the inevitable errors in this work is entirely mine, and of course, I shall endeavour to make corrections and improvements in future editions.

John-Peter Castagnino
London, 2008

---

[6] *The Man with the Golden Gun* (1974), screenplay by Richard Maibaum and Tom Mankiewicz, from the novel by Ian Fleming. In the film, Lazar fabricated the 4.2mm single-shot gold pistol and its 23-carat gold bullets used by the assassin Scaramanga (played by Christopher Lee); the pistol could be dismantled into and disguised as a cigarette case, a lighter, a pen, and cufflink.

CONTENTS—SUMMARY

Table of Cases	xv
Table of Statutes	xvii
Table of Statutory Instruments	xxi
Table of EU Directives	xxiii
FSA Handbook of Rules and Guidance	xxv

1. An Overview	1
2. The Two Principal Market Structures	11
3. Key Concepts	25
4. Products	31
5. The Legal Framework	127
6. Risk, Documents, and the Exchange-Based Market	169
7. Risk, Documents, and the OTC Market	183
8. Legal Issues	289
9. End-Users	363
10. Capital	383
11. Accounting and Tax	399
12. Defining the Risk Map	419

Selected Glossary	431
Bibliography	445
Index	447

CONTENTS

Table of Cases — xv
Table of Statutes — xvii
Table of Statutory Instruments — xxi
Table of EU Directives — xxiii
FSA Handbook of Rules and Guidance — xxv

1. An Overview

    1.1 What is a Derivative? — 1.01

    1.2 Why? — 1.04

    1.3 How? — 1.08

    1.4 Where and Who? — 1.15

    1.5 When? — 1.18

2. The Two Principal Market Structures

    2.1 The Participants in the Markets — 2.01

    2.2 The Exchange-based Market — 2.07

    2.3 The OTC Market — 2.19

    2.4 Market Service Providers — 2.22

    2.5 Derivative Exchanges — 2.27

3. Key Concepts

    3.1 'Long' and 'Short' — 3.01

    3.2 The Bid and Offer Spread — 3.03

    3.3 Tick and Basis Point — 3.04

    3.4 Margin — 3.05

4. Products

4.1	Introduction	4.01
4.2	Forward Contract	4.10
4.3	Futures Contract	4.17
4.4	Option Contract	4.32
4.5	Warrant	4.60
4.6	Forward Rate Agreement	4.63
4.7	Swap	4.69
4.8	Cap, Floor, and Collar Contracts	4.125
4.9	CPPI	4.132
4.10	Derivatives used as Financing Tools	4.148
4.11	Islamic-compliant Derivatives	4.158
4.12	Credit Derivatives	4.164
4.13	Multi-asset Derivatives	4.195
4.14	New Classes of Underlying	4.197
4.15	Valuations, Valuation Disruptions, and Adjustments	4.228
4.16	Different 'Wrappers' of Derivative Cash Flows	4.229
4.17	Repurchase and Reverse Repurchase Agreements	4.245
4.18	Financial Engineering	4.254

5. The Legal Framework

5.1	Introduction	5.01
5.2	Legislation and Regulation	5.02
5.3	The General Prohibition	5.48
5.4	Regulated Activities	5.56
5.5	Legal Market Structures	5.78
5.6	EU Legislation	5.87

6. Risk, Documents, And The Exchange-Based Market

6.1	Introduction	6.01
6.2	Recognized Investment Exchanges and Recognized Clearing Houses	6.02
6.3	Companies Act 1989	6.10
6.4	Give-up Agreements and Clearing Agreements	6.28

7. Risk, Documents, and the OTC Market

7.1	Introduction	7.01
7.2	OTC Derivative Documentation Generally	7.02
7.3	ISDA	7.11
7.4	The ISDA 2002 Master Agreement and its Schedule	7.19
7.5	ISDA Credit Support Documents	7.69
7.6	ISDA Confirmation	7.88
7.7	ISDA Definitions Generally	7.91
7.8	2002 ISDA Equity Derivatives Definitions	7.97
7.9	2003 ISDA Credit Derivatives Definitions	7.127
7.10	2005 ISDA Commodity Definitions	7.159
7.11	2006 ISDA Definitions	7.175
7.12	2006 ISDA Fund Derivatives Definitions	7.204

8. Legal Issues

8.1	Introduction	8.01
8.2	Unregulated Forwards and Regulated Futures	8.11
8.3	The Construction of the Terms of a Derivative Contract	8.28
8.4	Derivative Contracts Recharacterized as Other Contracts	8.33
8.5	The Doctrine of Ultra Vires	8.49
8.6	The Duty of Care: Selling and Misselling	8.94
8.7	Retail Offer of Derivatives and Issues Arising	8.142
8.8	The Swap Analysed as a Contract	8.182
8.9	Credit Derivatives Documentation	8.192

9. End-Users

9.1	The Investment Management Industry	9.01
9.2	Hedge Funds	9.25
9.3	Prime Brokerage	9.40
9.4	Corporate Treasuries	9.52

10. Capital

10.1	Introduction	10.01
10.2	Sources of Regulation	10.03
10.3	FSA Handbook	10.09
10.4	The Basel Committee	10.20
10.5	Basel 2	10.23
10.6	Credit Rating	10.33

11. Accounting and Tax

11.1	Financial reporting	11.01
11.2	The Taxation of Transactions: Hedging or Trading	11.19
11.3	The Taxation of Transactions: Income or Capital Gains	11.23
11.4	The Taxation of Transactions: Withholding Tax	11.41
11.5	The Substance of Transactions	11.46
11.6	'Accounting-driven' Transactions	11.50

12. Defining the Risk Map

12.1 Introduction	12.01
12.2 The Framework for Risk Control	12.02
12.3 The Risk Taxonomy	12.07

Selected Glossary	431
Bibliography	445
Index	447

TABLE OF CASES

Agnew and another v The Commissioner of Inland Revenue [2001] 2 AC 710, [2001] 3 WLR 454 .... 8.35
Bank of Credit and Commerce International (Overseas) Ltd (In Liquidation) v Price Waterhouse (No 2) [1998] Ch 84, [1998] PNLR 564 .... 8.152
Bank of Credit and Commerce International SA (In Liquidation) v Ali (No 1) [2001] UKHL 8, [2002] 1 AC 251, [2001] 2 WLR 735, [2001] 1 All ER 961 .... 8.34
Bankers Trust International PLC v PT Dharmala Sakti Sejahtera; PT Dharmala Sakti Sejahtera v Bankers Trust International PLC and another [1996] CLC 518 .... 8.07, 8.96-8.113, 8.123, 8.129, 8.130, 8.135, 8.136, 8.137
Barclay v Cousins (1802) 2 East 544 .... 8.41
Barclays Mercantile Business Finance Limited v Mawson (Her Majesty's Inspector of Taxes) [2004] UKHL 51 .... 11.37, 11.38
Bear Sterns Bank PLC v Forum Global Equity Limited [2007] EWHC 1576 (Comm), [2007] All ER (D) 103 (Jul) 7.08
British Eagle International Airlines Ltd v Compagnie Nationale Air France [1975] 1 WLR 758 .... 2.45
Caparo Industries PLC v Dickman [1990] 2 AC 605 .... 8.134, 8.151, 8.152
Chase Manhattan Bank NA v Israel-British Bank (London) Ltd [1981] Ch 105 .... 8.72
Commissioners of Customs & Excise v Barclays Bank PLC [2004] EWCA Civ 1555, [2005] 1 Lloyd's Rep 165 .... 8.124, 8.152
CR Sugar Trading Ltd (in administration) v China National Sugar & Alcohol Group Corporation [2003] EWHC 79 (Comm), [2003] All ER (D) 317 (Jan) 5.50, 8.13-8.27
De Beers Consolidated Mines Ltd v Howe [1906] AC 455 .... 11.25
Derry v Peek (1889) 14 App Cas 337 .... 8.131
Deutsche Bank AG v ANZ Banking Group Ltd, unreported 7.90, 8.28-8.32
Deutsche Morgan Grenfell PLC v Inland Revenue Commissioners [2006] UKHL 49, [2007] 1 AC 558 .... 8.93
Gibson Greetings v Bankers Trust Co, Orange County Investment Pool v Merrill Lynch & Co, and Proctor and Gamble v Bankers Trust Co 8.137
Guinness Mahon & Co Ltd v Kensington & Chelsea Royal London Borough Council [1998] 2 All ER 272 .... 8.190
Hazell v Hammersmith and Fulham London Borough Council [1992] 2 AC 1, [1991] 2 WLR 372, [1990] 2 QB 697, [1990] 2 WLR 1038 .... 8.06, 8.53-8.55, 8.56, 8.69, 8.77, 8.80, 8.86, 8.183
Hedley Byrne & Co Ltd v Heller & Partners [1964] AC 465, [1963] 2 All ER 575 .... 8.132, 8.133
Henderson v Merrett Syndicates [1995] 2 AC 145 .... 8.152
Her Majesty's Commissioners of Inland Revenue v Scottish Provident Institution [2004] UKHL 52 .... 11.38-11.40, 11.50
IFE Fund SA v Goldman Sachs International [2006] EWHC 2887 (Comm) 8.125
Inland Revenue Commissioners v McGuckian [1997] 1 WLR 991 .... 11.35
Interfoto v Stiletto [1989] 1 QB 433 .... 8.127, 8.167

Table of Cases

Jeancharm Ltd v Barnet Football Club Ltd [2003] EWCA Civ 58, [2003] All ER (D)
69 (Jan) 7.63
JP Morgan Chase Bank v Springwell Navigation Corporation [2008] EWHC 1186
(Comm) 8.07, 8.121-8.128, 8.129, 8.130, 8.132, 12.26
Kleinwort Benson Ltd v Lincoln City Council and others [1998]
3 WLR 1095 .... 8.77-8.81, 8.82, 8.84, 8.93
Kleinwort Benson Ltd v Sandwell Borough Council [1994] 4 All ER 890 .... 8.61
London, Chatham and Dover Railway Co v South Eastern Railway Co [1893] AC 429..... 8.92
Lordsvale Finance PLC v Bank of Zambia [1996] QB 752........................... 7.63
Lovell and Christmas Ltd v Wall (1911) 104 LT 85................................. 8.32
Lucena v Craufurd (1806) 127 ER 630... 8.41
MacNiven (Her Majesty's Inspector of Taxes) v Westmoreland Investments Limited [2001]
UKHL 6... 11.36
Matrix Securities Ltd v Theodore Goddard [1998] PNLR 290 .... 8.148
Morgan Stanley UK Group v Puglisi Cosentino [1998] CLC 481 .... 8.137
National Westminster Bank PLC v Spectrum Plus Limited and others [2005] UKHL 41, [2005]
4 All ER 209.. 6.26, 8.33
Nurdin & Peacock PLC v DB Ramsden & Co Ltd [1999] 1 WLR 1249 .... 8.82
Page v Newman (1829) 9 B & C 378 .... 8.92
Paradine v Jane (1647) Aleyn 26, Sty 47 [1558-1774] All ER Rep 172................... 7.45
Peekay Intermark Limited (1) Harish Pawani (2) v Australia and New Zealand Banking Group
Limited [2006] EWCA Civ 386, [2005] EWHC 830 (Comm)......... 8.07, 8.114-8.120,
8.123, 8.129, 8.130, 8.135, 8.164
Peregrine Fixed Income Limited (In Liquidation) v Robinson Department Store Public Company
Limited [2000] All ER (D) 1177... 8.02
Petromec Inc v Petroleo Brasileiro SA [2005] EWCA Civ 891, [2005] All ER (D)
209 (Jul).. 7.115
President of India v La Pintada Compania Navigacion SA [1985] AC 104............... 8.92
R & B Customs Brokers Co Ltd v United Dominions Trust Ltd (Saunders Abbott (1980) Ltd,
third party) [1988] 1 WLR 321, [1988] 1 All ER 847, Jones and Harland
2 JCL 266.. 8.174
Sempra Metals Limited (formerly Metallgesellschaft Limited) v Her Majesty's Commissioners of
Inland Revenue and another [2007] UKHL 34..................... 8.06, 8.91, 8.93
Seymour v Caroline Ockwell & Co; Zurich IFA Limited [2005] EWHC
1137 (QB) 8.145, 8.146-8.157, 8.158
Smith v Bridgend County Borough Council [2001] UKHL 58, [2001] 3 WLR 1347 ...... 8.35
Smith v Eric Bush [1990] 1 AC 831 .... 8.152
Trevor v Whitworth (1887) 12 App Cas 409....................................... 9.10
Vallejo v Wheeler (1774) 1 Cowp 143... 8.34
Valse Holdings SA v Merrill Lynch International Bank Ltd [2004] EWHC 2471
(Comm)... 8.137
Welsh Development Agency v Export Finance Co Ltd [1992]
BCLC 148.. 8.35
Westdeutsche Landesbank Girozentrale v Islington London Borough Council [1996]
AC 669, [1996] 2 WLR 802, [1994]
1 WLR 938 .... 8.06, 8.44, 8.47, 8.56-8.76, 8.77, 8.84, 8.86, 8.87, 8.90, 8.93, 8.188
Westminster Bank Executor & Trustee Co (Channel Islands) Ltd v National Bank of Greece SA
[1970] 46 TC 472 .... 11.41
White v Jones [1995] 2 AC 207, [1995] 1 All ER 691............................... 8.152
Wilson v Jones (1867) 2 Ex 150 .... 8.41
WT Ramsay Ltd v Inland Revenue Commissioners [1982] AC 300.......... 8.33, 11.35, 11.36

TABLE OF STATUTES

Arbitration Act 1996
  s 67 . . . . 8.25
  s 73 . . . . 8.25
Bank of England Act 1998
  Part III 5.83
    s 11(1) 5.83
    s 13(1) 5.83
Banking (Special Provisions) Act 2008
  (BSPA 2008) 10.06
  ss 2(2)(a), (b) 10.06
  s 2(6) 10.06
  s 3(1) 10.06
Capital Allowances Act 1990
  s 24(1) 11.37
Companies Act 1985
  s 395 . . . . 7.76, 7.77
  s 395(1) 7.76
  s 395(2) 7.76
  s 396 . . . . 7.76
  s 396(1) 7.76
  s 396(1)(e) 7.76
  s 396(1)(f) 7.76
Companies Act 1989 (CA 1989) . . 6.10–6.27
  Part VII 6.11, 6.12,
      6.13, 6.15, 6.18, 7.01, 7.24, 7.69
    s 154 . . . . 6.12
    s 155 . . . . 6.13
    s 155(2A) 6.13
    s 155(2)(b) 6.13
    s 155(3) 6.13
    s 158(1) 6.14
    s 158(2) 6.14
    s 158(3) 6.14
    ss 159–165 . . . . 6.14
    s 159(1) 6.15
    s 159(2) 6.16
    s 163 . . . . 7.21
    s 163(1) 6.17, 6.18
    s 164 . . . . 6.19
    s 164(1) 6.19
    s 164(3) 6.19
    s 173 . . . . 6.20

    s 173(1) 6.20
    s 174 . . . . 6.20
    s 174(1) 6.21
    s 175 . . . . 6.21
    s 175(1) 6.22
    s 175(1A) 6.22
    s 175(3) 6.23
    s 175(4) 6.23
    s 177 . . . . 6.25
    s 177(3) 6.25
    s 177(4) 6.25
    s 178 . . . . 6.26
    s 179 . . . . 6.26
    s 188(1) 6.13
Companies Act 2006
  (CA 2006) 7.76
  s 31(1) 8.49
  s 39(1) 8.49
  s 393(1) 11.02
  s 394 . . . . 11.02
  s 395(1) 11.02
  s 396(1) 11.02
  s 397 . . . . 11.02
  s 860 . . . . 7.76
Enterprise Act 2002
  (EA 2002) 6.10, 6.14, 6.22
Finance Act 1988
  s 66 . . . . 11.25
Finance Act 1994 . . . . 11.29
Finance Act 2002 (FA 2002) 11.29
  Sch 26 Derivative contracts
    rules 11.29–11.33
Financial Services Act 1986
  (FSA 1986) 5.05, 5.83, 5.84,
        5.85, 8.13, 8.19, 8.20, 8.26
  s 3 . . . . 8.14
  s 43 . . . . 5.83
  s 62 . . . . 8.150
  s 63 . . . . 8.36
  s 76(1) 8.150
  ss 76(1)(a), (b) 8.150
  Sch 1 . . . . 8.20, 8.21

Table of Statutes

Financial Services and Markets Act 2000
  (FSMA 2000)............ 5.02-5.77,
        5.83, 5.84, 5.87, 6.02, 6.12,
        8.11, 8.12, 8.13, 8.26, 8.38, 10.07
  Part IV.................... 5.17, 5.19,
        5.20, 5.21, 5.49, 8.38, 8.43
  Part VIII....................... 5.30
  Part XVI................ 8.169, 8.171
  s 1 .... 5.12
  s 2(1)(b) 8.143
  s 2(2) 5.12, 5.86, 6.05
  s 3(d) 8.143
  s 3(e) 8.143
  s 5 .... 8.143
  s 5(2) 8.143, 8.144
  s 19 .... 5.68, 5.77, 6.03
  s 19(1) 5.04, 5.48
  s 20 .... 8.43
  s 20(1) 5.49
  s 20(2) 5.49
  s 21 .... 5.34, 5.37, 5.77
  s 21(1) 5.33, 5.34, 5.35, 5.37, 5.38
  s 21(2) 5.33, 5.36
  s 21(3) 5.33
  s 21(8) 5.33
  s 21(9) 5.33
  s 21(10) 5.33
  s 22 .... 5.56, 5.57, 5.68, 5.77
  s 23 .... 5.54
  s 23(3) 5.54
  s 24 .... 5.54, 5.55
  s 24(1) 5.55
  s 24(2) 5.55
  s 24(3) 5.55
  s 24(4) 5.55
  s 25 .... 5.34
  s 25(2) 5.34
  s 26 .... 5.50, 5.52, 8.12, 8.43
  s 27 .... 5.50, 5.51, 5.52
  s 28 .... 5.50, 5.52
  s 29 .... 5.50, 5.51, 5.53
  s 30(1) 5.35
  s 30(2) 5.35
  s 30(3) 5.35
  s 30(4) 5.35
  s 40(4) 5.17
  s 41(2) 5.17
  s 102B 9.05
  s 118 .... 5.30
  s 118A 5.30
  s 118B 5.30
  s 118C 5.30
  s 138 .... 5.09
  s 138(7) 5.12
  s 229 .... 8.170
  s 229(4) 8.170
  s 229(8)(a) 8.170
  s 230 .... 8.171
  s 231 .... 8.170
  s 232 .... 8.170
  s 234 .... 8.171
  s 235 .... 9.06
  s 235(2) 9.06
  s 235(3) 9.06
  s 236 .... 9.08
  s 236(2) 9.08
  s 236(3) 9.08
  s 236(3)(a) 9.10
  s 262 .... 9.09
  s 264 .... 9.11, 9.12
  s 270 .... 9.12
  s 272 .... 9.12
  s 285(1) 6.04
  s 285(2) 6.04
  s 285(3) 6.04
  s 287 .... 6.06
  s 287(2) 6.06
  s 288 .... 6.07
  s 288(2) 6.07
  s 290(1) 6.06, 6.07
  s 292 .... 6.06, 6.07
  s 397 .... 5.26
  s 412 .... 8.36
  Sch 2 ..... 5.57, 5.58, 5.59, 5.61, 5.65,
     5.67, 5.69, 5.70, 5.71, 5.72, 5.73, 5.77
  Sch 6 .... 5.17, 5.18, 5.19
Gambling Act 2005 .... 8.36
  s 335(1) 8.36
  s 334(2) 8.36
Gaming Act 1845................... 8.36
Gaming Act 1892................... 8.36
Income and Corporation Taxes Act 1988
  (ICTA 1988) 11.24
Insolvency Act 1986 (IA 1986)
  s 43 .... 6.23
  s 127 .... 6.19, 6.24
  s 178 .... 6.19
  s 178(3)(a) 7.21, 7.24
  s 186 .... 6.19
  s 284 .... 6.19, 6.24
  s 315 .... 6.19
  s 323 .... 6.17
  s 345 .... 6.19
  Sch 6 .... 6.10
  Sch B1 .... 6.22
Insurance Companies Act
  1982......................... 8.38
Law of Property Act 1925............ 6.10

Law Reform (Miscellaneous Provisions) Act 1934
 s 3 .... 8.92
Limitation Act 1980 .... 8.78
Local Government Act 1972 .... 8.53
Misrepresentation Act 1967 ... 8.126, 8.133
 s 2(1) 8.133
National Debt Act 1972
 s 11(3) 5.66
National Loans Act 1968 .... 5.66
Pensions Act 2004 .... 5.02
Railway Clearing House Act 1830 ...... 2.45
Supreme Court Act 1981
 s 35A 8.59
Supreme Court of Judicature Act 1873 .. 8.60
Supreme Court of Judicature Act 1875 .. 8.60
Taxation of Chargeable Gains Act 1992
 (TCGA 1992) 11.24
 s 15(2) 11.26
 s 22 .... 11.26
 s 22(1)(d) 11.26
Unfair Contract Terms Act 1977 (UCTA 1977) 8.172–8.180
 s 2(1) 8.173
 s 2(2) 8.175
 s 3(2) 8.175
 s 4(1) 8.175
 s 11(1) 8.176
 s 12(1) 8.174
 Sch 1 .... 8.174

TABLE OF STATUTORY INSTRUMENTS

Capital Requirements Regulations 2006, SI 2006/3221 .... 10.35
Financial Collateral Arrangements (No 2) Regulations 2003, SI 2003/3226 (Collateral Regulations) 7.25–7.68, 7.77, 8.90
  s 2(a)(i)................... 7.26, 7.35
  s 2(c) 7.27–7.30
  s 3 .... 7.25, 7.31, 7.77
  s 4 .... 7.77
  s 5 .... 7.32–7.50
  s 5(1)(a) 7.35
  s 6 .... 7.51–7.65
  s 9(h) 7.66–7.68
  ss 9(h)(i)(2), (4) 7.35
  s 12 ....7.35
  s 12.1 ....7.25
  s 12.2 ....7.25
Financial Promotion Order: Financial Services and Markets Act 2000 (Financial Promotion) Order 2005, SI 2005/1529 (revoking SI 2001/1335) ... 5.37–5.47
  Part IV 5.40
  Part V........................5.40
  Part VI.......................5.40
    Art 4(1) 5.39
    Art 4(2) 5.39
    Art 5.......................5.38
    Art 12......................5.41
    Art 13......................5.43
    Art 14......................5.43
    Art 15......................5.43
    Art 16......................5.44
    Art 17......................5.43
    Art 17A 5.44
    Art 18......................5.44
    Art 19......................5.44
    Art 20......................5.44
    Art 20A 5.44
    Art 28......................5.45
    Art 28A 5.45
    Art 30......................5.42
    Art 30(2) 5.42
    Art 31......................5.42
    Art 32......................5.42
    Art 33......................5.42
    Art 48......................5.46
    Art 49......................5.46
    Art 50......................5.46
    Art 50A 5.46
    Art 51......................5.46
    Art 52......................5.47
    Art 53......................5.47
    Art 54......................5.47
    Art 55......................5.47
    Art 55A 5.47
    Art 58......................5.47
    Art 59......................5.47
    Art 60......................5.47
    Art 61......................5.47
    Art 62......................5.47
    Art 63......................5.47
    Art 64......................5.47
    Art 65......................5.47
    Art 66......................5.47
    Art 67......................5.47
    Art 68......................5.47
    Art 69......................5.47
    Art 70......................5.47
    Art 71......................5.47
    Art 72......................5.47
    Art 73......................5.47
    Sch 1 ....5.39
Financial Services (Designated Countries and Territories) (Overseas Collective Investment Schemes) (Bermuda) Order 1988, SI 1988/2284 ....9.12
Financial Services and Markets Act 2000 (Collective Investment Schemes) Order 2001 (Collective Investment Schemes Order), SI 2001/1062, as amended 9.06
Financial Services and Markets Act 2000 (Collective Investment Schemes) (Designated Countries and Territories) Order 2003, SI 2003/1181 ....9.11

Financial Services and Markets Act 2000 (Markets in Financial Instruments) Regulations 2007, SI 2007/126
   reg 4 . . . . 5.17
Insolvency Rules 1986, SI 1986/1925 as amended 6.10
   rule 4.90 . . . . 7.22, 7.23, 7.24, 7.25
   rule 4.90(1) 7.22
   rule 4.90(3) 7.22
Insolvency (Amendment) Rules 2005, SI 2005/527 . . . . 7.22
Loan Relationships and Derivative Contracts (Disregard and Bringing into Account of Profits and Losses) Regulations 2004 (Disregard Regulations), SI 2004/3256 . . . . 11.10, 11.11
Open-Ended Investment Companies Regulations 2001, SI 2001/1228 (OEIC Regulations) 9.09
Open-Ended Investment Companies (Investment Companies with variable Capital) Regulations 1996, SI 1996/2827 . . . . 9.09

Regulated Activities Order: Financial Services and Markets Act 2000 (Regulated Activities) Order 2001, SI 2001/544 . . . . . 5.57, 5.59, 5.76, 5.77
   Part II 5.67
   Part III 5.58, 5.59, 5.68
   Art 4(1) 5.68
   Art 14 . . . . 5.74, 5.75
   Art 16(1) 5.75
   Art 68(2) 5.74
   Art 84 . . . . 5.61, 8.26, 8.27
   Art 84(2) 5.62, 8.26
   Art 84(3) 5.63
   Art 84(4) 5.64
   Art 84(5) 5.64
   Art 84(6) 5.64
   Art 84(7) 5.63
   Art 85 . . . . 5.65
   Art 85(2) 5.66
Unfair Terms Regulations: Unfair Terms in Consumer Contracts Regulations 1999, SI 1999/2083 . . . . 8.172, 8.178, 8.179, 8.180

TABLE OF EU DIRECTIVES

Banking Consolidation (First): Dir 2000/12/EC on the taking up and pursuit of the business of credit institutions 5.96
Banking Consolidation (Second—recast): Dir 2006/48/EC relating to the taking up and pursuit of the business of credit institutions (recast) 5.96, 10.07
Banking Coordination (First) (BCD): Dir 77/780/EEC on the coordination of laws, regulations and administrative provisions relating to the taking up and pursuit of the business of credit institutions 5.96
 Art 12 .... 5.96
Banking Coordination (Second) (2BCD): Dir 89/646/EEC 5.96
Banking, Solvency Ratio and Capital Adequacy: Dir 98/33/EC, amending parts of Dirs 77/780/EEC, 89/647/EEC and 93/6/EEC 5.96
Capital Adequacy (First): Dir 93/6/EEC on the capital adequacy of investment firms and credit institutions 5.96
 Art 2 .... 5.96
 Annex II 5.96
Capital Adequacy (Second): Dir 98/31/EC, amending Dir 93/6/EEC on the capital adequacy of investment firms and credit institutions 5.96
Capital Adequacy: Capital Adequacy of investment firms and credit institutions (recast), Dir 2006/49/EC 10.07
Consolidated Supervision: Dir 92/30/EEC on the supervision of credit institutions on a consolidated basis 5.96
Financial Collateral Arrangements: Dir 2002/47/EC 7.25
Greenhouse Gas Emission Trading Scheme (ETS) within the Community, Dir 2003/87/EC, amending Dir 96/61/EC 4.222

Greenhouse Gas emission allowance trading, in respect of the Kyoto Protocol's project mechanisms (Linking Dir), Dir 2004/101/EC, amending Dir 2003/87/EC 4.222
Investment Services (ISD): Dir 93/22/EEC on investment services in the securities field 5.97
Large Exposures: Dir 92/121/EEC on the monitoring and control of large exposures of credit institutions 5.96
MiFID: Dir 2004/39/EC on Markets in Financial Instruments, amending Dirs 85/611/EEC, 93/6/EEC and 2001/12/EEC and repealing Dir 93/22/EEC 5.17, 5.22, 5.44, 5.57, 5.60, 5.79, 5.85, 5.86, 5.97, 5.98–5.102
 Art 4(1)(15) 5.80
 Annex I 5.59, 5.61, 5.65, 5.99
 Annex II 5.102
MiFID Implementing Directive: Dir 2006/73/EC implementing Dir 2004/39/EC 5.97
Own Funds: Dir 89/299/EEC on the own funds of credit institutions 5.96
Prospectus Directive: Dir 2003/71/EC on the prospectus to be published when securities are offered to the public or admitted to trading, amending Dir 2001/34/EC 2.07, 9.05
Solvency Ratio: Dir 77/780/EEC 5.96
Solvency Ratio: Dir 89/647/EEC on a solvency ratio for credit institutions 5.96
 Art 2 .... 5.96
 Art 5 .... 5.96
 Art 6 .... 5.96
 Art 7 .... 5.96
 Art 8 .... 5.96
 Annex II 5.96
 Annex III 5.96

UCITS I: Dir 85/611 on the coordination of laws, regulations and administrative provisions relating to undertakings for collective investment in transferable securities. 5.95, 5.97

UCITS 3: Dir 2001/107/EC, for the coordination of laws etc relating to Undertakings for Collective Investment in Transferable Securities, with a view to regulating management companies and simplified prospectuses, amending Dir 85/611/EEC (UCITS 1) 5.95, 9.03, 9.11, 9.12, 9.13, 9.20, 9.23

UCITS 3: Dir 2001/108/EC, for the coordination of laws etc relating to Undertakings for Collective Investment in Transferable Securities, with a view to investments of UCITS, amending Dir 85/611/EEC 5.95, 9.03, 9.11, 9.12, 9.13, 9.20, 9.23

Unfair Terms: Dir 93/13/EEC on unfair terms in consumer contracts. 8.178
  rec 16 . . . . 8.180

FSA HANDBOOK OF RULES AND GUIDANCE

FSA Handbook of Rules and
    Guidance 5.09, 5.13, 5.83,
        5.86, 9.09, 10.03–10.05, 10.07,
        10.09–10.19, 10.22, 10.35
Glossary 5.09, 5.81
Principles for Business 5.14, 8.137,
        8.157, 10.03
Principle 1 . . . . 5.14, 5.23
    PRIN 1.1.7G 5.15
    PRIN 1.1.9G 5.16
    PRIN 1.1.2G 5.14
Principle 2 . . . . 5.14, 5.23, 8.157
Principle 3 . . . . 5.14, 5.15, 8.157
Principle 4 . . . . 5.14, 10.03
Principle 5 . . . . 5.14
Principle 6 . . . . 5.14, 5.23, 8.137, 8.157
Principle 7 . . . . 5.14, 8.157
Principle 8 . . . . 5.14, 8.140
Principle 9 . . . . 5.14, 8.137
Principle 10 . . . . 5.14
Principle 11 . . . . 5.14
GEN 2.2.1G 5.10
Perimeter Guidance Manual (PERG)
    PERG 1.1.2G. 5.48
Threshold Conditions Manual
    (COND) 5.17, 5.94
    COND 1.3.1G. 5.19
    COND 1.3.2G. 5.19
    COND 2 . . . . 5.19
Collective Investment Schemes Specialist
    Sourcebook (COLL). 9.13
    COLL 5 . . . . 9.13, 9.15, 9.23
    COLL 5.1.2G 9.15
    COLL 5.2 . . . . 9.15
    COLL 5.2.7R. 9.15
    COLL 5.2.8R. 9.15
    COLL 5.2.10(3)R 9.17
    COLL 5.2.11R. 9.19
    COLL 5.2.20(1)R 9.17
    COLL 5.2.20(2)R 9.17
    COLL 5.2.20(3)R 9.17
    COLL 5.2.20(4)R 9.18
    COLL 5.2.20(5)R 9.18
    COLL 5.2.21R. 9.18
    COLL 5.2.22R. 9.18
    COLL 5.2.23R. 9.17
    COLL 5.2.24R. 9.21
    COLL 5.5 . . . . 9.15
    COLL 5.5.4R. 9.15
    COLL 5.6 . . . . 9.15
    COLL 5.6.4R. 9.15
    COLL 5.6.22R. 9.15
General Prudential Sourcebook
    (GENPRU) 10.03, 10.04,
        10.05, 10.08, 10.09
    GENPRU 1.2.13G. 10.03
    GENPRU 1.2.26R. 10.03
    GENPRU 1.2.30R. 10.19
    GENPRU 1.3. . . . . 10.18
    GENPRU 1.3.13R. 10.18
    GENPRU 2 . . . . 10.09
    GENPRU 2.1.40R. 10.09
    GENPRU 2.1.41R. 10.09
    GENPRU 2.1.43G. 10.09
    GENPRU 2.1.45R. 10.11
    GENPRU 2.1.48R. 10.10
    GENPRU 2.1.51R. 10.13
    GENPRU 2.1.52R. 10.14
    GENPRU 2.2. . . . . 10.17, 10.18
    GENPRU 2.2.8G. 10.17
    GENPRU 2.2.24G. 10.17
Market Conduct Sourcebook
    (MAR) 5.31, 5.86
    MAR 1 . . . . 5.30, 5.79
    MAR 3 . . . . 5.84, 5.85
    MAR 5 . . . . 5.80
    MAR 5.3.1R 5.80
    MAR 5.4.1R 5.80
    MAR 5.5.1R 5.80
    MAR 5.6.1R 5.80
    MAR 6 (s 6.3). 5.81
New Conduct of Business Sourcebook
    (COBS) 5.22, 5.29, 5.32
    COBS 1, Annex I 5.79
    COBS 1.1.1R. 5.79
    COBS 1.1.2R. 5.79

COBS 1.1.3R.	5.79
COBS 2	5.23
COBS 2.1.1R.	5.23
COBS 2.2.1R.	5.23
COBS 2.3.1R.	5.23
COBS 2.3.3G	5.23
COBS 2.4.3R.	5.23, 5.24
COBS 2.4.4R.	5.23
COBS 3	5.24
COBS 3.2.1R.	5.24
COBS 3.4.1R.	5.24
COBS 3.5.1R.	5.24
COBS 3.5.2R.	5.24
COBS 3.6.1R.	5.24
COBS 3.6.2R.	5.24
COBS 3.6.4R.	5.24
COBS 3.7.1R.	5.25
COBS 4	5.26, 5.36
COBS 4.2.1R.	5.26
COBS 4.2.4G	5.26
COBS 6	5.29
COBS 8	5.29
COBS 9	5.27, 5.85
COBS 9.2.1R.	5.27
COBS 10	5.28, 5.85
COBS 10.2.1R.	5.28
COBS 11	5.29
COBS 12	5.29
COBS 16	5.29
Prudential Sourcebook for Banks, Building Societies and Investment Firms (BIPRU).	10.05, 10.08, 10.09
BIPRU 3	10.13, 10.35
BIPRU 3.1.5R	10.13
BIPRU 3.2.1R	10.13
BIPRU 6	10.15, 10.19
BIPRU 6.1.3G	10.19
BIPRU 6.5.12R	10.15
BIPRU 6.5.25R	10.15
BIPRU 7	10.14
BIPRU 13	10.16
BIPRU 13.3.3R	10.16
BIPRU 13.3.4R	10.16
BIPRU 13.7	10.16
BIPRU Rule 13.7.6R	10.16
Sourcebook for non-investment insurance business (ICOBS).	5.22
Sourcebook for mortgage and home finance business (MCOB).	5.22
Sourcebook—Recognised Investment Exchanges and Recognised Clearing Houses (REC)	6.08
REC 2	6.08
Regulatory Guide on the Responsibilities of Providers and Distributors for the Fair Treatment of Customers	8.157

1

AN OVERVIEW

1.1 What is a Derivative?	1.01
1.2 Why?	1.04
1.3 How?	1.08
1.4 Where and Who?	1.15
1.5 When?	1.18

1.1 What is a Derivative?[1]

A derivative is a contract which gives rise to rights and obligations in respect of an underlying asset or other factor, which is usually referred to as just the 'underlying'. It is possible to write a derivative contract on any type of underlying. The underlying might be: **1.01**

- equity securities,
- debt securities,
- interests in funds,
- indices of prices or values,
- currencies,
- interest rates,
- credit risk,
- 'hard' commodities, which comprise both base metals and precious metals (gold and silver bullion, together with platinum and palladium),
- 'soft' commodities, such as agricultural produce (including cocoa, live hogs, pulp, and orange juice),
- energy, such as oil, gas, and electricity,

---

[1] As to derivative products and their pricing, see amongst others Das, *Swaps/Financial Derivatives* (John Wiley & Sons Inc., 2005), and Hull, *Options, Futures, and Other Derivatives* (Prentice Hall, 2007). As to the legal and regulatory treatment of derivatives, see amongst others Firth, *Derivatives Law and Practice* (Sweet & Maxwell, 2003), Henderson, *Henderson on Derivatives* (Lexis Nexis, 2003), and Hudson, *The Law on Financial Derivatives* (Sweet & Maxwell, 2006).

- more exotic types of underlying, such as emission rights, and
- other derivative instruments.

1.02 The right of a party conferred under a derivative contract might be the right to buy or to sell a specified quantity of the underlying at a specified price at a specified time, or the right to receive one or more payments (such as interest, the amount of which is calculated with reference to an underlying notional amount of money). Exercise of a right by a party can result in that party assuming obligations, for example the exercise of the right to buy the underlying gives rise to the obligation to pay the specified price for that underlying. The right of one party is the obligation of the other, hence the right of one party to choose whether or not to buy a specified quantity of the underlying (and thereby assume the obligation to pay the specified price) becomes the obligation of the other party to sell that specified quantity if that right is exercised, and that other party of course then has the right to receive payment of the specified price.

1.03 In very general terms, a derivative contract is a contract which contains a quantification of the future price or value of the underlying, irrespective of whether a delivery of the underlying is made. The future price or value of the underlying is quantified by the contractual counterparties when they enter into their derivative contract. This general analysis accords with every type of derivative, and it encapsulates the entire purpose of the derivative markets.

1.2 Why?

1.04 A derivative gives economic exposure to the underlying, and this property of a derivative indicates its purpose. A derivative is designed primarily to be used as a risk management tool, and therefore the derivative industry is sometimes referred to as being a part of the risk management industry.

1.05 The end-user of a derivative can use the derivative to decrease exposure to movements in the market for the underlying. That is, the end-user is acquiring protection from (hedging against) the risk of an unfavourable movement in the market for the underlying, whether that unfavourable movement is an increase or a decrease in the price of the underlying. This risk is usually referred to as price risk or market risk. A derivative used in this manner is used to reduce or to control market risk. The end-user pays a price for acquiring this protection. Depending on the type of derivative used, this price may be paid at the outset of the derivative transaction, or it may be paid in instalments over the duration of the derivative transaction. Sometimes this price is referred to as a premium. The derivative transfers the market risk from the end-user to the person selling the hedging protection. Other types of derivative transfer credit risk, which is the risk that a debtor who owes a payment obligation fails to make that payment, or the payment obligation is restructured, or the debtor suffers some form of insolvency. Again, the derivative transfers risk (this time, credit risk) from the end-user, who pays a premium to acquire the hedging protection, to the person selling the hedging protection.

1.06 The end-user of a derivative can also use the derivative to increase exposure to movements in the market for the underlying. The end-user is using the derivative to magnify any potential gains from favourable movements in the market for the underlying, whether that favourable movement is an increase or a decrease in the price of the underlying. A derivative used in this manner for speculative purposes is used to express an investment view.[2] However, of course a derivative used in this manner also magnifies any potential loss from an unfavourable movement in the market for the underlying.

1.07 As a derivative is a contract which contains a quantification of the future price or value of the underlying, the derivative market can also be used to discover the probable future price or value of the underlying. Participants in the derivative market make their own assessment as to this probable future price or value, and the terms of the derivative contracts that are struck indicate the consensus of the market. The statistics published by exchanges are therefore particularly important, as these data can indicate probable future prices and values, and therefore of equal importance are the regulatory obligations incumbent on trading members of exchanges to report to exchanges details of their transactions.

1.3 How?

1.08 Broadly, there are two markets for the underlying: the cash market (or 'spot' market), in which delivery of the underlying and payment for the underlying take place immediately, and the derivative market, in which delivery of the underlying and payment for the underlying take place in the future (although payment to buy the derivative contract, that is, payment to buy the rights conferred by the derivative, might be made in the present, when the derivative contract is made). Derivative contracts, under which actual delivery of the underlying is made, are described as being settled physically. Under some types of derivative contract, a payment is made instead of delivery of the underlying, and these derivative

---

[2] Certain derivatives can also be used to create a leveraged exposure to the underlying. The seller of the derivative exposure effectively provides financing to the buyer of the derivative exposure, whereby the buyer acquires more exposure than would have been achieved through a direct purchase of the underlying. Critically, the buyer pays interest on the financing made available. This is a more specialized form of derivative transaction, which is explored in greater depth in part 4.10 of Chapter 4.

contracts are described as being cash-settled. No delivery of the underlying is made under a cash-settled derivative contract.

1.09 The key characteristic of a derivative contract is that it creates an economic exposure to the underlying, whether the right under the derivative contract is the right to buy the underlying, the right to sell the underlying, or the right to receive a payment, the amount of which is calculated with reference to an underlying notional amount of money or an underlying notional amount of an asset. The derivative itself has its own price or value, which is different from the price of the underlying but which is linked to the price of the underlying. The term 'derivative' stems from this link between the price of the underlying and the price or value of the derivative, with its connotation that the derivative contract is 'derived from' its corresponding underlying.

1.10 One of the important attributes of a derivative contract is the ability it confers to control a disproportionately large quantity of the underlying, and this attribute makes a derivative an extremely flexible tool for both risk management and speculation. For example, the price paid to buy a derivative contract which creates rights in respect of a certain quantity of the underlying (say, the right to buy that same quantity of the underlying) may very well be significantly lower than the price that would be paid actually to buy that same quantity of the underlying in the market for the underlying. Crucially, the derivative creates an economic exposure to that same quantity of the underlying, and through the derivative, the buyer of the derivative has the same exposure to that particular quantity and yet does not pay the full price for that quantity in the market for the underlying. This attribute of the derivative is referred to as 'gearing',[3] and gearing is a measure of the extent of the economic exposure to the underlying that the derivative creates. A derivative which has high gearing creates a high level of economic exposure to the underlying. The buyer of the derivative experiences the movements of the price of the underlying through changes in the price of the derivative (which can be bought and sold independently of the underlying) without having actually to buy the underlying. It is because the buyer of the derivative does not need to buy the underlying to gain an exposure to the underlying that the derivative is said to create a synthetic exposure to the underlying.

1.11 Further, because the derivative has its own price or value, which is independent from but linked with the price of the underlying, rights under the derivative

---

[3] The term 'gearing' has different meanings, depending on the context in which it is used. In the context of corporate finance, 'gearing' means the level of debt that a company assumes relative to its share capital, expressed as a percentage of the share capital. In the United States, this percentage is referred to as 'leverage'.

contract can be created, extinguished or transferred, or indeed traded, separately from transactions in the underlying.

A key calculation in derivative mathematics is the ratio between the magnitude of movements in the price of a derivative and the magnitude of movements in the price of the underlying. This ratio, which may change over the life of the derivative contract, affects the extent of the economic exposure to the underlying that the derivative creates. **1.12**

As the price of a derivative is separate from, although linked to, the price of the underlying, and the price of the underlying changes over time (or exhibits volatility), the pricing or valuation of a derivative requires, as an input to the calculation, a prediction of the extent to which changes in the price of the underlying will occur. Derivatives are useful because the future price of the underlying is uncertain, and participants in the derivative markets either wish to decrease their exposures to these uncertain prices, because they wish to hedge against the risk of unfavourable movements, or to increase their exposures to these uncertain prices, because they wish to speculate on favourable movements. **1.13**

Derivative pricing and its associated mathematics is an immense and complex subject, to which an extensive and ever-growing body of study is devoted. Although derivative pricing is largely outside the scope of this book, a brief introduction to the basic concepts is provided in respect of each derivative product described.[4] **1.14**

1.4 Where and Who?

Trading in derivatives today generally takes place in two principal forums.[5] One, trading might take place on an exchange in accordance with the rules of that exchange. Standard contracts are bought and sold by the participants in the market, within the framework of the exchange. Exchanges used to be actual places where buyers and sellers would meet, but increasingly exchanges are electronic trading platforms accessed by participants through computer links. Two, trading might take place directly between contractual counterparties in the over-the-counter market (the 'OTC market'), which does not involve the infrastructure of an exchange. OTC derivative **1.15**

---

[4] See Chapter 4.
[5] A third forum for trading derivatives is the market made available by a market service provider (or electronic communication network), which functions very much like an exchange, in that buyers and sellers are put in touch with each other, but, unlike an exchange, performance of the contracts dealt through a market service provider is not guaranteed by any form of clearing system. The regulatory treatment of market service providers differs from the regulatory treatment of exchanges, and depends on the business model of the market service provider. For example, see the introduction in Chapter 5 to the treatment of multilateral trading facilities under the regulatory system applied in the EU.

contracts are individually and privately negotiated by the contractual counterparties, although certain standard forms of contract have been developed over the last quarter of a century or so, which assists the liquidity of the OTC market.[6]

1.16 Many different types of counterparty participate in the derivative markets, including:

- investment banks,
- commercial banks,
- specialist brokers and other financial institutions,
- investment managers and the funds under management,
- building societies,
- insurance companies,
- the treasury departments of commercial companies,
- public authorities, and
- (in respect of the more simple derivative products) retail investors.

1.17 Some of these counterparties are end-users who buy derivatives, and some of these counterparties sell derivatives to end-users; others intermediate between the ultimate buyers and sellers. Buying and selling a derivative is not the same as buying and selling assets or other financial instruments. How derivatives are bought and sold is explained in greater detail in the following pages.

1.5 When?

1.18 Although the derivative industry seems very much a feature of modern commercial life, derivative techniques were known and used in the ancient world. For example, forward contracts and option contracts were used by merchants, traders, and farmers living and working in the Roman Empire, and before that, in the time of the Greek city states, centuries before the birth of Christ. However, the development of the more formal market structures that are an important part of today's derivative markets took place after the 17th century, with the establishment of the first exchanges.

1.19 Indeed, Chapter 2 describes a little of the history of various derivative markets in London, and it can be seen that derivative markets such as the London Metal Exchange were an integral part of the development of today's society, facilitating the trade and commerce which allowed for economic and social expansion.

---

[6] See Chapter 7.

1.20 Later, the discovery of modern mathematical and computational techniques enabled a theoretical foundation to be established to explain the transactions that traders in the ancient world entered into as a matter of intuition. It is the establishment of a formal theoretical foundation that has unlocked the potential of the derivative markets, as participants are now able to understand and better control the transactions they enter into.

1.21 The complexity of derivative pricing, which for many observers defines and characterizes the derivative markets, often obscures the fact that derivatives are contracts, and therefore derivatives are governed by legal systems. As commercial dealings involving derivatives have become more intricate, English law is evolving to promote contractual certainty by establishing how these specialized forms of contract are enforced. The local authority swap cases throughout the 1990s provided the impetus for the clarification of several important elements of English law (such as the law of trusts and restitution), and the effect of these cases therefore resonated more widely than the financial markets. Indeed, from both a practical commercial perspective and a more theoretical academic perspective, one of the most dynamic areas of English law is the application of classical legal concepts to derivative contracts. Many elements of English law, including the law of contract, have evolved over several centuries, and yet certain derivative contracts (such as swaps) were devised towards the end of the 20th century, and these contracts are not readily accommodated by the existing legal system.

1.22 The derivative markets are evolving all the time, and new contracts are being devised to provide the opportunity to hedge against or to speculate on different types of risk. The markets are growing rapidly. Recent developments[7] include the innovation of:

- weather derivatives, which are designed to give an economic exposure to variations in temperature and rainfall,
- derivatives on emission rights, which are rights to emit no more than a specified volume of pollutants into the atmosphere during an industrial process,[8]

---

[7] Derivatives on communications bandwidth and computer memory seemed a distinct possibility at the beginning of the 21st century, when demand for such facilities began to outpace supply as the e-commerce economy burgeoned, and derivatives were regarded as a means of efficiently matching demand and supply. However, technological innovation and the corresponding increase in supply, and lower prices, resulted in supply remaining greater than demand. Consequently, these derivatives did not enter general use despite their initial promise.

[8] The trading of emission rights has assumed greater importance with the ever-increasing awareness of environmental issues and the introduction of formal frameworks for regulating emissions of greenhouse gases, such as the Kyoto Protocol. See part 4.14 of Chapter 4.

- derivatives on property (interests in real property),[9] and
- water.[10]

1.23 An important phenomenon of the modern derivative markets is the growing erosion of the distinctions between the different market structures. One, increasingly the same economic effect can be achieved using different derivative products traded in the different types of market. For example, the economic effect of entering into a swap contract, which was developed in the OTC market, can be achieved by using one of the futures contracts traded on an exchange. Two, certain elements of the infrastructure of the exchange market, principally the involvement of a clearing house which acts as a central counterparty and which thereby effectively ensures the performance of contracts, are being introduced in the OTC market, imparting greater stability and reducing counterparty risk.[11] Three, counterparties in certain types of trading relationship, such as prime brokerage (see Chapter 9), treat the exchange market and the OTC market as part of one exposure for the purposes of the control of risk.

1.24 The increasing prevalence of derivatives might be observed in the context of mortgage lending. Lenders compete for business, and one way of attracting borrowers is to offer loans which feature repayments that are made at a fixed rate of interest. Borrowers benefit from taking up fixed rate loans instead of variable rate loans because they know in advance the amount of their repayments, and they can budget accordingly, and not worry unduly whenever the Bank of England's Monetary Policy Committee considers the next move in interest rates.

---

[9] The generally illiquid nature of the real property market (in which sales and purchases tend to be effected at a significantly slower pace than in the markets for other assets) has tended to hinder the development of property derivatives, as potential participants in the property derivative market have been deterred by the lack of hedging opportunities. Nonetheless, indices of property prices are published, and the strong volume of derivative business linked to these indices, and not to actual interests in land, particularly in the United Kingdom, has been sufficient to prompt ISDA to publish the 2007 ISDA Property Index Derivatives Definitions.

[10] The suggestion that water is a class of commodity to be traded is highly controversial, because water is the one natural resource without which life is impossible. Proponents of trading water (and exchange-based water derivative contracts have been mooted) argue that the increasing scarcity of water requires the discipline of market forces to distribute it efficiently, pointing to an existing, albeit little-publicized, system for trading and allocating supplies in Australia and west Texas. Opponents argue that water is a basic human right and to expose supply of it to market forces would be to expose a significant proportion of the world's population to the risk of deprivation, particularly if regulators lacked strength. It is absolutely clear that any system for trading water must be accompanied by strong government regulation and control, and safeguards for the interests of the poor. Water cannot be denied to anybody on the strength of market forces; to allow otherwise would be criminal.

[11] LIFFE, which is at the time of writing a part of the NYSE Euronext franchise, offers three trade-matching and trade-processing services ('Afirm', 'Bclear', and 'Cscreen') to participants in the wholesale OTC equity derivative market. 'SwapClear' is a clearing service offered by the LCH.Clearnet to participants in the OTC swap market.

1.5 When?

1.25 A lender wishes to offer fixed rate loans to domestic borrowers. The lender must obtain funding to establish its loan book. As a financial institution, the lender obtains funding in the wholesale capital markets, usually paying a variable (or floating) rate of interest. However, crucially, the lender receives a fixed rate of interest from each individual borrower.

1.26 The lender becomes exposed to interest rate risk. On some occasions, the outgoing floating rate that the lender pays to obtain funding is greater than the incoming fixed rate that the lender receives from each individual borrower. Of course, on some occasions, the outgoing floating rate paid by the lender will be less than the incoming fixed rate received by the lender. The lender is said to have an exposure to interest rate risk, and this risk occasionally crystallizes. The lender will neutralize its exposure by using an interest rate derivative product (such as an interest rate swap) bought from a swap counterparty. The swap converts the lender's exposure to an obligation to make floating rate payments to an exposure to an obligation to make fixed rate payments. It is important to appreciate that the swap operates alongside the lender's underlying funding transaction; the swap does not extinguish that underlying funding transaction. The lender should of course ensure that the outgoing fixed rate that it pays (under the combined underlying funding transaction and the swap) is less than the incoming fixed rate that it receives from each individual borrower.

1.27 The benefit to the lender of using the swap is that the fluctuations in the profitability of the lender's loan book are smoothed out. The lender is no longer exposed to interest rate risk. This risk has been transferred to the swap counterparty, whose business is to trade interest rate risk. The trading of interest rate risk can become fairly complex. The individual domestic borrowers benefit because the lender is able to offer them a mortgage product which features fixed interest payments, and the borrowers are insulated from rises in interest rates. Therefore, anyone borrowing a home loan at a fixed rate is (indirectly through the lender) a user of an interest rate derivative product. This example illustrates how derivatives are an important, yet often hidden, part of modern society.

2

THE TWO PRINCIPAL MARKET STRUCTURES

2.1 The Participants in the Markets	2.01
2.2 The Exchange-based Market	2.07
2.3 The OTC Market	2.19
2.4 Market Service Providers	2.22
2.5 Derivative Exchanges	2.27

2.1 The Participants in the Markets

A participant in the derivative markets might be engaged in: **2.01**

- trading,
- the sell side (making a market), or
- the buy side (as an end-user).

Trading

Traders speculate. That is, traders seek to secure a profit through movements in the relevant market in which trading takes place. A trader secures a profit either by buying low and subsequently selling high, or by selling high and subsequently buying low, assuming market risk in doing so, and thereby expressing a view as to the direction in which the market will hopefully move. **2.02**

The sell side and making a market

Making a market in a derivative contract involves offering to buy and to sell that derivative contract without actually becoming exposed to movements in either the market for that derivative contract or the market for the underlying. In other words, the sale of 40 contracts to A and the sale of 60 contracts to B is balanced by the purchase of 30 contracts from C and the purchase of 70 contracts from D. Market-makers generate a revenue by buying contracts at a slightly lower price than the price at which they sell contracts. Market-makers seek to maintain an internal hedge. That is, market-makers seek to balance the total number of sales **2.03** they make with the total number of purchases they make, and they enter into external hedging arrangements if they cannot maintain their internal hedges. Market-makers do not trade in the pure sense of the word, as they do not form a view of the direction in which the market may move.

2.04 Notwithstanding that making a market involves both the sale and purchase of derivative contracts, this activity is described as the sell side because market-makers sell the facility to end-users to buy and to sell derivative contracts.

The buy side

2.05 The buy side of the derivative market comprises the end-users of derivatives. Any of the different types of counterparty described in paragraph 1.16 can potentially use a derivative, whether to decrease exposure to movements in the price of the underlying or to increase that exposure. Essentially, risk is either reduced or increased, depending on the end-user's objective (whether to hedge or to express an investment view) and overall tolerance to risk. It is important to appreciate that the use of derivatives by certain types of counterparty (for example, investment funds[1]) is governed very carefully by one set of regulations and the sale of derivatives to certain types of counterparty (for example, retail investors[2]) is controlled by another set of regulations. Certain types of derivatives, credit derivatives, were actually created and developed in response to yet another set of regulations.[3]

Liquidity

2.06 Both traders and market-makers provide liquidity to the market. A liquid market is a market in which it is easy to find a buyer or a seller who is prepared to transact at reasonable prices. A liquid market is a successful market. A liquid market also acts as a more efficient mechanism to discover prices. Tight spreads indicate that a market is liquid. A spread is quoted by a trader or a market-maker, and it is the difference between the lower price at which the trader or market-maker buys and the slightly higher price at which the trader or market-maker sells. A market-maker must assess the liquidity of the market in order to be able to quote spreads which generate both a flow of business and a profit.

2.2 The Exchange-based Market

2.07 Figure 2.1 illustrates the participants in the exchange-based market. The exchange itself is the forum where trading is conducted. The exchange draws up, or designs,

---

[1] See part 9.1 of Chapter 9.
[2] See part 8.7 of Chapter 8.
[3] See part 4.12 of Chapter 4.

2.2 The Exchange-based Market

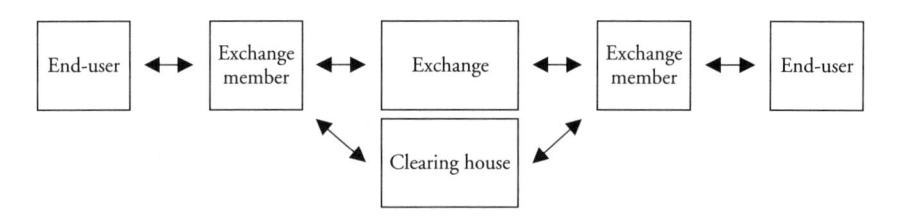

Figure 2.1 Elements of the exchange-based market

the standard contracts that are traded.[4] A fee is paid to the exchange in respect of each transaction dealt on the exchange. Therefore the exchange's revenues increase if it is able to design contracts that are considered to be useful and that are therefore actively traded. Exchanges are run as businesses,[5] and must compete with other exchanges, and indeed with the OTC markets more generally.

2.08 The standard contracts that are traded on an exchange contain terms that are never varied. Only the price at which the contracts are bought and sold changes during the course of trading. The exchange also administers the process of trading, including the system of clearing and margining. The clearing and margining system is fundamental to the operation of the exchange-based market and the different aspects of clearing and margining are explained elsewhere as relevant in this book; cash flows are considered in Chapter 3, and documentation is considered in Chapter 6. Nonetheless, an outline is provided here to introduce the concepts of exchange-based trading.

2.09 All exchange-based trading is conducted between members of the exchange. An exchange member may trade on the exchange using its own capital, or it may make a market, or it may act as a broker and enable an end-user which is not a member of the exchange to access the market. Certain end-users are themselves members of exchanges in order to enable them to trade without the expense of using a broker. For example, the treasury department of an oil company may become a member of an exchange in order to enable it to access the oil futures that are traded on that exchange. The oil company should spend less on exchange

---

[4] Derivatives that are traded on an exchange are sometimes referred to as 'listed derivative contracts', as they are contained in the list of instruments that are traded on a particular derivative exchange. Of course, securities (whether debt or equity) which contain an embedded derivative can also be listed on an investment exchange as listed securities and traded on that exchange. Special rules apply to disclosure of their derivative nature (see, for example, the prospectus directive, 2003/71/EC of the European Parliament and of the Council on the prospectus to be published when securities are offered to the public or admitted to trading and amending Directive 2001/34/EC, and its national implementation).

[5] As with any other industry, derivative exchanges are subject to a trend of globalization and consolidation, as evidenced by the change in the ownership and control of LIFFE since its inception in 1984.

membership than it would on brokerage fees to realize the benefits of exchange membership.

2.10 If an end-user which is not an exchange member wishes to enter into a transaction, then the end-user contacts a broker, which is an exchange member, to find out the price at which the contract is trading on the exchange. The end-user is the broker's customer. The end-user will then place an order with the broker if the end-user wishes to trade at the price quoted by the broker. For example, the end-user wishes to buy five futures contracts. The broker might fill this order by entering into two transactions:

- buying five futures contracts from a counterparty which is another exchange member, and
- selling five futures contracts to the end-user.

2.11 The overall effect of the two transactions is that the end-user buys five futures contracts from the counterparty. The end-user has accessed the market. The purchase by the broker of five futures contracts is said to be on-exchange, and the sale by the broker to the end-user is said to be off-exchange (all on-exchange trading is conducted between the members of the exchange). However, both the on-exchange and the off-exchange transactions are exchange-based and are subject to the rules of the exchange. Conversely, if the end-user wishes to sell, say, three futures contracts, the broker might fill this order by selling on-exchange three futures contracts to the counterparty and buying off-exchange three futures contracts from the end-user.

2.12 The broker is exposed to two risks. The first risk is that the end-user might fail to fulfil the obligation it owes to the broker, and the second risk is that the counterparty might fail to fulfil the obligations it owes to the broker. The broker controls the first risk by controlling the customer relationship it has with the end-user. For example, the broker may reserve the right not to enter into transactions with and for the end-user if the end-user fails to maintain an account with the broker which is sufficiently in credit or if the end-user fails to provide sufficient collateral to the broker. The second risk (that the counterparty might fail to fulfil its obligations) is controlled by the guarantee that is effectively given by the clearing house of the performance of every transaction that is dealt on-exchange. The clearing house gives this guarantee by acting as the central counterparty, that is, by being the seller to every buyer on the exchange and being the buyer to every seller on the exchange.

2.13 The clearing house becomes the seller to every buyer on the exchange and the buyer to every seller on the exchange through the transfer to it of all transactions that are dealt on the exchange. Once a transaction has been entered into by a buyer and a seller, details of that transaction are transmitted to the clearing house for registration. The transaction is a matched transaction if the purchase details

2.2 The Exchange-based Market

conform with the sale details (in terms of the particular contract that has been bought and sold, the quantity of the contract and the price). The matched transaction is then novated to the clearing house. Novation is a process under English law by which the rights and obligations under a contract entered into between A and B are transferred from B to C, so that C replaces B as A's contractual counterparty. Novation actually involves the cancellation of the first contract between A and B and the creation of a second contract between B and C. Crucially, A agrees that B is released from the obligations that B owed to A and instead C owes those obligations. As Figure 2.2 demonstrates, in the context of a derivative exchange, two new contracts are created, one between the seller and the clearing house and one between the buyer and the clearing house.

2.14 Through the novation of transactions to the clearing house, the counterparty risk that the exchange members would otherwise have to each other is eliminated. The elimination of counterparty risk generally allows contracts to be traded more freely and this promotes greater liquidity. The clearing house assumes the risk of a default by an exchange member. Each sale that has been novated to the clearing house should be balanced by a corresponding purchase. Although this balance should minimize the risk to which the clearing house is exposed, the clearing house also administers a payment system to avoid the risky accumulation of exposures. Generally, at the close of each trading session on the exchange, the exchange members whose positions remain open and have lost value during the session pay the amount of the loss to the clearing house. The exchange members whose positions remain open and have gained value during the session are paid the amount of that gain by the clearing house. Therefore profits flow from the losers at the end of the session through the clearing house to the winners at the end of the session.

2.15 The clearing process comprises the initial registration of a matched transaction with the clearing house, the novation of the transaction to the clearing house, and the subsequent payments of profits and losses.

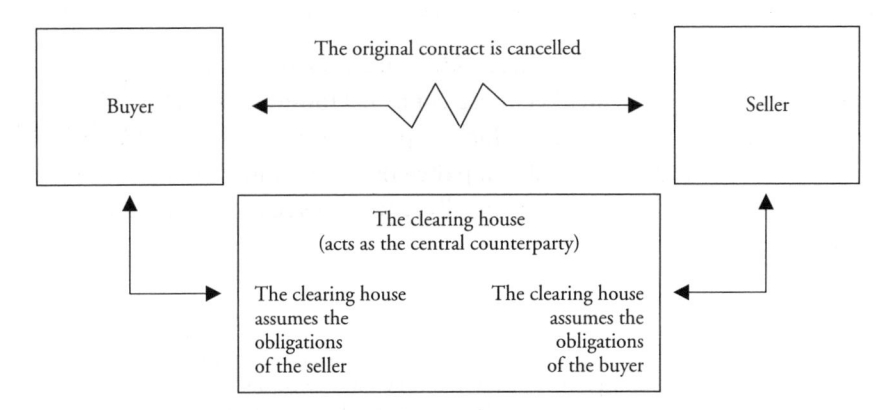

Figure 2.2 The novation of contracts

2.16 The clearing house also administers a system under which collateral is paid to minimize its risk: this is the margining system, which is examined in more depth in Chapter 3. Payments to and from the clearing house are made on a net basis, further simplifying the process and further reducing risk.

2.17 Usually, the clearing house supporting an exchange is owned by the major members of the exchange. Arrangements are usually made that the clearing house has sufficient capital to ensure that it remains financially stable.

2.18 All exchanges used to be physical places, where trading was conducted face-to-face between exchange members. Face-to-face trading is usually referred to as open-outcry. However, during the late 1990s, virtual exchanges were established, trading being conducted through a computer link as opposed to face-to-face in a physical forum. Some of these virtual exchanges have been established by the existing exchanges, seeking to capitalize on the IT revolution by controlling their costs and expanding access to their market and thereby increasing their revenue.

2.3 The OTC Market

2.19 The OTC market is the market in which derivatives are traded directly between counterparties without the infrastructure of an exchange. Generally, only professional participants such as dealers and sophisticated end-users, such as investment managers and corporate treasuries, participate in the OTC market. OTC derivative contracts[6] are potentially very much more complex than exchange-based contracts, involving very substantial cash flows, and these contracts are therefore suitable only for sophisticated end-users.

2.20 As Figure 2.3 illustrates, the OTC market has no rigid structure. However, the complexity of many OTC derivative contracts restricts the liquidity of the market for these contracts, and therefore certain market participants act as brokers, bringing together the contractual counterparties.

2.21 The risks that the OTC market must address are fundamentally the same as those that the exchange-based market must control. However, as the OTC market largely lacks the infrastructure which supports the exchange-based market, OTC market participants must develop their own risk control policies and procedures.[7] OTC market participants generally require their counterparties to provide

---

[6] See Chapter 7.
[7] However, in recognition of the value of the contribution made by a clearing house to the stability of a market, certain major participants in the OTC market collaborate to establish clearing systems for contracts that are commonly dealt, for example SwapClear, which was established to support the OTC swap market.

2.4 Market Service Providers

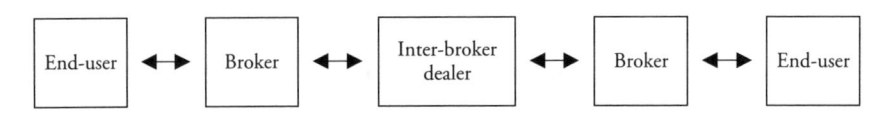

```
[End-user] ⟷ [Broker] ⟷ [Inter-broker dealer] ⟷ [Broker] ⟷ [End-user]
```

Figure 2.3 Elements of the OTC market

collateral and a system of margin is applied. The extensive documentation used in the OTC market reflects the reliance that participants must place on their own risk control policies and processes.

2.4 Market Service Providers

2.22 The market made available by a market service provider is a hybrid between the exchange-based market and the OTC market. The term 'electronic communication network' is used in the North American markets to refer to market service providers, and highlights the fact that the system made available by a market service provider is essentially a computer network. Generally, the market made available by a market service provider operates in one of two ways.

2.23 First, the market service provider might make a market in the derivative contracts that are traded. The term 'making a market' is explained in paragraph 2.03. End-user A wishes to buy and end-user B wishes to sell. On the basis that A's order to buy matches B's order to sell, the market service provider sells to A and buys from B. The market service provider therefore acts as the central counterparty, in a similar manner to the role played by the clearing house to an exchange. However, A and B do not initially actually enter into a transaction with each other, and there is therefore no novation of contracts. Figure 2.4 illustrates this type of market made available by a market service provider (MSP).

2.24 Second, the market service provider might operate an order matching system. End-user A wishes to buy and end-user B wishes to sell. A and B enter their respective orders into the market service provider's system. On the basis that A's order to buy matches B's order to sell, A buys from B through the market service provider's system. The market service provider itself does not actually enter into a transaction with either A or B. Figure 2.5 illustrates this type of market made available by a market service provider.

```
[End-user] ⟷ [MSP (as counterparty)] ⟷ [End-user]
```

Figure 2.4 A market service provider as buyer or seller

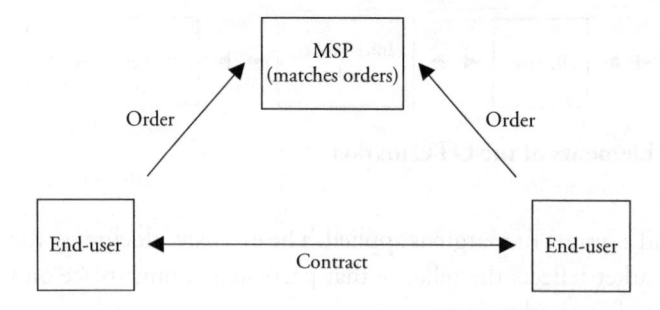

```
                    ┌──────────────┐
                    │     MSP      │
                    │(matches orders)│
                    └──────────────┘
                   ↗                ↖
             Order                    Order
           ↗                              ↖
  ┌──────────┐                        ┌──────────┐
  │ End-user │ ◄─────────────────►    │ End-user │
  └──────────┘       Contract         └──────────┘
```

Figure 2.5 A market service provider as order matching system

2.25 The same basic risk of counterparty default which arises in the exchange-based market and the OTC market arises in the market made available by a market service provider, whether the market service provider makes a market or operates an order-matching system. Therefore the same measures which might be used to control this risk, such as clearing or collateralization, might be used.

2.26 The regulatory treatment of a market service provider differs from that of an exchange. Special regulatory requirements apply to exchanges (which generally require the maintenance of an orderly market with clear, fair, and transparent rules), whereas a market service provider will require a different category of regulatory permission to transact its business. Chapter 5 contains a discussion of the legal and regulatory issues which arise, including regulation.

2.5 Derivative Exchanges

2.27 The following paragraphs describe certain derivative exchanges which operate within the United Kingdom. A theme which emerges is that although these exchanges were established for the market within the United Kingdom, the overall trend of globalization in all aspects of commerce has resulted in these exchanges becoming parts of larger multinational organizations, providing markets and associated services across borders and jurisdictions. This trend has been in part facilitated by the increasing power of IT systems, making the 'virtual' exchange a viable alternative to the physical forum which preceded it.

NYSE Euronext LIFFE

2.28 The London International Financial Futures and Options Exchange (LIFFE) was originally established in September 1982 as the London International Financial Futures Exchange. The establishment of LIFFE coincided with the introduction of the FTSE 100 index by the London Stock Exchange and the Financial Times in a joint venture. The FTSE 100 index was first calculated as of 3 January 1984 with a base value of 1,000. Amongst the first contracts listed and traded on LIFFE were FTSE 100 index futures of varying maturities.

2.29 Through a series of mergers, LIFFE now incorporates several of the derivative markets that were separately traded in London. In 1992, LIFFE merged with the London Traded Options Market, which had originally been established by the London Stock Exchange, and the new exchange was styled the London International Financial Futures and Option Exchange, although the acronym LIFFE was retained. Commodity derivatives have been traded on LIFFE since the merger between LIFFE and the London Commodities Exchange on 16 September 1996. The London Commodities Exchange had been established in 1954 as the successor to the London Sale Rooms, and it had merged with the Soft Commodity Futures Trade Association. The London Commodities Exchange adopted the name London Fox (the London Futures and Options Exchange) in 1987, but later reverted to being styled the London Commodities Exchange. The London Commodities Exchange merged with the Baltic International Freight Futures Exchange (BIFFEX) in 1991.

2.30 Until recently, trading on LIFFE was conducted on an open-outcry basis at the exchange's premises at Cannon Bridge in the City of London. Traders, who wore brightly coloured jackets to identify their different roles in the market, would transact business fact-to-face in special pits. Particular contracts would be traded in particular pits. The traders would be surrounded by runners, who would pass orders to the traders, and exchange officials who supervised trading. The energy of open-outcry trading at LIFFE quickly became a very visible emblem of the financial markets in London. However, trading on LIFFE is now conducted exclusively through computer link.

2.31 Apart from the replacement of open-outcry trading by screen-based trading, LIFFE has undergone other significant changes. The structure of LIFFE's governance changed when the exchange underwent demutualization in April 1999. Previously, LIFFE had been owned and managed by the major participants in its market, but following demutualization, the exchange passed into the ownership of a holding company. A board of directors responding to the policy determined by the shareholders manages the exchange. Many other exchanges around the world, whether derivative exchanges or other types of exchange, are undergoing a similar process of demutualization, which of course facilitates the ongoing process of consolidation through mergers and acquisitions.

2.32 In 2002, LIFFE was bought by Euronext, the pan-European organization of exchanges based in Paris. Euronext provides not only equity and derivative markets, but also clearing and settlement services and it publishes various indices of equity prices. Euronext's merger in 2007 with the New York Stock Exchange (NYSE)

London Metal Exchange

2.33 In 1571, during the reign of Queen Elizabeth I, the Royal Exchange opened in London, and over centuries it would develop into the London Metal Exchange (LME). The Royal Exchange was founded by Sir Thomas Gresham,[8] the Elizabethan financier. Gresham served as the royal agent in the Netherlands of Queen Elizabeth I, and in 1565 his vision was realized that the Corporation of the City of London and the Mercers' Company, an association of textiles merchants of which he was a member, should jointly establish an exchange to facilitate the transaction of business in London. The Royal Exchange was duly opened by Queen Elizabeth I. However, this building was destroyed in the Great Fire of London in 1666, and was subsequently rebuilt by Jarman. This second building was also destroyed by fire. The Royal Exchange building which still stands today on the same site at the junction of Cornhill and Threadneedle Street in the City of London was built by Tite from 1842 to 1844 but now it houses offices, restaurants, and exclusive shops.

2.34 Metals merchants and indeed merchants buying and selling other commodities would meet at the Royal Exchange to transact their business. European merchants began to participate in these markets, and by the early 19th century, the Royal Exchange was too small to accommodate all of those congregating to transact their business, whether buying and selling commodities or providing trade finance to the market. The various groups of merchants therefore began to find other places to meet and to arrange their business. The coffee shops in the City of London increasingly became venues for the different markets. In particular, the Jerusalem Coffee House near Cornhill became popular with metals merchants, just as Edward Lloyd's Coffee House was the venue of those participating in the early shipping and insurance markets. Of course, today the name Lloyd's is synonymous with the London insurance markets.

2.35 The Industrial Revolution in the 19th century drove demand for metals of all types. Large-scale use of metals was made by the engineering industries of the modern technological age which started to emerge, such as mass production in factories, steam engines to power society, the development of a railway network and rolling stock, iron-clad ships powered by steam, and construction generally. The refinement of metallurgical techniques, which gave rise to the development of new alloys, prompted further demand for metals. The increased demand for

---

[8] *c.*1518/19–1579.

2.5 Derivative Exchanges

metals was met by increased supply from outside Europe. Merchants established a formal and regular system of importing cargoes of metals.

Copper was imported into Europe from South America, principally from Chile, and tin was imported into Europe from Malaysia. Merchants buying and selling metals were exposed to the risk that the price of metal would fluctuate while the cargo was in transit. Therefore merchants began to buy and to sell their parcels of metal on a forward basis. A buyer and a seller would enter into a forward contract, agreeing the price that would be paid by the buyer against delivery by the seller of a specified quantity of metal some months later. Generally, under these forward contracts, delivery of the metal by the seller and payment of the forward price by the buyer would take place three months after the contract was struck. The three month duration of these forward contracts reflected the average duration of the voyage by sea from Chile, the source of copper, and, following the opening of the Suez Canal in 1869, from Malaysia, the source of tin. The development of the telegraph allowed news of shipping movements, and delays in shipping and disasters at sea, to be factored into the price of the forward contracts. Therefore the forward prices of metals began to reflect more accurately the difference between the cost of acquiring an asset in the present and the usually higher cost of acquiring an asset in the future, the difference representing factors such as shipping costs, insurance costs, storage costs, and financing. This is the concept of the cost-of-carry, which is intrinsic to the pricing of forward contracts and futures contracts.[9] **2.36**

Merchants began to meet at regular times to trade metals, and they would agree the sale and purchase of standard quantities of metals, conforming to standard qualities of purity, in order to simplify their negotiations. They would merely find the price representing the equilibrium between supply and demand. Trading would be conducted in a circle drawn on the floor of the coffee house in which they conducted business. This is the origin of today's trading in the ring of the LME. **2.37**

The direct precursor to the LME was the London Metals and Mining Company, which was formed in 1877 by metals merchants who wished to establish some formal structure for their market. Trading first took place at Lombard Court over a hat shop. Growth in membership soon prompted a move to a purpose-built exchange in Whittington Avenue. The LME has evolved since its establishment, with a hiatus between 1939 and 1952 caused by the Second World War. **2.38**

Today, the LME is the derivative market for a variety of metals. The LME also calculates an index of the price of metals. The derivative contracts traded on the LME include futures, options, and traded average price options, which are options based on the average price of the underlying metal over one month. Curiously, the LME **2.39**

---

[9] See paragraph 4.28.

has also recently in 2005 introduced futures contracts on plastics. The LME retains open-outcry trading, which takes place during brief 'ring' trading sessions throughout the day at the exchange's premises at Leadenhall Street in the City of London. Members of the LME also conduct trading in a telephone-based market, which is subject to the exchange's rules, which is permanently available. In line with other exchanges, the LME has also introduced an electronic trading platform, which allows transactions to be executed electronically and then matched and cleared through the LCH.Clearnet system, which is introduced in the following paragraphs.

2.40 It is interesting and significant to note that the LME is included in this book because in addition to being a derivative market it is also the market for trading physical metal, which is metal that is sold for immediate delivery without the formation of any derivative contract. The LME, working with the London Clearing House, has developed an electronic system called SWORD to effect the transfer of warrants which demonstrate ownership of metal held in warehouses approved by the LME. SWORD is effectively a database of warrants that have been issued, recording the ownership of particular warrants. The sale and purchase of metal is effected by changing the name of the owner of the relevant warrant in the database.

ICE Futures

2.41 ICE Futures was established in 1980 as the International Petroleum Exchange (IPE) by a group of energy companies. The price of oil was generally stable until the early 1970s. However, two oil price shocks reverberated around the global economy in the 1970s. The first oil price shock happened in 1973, when an embargo by oil-exporting countries forced the average price of oil up from approximately US$12 per barrel in 1973 to approximately US$40 per barrel in 1974. The second oil price shock happened in 1979 following the Iranian Revolution which saw the Shah of Persia deposed and his regime replaced by that of the Ayatollahs. The price of oil reached, very briefly, US$82 per barrel. Apart from contributing to stagflation in the 1970s, these oil price shocks increased volatility in the prices of various oil benchmarks, and this volatility gave rise to the need for a mechanism to hedge against unfavourable movements in price.

2.42 The first contract listed and traded on the IPE was a futures contract for gas oil. Today, futures, options, and swaps are traded on a variety of energy markets, such as oil (including the important benchmark Brent Crude futures contract), the various distillations of oil (including petroleum), gas, and electricity. Open-outcry trading used to take place at the IPE's premises, which most recently were at Commodity Quay in St Katherine Docks, near Tower Bridge in the south-east corner of the City of London.[10]

---

[10] Coincidentally, Commodity Quay has also previously been occupied by the London Commodities Exchange.

2.5 Derivative Exchanges

The IPE was acquired by the IntercontinentalExchange (ICE) in June 2001, and the IPE was subsequently renamed ICE Futures in 2006. Like other exchanges, the market that was traded on the IPE has migrated onto an electronic trading platform.

2.43

Other exchanges

Of course, the IT revolution has enabled many 'virtual' exchanges in different jurisdictions to be established, all of which can be accessed from anywhere in the world using computers. Indeed, some exchanges that have been established in recent years appear to have been set up specifically to offer price hedging and price speculation opportunities in very specific markets.[11] Although market participants with the appropriate software and security clearance are able to access these exchanges, it is important that these market participants satisfy themselves thoroughly as to the clearing and settlement procedures which apply, and as to the special risk of a communications failure which may prevent access to the market at a critical time. By way of interesting background, the world's first purely electronic derivative exchange was the Swiss Options and Futures Exchange, which opened in 1988.

2.44

Clearing and LCH.Clearnet

A number of clearing houses had evolved in London during the 18th and 19th centuries. Between 1750 and 1770, bankers would settle accounts between themselves on a net basis in an early form of clearing system, and in 1775 premises at Change Alley became the usual forum where clearing would take place. Different premises have been used. Banks continued to send clerks to the clearing house to sort and to distribute cheques under the bank clearing system until the 1980s, when the Clearing House Automated Payments System (CHAPS) was established. CHAPS was developed in 1984 to serve as an electronic system to transmit value between banks and thereby to facilitate payments. Other industries also use clearing systems. For example, a number of separate independent companies operated the railway network in the United Kingdom in the 19th century, in much the same manner as today's railway network is managed, and the Railway Clearing House was established in 1842 under the Railway Clearing House Act 1830, to allocate receipts between the relevant companies. The International Air Transport Association provided a clearing system to participating airlines, allowing airlines to settle debts through the payment of differences.[12]

2.45

---

[11] For example, FishEX, which is based in Tromsø in Norway above the Arctic Circle, offers an electronic platform for the trading of salmon futures contracts, with a view to expanding the range of contracts offered to other fish.

[12] See *British Eagle International Airlines Ltd v Compagnie Nationale Air France* [1975] 1 WLR 758.

2.46 The London Clearing House (LCH), which provides clearing services to derivative exchanges in the United Kingdom, began as an organization to clear commodity transactions. The forerunner to the LCH, the London Produce Clearing House, was established in 1888 to provide a guarantee to buyers and sellers of agricultural produce that their forward contracts would be performed. The provision of such a guarantee is of course the principal purpose of a clearing function. The amounts owed by the clearing participants to each other were settled each month. The Beetroot Sugar Association was established in 1888 to clear transactions in beetroot sugar, which was traded in lots of 500 bags of a specified weight, and the right to take delivery of sugar was evidenced by a form which was stamped and passed to the buyer as each transaction was concluded.

2.47 During the 1980s, the LCH's business expanded to providing clearing services to the IPE in 1981, LIFFE in 1982, and the LME in 1987. During the late 1990s, the LCH began to offer clearing services for a variety of OTC markets, including repo and interest rate swaps.

2.48 The LCH and Clearnet SA merged in December 2003 to form LCH.Clearnet. Clearnet SA was formed in 1969 in order to clear commodity transactions in Paris. LCH.Clearnet Ltd and LCH.Clearnet SA are separate entities providing different clearing services under separate rulebooks and processes.

3

KEY CONCEPTS

3.1 'Long' and 'Short'	3.01
3.2 The Bid and Offer Spread	3.03
3.3 Tick and Basis Point	3.04
3.4 Margin	3.05

3.1 'Long' and 'Short'

A party to a derivative contract is said to open a position when entering into the contract. A position can be opened either by buying the derivative contract or by selling the derivative contract. A position that has been opened by buying is a long position, and a position that has been opened by selling is a short position. **3.01**

An open position is closed by entering into a transaction equal and opposite to the transaction in which the position was opened, although of course the opening price and the closing price will tend to differ (this difference of course generating the profit or the loss made). For example, a trader opens a position by selling five lots of the March FTSE 100 index future, and the trader is therefore short five lots of the December future. The trader would subsequently close this position by buying five lots of the December future. **3.02**

3.2 The Bid and Offer Spread

The price of a derivative contract is expressed as a bid and offer spread. For example, the quote for a futures contract might be 6,195–6,205. A trader or market-maker quoting the spread will buy the contract for the bid price 6,195 per contract and sell the contract for the offer price 6,205 per contract. The difference 10 is the spread. The spread is the profit made by the market-maker (the trader's profit derives from opening and closing positions to capture profitably market movements). **3.03**

3.3 Tick and Basis Point

3.04 The term 'tick' is usually encountered in the exchange-based market, and its equivalent in the OTC market is the 'basis point'[1] (which is often abbreviated to 'bip'). A tick is the smallest amount by which the quote for a derivative contract moves. The purpose of a tick is to avoid potentially infinitesimal movements in the price of a derivative contract, thereby facilitating the administration of dealing on an exchange. The benefit of easy administration of dealing is that liquidity is enhanced. For example, the tick for the FTSE 100 index future is 0.5 of an index point. Therefore a market-maker that quotes a bid price of 6,195 and now wishes to quote a different price can only change the bid price by 0.5 of an index point or more. The tick is represented by a monetary value. Therefore the profit or loss (P&L) of a position can be calculated with reference to the number of ticks by which the quote for a derivative contract moves.

3.4 Margin

3.05 Paragraph 2.14 introduces the principle that payments flow from the losers at the end of each trading session through the clearing house to the winners at the end of the session. Crucially, at the end of the session, all exchange members whose positions remain open and have lost value during the session pay the amount of that loss to the clearing house, and all exchange members whose positions remain open and have gained value during the session are paid the amount of that gain by the clearing house.

3.06 However, only certain larger and more capitalized members of the exchange (clearing members) have accounts with the clearing house. All payments flow through the accounts held by the clearing members with the clearing house. Non-clearing members access the clearing system through accounts held with clearing members. A clearing member is responsible to the clearing house for the payments that a non-clearing member, which holds an account with the clearing member, is required to make. Figure 3.1 illustrates the flow of payments through the clearing house from the losers to the winners on the exchange.

3.07 As the central counterparty, the clearing house must ensure that it can pay profits to the winners even if it does not receive the corresponding payments from the losers. The clearing house therefore administers a margining system to provide sufficient collateral to enable it to pay profits to the winners even if it does not receive the corresponding payments from the losers.

---

[1] The term 'basis point' is also used to refer to 1/100 of 1%, which is 0.01%.

3.4 Margin

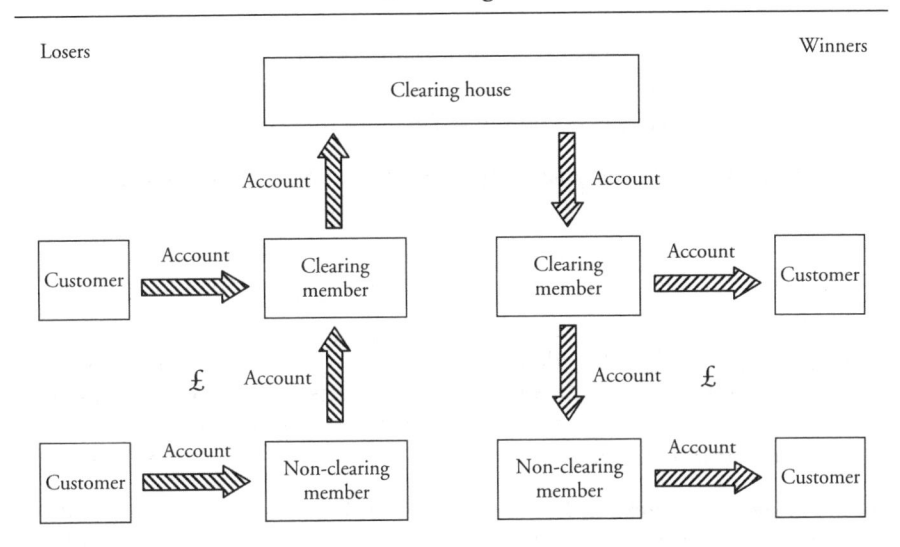

Figure 3.1 The flow of payments in an exchange-based market

Initial margin

Initial margin is collateral that is required when a position is opened. The amount of initial margin that is required for a position is calculated to protect the clearing house against the maximum amount of loss that can be expected to be made in respect of that position in one trading session (which is usually one day). The amount of initial margin varies from contract to contract. The clearing house and the exchange determine the amount of initial margin required in respect of each contract with reference to factors such as the volatility of the movements in the price of the contract and the volume of contracts being traded. The initial margin is retained until the position is closed, whereupon it is repaid.

3.08

Variation margin

Each position that is open at the end of a trading session is marked to market. Marking to market a position at the end of a trading session generally involves calculating the gain or loss made by that position during the trading session. The settlement price of the contract is used to mark to market the position. The settlement price of the contract is generally calculated with reference to a selection of prices, including the closing bid and offer price, the last actual price traded, and a weighted average of the prices traded during a specified period immediately prior to the close of trading. The rules of the exchange define in detail how the settlement price is calculated.

3.09

If the amount of margin already paid is insufficient to cover any loss made, variation margin (which is also known as daily margin) becomes payable to make up the shortfall. Although positions are marked to market at the close of a trading

3.10

session, clearing houses usually reserve the right to require the payment of margin (or make margin calls) more frequently during a trading session in order to avoid the accumulation of large exposures in fast-moving and volatile markets.

3.11 The purpose of margin is to enable positions to be opened at low cost, and variation margin contributes to the control of the risk of default. Margin is generally not required in respect of long option positions, because the maximum loss that holders of options can incur is the premium that they pay to buy the option. Of course, on some exchanges, the premium is not paid immediately in respect of certain options, and therefore margin may be required. The specification of a particular contract will indicate the margin requirements in respect of that contract.

Example of tick and margin

3.12 For the purpose of this example, the tick of a share index future is 0.5, the value of one index point is £10 and therefore the value of one tick is £5. The futures contract is cash-settled (that is, no delivery of shares constituting the underlying index is made, and instead one party makes a payment to the other to reflect the change in the value of the index). To maintain clarity, this example does not reflect the flow of payments through clearing members and non-clearing members.

3.13 On day 1, a trader sells five futures contracts at 6,195. The trader opens a short position. Assume that the initial margin requirement, set by the clearing house and the exchange, is £2,500 per contract. Therefore the initial margin requirement for five contracts is £12,500. The trader is required to pay the initial margin of £12,500 into a margin account held with the clearing house. The balance of the margin account is £12,500 in credit. The trader is required to maintain a balance in the margin trading account of not less than £12,500 in credit while the position is open. The policy of the clearing house and the exchange is that £12,500 is the maximum amount of loss that can be expected to be made in one trading session in respect of a position comprising five lots of the share index future, and therefore this amount must be available to the clearing house to meet that potential loss.

Initial margin requirement = £2,500 * 5 = £12,500

3.14 On day 2, the settlement price of the futures contract is 6,250. The price of the futures contract has increased by 55 points, which is 110 ticks. The position has lost £2,750. The amount of the loss £2,750 is paid from the trader's margin account to the clearing house. (The clearing house uses the amount paid from the trader's margin account, and amounts it receives from other losers, to pay profits to exchange members whose positions have gained value.) The balance of the clearing account is now £9,750 in credit. The trader is required to pay variation margin of £2,750 to maintain the balance of the margin account at £12,500 in credit.

Loss = ticks * tick value * number of contracts
Loss = 110 * £5 * 5 = £2,750

3.4 Margin

On day 3, the settlement price of the futures contract is 6,150. The price of the futures contract has decreased by 100 points, which is 200 ticks. The position has gained £5,000. The amount of the gain £5,000 is paid into the margin account from the clearing house. (The clearing house uses amounts it receives from losers to pay profits into the trader's margin account and to other winners.) The balance of the trader's margin account is £17,500 in credit. The trader is therefore able to withdraw £5,000 from the margin account and still leave the required balance of £12,500 in credit. **3.15**

Gain = ticks * tick value * number of contracts
Gain = 200 * £5 * 5 = £5,000

On day 4, the trader buys five futures contracts at 6,115 thereby closing the position. The price of the futures contract has decreased by 35 points, which is 70 ticks. The position has gained £1,750 since it was last marked to market. The amount of the gain £1,750 is paid into the margin account by the clearing house. The balance of the account is £14,250 in credit. As the position has been closed, the trader is able to withdraw £14,250 from the margin account, which includes the initial margin paid when the position was opened. **3.16**

Gain = ticks * tick value * number of contracts
Gain = 70 * £5 * 5 = £1,750

The trader has made a trading profit of £4,000 by selling five futures contracts at 6,195 and subsequently buying back five futures contracts at 6,115. The amount of the trader's profit is 80 points, which is 160 ticks. **3.17**

Trading profit = ticks * tick value * number of contracts
Trading profit = 160 * £5 * 5 = £4,000

The trader's cash flow, as set out in the summary below, indicates how the trading profit £4,000 has been made. The balance is 0 at the start of trading and the balance of £4,000 at the end of trading is the trading profit. **3.18**

	Movement	Pay	Receive	Balance
Start				£0
Day 1	To margin account (initial margin)	£12,500		−£12,500
Day 2	To margin account (variation margin)	£2,750		−£12,250
Day 3	From margin account (variation margin)		£5,000	−£10,250
Day 4	From margin account (variation margin)		£14,250	£4,000

4

PRODUCTS

4.1 Introduction	4.01	4.11 Islamic-compliant Derivatives	4.158
4.2 Forward Contract	4.10	4.12 Credit Derivatives	4.164
4.3 Futures Contract	4.17	4.13 Multi-asset Derivatives	4.195
4.4 Option Contract	4.32	4.14 New Classes of Underlying	4.197
4.5 Warrant	4.60	4.15 Valuations, Valuation Disruptions, and Adjustments	4.228
4.6 Forward Rate Agreement	4.63		
4.7 Swap	4.69	4.16 Different 'Wrappers' of Derivative Cash Flows	4.229
4.8 Cap, Floor, and Collar Contracts	4.125	4.17 Repurchase and Reverse Repurchase Agreements	4.245
4.9 CPPI	4.132	4.18 Financial Engineering	4.254
4.10 Derivatives used as Financing Tools	4.148		

4.1 Introduction

This chapter introduces the more common derivative products: this group of the more common products comprises the forward contract, the futures contract, the option contract, the warrant, the forward rate agreement, the swap, and cap, floor, and collar contracts. A basic explanation is provided of how each product works and how it is used in terms of the cash flows that it creates. In addition, some history and background is provided to place each product in its proper context. Swaps are given some prominence in this chapter, because they are conceptually the most difficult to analyse. In particular, although the idea of the swap is almost beguilingly easy, the actual operation of a swap must be carefully considered, as this operation requires very particular documentation, and gives rise to a number of interesting economic and legal issues. **4.01**

This chapter next considers the constant proportion portfolio insurance (CPPI) structure, which both creates an exposure to the underlying, which increases if the underlying performs in an advantageous manner, and also provides protection of the amount invested. Crucially, the construction of a CPPI index involves derivative structuring techniques, and a CPPI index can also itself form the underlying of **4.02** another derivative contract. A specialized use of derivative techniques is the provision of acquisition financing in a derivative format, which is also explored in this chapter.

4.03 Credit derivatives are distinguished from other derivatives in that the underlying is a different type of risk: the underlying of other derivatives is essentially movements in the price of the underlying, whether that underlying is a commodity or a financial instrument, whereas the underlying of a credit derivative is credit risk. This distinction informs the contractual treatment of the underlying in each case. However, the actual transaction structures that are created to give the exposure to the different types of risk, whether price risk or credit risk, are substantially similar.

4.04 At first glance, derivative structuring techniques are not easily compatible with the principles of Islamic financing, which has evolved to complement the Shari'a. However, Islamic financing techniques have evolved in tandem with the conventional financing industry, and an introduction is provided to certain of the Islamic financing techniques which find a ready application in the derivative markets.

4.05 In recent years, a number of new classes of underlying have emerged, such as the multi-asset exposure and the hedge fund. Although exposures to these new classes of underlying tend to be created using familiar derivative structures, the novelty of the characteristics and practices of these emerging classes of underlying and their markets merit some consideration. In particular, electricity and power trading, and carbon trading, require an introduction given their growing importance in a global society which faces significant challenges.

4.06 In particular, all derivative contracts are required to set out a process for valuing the underlying, and these processes must accommodate disruptions to valuations. All derivative contracts are also required to provide for the consequences of certain events which may affect the underlying, or even result in the underlying no longer being available, whether for the purposes of valuation or for the purposes of hedging exposures that are assumed by selling the derivative product. Different classes of underlying give rise to unique requirements, and this chapter introduces what these requirements are, laying the foundation for a closer consideration of the relevant contractual treatments in Chapter 7.

4.07 An introduction is given to the different formats or 'wrappers' in which a derivative exposure can be delivered, with a particular emphasis on the securitization of derivative cash flows, the purpose of which is to place in the hands of the investor a transferable security which creates the derivative exposure to the underlying and which brings all the benefits and convenience of an investment in a security.

4.08 This chapter concludes with a necessarily brief introduction to the topic of financial engineering, which is generally the process of combining different derivative products to achieve a particular required economic effect. This chapter sets the conceptual foundation for a consideration in subsequent chapters of the legal and regulatory framework in which the derivative industry operates and the documentation that is used.

4.09 There are two different broad categories of derivative cash flow: the forward cash flow and the option cash flow. The swap cash flow actually properly comprises a series of forward cash flows. These are the building blocks out of which more complex derivative structures are created, and it is recollected that the fundamental principle of a derivative transaction is the assessment that is made in the present of the probable future price or value of the underlying.

4.2 Forward Contract

4.10 A forward contract is a contract to buy and to sell the underlying. Both the delivery of the underlying by the seller and the payment for the underlying by the buyer do not take place when they enter into the contract; instead, delivery and payment take place on a future date which is called the delivery date. The buyer and the seller agree, when they first enter into the contract, the forward price that is to be paid by the buyer on the delivery date and the quantity of the underlying that is to be delivered by the seller on the delivery date. Alternatively, the forward price to be paid by the buyer might be calculated on the delivery date in accordance with a formula that is set out in the forward contract. The forward contract also contains particulars of how delivery of the underlying is to be effected.

4.11 The forward contract creates a binding obligation on both the buyer and the seller. The effect of the forward contract is that the buyer and the seller lock the price of the underlying when they first enter into the contract and thereby insulate themselves from an unfavourable movement in the spot price of the underlying. The spot price of an asset is the price of that asset for immediate delivery, as opposed to delivery at some future time. The spot market for an asset is the market for immediate delivery of that asset.

4.12 By entering into the forward contract, the buyer guarantees the forward price that the buyer pays and the seller guarantees the forward price that the seller receives. By guaranteeing the forward price, the buyer is protected from any increase in the spot price of the underlying which may occur during the period between the time when the contract is struck and the delivery date, but the buyer gives up the possibility of benefitting from any decrease in the spot price which may occur during that period. Similarly, by guaranteeing the forward price, the seller is protected from any decrease in the spot price of the underlying which may occur during that period, but the seller also gives up the possibility of benefitting from any increase

Chapter 4: Products

in the spot price which may occur during that period. The price of the contract (the locked price) is the buyer's and the seller's estimation of the spot price of the underlying on the delivery date.

4.13 In Europe, forward contracts were increasingly used in the 17th century in agricultural markets. Farmers and merchants would agree the forward sale and purchase of agricultural produce, and they would negotiate their forward contracts on the basis of their expectations of harvest. By using forward contracts, they insulated themselves from unfavourable variations in the spot price for the underlying produce, which might be caused by any one of a number of factors, including the success or failure of the harvest.

4.14 Figure 4.1 illustrates the payment profile of a forward contract. At time T1, the harvest of the underlying produce has not taken place. The farmer forward sells produce to the merchant. The farmer and the merchant agree the terms of their forward contract, including the quantity of the produce being sold forward, the quality of the produce being sold, the delivery date, the locked forward price and how delivery will be effected. The locked forward price of the forward contract, which the merchant will pay on the delivery date, is the horizontal dotted line. At time T2, which is the delivery date, the farmer is obliged to deliver to the merchant the specified quantity of produce and the merchant is obliged to pay the forward price to the farmer. If the farmer and the merchant do not enter into the forward contract, then the farmer (the seller) is exposed to the risk that the spot price of the produce is P2 at time T2, and the merchant (the buyer) is exposed to

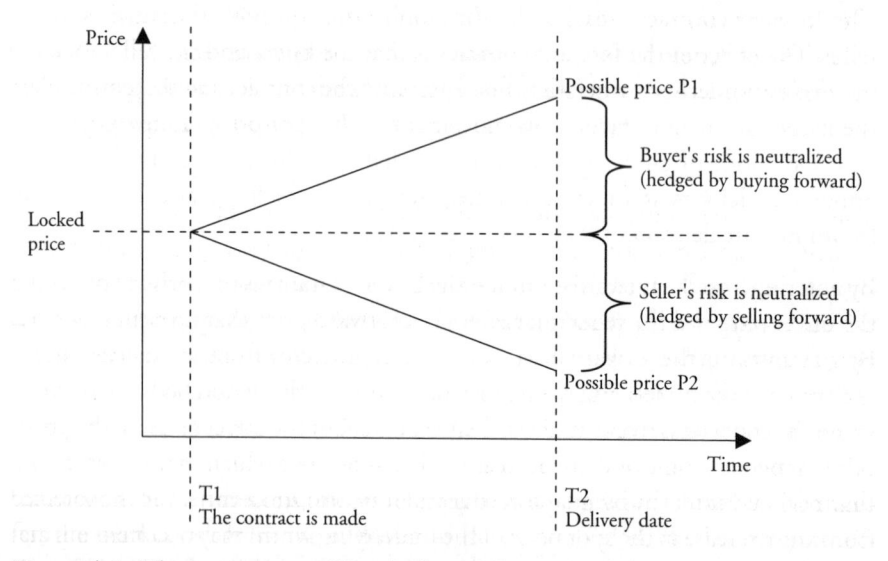

Figure 4.1 The payment profile of a forward contract

the risk that the spot price of the produce is P1 at time T2. By entering into the forward contract, the farmer neutralizes the price risk that the spot price of the produce decreases to P2 at time T2 but gives up the possibility of selling the produce at the higher price P1 at time T2. Similarly, by entering into the forward contract, the merchant neutralizes the price risk that the spot price of the produce increases to P1 at time T2 but gives up the possibility of buying the produce at the lower price P1 at time T2.

4.15 Of course, crucially, the spot price of the produce at time T2 is not known at time T1. The farmer and the merchant are exposed to equal and opposite price risks at time T1, and they can neutralize their respective price risks by entering into their forward contract.

4.16 All manner of underlying used to be bought and sold using forward contracts, including, in addition to agricultural produce such as wheat and livestock, precious metals and base metals. In the modern markets, the largest volumes of forward contracts are traded in the OTC interest rate and foreign exchange markets, but forward contracts continue to constitute a significant part of the commodity markets.

4.3 Futures Contract

4.17 A futures contract is a contract to buy and to sell the underlying. Both the delivery of the underlying by the seller and the payment for the underlying by the buyer do not take place when they enter into the contract; instead, delivery and payment take place on a future date which is called the delivery date. The buyer and the seller agree, when they first enter into the contract, the forward price that is to be paid by the buyer on the delivery date and the quantity of the underlying that is to be delivered by the seller on the delivery date. Alternatively, the forward price to be paid by the buyer might be calculated on the delivery date in accordance with a formula that is set out in the futures contract. The futures contract also contains particulars of how delivery of the underlying is to be effected.

4.18 As the definition of a futures contract set out in the preceding paragraph indicates, a futures contract is essentially similar to a forward contract. Indeed, the payment profile of a futures contract, which is illustrated in Figure 4.2, is the same as that for the forward contract illustrated in Figure 4.1. However, there is an important distinction between a futures contract and a forward contract. Whereas a forward contract is individually negotiated between the seller and the buyer, a futures contract contains standard terms. The only term of a futures contract that the seller and the buyer negotiate is the futures price of the contract. The rapid-fire trading of futures contracts on an exchange therefore becomes possible. Forward contracts became standardized during the 19th century. First, the contractual terms governing the quantity and the quality of the underlying being bought and sold became standardized, and then a calendar of delivery dates became established. Standardization of contractual terms enabled the first derivative exchanges to be established. In the United States of America, the Chicago Board of Trade (CBOT) was established in 1848, and the Chicago Produce Exchange was established in 1874. The Chicago Produce Exchange, together with the Butter and Egg Board, became the Chicago Mercantile Exchange (CME) in 1919. Today, futures contracts on soft commodities as well as equity indices and interest rates are traded on these exchanges, the CBOT and the CME competing healthily with each other.

4.19 Paragraph 1.07 indicates that one of the important functions of an exchange is the discovery of prices. The futures price of the underlying is openly negotiated and disseminated to interested parties on an exchange, and therefore the consensus of the market as to the spot price of the underlying on the future delivery date is readily observed. Some indication is thereby given by the futures market as to expectations of movements in the spot price. The number of futures contracts at the end of a trading session which are open is the 'open interest' of that particular futures contract. Open interest is a useful statistic of the supply and demand of that particular futures contract, and can be used to refine an estimation of the spot price of the underlying at the future delivery date. Generally more confidence can be placed on the estimation if open interest is high.

Example of the use of a futures contract

4.20 A futures contract can be used to hedge against an increase in the underlying spot price. On day 1, the underlying spot price is £4,950. The price of the futures contract is £5,000 (to maintain clarity, this example omits the concepts of ticks and tick value). The buyer believes that on day 30, which is the delivery date of the contract, the underlying spot price will be more than £5,000. The buyer therefore buys one futures contract (the buyer goes long one futures contract). The buyer's motivation for doing so might be either that the buyer prefers to lock a futures price of £5,000 on day 30 rather than risk paying more than £5,000 on day 30, or that the buyer prefers to pay £5,000 on day 30 instead of £4,950 on day 1, because the buyer does not have available funds on day 1 but expects to do so on day 30.

4.21 A futures contract can be used to hedge against a decrease in the underlying spot price. On day 1 the underlying spot price is £4,950. The price of the futures contract is £5,000. The seller believes that on day 30 the underlying spot price will be less than £5,000. The seller therefore sells one futures contract (the seller goes short one futures contract). The seller's motivation for doing so might be either that the seller prefers to lock a futures price of £5,000 on day 30 rather than risk receiving less than £5,000 on day 30, or that the seller prefers to receive a better price on day 30 than the price available on day 1.

4.3 Futures Contract

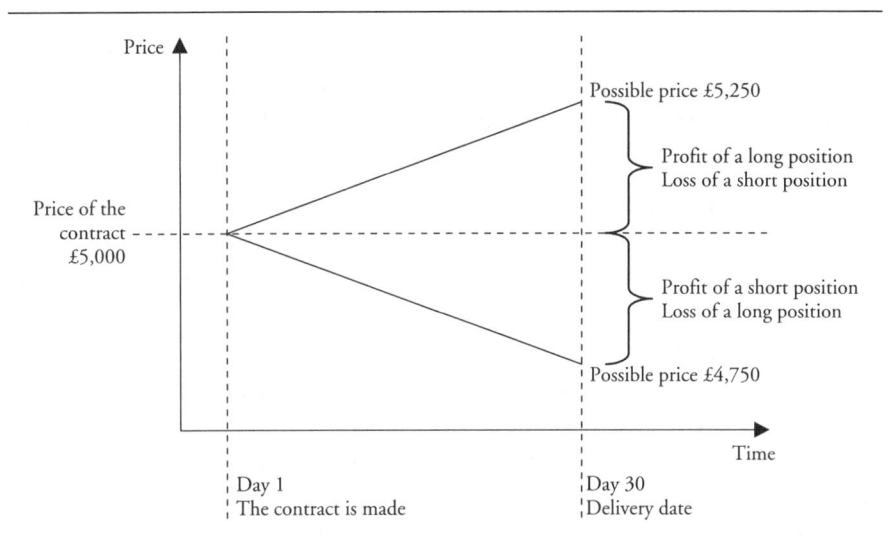

Figure 4.2 The payment profile of a futures contract

Figure 4.2 illustrates the payment profile of the futures contract in this example. **4.22**
Two possible underlying spot prices on day 30 are indicated: £5,250 and £4,750.
The futures price £5,000 is the horizontal dotted line.

The long futures position opened by the buyer in paragraph 4.20 would make a **4.23**
profit if the underlying spot price on day 30 is £5,250. The amount of the buyer's
profit will be £250. On day 30, the buyer will be obliged to take delivery of the
underlying and pay the futures price £5,000, which is £250 less than the spot price
£5,250. If, however, the underlying spot price on day 30 is £4,750, then the buyer
will make a loss. The buyer will be obliged to take delivery of the underlying and
pay the futures price £5,000, which is £250 more than the spot price £4,750.

The short futures position opened by the seller in paragraph 4.21 would make a **4.24**
profit if the underlying spot price on day 30 is £4,750. The amount of the seller's
profit will be £250. On day 30, the seller will be obliged to deliver the underlying
and the seller will receive the futures price £5,000, which is £250 more than the
spot price £4,750. If, however, the underlying spot price on day 30 is £5,250, then
the seller will make a loss. The seller will be obliged to deliver the underlying and
the seller will receive the futures price £5,000, which is £250 less than the futures
price £5,000.

At any possible underlying spot price on the delivery date, the amount of profit **4.25**
made by the buyer will be the same as the amount of the corresponding loss made
by the seller, and the amount of any loss made by the buyer will be the same as the
amount of the corresponding profit made by the seller. Trading derivatives has

sometimes been described as a zero-sum game,[1] and this soubriquet is somewhat justified in the context of the direct relationship between the amounts of the buyer's profit and the seller's loss or the buyer's loss and the seller's profit. There is only one winner who gains at the expense of the loser.

4.26 To maintain clarity, the example set out in the preceding paragraphs does not reflect the incremental payment of losses or the incremental receipt of profits which characterize the margining system that is applied on exchanges. As paragraph 2.14 indicates, on each day that the futures position is open between day 1 and day 30, generally each of the buyer and the seller receives from the clearing house any profit made on that day, and pays to the clearing house any loss made on that day. The two benefits of the clearing system become apparent. One, losses are not paid in one amount on one day, but instead are spread over the period during which the position is open. A person making a loss can close out the position (provided of course that the market is sufficiently liquid) before the loss becomes unbearable. Two, the buyer and the seller do not have a direct exposure to each other. They receive payments from, and make payments to, the clearing house. This second benefit enables futures to be traded very easily.

Trading futures

4.27 After day 1, and before the delivery date day 30, the buyer can close the long position by selling one futures contract into the market, and the seller can close the short position by buying one futures contract from the market. For example, on day 20, the underlying spot price has increased to £5,100 and the price of the futures contract, with the delivery date day 30, has correspondingly increased to £5,200. On day 20, the buyer might sell one futures contract (which cancels the one futures contract the buyer originally bought on day 1, and which therefore closes the long position), having made a profit of £100 (which is the increase in the price of the futures contract). On day 20, the seller might buy one futures contract (which cancels the one futures contract the seller originally sold on day 1, and which therefore closes the short position), having made a loss of £100 (which is the increase in the price of the futures contract). Closing positions by selling and buying further futures contracts is made possible because the contracts are standardized. The futures contract that the buyer originally buys on day 1 is the same as the contract that the buyer subsequently sells on day 20 (both contracts require the payment of the futures price and the delivery of the underlying

---

[1] The term 'zero-sum game' derives from game theory. A zero-sum game is a model of behaviour which postulates that one player's win is made at the expense of another player's loss, and the system in which the players compete is closed, in that the aggregate of all wins and all losses is zero. See paragraph 4.27 for a discussion as to whether or not it is entirely appropriate to use the label 'zero-sum game'.

on day 30); the only difference between the two contracts is the futures price itself. The exchange member who buys from the original buyer (who is selling to close the long position) or who sells to the original seller (who is buying to close the short position) enters into a position with the clearing house after the novation of the transaction to the clearing house. The exchange member's profit or loss will be calculated from a base futures price £5,200, which is the price at which the exchange member buys or sells. The reality of trading futures and the clearing function which supports the exchange tends to disprove the analysis in paragraph 4.25 that trading derivatives is a zero-sum game.[2] The two parties to a transaction usually have different investment horizons and different tolerances to risk, and therefore they will close out their positions at different times. Any loss made by an original buyer is not necessarily the same as any profit made by an original seller, and vice versa.

Futures pricing

4.28 A futures contract is priced using the cost-of-carry model. Carrying an asset is holding that asset from one point in time to the next. Costs are incurred in carrying an asset, and these costs are reflected in the model. The model is based on the assumption that the purchase of a futures contract is equivalent to the purchase of the underlying in the spot market and financing (that is, carrying) that underlying to the delivery date of the futures contract. For example, the underlying spot price is £1,000. The financing rate is 8% per annum. Therefore the price of the three month futures contract is £1,020, which is calculated as £1,000 + (£1,000 * (8% * 0.25)). Three months is 0.25 of one year.

4.29 The financing rate depends on the underlying. For example, the financing rate of a physical commodity reflects the costs of practical necessities such as warehousing, transport, insurance and interest charges, and perhaps a deduction might be made to accommodate any deterioration in the quality of that commodity and therefore any decrease in its value. Different financing rates are used for different types of underlying, and the calculation must be refined to reflect any return made by the underlying during the period when it is carried. This is particularly important in the context of financial futures: financial assets generate a yield (interest is paid in respect of debt securities and dividends are paid in respect of equity securities), which must be reflected in the cost-of-carry model that is used.

---

[2] This analysis supports the observation that the distinction between a zero-sum game and a non-zero-sum game is that a zero-sum game for a particular number of players is a non-zero-sum game for that same number of players plus an extra player, the extra player representing the loss or the gain of the system within which the players compete. See von Neumann and Morgenstern, *Theory of Games and Economic Behaviour* (Princeton University, 60th anniversary edition, 2007).

4.30 The underlying spot price converges with the price of the futures contract during the period up to the delivery date of the futures contract, and on the delivery date of the futures contract, the underlying spot price should be the same as the futures price. Before the delivery date, the usual market condition is that the futures price is higher than the underlying spot price, and this is called contango. However, sometimes the underlying spot price is higher than the futures price, and this is called backwardation. Backwardation occurs when the underlying is scarce in the short term, and this scarcity drives the spot price up. The usual market condition contango is restored as the expectation grows that more of the underlying will become available in the longer term. The practicalities of the commodities market often give rise to the disconnection of the futures price from the level suggested by adjusting the spot price by the appropriate cost-of-carry model. For example, the underlying spot price might be driven down to a low level by a significant surplus of the underlying in the short term, but the futures price does not respond to the same extent. Factors such as warehousing costs, transportation costs, and even the cost of certain industrial processes (for example, the availability of the facilities to refine sugar) become relevant. The costs of these facilities (warehousing, transportation, and industrial processes) are determined by supply and demand for these facilities.

4.31 The first futures contracts evolved from agricultural and commodity forward contracts, and enabled the first exchanges to be established, both in Europe and in the United States of America. Financial futures contracts were developed in the 20th century, on shares, indices, bonds, money market instruments, interest rates and (on a limited number of exchanges) currencies. In the United Kingdom, the FTSE 100 share index was created in 1984 (with a base value of 1,000) specifically in order to enable the trading of share index futures on LIFFE, which was then newly established (see Chapter 2).

4.4 Option Contract

4.32 The holder (or buyer) of an option decides whether or not to exercise the right that is conferred by the option contract. If the holder decides to exercise the right, then both the holder and the writer (the seller) of the option owe to each other the obligations set out in the option contract. It is important to appreciate that the writer of the option contract has no choice as to whether or not the option is exercised: this is entirely the decision of the holder of the option. The holder pays a premium to the writer to buy the option from the buyer.

4.33 A call option gives the holder the right to buy (to call) from the writer the specified underlying at the specified exercise price.[3] A put option gives the holder the right

---

[3] The term 'exercise price' is used interchangeably with the term 'strike price'.

4.4 Option Contract

to sell (to put) to the writer the specified underlying at the specified exercise price. An option, whether a call or a put, expires on the specified expiry date. Any right conferred by the option contract can only be exercised by the holder before or on the specified expiry date. The two most common options are the American-style option and the European-style option. An American-style option can generally be exercised at any time before and including its expiry date, whereas a European-style option can only be exercised on its expiry date. The options described in this paragraph are usually referred to as 'vanilla' options, in that they have no special features.

There are many types of 'exotic' option which have special features that vanilla options do not have, and these exotic options tend to be found in the OTC market. An Asian option (which is also known as an average rate option) is an option the exercise price of which is the average price of the underlying over a specified period. An Asian option is a path-dependant option.[4] The rights under a barrier option[5] are either switched on or switched off, as it were, if and when the price of the underlying reaches a prescribed threshold or 'barrier'. A Bermudan option can be exercised only on one of a series of specified dates before its expiry date. A cliquet option (which is also known as a ratchet option) is an option the exercise price of which is reset periodically before its expiry date, usually so that advantageous movements in the underlying are effectively secured. A digital option is an option which pays out a specified amount in the event that the price or level of the underlying reaches a specified threshold[6] but pays out nothing if that specified threshold is not reached. A lookback option gives the holder the right to exercise at the most favourable price that the underlying achieves during a specified price. A rainbow option gives the holder the right to choose which asset to buy, in the case of a call rainbow option, or to sell, in the case of a put rainbow option, out of a specified selection. **4.34**

Options are dealt OTC as well as on exchanges, and the basic principles are the same, whether the option is individually and privately negotiated between the writer and the holder in the OTC market or whether the option is a standard contract that is listed and traded on an exchange. **4.35**

---

[4] An option is path-dependent if its operation and the pay-off it generates depend on the performance of the underlying over a period, that is, the path taken by the underlying.
[5] The right to buy or to sell the underlying under a knock-in barrier option only becomes available if the price of the underlying reaches the prescribed knock-in threshold. The right to buy or to sell the underlying under a knock-out barrier option only remains available if the price of the underlying never reaches the prescribed knock-out threshold.
[6] An all-or-nothing digital option pays out a specified amount in the event that the price or level of the underlying is either above or below a specified threshold on its expiry date. A one-touch option pays out a specified amount in the event that the price or level of the underlying reaches a specified threshold at any time before its expiry date.

Chapter 4: Products

4.36 In the following analyses, U is the underlying spot price, E is the exercise price specified in the option contract, and P is the premium paid by the holder to the writer to buy the option.

Analysing a long call position

4.37 Figure 4.3 illustrates the P&L on the expiry date of a call option that has been bought. The cost to the holder of buying the underlying (at or before the expiry date) through exercising the option is an amount X, which is E plus P. The holder first pays P to buy the option, then pays E if the holder exercises the option and buys the underlying under the terms of the option contract. Whether or not the holder would make a profit through exercising the option depends on U. If U is more than X, then the holder would make a profit through exercising the option. The amount of the holder's profit would be the amount by which U is more than X. The amount of the holder's profit is potentially unlimited. If U is between X and E, then the holder would make a loss through exercising the option. The amount of the holder's loss would be the amount by which U is less than X. The holder would make less of a loss through exercising the option than not exercising the option. If U is less than E, then the holder would not exercise the option because the holder can buy the underlying more cheaply in the spot market without exercising the option. The holder would lose the entire premium.

4.38 It is important to note that an option which cannot be exercised profitably is not necessarily without value during its life to the expiry date. Indeed, the concept that an option which cannot be exercised profitably at a particular time before its expiry nonetheless retains some value at that time is a key element of option pricing theory, which is introduced below.

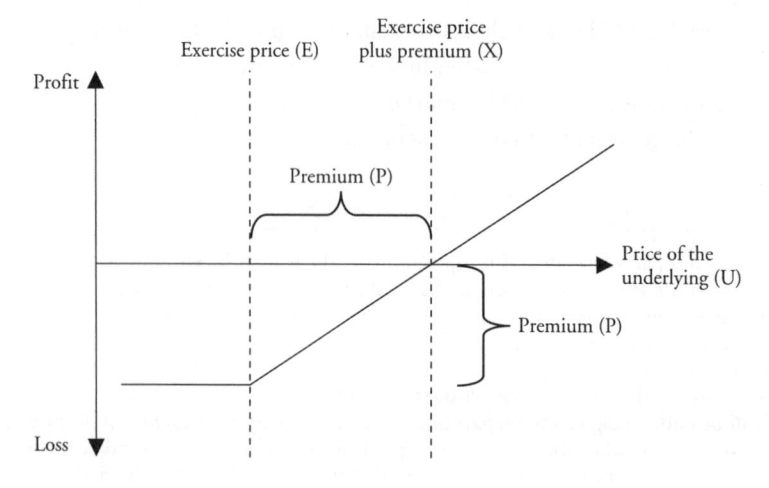

Figure 4.3 Long call

4.4 Option Contract

Analysing a short call position

Figure 4.4 illustrates the P&L on the expiry date of a call option that has been sold. Whether or not the writer would make a profit if the holder exercises the option depends on U. The cost to the holder of buying the underlying (at or before the expiry date) through exercising the option is an amount X, which is E plus P. If U is more than X, then the writer would make a loss if the holder exercises the option. The amount of the writer's loss would be the amount by which U is more than X. The amount of the writer's loss is potentially unlimited. If U is between E and X, then the writer would make a profit if the holder exercises the option. The amount of the writer's profit would be the amount by which U is less than X. If U is less than E, then the holder would not exercise the option, because the holder can buy the underlying more cheaply in the spot market without exercising the option (under the terms of which the holder would pay E) and the writer's entire profit is P. **4.39**

These analyses again illustrate that trading derivatives is from one perspective a zero-sum game. Again, there is a direct relationship between the amount of the holder's profit and the writer's loss, or between the holder's loss and the writer's profit. There is only one winner. **4.40**

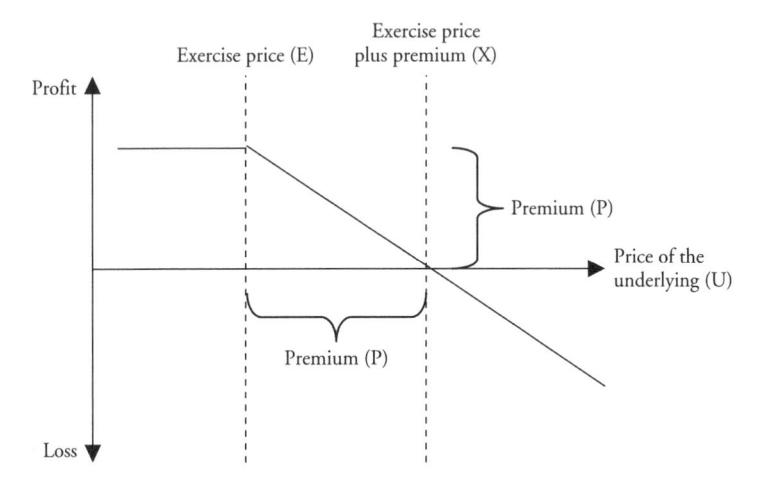

Figure 4.4 Short call

Analysing a long put position

Figure 4.5 illustrates the P&L on the expiry date of a put option that has been bought. The amount that the holder receives for selling the underlying (at or before the expiry date) through exercising the option is an amount X, which is E minus P. The holder first pays P to buy the option, and then receives E if he exercises the option and sells the underlying under the terms of the option **4.41**

Chapter 4: Products

contract. Whether or not the holder would make a profit through exercising the option depends on U. If U is more than E, then the holder would not exercise the option because he can sell the underlying for a higher price in the spot market without exercising the option. The holder would lose the entire premium. If U is between X and E, then the holder would make a loss through exercising the option. The amount of the holder's loss would be the amount by which U is more than X. The holder would make less of loss through exercising the option than not exercising the option. If U is less than X, then the holder would make a profit through exercising the option. The amount of the holder's profit would be the amount by which U is less than X. The amount of the holder's profit is potentially X (the holder's potential profit is of course limited by the fact that U can decrease to zero and not lower).

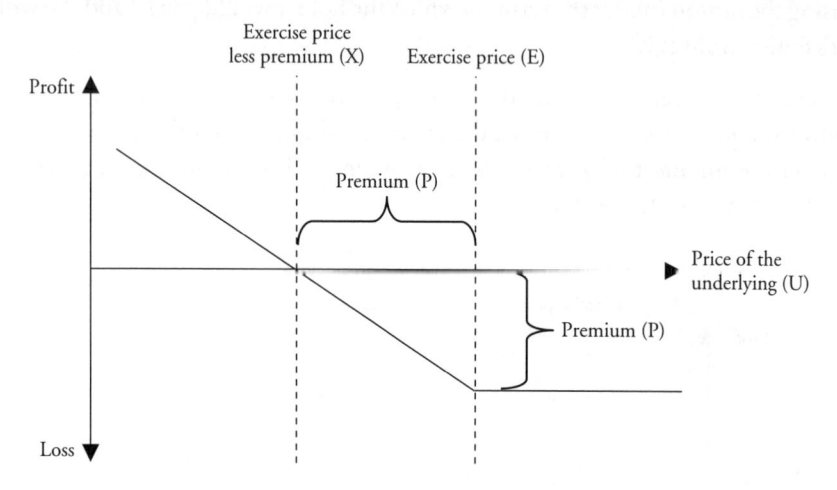

Figure 4.5 Long put

Analysing a short put position

4.42 Figure 4.6 illustrates the P&L on the expiry date of a put option that has been sold. Whether or not the writer would make a profit if the holder exercises the option depends on U. The amount that the holder receives for selling the underlying (at or before the expiry date) through exercising the option is an amount X, which is E minus P. If U is more than E, then the holder would not exercise the option, because the holder can sell the underlying for a higher price in the spot market without exercising the option (under the terms of which the holder would receive E) and the writer's entire profit is P. If U is between X and E, then the writer would make a profit if the holder exercises the option. The amount of the writer's profit would be the amount by which U is more than X. If U is less than X, then the writer would make a loss if the holder exercises the option. The amount of the writer's loss would be the amount by which U is less than X. The amount of the

4.4 Option Contract

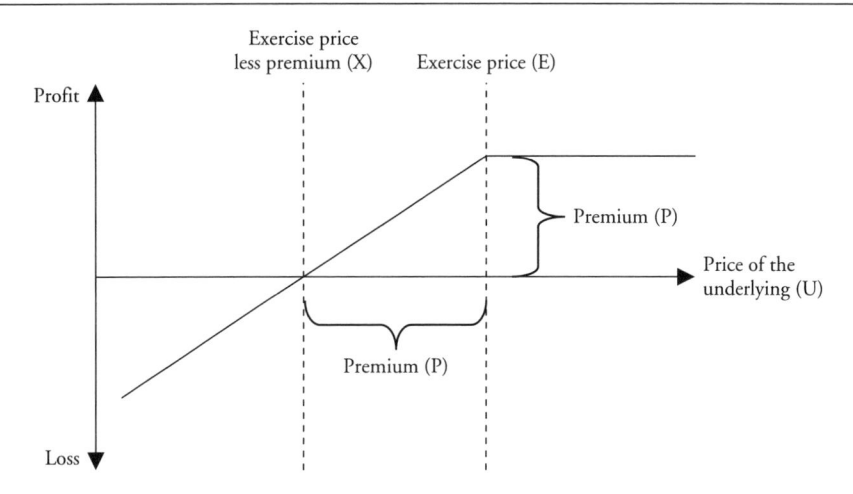

Figure 4.6 Short put

writer's loss is potentially X (the writer's potential loss is of course limited by the fact that U can decrease to zero and not lower).

Option strategies

An option strategy may employ combinations of call options and put options, comprising short positions and long positions of options, and depending on the strategy, perhaps even with different exercise prices and different expiry dates. These strategies can create sophisticated exposures to the underlying. **4.43**

Option pricing[7]

The holder decides whether or not to exercise the option on the basis of whether or not exercising the option would be profitable. As the previous paragraphs demonstrate, the pay-off generated by an option is determined, at an intrinsic level, by the relationship between U and E. A call option is in-the-money if U is more than E. Exercise of the option by the holder would enable the holder to buy the underlying for a lower price than the holder would pay in the spot market. Such an option has intrinsic value, which is the amount by which U is more than E. A call option is out-of-the-money if U is less than E. The holder would not exercise the option because the holder can buy the underlying in the spot market for a lower price than the holder would pay if the holder exercised the option and bought the underlying under the terms of the option. A put option is in-the-money if U is less than E. Exercise of the option by the holder would enable the holder to sell the underlying **4.44**

---

[7] See Das, *Swaps/Financial Derivatives* (John Wiley & Sons Inc., 2005), and Hull, *Options, Futures, and Other Derivatives* (Prentice Hall, 2008).

Chapter 4: Products

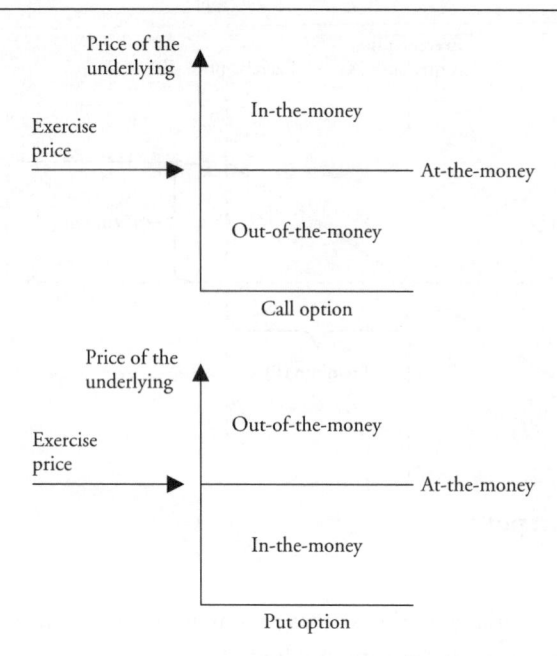

Figure 4.7 In-the money, at-the-money, and out-of-the-money

for a higher price than the holder would receive in the spot market. Such an option has intrinsic value, which is the amount by which U is less than E. A put option is out-of-the-money if U is more than E. The holder would not exercise the option because the holder can sell the underlying in the spot market for a higher price than the holder would receive if the holder exercised the option and sold the underlying under the terms of the option. An option might be deeply in-the-money or deeply out-of-the-money. An option, whether a call option or a put option, is at-the-money if U is equal to E. Figure 4.7 illustrates how an option might be in-the-money, at-the-money or out-of-the-money.

4.45 In comparison with futures pricing, option pricing is extremely complex and is largely outside the scope of this book. Mathematical pricing models have been developed to calculate the theoretical value of different types of option written on different types of underlying. The fundamental concept of option pricing is the calculation of the pay-off generated by the relationship between U and E. E usually remains the same during the life of the option, whereas U changes, or exhibits volatility.[8]

---

[8] Of course, certain types of option feature the complexity that E changes over the life of the option, such as cliquet or ratchet options, and barrier options feature the complexity that the right conferred by the option contract, whether to buy or to sell the underlying, is either switched on or switched off, as it were, if and when U reaches prescribed barriers.

4.4 Option Contract

4.46 Volatility is the measurement of the variability, but not the direction, of movements in U.[9] That is, volatility is the measurement of the extent to which U fluctuates. Volatility is the most important variable in the calculation of the price of an option. The price of an option is almost (but not exactly) directly proportional to the level of volatility exhibited by U. The price of an option increases if volatility increases, and the price of an option decreases if volatility decreases. The writer of an option may wish to hedge against the possibility that the option is exercised by the holder. In order to remain perfectly hedged, that is, neither over-hedged nor under-hedged, the writer enters into transactions to buy and to sell the underlying as required. Thus, if the spot market for the underlying is more volatile, then the price of the option increases in order to compensate the writer for the more frequent adjustments that the writer must make to maintain the perfect hedge, by trading the underlying and incurring costs in doing so. Therefore the observation is made that option pricing theory is in part built on the dynamic hedging of the underlying.

4.47 There are two measures of volatility. Historical volatility is calculated with reference to an existing data population of past movements in U. Implied volatility is the volatility of the movements in U which gives rise to a particular price of an option. The market for an option indicates a particular price for that option, and that price is the result of a particular degree of volatility, the implied volatility, which is the consensus of the market as to the volatility of the movements in the underlying. Therefore, implied volatility can be extracted from an option pricing model into which the market price of the option is fed.

4.48 An option which is out-of-the-money might nonetheless have some value depending on the time remaining before the expiry date and the level of volatility exhibited by U. Such an option has the potential to move in-the-money before the expiry date and therefore increase in value. An element of the value of an option is therefore time value. Of course, an option which is in-the-money also has time value. An option loses time value as the expiry date draws near. This phenomenon is known as time decay. Time decay operates to the disadvantage of the holder and to the advantage of the writer.

4.49 An option pricing model must simulate the movements in U within boundaries that are determined by both the volatility exhibited by U and the life of the option. The simulation of the movement of U within these boundaries over the life of the option is achieved by applying probability theory. Generally, the distribution of movements in U should be such that it is less likely that U moves along the

---

[9] Volatility is usually measured as the annualized standard deviation of the daily movements in the price of the underlying. Variance is volatility squared, and forms the underlying of the variance swap, which is a new type of derivative. See part 4.14 of this chapter.

boundaries and more likely that U moves between the boundaries. Whether or not the movements in U demonstrate a normal distribution should be reflected by the option pricing model.

4.50 It is important to monitor the performance of an open option position, whether a long position or a short position, and to manage that position. Knowing the theoretical value of the option is not enough: it is important to model the sensitivity of the price of the option to various factors, in order to refine the strategy. An option pricing model, if manipulated, provides data other than the theoretical value of the option. These data include the five Option Greeks, which demonstrate the sensitivity of certain values to changes in other values. The Option Greeks and other option metrics generally comprise the following.

- Delta indicates the sensitivity of P to movements in U. The value of delta is between 0 and 1. Delta of 1 indicates that P changes at the same rate as U, whereas delta of 0 indicates that P does not change in response to changes in U. Charm indicates how delta changes over time.
- Gamma indicates the sensitivity of delta to movements in U. Colour indicates how gamma changes over time.
- Lambda (or kappa or vega) indicates the sensitivity of P to changes in the volatility exhibited by U.
- Rho indicates the sensitivity of P to changes in the rate of return achieved by a theoretical risk-free investment.
- Theta indicates the sensitivity of P to the passage of time to the expiry date.

4.51 It is important to appreciate that the inter-dependencies of the various factors which determine the price of the option[10] may mean that even if the trader correctly forecasts the performance of one of the factors (say, the movements in U), the combined effect of that factor and the others (say, the volatility of the movements in U) may mean that the trader nonetheless makes a loss.

Automatic exercise

4.52 Some option contracts are exercised automatically on their expiry date. An option that is subject to automatic exercise is deemed to be exercised by the holder on its expiry date if it is in-the-money from the perspective of the holder, and any payment or delivery under that option contract is then required to be made. The principal benefit for the holder of the option is that the holder does not need to serve an exercise notice. Another type of option is the 'autocall' option.

---

[10] Different option pricing models require different inputs, depending on the features of the option. The Black Scholes Equation requires the input of values for U, E, expected volatility, the risk-free interest rate, and the time remaining before expiry. The underlying is not assumed to pay dividends, therefore no dividend amount is required.

An autocall option (or barrier option) is exercised automatically at any time before its expiry date if U increases to a specified threshold, or barrier.

The Black Scholes Equation

The most important option pricing model, because it was the first for which a mathematical proof was formally set out, is the Black Scholes Equation, which was proved by Fischer Black and Myron Scholes in 1973.[11] Black and Scholes, with Robert Merton, developed a mathematical proof which demonstrated that a formula which had been drawn up earlier in 1962 by A. James Boness in a Ph.D. dissertation at the University of Chicago[12] has a valid application in modern finance. The Black Scholes Equation is an adaptation and improvement on Boness's formula. In recognition of the importance of the equation to modern finance, Myron Scholes and Robert Merton were awarded the Nobel Prize in economics by the Royal Swedish Academy of Sciences on 14 October 1997. Fischer Black had passed away in 1995. The Black Scholes Equation was originally formulated to calculate the theoretical value of a European option on an equity security in respect of which no dividend is paid. The Black Scholes economy is based on the simplifying assumption that interest rates are constant during the life of the option. Later pricing models include refinements to predict the movement of interest rates over the life of the option.

4.53

The origin and development of option technique

Greek, Roman and Phoenician traders in the ancient world were known to have made use of option techniques as they bought and sold cargoes. Commentators also believe that Thales, the Greek philosopher and mathematician,[13] was one of the world's first option speculators. Thales predicted one year that the harvest for olives would be particularly good and that therefore there would be strong demand for olive presses. He therefore bought options to buy the rights to use olive presses. Thales bought these options, on olive press capacity, during the off-season when there was little demand for olive presses and when therefore the price of the use of olive presses was low and the options were correspondingly cheap. However, during the harvest, which was good as Thales had predicted, demand for olive presses became very strong. Thales exercised his options and bought olive press capacity, paying the exercise price of the options, which was less than the prevailing price of the use of olive presses. He was then able to lease out to farmers at the prevailing market rate the use of the presses of which he gained control through the exercise

4.54

---

[11] 'Journal of Finance', 1973.
[12] *A Theory and Measurement of Stock Option Value*, 1962.
[13] Thales is believed to have been born in Miletus in about 624 BC. He is known for predicting an eclipse of the sun, and in his mathematics he sought to enumerate natural laws.

of his options, and he realized a profit, which was the difference between the lower exercise price of his options and the higher prevailing market rate.

4.55 Almost two millennia later, the business of offering option contracts was well developed in the 19th century, with put and call brokers making available options written on a limited number of shares. Put and call option contracts became known as 'privileges' in the United States of America. There was no formal market for these options, which were individually negotiated by the writers and the holders. These options were tailored to individual transactions, and therefore brokers tried to generate liquidity by soliciting advertisements in newspapers. In London, traditional options were offered by stockbrokers to their customers. Like privileges in the US market, traditional options, whether call options or put options, are contracts that are entered into on an individual basis and therefore they lack the liquidity of standard contracts that are listed and traded on an exchange. This activity in the 19th century was observed by Charles Castelli, who wrote a book in 1877 called *The Theory of Options in Stocks and Shares*. Castelli's work did not seek to lay any theoretical foundation, but instead explored and explained the hedging and speculative uses of options. Early option trading was somewhat cumbersome, as market participants had no reliable means of valuing their contracts, and they certainly had no access to the modern analytical techniques described in the preceding paragraphs. Only the innovation in the 20th century of exchange-based option trading and the parallel development of modern computational techniques unlocked the potential of option trading.

4.56 Perhaps the seminal work in option pricing was developed by Louis Bachelier in 1900, in his dissertation *Théorie de la Spéculation*, written at the Sorbonne. Bachelier was truly ahead of his time. He predicted the random walk of asset prices and developed the concept of using the Brownian[14] analysis of particle movements to model the movements in asset prices. Although the option pricing model that he proposed allowed in theory the price of an option to exceed the price of the underlying, Bachelier's work is nonetheless significant, although his work was overlooked for nearly 50 years. After developing his work on option pricing, Bachelier spent the remainder of his career in obscurity.

4.57 However, in 1955, Paul Samuelson at the Massachusetts Institute of Technology, having read Bachelier's work, wrote a paper, *Brownian Motion in the Stock Market*. In the same year, Kruizenga, one of Samuelson's students, cited Bachelier's

---

[14] Brownian motion is the random movement of particles suspended in a fluid, whether a liquid or a gas, and is named after the botanist Robert Brown (1773–1858), who observed and described the random movement of particles suspended within pollen grains. Models have been developed to capture this random movement, using probability theory. The application of Brownian analysis to asset prices seeks to identify parallels between random movements of particles and random movements in asset prices.

work in his paper, *Put and Call Options: A Theoretical Market Analysis*. It was Boness who, refining this earlier work, in 1962 developed the pricing model which Black and Scholes would build on and mathematically prove in 1973, thereby laying the foundation for modern option mathematics.

The exponential growth in computing power[15] since the 1960s has facilitated the development of option pricing techniques,[16] and undoubtedly the prototype spreadsheets which became available during the 1970s allowed the complexities of American options (and their ability to be exercised at generally any time before expiry) to be explored more easily than was previously possible.   **4.58**

Many other option pricing models have been developed since the Black Scholes Equation, although the Black Scholes Equation remains a solid foundation for option pricing, and indeed the equation has found use in other fields of financial mathematics. These other pricing models are specific to different types of underlying and to different types of option rights. Option pricing mathematics is a very fruitful and dynamic branch of financial mathematics, and this book only identifies a few of the many models that have been devised. Paragraph 4.34 identifies only some of the many types of option contract that have been devised, and each type of option presents the financial engineer with the task of developing a robust and appropriate pricing and valuation methodology. Many different pricing models have been formulated, and the following list is only representative of the growing universe of models. The Black model (1976) was formulated to price commodity options and commodity forward contracts. The Garman and Kohlhagen model (1983) was formulated to price foreign exchange options. The Grabbe model (1983) was formulated to price foreign exchange options. The Cox, Ingersoll, and Ross model (1985) was formulated to price bonds and bond options. The Heath, Jarrow, and Morton model (1992) was formulated to price bonds and bond options. The Chiang and Okunev model (1995) was formulated to price foreign exchange options.   **4.59**

4.5 Warrant

A call warrant, which is usually referred to simply as a 'warrant', is similar to a call option, in that the holder has the right, but not the obligation, to buy the underlying equity or debt securities at the specified exercise price. However, a warrant is   **4.60**

---

[15] The growth in computing power is said to observe Moore's law, after Gordon Moore, one of the co-founders of microprocessor manufacturer Intel, who in 1965 theorized that the processing capability of microprocessor circuitry doubles every two years.

[16] Manufacturers of early electronic pocket calculators in the mid-1970s included option pricing functions in their equipment.

itself a security that is traded on an exchange in the same manner as the underlying equity or debt securities. The pay-off generated by a warrant is determined, like the pay-off generated by an option, at an intrinsic level by the relationship between the underlying spot price and the exercise price specified in the terms and conditions of the warrant. The market for warrants is separate from, but linked to, the market for the underlying securities.

4.61 There are important distinctions between a warrant and an option. Whereas an option is written by an investor or a trader, a warrant is only issued by the entity which issues the underlying securities. Whereas exchange-based options tend to be listed and traded on specialist derivative exchanges, warrants tend to be listed and traded on stock exchanges. Warrants tend to have longer lives to expiry than options.

4.62 Put warrants also exist, and these are similar to put options, subject to the same distinctions which are made in the preceding paragraph.

4.6 Forward Rate Agreement

4.63 A forward rate agreement (FRA) specifies the rate of interest that is applied to a notional underlying loan or a notional underlying deposit. The FRA contract also specifies the underlying notional amount of money to which the rate of interest is applied, the start date of the notional underlying loan or deposit, and the end date of the notional underlying loan or deposit. An FRA can be used to hedge against exposures to unfavourable movements in interest rates arising in respect of loans and deposits.

Hedging in respect of a loan

4.64 For example, on 1 June a borrower enters into a three month loan facility, under which the borrower will draw down funds on 1 July. The loan will be repaid on 30 September. Interest on the loan will be paid at the rate known as three month sterling LIBOR and the rate will be fixed when the loan is drawn down on 1 July. The rate will change between 1 June and 1 July. The borrower is concerned that the rate will increase during this period, increasing the funding costs of the loan. The borrower might therefore enter into an FRA with a dealer to hedge against this potential increase in funding costs.

4.65 The particular FRA that the borrower requires on 1 June is the 1x4 FRA, which is the FRA for a notional loan or deposit starting in one month and maturing in four months. The dealer quotes a bid and offer spread of 3.25–3.28 for the FRA. The borrower pays the offer rate 3.28% for the FRA because the borrower is buying the FRA from the dealer. Under the FRA, on the settlement date 1 July, if the rate

4.6 Forward Rate Agreement

is more than 3.28%, then the dealer pays the borrower the amount by which the rate is more than 3.28%, and if the rate is less than 3.28%, then the borrower pays the dealer the amount by which the rate is less than 3.28%. By using the FRA, the borrower has replaced an uncertain liability to pay interest by a certain liability which is known in advance, but foregoing any decrease in the rate below the fixed 3.28%. The operation of the FRA recollects the operation of a forward contract examined above.

Hedging in respect of a deposit

For example, on 1 June a depositor proposes to place funds on deposit for five months starting on 1 July. The deposit will mature on 30 November. Interest on the deposit will be paid at the rate known as five month sterling LIBOR and the rate will be fixed when the deposit is made on 1 July. The rate will change between 1 June and 1 July. The depositor is concerned that the rate will decrease during this period, decreasing the interest that will be earned on the deposit. The depositor might therefore enter into an FRA with a dealer to hedge against this potential decrease in interest earned. **4.66**

The particular FRA that the depositor requires on 1 June is the 1x6 FRA, which is the FRA for a notional loan or deposit starting in one month and maturing in six months. The dealer quotes a bid and offer spread of 3.26–3.29 for the FRA. The depositor receives the bid rate 3.26% because the depositor is selling the FRA to the dealer. Under the FRA, on the settlement date 1 July, if the rate is less than 3.26%, then the dealer pays to the depositor the amount by which the rate is less then 3.26%, and if the rate is more than 3.26%, then the depositor will pay to the dealer the amount by which the rate is more than 3.26%. By using the FRA, the depositor has replaced an uncertain return of interest received by a certain return which is known in advance, but foregoing any increase in the rate above the fixed 3.26%. Again, the operation of the FRA recollects the operation of a forward contract examined above. **4.67**

Discounting funds

An amount that is paid by the dealer, by the borrower, or by the depositor in the examples set out in the preceding paragraphs is discounted to reflect the return that would be earned on that amount during the term of the loan or the deposit. The reason for discounting is that a recipient of a particular amount that is scheduled to be paid at a specified future time should be indifferent as to whether that particular amount is received at that specified future time or a lesser amount is received now, provided that the lesser amount received now will grow, if invested according to a benchmark, to equal or exceed that particular amount at that specified future time. **4.68**

4.7 Swap

4.69 Although swaps have attracted many complex and sometimes not immediately helpful definitions, a swap is most simply a contract which gives rise to the rights and obligations of each party to receive from the other party, or to make to the other party, a series of payments in accordance with a specified timetable. Whether a party makes or receives a payment on a particular date in that timetable will be determined by the movement of a particular underlying rate or price. A swap is therefore a series of forward payments. A swap might last for several years, or even decades. The amount of each payment is calculated with reference to an underlying notional amount, whether an amount of money (in the case of an interest rate swap), a quantity of a commodity (in the case of a commodity swap), a number of shares or share indices (in the case of an equity swap), or a number of bonds (in the case of a bond swap). It is important to appreciate that a swap does not give rise to an obligation to pay or to deliver the notional underlying.

4.70 The operation of a swap is most usefully illustrated by considering an interest rate swap. An interest rate swap can be used either to hedge against an unfavourable movement in interest rates, or it can be used to obtain better funding costs.

Hedging using an interest rate swap

4.71 A borrower has borrowed funds under a loan agreement. Under the loan, the borrower is required to make payments of interest at the loan rate, which is a variable (or floating) rate of interest. The borrower is therefore exposed to the interest rate risk that the loan floating rate might increase, thereby increasing its funding costs. The borrower might therefore use a swap to hedge against this interest rate risk. The borrower would buy a swap from a dealer (its swap counterparty). Under the swap, the borrower makes payments to the dealer of swap fixed amounts. Each fixed amount is calculated with reference to the underlying notional amount of the swap and the swap fixed rate. Under the swap, the dealer makes payments to the borrower of swap floating amounts. Each floating amount is calculated with reference to the underlying notional amount of the swap and the swap floating rate. From a broader perspective, it is useful to note that the parties are said to make payments of 'interest' under an interest rate swap. The amount of a payment is calculated with reference to the underlying notional amount of money and the specified interest rate. The character of the payments made under a swap contract can be very important in determining the tax treatment of the transaction.[17]

---

[17] See Chapter 11.

4.7 Swap

Crucially, the swap does not cancel the borrower's obligation to make payments of interest under the loan. Instead, the swap operates alongside the borrower's underlying borrowing transaction. The effect of the swap is that the borrower's exposure to an obligation to make payments of interest at the loan floating rate is neutralized and replaced by an exposure to an obligation to make payments of interest at the swap fixed rate. As Figure 4.8 demonstrates, the swap is effectively superimposed over the borrower's underlying borrowing transaction and it changes the borrower's exposure to movements in the loan floating rate. The swap floating rate that the borrower receives from the dealer offsets the loan floating rate the borrower pays to the lender. The borrower thus has an exposure only to the obligation to make payments of interest at the swap fixed rate. **4.72**

It is therefore important that there is a precise correlation between the loan floating rate paid by the borrower and the swap floating rate received by the borrower, and from time to time between the amount outstanding in respect of the loan and the underlying notional amount of the swap, in order that the borrower's interest rate risk is fully hedged. **4.73**

In order to develop a numerical example of the operation of the swap, assume that the borrower has borrowed £100 million on 1 January at a floating rate of interest which is set with reference to one of the LIBOR rates determined by the British Bankers' Association. The borrower pays interest in arrears on the principal of the loan outstanding every three months, at a rate of three month sterling LIBOR, which is just referred to in this example as 'LIBOR'. The borrower also pays back **4.74**

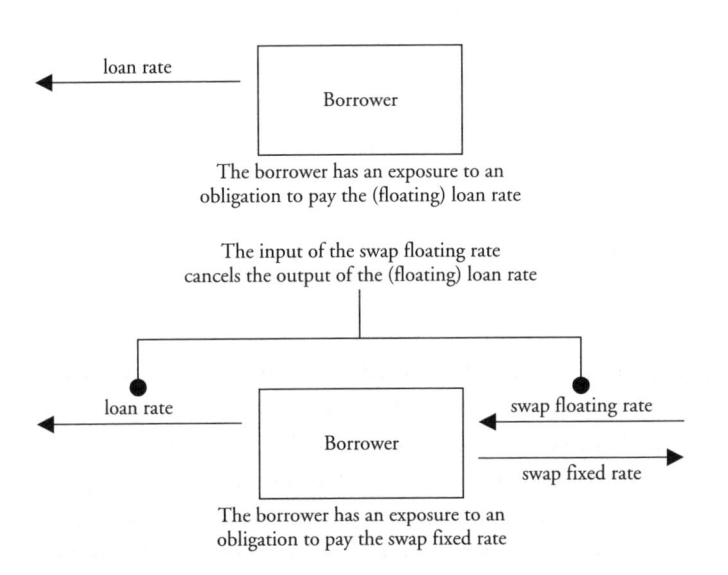

Figure 4.8 The offsetting between the swap floating rate and the loan floating rate, leaving the swap fixed rate

£10 million of the principal of the loan on each interest payment date. The schedule of payments made by the borrower under the loan is therefore set out in the following table.

Interest payment date	Principal of loan outstanding (£ million)	Repayment of principal (£ million)
31 March	100	10
30 June	90	10
30 September	80	10
31 December	70	10
etc.		

4.75 The borrower determines that it does not wish to pay more than 7% interest on the loan. Therefore the borrower buys an interest rate swap from a dealer, the purpose of which is to establish a protected rate of 7% for the borrower's cost of borrowing under the loan. Under the swap, the borrower pays the dealer the swap fixed rate of 7% and the dealer pays the borrower the swap floating rate, which is LIBOR. The borrower and the dealer enter into the swap on 1 January, and each interest payment date under the loan has a corresponding swap payment date, on which the borrower and the dealer make their payments. The schedule of payments made by the borrower and the dealer under the swap is therefore as set out in the following table. Paragraph 4.73 draws attention to the requirement that there is a precise correlation between the amount outstanding in respect of the loan and the underlying notional amount of the swap. The table set out below demonstrates that the underlying notional amount of the swap amortizes in synchrony with the principal amount of the loan.

Swap payment date	Underlying notional amount (£ million)
31 March	100
30 June	90
30 September	80
31 December	70
etc.	

4.76 On the first interest payment date (31 March), LIBOR is 8%. Under the loan, the borrower pays an excess of 1% more than the 7% protected rate. The interest rate risk to which the borrower is exposed crystallizes. However, under the swap, the swap floating rate paid by the dealer to the borrower is 8%, the swap fixed rate paid by the borrower to the dealer is 7%, and a net payment of 1% is made by the dealer to the borrower. The 1% that the borrower receives from the dealer under the swap offsets the excess of 1% that the borrower pays under the loan. The combined effect of the loan and the swap is that the borrower pays the protected rate 7%.

4.7 Swap

The swap is in-the-money from the borrower's perspective. The swap has value because it operates to neutralize the crystallization of the interest rate risk.

4.77 On the second interest payment date (30 June), LIBOR is 5%. The borrower pays a shortfall of 2% less than the 7% protected rate. The interest rate risk to which the borrower is exposed does not crystallize. However, under the swap, the swap floating rate paid by the dealer to the borrower is 5%, the swap fixed rate paid by the borrower to the dealer is 7%, and a net payment of 2% is made by the borrower to the dealer. The 2% that the borrower pays to the dealer under the swap offsets the shortfall of 2% that the borrower pays under the loan. The combined effect of the loan and the swap is that the borrower pays the protected rate 7%. The swap is out-of-the-money from the borrower's perspective.

4.78 On the third interest payment date (30 June), LIBOR is 7%. The borrower pays the protected rate 7%. The interest rate risk to which the borrower is exposed does not crystallize. However, under the swap, the floating rate paid by the dealer to the borrower is 7%, the swap fixed rate paid by the borrower to the dealer is 7%, and no net payment is made. No payment is made under the swap, but as the borrower already pays the protected rate under the loan, no payment under the swap is required. The swap is at-the-money from the borrower's perspective.

4.79 On the first interest payment date, which is considered at paragraph 4.76, the advantage to the borrower of using the swap is evident. Without the swap, the borrower would have been required to pay interest at 8% under the loan, which is more than the protected rate 7%. The effect of the swap is that the borrower pays interest at the protected rate. The second interest payment date, which is considered at paragraph 4.77, demonstrates the cost to the borrower of using the swap. Without the swap, the borrower would have been required to pay interest at 5% under the loan, which is 2% less than the protected rate 7%. However, the effect of the swap is that the borrower pays interest at the protected rate. Therefore on some occasions, such as the first interest payment date, the borrower benefits from the swap, because the swap limits the borrower's overall obligation to pay interest at the protected rate. The swap is in-the-money from the borrower's perspective. On other occasions, such as the second interest payment date, the borrower does not benefit from the swap, as the swap increases the borrower's overall obligation to pay interest at the protected rate. The swap is out-of-the-money from the borrower's perspective. Therefore the effect of the swap over the life of the loan and the swap is to smooth out the fluctuations in the borrower's exposure to the cost of borrowing under the loan.

4.80 When the swap is out-of-the-money from the borrower's perspective, the borrower is effectively paying for it. The exposure that the borrower has to fluctuations in its cost of borrowing under the loan might be represented by a wave, as illustrated in Figure 4.9. The peaks of the wave are the occasions when the borrower's cost of borrowing is high because of an unfavourable movement in LIBOR. The troughs of the wave are the occasions when the borrower's cost of borrowing is low because of a favourable movement in LIBOR. The borrower uses the swap to neutralize its exposure. The swap might be represented by a second wave, as illustrated in Figure 4.10. Crucially, the shape of the swap is equal and opposite to the shape of the exposure. Figure 4.11 illustrates the effect of combining the exposure with the swap. The two waves cancel each other out. Each peak in the exposure wave is offset by a corresponding trough in the swap wave, and each trough in the exposure wave is offset by a corresponding peak in the hedge wave.

4.81 It is important to note that the obligation of the borrower to make payments at the swap fixed rate and the obligation of the dealer to make payments at the swap floating rate are netted. That is, on each swap payment date, the existing obligations of each of the borrower and the dealer are cancelled and replaced by a new third obligation owed by the party which owes the higher amount to pay the difference to the other party. The effect of the swap to hedge the borrower's exposure to interest rate risk becomes apparent when the net payment made under the swap is applied to the borrower's exposure.

Achieving cheaper funding costs using an interest rate swap

4.82 The use of an interest rate swap to achieve cheaper funding costs is predicated on the theory of comparative advantage. The theory of comparative advantage postulates that a party should specialize in the activity in which it has an advantage relative to the other party. A transaction between the parties would then allow both parties to share the benefit of that comparative advantage. In the interest rate swap market, the theory of comparative advantage is applied to the cost of borrowing, whether borrowing is undertaken at a floating rate of interest or a fixed rate of interest.

4.83 Two borrowers A and B can borrow at different rates. The rates at which they can borrow are largely determined by their credit ratings, although the currency and term of the required borrowing are also relevant. A can borrow at either a floating rate LIBOR plus 0.1% or a fixed rate 6.5%. A requires floating rate financing and therefore A would be expected to borrow at its floating rate LIBOR plus 0.1%. B can borrow at either a floating rate LIBOR plus 0.8% or a fixed rate 8%. B requires fixed rate financing and therefore B would be expected to borrow at its fixed rate 8%.

4.84 However, the cost to both A and B of their respective borrowings can be reduced if they use a swap. A borrows at its fixed rate 6.5%. B borrows at its floating rate LIBOR plus 0.8%. Under the swap, A pays LIBOR (which is a floating rate) to B, and B pays a fixed rate 6.8% to A. The swap fixed rate 6.8% paid by B is the result of financial engineering which is undertaken during the negotiation of the terms of the swap.

4.85 In absolute terms, A has the advantage over B in respect of both floating rate borrowing and fixed rate borrowing. A is able to borrow at either rate more cheaply

4.7 Swap

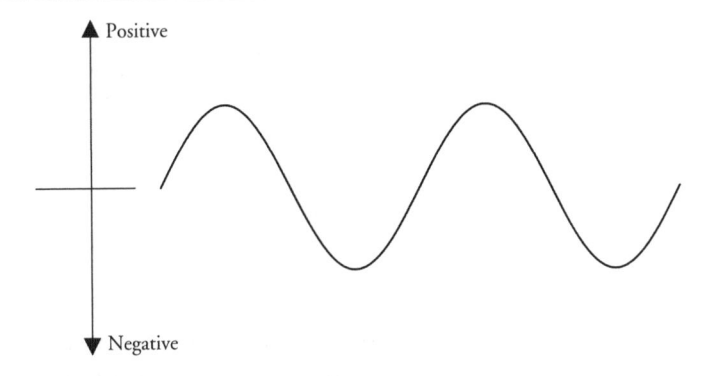

Figure 4.9 **The exposure wave**

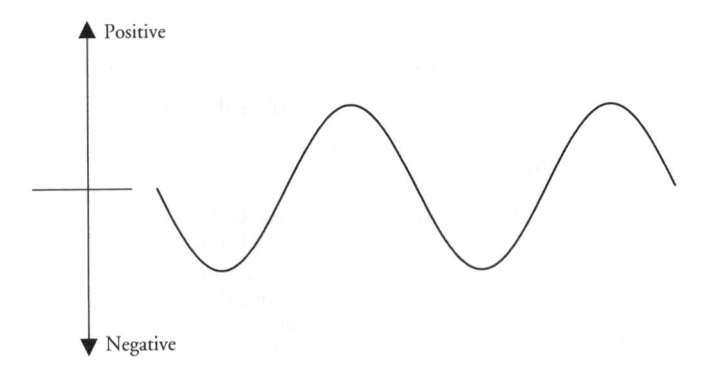

Figure 4.10 **The swap wave**

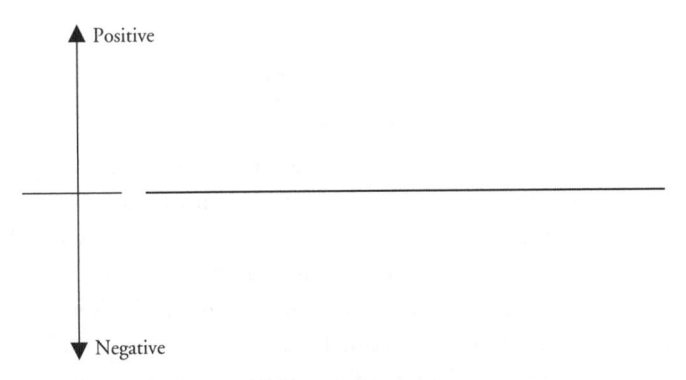

Figure 4.11 **The two waves offset and cancel each other**

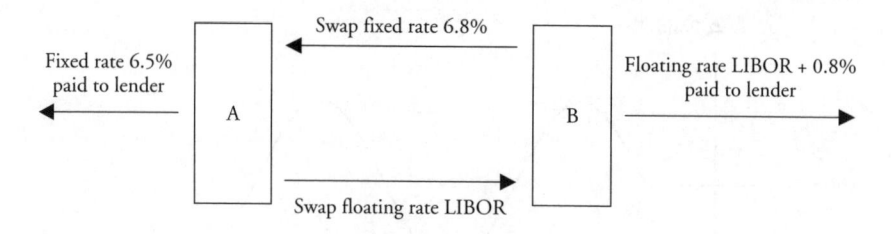

Figure 4.12. A funding swap making use of comparative advantage

than B can, perhaps because A has a stronger balance sheet and more stable earnings, and therefore A has a better credit rating. A's advantage in fixed rate borrowing is 8% minus 6.5% which is 1.5%. A's advantage in floating rate borrowing is (LIBOR plus 0.8%) minus (LIBOR plus 0.1%) which is 0.7%. Therefore A has the comparative advantage, that is, the greater advantage over B in fixed rate borrowing. It is A's comparative advantage in fixed rate borrowing that A and B share to their mutual benefit. Figure 4.12 illustrates the swap that A and B use.

4.86 The combined effect of A's borrowing and the swap is that A pays a floating rate LIBOR minus 0.3%. This rate is calculated in the following manner.

	Receive	Pay	Net
Fixed rate	6.8%	6.5%	Receive 0.3%
Floating rate	Nil	LIBOR	Pay LIBOR
Net rate			Pay LIBOR minus 0.3% Floating

4.87 The combined effect of B's borrowing and the swap is that B pays a fixed rate 7.6%. This rate is calculated in the following manner.

	Receive	Pay	Net
Fixed rate	Nil	6.8%	Pay 6.8%
Floating rate	LIBOR	LIBOR plus 0.8%	Pay 0.8%
Net rate			Pay 7.6% Fixed

4.88 The combined effect for A of its borrowing and the swap is that A pays interest at a floating rate, as originally required, which is lower at LIBOR minus 0.3% than the rate that A would have obtained without the swap, which would have been LIBOR plus 0.1%. The combined effect for B of its borrowing and the swap is that B pays interest at a fixed rate, as originally required, which is lower at 7.6% than the rate that B would have obtained without the swap, which would have been 8%. The swap is the key element of this swap funding structure, and the swap is built around the swap fixed rate.

4.7 Swap

4.89 In practice, a dealer would design the structure and arrange the participation in the structure of both A and B. The dealer would act as an intermediary. It is important to appreciate that A and B would not actually enter into the swap with each other. The swap has been illustrated in Figure 4.12 without the involvement of the dealer merely for the purposes of developing a clear explanation of the principle that A's comparative advantage in fixed rate borrowing is shared by both A and B to their mutual benefit. Instead, more realistically, A would enter into one swap with the dealer, and B would enter into another swap with the dealer. The dealer would act as a conduit of funds between A and B. Figure 4.13 illustrates how the dealer acts as a conduit of funds.

4.90 The dealer earns a spread between the higher swap fixed rate 6.9% that it receives from B and the lower swap fixed rate 6.7% that it pays to A. The dealer might also charge a fee to either or both of A and B for arranging the funding swap structure.

4.91 A bid and offer spread is quoted for almost any asset that is bought and sold in commerce, and a funding structure is no exception. The bid and offer spread of the funding swap structure in this example is 6.7%–6.9%. The dealers pays the bid price 6.7% and receives the offer price 6.9%. The dealer makes a profit of 0.2%, which is the spread, by buying a swap from A and selling a swap to B.

4.92 The dealer is able to act as an intermediary because the dealer has market knowledge and the ability to trade swaps and to warehouse funds. The dealer would also have the strong balance sheet and credit rating which would make the dealer an attractive swap counterparty for both A and B. A and B are both customers of the dealer, and may well be involved in different commercial activities (A might be a car manufacturer and B might be the owner and operator of a chain of hotels), and therefore in all probability they would not necessarily have the close relationship that would enable them to identify the opportunities afforded by the funding swap structure. The dealer is able to design the structure to the advantage of both A and B because the dealer is acquainted with the resources (including the balance

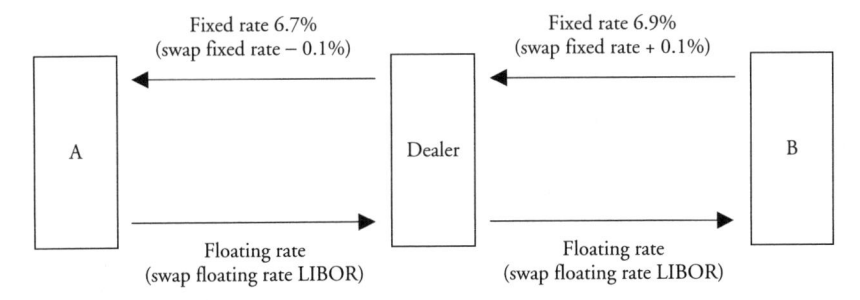

Figure 4.13 The involvement of the dealer in a funding swap structure

sheet and cash flow) and objectives (including the required type of funding) of each of them. Of course, neither A nor B would be aware of the involvement of the other in the structure; the preservation of customer confidentiality is a key requirement of the legal and regulatory system.

4.93 It is possible that A and B do not need to borrow for the same term. Either A or B might decline to use the funding swap structure if the duration of its particular swap is not of the appropriate duration. By entering into a swap with the dealer, each of A and B is able to enter into a swap the duration of which is suitable, and this would in all probability not be the case if A and B were to transact directly with each other. The dealer uses its market knowledge and trading opportunities to enter into a third swap with a third party C to offset, hopefully for a profit, any exposure it has from any difference between the swaps it has entered into with A and B. To continue the example, assume that the swap that the dealer enters into with A comes to an end two years before the swap that the dealer enters into with B. The dealer must obtain a stream of payments at LIBOR that it can pay to B for the remaining two years, and therefore the dealer would enter into a third swap from C, hopefully paying to C a swap fixed rate which is less than the swap fixed rate 6.9% that the dealer receives from B. The strength of the dealer's balance sheet should enable the dealer to assume two risks. The first risk is that the dealer does not immediately enter into the third swap. Under this circumstance, the dealer is said to warehouse funds. The second risk is that the dealer only manages to enter into the third swap on unfavourable terms.

Terminology

4.94 Terminology in the swap market observes the following convention. The swap fixed rate payer pays the fixed rate under the swap, receives the floating rate under the swap, is long the swap (that is, buys the swap), and buys the fixed rate. The swap floating rate payer pays the floating rate under the swap, receives the floating rate under the swap, is short the swap (that is, sells the swap), and sells the floating rate. The dealer sells one swap and receives the offer price, which is a higher swap fixed rate, and the dealer sells a swap and pays the bid price, which is a lower swap fixed rate.

Pricing an interest rate swap

4.95 The key element to pricing an interest rate swap is establishing the swap fixed rate. The swap floating rate is determined by the swap's purpose. For example, the floating rate of a swap that is bought to hedge an exposure to fluctuations in a particular variable interest rate will be that variable interest rate. The calculation of the swap fixed rate is the result of the financial engineering which is undertaken during the negotiation of the terms of the swap. The factors which determine the price of a swap include one, the customer's requirements (whether the swap is to be used for hedging or for speculation, the cost that the customer is prepared to pay, the required timing of the transaction, and the customer's existing exposures), two, the dealer's own business (the availability of capital, the availability of appropriate transaction structures, the customer's credit ratings, and the availability of liquidity in order for the dealer to hedge its obligations under the swap), and three, the environment in which the dealer conducts its business (the level of interest rates, foreign exchange rates, capital market yields, and the levels of bids and offers in the market). From a broad perspective, the swap fixed rate is the price of the swap, and this rate therefore represents the cost to the dealer of providing the product together with an element of profit. These are the internal factors. The pressure of market efficiency generally moves the swap fixed rate quoted by the dealer to a level which competes with the rates quoted by other dealers and the cost of using alternative structures. These are the external factors.

4.96 The preceding paragraph indicates the broad framework for the pricing of swaps. There are two distinct methodologies within this broad framework. The first methodology involves the aggregation of a series of financial forwards to create the swap. The second methodology involves pricing the swap with reference to the cost of using alternative capital market instruments and structures.

4.97 Satyajit Das writes of the decomposition of a swap into a series of financial forwards.[18] To develop the definition of a swap set out in paragraph 4.69, in the context of the application of netting which is described in paragraph 4.76, a swap is a series of pairs of payment obligations: one obligation of a pair is the obligation of one party to pay a fixed amount and the other obligation of a pair is the obligation of the other party to pay a floating amount. Returning to the example of the interest rate swap used for hedging, the schedule of payments made under that swap is set out in paragraph 4.75. Under that swap, the first pair of payment obligations arises on 31 March, the second on 30 June, and so on. Therefore, each pair of payment obligations under a swap is a forward contract, under which the difference between a fixed amount and a floating amount is paid under a netting arrangement. A pair of payment obligations is therefore a forward rate agreement (see paragraph 4.63). A party to an FRA makes a payment if the FRA is out-of-the-money and receives a payment if the FRA is in-the-money, and in a similar fashion, a party to a swap makes a payment if on the relevant swap payment date the swap is out-of-the-money and receives a payment if the swap is in-the-money. A swap is therefore a series, or strip, of FRAs. Returning to the example of the swap used for hedging, on 1 January, when the borrower and the dealer enter into the swap, the three FRAs which would match the schedule of payments under the swap would be the 0x3 FRA (for the period to the first swap

---

[18] *Swaps/Financial Derivatives* (John Wiley & Sons Inc., 2005).

payment date 31 March), the 3x6 FRA (for the period to the second swap payment date 31 March), and the 6x9 FRA (for the period to the third swap payment date 30 September). The financial engineer pricing the swap would break the swap down into discrete pairs of payment obligations, and then calculate the fixed rate of each pair with reference to the analogous FRA, and then calculate the swap fixed rate as a blend of the fixed rates of the various pairs. It is evident that the decomposition of a swap into a series of FRAs for pricing purposes depends on the availability of suitable FRAs.

4.98 The second methodology involves the relative value approach of the modern global financial markets. The yield generated by one investment must compete against the yield generated by another investment. The corollary of competing yields is that the cost of acquiring funding through the issue of one investment must compete against the cost of acquiring funding through the issue of another investment. Returning to the example of the interest rate swap used for hedging, the cost to the borrower of borrowing at a floating rate and using the swap to fix that cost at a protected rate must compete with the cost that the borrower would incur through acquiring funding by another method, such as issuing debt which pays a fixed rate of interest (or coupon).

4.99 One of the early pioneers of swap pricing is Rod Beckström, who worked for the Oklahoma-based financial institution Sooner Federal Savings and Loan in the early 1980s. His profile in *Risk* magazine[19] recalls how he developed a way of pricing an interest rate swap using a 'Visicalc' spreadsheet running on an Apple II domestic computer. Beckström moved to Morgan Stanley, where he was one of the first swap traders and where he continued to develop pricing techniques for interest rate swaps and currency swaps, now using a 'Lotus 1-2-3' spreadsheet running on an IBM PC. As pricing became more efficient, competitive pressures drove down the margins made by the dealers selling swap structures, and today hedging swaps are said to be 'plain vanilla' and are executed simply and easily, with a largely automated documentation process. A key element to interest rate swap pricing is the modelling of movements in the relative rates. Different types of underlying behave differently. For example, whereas a particular foreign exchange rate or the price of a particular commodity might reach a certain level and remain at that level, interest rates generally tend to move around, and to revert to a mean (or average). Therefore modelling movements in the relevant rates should ideally reflect mean reversion, otherwise the probability that high rates or low rates will be maintained will be overstated. Movements in interest rates are said to be path-dependent; the probability that a particular rate will move in a particular direction during a particular period is determined in part by the movements in that rate

---

[19] *Risk*, 15/12, December 2002, p. 25.

before that period. The Monte-Carlo simulation has been developed as an analytical technique which calculates path-dependent probabilities and captures mean reversion. A Monte-Carlo simulation operates by generating a number of different individual tracks of how the rate might move. Enough tracks are generated to develop a sensible view of the probable movement of the rate, which will be the mean path within the probability envelope that is created by the various simulations.

Different interest rate swaps

There are different types of interest rate swap. A fixed interest swap converts an exposure to an obligation to make floating rate payments to an exposure to an obligation to make fixed rate payments. A floating interest swap converts an exposure to an obligation to make fixed rate payments to an exposure to an obligation to make floating rate payments. A basis swap converts an exposure to an obligation to make floating rate payments to an exposure to make other floating rate payments. **4.100**

Currency swaps

A currency swap is essentially the same as an interest rate swap. The only difference is that whereas an interest rate swap involves one currency, a currency swap involves two or more currencies. A person might receive a cash flow in one currency, but requires an income in a second currency, perhaps to meet payment obligations denominated in that second currency. A currency swap would therefore be the most elegant and efficient mechanism by which the necessary conversion is achieved. The currency swap also offers the advantage of incorporating interest rate hedging if this hedging is also required. **4.101**

Commodity swaps

The purpose of a commodity swap is that the parties exchange their respective exposures to movements in the price of the underlying commodity. The structure of the commodity swap is a usual swap structure. The swap comprises a series of payment dates. On each payment date, each party has an obligation to make a payment to the other. These pairs of obligations are usually netted, with the result that both obligations are cancelled and replaced by a third obligation of the party which owes the higher amount to pay the difference. The amount of each payment is calculated with reference to the underlying notional amount of the commodity and the price of that commodity. **4.102**

Commodity swaps have diverse applications. The underlying might be an amount of any soft or hard commodity for which prices are readily available, or the underlying might be the price of freight (such as the BIFFEX index, **4.103** see paragraph 4.205).[20] Counterparties to OTC commodity swaps often use the price of a futures contract that is traded on an exchange as the reference price of their swap, on the basis that the futures price is the market's consensual expectation of what the spot price of the commodity will be on the futures delivery date, reflecting the supply and demand factors which affect the price of the commodity.

4.104 By way of example, a producer of sugar (such as a refiner of raw sugar cane) is exposed to the risk that the price at which it sells sugar every month fluctuates. Whereas any increase in the price of sugar is favourable, any decrease in the price of sugar is not. The producer therefore enters into a commodity swap with a dealer, which might be a commodity trading house, to smoothe out the producer's exposure to the fluctuations in the price it receives for its monthly sales of sugar. Under the swap, which is sometimes referred to as a producer swap, the producer pays floating amounts to the dealer, and the dealer pays fixed amounts to the producer. The swap payment dates match the dates of the producer's sale of physical sugar. The net effect of these swap payments is that the price of sugar received by the producer is fixed. For the purpose of this example, the price of sugar fluctuates around £250 per net metric ton, and the producer wishes to fix the price it receives at a protected price of £250 per net metric ton. To maintain clarity, this example does not reflect the maintenance of an appropriate underlying notional amount of the swap.

4.105 The following table illustrates, from the producer's perspective, how the price of sugar received by the producer is fixed. On 1 January, the producer receives the spot price 252. Under the swap, the producer has the obligation to pay the floating price 252 to the dealer, and the dealer has the obligation to pay the fixed price 250 to the producer. The producer has the net obligation to pay 2 to the dealer. The combined effect of the spot price and the swap net payment is that the producer receives the protected price 250. The swap is out-of-the-money from the producer's perspective. On 1 February, the producer receives the spot price 248. Under the swap, the producer has the obligation to pay the floating price 248 to the dealer, and the dealer has the obligation to pay the fixed price 250 to the producer. The dealer has the net obligation to pay 2 to the producer. The combined effect of the spot price and the swap net payment is that the producer receives the protected price 250. The swap is in-the-money from the producer's perspective. The swap smoothes out the fluctuations in the price received by the producer.

---

[20] Certain types of derivative such as carbon trading derivatives, energy derivatives, and weather derivatives are not easily classified, hence these tend to be treated as commodity derivatives as a matter of convenience. Such treatment underlines the reality that a cash-settled derivative contract can easily be written on any changing data population.

4.7 Swap

Payment date	Spot in	Swap floating out	Swap fixed in	Swap net	Combined in
1 January	+252	−252	+250	−2	+250
1 February	+248	−248	+250	+2	+250
1 March	+246	−246	+250	+4	+250
1 April	+250	−250	+250	0	+250

The dealer has assumed the producer's exposure to fluctuations in the price of sugar. The swap has transferred the price risk to the dealer. The dealer might therefore enter into a second swap, a consumer swap, with an industrial consumer of sugar (such as a soft drinks manufacturer). The consumer is exposed to the risk that the price of sugar it buys every month fluctuates. Whereas any decrease in the price of sugar is favourable, any increase in the price of sugar is not. The consumer is therefore exposed to a price risk which is equal and opposite to the price risk to which the dealer is exposed, the dealer having assumed the producer's price risk. **4.106**

Under the swap, the consumer pays fixed amounts to the dealer, and the dealer pays floating amounts to the consumer. The swap payment dates match the dates of the consumer's purchases of physical sugar. The net effect of these swap payments is that the price of sugar paid by the consumer is fixed. For the purpose of this example, again the price of sugar fluctuates around £250 per net metric ton and the consumer wishes to fix the price it pays at a protected price of £250 per net metric ton. The following table illustrates, from the consumer's perspective, how the price of sugar paid by the consumer is fixed. **4.107**

Payment date	Spot out	Swap floating in	Swap fixed out	Swap net	Combined out
1 January	−252	+252	−250	+2	−250
1 February	−248	+248	−250	−2	−250
1 March	−246	+246	−250	−4	−250
1 April	−250	+250	−250	0	−250

On 1 January, the consumer pays the spot price 252. Under the swap, the consumer has the obligation to pay the fixed price 250 to the dealer, and the dealer has the obligation to pay the floating price 252 to the consumer. The dealer has the net obligation to pay 2 to the consumer. The combined effect of the spot price and the swap net payment is that the consumer pays the protected price 250. The swap is in-the-money from the consumer's perspective. On 1 February, the consumer pays the spot price 248. Under the swap, the consumer has the obligation to pay the fixed price 250 to the dealer, and the dealer has the obligation to pay the floating price 248 to the consumer. The consumer has the net obligation to pay 2 to the dealer. The combined effect of the spot price and the swap net payment is that the consumer **4.108**

pays the protected price 250. The swap is out-of-the-money from the consumer's perspective. The swap smoothes out the fluctuations in the price paid by the consumer.

4.109 The producer swap is always out-of-the-money from the producer's perspective when the consumer swap is in-the-money from the consumer's perspective (for example on 1 January), and the producer swap is always in-the-money from the producer's perspective when the consumer swap is out-of-the-money from the consumer's perspective (for example on 1 February). The producer swap is equal and opposite to the consumer swap because both swaps are used to neutralize equal and opposite price risks. In practice, of course, the dealer will charge a spread between the fixed price it pays to the producer and the slightly higher fixed price it receives from the consumer. The intermediation of the dealer is needed, because the producer may need the producer swap for a different period than the consumer needs the consumer swap, perhaps because of differences in their respective commercial operations. The dealer is able to trade the sugar price risk in the same manner as interest rate risk is traded, by occasionally warehousing funds.

Equity swaps

4.110 The purpose of an equity swap is that the parties exchange their respective exposures to movements in the price of the underlying shares or share index or indices. The structure of an equity swap is the usual swap structure. The swap comprises a series of payment dates. On each payment date, each party has an obligation to make a payment to the other. These pairs of payment obligations are usually netted, with the result that both obligations are cancelled and replaced by a third obligation of the party which owes the higher amount to pay the difference. The amount of each payment is calculated with reference to the underlying notional amount of the swap and the price of the underlying shares or the level of the underlying share index or indices. An equity swap operates in much the same manner as a commodity swap, in that the party paying the floating amount and receiving the fixed amount is smoothing out its exposure to movements in the price or level of the underlying. However, as Chapter 7 demonstrates, the underlying notional amount of an equity swap[21] is adjusted over the life of the swap.

The origin and development of the swap market

4.111 The swap market has experienced exponential growth since the 1980s. Both ISDA[22] and the BIS[23] collate statistics on a frequent basis which indicate the size

---

[21] The underlying notional amount of a commodity swap must also be adjusted over the life of the swap.
[22] International Swaps and Derivatives Association, Inc. See Chapter 7.
[23] The Bank for International Settlements. See Chapter 10.

and trends of the different parts of the international derivative markets, both exchange-based and OTC.

4.112 The history of the swap market can be traced back to the Second World War and the macroeconomic developments of the time. Unlike other derivative products, such as forwards, futures, and options, swaps are very much a modern innovation, and the true genesis of the swap market in the 1970s was a consequence of the emergence of a new type of risk.

4.113 During the Second World War, as the outcome of the conflict grew more certain and the contours of the post-war geopolitical landscape became more defined, attention turned to the need to rebuild international trade, the international exchange of currency, and the availability of credit. The Second World War had compounded the effect of the Depression of the 1930s, adding to the urgency of restoring international trade and finance. In July 1944, the International Monetary and Financial Conference of the United and Associated Nations was held at Bretton Woods, in New Hampshire. The Bretton Woods Agreement was signed by 44 nations, and the Agreement was mainly negotiated by Harry Dexter White, representing the United States of America, and John Maynard Keynes, representing the United Kingdom. The Agreement established the Bretton Woods System of fixed currency exchange rates.

4.114 The Bretton Woods System contained the following key elements. One, the International Monetary Fund (IMF) was established in Washington DC to lend foreign exchange to any member of the System whose foreign exchange reserves have been depleted. Any loan made by the IMF is generally conditional on the borrowing member adopting and maintaining an economic policy which is consistent with the Bretton Woods Agreement. Two, the US dollar and sterling were designated as reserve currencies; the US dollar was designated the principal reserve currency. Members of the System other than the United States and the United Kingdom would maintain their foreign exchange reserves as either US dollars or sterling. Three, the exchange rate between the US dollar and sterling was fixed at a specified dollar rate. The value of the US dollar was itself fixed to the price of gold, at US$35 per troy oz. The US dollar rate of the currency of each member was allowed to fluctuate within a narrow range, 1% of its specified US dollar rate. The value of the US dollar relative to the price of gold was maintained at the fixed US$35 per troy oz by the United States buying and selling gold as required in the settlement of financial transactions. Four, the specified US dollar rate of the currency of a member could be changed only if that member's balance of payments was in 'fundamental disequilibrium'. Five, after a transition period, currencies became convertible, that is, one currency could be bought and paid for using another currency. However, the conversion of currencies could only take place within the established framework of the specified US dollar rates of those currencies.

Six, members of the System subscribed to the IMF by paying gold and currency, which the IMF could then use to lend to members.

4.115 The maintenance of fixed exchange rates, which was one of the fundamental objectives of the Bretton Woods System, required members to adopt and to pursue coordinated economic policies. However, stresses in the System began to emerge in the 1960s. The economic policy of the United States began to diverge from that of Germany and Japan. Germany and Japan had began to assume greater importance within the System to reflect the growth of their economies. Further, during the mid-1960s, the United States experienced an increase in inflation as a consequence of its growing expenditure, including significant spending on defence items such as the Vietnam War and the rapid development of a nuclear deterrent, the race to achieve the first manned lunar landing, and the Great Society programme during the presidency of Lyndon B. Johnson, which was a programme of extensive expenditure on education, medical services, and the renewal of the justice system. Participants in the foreign exchange markets perceived that the US dollar had increased in response to increased inflation in the United States, and that the deutschmark and Japanese yen had become undervalued relative to the US dollar. Generally, participants in the foreign exchange markets attempted to buy deutschmarks and yen low with the expectation of later selling these currencies high. An excess of demand for deutschmarks and yen therefore emerged as a consequence of the perceived loss of value of these two currencies. The effect of this excess demand for these two currencies was that the price, expressed as US dollars, of these two currencies increased: that is, the market US dollar rate of each of the deutschmark and the yen was pushed down from its specified dollar rate; broadly, more US dollars would be needed to buy these two currencies as their market US dollar rate decreased.

4.116 Two courses of action were open to Germany and Japan. Under the first course of action, they could adjust the specified US dollar rate of their currencies in order to neutralize the excess demand for their currencies. Under the second course of action, they could increase supplies of deutschmarks and yen to meet the excess demand for their currencies, thereby forestalling any movement in the market US dollar rates of those currencies away from the specified rates. The first course of action would have involved changing the specified US dollar rates of the deutschmark and the yen within the Bretton Woods System. However, the Bretton Woods Agreement only permitted changing the specified US dollar rate of the currency of a member if that member's balance of payments was in a condition of 'fundamental disequilibrium'. Germany and Japan therefore elected to pursue the second course of action: intervention in the global foreign exchange markets to increase supplies of deutschmarks and yen.

4.117 Intervention required the purchase of US dollars and the sale of deutschmarks and yen, with the objective of pushing back the market US dollar rates of both deutschmarks and yen to their specified rates. The theory of intervention was that the increased supply of deutschmarks and yen would meet the demand for these two currencies. As demand for deutschmarks and yen was met, the prices expressed as US dollars of these two currencies would fall, and the market US dollar rates of these two currencies would be pushed back up to the specified US dollar rates; broadly, fewer US dollars would be needed to buy these two currencies as their US dollar rates increased.

4.118 Therefore the Bundesbank sold deutschmarks for US dollars and the Bank of Japan sold yen for US dollars. The scale of intervention was significant. The Bundesbank bought US$3 billion during April 1971. On 4 May 1971, the Bundesbank bought a further US$1 billion, and on 5 May 1971, the Bundesbank bought another US$1 billion in one hour. Despite these large-scale purchases of US dollars, intervention failed, and the Bundesbank halted its intervention. The deutschmark was allowed to float. On 15 August 1971, the US President Richard Nixon suspended the convertibility of the US dollar into gold and imposed a 10% tax on imports into the United States.

4.119 The G10 met at the Smithsonian Institution in Washington DC on 17 and 18 December 1971 and formulated the Smithsonian Agreement, which was a revision to the Bretton Woods Agreement. Under the Smithsonian Agreement, the specified US dollar rates of the currencies of members would be reset, the market US dollar rate of each member's currency was allowed to fluctuate within a broader range, 2.25% of its specified US dollar rate, and the value of gold within the mechanism was increased to US$38 per troy oz. However, the Smithsonian Agreement failed during early February 1973. As a consequence, on 12 February 1973, the US dollar was devalued by 10% and exchange rates were allowed to float. Economists have commented that the loss of monetary control by the world's leading industrialized powers during the early 1970s and the abandonment of the Bretton Woods System prompted the high levels of inflation experienced during the 1970s. The background was therefore established during the 1970s for the increased interest rate risk and foreign exchange risk to which corporate treasuries and indeed governments became exposed. The emergence and increasing prominence of these two risks prompted the formulation of new risk control products, that is, modern swap contracts.

4.120 The first currency swap was arranged in 1976 by two investment banks, Goldman Sachs and Continental Illinois Limited. This swap represented a refinement of the techniques which had been rehearsed in the market for parallel loans and back-to-back loans which emerged after the Second World War as a mechanism to achieve funding in varying currencies without breaching the exchange controls that were put in place after the Second World War. Both types of loan can be broken down into spot and forward payments, and therefore the forward cash flows inherent in a modern swap can be discerned. This transaction, which involved swapping exposures to obligations denominated in sterling and Dutch guilders, was arranged between the Dutch entity Bos Kalis Westminster and the English entity ICI Finance.

4.121 The first currency swap to complement a debt capital market issue was arranged in 1979. Roylease, the leasing subsidiary of the Royal Bank of Canada, issued a five year bond denominated in deutschmarks and paying a coupon of 6.75%. Roylease swapped its exposure to pay an obligation denominated in deutschmarks, the denomination of the bonds, to an exposure to an obligation to pay Canadian dollars, presumably to match the currency of its income. The structure of the transaction was a series of forward foreign exchange contracts, first converting deutschmark obligations into US dollar obligations, and then converting the US dollar obligations into Canadian dollar obligations.

4.122 In August 1981, Salomon Brothers arranged a currency swap between the World Bank and the International Business Machines (IBM). The transaction is widely seen as the transaction which established the currency swap market. IBM had borrowed deutschmarks and Swiss francs and therefore owed interest payment obligations denominated in these two currencies. Under a separate borrowing, the World Bank had raised US$290 million through issuing bonds, and therefore owed interest payment obligations denominated in US dollars. Under the swap, IBM paid the World Bank the US dollars that the World Bank needed to meet its US dollar interest payment obligations, and the World Bank paid IBM the deutschmarks and Swiss francs that IBM needed. IBM required US dollar funding, but it could borrow more cheaply in deutschmarks and Swiss francs. Accordingly, it borrowed in those two currencies, and used the amount borrowed to buy the US dollars it needed. The US dollar then appreciated in value relative to the deutschmark and the Swiss franc during the terms of the swap, and IBM therefore made a profit. Over the term of the swap, IBM was effectively selling US dollars (which it paid to the World Bank) and buying deutschmarks and Swiss francs (which it received from the World Bank). This currency swap demonstrated the fundamental purpose of the currency swap. Jessica Einhorn, who worked on the swap during the early stages of her career with the World Bank, commented in *Risk* magazine[24] on the significance of the transaction. 'The basic concept of the currency swap market meant you could go to any market in the world where you had the most efficient credit to borrow, take that efficiency and swap it into any currency you wanted.'

4.123 In 1981, Deutsche Bank arranged what is seen as the first widely publicized interest rate swap. Deutsche Bank had issued a seven year US$300 million bond, and swapped its exposure to pay a fixed rate coupon into an exposure to pay a floating rate coupon.

---

[24] *Risk*, 15/12, December 2002, p. 36.

4.8 Cap, Floor, and Collar Contracts

4.124 During the 1980s, the development of standardized transaction structures and transaction implementation techniques, including documentation processes, contributed to the increasing efficiency of the swap market. In turn, increasing demand for transactions was driven by, one, increasing volatility in interest rates, currency exchange rates, commodity prices, and equity prices, and two, the increasingly international character of the global markets, a trend which has increased demand for cross-border funding and investment opportunities. The modern swap market has matured into a broad and liquid resource for treasury managers. Investment banks now regard swaps as financial instruments to be traded, and have supported the development of standard contracts and market practices, such as those developed under the auspices of ISDA. Part 4.12 of this chapter also considers credit derivatives, which are the latest major class of product to be developed by the global derivative industry. Although the underlying of the credit derivative market is credit risk, and not price risk, credit derivative transactions are built on the foundation of swap techniques, and this heritage is discernible in the structure of the industry-standard documentation that is used.

4.8 Cap, Floor, and Collar Contracts

Interest rate cap

4.125 The buyer of an interest rate cap fixes the rate of interest on a notional loan at a protected rate for the period specified in the cap contract. The buyer of the cap is acquiring protection from the risk of an increase in the cost of borrowing above the protected rate. A borrower has borrowed funds under a loan agreement. Under the loan, the borrower is required to make payments of interest at the loan rate, which is a fluctuating rate. The borrower might use a cap to hedge against the risk that the loan rate might increase. The borrower buys a cap from a dealer. The borrower makes one payment of premium to the dealer at the outset of their transaction. During the term of the cap transaction, on each cap payment date, which should correspond with an interest payment date under the loan, if the reference loan rate is above the protected cap rate, then the dealer pays the difference to the borrower. The borrower's funding cost is capped at the protected cap rate. Figure 4.14 illustrates the payment profile of a cap.

4.126 Two observations can be made. One, the hedge acquired by buying a cap is very much like the hedge conferred by buying a call option. The party buying the cap (the borrower) pays a fixed amount (the premium) to the seller (the dealer), and the seller then pays floating amounts to the borrower whenever the cap is in-the-money from the buyer's perspective. Each floating amount is the difference between the protected cap rate and the higher reference loan rate. Two, therefore the payment profile of a cap, as illustrated in Figure 4.14, is identical to the payment profile of a long call option (see Figure 4.3).

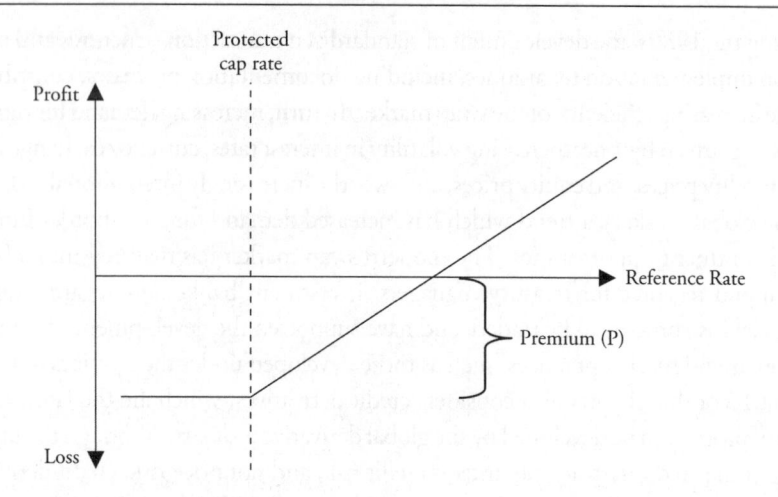

Figure 4.14 The payment profile of a cap

Interest rate floor

4.127 The buyer of an interest rate floor fixes the return on an investment at a protected rate for the period specified in the floor contract. The buyer of the floor is acquiring protection from the risk of a decrease in the return earned below the protected rate. A depositor has placed funds on deposit and receives a variable deposit rate. The depositor might use a floor to hedge against the risk that the deposit rate might decrease. The depositor buys a floor from a dealer. The depositor makes one payment of premium to the dealer at the outset of their transaction. During the term of the floor transaction, on each floor payment date, which should correspond with each date on which interest is paid on the deposit, if the reference deposit rate is below the protected floor rate, then the dealer pays the difference to the depositor. Therefore a floor is imposed below which the depositor's return does not decline. Figure 4.15 illustrates the payment profile of a floor.

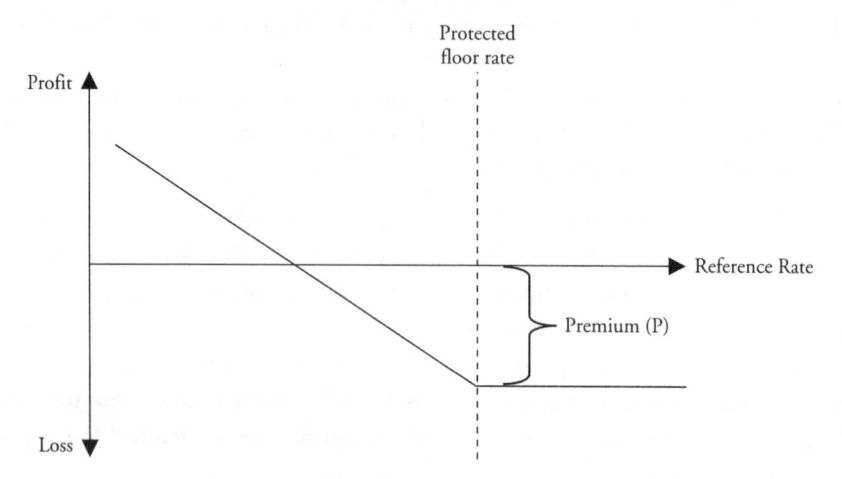

Figure 4.15 The payment profile of a floor

4.8 Cap, Floor, and Collar Contracts

Again, two observations can be made. One, the hedge acquired by buying a floor is very much like the hedge conferred by buying a put option. The party buying the floor (the depositor) pays a fixed amount (the premium) to the seller (the dealer), and the seller then pays floating amounts to the buyer whenever the floor is in-the-money from the buyer's perspective. Each floating amount is the difference between the protected floor rate and the lower reference deposit rate. Two, therefore the payment profile of a floor, as illustrated in Figure 4.15, is identical to the payment profile of a long put option position (see Figure 4.5). **4.128**

Interest rate collar

The buyer of an interest rate collar fixes the rate of interest on a notional loan at a protected rate for the period specified in the collar contract. A collar therefore resembles a cap, in that both contracts confer protection against an increase in the reference floating rate. However, the collar contract specifies two rates, a collar upper rate and a collar lower rate. The buyer of the collar is acquiring protection from the risk of an increase in the cost of borrowing above the protected collar upper rate. A borrower has borrowed funds under a loan agreement. Under the loan, the borrower is required to make payments of interest at the loan rate, which is a floating rate. The borrower might use a collar to hedge against the risk that the loan rate might increase. The borrower buys a collar from a dealer. During the term of the collar transaction, on each collar payment date (which should correspond with an interest payment date under the loan), if the reference loan rate is above the protected collar upper rate, then the dealer pays the difference to the borrower, and if the loan rate is below the collar lower rate, then the borrower pays the difference to the dealer. The effect of the collar only becomes fully apparent when the cash flow of the collar is combined with the cash flow of the underlying loan. The combined cash flow of the collar and the loan is that the borrower's overall funding cost is not lower than the collar lower rate, but not higher than the protected collar upper rate. Figure 4.16 illustrates the payment profile of a collar. **4.129**

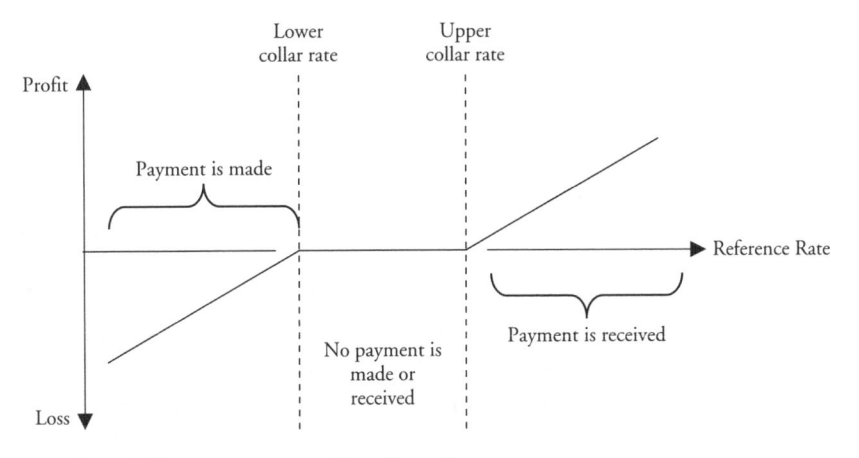

Figure 4.16 The payment profile of a collar

4.130 The operation of a collar is therefore almost identical to the operation of a swap. However, the key difference between a collar and a swap is that the collar features two rates, the lower rate and the upper rate. The reference rate can move between the lower rate and the upper rate without giving rise to a payment under the collar contract.

4.131 Although a collar and a cap both confer protection against the risk of an increase in the reference loan rate, there are three important differences. One, whereas the borrower makes an initial payment of premium to buy the cap, the borrower does not make any initial payment of premium to buy the collar. Two, whereas the borrower makes no further payment during the term of the cap, the borrower might be required to make a payment on a collar payment date if the collar on that date is out-of-the-money from the borrower's perspective (on such occasions, the reference loan rate is below the collar lower rate). Three, whereas the borrower's liability under the cap is limited to the premium paid to buy the cap, the borrower has potentially much greater liability under the collar, although if the collar is used properly to hedge against unfavourable movements in the reference loan rate, any loss under the collar should be offset by a corresponding gain under the loan.

4.9 CPPI

4.132 CPPI is an acronym for constant proportion portfolio insurance. CPPI is a technique for calculating the values of a specialized form of index, which creates a magnified investment exposure to an underlying and which also offers protection of a proportion of the capital that is invested. There are two ways in which CPPI might be used. An investor might receive payments that are linked directly to the performance of the index. Alternatively, given that the index creates a data population on which a derivative contract can be written, the investor might receive payments under a derivative transaction, the underlying of which is the index. For example, a derivative transaction might be a cash-settled swap linked to the performance of a CPPI index. As the level of the index itself is calculated with reference to the underlying, which might be any asset, instrument or data population on which a derivative can be written, as a matter of nomenclature the index itself might be considered to constitute a specialized form of derivative payout. The index might therefore also be described, admittedly a little fancifully, as a lens through which the underlying is viewed. Crucially, the amount of exposure that is created by the index is changed from time to time, in response to changes in the price or value of the underlying. The index describes the performance of the underlying, and in contrast to other forms of index encountered, it does not directly describe prices. The index must of course be placed in a contractual 'wrapper' which actually creates the obligations to make payments.

4.9 CPPI

4.133 There are two key principles which underpin the index. The first principle is that the level of the index at any particular time is allocated between a so-called risky asset and a so-called risk-free asset. The risky asset is the actual underlying to which the investment exposure is created. The underlying is described as the 'risky' asset because an investment in the CPPI structure is an investment in the risk of this asset. The risk-free asset is an asset which generates a low investment return but which gives rise theoretically to no risk, and which therefore offers a more stable and safe investment. The risk-free asset is therefore occasionally referred to as the 'reserve' asset, because when the risky asset performs badly, increasing exposure is allocated to the risk-free asset. The risk-free asset is often set to mimic a cash deposit and it earns an appropriate interest rate. The amounts of the level of the index that are allocated to the risky asset and the risk-free asset are rebalanced through the life of the transaction, in order that the exposure of the index to the risky asset increases when the risky asset performs well, and the exposure of the index to the risky asset decreases when the risky asset performs badly. When the exposure of the index to the risky asset decreases, the exposure of the index to the risk-free asset increases, such that at any time the level of the index is allocated between the risky asset and the risk-free asset. By way of example, at a particular time the level of the index might be 110. The 110 would be made up of an allocation to the risky asset of 65 and an allocation to the risk-free asset of 45. One of the key reasons for using a CPPI structure is therefore indicated: a CPPI structure is intended to deliver to the investor a form of capital protection. The operation of the index effectively moves the investor's investment capital away from the risky asset and towards the risk-free 'reserve' asset if the risky asset performs badly.

4.134 The second principle is that the allocation at any particular time of the level of the index between the risky asset and the risk-free asset is driven by the relationship between the level of the index at that time and the present value at that time of a protected amount. The protected amount is specified at the outset of a transaction. From time to time during the life of the transaction, the present value of the protected amount is the part of the level of the index that should not be allocated to the risky asset, and the protected amount is therefore the part of the level of the index that should be allocated to the risk-free asset. Following from this, the present value of the protected amount from time to time during the life of the transaction is said to represent a floor, and it is calculated on the basis of a notional investment in a zero-coupon bond. Accordingly, the present value through the life of the transaction of the protected amount is referred to as the 'bond floor'. The protection of the investor's capital is achieved through the structure tracking the bond floor, and thereby an optimal balance is maintained between maximizing the exposure to the risky asset while retaining the required element of a guaranteed return. As the index is rebalanced periodically, it is usually referred to as a 'dynamic' index, although just the term 'index' is used in this book for the sake of brevity.

4.135 By way of necessary introductory explanation, a zero-coupon bond, as its description suggests, does not pay interest (or coupon) and instead only repays its principal value on maturity, yet crucially the investor in the zero-coupon bond is required only to pay a discounted price for it.[25] The discounted price paid by the investor gives rise to the inbuilt effective interest rate. For example, a £100 three-year zero-coupon bond is priced to deliver an inbuilt effective interest rate of 4.5% per annum. On day 1, the investor pays the present value on day 1 of £100, which is £100 discounted by 4.5% per annum for three years. The investor therefore pays just £87.63 on day 1. However, the investor is repaid £100 at the end of the three year period of the zero-coupon bond. £87.63 compounds at 4.5% annually to give £100 after three years.

4.136 The level of the index on any particular calculation day T is calculated using the first core CPPI formula, which is typically expressed in the manner set out below. At a purely conceptual level, the allocation of the level of the index between the risky asset and the risk-free asset is discernible. This allocation is achieved using the concept of the current exposure, which is represented in the formula by CE. The current exposure is the percentage of the level of the index that is actually to be allocated to the risky asset, and therefore 1 minus the current exposure is the percentage of the level of the index that is to be allocated to the risk-free asset. A cursory glance at the formula also informs that the level of the index on T is calculated with reference to the level of the index on T−1, which is the calculation day immediately preceding T, the performance of the risky asset between T−1 and T, the performance of the risk-free asset between T−1 and T, and the current exposure that is determined on T−1. It is important to appreciate that this is a simple example of the core CPPI formula, and to maintain clarity this example does not include certain features that are commonly encountered, including adjustments which allow for illiquidity in the risky asset and various adjustments to extract fees from the structure.

$$I_T = I_{T-1} * [1 + (CE_{T-1} * \text{Risky performance}) + ((1 - CE_{T-1}) * \text{Risk-free performance})]$$

4.137 The formula operates in a subtle manner, and a simple example of a CPPI transaction with a maturity of one year is the most helpful way of exploring it. The inbuilt effective interest rate of the bond floor is assumed to be 4.5% per annum. The value of the risk-free asset is assumed to grow by a stable 5% per annum. One year is assumed to comprise 12 months of 30 days each. The first calculation day of the transaction is day 30, and calculation days occur at intervals of 30 days. The index is given a base level of 100. The protected amount is set at 80. Therefore on day 1, the level of the index is 100 and the present value of the bond floor is 76.56, which is 80 discounted for one year at 4.5% per annum. The percentage allocated to the

---

[25] Discounting funds is introduced at paragraph 4.68.

4.9 CPPI

risky asset on day 1 is equal to the target percentage on day 1. The target percentage on any particular calculation day T is broadly the percentage of the level of the index on T which is above the bond floor on T, and this percentage is calculated using the second core CPPI formula, which is typically expressed in the manner set out below. Target percentage is represented in the formula by TP and the present value of the bond floor is represented in the formula by Floor.

$$TP_T = (I_T - Floor_T) / I_T$$

4.138 Therefore, on day 1, the target percentage is equal to (100 minus 76.56) divided by 100, which is 23.81%. Thus 23.81% of the initial level of the index 100 is allocated to the risky asset, which is 23.81. The remaining 76.19 of the initial level of the index is allocated to the risk-free asset. The current exposure for day 1, the first day of the transaction, is also set to equal the day 1 target percentage. The day 1 current exposure is used in the calculations performed on day 30, as the following paragraphs illustrate.

4.139 The level of the index is first calculated on day 30 of the transaction, which is the first calculation day. The day 30 level of the index is calculated, using the first core CPPI formula set out above, with reference to the day 1 level of the index, the performance of the risky asset since day 1, the performance of the risk-free asset since day 1, and the day 1 current exposure. The performance of the risk-free asset is 5% per annum, for one month.

4.140 Once the day 30 level of the index has been calculated, the actual exposure of the day 30 level of the index to the risky asset as at day 30 is calculated. The day 30 actual exposure, is calculated with reference to the day 1 index level, the day 1 current exposure, and the performance of the risky asset since day 1. The day 30 actual exposure will differ from the day 1 current exposure (the day 1 current exposure having been used to calculate the day 30 level of the index). The day 30 actual exposure is then compared with the day 30 target exposure. It is recollected that the target exposure on a particular day is calculated, using the second core CPPI formula, as the difference between the level of the index on that day and the bond floor on that day, expressed as a percentage of the level of the index on that day. The day 30 target exposure is therefore calculated with reference to the day 30 bond floor and the day 30 level of the index. The day 30 bond floor is the present value on day 30 of the protected amount, which is 76.83. If the difference between the day 30 actual exposure and the day 30 target exposure is greater than a specified threshold, then the day 30 current exposure is reset to equal the day 30 target exposure. This specified threshold therefore determines the sensitivity of the CPPI structure; a lower threshold results in the index being rebalanced more frequently.

4.141 The resetting of the current exposure to equal the target exposure is how the allocation of the level of the index between the risky asset and the risk-free asset is rebalanced such that the percentage of the index that should be exposed to the risky asset after the rebalancing is limited to the target percentage. This is the critical part of the operation of a CPPI structure, which delivers the capital protection referred to above.

4.142 The next calculation day is day 60 of the transaction. The day 60 level of the index is calculated with reference to the day 30 level of the index (day 30 is the immediately preceding calculation day), the performance of the risky asset since day 30, the performance of the risk-free asset since day 30, and the day 30 current exposure. It is important to recollect that the day 30 current exposure would have been reset to the day 30 target exposure if the difference between the day 30 actual exposure and the day 30 target exposure was greater than the specified threshold.

4.143 Again, once the day 60 level of the index has been calculated, the actual exposure of the day 60 level of the index to the risky asset is calculated, and the day 60 actual exposure is compared with the day 60 target exposure. Again, the day 60 actual exposure is calculated with reference to the day 30 level of the index, the day 30 current exposure and the performance of the risky asset since day 30. Again, if the difference between the day 60 actual exposure and the day 60 target exposure is greater than a specified threshold, then the day 60 current exposure is reset to equal the day 60 target exposure. And thus the level of the index is calculated on succeeding calculation days.

4.144 Two refinements might be made to the operation of the index. One, a multiplier can be used to magnify the exposure to the risky asset by increasing the amount of the index that is allocated to the risky asset, although the use of a multiplier would tend to accelerate the effects of disadvantageous movements in the price or value of the risky asset. Two, the current exposure can be allowed to be greater than 100%, under which circumstance the investor effectively has a leveraged exposure to the risky asset. The investor effectively borrows in order to acquire the extent of the exposure to the risky asset which exceeds 100%. To maintain clarity, the example of the formula set out above omits the payment of interest on the amount of this borrowing, although commercially clearly such interest would be extracted from the structure.

4.145 In actual use, there is a tension in the assembly of a CPPI structure. On the one hand, the calendar of calculation days should be set to optimize the rebalancing of the index. As rebalancing the index involves taking observations or valuations of the risky asset, the frequency at which rebalancing is carried out should synchronize with the frequency at which these observations or valuations can be made. Certain types of asset are valued less frequently than other types of asset. For example, whereas a price for a share that is listed and traded on an investment exchange is refreshed more or less continuously through the trading session on that exchange, the equivalent price of a share in a hedge fund, the net asset value of that hedge fund share, might be determined only on a monthly basis.

Accordingly, the rebalancing of a dynamic index giving an exposure to such a hedge fund share might only be carried out on a monthly basis.

However, on the other hand, the illustration set out in the preceding paragraphs of the use of a CPPI index demonstrates that the level of the index on a particular calculation day is determined by an allocation of exposure that is made on the immediately preceding calculation day. This allocation of exposure reflects the relationship on that immediately preceding calculation day of the present value on that day of the bond floor and the level of the index on that day. A risk can emerge that the index is not sufficiently insulated from any sudden sharp adverse movement in the price or value of the risky asset which might happen after this allocation. The crux of the tension is that rebalancing often would help to achieve this insulation, but frequent rebalancing might be precluded by the structure of the market for the underlying. Resolving this tension is a structural difficulty that those developing CPPI transactions must address. One way to control this risk might be to build into the structure the right to rebalance between calculation days on an ad hoc basis if the volatility of the movements in the price or value of the underlying exceeds a specified threshold. At a more fundamental level, this risk prompts the observation that there is no reward without risk, even in a structure which has been developed to mitigate risk. Setting the protected amount high relative to the initial level of the index would tend to diminish the performance of the index as more of it is made up of the bond floor, and a multiplier would tend to increase the sensitivity of the index to the performance of the risky asset, but with the increased upside potential there is the countervailing increased downside risk. **4.146**

CPPI structures were first developed during the late 1980s, and since that time their use has expanded to encompass all types of underlying asset. The principal attraction of the CPPI structure is that it offers capital protection of an investment, but without stifling the ability of the structure to benefit from the performance of the underlying. The term 'portfolio insurance' is a generic term which applies to all investment structures which feature some rebalancing mechanism the purpose of which is to confer capital protection of an investment by dynamically rebalancing a synthetic index between a reference risky asset and a risk-free asset. Other variants include TIPP, which is time-invariant portfolio protection, and OBPI, which is option-based portfolio insurance. **4.147**

4.10 Derivatives used as Financing Tools

The two most common applications of derivatives are to hedge against certain risks (whether price risk or credit risk, which is considered below) or to speculate on the increase in the price of the transfer of such risks. A third, and significantly more specialized, application of derivative techniques is the provision of financing **4.148** through a derivative transaction. Under such a derivative financing transaction, a leveraged exposure to the underlying is created and sold by one party to the other. As a matter of convenience, the parties to a derivative financing transaction are said to be a buyer and a seller.

4.149 A clear example of a financing derivative transaction is a call option contract which has an accreting strike price. The buyer wishes to acquire an exposure to certain shares, and clearly the buyer's potential profit is higher if the buyer is able to acquire an exposure to more shares, although of course the buyer is exposed to greater downside risk. The buyer has £50 to invest.

4.150 The seller sells to the buyer an accreting strike call option written over 50 shares. The option is specified to expire on day 180. On day 1, the spot price of the shares is £5 and therefore the value of the underlying is 50 shares multiplied by £5, which is £250. The strike price is set; in this example, the strike price is £200. The strike price that is set on day 1 is the amount of financing provided by the seller under the transaction. The premium, which is paid by the buyer on day 1, is the value of the underlying on day 1 minus the strike price on day 1. The premium is therefore £250 minus £200, which is the £50 that the buyer wishes to invest. The option is deeply in-the-money, because the underlying value is significantly higher than the strike price. Over the life of the transaction, the strike price increases (or accretes) by the specified rate of interest, which in this example is 10% per annum. However, the expectation of the buyer is that the underlying value will increase by more over the life of the option.

4.151 On day 180, the spot price of the shares is £7 and therefore the value of the underlying is 50 shares multiplied by £7, which is £350. The strike price has increased to £210, having accreted by the specified rate of interest over 180 days. The amount of interest £10 is calculated as £200 + (£200 * (10% * 0.5)). 180 days is treated as 0.5 of one year. The option is further in-the-money. The option expires automatically, and the buyer receives the cash settlement amount. The cash settlement amount is the value of the underlying on the expiry date minus the strike price on the expiry date, which is £350 minus £210, which is £140. The profit made by the buyer is the cash settlement amount minus the premium that had been paid on day 1, which is £140 minus £50, which is £90.

4.152 The buyer has made a higher profit by using the accreting strike call option than the buyer would have made by investing just the amount of the premium directly in shares. An investment of £50 would have bought just ten shares on day 1 at £5 per share. The holding of ten shares would have increased in value to £70 on day 30, giving rise to a profit of just £20. By contrast, the £90 profit made by the buyer through using the accreting strike call option is 450% as much as the £20 profit that would have been made through a direct shareholding. The buyer therefore acquired a leveraged exposure to the shares; the buyer acquired an exposure to the potential increase in value of 50 shares instead of just ten shares.

4.10 Derivatives used as Financing Tools

The seller's return for providing the leveraged exposure through selling the accreting strike call option is the amount of interest by which the strike price accreted. In order to be able to pay the cash settlement amount on day 180, the seller buys the required number of shares on day 1 for £250. This shareholding is the seller's hedge for its obligations under the accreting strike call option contract (the seller's principal obligation is of course to pay the cash settlement amount). Of the £250 paid by the seller to acquire the hedging shareholding, £50 are funded through the receipt of the premium from the buyer and the remaining £200 are funded by the seller itself. On day 180, the seller sells the hedging shareholding for £350. Of the £350 received by the seller on its disposal of the hedging shareholding, the seller pays £140 to the buyer as the cash settlement amount and retains £210. Through selling the accreting strike call option, the seller has employed £200 of its capital and earned £10 over the life of the transaction, which represents the return on that capital. **4.153**

A number of observations can be made. First, both the seller and the buyer are exposed to the price risk that the shares decrease in value instead of increasing in value. The seller has used £200 of its own capital to create the exposure to the shares. Accordingly, over the life of the transaction, the seller would monitor the ratio of the strike price to the underlying value. On day 1, the ratio is £200 to £250, which equates to 80% leverage being provided. The seller may require the accreting strike call option contract to provide that the transaction ends before its scheduled expiry date if the ratio exceeds a threshold. The ratio would increase if the underlying value decreases towards the strike price, and of course a subtlety is that the strike price itself is accreting upwards towards the underlying value at the specified rate of interest. As the ratio approaches the specified threshold, the seller's risk is greater that the underlying value might decrease to less than the strike price. Further, the seller may require the accreting strike call option contract to provide that the seller has the right to require the buyer to reduce the amount of leverage (or 'de-lever') provided under the contract by repaying some of the financing; such a repayment would have the effect of reducing the strike price and thereby reducing the ratio. **4.154**

Second, from the perspective purely of the economics of the transaction, the seller is effectively lending to the buyer the £200 of financing and charging a rate of interest on that amount. The risk to which the seller is exposed is collateralized in that one, the seller has legal title to the assets in respect of which the financing is provided, and the seller may therefore liquidate those assets and retain the sale proceeds without first taking enforcement action, and two, the terms of the contract are such that the seller's obligation to pay the cash settlement amount is an obligation to pay the amount by which the value of the collateral (that is, the underlying value) exceeds the amount of the financing that must be repaid (that is, the strike price). In the event that the value of the collateral is less than the **4.155** amount of the financing, the seller has no obligation to make a payment. However, monitoring the ratio and reserving the ability to respond, as discussed in the preceding paragraph, control this risk.

4.156 Third, and flowing on from the second issue, the seller and the buyer are expressed to enter into a derivative transaction, and therefore the risk which arises is that the accreting strike call option contract is more properly characterized as a secured loan instead of a derivative.[26] One of the consequences of any such recharacterization of the contract is that the accounting treatment and tax treatment of the contract might be challenged. An additional consequence might be that an insolvency practitioner winding up the buyer in the event of the buyer's insolvency may seek to set aside the derivative financing transaction on the grounds that it was improperly entered into. It is therefore important that the character of the accreting strike call option transaction as a derivative is preserved. For example, the seller should be at liberty to determine whether or not it hedges its obligations under the contract; counterparties to derivative transactions do not have an obligation to hedge their obligations, whereas the essential characteristic of a secured loan is that the lender takes security.

4.157 The preceding paragraphs demonstrate the great flexibility of derivative techniques. In this particular example, a derivative is used to provide acquisition financing on a collateralized basis, and as such, derivatives are increasingly being used in a variety of corporate solution transactions.

4.11 Islamic-compliant Derivatives

4.158 Established derivative techniques are now being adapted for use within the Shari'a. The Shari'a is the Islamic legal system which is applied within the Muslim faith, providing Muslims with certain values and principles to govern every aspect of their lives, including their financial relationships. The importance of the Shari'a is growing rapidly in the financial markets, both within the United Kingdom and internationally,[27] as members of the Muslim faith seek to access in a manner which does not contradict their beliefs the conventional financial systems which have evolved.

4.159 The Shari'a is built up from five sources. First, the Qur'an is the written record of the word of God made by the Prophet Mohammed, and the Sunna consists of the traditional account of the life and teachings of the Prophet Mohammed.

---

[26] The recharacterization of contracts is discussed more generally at part 8.4 of Chapter 8.

[27] For example, in the United Kingdom, which has a sizeable Muslim population, commercial banks have started to offer Shari'a-compliant savings and loans products, and from a global perspective, ISDA is publishing a form of its master agreement for Shari'a trading relationships.

4.11 Islamic-compliant Derivatives

The qiyas is a process by which new circumstances and situations are explained and analysed within the framework of accepted principles. The ijma is the consensus reached on a particular question, and the ijtihad is the opinion of Islamic jurists on a particular question. In this way, the Shari'a is capable of evolving as new questions arise and are considered. Legal opinions are given by religious leaders, or mufti. Such a legal opinion is a fatwa.

4.160 Of great importance to the establishment of financing techniques which do not contradict the Shari'a therefore are certain prohibitions on various activities which are accepted within the conventional financial systems. Three key principles of the Shari'a should be considered. One, according to the Shari'a, money is not a commodity. From this principle flows the proposition that money cannot have value and money cannot be bought and sold, and therefore charging interest (or riba) on money is forbidden. Two, as charging interest on money is forbidden, distributing an investment return in the form of income is forbidden. Three, there should be no uncertainty (or gharar) in contracts made under Islamic law; that is, the amount of a payment obligation should be fixed at the time the contract is made. Some difficulty is therefore posed by a conventional derivative contract, which by its very nature connotes the making of payments at a time after the contract is made, of amounts that are not known until events have occurred in a manner not known when the contract is made. By extension, therefore, gambling and speculation (maisar) are also strictly contrary to the Shari'a. Four, the Shari'a prohibits any trade in or use of certain commodities such as pork, alcohol, and weaponry.

4.161 A number of Islamic-compliant financing techniques have evolved. One, partnership financing (mudaraba) involves the financier making available funds that are invested, and agreeing with the borrower the division of any profit made from the investment. The financier also retains from any profit a fee for the service it provides of identifying the investment that is made. Any loss is borne by the financier. There is a strong element of trust; the borrower relies on the financier to make the investment decision. Two, equity financing (musharaka) involves both the financier and the borrower making available funds that are invested, and agreeing the division between them of any profit. Again, the financier also retains from any profit a fee for the service it provides of identifying the investment that is made. However, any loss is borne by each of the financier and the borrower in direct proportion to the funds they make available. Three, added cost financing (murabaha) involves the borrower instructing the financier to buy the asset the acquisition of which is financed. The financier then sells the asset to the borrower at the initial cost of acquisition plus an amount of profit that the financier and the borrower agree that the financier should make. By acquiring title to the asset, the financier assumes the benefits and risks of ownership, and therefore is entitled to obtain a profit from such ownership. Four, sukuks resemble conventional debt securities, but are structured in a manner which is harmonious with the Shari'a. As the Shari'a permits debt to be traded only at its par value, sukuks are backed by assets, and therefore in place of interest, sukuks confer the right to share in the income generated by the assets.

4.162 Of particular relevance to this book is the Islamic form of the option contract known as the bei al-arboun. The investor enters into a contract with the Islamic financial institution under which the financial institution buys an asset on behalf of the investor and the investor pays to the financial institution a deposit. Under the terms of the contract, the investor has the right to decide whether or not to buy the asset from the financial institution, paying a specified price. If the investor does not proceed with the full purchase, the financial institution retains the deposit.

4.163 The process of developing an Islamic-compliant product involves seeking a legal pronouncement, or fatwa. It is important to realize that different Islamic scholars may individually reach different conclusions as to the application of the Shari'a, depending on their interpretations and the particular school of Islamic jurisprudence to which they belong.

4.12 Credit Derivatives

Credit risk

4.164 Credit risk is generally the risk that a party which owes an obligation to make a payment, the obligor, either fails to make that payment or becomes insolvent, or that the terms of the obligation are changed, such as a restructuring of the obligation. The insolvency of the obligor clearly reduces significantly the probability that the payment obligation will be completely fulfilled, as the party to whom the payment obligation is owed would rank as a creditor of the obligor and would therefore only receive a percentage of the amount of the payment, if anything, and subject to whether or not that party had taken security and the ranking of any security taken by any other creditor. Although credit risk can be controlled by taking security, or otherwise obtaining collateral,[28] in the final analysis the efficacy of a security device depends on its proper implementation (and this would include its proper characterization, such as whether or not it is a fixed charge or a floating charge, and perfection, such as registration) and the availability of funds available for distribution. The efficacy of a more general collateral arrangement depends on

---

[28] The term 'security' describes the various devices available under law to secure an obligation, whereas the term 'collateral' has a wider meaning which connotes putting in place arrangements which may not properly constitute a security device but which have the same purpose, to ameliorate concerns of creditworthiness.

4.12 Credit Derivatives

the amount of collateral that is used (it is common for the amount of collateral posted to equal only a percentage of the obligation covered, and the risk therefore remains of a loss to the extent of the uncovered percentage; full collateralization of the obligation may not always be possible because it would require the obligor effectively to make available funds equal to the full amount of the obligation and this requirement may very well distort the economics of the relationship between the obligor and its counterparty). Credit risk can be controlled by obtaining a guarantee from a third party guarantor, whose own ability to pay under the guarantee should be unaffected by the insolvency of the obligor. However, a credit risk would also emanate from the guarantor.

Credit derivative transaction

Under a credit derivative transaction, the credit risk which arises in respect of a particular obligor or obligation is isolated. Under a credit derivative contract, the protection buyer pays a protection fee or premium to the protection seller, and the protection seller assumes the credit risk. As a matter of intuition, the terms 'protection buyer' and 'protection seller' indicate that the protection buyer is buying protection against the credit risk because the protection buyer is exposed to that credit risk through some relationship that it has with the relevant obligor or some exposure that it has to the obligation in question. By extension, if the credit risk crystallizes, then under the terms of the credit derivative contract, the protection seller makes a payment to the protection buyer to offset the loss caused to the protection buyer. However, crucially, a credit derivative contract can be entered into whether or not the protection buyer is actually exposed to the relevant obligor or obligation.[29] There is no requirement under a credit derivative contract that the protection buyer has an interest in the reference obligation, and indeed there is no requirement that the obligor is even aware of the credit derivative transaction. The cash settlement amount that is paid on the settlement of a credit derivative transaction is not usually determined with reference to any loss that the protection buyer might actually suffer; that amount might instead be determined by another process, such as obtaining market valuations of the relevant payment obligation. Therefore, although clearly a credit derivative transaction can be used by the protection buyer in order to obtain protection from a loss that the protection buyer might actually suffer if the credit risk crystallizes, a credit derivative transaction can also be used to trade, and therefore to speculate on, credit risk. In this way, credit risk has become a discrete class of asset. In selling protection, the protection seller receives the protection fee or premium in the expectation that the credit

4.165

---

[29] In this way, a credit derivative contract is distinguished from an insurance contract, which it resembles at first glance. The difference between a credit derivative contract and an insurance contract is discussed in more detail in part 8.4 of Chapter 8.

risk will not crystallize. The premium is the protection seller's reward for assuming the risk. Alternatively, the protection seller might in turn buy its own offsetting protection in respect of that credit risk, paying less premium than it receives, and making a profit on the difference. The credit risk has become detached from any underlying transaction or relationship and can be transferred for a price and indeed traded.

4.166 Under the credit derivative transaction, the credit risk which gives rise to settlement of the transaction is the risk that a credit event occurs. Six different types of credit event[30] form the basis of the credit derivative market, and one or more of them will apply to any particular credit derivative transaction. One, a bankruptcy of the reference entity occurs. Two, a debt obligation owed by the reference entity is accelerated as a result of a default. Three, a debt obligation becomes capable of being accelerated as a result of a default. Four, the reference entity fails to make a payment under a debt obligation. Five, the reference entity or a governmental authority repudiates or otherwise imposes a moratorium on a debt obligation. Six, a debt obligation is restructured. In each case, the reference obligation of the credit derivative contract in respect of which the credit event occurs is either specifically identified in the contract (for example, an issue of debt securities bearing a particular ISIN[31]) or is a debt obligation which is not so specified but which has certain characteristics that are specified in the credit derivative contract.

4.167 Either party has the right, but not the obligation, to notify the other party that the credit event has occurred. Following notification, the credit event is quantified and the transaction is then settled. Cash settlement entails the payment by the protection seller to the protection buyer of a cash settlement amount. Physical settlement entails both the payment by the protection seller to the protection buyer of a physical settlement amount, and the delivery by the protection buyer to the protection seller of a delivery obligation (again, the debt obligation that the protection buyer delivers is either specifically identified in the credit derivative contract or it is a debt obligation that is selected by the protection buyer and which merely has certain characteristics that are specified in the credit derivative contract). The protection seller, having taken delivery of the delivery obligation, would then be able to seek to recover some value from that delivery obligation to offset at least partially the amount of the payment made to the protection buyer.

---

[30] Article IV of the 2003 ISDA Credit Derivatives Definitions. See Chapter 7.

[31] An ISIN is an International Securities Identification Number, which is a means of identifying a particular issue of securities. The International Standards Organization developed the ISIN system to catalogue and readily identify issues of securities.

4.12 Credit Derivatives

The credit event must be defined very carefully in order to achieve the transfer of credit risk to the protection seller.[32] The exact definition of the credit event becomes even more crucial for certain end-users of credit derivatives, such as commercial banks, which use credit derivatives actually to buy protection against credit risk. Commercial banks using credit derivatives for this purpose are constrained by the applicable banking regulations as to how they use credit derivatives. A bank's motivation for buying credit protection is not only to control the credit risk to which it is exposed, but also to use its capital more efficiently. A lending bank is exposed to the basic credit risk that its borrower might fail to make the payments of interest and repayments of principal under a loan. The bank is required by banking regulations[33] to hold aside an element of its capital to cushion it against the crystallization of certain risks which arise in its business, such as credit risk. The amount of capital that a bank is required to hold in this manner is usually referred to as regulatory capital, and generally the amount of regulatory capital that a bank is required to hold aside is determined by a complex set of banking regulations and quantified as a specified percentage of the bank's capital base. The bank achieves compliance with the applicable banking regulations by defining internal credit exposure policies which restrict the amount of business written by the bank to credit lines which are full or exhausted when the amount of regulatory capital that the bank is required to hold aside amounts to that specified percentage. The amount of regulatory capital that the bank is required to hold aside in respect of its business is determined in part by the credit risk arising under that business. The amount of credit risk arising under a particular transaction determines the amount of regulatory capital that the bank is required to hold aside in respect of that transaction, and the amount of credit risk is generally determined by the amount of the obligation owed to the bank under that transaction (such as the principal outstanding of a loan) and the type of obligor. If the bank is able to transfer away the credit risk arising under one line of business, then the

4.168

---

[32] This prompts the observation that the structuring and maintenance of credit derivative transactions involve significantly more contractual analysis than other types of derivative transaction. Under a derivative transaction other than a credit derivative, the payout is triggered by the price or value of the underlying performing in a specified manner, whereas under a credit derivative transaction, the payout is triggered if events or circumstances fall within the contractual definition of a credit event. Chapter 7 examines how the quality of information that is available to support a claim that a credit event has occurred is critical, and indeed doubt as to whether or not a particular event properly constitutes a credit event has been the cause of litigation (a protection buyer would seek to show that a credit event has taken place; the protection seller would resist this claim). A potential difficulty is the confidentiality of the information that is disclosed to support the claim that a credit event has occurred. This difficulty can arise in particular in the context of a bank as protection buyer buying protection in respect of a reference entity to which it has made loans. The bank has a duty to keep confidential its relationship with its customer, the reference entity. A possible solution is for the reference entity to give its consent in advance, in the relevant loan document, for the bank to disclose the required information, although of course this consent may not always be forthcoming.

[33] See Chapter 10.

bank is generally required to hold aside less regulatory capital in respect of that line of business. The credit lines limiting the amount of business that the bank can write are therefore recycled, and the bank can write a further amount of business. By writing more business than the first line on its existing capital base, the bank has generated an enhanced return on its use of its capital. Credit derivatives therefore generally allow a bank to manage its assets and liabilities in a more flexible manner. However, it is important to appreciate that banking regulations set detailed criteria which must be satisfied in order for the transfer of credit risk by a bank as a protection buyer to be recognized for the purpose of calculating whether or not the bank is holding sufficient regulatory capital.[34]

4.169 Of course, banks are not the only buyers of credit protection. An entity other than a bank might be subject to its own internal rules that it has established in order to manage its operations prudently, governing the extent of the credit risk that it is prepared to assume, such as credit limits applied to trade creditors. Such an entity might use credit derivatives to transfer away the credit risk arising from a particular amount of business, allowing a greater amount of business to be entered into without breaching the defined credit limits.

4.170 Certain investment funds invest in traded debt, and such an investment fund might use credit derivatives to transfer away the credit risk arising from a holding of traded debt, particularly if the debt has been bought to provide a stable cash flow of interest earnings.

4.171 The price of the credit protection that is bought and sold in respect of an entity and its obligations has become a proxy for assessing the creditworthiness of that entity, complementing the more usual references that are made to the formal credit ratings that are assigned by the credit rating agencies. The price paid under credit default swap transactions is the usual statistic that is quoted, and high credit default swap premiums, expressed as basis points, indicate that the market perception is that the quality of a particular name's creditworthiness is deteriorating. Credit default swap prices are quoted on an ongoing basis, and therefore constitute a more responsive and consensual assessment of the creditworthiness of a particular name.

4.172 The most common credit derivative products are OTC credit default swap contracts, although OTC total return swap contracts and OTC credit spread option contracts have also been traded. Further, the cash flows of OTC credit default swaps are commonly securitized under synthetic collateralized debt obligation (synthetic CDO) issues. These products are introduced in the following paragraphs.

---

[34] See Chapter 10.

4.12 Credit Derivatives

Credit default swap

4.173 The protection buyer pays a premium to the protection seller, usually by way of periodic payments on specified payment dates of an amount equal to a percentage of the notional amount of credit risk that is traded. Following the occurrence of an event or circumstance which falls within the definition of the credit event set out in the credit default swap contract, and verification that the definition has been satisfied, the transaction is settled, whether by cash settlement or physical settlement. Credit default swaps are described as unfunded credit derivative transactions, as they are bilateral OTC contracts entered into between the protection buyer and the protection seller.

4.174 Credit default swaps are the most common type of credit derivative transaction, with single-name credit default swap transactions accounting for one-third of the credit derivative market, and as such, as mentioned in paragraph 4.171, the percentage premium paid by protection buyers in respect of a particular name has become a proxy for published credit ratings in respect of such name.

Total return swap[35]

4.175 As the word swap suggests, a total return swap involves an exchange of cash flows. The protection buyer and the protection seller make a series of payments to each other, and the transfer of credit risk is achieved through the difference between the amounts of the two cash flows. At specified intervals, the protection seller pays to the protection buyer the total return that a person to whom the reference obligation is owed should receive in respect of the reference obligation, and the protection buyer pays to the protection seller the actual amount that is received in respect of the reference obligation. The payments under the total return swap contract are in synchrony with the payments that are scheduled to be made under the reference obligation.

4.176 By way of example, the total return that should be paid under the reference obligation is £100. However, the reference entity only pays £80 under the reference obligation. A loss of £20 therefore occurs. Under the total return swap contract, the protection buyer pays to the protection seller the £80 that is actually paid under the reference obligation, and the protection seller pays to the protection buyer the total return £100 that should have been paid under the reference obligation. In this way, the protection buyer receives the £100 that should be paid. The protection buyer pays for the credit protection by making periodic payments on

---

[35] The total return structure is used for other types of underlying in addition to credit risk, but the principle remains the same: one party, the protection buyer, is insulated from any decrease in the return that the underlying asset is scheduled to generate, whether through the crystallization of credit risk or, in the case of other types of underlying, price or market risk.

specified payment dates of an amount equal to a percentage of the notional amount of credit risk that is traded.

4.177 It is evident that a total return swap contract does not rely as heavily on a contractual interpretation of whether or not a credit event occurs (in contrast with a credit default swap contract). Instead, the amounts paid under the total return swap are determined by amounts that are owed and amounts that are actually paid. The total return swap contract is therefore a less difficult contract to put in place and operate.

Credit spread option

4.178 A credit spread option confers credit protection in respect of an investment in a debt security. The reference entity is the issuer of the debt security. In order to develop an explanation of a credit spread option, it is necessary to consider how the yield of a debt security is calculated, and how this calculation of yield is used. Yield is generally the function of the rate of coupon (or interest) that is paid on a debt security and the price of that debt security. The risk of holding a debt security is that the issuer defaults under its obligations to make payments or more generally fails and enters into insolvency. A low-risk debt security generates a low yield, and a high-risk debt security generates a high yield. The high yield compensates the holder of the debt security for the greater risk of a default or failure of the issuer of the debt security. When a debt security is sold, whether on its initial issue into the primary market or on a subsequent sale from one investor to another in the secondary market, its yield is selected to attract a buyer. Essentially, the yield must be better than that of competing investments. When a debt security is initially issued into the primary market, the selected yield is achieved by adjusting both the coupon and the price. When a debt security is sold in the secondary market, the selected yield is achieved only by adjusting the price. Therefore if the market of buyers and sellers perceives that the risk of a default or failure by the issuer has increased, then the yield of the debt security must be increased to attract buyers. Generally, in the mathematics underpinning debt securities, yield equals (coupon / price) * 100, and price equals (coupon / yield) * 100.

4.179 The first equation is the key equation of elementary debt securities mathematics, and indicates that the yield of a debt security increases only if price decreases, if coupon is held constant. The first equation can be rearranged to give the second equation, which is used to calculate the price at which a debt security must be sold in order to achieve the yield that has been selected. The second equation indicates that price decreases if yield increases and coupon is held constant.

4.180 By way of illustration, a debt security has been bought by an investor, on the basis that it generates a particular yield. The risk increases that the issuer might default. The investor now wishes to sell the debt security. In order to attract a buyer, the investor must offer to sell the debt security at a price which generates a higher yield. The second equation indicates that the higher yield is only achieved if the price of the debt security is reduced. The reduction in price of the debt security is detrimental to the investor.

The yield of a debt security is sometimes expressed as a spread over a selected benchmark. The benchmark is usually the yield generated from time to time by government debt, such as US Treasuries or UK gilts, which is deemed to be free of risk. The spread of a debt security might for example be 50 basis points, which means that the yield of the debt security is 50 basis points higher than the yield of the selected benchmark. If the yield of a debt security increases, then the spread widens, and the widening of a spread indicates that the market is beginning to build into the price of the debt security certain unfavourable factors, such as a perceived diminution in the creditworthiness of the issuer. The benchmark does not give rise to credit risk, and therefore a widening of the spread is considered to be due to the deterioration of the creditworthiness of the issuer. **4.181**

The widening of the spread over a selected benchmark is the credit event of a credit spread option. Upon the occurrence of the credit event, the protection seller makes a payment to the protection buyer of a cash settlement amount. Again, the observation is made that a credit spread option contract does not rely as heavily on a contractual interpretation of whether or not a credit event occurs (in contrast with a credit default swap contract). Whether or not a credit event occurs is determined with reference to numerical market data. **4.182**

Synthetic collateralized debt obligation

The synthetic collateralized debt obligation[36] is essentially a securitization of the cash flow of a credit default swap, and broadly it replicates through the use of derivative techniques the economic effect of a more traditional structure based on actual debt and loan obligations (hence the tag 'synthetic'). The more traditional structure based on actual debt and loan obligations is usually known as a 'cash CDO'.[37] The purpose of a CDO, whether cash or synthetic, is to place in the hands of the investor a debt security which creates in one transferable package an exposure to, and thereby delivers a return based on, a pool of reference debt or loan obligations. A CDO therefore comprises an issue of debt securities which are usually of shorter maturity, and therefore the term 'notes' is used to describe them. **4.183**

---

[36] Synthetic CDO or CSO.
[37] The forerunners of the cash CDO include the collateralized bond obligation (which creates an investment exposure to a pool of traded debt securities) and collateralized mortgage obligation (which creates an investment exposure to a pool of residential and commercial mortgages). The techniques developed for CBO and CMO were then applied to collateralized loan obligation issues. However, the basic structure of each is similar.

Synthetic CDOs are described as funded credit derivative transactions, as the credit default swap is contained in a structured finance 'wrapper'.

4.184 The CDO notes are usually issued by a special purpose vehicle which is established by the arranging bank in a jurisdiction which either levies little or no tax (such as the Cayman Islands), or which has established a low tax regime for structured finance transactions (such as the Republic of Ireland or the Netherlands). The investor subscribes for the CDO notes, which operate to transfer to the investor the credit risk that a default or other failure occurs in the reference pool. The investor earns a superior return relative to the prevailing investment benchmarks in return for assuming the credit risk emanating from the reference pool. The terms on which the investor assumes the credit risk are set out in the conditions of the CDO notes.[38]

4.185 The issuer receives the principal paid by the investor on the issue of the CDO notes, and sets this aside as collateral. The collateral might be held by the issuer in a guaranteed investment contract (GIC) with a highly rated counterparty or in a holding of highly rated debt. The collateral held by the issuer should match the issuer's obligations to repay the principal of the CDO notes to the investor, and so the GIC or the highly rated debt should be selected to mature when the CDO notes are scheduled for repayment. The issuer also enters into a credit default swap as protection seller with its credit default swap counterparty, which is usually the arranging bank. The credit default swap is usually a portfolio transaction, in that it operates with reference to a portfolio of reference entities, although single name credit default swap transactions are also encountered.

4.186 Under the terms of the CDO notes, the issuer pays to the investor interest (or coupon) which is made up of the return earned by the issuer on the collateral, whether a GIC or highly rated debt, plus the premium received by the issuer under the credit default swap transaction. In this way, the CDO notes are able to deliver to the investor a superior investment return.

4.187 If a credit event occurs, then the issuer pays to the arranging bank a cash settlement amount, and the principal outstanding of the CDO notes is correspondingly reduced by the amount of that cash settlement amount. In this way, the credit risk has been passed through to the investor. Of course, it is important that the terms of the CDO notes operate to pass to the investor the same credit risk that is passed to the issuer under the credit default swap contract. The occurrence

---

[38] The CDO notes are issued as a structured finance transaction, and the usual elements of such a structure are present, including a prospectus to describe the investment and the operation of the CDO notes, a trust deed by which the issuer settles a trust of its assets and rights on a trustee which safeguards the investor's interests, and various ancillary arrangements for the administration of the transaction, such as a paying agency.

4.12 Credit Derivatives

of a credit event should have no effect on the issuer. The issuer is usually a thinly capitalized entity which has been established for the purposes of issuing structured finance securities, and each issue of securities is made on a limited recourse basis, which means that the only assets of the issuer that are available to meet the issuer's obligations under a particular issue of securities are those assets specified for that purpose; these assets are usually held subject to the terms of a trust created in favour of the trustee for the benefit of the holders from time to time of the securities. Further, any rating agency retained by the arranging bank to provide a rating of the CDO notes would need to be satisfied that a credit event would have no effect on the issuer's ability to pay amounts, and the documentation of both the CDO notes and the underlying credit default swap are therefore carefully analysed.

4.188 The arranging bank funds the payments of premium it makes under the credit default swap it enters into with the issuer by selling credit protection, and receiving the corresponding premium, from the credit risk market. Ideally, the arranging bank pays a lower premium to the issuer than it receives from the credit risk market, in order to be able to earn a spread on passing through the credit risk to the issuer. Figure 4.17 illustrates the structure of a synthetic CDO.

4.189 To maintain clarity, this example purposely disregards the detail of any tranching. Tranching generally involves the issue to investors of different ranks of CDO notes, from senior through to mezzanine down to junior. Below the junior rank is

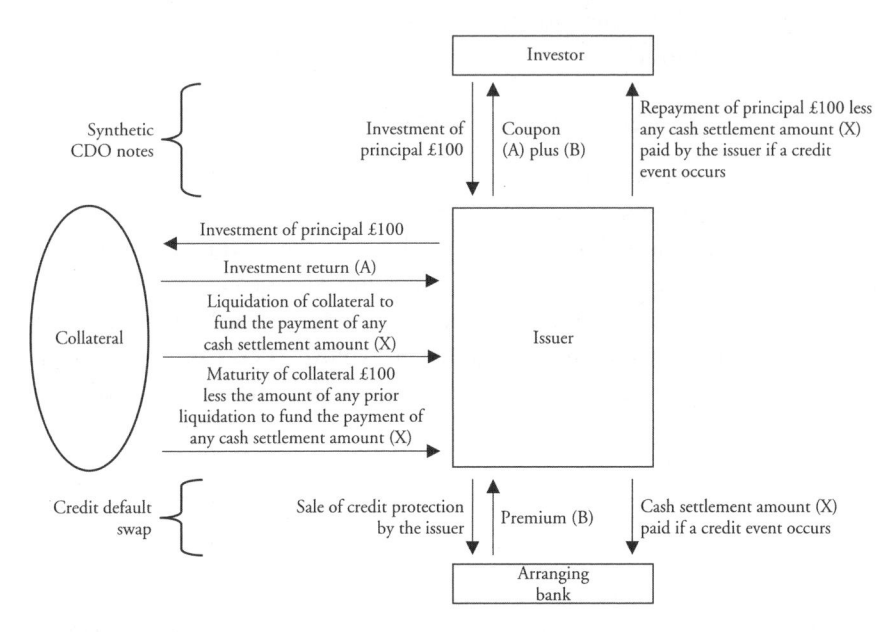

Figure 4.17 The structure of a synthetic CDO

the 'equity piece'.[39] Each rank, other than the equity, may be rated. The general principle is that the lower ranks absorb losses before the higher ranks, hence the higher ranks enjoy higher ratings and pay less interest (or coupon). A subtlety is that each rank absorbs no more than a percentage of a loss, and losses may be sustained more than once, subject to a total ceiling on losses that might be imposed. Accordingly, both the terms of the CDO notes and the credit default swap contract would also need to provide that credit events can take place more than once. The structure of a synthetic CDO is therefore extremely flexible, and can be calibrated quite precisely to the investor's required balance of risk and reward.

4.190 A managed synthetic CDO offers further advantages to the investor. The composition of the reference portfolio of the credit default swap is managed through the life of the CDO transaction, in order that particular reference obligations which might default, and which might therefore ultimately cause loss to the investor, are identified and replaced by other reference obligations which give rise to a lower risk. The credit default swap contract and other transaction documentation contain extensive criteria for the selection and replacement of reference obligations. A managed synthetic CDO should therefore operate in much the same manner as a pooled investment debt, and this gives rise to a further potential difficulty. Managing investments is in many jurisdictions an activity for which a regulatory licence must be held, and the regulatory analysis of a managed CDO structure therefore becomes critical. An alternative might be to include detailed rules governing the removal and replacement of reference obligations, in order that no active management of the portfolio takes place, and instead reference obligations are removed or added mechanically in response to the rules. However, it is extremely difficult to achieve the necessary precision in the drafting.

Development of the credit derivative market

4.191 The first credit derivative transactions were entered into during 1993 by the investment banks Credit Suisse Financial Products (the derivatives operation at that time of Credit Suisse First Boston) and Bankers Trust, which marketed debt securities the repayment amounts of which were linked to specific events of default in respect of the reference entities. The motivation for the early credit derivative transactions was the requirement of banks to remove assets from their balance sheets and thereby recycle the credit lines they made available, as explained in paragraph 4.168.

---

[39] In this context, the term 'equity piece' is something of a misnomer, as the securities in this rank are also debt securities. The term 'equity' is a reference to the fact that this lowest rank of debt securities operates like equity in that the holder is exposed entirely to the credit risk.

4.12 Credit Derivatives

4.192 The credit derivative market gained momentum rapidly through the late 1990s, and by the early 2000s, synthetic CDO issues became prominent, and grew in complexity. The first synthetic CDOs were driven by the usual form of credit default swap, but later structures were driven by credit default swaps which had as their underlying not a portfolio of reference entities and their obligations but a second layer of credit default swaps. These structures are termed synthetic CDO squared transactions, which is sometimes written as CDO^2. A further iteration is the synthetic CDO cubed transaction, which introduces a third layer of credit default swaps. The CDO cubed structure has not been as widespread as the CDO squared structure. These structures pose obvious challenges in terms of the complexity of documentation required and, at a more fundamental level, the modelling of the credit risk being packaged and passed on. Each layer of credit default swaps introduces further leverage within the structure, which means that there is a non-linear relationship between the amount of a loss generated at the level of the reference entity and the reference obligation and the amount by which the CDO notes are written down. The principal motivation for structuring a CDO squared or even a CDO cubed transaction might include the availability in the arranging bank's inventory of existing residual credit default swap positions which were opened in respect of previous transactions, parts of which were not sold. These residual elements can be repackaged into investments that can be sold. The attraction of a CDO squared transaction for the investor is that the effect of a credit event at the lower layer of credit default swap may be diluted at the level of the CDO notes. In this way, more credit events can occur before the CDO notes themselves are written down significantly. However, the risk remains that the pattern of credit events, in terms of the particular reference entities and reference obligations involved and the amounts of the losses which occur, may deviate from the assumptions underpinning the modelling of the transaction. The leverage implicit in the structure would exacerbate the effect on the CDO notes of these losses. Nonetheless, the ever-increasing complexity of these products in itself brings considerable risks, and there is a level of complexity beyond which even the most sophisticated investors will be unwilling to venture.[40]

4.193 Other developments within the credit derivative market include the establishment of various credit indices and the publication of standard contractual provisions for different types of credit derivative transaction and reference entity. Essentially, a credit index tracks the premiums paid for credit derivative

---

[40] By way of an aside, Warren Buffet, who is one of the world's most successful investors, has remarked, in a conversation which took place on 17 February 2006 with a group of students from Wharton University and reported on that university's website, that he refers to three boxes when considering whether or not an investment opportunity should be included in a portfolio, one labelled 'yes', one labelled 'no', and one labelled 'too difficult' (Warren Buffet was speaking generally and not with reference to synthetic CDOs).

protection, and the inclusion of a reference entity in such an index is subject to detailed rules, including the jurisdiction of establishment of the reference entity, its commercial activity (that is, the industrial sector in which it is properly categorized), the volume of credit protection traded in respect of it, and the record of its creditworthiness. A credit index can be used either as the underlying of a credit derivative transaction, in much the same way as an index of share prices can be used as the underlying of an equity-linked derivative transaction, or as a determinant of amounts payable under a credit derivative transaction by way of premium. ISDA has published a broad variety of standard contractual definitions and provisions for different types of credit derivative transaction, reference entity, and reference obligation, including asset-backed securities[41] which have certain characteristics that are very distinct from those of other types of reference entity such as industrial companies. The considerable detail that these developments all involve is outside the scope of an introductory text such as this.[42]

4.194 Further innovations have included the synthetic CPPI structure, which is based on the more usual CPPI structure described in part 4.9 of this chapter, and the CPDO structure which evolved from CPPI during 2006. CPDO transactions involve yet higher levels of gearing. It remains to be seen how the credit derivative market evolves following the difficulties caused by the sub-prime losses of the second half of 2007.

4.13 Multi-asset Derivatives

4.195 Multi-asset derivative products are investment products which use derivative techniques to create investment exposures to two or more classes of underlying within the same product. Each class of underlying within the same product is sometimes labelled a 'silo'. One purpose of such an investment product might be to enhance the return generated by one class of underlying with the return generated by another class of underlying. A second purpose of such an investment product might be to develop an investment exposure which captures the correlation between different classes of underlying, including any divergence or convergence between the different classes of underlying. Different classes of underlying are susceptible to different stimuli. For example, more factors might potentially affect the price performance of commodities and energy than might potentially affect the price performance of financial instruments; factors which might potentially affect the price performance of commodities and energy include the

---

[41] The debt securities created and issued under a securitization.
[42] See Parker, *Credit Derivatives: Documenting and Understanding Credit Derivative Products* (Globe Law and Business, 2007).

weather and geopolitical developments. Different classes of asset respond differently to the same stimuli and the effect on different classes of asset endure for different periods. These differences have implications for the pricing assumptions underpinning the structuring of multi-asset derivative products. A third purpose of such an investment product might be to enable the investor to gain from an uncertain market, through a payout formula which operates with reference to the best performing class of underlying.

Given that two or more classes of underlying are blended within one transaction, documentation must be prepared on a bespoke basis. The industry-standard documentation[43] does not easily accommodate combining the treatments of different classes of underlying within one contract, and the difficulty can be particularly acute in the context of legislating within the contract for the consequences for the transaction as a whole of a disruption to the valuation of any particular underlying or the occurrence of a particular event in respect of any particular underlying which requires some adjustment to the terms of the contract. **4.196**

4.14 New Classes of Underlying

New classes of underlying have emerged within recent years, including hedge fund interests, interests in other forms of fund such as mutual funds, certain new classes of commodity underlying such as freight prices, and, of growing interest in the early 21st century, power trading and carbon emissions. Further, the exploration of the mathematical properties of derivative exposures also represents new opportunities to develop new products. These new classes of underlying give rise to certain interesting observations. First, hedge fund interests are growing in importance as more investors are attracted to the absolute returns hedge funds offer, and this has the effect of increasing the assets under management within the hedge fund, or alternative investment, sector.[44] In addition, other investment products which create exposures to hedge funds are being created, further effectively increasing the distribution of hedge funds. However, as the following paragraphs illustrate, hedge funds constitute a difficult class of asset over which to write derivative contracts. Second, freight derivative contracts have been traded on various derivative exchanges for some years; however, this particular segment of the derivative market has recently witnessed some structural change and significant enlargement. Third, an extremely important class of underlying might be termed computed data. This class of underlying does not strictly comprise any **4.197**

---

[43] See the various sets of ISDA definitions, which are introduced in Chapter 7.
[44] Hedge funds are introduced in Chapter 9, from the perspective of the hedge fund as an end-user of a derivative.

new class of asset, but instead consists of the results of mathematical calculations that are performed in respect of an existing class of underlying. Within this class are included, by way of illustration, convergence transactions, divergence transactions, and volatility swaps.[45] Doubtless other varieties will emerge, and it is beyond the scope of this introductory book to catalogue each of them. The actual reference asset of a derivative contract written over computed data might well be a familiar and common asset, such as a share. The writing of a derivative contract over computed data illustrates one of the key principles of derivative transactions: it is possible to write a derivative contract over any fluctuating data population. The emergence of new forms of data computed from existing classes of asset illustrates how different risks can be isolated and either hedged against or speculated on using derivatives. Fourth, electricity and power trading and carbon trading are included, as these activities constitute markets which are readily adapted to the overlay of the creation and trading of derivative exposures. In particular, electricity and power trading represents a more liquid and less controversial base for the development of a new class of underlying, and these types of contract seemingly have a conceptual connection with existing energy and chemical derivatives such as oil futures contracts. Indeed, the mechanisms for buying and selling electricity that have emerged include a forward component. However, in the case of the nascent carbon trading market, although the structures and cash flows which are familiar within other types of market are already discernible, and therefore the derivative overlay connoted above is feasible, the underlying market yet lacks certainty and liquidity. Nonetheless, conceptually, this market, whether cash or derivative, would operate to reallocate a finite volume of resource efficiently. In the case of carbon trading, or emissions trading, the resource being reallocated efficiently is the right to emit during an industrial process a specified quantity of greenhouse gas. Nonetheless, as indicated above, carbon trading is one facet of an emotive and controversial subject and the importance of the reactions the topic attracts cannot be understated.

4.198 One of the key themes underlying this discussion of new classes of underlying is that although the underlying examined are novel, the techniques used to create an economic exposure to each of them are already well rehearsed within the derivative industry. Indeed, although an individual new class of underlying might give rise to particular difficulties in the contractual treatment of that class, in terms of valuations, disruptions to valuations, and adjustments and extraordinary events, the overall methodology is again well rehearsed.

---

[45] The term 'variance' is used to describe a transaction or contract which creates an exposure to changes in the magnitude of movements in a data population.

4.14 *New Classes of Underlying*

Hedge funds and other funds

4.199 Hedge funds[46] are mentioned in different contexts in this book. The focus of this part of this chapter is the hedge fund interest as the underlying of a derivative exposure, irrespective of the 'wrapper' which contains that exposure. The term 'hedge fund interest' is used because generally a hedge fund might be constituted as a form of corporation, which issues shares, or as a form of partnership, in which investors have partnership interests. Certain difficulties and risks emerge from the particular characteristics of hedge funds as an asset class.[47]

4.200 First, a hedge fund interest is usually valued by an agent appointed by the fund for that purpose.[48] This process is diametrically different from the discovery of prices which takes place in respect of most other classes of asset that underlie derivative contracts. For example, the discovery of the price of a share traded on an investment exchange is achieved merely by obtaining the price of that share published by the exchange, usually through an electronic price feed. The price of the share is published throughout the trading session, and a settlement price is determined at the end of the trading session in accordance with the rules of the exchange. The prices of the share that are published by the exchange reflect the buying and selling pressure exerted on that share. Prices for the exchange-traded share are therefore available almost continuously, whereas the value of a fund interest is only available when the valuation agent publishes the value. A related risk is that whereas prices for the exchange-traded share should accurately represent the market's overall perception of that share and the entity which issued it, the value of a fund interest may be calculated by a person who is too closely connected with the fund or with the investment advisers or investment managers of the fund, and who therefore has a vested interest in overstating that value. Of course, many hedge funds appoint an independent third party to perform valuations, and such an appointment considerably mitigates the risk of valuation fraud. A further risk is the risk that the valuation agent may have the right to suspend valuations, perhaps in response to events or circumstances in the markets in which the hedge fund invests.

4.201 Second, a party writing a derivative contract the underlying of which is a hedge fund interest, or selling an investment product which offers a derivative exposure to a hedge fund interest, would usually seek to hedge its own exposure to that hedge fund interest by subscribing for and holding it. An important constraint to

---

[46] Despite the increasing prominence of hedge funds, no definition of 'hedge fund' exists.
[47] For example, as a structural issue, hedge funds often employ leverage, and therefore an accurate assessment of a fund's value, and the extraction of that value, can pose significant difficulties.
[48] The value of a hedge fund interest is usually expressed as the net asset value of the fund, which is generally the net assets of the fund (after deducting liabilities) divided by the number of hedge fund interests issued. However, hedge funds also publish other measurements of their performance.

this hedging activity is the liquidity offered by the hedge fund. Generally, subscriptions and redemptions of hedge fund interests can only take place at the frequency, or within the liquidity cycle, prescribed by the internal regulations governing the hedge fund, for example its articles of association or by-laws. Liquidity cycles of one month are quite common, and quarterly, half-yearly, or even annual liquidity cycles are not unheard of. Further, hedge funds sometimes reserve a 'lock-up' right which effectively locks the investor's capital in the fund for a specified period. Clearly hedging an exposure to an interest in a hedge fund which has an infrequent liquidity cycle or which invokes a 'lock-up' right will create some difficulty. An associated risk to hedging is the right reserved by the fund or its manager to suspend liquidity or to impose some form of 'gating' in response to any cash flow difficulty that the fund may be experiencing. By way of background, if a hedge fund does not have cash readily available, it may be required to liquidate the relevant amount of its own investment portfolio in order to meet its obligation to pay investors who are redeeming their interests. The term 'gating' describes the process by which a hedge fund fulfils only a proportion of the redemption orders placed, whether by fulfilling the redemption orders of a proportion of the investors placing those orders, or by fulfilling only a proportion of each redemption order placed. Of course, hedging activity will be compromised however the gating is applied. A further related risk is the risk that the amount received on the redemption of a position held for hedging purposes is less than anticipated. Such a shortfall may be caused by the hedge fund receiving less on the liquidation of the relevant amount of its own investment portfolio. The hedge fund would only begin liquidating a part of its own investment portfolio when it receives redemption orders, and of course the hedge fund will pay out to redeeming investors only after it has completed these liquidations, and there is every possibility that the proceeds of these liquidations will be less than anticipated. Sometimes redemption proceeds are paid to redeeming investors some months after they place their redemption orders and are taken 'off risk', and sometimes the hedge fund has the right to keep back a proportion of the redemption proceeds it pays pending finalization of the relevant valuations and accounts.

4.202 A further potential risk is the risk that the investment portfolio of the hedge fund is no longer managed in accordance with the strategy prescribed for the fund, whether in terms of the types of asset in which investments are made, or the diversification of the assets in which investments are made. This phenomenon is sometimes referred to as 'style drift'. Further, the appointment of the investment manager or adviser might come to an end. A related risk is the risk that the involvement in the management of the hedge fund's investment portfolio of a key individual might come to an end. Investment management firms in the more mainstream investment management sector employ teams of investment managers, traders and research analysts, and the investment strategy sold to the investor is the house strategy. By contrast, the investment strategy of a hedge fund might well be informed by the views and insights of a particular star investment manager, and indeed the fund may well be marketed on the strength of the theories and performance of this manager, and the departure of that manager would have an obvious effect on the performance of the fund.

4.203 Although the hedge fund vehicle itself is unlikely to be regulated, the various service providers performing various functions for and on behalf of the fund, such as investment managers and advisers and valuation agents, will tend to be regulated. The withdrawal of a regulatory licence would affect at least the administration of the fund, and may well even affect the performance and stability of the fund.

4.204 Similar risks generally arise in the context of mutual funds. However, mutual funds tend to be more regulated than hedge funds, and the regulatory supervision to which mutual funds are subject generally ameliorates many of these risks. Accordingly, OTC contracts which have as their underlying mutual fund interests tend to omit many of the provisions which are included within contracts which have as their underlying hedge fund interests. Chapter 7 explores in outline how these risks are controlled in OTC derivative contracts.

Freight derivatives

4.205 Freight derivatives are derivative transactions, the underlying of which are freight prices. Freight derivatives are increasingly dealt in the OTC derivative market, although exchange-based contracts have been traded for longer. For example, the New York Mercantile Exchange currently offers a variety of contracts based on the price of freight on major shipping routes,[49] and following its merger with the London Commodities Exchange, the LIFFE exchange in London previously offered futures contracts and options contracts on the BIFFEX index.[50] Today, the Baltic Exchange, which publishes maritime market information for the trading and settlement of various contracts, calculates and publishes its Baltic indices,[51]

---

[49] These routes are: Ras Tanura to Yokohama by freighter, Ras Tanura to Yokohama by tanker, Singapore to Japan by tanker, Middle Eastern Gulf to Japan by freighter, West Africa to the US Atlantic Coast by freighter, North Sea to Europe by freighter, Caribbean to US Gulf by freighter, and Caribbean to US Atlantic Coast by freighter.

[50] The BIFFEX index was an index which was based on the Baltic Panamax Index, which reflects the spot freight rate on seven shipping routes. These shipping routes represent the international trade in grain, oil, coal and iron ore, and the freight rates are based on the cost of freight in a standard 50,000 tonne 'Panamax' vessel, which is a class of ship able to navigate the Panama Canal. The Baltic Panamax Index continues to be calculated by the Baltic Exchange.

[51] The principal Baltic indices published by the Baltic Exchange are: the Baltic Exchange Capesize Index, the Baltic Exchange Panamax Index (from which the BIFFEX Index was calculated, see above), the Baltic Exchange Supramax Index, and the Baltic Exchange Handymax Index. Other indices published by the Baltic Exchange reflect the price of shipping on tanker routes and liquid petroleum gas (LPG) routes.

which measure the price of shipping on various routes different bulk cargoes by sea. These cargoes comprise both wet cargoes, such as crude oil and oil distillates, and dry cargoes, such as coal and iron ore. The indices are determined with reference to the rates quoted for the relevant routes by ship-broking houses. The various indices are used by the participants in the freight industry, including charterers and shipowners. The indices form the underlying of various derivative contracts, which enable shipowners and cargo owners to smooth out their respective exposures to the fluctuating price of shipping.[52] To support this hedging activity, the Baltic Exchange also calculates forward curves and settlement prices for forward freight agreements. The Baltic Exchange continues to monitor existing indices and how they are used, whether to improve existing indices, to delete indices, or to introduce new indices. The forward freight agreement is a forward contract to fix the price of freight on a particular shipping route for a specified tonnage of a specified cargo, and operates in the same manner as any other forward contract.[53] The shipping industry uses a standard contract which is maintained by the Forward Freight Agreement Brokers' Association.

4.206 The expanded ISDA Commodity Definitions published in 2005[54] include OTC freight price derivative contracts. The inclusion of freight price derivative contracts within the framework of the ISDA Commodity Definitions illustrates that, although freight prices do not represent a new class of underlying, the means by which derivative exposures to freight prices are created and traded is subject to competitive pressure and therefore change. Indeed, the freight derivative market has expanded significantly during 2007, as financial institutions and hedge funds have been attracted to the opportunities afforded by increasing volatility and a rise in shipping prices. Adverse weather causing port closures and energy supply difficulties have contributed to uncertainty over future shipping prices, and this uncertainty in turn has given rise to the hedging and speculative use of freight derivatives.

Computed data

4.207 'Computed data' is the term adopted in this book to refer to data that is calculated or otherwise determined in respect of a particular asset and which itself forms the underlying of a derivative contract. For example, a derivative contract can be written on the volatility exhibited by the spot price of an asset, and the underlying of that derivative contract is not strictly the asset itself, but the fluctuating volatility data population. By way of illustration, under a volatility swap, an amount is paid which is calculated with reference to the change in the volatility of the reference asset.

---

[52] The annual freight market is worth some US$150 billion.
[53] See part 4.2 of this chapter.
[54] See Chapter 7.

The volatility of the reference asset is measured on the strike date, and again on the subsequent measurement date, and volatility might be determined either on the basis of preceding price observations or from an option pricing model. The change in volatility is given a monetary value by multiplying it by the notional amount of the swap. Indeed, in common with other varieties of swap, the notional amount itself is not paid. Volatility emerged as a distinct asset class during the late 1970s, as financial techniques were developed to perform the necessary analysis. In addition to the definition of how the two different measurements of volatility are calculated, the contract would of course need to contain the usual provisions governing how valuations of the reference asset are obtained and how the transaction responds to the occurrence of valuation disruptions, adjustments, and extraordinary events in respect of that reference asset.

4.208 Two further examples of computed data used as underlying asset classes are correlation and dispersion. Correlation is the measure of the extent to which the price or level of one asset moves in the same direction as the price or level of another asset. A high correlation indicates that there is a strong relationship between the movements in the prices of the two assets, and a low correlation indicates the opposite. Dispersion is the measure of the extent to which the volatility exhibited by the price or level of one asset moves in the same direction as the volatility exhibited by the price or level of another asset. Again, a high correlation indicates that there is a strong relationship, and a low correlation indicates the opposite. The correlation and dispersion data constitute a fluctuating data population over which the relevant derivative contract can be written. Again, in addition to the definition of how the correlation or dispersion data are calculated, the contract would need to legislate for valuations, disruptions to valuations, adjustments, and extraordinary events in respect of the two assets. Dispersion and correlation transactions have become more commonplace in recent years as investment managers have sought to capture the relationships between different industry sectors. Whereas companies within a particular industry sector, such as energy companies, might perform better, companies in another industry sector, such as consumer-oriented companies, might perform less well. Broad market indices may not capture the relationship between the two sectors in as detailed a fashion as a derivative contract written on the particular correlation or dispersion data.

Electricity and power trading[55]

4.209 Within Great Britain, the framework for electricity trading is administered by ELEXON,[56] in its capacity as the Balancing and Settlement Code Company

---

[55] The licensing and regulation of the electricity industry is outside the scope of this book.
[56] ELEXON is a wholly owned subsidiary of the National Grid Company, but it is independently managed and has a separate board of directors.

for Great Britain. The Balancing and Settlement Code contains the rules and procedures for trading between the generators of electricity and the suppliers of electricity, and was drawn up by the National Grid. All licensed electricity companies are required to sign the Code, and other interested parties, for example energy trading companies, may sign it. The Code is given contractual force by the BSC Framework Agreement. The generators of electricity sell into the wholesale market which comprises the suppliers, and the suppliers in turn sell electricity in the retail market to public and private consumers. ELEXON administers a surprisingly complex system under which details of electricity sale and purchase contracts are matched and cleared, and payments are netted and settled.[57] As the following paragraphs demonstrate, in necessarily broad terms, this process is substantially familiar from the clearing and settlement of exchange-based derivative contracts already covered in previous chapters. The generators and suppliers are referred to as BSC Trading Parties, as they must adhere to the Balancing and Settlement Code. The National Grid itself administers the actual physical electricity transmission system, that is, the extensive network of relay stations, electricity lines, and related infrastructure.

4.210 Generators and suppliers enter into contracts for the supply and payment of electricity for periods or blocks of 30 minutes. These contracts are struck in either the OTC market directly between generators and suppliers or on power exchanges such as the IntercontinentalExchange ICE. However, the complexity of electricity as a class of underlying asset is that the actual amount generated and consumed inevitably differs from the amount for which contracts have been struck, and storing electricity is not a practical proposition. Accordingly, a system for the payment of the imbalances has been introduced.

4.211 The purpose of the clearing and settlement system is to smooth out imbalances between the amount of electricity that is contracted to be bought and sold and the amount of electricity that is actually delivered within each half-hour period, in order that the retail demand for electricity is always met. The concept of the imbalance is the foundation of the system pricing process. Generators may actually generate more or less electricity than they have contracted to sell, and suppliers may buy more or less electricity than their customers actually use. The term 'system' refers to the whole system for the wholesale transmission of electricity from the generators to the suppliers, and therefore electricity effectively is put into the system by the generators, and taken out of the system and transmitted to the ultimate consumers by the suppliers. Accordingly, the system itself records an energy imbalance if the totals represented by the various contracts for the sale and

---

[57] ELEXON's other functions are to provide advice and assurance as to the processes of the Balancing and Settlement Code and to provide advice and support to the committees supporting the Code.

purchase of electricity do not match the totals of the electricity actually generated and used. In short, therefore, the system identifies imbalances between electricity generation and demand for each half-hour period. The system as a whole is long electricity when the amount of generation is higher than the amount of demand, and conversely the system as a whole is short electricity when the amount of generation is less than the amount of demand. In addition, certain BSC Trading Parties will have either a net surplus of electricity or a net deficit of electricity following each half-hourly assessment of imbalances.

The National Grid operates the transmission system and balances the flow of electricity within the system. The National Grid seeks to balance the transmission of electricity through the system by buying from generators additional electricity to put into the system, and by selling to suppliers additional electricity for delivery out of the system for retail distribution. Certain BSC Trading Parties are able, if they wish, to buy and to sell additional electricity within this balancing mechanism. The National Grid seeks to balance the overall supply of electricity with the overall demand for electricity. The involvement of BSC Trading Parties in buying and selling additional electricity is very important as this adds the necessary liquidity to the market and enables fluctuations in demand for electricity to be met. National Grid also receives information from BSC Trading Parties to enable it to assess whether or not there is likely to be equilibrium between electricity supply and demand and whether or not the system as a whole will be long or short. By showing bid and offer prices for electricity, the National Grid is able to influence the buying and selling of BSC Trading Parties and thereby maintain the required equilibrium between electricity supply and demand. The National Grid also has the ability to take urgent remedial short-term action to respond to sudden spikes in demand or sudden decreases in supply, perhaps caused by malfunction in any component of the physical network. **4.212**

In addition, spot and forward sales and purchases of electricity are made for each half-hour period. Forward sales and purchases take place up to three business days prior to the particular relevant half-hour period. All BSC Trading Parties are able to submit bids and offers for electricity before the deadline, which is referred to as Gate Closure, for each half-hour period during which the relevant amount of electricity is scheduled to be delivered. **4.213**

Energy Imbalance Prices are calculated on the basis of both the prices discovered in the course of the National Grid's balancing actions and the prices discovered in the course of the spot and forward sales and purchases prior to Gate Closure for each half-hour period. Imbalances in the amount of electricity can occur either in the direction of the transmission system (that is, the flow of electricity in direction from the generators to the suppliers) or in the opposite direction. Two different prices, System Sell Prices and System Buy Prices, are calculated with reference to Energy Imbalance Prices. **4.214**

4.215 Imbalances in the same direction of the transmission system are smoothed out using Energy Imbalance Prices calculated from the National Grid's balancing actions. On each half-hourly assessment of the imbalance within the system, if the system as a whole is long (that is, a surplus of electricity has been put into the system), then BSC Trading Parties which are long are paid the System Sell Price, and if the system as a whole is short (that is, there is a shortfall in the amount of electricity that has been put into the system), then BSC Trading Parties which are short pay the System Buy Price.

4.216 Imbalances in the opposite direction to the transmission system are smoothed out using Energy Imbalance Prices calculated from the spot and forward sales and purchases of electricity prior to Gate Closure. On each half-hourly assessment of the imbalance within the system, if the system as a whole is long (that is, a surplus of electricity has been put into the system), then BSC Trading Parties which are short pay the System Buy Price, and if the system as a whole is short (that is, there is a shortfall in the amount of electricity that has been put into the system), then BSC Trading Parties which are long are paid the System Sell Price.

4.217 The overall principle is that an individual BSC Trading Party either pays if it is long electricity (whether because it is a generator and it has generated more than it has contracted to sell, or because it is a supplier and its customers have consumed less than it has contracted to buy from generators), or is paid if it is short electricity (whether because it is a generator and has generated less than it has contracted to sell, or because it is a supplier and its customers have consumed more than it has contracted to buy from generators). To maintain clarity, the explanations set out in the preceding paragraphs do not include the adjustments made to the various calculations to reflect weightings for volumes, the process by which minimum amounts of electricity are bought and sold, or the treatment of transmission losses.[58]

4.218 Familiar clearing and settlement concepts are discernible within the mechanism for electricity generation and transmission. Moreover, the spot and forward trading of electricity already takes place within the system, and there is scope for further intermediation through the use of derivative contracts. Interestingly, from a broader perspective, electricity generation and transmission are now being made economically more efficient by the intervention of derivative techniques at

---

[58] Transmission losses consist of fixed losses and variable losses. Certain losses of electricity are fixed because they occur in iron components that are subject to a magnetic field, which is created by a voltage. Voltage is broadly constant and therefore the loss of electricity caused by the magnetic field created by voltage is also broadly constant. Other losses of electricity are variable because they occur in components which heat up and dissipate electricity as a consequence of the flow of current. Current fluctuates depending on the amount of electricity being transmitted, and therefore variable losses of electricity increase as the distance increases over which the electricity is transmitted.

different levels: first, at the level of the price paid for the raw commodities that are combusted to generate electricity, such as oil, gas, and coal; second, at the level of the price paid for the shipping of these raw commodities; and third, at the level of the price paid for the sale of the electricity to the end consumer through the transmission from the wholesale to the retail power market. Indeed, a fourth level may be some form of fixed price contract paid by the end consumer of the electricity, which would itself constitute a form of derivative contract. The equivalent of the domestic fixed price energy contract is the fixed rate home loan discussed in Chapter 1. Indeed the observation made in Chapter 1 is recollected, that derivatives are a hidden yet increasingly important part of modern society, and derivative techniques are being applied in diverse activities which at first glance have little to do with the financial markets.

Carbon trading

Carbon trading at once represents an intensely emotive subject[59] and potentially new ground for the derivative industry. Carbon trading is broadly the mechanism by which regulatory permits or allowances to emit greenhouse gases[60] into the atmosphere can be reallocated between the components of global industry so as to promote industrial efficiency and yet restrict the overall emission of greenhouse gases to a level deemed by international consensus to not pose a threat to the global climate system. The most important greenhouse gas is carbon dioxide, and other greenhouse gases can be converted into their carbon dioxide equivalents, which is the unit upon which carbon trading is based. Conversion of another greenhouse gas into its carbon dioxide equivalent is based on a calculation, an input of which is the global warming potential of that other greenhouse gas, as assessed by the Intergovernmental Panel on Climate Change. The key element of the various initiatives to combat global warming is the agreement between the relevant participating states to reduce emissions of greenhouse gases by a specified percentage of the emissions recorded in respect of a base year. The total volume of greenhouse gases that can be emitted under an agreement is therefore restricted,

4.219

---

[59] Intense and sometimes polemic scientific debate continues as to whether or not the phenomenon of increasing temperatures, global warming, is due to human activity or is a part of a natural cycle. For both perspectives, see Gore, *An Inconvenient Truth* (Bloomsbury Publishing Plc, 2006) and *The Great Global Warming Swindle*, a film by Martin Durkin broadcast on Channel 4, 8 March 2007, and which has attracted some controversy.

[60] Greenhouse gases are gases which tend to promote the greenhouse effect, which is the introduction into the atmosphere of gases which block heat from radiating away from the planet's surface, thereby causing the temperature of the planet's surface to rise above levels perceived to be normal. See Lovelock, *Gaia* (Gaia Books Limited, 1991). The six principal greenhouse gases identified in Annex A of the Kyoto Protocol are carbon dioxide, hydrofluorocarbons, methane, nitrous oxide, perfluorocarbons, and sulphur hexafluoride. Chlorofluorocarbons (CFCs) are outside the scope of the Kyoto Protocol; instead they are covered by the Montreal Protocol on Substances that Deplete the Ozone Layer, adopted in Montreal on 16 September 1987.

yet this total volume can be reallocated between commercial actors in ways which do not restrict economic and technological growth. One of the tensions in developing international agreements to control emissions is the stance by some developing countries that their own economic growth should not be curtailed as a part of a process to repair the environmental damage caused by other more developed countries which have already achieved greater economic development and industrialization. Great sensitivity is therefore required.

4.220 The Kyoto Protocol, which has achieved familiarity through media coverage, is one of the protocols adopted under the United Nations Framework Convention on Climate Change (UNFCC). The UNFCC itself was adopted in New York on 9 May 1992, and the Kyoto Protocol itself was adopted at the third Conference of the Parties to the UNFCC in Kyoto, Japan, on 11 December 1997. The purpose of the Kyoto Protocol[61] is to create legal obligations on its signatories to restrict the emission of greenhouse gases to specified targets, and the legal obligations under the Kyoto Protocol have been developed to reflect the principles originally established under the UNFCC. Whereas the UNFCC merely encourages signatories to stabilize their emissions of greenhouse gases, the Kyoto Protocol commits them to do so. There are three categories of signatory to the Kyoto Protocol. These categories are derived from the categories of signatory to the UNFCC, and they are Annex I Parties, Non-Annex I Parties, and Economies in Transition. Annex I Parties are industrialized countries which were members in 1992 of the Organisation for Economic Co-operation and Development. Broadly under the Kyoto Protocol, the Annex I Parties aim to reduce during the commitment period 2008 to 2012 their aggregate anthropogenic carbon dioxide equivalent emissions of the six greenhouse gases to less than 5% below the base level of emissions recorded in 1990.

4.221 The controversy that has surrounded the adoption and ratification of the Kyoto Protocol by various states is outside the scope of this book.[62] Three main initiatives are contemplated by the Kyoto Protocol. First, the Annex I Parties are required to participate in joint implementation with each other of the standards of the Kyoto Protocol.[63] Joint implementation involves Annex I Parties cooperating to share the technologies required to reduce emissions of greenhouse gases. One Annex I Party invests capital and technology in an enterprise or project in a second Annex I Party. The recipient Annex I Party achieves reduced emissions, and this reduction

---

[61] See Article 2 and Article 3 of the Kyoto Protocol.
[62] The condition for entry into force of the Kyoto Protocol was ratification of the Kyoto Protocol both by at least 55 signatories to the UNFCC and by the number of Annex I Parties which represent 55% of the total carbon dioxide emissions of all of the Annex I Parties as at 1990. See Article 25(1) of the Kyoto Protocol. Following ratification by Russia in November 2004, the Kyoto Protocol subsequently came into force on 16 February 2005.
[63] See Article 6 of the Kyoto Protocol.

can be used by the investing Annex I Party to offset its own emissions and thereby avoid emitting greenhouse gases beyond its own targets. Second, the clean development mechanism is a framework for the implementation by Annex I Parties of projects in Non-Annex I Parties with the objective of securing reduced emissions.[64] Again, this reduction can be used by the investing Annex I Party to offset its own emissions and thereby avoid emitting greenhouse gases beyond its own targets. Third, and of most relevance to this book, the Kyoto Protocol permits signatories to participate in emissions trading.[65] Extremely detailed rules and guidelines have been adopted under the Marrakesh Accords, governing how regulatory permits to emit greenhouse gases should be allocated, traded, and transferred between signatories to the Kyoto Protocol. The key concept underpinning emissions trading under the Kyoto Protocol is the treatment of 'assigned amounts', which are the individual emissions targets and the group emissions targets set out in Annex B to the Kyoto Protocol. Assigned Amount Units are the rights that are traded and transferred.

Carbon trading has already taken place within the European Union, which has developed an emission trading scheme known by its acronym EU ETS,[66] which came into effect on 1 January 2005. Under the first phase of the EU ETS, which was from 2005 to 2008, each member state was required to determine targets for its total emissions of greenhouse gases and to allocate emissions allowances to operators of relevant installations, in accordance with its national allocation plan. A relevant installation is an energy-intensive installation which emits a volume of greenhouse gas above a specified threshold, and any installation is potentially included, such as a power station burning fossil fuels and factories engaged in various processes. Under the second phase of the EU ETS, from 2008 to 2012, more stringent financial penalties are levied on operators of relevant installations which exceed the volumes of emissions permitted under the emissions allowances that have been allocated to them. There is a clear interface between the Kyoto Protocol and the EU ETS, and the European Union has therefore taken measures to ensure that its response is as consistent as possible with the Kyoto Protocol by amending the Directive which established the EU ETS. The Directive by which this amendment is achieved is referred to as the 'Linking Directive'.[67] **4.222**

---

[64] See Article 12 of the Kyoto Protocol.
[65] See Article 17 of the Kyoto Protocol.
[66] The EU ETS was established under Directive 2003/87/EC of the European Parliament and of the Council of 13 October 2003 establishing a scheme for greenhouse gas emission allowance trading within the Community and amending Council Directive 96/61/EC.
[67] Directive 2004/101/EC of the European Parliament and of the Council of 27 October 2004 amending Directive 2003/87/EC establishing a scheme for greenhouse gas emission allowance trading within the Community, in respect of the Kyoto Protocol's project mechanisms.

4.223 Although the first forward trade within the European Union in EU emissions allowances took place in February 2003, under which Shell Trading sold a significant volume of emissions allowances to Nuon Energy Trade and Wholesale,[68] the EU ETS provides a framework within which the requisite market structures might be developed for trading standardized contracts written on EU ETS emissions allowances. Notwithstanding the novelty of the underlying, the familiar processes of developing standardized contracts and establishing market procedures such as trade matching, clearing, settlement, and the application of a margin payment system, are required.

4.224 Several exchanges have been established on which EU ETS emissions allowances are traded, including Energy Exchange Austria, the European Energy Exchange (which is based in Germany), the European Climate Exchange (which is a subsidiary of the Chicago Climate Exchange), Nord Pool (which is based in Norway), and Powernext Carbon (which is the emissions spot market established by the French energy exchange Powernext). The development of derivative trading in emissions allowances is facilitated by the standardization of the allowance and the conversion where necessary of allowances into their carbon dioxide equivalents. Standardization of contracts is a key step in the development of derivative exchanges, as part 4.2 and part 4.3 of this chapter illustrate, with reference to the transition from forward contracts struck privately to standardized futures contracts dealt on an exchange. The European Climate Exchange has achieved the distinction of introducing the first exchange-based futures contract based on EU ETS emissions allowances. This futures contract is the ECX CFI, or Carbon Financial Instrument. Although the initial participants in the various emissions markets are governments and operators of installations, financial intermediaries are expected to participate, bringing with them the experience and balance sheet to allow more tailored transactions to be structured. It is important that the emerging emissions markets have the necessary liquidity to attract participants, and the involvement of financial institutions will help to secure this liquidity.

4.225 Carbon trading gives rise to the familiar requirements for an enforceable contract, including certainty of the terms of the contract. The standardization of derivative contracts based on emissions, such as the EXC CFI futures contract, and the introduction of exchanges, with their concomitant processes and support infrastructure, ameliorate significantly many of the risks associated with contracting for the transfer of emissions allowances. Transactions can take place easily and swiftly on the basis of established definitions of the underlying and established descriptions of the rights and obligations of the parties.

---

[68] See a press release issued by Shell on 27 February 2003.

4.14 New Classes of Underlying

4.226 However, preparation of OTC derivative contracts will require the usual detailed specification of the underlying and the parties' rights and obligations in respect of the underlying. The foregoing paragraphs demonstrate that the various initiatives to combat global warming take place at different supranational and national levels. Consequently, an OTC contract which is written on an emissions allowance must clearly identify that allowance, whether it is an allowance allocated under the implementation of the Kyoto Protocol, such as an Assigned Amount Unit, or an allowance allocated under the EU ETS. It is also important to build into the contract a process for the valuation of the allowance to which the economic exposure is created. As with other classes of underlying, a liquid and transparent market for the underlying greatly facilitates the valuation of the underlying for the purposes of the contract. The contract must also legislate for the settlement of the transaction, whether settlement is effected through a payment made by one party to the other, or through the delivery by one party to the other of the emissions allowances governing the requisite volume of emissions. An ancillary issue which arises in the context of physical settlement of a transaction through the delivery of documents is the need to integrate the operation of the contract with the processes of the registry which records the persons entitled to the various emissions allowances. For example, member states of the European Union are required to establish and maintain registries of the emissions allowances they allocate in accordance with their national allocation plans, and entries in these national registries are cross-checked against a central registry known as the 'Community independent transaction log'. Other issues which arise are in fact the usual issues which must be addressed in the administration of any OTC derivative trading relationship, such as the appropriate representations and warranties to be given by each party to the other, including the maintenance of any relevant trading licence or permit in addition to the usual financial services licensing, the consequences of a default by a party, the provision of collateral to minimize credit risk, and dispute resolution. One area of potential complexity is the effect on the transaction of a change in the legal or regulatory treatment of the emissions trading scheme to which the contract is linked. OTC derivative contracts usually include provisions to regulate the effect on the transaction of a change in law,[69] but there is a need in the context of carbon trading to anticipate the potentially dramatic effect that a change in the international agreements governing carbon trading might have on privately-negotiated contracts. Different provisions within the contract may appear to apply, and care must be taken to ensure that the contract operates without ambiguity in certain prescribed circumstances. Finally, issues may arise where carbon trading is being undertaken as an adjunct to a project within the auspices of the Kyoto Protocol, such as a joint implementation project between two Annex I Parties or a project within the clean

---

[69] See Chapter 7.

development mechanism between an Annex I Party and a Non-Annex I Party. For example, transfer of the resulting emissions allowance is contingent on the relevant regulatory authorities approving the outcome of the project.

4.227 Therefore, in parallel with the establishment of exchange-based carbon trading, the OTC market has began to develop the necessary standard-form documentation. For example, ISDA has set up its Emissions Working Group to consider the appropriate treatment, and has already published its first generation of documents, including an allowances index, and a template confirmation for transactions the underlying of which are EU emissions allowances. Other bodies such as the International Emissions Trading Association and the European Federation of Energy Traders have also published forms of documents, and clearly progress in the development of the nascent OTC carbon trading market will depend on harmonization and the adoption of common standards. In this way, parallels can be drawn between carbon trading and the evolution of the derivative markets for other classes of underlying, and this underscores the observation that new classes of underlying are broadly accommodated within existing frameworks.

4.15 Valuations, Valuation Disruptions, and Adjustments

4.228 Derivative contracts feature inherent complexities which stem from the nature of the underlying asset. Certain of these complexities have been introduced in the foregoing paragraphs, particularly in respect of the emerging classes of underlying. The calculations of the various amounts payable under a derivative contract are made with reference to the prices of actual assets or instruments, or with reference to indices of the prices of actual assets or instruments. In the case of a credit derivative contract, a means of identifying and verifying the occurrence of a credit event is also required. The contract must therefore legislate for obtaining the valuations or market observations upon which the calculations and determinations are made, and the contractual provisions must be drafted with an awareness of the relevant market for the underlying. Necessarily, the contract must also provide for the consequences of any disruption to these valuations and observations, including various fallbacks and the consequences of a fallback itself being ineffective. Further, the contract must consider the consequences of certain events which may affect the underlying of the contract and thereby change the economics of the transaction. The effect on the transaction can be dramatic, for example, certain events and circumstances may result in the underlying of the transaction disappearing. Other consequences flow from events which may affect the ability of the contractual counterparties to perform their obligations under the contract or their ability to hedge the exposures that they assume by entering into the contract. As intimated above, much depends on the nature of the underlying assets themselves, and the conventions of the relevant market. These considerations apply to both exchange-based and OTC derivative contracts. However, whereas the rules of the relevant exchange and associated clearing house as much as the actual listed contracts themselves contain the required provisions in the case of exchange-based contracts, only the contracts making up an OTC relationship can contain all of the required provisions. These aspects of the contracts are considered in Chapter 7.

4.16 Different 'Wrappers' of Derivative Cash Flows

4.229 A derivative product is properly the payout that is determined with reference to the movement in the price of the underlying or the occurrence of a credit event and the quantification of the loss that the credit event gives rise to. A derivative product is therefore essentially a cash flow, and a particular derivative product can be delivered to the end-user in a number of different formats or 'wrappers'. The observation is made in Chapter 1 that a derivative creates an economic exposure to the underlying, and the concept that is developed in this chapter is that the derivative contract legislates for the valuation or other observation of the underlying and the conversion of those valuations or other observations into amounts that are paid by the participants, with perhaps delivery of an asset if that is required under the terms of the derivative contract. The contractual terms of the derivative product can be placed inside different 'wrappers'. For example, an investor can acquire a derivative exposure to a basket of shares by entering into an OTC contract the underlying of which comprises those shares, or by buying a debt security the repayment of which is determined with reference to the performance of those shares, or by buying an equity security the valuation of which is determined with reference to the performance of those shares, or even by making a market-linked deposit under the terms of which the balance repaid by the deposit-taking institution is determined with reference to the performance of those shares. Of course, the investor might also be able to identify exchange-based contracts which create the required investment exposure.[70] The different 'wrappers' involve different contractual structures and therefore different costs and risks, and therefore selection of the 'wrapper' will be a balance between those costs and risks, and the requirements of the contractual participants. By way of illustration, an OTC structure, which is a privately negotiated bilateral contract, exposes the investor to the risk that the seller of the exposure defaults or otherwise fails, although counterparty credit risk might be mitigated through collateralization, but the cost of

---

[70] The benefits of the exchange-based market are convenience and the clearing system which ensures the performance of contracts, and its disadvantages include primarily its inflexibility; participants are constrained to using only the listed contracts. However, the range of listed contracts that are available is growing, for example, single stock futures have been introduced in recent years.

such a structure would be less than that of a structure which involves the issue of debt or equity securities by a vehicle, sometimes purposely established for the business of issuing such securities, which is insulated from certain risks. The following paragraphs consider the different 'wrappers' that are more commonly encountered.

The securitization of derivative cash flows

4.230 The purpose of the securitization of a derivative cash flow is to place in the hands of the investor a transferable security which creates the required derivative exposure to the underlying, but delivered in a more convenient package. The synthetic collateralized debt obligation that is considered in part 4.11 of this chapter is an example of the securitization of a derivative cash flow. Of course, the technique is not confined to the securitization of credit default swap payments, and a significant market has developed for the creation of debt securities which offer the investor a precise exposure to almost any class of underlying,[71] and the exposure might be leveraged or subject to another mathematical relationship which creates a non-linear exposure to the underlying. The delivery of an investment in the form of a debt security offers certain advantages. One, the investor holds convenient transferable securities that the investor can, in theory, sell if a satisfactory secondary market exists.[72] Two, the jurisdiction in which the issuer issues the securities might offer certain tax advantages, usually the payment of interest on a gross basis with no deduction or withholding for or on account of tax. Three, the issue might be made with the benefit of the involvement of a corporate trustee, the role of which is to monitor the performance by the issuer of its obligations under the conditions of the securities and if necessary to enforce those obligations, having recourse to the security devices, such as fixed and floating charges, that the issuer creates in favour of the trustee. Four, for certain categories of investor, there are fewer regulatory impediments to holding transferable securities than entering into another form of investment, such as an OTC contract.

4.231 The actual derivative payout is contained within the conditions of the securities. The conditions of the security must also, in the usual way, legislate for the valuation of the underlying, the consequences of disruptions to the valuation of the underlying, and the consequences of certain adjustment and extraordinary events which might occur in respect of the underlying, such as corporate actions.

---

[71] Commonly exposures to the equity markets, commodity markets, and various funds are structured.

[72] Of course, the more structured securities which are tailored to a particular investor's requirements are not easily sold precisely because of their bespoke nature, and indeed the offering material prepared for such issues explicitly warns that the investor should be prepared to hold the securities to maturity and that no liquid secondary market is expected to develop. Nonetheless, in theory at least, and from a purely mechanical perspective, the securities are transferable.

4.16 'Wrappers'

4.232 The following example of the issue of structured debt securities which is linked to the performance of a basket of shares is provided to illustrate how a securitized derivative cash flow is arranged. An investor wishes to acquire an investment which is linked to the value of a particular basket of shares. That is, the investor's requirement is that the value of the investment increases in a particular proportion to increases in the value of the underlying basket of shares. The investor is therefore seeking a long exposure to the underlying basket. The investor might obtain this long exposure by entering into an equity swap; however, the alternative available to the investor is to invest instead in equity-linked debt securities that have been structured to give the investor the required exposure. Of course, instead of equity-linked debt securities, the investor may wish to invest in equity securities which give the same exposure. These are considered presently.

4.233 The investor and the arranging bank discuss ways in which the investment might be structured; the arranging bank might well have several entities available to issue the securities. One entity might be used to issue debt, another might be used to issue equity, a third might be used to issue debt securities listed on a particular investment exchange, and so on. Selection of a debt issue or an equity issue, and indeed the issuer itself, will be a part of the structuring discussions. Further discussions might explore whether investment gains should be delivered as capital gains or as income.

4.234 In the case of an issue of debt securities, the investor subscribes for notes[73] issued by the selected issuing entity. On the issue date, the investor pays the issue price for each note, which is expressed either as a percentage of the denomination per note or as an amount per note. On the repayment date, the issuer repays each note. The repayment amount per note is the denomination per note plus an amount to reflect any investment gain or minus an amount to reflect any investment loss. If the investment is principal protected, then the repayment amount per note is not less than the amount paid, and if the investment offers only partial principal protection, then the repayment amount per note is not less than a high percentage of the amount paid.

4.235 In the example of the long exposure to the underlying basket, an investment gain is made if the underlying basket increases in value over the valuation period, and an investment loss is realized if the underlying basket decreases in value over the valuation period. The valuation period starts on the strike date, which for this example is the issue date, and ends on the valuation date, which for this example is specified to be five days prior to the repayment date. The valuation date is

---

[73] The term 'note' tends to be used to describe debt securities of shorter maturities, and the term 'bond' tends to be used to describe debt securities of longer maturities. The distinction is purely a matter of terminology.

purposely scheduled to occur five days prior to the repayment date in order that the effect on the transaction of any disruption to the valuation of the underlying basket can be resolved before the issuer is required to perform its obligation to make a repayment of principal.

4.236 The repayment amount per note is calculated in accordance with a formula which captures the performance of the underlying basket over the valuation period. By way of example, the value of the underlying basket at any particular time is merely the arithmetic mean of the price at that time of each share contained in the basket; on the assumption that the shares are equally represented in the basket, the prices are not weighted for the purposes of this calculation. The performance of the underlying basket might be calculated as the value of the underlying basket on the valuation date divided by the value of the underlying basket, minus 1. In one scenario, the value of the underlying basket on the strike date is 200, the value of the underlying basket on the valuation date is 220, thus the performance of the underlying basket is (220 divided by 200) minus 1, which is 0.1. From another perspective, 0.1 equates to an increase in the value of the underlying basket of 10%. In another scenario, the value of the underlying basket on the strike date is 200, the value of the underlying basket on the valuation date is 170, thus the performance of the underlying basket is (170 divided by 200) minus 1, which is – 0.15. Again, from another perspective, –0.15 equates to a decrease in the value of the underlying basket of 15%. Thus the repayment amount per note would be equal to the denomination per note multiplied by 1 plus the performance of the underlying basket. Assume that the denomination per note is £1,000 and the issue price is 101%. The amount per note paid by the investor on the issue date is £1,000 multiplied by 101%, which is £1,010. The performance of the underlying basket is 0.1, as in the first scenario described above. Therefore, the amount per note paid by the issuer on the repayment date is £1,000 multiplied by 1 plus the performance, which is £1,100.

4.237 In the case of an issue of equity securities, the investor subscribes for shares issued by the selected issuing entity. The value of the shares might be determined by a formula in a manner similar to the formula presented above in respect of the analogous issue of debt securities, and certainly this approach would be the most straightforward. Alternatively, the net asset value per share might be calculated to determine the performance of the investment.

4.238 The investor might have the opportunity to select whether the investment should be structured to deliver a capital gain or an income. The treatment of capital gains and income differs in many jurisdictions, in that different reliefs and exemptions are available in respect of either,[74] which prompts the need from time to time to

---

[74] See Chapter 11.

develop different structures. Generally, if capital gains are required, then the value of the investment is increased by any investment gain, and if income is required, then the value of the investment is not increased by any investment gain, and instead the investment gain is paid to the investor separately, in order that this separate payment stream is taxed separately. Of course, analysing the detail of the applicable tax legislation and regulation, and the interpretation of the legislation and regulation, is of critical importance in developing such structures.

4.239 The issuing entity, whether it is issuing debt securities or equity securities, usually hedges itself in order that it does not itself assume any exposure to the underlying. It is particularly important for the issuing entity to be hedged if it is a special purpose vehicle which has been established to issue many different series of securities under a programme. The issuing entity would therefore buy its hedge from the arranging bank, usually in the form of an OTC derivative contract. In this way, the market or price exposure to the underlying is passed to the arranging bank, which might decide either to trade that risk or, more usually, to hedge that risk. One of the most important determinants of the price of the structure that the investor pays is the cost to the arranging bank of putting in place its hedge. It is recollected, in the example set out in the preceding paragraphs of the issue of equity-linked debt, that the investor pays an issue price of 101% of the denomination per note. Leaving aside the performance of the underlying basket, the investor pays £1,010 to buy the right to be repaid £1,000. The £10 difference is a part of the price of the structure to the investor and would pay towards the cost of hedging. Other costs might include the percentage earned by any distributor or other intermediary.

Embedded derivatives

4.240 A more straightforward type of structured debt security is one which contains an embedded option. The embedded option within such a security governs whether or not the issue is redeemed early. An embedded call option gives the issuer of the debt the right to redeem the debt before its scheduled maturity. The purpose of an embedded call option might be to enable the issuer of fixed rate debt to benefit from a decrease in interest rates after the debt is issued. If interest rates decrease, then the issuer would exercise the embedded call option, redeem the debt, and then issue new debt which pays a lower rate of interest, thereby refinancing the borrowing. An embedded put option gives the holder of the debt the right to require the issuer to redeem the debt before its scheduled maturity. The purpose of an embedded put option might to be to enable the holder of fixed rate debt to benefit from an increase in interest rates after the debt is issued. If interest rates increase, then the issuer would exercise the embedded put option. The issuer would then be able to reinvest the redemption proceeds in an environment characterized by higher yields.

Convertible and exchangeable debt[75]

4.241 A convertible debt security entitles the holder to convert the debt into the equity of either the issuer or a company related to the issuer. The holder decides whether or not to convert the debt into equity, and the conditions of the debt prescribe the ratio, or 'conversion price', at which conversion takes place. Prior to conversion, the convertible security operates as a debt security and confers the usual rights to repayment of principal and perhaps payment of interest. The mechanics of conversion are fairly involved. The debt is deemed to be redeemed and the holder is deemed to subscribe for new shares issued by the issuer or a company related to the issuer. The obligation of the issuer to pay the redemption proceeds of the debt to the holder is offset against the obligation of the holder to pay the subscription amount to the issuer (or the related company) in respect of the new shares. Thus no amount is actually paid by the issuer, other than incidental transaction costs, which may include stamp taxes.

4.242 Exchangeable debt is similar to convertible debt, although an exchangeable debt security entitles the holder to convert the debt into the equity of a company unrelated to the issuer. In order to facilitate the exchange, the equity of the unrelated company is already in existence and held by the issuer of the exchangeable debt pending exercise of the right to exchange. This is fairly logical: the right to exchange the exchangeable debt can only be exercised against the issuer of the exchangeable debt and not the unrelated company. After exchange, the holder no longer holds debt in the issuer of the exchangeable debt, and instead holds equity in the unrelated company. Again, the holder of the debt makes no payment on exchange of the debt into the equity. On exchange, the debt is deemed to be redeemed, and the issuer transfers the existing equity that it holds in the unrelated company to the holder, and the obligation of the issuer to pay the redemption proceeds of the debt to the holder is offset against the obligation of the holder to pay the acquisition cost to the issuer in respect of the relevant shares.

4.243 An investment in convertible or exchangeable debt is essentially an investment linked to the performance of the relevant shares. The right to convert or to exchange is analogous with a call option, although there is one key difference. Although the buyer of a call option pays a premium to buy the option and then pays the exercise price if the buyer subsequently exercises the option, the holder of the debt pays the subscription amount to the issuer of the debt but does not make any further payment if the holder exercises the right to convert or to exchange.

---

[75] Convertible and exchangeable debt are sometimes referred to as 'hybrid' securities, as they combine the legal and economic features of both debt securities and equity securities.

4.244 The holder of the debt anticipates that the relevant share price increases to above the conversion or exchange price specified in the conditions of the debt. If the relevant share price indeed increases above the specified conversion or exchange price, then the holder exercises the right to convert or to exchange, and is then able to sell the shares thus acquired and realize a profit, subject to the amount paid initially to subscribe for the debt. If the relevant share price does not increase, then the holder retains the debt and continues to receive any interest and, on maturity, receives the repayment of principal.

4.17 Repurchase and Reverse Repurchase Agreements

4.245 A repurchase agreement (or repo) is more fully a sale and repurchase agreement. Repo is included in this book as technically it is a derivative: the repo transaction contains a forward contract, which is an integral part of the structure of the transaction. Repo transactions tend to be entered into in respect of underlying debt securities. The repo markets are broad and an important component of the global debt capital markets.

4.246 A basic or 'classic' repo takes place in two stages, an initial sale and the subsequent repurchase. Under the initial sale, A sells debt securities to B and B pays to A the initial sale price. Simultaneously, A and B agree a forward contract, which is the subsequent repurchase, and which takes place on the repurchase date. Under the forward leg of the repo, A buys back the debt securities from B, paying to B the repurchase price. Crucially, the repurchase price is slightly higher than the initial sale price. The repurchase price is the sale price plus an amount calculated with reference to the repo rate. B's obligation to deliver debt securities to A under the subsequent repurchase is actually an obligation to deliver back to A debt securities which are equivalent to those that A originally delivered to B under the initial sale. The concept that the debt securities are equivalent (or 'fungible') is fundamental.

4.247 From A's perspective, the repo transaction allows A to borrow funds from B. The repo rate is effectively the rate of interest charged by B on the borrowing and should compete with the rate of interest charged on more traditional forms of lending. A might use a repo transaction to borrow funds because A has exhausted credit lines made available by its usual lenders, but A has in its inventory debt securities that can be used as collateral. From B's perspective, the repo transaction allows B to lend to A with the benefit of collateral and without the complexities of taking security from A and perfecting that security, for example, through registration of a charge. Conversely, A would not require any security to secure B's obligation to deliver the equivalent debt securities under the subsequent repurchase, as

A would only pay the repurchase price on a delivery versus payment basis.[76] Therefore a repo transaction operates in the same manner as a secured lending, from the perspective of the management of counterparty risk.

4.248 Further, the general repo technique allows A to lend the debt securities to B, and allows B to borrow the debt securities from A. This type of transaction is actually referred to as a securities lending transaction, or a stock lending transaction. However, although the participants in the structure A and B are the same, their motivations are different. B might require the debt securities to settle an immediate obligation to deliver those securities under another transaction, and A might have the debt securities immediately available in its inventory. Therefore A would sell the debt securities to B to enable B to meet its obligation for immediate delivery of those debt securities, B would pay cash to A (this cash would serve as collateral for what is effectively a loan of the debt securities), and B would subsequently source and sell back to A equivalent debt securities under the second leg of the securities lending transaction. There is no repurchase price under a securities lending transaction. Instead, under the second leg of a securities lending transaction, B has the obligation to deliver equivalent debt securities to A, and A has the obligation to pay an amount equal to the amount of the initial payment made by B. A might charge a fee to B for the loan of the debt securities, and this fee may be deducted from the amount paid by A.

4.249 As debt securities are delivered by A to B under the initial sale, and equivalent debt securities are delivered by B to A under the subsequent repurchase, the repo rate reflects any income generated by the debt securities underlying the repo that are in B's ownership. A is said to retain the economic risk or benefit of owing the debt securities, because movements in the price of the debt securities are reflected in the repurchase price. The repurchase price is agreed when the transaction is first entered into. The same principle applies to securities lending transactions. Of course, the tax implications of a repo transaction or a securities lending transaction must be carefully considered. For example, the initial sale by A to B might give rise to a liability to capital gains tax.

4.250 A reverse repo operates in the same manner as a repo, and the term 'reverse repo' is purely a matter of terminology. Whether or not a transaction is a repo or a reverse repo from a particular party's perspective depends entirely on whether that

---

[76] Delivery versus payment, or DVP, is a method for the settlement of the sale and purchase of an asset. Payment and delivery of the asset take place simultaneously. In the case of debt securities, investors' interests in debt securities are commonly bought and sold in a clearing system, permitting the actual security (the physical document) evidencing the indebtedness of the issuer to be held securely by a custodian at all times, without the inconvenience and risk of moving that document. These sales and purchases by investors are settled on a DVP basis merely by making adjustments of the relevant investors' cash and securities accounts.

Fungible instruments

4.251 The term fungible actually has no definition in English law, although it is in common use. The term describes the quality that certain instruments have of being completely interchangeable with each other, in that each instrument confers the same rights and creates the same benefits as another instrument of the same type or series. For example, banknotes of the same currency and denomination are fungible; it is a matter of indifference whether one particular £5 banknote is held or another particular £5 banknote is held.

4.252 Under the US Uniform Commercial Code,[77] the connotation of equivalence inherent in the term 'fungible' is apparent; goods and securities are fungible if they are 'goods or securities of which any unit is, by nature or usage of trade, the equivalent of any other like unit'. Items can be fungible if they are identical and therefore indistinguishable, such as commodities, or items can be fungible if they are nearly identical, such as banknotes of the same currency and denomination which differ only in the serial numbers they bear.

The origins of the repo market

4.253 The repo market evolved in the US debt capital markets, and the first transactions were denominated in US dollars. Repo techniques were first introduced in 1918 by the US Federal Reserve Board as a means of controlling the money supply, and therefore as a means of controlling inflation in accordance with monetary theory,[78] whether by removing surplus funds or by adding funds to adjust the liquidity of the economy. Repo techniques are now applied in most global financial centres, including London, where repo trading generally started in 1986, and a variety of currencies are used. The repo market contributes liquidity to the debt capital markets more generally, and the development and growth of the repo market is a response to increasing demand for both sources of funding and investment opportunities. Apart from the classic repo structure and securities lending facility, the market also includes more simple sell/buy-back structures and more complex tripartite repo transactions. Many banks have substantial repo businesses to provide the liquidity and cash flow to drive other elements of their trading. Sale and

---

[77] UCC § 1–201(17).
[78] Monetary theory postulates that inflation can be controlled through regulating demand in an economy by regulating interest rates and the amount of money in the economy.

repurchase techniques can be applied to other assets, including equities and commodities.

4.18 Financial Engineering

4.254 'Financial engineering' is the term that is used to describe the process of using one or more derivative exposures to create a particular economic effect. All of the derivative products described in this book share one common characteristic; each of them can be analysed from the perspective of the cash flow it generates. Each cash flow that a derivative generates can be described as a building block, and various building blocks can be assembled to create an overall structure. A derivative structure is therefore an assemblage of the different cash flows that are required to achieve the particular economic effect that the structure is designed to have.

4.255 A cash flow is essentially a coordinate of funds. For these purposes, a cash flow is most usefully described as one or more specified payments made in accordance with a specified schedule. To develop this definition of a cash flow, the amount of each payment might either be specified in the derivative contract, or it might be calculated using a formula that is specified in the derivative contract. Therefore, from one analytical perspective, a derivative is one or more cash flows, like any other financial instrument, and from another analytical perspective, a derivative is a contract which gives rise to rights and obligations in respect of the underlying. In the same way, although from one perspective a debt security is an investment which gives rise to a certain cash flow, which comprises the repayment of principal, whether in one amount or by instalments, and perhaps the payment of interest, from another perspective a debt security is a contract,[79] which gives rise to certain obligations of the issuer which include the obligation to repay the principal and to pay any interest. Indeed, all assets can be analysed in this multiple fashion.

4.256 The observation is made at the beginning of this chapter that there are two fundamental types of derivative obligation. The first type of derivative cash flow is the forward obligation, whether this is an obligation to make a payment or to make a delivery. The second type of obligation is the optional obligation, again whether this is an obligation to make a payment or to make a delivery, depending on whether or not the option is exercised. These two types of obligation, or building block, form the foundation of derivative structuring, and the price of a structure is determined in part by whether or not the structure incorporates an option.

---

[79] A debt security is in essence a contract, whether made between the issuer and the holder from time to time of the security, or made between the issuer, the holder from time to time of the security, and the trustee of the issue.

4.18 Financial Engineering

The payment profiles, and therefore the cash flows, of certain derivatives are the same, and this homogeneity assists the financial engineer. This chapter contains certain examples of this homogeneity. One, the payment profile of a futures contract is the same as the payment profile of a forward contract. Both contracts govern the forward sale and purchase of the underlying, comprising delivery and payment. Two, the payment profile of an interest rate cap is the same as the payment profile of a long call option position. A premium is paid to acquire both a cap and a call option. Both a cap and a call option increase in usefulness, and therefore in value, as the underlying increases. As the underlying increases above a certain level, there is certainty that the call option will be exercised. Three, the payment profile of an interest rate floor is the same as the payment profile of a long put option position. A premium is paid to acquire both a floor and a put option. Both a floor and a put option increase in usefulness, and therefore in value, as the underlying decreases. As the underlying decreases below a certain level, there is certainty that the put option will be exercised. Four, the payment profile of a swap is the same as the payment profile of both a futures contract and a forward contract, because a swap is a series, or 'strip', of forward payments. **4.257**

One of the themes which runs through this book is the close interaction between the different components of the financial markets. Aside from the obvious link between a particular derivative market and its related underlying market, the links between the different components of the financial markets are also discernible in the pricing of different instruments. **4.258**

The yield achieved by investing in one particular market must generally compete with the yield achieved by investing in another market.[80] Therefore, for example, the yield of deploying capital in the swap market must compete with the yield of deploying capital in the debt capital market. The relative value approach to investing is predicated on the analysis of competing yields, and indeed one of the alternative means of pricing a hedging swap relies on calibrating the yield achieved using a swap to complement its underlying transaction, so that the cost of the combination of the underlying transaction and the swap equates to the cost of an alternative structure which achieves the same economic effect. For example, the cost to a borrower of borrowing at a floating rate and using an interest rate swap to fix the interest paid should equate to the cost of borrowing at a fixed rate. Many swap rates are quoted, for different currencies and for different tenors. **4.259**

---

[80] Of course, homogenous yet separate markets which co-exist do not generate precisely the same yields, and arbitrage is the process of exploiting for profit any discrepancy between markets.

5

THE LEGAL FRAMEWORK

5.1 Introduction	5.01
5.2 Legislation and Regulation	5.02
5.3 The General Prohibition	5.48
5.4 Regulated Activities	5.56
5.5 Legal Market Structures	5.78
5.6 EU Legislation	5.87

5.1 Introduction

5.01 Financial services legislation, and the regulation that is made under that legislation, together provide the legal framework for the financial markets, including of course the derivative markets. This legal framework establishes the system for the regulation of the derivative markets, provides a definition of each type of derivative market, and provides a definition of each type of derivative contract that is dealt. This chapter considers the sources of the applicable legislation and regulation, the regulatory concept of the general prohibition, the types of regulated activity which fall within the scope of the regulatory system, the different legal market structures, and the increasing volumes of EU legislation which set the overall standards that are implemented at the national level throughout the European Economic Area. Financial services regulation is a wide subject, and this chapter can only set out a brief survey of the more basic principles in the context of the subject matter of this book. However, these principles of course underpin the derivative markets, and accordingly some of the fundamental principles introduced in this chapter are examined in greater depth elsewhere, particularly in Chapter 8.

5.2 Legislation and Regulation

Financial Services and Markets Act 2000

5.02 The derivative markets, and indeed most of the financial services industry in the United Kingdom generally, with the notable exception of the provision of occupational pensions,[1] are now regulated under the scheme established by the Financial Services and Markets Act 2000, as amended (FSMA 2000). The FSMA 2000 received Royal Assent on Wednesday 14 June 2000, after the most protracted debate in the history of the United Kingdom's Parliament. Indeed, the Financial Services and Markets Bill 1998/99 was the first Government Bill to be carried over from one Parliamentary Session to the next to allow for greater pre-legislative scrutiny, under the refinement to Parliamentary procedure recommended by the Select Committee on the Modernization of the House of Lords in its first report *The Legislative Process*.[2] Accordingly, the Financial Services and Markets Bill was also debated during the 1999/2000 Parliamentary Session, and the FSMA 2000 finally became effective some one and a half years later at midnight on Friday 30 November 2001, the date known within the financial services industry as 'N2'.

5.03 The FSMA 2000 is a framework. The detail of how the FSMA 2000 operates is set out in voluminous secondary legislation, which comprises a significant number of statutory instruments made by HM Treasury as well as a complex set of regulatory rules.

5.04 Although the FSMA 2000 is made under English law, its territorial scope is the United Kingdom of Great Britain and Northern Ireland. The FSMA 2000 specifically refers to the United Kingdom.[3] The territorial scope of the FSMA 2000 does not include the Crown Dependencies, which are the Isle of Man and the Channel Islands. It is relevant to note the Crown Dependencies because of their prominent financial services industries, their offshore tax status, and their close political links with the United Kingdom.

5.05 The FSMA 2000 and the unified regulatory structure that it creates supersede the Financial Services Act 1986 and the diverse regulatory organs which operated under the Financial Services Act 1986, including the self-regulating organizations such as the Securities and Futures Authority (SFA), the Investment Management Regulatory Organization (IMRO), and the Personal Investment Authority (PIA) which were established under that Act and sanctioned by the Securities and Investment Board (SIB).

5.06 In very broad terms, the FSMA 2000 and the secondary legislation made under it define a perimeter. The actual definition of the perimeter by the FSMA 2000 and certain pieces of secondary legislation is complex, but extremely important.

---

[1] The provision of occupational pensions is regulated by the Pensions Regulator, which operates within the framework established under the Pensions Act 2004.
[2] HC 190 1997–98.
[3] See s 19(1) of the FSMA 2000, which establishes the general prohibition.

Regulatory consequences, including under many circumstances the principal requirement to be authorized, flow from undertaking certain activities within the perimeter, and regulatory, civil, and criminal sanctions may be applied to persons who contravene this basic requirement to be authorized. The detail of this requirement, and the exemptions which might apply, are considered in the following paragraphs.

5.07 The policy underpinning the establishment of the perimeter is, using general terminology, to include investment activities within the perimeter and to exclude commercial activities from the perimeter. Investment activities within the perimeter are referred to as regulated activities. Derivatives are an extremely useful example of how differences arise between investment activities and commercial activities, as this chapter demonstrates.

5.08 Authorization to carry on certain regulated activities within the perimeter is given by the Financial Services Authority (FSA). The conferring of various powers and duties on the FSA is one of the visible manifestations of the regulatory structure created under the FSMA 2000. The assumption by the FSA of its responsibilities was announced on 20 May 1997 as the headline for the change to the United Kingdom's regulatory system put into motion at that time. The FSA is the unified regulator of much of the United Kingdom's financial services industry, including the derivative markets.[4] The FSA is usually referred to by that acronym, both colloquially and within its own materials, although it is referred to in primary legislation as the 'Authority'.

Financial Services Authority

5.09 As well as defining the legal framework for the United Kingdom's financial services industry, the FSMA 2000 establishes the system for the regulation of the industry by the FSA. The FSA applies its *Handbook of Rules and Guidance* (FSA Handbook) as the practical manual of how regulation is achieved within the parameters established by the FSMA 2000.[5] The FSA Handbook sets out the minute detail by which the FSA achieves regulation.[6] The FSA Handbook generally contains rules, formal guidance, and other evidential provisions which indicate how compliance with the detail of the rules and the overall philosophy of

---

[4] The FSA is the same corporate entity as the SIB, which was restyled the 'Financial Services Authority'. The FSA assumed the supervisory and regulatory responsibilities of the SFA, the IMRO, and the PIA, and adopted the rules of these organizations, prior to establishing its own set of rules.

[5] The FSA's general rule-making power is set out in s 138 of the FSMA 2000.

[6] The extensive volume of the FSA Handbook, which is updated continuously, necessarily entails that only the pertinent aspects of it are discussed in this book.

regulation is achieved. The FSA Handbook is divided into various blocks,[7] which contain convenient groups of various sourcebooks and manuals. The FSA Handbook is available online at the FSA's website, which is useful given that the FSA Handbook occupies a substantial number of A4 lever arch files when printed, extending to thousands of pages.

Style of regulation

5.10 The approach of the FSA is said to be increasingly 'principles-based' instead of 'rules-based'. A rules-based approach to regulation would seek to determine whether or not a particular act or omission to act contravenes a particular regulatory provision through a close analysis of the wording of that provision. A rules-based approach might well result in particular acts or omissions satisfying the precise wording of a particular regulatory provision on a technical reading of that provision despite not fulfilling the intention underpinning that provision. By contrast, a principles-based approach to regulation would also include a consideration as to whether or not the intention underpinning the relevant regulatory provision has been fulfilled; thus it is said that both the letter and the spirit of regulation must be observed.[8] By moving towards a principles-based approach, the FSA is reserving to itself considerable discretion as to how regulation is achieved. Although a principles-based approach should benefit the financial services industry as a whole, as the senior management of financial services institutions might focus more on the systems and processes they put in place because they will be required to consider the purpose underpinning the various applicable regulation as opposed merely to ensuring that the relevant sets of rules are complied with, a criticism of a principles-based approach is that there is a risk of inconsistency in the manner in which the FSA regulates the industry. In particular, enforcement based on principles might lead to a de facto expansion of the rules that are published. In practice, however, it seems likely that regulation will consist of the application of a combination of rules and principles.

---

[7] The blocks are: Glossary (which sets out the terms used throughout the FSA Handbook), High Level Standards (which contains the standards which apply to all firms and approved persons), Prudential Standards (which contains the prudential requirements for firms), Business Standards (which contains the detailed requirements relating to the day-to-day business of firms), Regulatory Processes (which describes how the FSA performs its authorization, supervision, and disciplinary functions), Redress (which contains the processes for handling complaints and compensation), the Specialist sourcebooks (which variously set out the requirements which apply to individual business sectors), Listing Prospectus and Disclosure (which contains the rules made by the FSA in its capacity as the United Kingdom Listing Authority), Handbook Guides (which variously provide a basic overview of certain topics), and Regulatory Guides (which variously provide guides to regulatory topics).

[8] GEN 2.2.1G provides that every provision in the FSA Handbook must be interpreted in the light of its purpose.

5.11 The FSA complements its principles-based approach to regulation by consulting with participants in the financial services industry to address its concerns, with enforcement action generally being seen as a last resort. The *Financial Times*[9] suggests that an emphasis on consultation has resulted in the FSA being regarded as not having any meaningful record of enforcement action to point to, and certain commentators believe that this shows that the FSA cannot easily prove that it is policing the financial services industry as effectively as the regulators in other jurisdictions. In turn, the FSA draws a distinction between its approach and the experience of its equivalent regulator in the United States for the purposes of the relevant markets,[10] noting that the US regulator has not yet succeeded in proving any manipulation of prices in those particular markets. However, analysis suggests that the ability of the US regulator to plea bargain is a significant factor, with the inference that focusing on the number of actions brought in court, and the number of those actions which are successful, does not accurately show the effectiveness of the US model of regulation, and consequently it seems that the power to enter into plea bargains would be a useful addition to the FSA's general powers. As a final observation, the debate does highlight the differences in the understanding of the different regulators of the markets.

Statutory objectives of regulation

5.12 The FSA is identified as the regulator in the FSMA 2000[11] which is one of the innovations of the FSMA 2000. All of the FSMA 2000 and the secondary legislation made under it should be read in the context of the regulatory objectives of the FSA. Section 2(2) of the FSMA 2000 provides that the FSA's regulatory objectives are market confidence, public awareness, the protection of consumers, and the reduction of financial crime. The promotion of confidence in the financial system, which comprises financial markets and exchanges, regulated activities, and other activities connected with financial markets and exchanges, is an important objective, as the financial services industry can only attract consumers and the industry participants necessary to foster liquidity and competition if all such stakeholders are confident as to their rights and remedies in transparent and fair markets. Public awareness connotes the efforts made to ensure that members of the investing public understand the terms and risks of the financial products they buy. This regulatory objective resonates through the rules made governing financial

---

[9] 'FSA faces scrutiny on role of "speculation"', 24 July 2008. The context of this reportage is the concern expressed by certain politicians in both the United States and the United Kingdom that the volatility that has been observed in the price of oil can be attributed to speculation in the financial markets that has been made possible by regulators having an insufficient understanding of the markets to detect the manipulation of prices.
[10] The Commodity Futures Trading Commission (CFTC).
[11] See s 1 of the FSMA 2000.

promotions, which are broadly advertisements for investment products and services, and the preparation of the formal materials, such as prospectuses upon which investment decisions should be based, as well as the rules governing the provision of appropriate information and advice. Other measures more readily familiar perhaps include the requirement that the interest rates paid on savings products are converted into an Annual Equivalent Rate to enable prospective depositors and savers to assess different products using a common yardstick. The third regulatory objective is to secure the appropriate degree of protection for consumers. The term 'consumer' has a wide definition[12] and broadly refers to all classes of person who use any financial services, have rights or interests which derive from or are attributable to the use of financial services, or who have rights or interests that may be adversely affected by the use of financial services by persons acting on their behalf or in a fiduciary relation to them. A consumer might be a natural person, a partner in a partnership, a corporate entity, or another body, and this term emphasizes that no class of user is any less deserving of the basic protections afforded by the regulatory system, although the regulatory system does recognize that certain more sophisticated users enjoying greater resources should be capable of making more rigorous enquiry and investigation into financial services products than other less sophisticated users.[13] Nonetheless, the fact that a customer is sophisticated would not excuse a provider of financial services from fulfilling certain fundamental obligations, such as acting with integrity. The reduction of financial crime embraces fraud and dishonesty, misconduct in a financial market, misuse of information relating to a financial market, and handling the proceeds of crime. On one level, the risk of fraud and dishonesty threatens not just the various organizations providing financial services, and therefore the stability of the financial system, but also the consumers of financial services. On another level, the risk of misconduct in, or misuse of information relating to, a financial market erodes confidence in the financial system. On yet another level, denying criminals the opportunity to launder and therefore make use of the proceeds of their crime has the powerful potential both to deter crime and to reduce the flow of funds that might be used to finance further acts of terrorism.

Terminology

5.13 The FSA Handbook uses the term 'firm' to refer to a person or organization which is authorized to carry on regulated activities, whether an individual, a body corporate, a partnership, or an unincorporated association. The FSA Handbook uses the term 'approved person' to refer to a person or, more rarely, organization which performs on behalf of a firm certain activities in the course of the firm's business.

---

[12] See s 138(7) of the FSMA 2000.
[13] See part 8.7 of Chapter 8 for a discussion of the retail offer of derivatives.

5.2 Legislation and Regulation

The FSA Handbook uses the term 'controlled function' to refer to each such activity performed by an approved person. Therefore, firms tend to be organizations such as banks, building societies, insurers, and investment firms which carry on business, and approved persons tend to be the individuals who perform certain roles within firms, such as directors, officers, employees, or (in the case of firms organized as partnerships) partners. A controlled function is a role within a firm which is relevant to each regulated activity undertaken by the firm, such as acting as an investment advisor, acting as a compliance officer, or being involved in risk management or senior management. Not every role is a controlled function; for example, in-house counsel working as lawyers do not perform controlled functions. As indicated above, although in the majority of cases the approved persons acting for firms are individuals, it is possible for organizations to perform controlled functions for a firm; for example, a small investment firm might find it easier to engage the services of a specialized consultancy to perform certain controlled functions for it, although of course the senior management of that investment firm remain accountable for the conduct of that investment firm's business and its systems and controls. Indeed, recent changes in regulation have demonstrated a particular focus on outsourcing.[14]

The Principles

5.14 The FSA has established its Principles for Businesses, which are usually known as the Principles. The stated purpose of the Principles[15] is that they 'are a general statement of the fundamental obligations of firms under the regulatory system. This includes provisions which implement the Single Market Directives. They derive their authority from the FSA's rule-making powers as set out in the Act and reflect the regulatory objectives.' The 11 Principles are general statements of the standards that a firm must observe. Given their intrinsic importance to the scheme of regulation, it is appropriate to reproduce each of the 11 Principles.

- Principle 1. Integrity. 'A firm must conduct its business with integrity.'
- Principle 2. Skill, care, and diligence. 'A firm must conduct its business with due skill, care and diligence.'
- Principle 3. Management and control. 'A firm must take reasonable care to organise and control its affairs responsibly and effectively, with adequate risk management systems.'
- Principle 4. Financial prudence. 'A firm must maintain adequate financial resources.'

---

[14] See the discussion below in respect of MiFID.
[15] PRIN 1.1.2G.

- Principle 5. Market conduct. 'A firm must observe proper standards of market conduct.'

- Principle 6. Customers' interests. 'A firm must pay due regard to the interests of its customers and treat them fairly.'

- Principle 7. Communications with clients. 'A firm must pay due regard to the information needs of its clients, and communicate information to them in a way which is clear, fair and not misleading.'

- Principle 8. Conflicts of interest. 'A firm must manage conflicts of interest fairly, both between itself and its customers and between a customer and another client.'

- Principle 9. Customers: relationships of trust. 'A firm must take reasonable care to ensure the suitability of its advice and discretionary decisions for any customer who is entitled to rely upon its judgment.'

- Principle 10. Clients' assets. 'A firm must arrange adequate protection for clients' assets when it is responsible for them.'

- Principle 11. Relations with regulators. 'A firm must deal with its regulators in an open and cooperative way, and must disclose to the FSA appropriately anything relating to the firm of which the FSA would reasonably expect notice.'

5.15 A firm becomes liable to disciplinary sanctions if it breaches a Principle,[16] and whether or not a firm has breached a Principle is determined with reference to the standard of conduct required under that Principle. The burden of proof lies on the FSA to demonstrate that the firm has been at fault. A precise reading of the language of the relevant Principle indicates the standard of conduct required. For example, Principle 3 requires a firm to take reasonable care to organize and control its affairs responsibly and effectively, with adequate risk management systems. A firm would not be in breach of this Principle if it had failed to control or to prevent risks that it could not have foreseen; however, the firm would breach this Principle if it fails to organize or to control its affairs responsibly or effectively.

5.16 The principles-based approach followed by the FSA is made explicit in PRIN 1.1.9G. The Principles are described as constituting a general statement of the regulatory requirements which apply in new or unforeseen circumstances. In addition, and pertinently, the actual rules and guidance set out elsewhere in the FSA Handbook do not exhaust the implications of the Principles in circumstances which are not covered by specific guidance. It is therefore evident that even if a firm does not breach a specific rule or does not follow specific guidance, the firm may nonetheless breach a Principle if its conduct falls short of the standard required.[17]

---

[16] PRIN 1.1.7G.
[17] See paragraph 5.10.

5.2 Legislation and Regulation

The FSA has a wide discretion to take action against a member of the regulated community, whether a firm or an individual, in response to transgressions of both the spirit and the letter of the regulations.

Permission

Part IV of the FSMA 2000 sets out provisions relating to the permission granted by the FSA to carry on regulated activities. A permission given by the FSA is referred to as 'a Part IV permission'.[18] Schedule 6 to the FSMA 2000 sets out 'threshold conditions', which are the minimum standards that an applicant seeking permission must attain in order to be eligible for that permission. The FSA has a statutory duty to ensure that the person seeking or holding a Part IV permission will satisfy and continue to satisfy the threshold conditions in relation to all of the regulated activities within the scope of that permission, whether in giving or varying that permission, or imposing or varying any requirement in respect of that permission.[19] The FSA Handbook contains the practical approach to applying the statutory threshold conditions, and this practical approach is set out in the Threshold Conditions manual of the FSA Handbook (COND). Moreover, since the implementation in the United Kingdom of the Market in Financial Instruments Directive,[20] which is almost universally referred to as MiFID, the FSA also requires that the authorization requirements of MiFID are met before giving a Part IV permission to an investment firm.[21] **5.17**

In overall terms, an applicant for a Part IV permission must demonstrate that it is fit and proper having regard to all the circumstances to be authorized to carry on the particular relevant regulated activities. Part I of Schedule 6 to the FSMA 2000 sets out the threshold conditions that must be satisfied. The applicant must have appropriate legal status. If the applicant is a body corporate constituted under the law of any part of the United Kingdom, it must maintain its head office or its registered office within the United Kingdom. If the applicant is not a body corporate, but has its head office within the United Kingdom, it must carry on business in the United Kingdom. If the applicant has 'close links' with another person, the FSA must be satisfied that those close links are not likely to prevent the FSA's effective supervision of the applicant. If the other person with which the applicant has close links appears to be subject to the laws, regulations, or administrative provisions of territory which is not an EEA State, the FSA must be satisfied that neither **5.18**

---

[18] Section 40(4) of the FSMA 2000.
[19] Section 41(2) of the FSMA 2000.
[20] 2004/39/EC Directive of the European Parliament and of the Council on markets in financial instruments, amending Council Directives 85/611/EEC and 93/6/EEC and Directive 2001/12/EEC of the European Parliament and of the Council and repealing Council Directive 93/22/EEC.
[21] Regulation 4 of the Financial Services and Markets Act 2000 (Markets in Financial Instruments) Regulations 2007, SI 2007/126.

those foreign provisions nor any deficiency in their enforcement would prevent the FSA's effective supervision of the applicant. The applicant must have resources that are adequate in relation to the relevant regulated activities. It is important to note that the term 'resources' is used; the absence of any qualification indicates that resources in this context are both financial and non-financial, such as systems and controls and organizational structure. The FSA may take into consideration any group to which the applicant belongs and the effect that membership may have on the applicant, including the extent to which other members of the group may create obligations on the applicant.

5.19 The applicant makes its application to the FSA for a Part IV permission using a detailed set of forms which are designed to elicit all the relevant information from the applicant in respect of the applicant's proposed business, the applicant's infrastructure (its systems and controls), and the applicant's financial resources. An independent auditor is required to verify the applicant's responses as to its financial resources. COND 2 repeats each of the threshold conditions set out in Schedule 6 to the FSMA 2000 (replacing references to 'the Authority' with references to 'FSA') and sets out guidance indicating how the FSA will interpret each such threshold condition. The guidance is described as not being exhaustive and being written in very general terms.[22] The FSA will consider whether or not a firm satisfies and will continue to satisfy the threshold conditions in the context of the size, nature, scale, and complexity of the business that the firm carries on or will carry on if the relevant application is granted.[23]

5.20 The scope of the firm's Part IV permission is important. The firm can only carry on regulated activities in the United Kingdom within the scope of its Part IV permission, which is defined with reference to categories of activities and categories of investment. The various categories of activities and investments are examined in more detail in the following paragraphs.

5.21 The firm is required to maintain its Part IV permission by ensuring that it meets on a continuing basis the relevant threshold conditions applicable to it. The requirement that the firm maintains adequate financial resources is particularly important. The topic of financial resources (or capital) is examined in more depth in Chapter 10.

The conduct of business

5.22 The FSA Handbook contains extensive rules which govern the manner in which a firm is required to carry on its business. Most of these rules are contained in the New Conduct of Business Sourcebook (COBS), which is contained in the Business

---

[22] COND 1.3.1G.
[23] COND 1.3.2G.

5.2 *Legislation and Regulation*

Standards Block.[24] COBS sets out the conduct of business requirements which apply to firms with effect from 1 November 2007. COBS is of relevance to this book, as the institutions which participate in the derivative markets fall within its scope.[25] In keeping with the introductory nature of this book, only the key rules are introduced. For each key rule, COBS sets out ancillary rules and guidance indicating how the FSA expects the firm to comply with that rule. One ancillary rule which should be noted in particular is the requirement for the firm to keep accurate records for the prescribed period. Individual rules are supported by record-keeping requirements.

COBS 2 sets out the fundamental obligations for the conduct of business. A firm must act honestly, fairly, and professionally in accordance with the best interests of its client.[26] A firm must provide appropriate information in a comprehensible form to a client about the firm and its services, the investment products and the investment services being offered, the venues where services are provided from, and costs and associated charges, so that the client is reasonably able to understand the nature and risks of the services being offered and the client is consequently reasonably able to take investment decisions on an informed basis.[27] A firm must not pay or accept any fee or commission, or provide or receive any non-monetary benefit, in relation to the investment business carried on for a client.[28] There are exceptions. The firm is of course able to accept fees, commissions, and benefits paid or provided by its client or on behalf of its client. The firm is also able to accept fees, commissions, and benefits paid or provided by or on behalf of a third party, provided that this does not impair the firm's ability to act in the best interests of its client and provided that the firm discloses to its client its receipt of the fees, commissions, or benefits. The relevance of Principles 1 (the requirement to conduct business with integrity), 2 (the requirement to conduct business with skill, care, and diligence), and 6 (the requirement to pay due regard to the interests of customers and to treat them fairly) is emphasized in the guidance.[29] Where a firm is providing services to a person who is acting as an agent for a principal, then the firm must generally treat the agent as its client, and not the principal.[30] Of course, the firm and the agent and the principal are free to agree otherwise in writing. A firm is entitled to rely on information or instructions given to it by a second firm, provided that the second firm is itself authorized within

5.23

---

[24] COBS reflects the requirements of MiFID. The FSA Handbook uses the concepts of 'designated investment business' and 'MiFID or equivalent third country business'.
[25] ICOBS is the new sourcebook for non-investment insurance business and MCOB is the sourcebook for mortgage and home finance business.
[26] COBS 2.1.1R.
[27] COBS 2.2.1R.
[28] COBS 2.3.1R.
[29] COBS 2.3.3G.
[30] COBS 2.4.3R.

the European Economic Area or subject to equivalent relevant requirements.[31] Crucially, the second firm is responsible for the completeness and accuracy of any information transmitted to the first firm and for the appropriateness of any advice or recommendation provided to the client, and the first firm is responsible for concluding the services or transactions based on that information or advice in accordance with the applicable regulatory requirements.

5.24 COBS 3 sets out the obligation that a firm categorizes its clients. This obligation is intrinsic to the regulatory scheme, as the extent to which a firm is required to provide information and to observe certain standards is determined by the categorization of the particular client. It is to be stressed that the purpose of the categorization of clients is to ensure that all clients are treated appropriately and fairly[32] under the Principles. A client[33] is a person to whom a firm provides, intends to provide, or has provided a service in the course of carrying on a regulated activity or an ancillary service in the case of MiFID or equivalent third country business. A client can also be a potential client. A client can also be a person to whom a financial promotion is communicated or is likely to communicated, where the firm communicates or approves that financial promotion. COBS 2.4.3R identifies who should be treated as the client if the firm is transacting or otherwise dealing with a person who is acting as agent of another person. The different categories of client are retail clients, professional clients, and eligible counterparties. A retail client is a client who is not a professional client or an eligible counterparty.[34] A professional client is a client which is either a per se professional client or an elective professional client.[35] A per se professional client is a client which falls within one of the categories listed in COBS 3.5.2R, unless a different categorization applies. The provisions of this Rule are detailed, and the application of the different categories is determined by the nature of the investment business involved and the client and its financial resources and size. An elective professional client is a client that the firm decides to treat as a professional client. Generally, the firm can only treat as elective clients persons of requisite expertise, experience, and knowledge, and before treating a person as an elective professional client, the firm must state its intention to do so, the firm must provide a clear written warning of the protections and investor compensation rights that may be lost through such categorization, and that person must state in writing in a separate document that it is aware of the consequences of losing such protections and investor compensation rights.

---

[31] COBS 2.4.4R.
[32] Treating customers fairly has become a key imperative of the regulatory system, and the requirement to treat customers fairly is explored in more depth in part 8.7 of Chapter 8, in the context of the retail offer of derivatives.
[33] COBS 3.2.1R.
[34] COBS 3.4.1R.
[35] COBS 3.5.1R.

An eligible counterparty is a client which is either a per se eligible counterparty or an elective eligible counterparty.[36] A per se eligible counterparty is a client which falls within one of the categories listed in COBS 3.6.2R. These categories comprise investment firms, credit institutions, insurance companies, collective investment schemes, pension funds and their management companies, other regulated financial services institutions, certain types of dealer in commodities and commodity derivatives, public bodies, central banks, and supranational organizations. An elective eligible counterparty is a client that the firm decides to treat as an eligible counterparty. Generally, the firm can only treat as eligible counterparties organizations, and not individuals, which satisfy the criteria prescribed in COBS 3.6.4R. A prospective client can request to be categorized as an eligible counterparty, but the firm can only treat that prospective counterparty as an eligible counterparty if the relevant criteria have been satisfied.

5.25 Broadly, the different categorizations of client attract different degrees of protection, with retail clients enjoying the highest degree of protection. Again, it is worth emphasizing that a firm is not absolved of its obligations under the principles of regulation or under the applicable legislation and regulation merely because it is dealing with a client that has been categorized so as to receive a lower degree of protection. Indeed, a firm must allow a professional client or an eligible counterparty to request re-categorization as a client that benefits from a higher degree of protection.[37]

5.26 COBS 4 sets out the obligation that a firm must ensure that a communication or a financial promotion[38] is fair, clear, and not misleading.[39] The requirement under the FSA Handbook for communications which are fair, clear, and not misleading is reinforced by the criminal offence defined under the FSMA 2000. Section 397 of the FSMA 2000 provides that a person is guilty of a criminal offence if he makes a statement, promise, or forecast which he knows to be misleading, false, or deceptive in a material particular; if he dishonestly conceals any material facts whether in connection with a statement, promise, or forecast made by him or otherwise; or if he recklessly makes (dishonestly or otherwise) a statement, promise, or forecast which is misleading, false, or deceptive in a material particular. COBS 4.2.4G sets out the information that the FSA expects a communication to include if relevant, such as a statement that the client's capital is at risk, and a balanced impression of both the short-term and long-term prospects of the relevant investment. Different risk warnings and different amounts of information are to be provided to the different categories of client; the rationale of this principle is that more

---

[36] COBS 3.6.1R.
[37] COBS 3.7.1R.
[38] See paragraphs 5.32 ff.
[39] COBS 4.2.1R.

sophisticated and professional investors will require less information in order to be able to assess the merits and risks of a particular investment, because they possess experience, expertise, and resources.[40]

5.27 COBS 9 sets out the obligation that a firm must assess the suitability of a particular investment for its clients if the firm makes a personal recommendation in relation to a designated investment or if the firm manages investments. A firm must take reasonable steps to ensure that a personal recommendation, or a decision to trade, is suitable for its client, and the firm must obtain the necessary information regarding the client's knowledge and experience in the relevant investment field, financial situation, and investment objectives.[41] The detailed application of the requirements under COBS 9 are in part determined by the type of client and the type of business.[42]

5.28 COBS 10 sets out the obligation that a firm must assess the appropriateness of a particular investment for its clients if the firm neither makes investment recommendations nor otherwise provides investment advice. When assessing appropriateness, a firm must determine whether the client has the necessary experience and knowledge in order to understand the risks involved in relation to the product or service offered or demanded, and may assume that a professional client has the necessary experience and knowledge in order to understand the risks involved in relation to those particular investment services or transactions, or types of transaction or product, for which the client is classified as a professional client.[43] The detailed application of the requirements under COBS 10 are in part determined by the type of client and the type of business.[44]

5.29 Other parts of COBS of particular relevance provide for the provision of information about the firm, its services and remuneration,[45] client agreements,[46] dealing and managing, including the requirements to give best execution,[47] investment research,[48] and reporting information to clients.[49]

5.30 The firm is also required to observe the requirements of other parts of the FSA Handbook, such as the Market Conduct sourcebook (MAR). MAR 1 generally explains the standards of conduct that are required in the financial markets, with

---

[40] See part 8.7 of Chapter 8 for a discussion of the nature and quality of the information that must be provided in the context of the retail offer of derivatives.
[41] COBS 9.2.1R.
[42] See part 5.5 of this Chapter.
[43] COBS 10.2.1R.
[44] See part 5.5 of this Chapter.
[45] COBS 6.
[46] COBS 8.
[47] COBS 11.
[48] COBS 12.
[49] COBS 16.

the overall objective of providing guidance as to what activity constitutes market abuse and what activity does not. Part VIII of the FSMA 2000 contains the statutory provisions relating to the penalties for market abuse. The definition of market abuse is broad[50] and generally consists of one, dealing or attempting to deal by an insider on the basis of inside information;[51] two, the disclosure by an insider of inside information otherwise than in the proper course of the exercise of his employment, profession, or duties; three, other behaviour which is likely to be regarded by a regular user of the market in question as a failure to observe the standard of behaviour reasonably expected of a person in the relevant position in relation to the market; four, effecting transactions or orders to trade which give or are likely to give a false or misleading impression as to the supply and demand or price of the investment in question; five, effecting transactions or orders to trade which employ fictitious devices or any other form of deception or contrivance; six, the dissemination of information which gives or is likely to give a false or misleading impression as to the supply and demand or price of the investment in question; and seven, other behaviour which is likely to give a regular user of the market in question a false or misleading impression as to the supply and demand or price of the investment in question or which is likely to be regarded by such a regular user as behaviour that would distort or is likely to distort the market in that investment, and the behaviour is likely to be regarded by such regular user as a failure to observe the standard of behaviour reasonably expected of a person in the relevant position in relation to the market.

5.31 MAR also contains chapters which address different segments of the financial markets, and these are more properly introduced below in part 5.5 of this chapter in the discussion of legal market structures.

Financial promotion

5.32 It is important to appreciate that the regulation of financial promotions or making investment advertisements, which has already been mentioned above in the context of COBS, under the FSMA 2000 is separate from the regulation of the perimeter. Generally, a person might not carry on a regulated activity and therefore avoid the regulatory consequences of doing so, but might nonetheless communicate a financial promotion within the meaning of the FSMA 2000 and the relevant secondary legislation.

5.33 Section 21(1) of the FSMA 2000 provides that a person must not, in the course of a business, communicate an invitation or inducement to engage in investment activity. Section 21(2) of the FSMA 2000 provides that sub-section (1) does not

---

[50] See ss 118 and 118A of the FSMA 2000.
[51] See s 118B of the FSMA 2000 for the definition of an 'insider' and s 118C of the FSMA 2000 for the definition of 'inside information'.

apply if that person is authorized or the content of the communication has been approved by an authorized person. Section 21(3) of the FSMA 2000 has the effect that the restriction set out in sub-section (1) also applies to a communication originating outside the United Kingdom and which is capable of having an effect in the United Kingdom. Again, regulatory, civil, and criminal sanctions may be applied to persons who contravene the restriction on financial promotion. The expression 'engaging in investment activity' is defined[52] as entering or offering to enter into an agreement the making or performance of which by either party constitutes a controlled activity, or exercising any rights conferred by a controlled investment to acquire, dispose of, underwrite or convert a controlled investment. The term 'controlled activity' is effectively defined[53] as an activity specified in an order made by the Treasury, and similarly the term 'controlled investment' is effectively defined[54] as an investment specified in an order made by the Treasury.

5.34 Section 25 of the FSMA 2000 sets out the criminal sanctions that may be applied, and provides that a person who contravenes section 21(1) is guilty of an offence and liable on summary conviction to imprisonment for a term not exceeding six months or a fine not exceeding the statutory maximum or both, and on conviction on indictment, to imprisonment for a term not exceeding two years or a fine or both. The fine that may be imposed following a conviction on indictment is unlimited. A statutory defence is set out at section 25(2) of the FSMA 2000. A person accused of contravening section 21(1) is able to raise the defence that he believed on reasonable grounds that the content of the communication was prepared or approved for the purposes of section 21 by an authorized person or that he took all reasonable precautions and exercised all due diligence to avoid committing the offence. It is important to note that the word 'all' indicates on a natural reading that an accused raising such a defence should be able to show that there was nothing further he could have done.

5.35 Section 30(2) of the FSMA 2000 provides that if in consequence of an unlawful communication (which is a communication made in contravention of section 21(1) of the FSMA 2000) a person enters as a customer into a controlled agreement, it is unenforceable against him and he is entitled to recover any money or other property paid or transferred by him under the agreement and compensation for any loss sustained by him as a result of having parted with that money or other property. The term 'controlled agreement' is defined[55] as an agreement the making or performance of which by either party constitutes a controlled activity. Section 30(3) of the FSMA 2000 provides that if in consequence of an unlawful

---

[52] Section 21(8) of the FSMA 2000.
[53] Section 21(9) of the FSMA 2000.
[54] Section 21(10) of the FSMA 2000.
[55] Section 30(1) of the FSMA 2000.

communication a person exercises any rights conferred by a controlled investment, no obligation to which he is subject as a result of exercising them is enforceable against him and he is entitled to recover any money or other property paid or transferred by him under the obligation and compensation for any loss sustained by him as a result of having parted with that money or other property. Under section 30(4) of the FSMA 2000, the court may allow the agreement or obligation to be enforced or money or property paid or transferred to be retained, if it is satisfied that it is just and equitable in the circumstances of the case, having regard to the relevant facts and circumstances.

5.36 The purpose of section 21(2) of the FSMA 2000 is to ensure that any financial promotion is either made by a person who is within the regulated community or approved by a person who is within the regulated community, and therefore that any financial promotion is subject to the FSA's rules and principles governing the nature and quality of information and of course behaviour more generally. COBS 4[56] sets out the regulatory obligations in respect of making or approving financial promotions.

5.37 Although the broad definition of a financial promotion is set out in section 21(1) of the FSMA 2000 as an invitation or an inducement to engage in investment activity, section 21 of the FSMA is very much a framework, which empowers the Treasury to specify by order the necessary detail. The Financial Services and Markets Act 2000 (Financial Promotion) Order 2005,[57] as amended (Financial Promotion Order) contains the necessary and very extensive detail.

5.38 The scheme of the Financial Promotion Order is to set out the detail of the financial promotion restriction and the exemptions which are available. The financial promotion restriction is the restriction in section 21(1) of the FSMA 2000.[58] The Financial Promotion Order distinguishes between real time communications (such as conversations) and non-real time communications (such as printed advertisements), and between communications that are solicited and unsolicited, and embraces the different means by which a communication can be made, including electronic means such as e-mail.

5.39 The Financial Promotion Order uses the term 'controlled activity' to refer to the investment activities in respect of which the financial promotion restriction applies, and the term 'controlled investment' to refer to the investments in respect of which the financial promotion restriction applies. A controlled activity is an activity which falls within any of paragraphs 1 to 11 of Schedule 1 to the Financial

---

[56] See paragraph 5.24.
[57] SI 2005/1529. The original statutory instrument was SI 2001/1335, which SI 2005/1529 revokes and re-enacts with certain amendments.
[58] Article 5 of the Financial Promotion Order.

Promotion Order.[59] A controlled investment is an investment which falls within any of paragraphs 12 to 27 of Schedule 1 to the Financial Promotion Order.[60]

5.40 The exemptions from the financial promotion restriction that are potentially available are set out in Parts IV, V, and VI of the Financial Promotion Order. Part IV of the Financial Promotion Order sets out the exemptions that are potentially available in respect of all controlled activities. Part V of the Financial Promotion Order sets out the exemptions in respect of deposits and insurance. Part VI of the Financial Promotion Order sets out the exemptions in respect of certain controlled activities only. The detail of the many and various exemptions is outside the scope of this book, although certain of them are examined in order that the overall policy informing the scope of the regulation of financial promotion becomes evident.

5.41 Broadly, the objective of the Financial Promotion Order is to regulate communications that are made for the purposes of a business in the United Kingdom and which can have an effect either in the United Kingdom or outside the United Kingdom, and communications that are made outside the United Kingdom and which can have an effect in the United Kingdom. Accordingly, article 12 of the Financial Promotion Order provides that the financial promotion restriction does not apply to any communication which is made to a person who receives it outside the United Kingdom or which is directed only at persons outside the United Kingdom, whether or not that communication is made from inside or outside the United Kingdom. Crucially, an unsolicited real time communication will be subject to the financial promotion restriction if it is made from a place within the United Kingdom and it is made for the purposes of a business which is carried on in the United Kingdom. The territorial scope of the Financial Promotion Order therefore becomes clear.

---

[59] Article 4(1) of the Financial Promotion Order. The controlled activities are: accepting deposits, effecting or carrying out contracts of insurance, dealing in securities and contractually based investments, arranging deals in investments, operating a multilateral trading facility, managing investments, safeguarding and administering investments, advising on investments, advising on syndicate participation at Lloyd's, providing funeral plan contracts, providing qualifying credit, arranging qualifying credit, advising on qualifying credit, providing a regulated home reversion plan, arranging a regulated home reversion plan, advising on a regulated home reversion plan, providing a regulated home purchase plan, arranging a regulated home purchase plan, advising on a regulated home purchase plan, and agreeing to carry on specified kinds of activity.

[60] Article 4(2) of the Financial Promotion Order. The controlled investments are: a deposit, rights under a contract of insurance, shares and stock, instruments creating or acknowledging indebtedness, government and public securities, instruments giving entitlements to investments, certificates representing certain securities, units in a collective investment scheme, rights under a stakeholder pension scheme, options, futures, contracts for differences, Lloyd's syndicate capacity and syndicate membership, funeral plan contracts, agreements for qualifying credit, regulated home reversion plans, regulated home purchase plans, and rights to or interests in investments.

5.2 Legislation and Regulation

Communications that are made by an overseas communicator are potentially exempt from the financial promotion restriction.[61] An overseas communicator is a person who carries on the relevant investment activities outside the United Kingdom, but does not carry on any such activity from a permanent place of business in the United Kingdom.[62] **5.42**

Communications that are made for a purpose other than to invite or to induce the recipient to engage in investment activity are potentially exempt from the financial promotion restriction.[63] **5.43**

Communications that are made by or to certain categories of person are potentially exempt from the financial promotion restriction, on the basis broadly that such communications are made in a context other than an invitation or inducement to engage in investment activity.[64] **5.44**

Notably, articles 28 and 28A of the Financial Promotion Order provide that the financial promotion restriction does not apply to a 'one off' communication if certain conditions are met. **5.45**

The regulation of financial promotions potentially excludes communications made to persons deemed to have the necessary expertise and experience to make their own assessment as to the merits and demerits of a financial promotion, or the necessary resources to obtain such advice as they might require to make such an assessment. Numerous categories of such expert and experienced persons are specified.[65] Again, it is to be noted that these exemptions are available only in respect of certain controlled activities. **5.46**

Other exemptions exclude from the financial promotion restriction communications made in circumstances in which the apparent inducement or invitation to **5.47**

---

[61] See articles 30 (Solicited real time communications), 31 (Non-real time communications to previously overseas customers), 32 (Unsolicited real time communications to previously overseas customers), and 33 (Unsolicited real time communications to knowledgeable customers) of the Financial Promotion Order.

[62] Article 30(2) of the Financial Promotion Order.

[63] See articles 13 (Communications from customers and potential customers), 14 (Follow up non-real time communications and solicited real time communications), 15 (Introductions), and 17 (Generic promotions) of the Financial Promotion Order.

[64] See articles 16 (Exempt persons), 17A (Communications caused to be made or directed by unauthorised persons), 18 (Mere conduits), 19 (Investment professionals), 20 (Communications by journalists), and 20A (Promotion broadcast by a company director etc). It is to be noted that the implementation of MiFID has curtailed the availability of article 18, which is a development that should be seen in the context of the regulatory initiative to ensure that all of the actors involved in providing and distributing financial products retain responsibility to the consumer. See part 8.7 of Chapter 8.

[65] See articles 48 (Certified high net worth individuals), 49 (High net worth companies, unincorporated associations etc.), 50 (Sophisticated investors), 50A (Self-certified sophisticated investors), and 51 (Associations of high net worth or sophisticated investors) of the Financial Promotion Order.

engage in investment activity is ancillary to another activity or agreed course of action. Numerous circumstances are specified.[66]

5.3 The General Prohibition

5.48 The general prohibition is one of the key concepts of the system for financial services regulation in the United Kingdom. No person may carry on a regulated activity in the United Kingdom, or purport to do so, unless he is an authorized person or an exempt person.[67] Two observations are made. One, the territorial scope of the FSMA 2000 is that the perimeter is defined with reference to the United Kingdom. Therefore any regulated activity which takes place in the United Kingdom falls within the scope of the perimeter, and any regulated activity which takes place outside the United Kingdom falls outside the perimeter. Two, the perimeter is defined with reference to a regulated activity. The term 'regulated activity' bears a very specific meaning, as the following paragraphs indicate. Regulatory, civil, and criminal sanctions may be applied to persons who contravene the general prohibition. One of the functions of the FSA is to police the perimeter, and the FSA has published guidance as part of the FSA Handbook.[68]

Regulatory sanctions

5.49 The regulatory sanctions are set out in part in section 20(1) of the FSMA 2000, which provides that if an authorized person carries on a regulated activity in the United Kingdom, or purports to do so, otherwise than in accordance with permission given to him by the FSA under Part IV, or resulting from any other provision of the FSMA 2000, then he is taken to have contravened a requirement imposed on him by the FSA under the FSMA 2000. Critically, a regulatory sanction can

---

[66] See articles 52 (Common interest group of a company), 53 (Settlors, trustees and personal representatives), 54 (Beneficiaries of trust, will or intestacy), 55 (Communications by members of professions), 55A (Non-real time communications by members of professions), 58 (Acquisition of interest in premises run by management companies), 59 (Annual accounts and directors' report), 60 (Participation in employee share schemes), 61 (Sale of goods and supply of services), 62 (Sale of body corporate), 63 (Takeovers of relevant unlisted companies: interpretation), 64 (Takeovers of relevant unlisted companies), 65 (Takeovers of relevant unlisted companies: warrants etc.), 66 (Takeovers of relevant unlisted companies: application forms), 67 (Promotions required or permitted by market rules), 68 (Promotions in connection with admission to certain EEA markets), 69 (Promotions of securities already admitted to certain markets), 70 (Promotions included in listing particulars etc.), 71 (Material relating to prospectus for public offer of unlisted securities), 72 (Pension products offered by employers), and 73 (Advice centres) of the Financial Promotion Order.

[67] Section 19(1) of the FSMA 2000.

[68] Perimeter Guidance Manual (PERG). PERG 1.1.2G provides that the purpose of PERG is to give guidance about the circumstances in which authorization is required, or exempt person status is available, including guidance on the activities which are regulated under the FSMA 2000 and the exclusions which are available.

only be applied by the FSA to an authorized person, that is, to a person already within the regulatory system, and moreover, the FSA determines the regulatory response to the contravention, such as an investigation or enforcement action, which may amount to censure, a fine or even withdrawal of authorization. Moreover, the authorized person's record with the FSA will become tainted, and this will colour its future relationship with the regulator. In particular, section 20(2) of the FSMA 2000 provides that such a contravention does not make the authorized person guilty of an offence, does not make any transaction void or unenforceable, and does not give rise to any right of action for breach of statutory duty, although in prescribed circumstances a person who suffers loss as a result of that contravention may bring an action. Therefore, the effect of section 20(2) of the FSMA 2000 is that the civil and criminal sanctions do not apply to an authorized person.

Civil sanctions

5.50 The civil sanctions are set out in sections 26, 27, 28, and 29 of the FSMA 2000. Section 26 of the FSMA provides that an agreement made by a person in the course of carrying on a regulated activity in contravention of the general prohibition is unenforceable against the other party, and the other party is entitled to recover any money or property paid or transferred by him under the agreement and compensation for any loss sustained by him as a result of having parted with that money or property. The case *CR Sugar Trading Ltd (in administration) v China National Sugar & Alcohol Group Corporation*,[69] which is more fully discussed in Chapter 8, illustrates the significant risk that an agreement entered into in contravention of the general prohibition is unenforceable. The case also illustrates the urgent need in some areas of commerce to establish that a particular business or activity does not fall within the perimeter. Section 26 does not apply if the regulated activity concerned is accepting deposits: instead section 29 applies to the activity of accepting deposits in breach of the general prohibition.

5.51 Section 27 of the FSMA 2000 similarly provides that an agreement made by an authorized person in the course of carrying on a regulated activity, not in contravention of the general prohibition but in consequence of something said or done by a third party acting in the course of a regulated activity in contravention of the general prohibition, is unenforceable against the other party to the agreement, and the other party to the agreement is entitled to recover any money or property paid or transferred by him under the agreement and compensation for any loss sustained by him as a result of having parted with that money or property. Again, section 27 does not apply if the regulated activity concerned is

---

[69] [2003] EWHC 79 (Comm).

accepting deposits: instead section 29 applies to the activity of accepting deposits in breach of the general prohibition.

5.52 Section 28 of the FSMA 2000 provides for agreements made unenforceable by sections 26 or 27. Broadly, under section 28 of the FSMA 2000, the amount of compensation recoverable for an agreement made unenforceable is either the amount agreed by the parties or by the court. Further, the court may determine in its discretion either to allow the agreement to be enforced or money and property paid under the agreement to be retained if it is just and equitable to do so, having regard to the relevant facts and circumstances.

5.53 Section 29 of the FSMA 2000 provides that if a deposit-taker accepts a deposit in contravention of the general prohibition, the depositor may apply to the court for an order directing the deposit-taker to return the money to the depositor if the depositor is not entitled, under the relevant agreement, to recover without delay that money, and the court need not make such an order if it is satisfied that it would not be just and equitable for that money to be returned.

Criminal sanctions

5.54 The criminal sanctions are set out in sections 23 and 24 of the FSMA 2000. Section 23 of the FSMA 2000 provides that a person who contravenes the general prohibition is guilty of an offence and liable on summary conviction to imprisonment for a term not exceeding six months or a fine not exceeding the statutory maximum or both, and on conviction on indictment, to imprisonment for a term not exceeding two years or a fine or both. The fine that may be imposed following a conviction on indictment is unlimited. A statutory defence is set out at section 23(3) of the FSMA 2000. A person accused of contravening the general prohibition is able to raise the defence that he took all reasonable precautions and exercised all due diligence to avoid committing the offence. For example, obtaining a legal opinion letter from a properly instructed law firm as to whether or not a particular business or activity falls within the perimeter should constitute a reasonable precaution, although again it is important to note that the word 'all' indicates on a natural reading that an accused raising such a defence should be able to show that there was nothing further he could have done.

5.55 Section 24 of the FSMA 2000 provides that a person who is neither an authorized person nor, in relation to the regulated activity in question, an exempt person is guilty of an offence if he describes himself (in whatever terms) as an authorized person, or describes himself (in whatever terms) as an exempt person in relation to the regulated activity, or behaves or otherwise holds himself out in a manner which indicates (or is reasonably likely to be understood as indicating) that he is an authorized person or an exempt person in relation to the regulated activity. Section 24(3) of the FSMA 2000 provides that a person guilty of an offence under section 24(1) of the FSMA 2000 is liable on summary conviction to imprisonment for a term not exceeding six months or a fine not exceeding level 5 on the standard scale or both. Section 24(4) of the FSMA 2000 increases the maximum fine that may be imposed by multiplying the amount of the standard fine by the number of days for which there is a public display of material in contravention of section 24(1). A statutory defence is set out at section 24(2) of the FSMA 2000. A person accused of contravening section 24(1) of the FSMA 2000 is able to raise the defence that he took all reasonable precautions and exercised all due diligence to avoid committing the offence. Again, it is important to note that the word 'all' indicates on a natural reading that an accused raising such a defence should be able to show that there was nothing further he could have done.

5.4 Regulated Activities

5.56 Section 22 of the FSMA 2000 provides that an activity is a regulated activity if it is an activity of a specified kind which is carried on by way of business and which relates to an investment of a specified kind or, in the case of an activity which is also specified for the purpose of section 22 of the FSMA 2000, to property of any kind. The expression 'investment of a specified kind' means an investment specified in an order made by the Treasury.

5.57 Schedule 2 to the FSMA 2000 contains Part I (Regulated activities), Part II (Investments), and Part III (Supplemental provisions). Schedule 2 to the FSMA 2000 is very much a framework, describing activities and investments in general terms, and the Treasury is expressly authorized[70] to make regulations or other instruments for the purposes of or in connection with any relevant provision of the FSMA 2000. The broad definition of each type of derivative contract is found in Part II of Schedule 2 to the FSMA 2000, and the definition of each regulated activity is found in Part I of Schedule 2 to the FSMA 2000. The detail of each regulation is amplified in the Financial Services and Markets Act 2000 (Regulated Activities) Order 2001,[71] as amended (Regulated Activities Order). Whether or not a particular activity is a regulated activity, and therefore potentially within the perimeter, depending on whether or not that activity is carried on within the United Kingdom, is determined by the following factors. One, is the activity an activity of a specified kind? Two, is an investment of a specified kind involved? Three, is the activity carried on by way of a business? Section 22 of the FSMA 2000 Act,

---

[70] Paragraph 25(1)(c) of Part III of Schedule 2 to the FSMA 2000.
[71] SI 2001/544. The Regulated Activities Order has most recently been amended to reflect the transposition of MiFID into English law.

in conjunction with the Regulated Activities Order, achieves the differentiation between investment activities and commercial activities.

Investments of a specified kind

5.58 From a regulatory perspective, there are three categories of derivative: options, futures, and contracts for differences. The observation is made in paragraph 4.09 that there are two categories of derivative cash flow, and therefore a link is discernible between the classification of derivative cash flows and the legal and regulatory definitions of the contracts. Each category of derivative contract is defined in outline in Part II of Schedule 2 to the FSMA 2000 (Investments), and each definition is given more substance in Part III of the Regulated Activities Order (Specified Investments). Part III of the Regulated Activities Order defines which investments are specified for the purposes of the FSMA 2000.

Options

5.59 Options are described in the FSMA 2000[72] as options to acquire or dispose of property. Options are specified under the Regulated Activities Order[73] broadly as:

- options to acquire or dispose of a security or contractually based investment other than another option;
- options to acquire or dispose of currency of the United Kingdom or any other country or territory;
- options to acquire or dispose of palladium, platinum, gold or silver;
- options to acquire or dispose of an option to acquire or dispose of any of the above (that is, another option);
- options to acquire or dispose of an option to acquire or dispose of certain derivative contracts listed in Section C of Annex I of MiFID, but only if certain types of counterparty are involved;
- options which relate to commodities, may be physically settled, are not for commercial purposes, and are to be considered as having the characteristics of other derivative financial instruments, but only if certain types of counterparty are involved; and
- certain other options which may be physically settled and which have certain characteristics specified in paragraph 10 of Section C of Annex I of MiFID, but only if certain types of counterparty are involved.

5.60 MiFID has extended the definition of 'option' to include options written on commodities.

---

[72] Paragraph 17 of Part II of Schedule 2 to the FSMA 2000.
[73] Article 83 of Part III of the Regulated Activities Order.

5.4 Regulated Activities

Futures

5.61 Futures are described in the FSMA 2000[74] as rights under a contract for the sale of a commodity or property of any other description under which delivery is to be made at a future date and at a price agreed on when the contract is made. Futures are specified in the Regulated Activities Order[75] as:

- rights under a contract for the sale of a commodity or property of any other description under which delivery is to be made at a future date and at a price agreed on when the contract is made;
- futures which relate to commodities and which may be physically settled, but only if certain types of counterparty are involved;
- futures and forwards which relate to commodities, may be physically settled, are not for commercial purposes, and are to be considered as having the characteristics of other derivative financial instruments, but only if certain types of counterparty are involved; and
- futures which may be physically settled and which have certain characteristics specified in paragraph 10 of Section C of Annex I of MiFID, but only if certain types of counterparty are involved.

5.62 Article 84(2) of the Regulated Activities Order specifically excludes from the definition of 'futures' rights under any contract which is made for commercial and not investment purposes. The overall policy of the FSMA 2000 is discernible, to include within the perimeter certain activities undertaken in respect of a contract that is made for investment purposes, and to exclude from the perimeter other activities undertaken in respect of a contract that is made for commercial purposes. Chapter 8 explores the consequences of the distinction that is drawn between investment futures and commercial forward contracts.

5.63 Article 84(3) of the Regulated Activities Order provides broadly that a contract is to be regarded as made for investment purposes if it is either made or traded on a recognized investment exchange or not made or traded on a recognized investment exchange but expressed to be as traded on such an exchange or on the same terms as an equivalent contract made on such an exchange. Article 84(7) of the Regulated Activities Order sets out the indications that a contract is made for investment purposes: it is expressed to be as traded on an investment exchange, its performance is ensured by an investment exchange or a clearing house, or there are arrangements for the payment or provision of margin.

5.64 Article 84(4) of the Regulated Activities Order provides broadly that a contract is to be regarded as made for commercial purposes if under its terms delivery is to be

---

[74] Paragraph 18 of Part II of Schedule 2 to the FSMA 2000.
[75] Article 84 of Part III of the Regulated Activities Order.

made within seven days. The second limb of article 84(4) is that a contract is to be regarded as made for investment purposes, notwithstanding its express terms, if it can be shown that the parties intended that delivery is made after seven days. The purpose of this second limb of article 84(4) is to bring within the perimeter contracts that are made for investment purposes but which are expressed to be made for commercial purposes, presumably in order to avoid the requirement for regulatory oversight. Article 84(5) of the Regulated Activities Order sets out the indications that a contract, which does not fall within the scope of article 84(4), is made for commercial purposes, and the absence of them is an indication that it is made for investment purposes: one or more of the parties is a producer of the commodity or other property and uses it in his business, and the seller delivers or intends to deliver the property or the purchaser takes or intends to take delivery of it. Although the word 'and' joining the two indications is absent in the original order, the context strongly suggests that both indications must be present for the contract to be treated as made for commercial purposes. Article 85(6) of the Regulated Activities Order sets out a further indication that a contract is made for commercial purposes: the prices, the lot, the delivery date, or the other terms of it are determined by the parties for the purposes of the particular contract and not solely by reference to regularly published prices, standard lots, standard delivery dates, or standard terms.

Contracts for differences

5.65 Contracts for differences are described in the FSMA 2000[76] as rights under a contract for differences or any other contract the purpose or pretended purpose of which is to secure a profit or avoid a loss by reference to fluctuations in the value or price of property of any description or an index or other factor designated for that purpose in the contract. Contracts for differences are specified in the Regulated Activities Order[77] as:

- rights under a contract for differences or any other contract the purpose or pretended purpose of which is to secure a profit or avoid a loss by reference to fluctuations in the value or price of property of any description or an index or other factor designated for that purpose in the contract; or
- derivative instruments for the transfer of credit risk and to which paragraph 8 of Section C of Annex I of MiFID applies, but only if certain types of counterparty are involved.

5.66 Article 85(2) of the Regulated Activities Order specifically excludes from the definition of 'contracts for differences' contracts under which the parties intend

---

[76] Paragraph 19 of Part II of Schedule 2 to the FSMA 2000.
[77] Article 85 of Part III of the Regulated Activities Order.

that the profit is secured or the loss is avoided by one or more of the parties taking delivery of any property to which the contract relates, contracts under which money is received by way of deposit on terms that any interest or return to be paid on the sum deposited will be calculated with reference to fluctuations in an index or other factor,[78] any contract under which money is received by the Director of Savings as deposits or otherwise in connection with the business of the National Savings Bank, any contract under which money is raised under the National Loans Act 1968 or treated as so raised by virtue of section 11(3) of the National Debt Act 1972, or rights under a qualifying contract of insurance.

Activities of a specified kind

5.67 There are several categories of regulated activities under the FSMA 2000, some of which are more relevant to derivatives than others. The categories are: dealing in investments, arranging deals in investments, deposit taking, safekeeping and administration of assets, managing investments, giving investment advice, establishing collective investment schemes, and using computer-based systems for giving investment instructions. Each category of activity is defined in outline in Part I of Schedule 2 to the FSMA 2000 (Regulated activities), and each definition is given more substance in Part II of the Regulated Activities Order (Specified activities). Part II of the Regulated Activities Order defines which activities are specified for the purposes of the FSMA 2000. Part II of the Regulated Activities Order is divided into chapters, each of which pertains to a particular activity. Generally, each chapter sets out the definition of the relevant activity, building on the definition set out in Part I of Schedule 2 to the FSMA 2000, and then sets out various exclusions. The intricacies of the many exclusions found are outside the scope of this book. The effect of an exclusion is that a particular activity, even if it involves a specified investment, is not an activity of a specified kind if certain prescribed conditions are met.

5.68 The overall purpose of the Regulated Activities Order is to differentiate between activities which constitute activities of a specified kind, and which therefore potentially fall within the perimeter, and activities which do not constitute activities of a specified kind, and which therefore fall outside the perimeter. The scheme of the FSMA 2000 and the Regulated Activities Order is set out succinctly in article 4(1) of the Regulated Activities Order. The Regulated Activities Order specifies kinds of activity for the purposes of section 22 of the FSMA 2000 (the classes of activity and categories of investment), and accordingly any such specified activity, which is carried on by way of business and which relates to an

---

[78] Such a deposit is a market-linked deposit, of the type discussed in part 4.16 of Chapter 4. The rationale for treating a market-linked deposit as a deposit and not as an investment for regulatory purposes is to ensure that the full protections required for deposit-taking activity are applied. The key characteristic of a market-linked deposit is that it is a deposit.

Chapter 5: The Legal Framework

investment of a kind specified by any provision of Part III of the Regulated Activities Order, is a regulated activity for the purposes of the FSMA 2000. Further, that regulated activity then falls within the scope of the general prohibition established by section 19 of the FSMA 2000 if that regulated activity is carried on in the United Kingdom.

Dealing in investments

5.69 Dealing in investments is described in the FSMA 2000[79] as buying, selling, subscribing for or underwriting investments or offering or agreeing to do so, either as a principal or as an agent.

Arranging deals in investments

5.70 Arranging deals in investments is described in the FSMA 2000[80] as making, or offering or agreeing to make arrangements with a view to another person buying, selling, subscribing for or underwriting a particular investment, or arrangements with a view to a person who participates in the arrangements buying, selling, subscribing for or underwriting investments.

Managing investments

5.71 Managing investments is described in the FSMA 2000[81] as managing, or offering or agreeing to manage, assets belonging to another person where the assets consist of or include investments, or the arrangements for their management are such that the assets may consist of or include investments at the discretion of the person managing or offering or agreeing to manage them.

Investment advice

5.72 Giving investment advice is described in the FSMA 2000[82] as giving or offering or agreeing to give advice to persons on buying, selling, subscribing for or underwriting an investment, or exercising any right conferred by an investment to acquire, dispose of, underwrite or convert an investment.

Using computer-based systems for giving investment instructions

5.73 Using computer-based systems for giving investment instructions is described in the FSMA 2000[83] as sending on behalf of another person instructions relating to

---

[79] Paragraph 2(1) of Part I of Schedule 2 to the FSMA 2000.
[80] Paragraph 3 of Part I of Schedule 2 to the FSMA 2000.
[81] Paragraph 6 of Part I of Schedule 2 to the FSMA 2000.
[82] Paragraph 7 of Part I of Schedule 2 to the FSMA 2000.
[83] Paragraph 9 of Part I of Schedule 2 to the FSMA 2000.

5.4 Regulated Activities

an investment by means of a computer-based system which enables investments to be transferred without a written instrument, offering or agreeing to send such instructions by such means on behalf of another person, causing such instructions to be sent by such means on behalf of another person, and offering or agreeing to cause such instructions to be sent by such means on behalf of another person.

The differentiation between investment activities and commercial activities

5.74 Two practical examples might be developed to illustrate how the Regulated Activities Order achieves the differentiation between investment activities which fall within the perimeter and commercial activities which fall outside the perimeter. In the first example, a producer of sugar (such as a refiner of raw sugar cane) and an industrial consumer of sugar (such as a soft drinks manufacturer) enter into a contract for the physical sale of sugar, under which the producer sells a quantity of sugar to the manufacturer every month. The producer and the consumer also enter into a swap to smooth out the fluctuations in the price of sugar over the term of the physical sale. The swap is a contract for differences (CFD) and therefore the swap is an investment of a kind specified in the Regulated Activities Order. Accordingly, by entering into the swap, the producer and the consumer carry on an activity which appears to be a specified kind of activity under article 14 of the Regulated Activities Order. Dealing in investments as principal means buying, selling, subscribing for, or underwriting securities or contractually based investments, other than funeral plan contracts or rights to or interests in investments. A CFD is a contractually based investment. However, article 68(2) of the Regulated Activities Order contains an exclusion from article 14: there is excluded from article 14 any transaction entered into by a supplier with a customer, if the transaction is entered into for the purposes of or in connection with the sale of goods or the supply of services, or a related sale or supply. The circumstances of the producer and the consumer entering into the swap are such that the exclusion contained in article 68(2) is available. The producer is the supplier and the consumer is the customer, and the swap is entered into for the purposes of or in connection with the sale of goods, which is the sale of sugar under the physical contract. The purpose of the swap is to hedge the exposure that the producer and the consumer have to fluctuations in the price of sugar that they sell and buy. The swap is therefore linked to the physical sale. Therefore the effect of article 68(2) is that the producer and the consumer do not carry on an activity of a specified kind, and their activity of entering into the swap falls outside the perimeter. In these circumstances, the swap is a contract that is made for commercial purposes, and not for investment purposes.

5.75 By contrast, in the second example, there is no physical sale. A commodities trading house and its counterparty enter into a swap to express their different investment views as to the fluctuations of the price of sugar. At first glance, the trading house and its counterparty appear to deal in investments as principals within the meaning of article 14 of the Regulated Activities Order, and therefore they appear to carry on an activity of a specified kind. In these circumstances, the swap is a contract that is made for investment purposes, and not for commercial purposes. Assuming that the commodities trading house is an authorized person, then the counterparty itself is able to avail itself of the exclusion set out in article 16(1) of the Regulated Activities Order, the effect of which is that a person who is not an authorized person does not carry on an activity of the kind specified in article 14 by entering into a transaction relating to a contractually based investment with or through an authorized person. Of course, as the commodities trading house is within the regulated community, activities undertaken by the commodities trading house in connection with the swap fall within the scope of regulation.

5.76 In both examples, the swap is a CFD and therefore an investment of a specified kind. However, the circumstances of each example determine whether or not the swap is entered into for investment purposes or for commercial purposes. These two examples are deliberately clear-cut in order to emphasize the operation of the Regulated Activities Order. It is stressed that this is a complex and subtle area of regulation, and a close analysis is required of any particular set of circumstances.

Terminology

5.77 It is useful to conclude this discussion on regulated activities with a summary of the different sets of terminology used at the different levels of the relevant legislation and regulation. The general prohibition is defined in section 19 of the FSMA 2000 with reference to a regulated activity. Regulated activity is defined in section 22 of the FSMA 2000 with reference to inter alia an activity of a specified kind which relates to an investment of a specified kind. Regulated activity is defined in Schedule 2 to the FSMA 2000 in general terms. Activities of a specified kind and investments of a specified kind are defined in detail in the Regulated Activities Order. The restriction on financial promotion is defined in section 21 of the FSMA 2000 with reference to engaging in investment activity. Engaging in investment activity is defined in section 21 of the FSMA 2000 with reference to controlled activities and controlled investments. Controlled activities and controlled investments are defined in detail in the Financial Promotion Order.

5.5 Legal Market Structures

5.78 Three different market structures are introduced in Chapter 2: the exchange-based market, the OTC market, and the market made available by a market service provider. These three different types of market are classified with reference to the type of connection between the counterparties. Counterparties in the

5.5 *Legal Market Structures*

exchange-based market are connected indirectly by the exchange and the clearing house, whether the exchange is a physical forum or an intangible computer network, and following the novation of transactions, all contracts are settled through the clearing house. By contrast, counterparties in the OTC market are connected directly by the communications between their branches and their offices, or indirectly by intermediating brokers, and contracts are settled between counterparties directly, under the terms of voluminous documentation put in place between them. These classifications are a matter of convenience and practicality, as the differences between the exchange-based market and the OTC market are discernible ultimately in the manner in which risk is controlled.

5.79 By contrast, legislation and regulation instead seek to differentiate between different categories of market participant, and not with reference to the forum in which business is dealt. Paragraph 5.24 explains the basis on which a firm authorized by the FSA is required to categorize its clients. The categorization of a particular client then determines the modification to the general conduct of business rules applicable to that client.[84] COBS 1.1.1R establishes that the New Conduct of Business Sourcebook applies to certain business and certain activities. This Rule is referred to as the 'general application rule'. COBS 1.1.2R provides that the general application rule is modified according to the activities of a firm and its location. The various modifications to the general application rule made pursuant to COBS 1.1.2R are set out in Annex 1 of COBS 1. COBS 1.1.3R provides that the general application rule is also modified for particular purposes, including purposes related to the type of firm, its activities or location, and for purposes relating to connected activities. The various modifications to the general application rule made pursuant to COBS 1.1.3R are made throughout COBS. Again, it is important to emphasize that notwithstanding the modification of particular rules, the fundamental standards expressed in the Principles must be observed at all times. It is telling that the provisions of MAR 1 do not seek to increase or decrease the protections conferred on different categories of client. In addition, MiFID has introduced into the regulatory scheme the concepts of a multilateral trading facility (MTF) and of a systematic internalizer. The former concept is of particular relevance to this book.

5.80 An MTF is a multilateral system, operated by an investment firm or a market operator, which brings together multiple third-party buying and selling interests in financial instruments, in accordance with non-discretionary rules, in a way that results in a contract.[85] The market service provider referred to in Chapter 1[86] is an MTF. MAR 5 refers to different types of market that can be offered by

---

[84] See paragraph 5.23.
[85] Article 4(1)(15) of MiFID.
[86] See paragraph 1.15.

an MTF: a continuous auction order book trading system (which continuously and automatically matches sell orders and buy orders without human intervention), a quote-driven trading system (under which transactions are concluded on the basis of firm quotes that are continuously made available by market makers), a periodic auction trading system (which periodically and automatically matches sell orders and buy orders without human intervention), and a fourth type in which prices are determined by a different process. MAR 5 requires a firm offering an MTF to have[87] one, transparent and non-discretionary rules and procedures for fair and orderly trading; two, objective criteria for the efficient execution of orders; three, transparent rules regarding the criteria for determining the financial instruments that can be traded under its systems; four, transparent rules based on objective criteria governing access to its facility and limiting access to, amongst others, persons who are fit and proper, who have a sufficient level of trading ability and competence, who have (where relevant) adequate organization arrangements, and who have sufficient financial resources; and five, either provide to users, or be satisfied that users have, sufficient publicly available information to form an investment judgment. Other requirements under MAR include the need for a firm operating an MTF to have in place arrangements to facilitate the efficient settlement of transactions,[88] to have in place arrangements and procedures for the regular monitoring of compliance by its users with its rules, and to monitor transactions undertaken by its users to identify breaches of its rules, disorderly trading conditions and conduct which may involve market abuse,[89] and to make reports to the FSA of significant breaches of the firm's rules, disorderly trading conditions, and conduct which may involve market abuse.[90] These requirements echo the requirements that investment exchanges must meet in order to be recognized under the regulatory system.[91] Potentially any financial instrument[92] can be traded under the systems of an MTF, including derivative contracts.

5.81 Although not directly relevant to this book, it is perhaps helpful to set out a little background to the concept of the systematic internalizer. Whether or not a firm is a systematic internalizer is determined in accordance with criteria set out in section 6.3 of MAR 6. The concept of the systematic internalizer applies only to cash business in shares, and not to business in derivatives. A firm is a systematic internalizer if it makes a market in shares that are admitted to trading on a regulated market (that is, it deals on its own account by executing client orders in these shares),

---

[87] MAR 5.3.1R.
[88] MAR 5.4.1R.
[89] MAR 5.5.1R.
[90] MAR 5.6.1R.
[91] See Chapter 6.
[92] See the Glossary to the FSA Handbook. The definition of financial instrument includes derivatives.

5.5 Legal Market Structures

and it does so outside a regulated market or an MTF, and it does so on an organized, frequent, and systematic basis, that is, as a part of its usual business model. MAR 6 requires a firm which is a systematic internalizer to publish a firm quote for each share admitted to trading on a regulated market for which it is a systematic internalizer. The purpose of the concept of the systematic internalizer therefore seems to be to ensure that an orderly market exists for listed shares beyond the regulated exchange on which those shares are listed.

Historical perspective

5.82 By way of background, the regulatory system has long sought to impose on a market between investment professionals a more light regime, and to impose on a market between investment professionals and their lay customers a more robust and prescriptive regime, but always subject to a fundamental set of principles describing best practice. The latest iteration of the system for financial regulation continues to create a distinction between the treatment of business between investment professionals and business between investment professionals and their lay clients, but as the following paragraphs demonstrate, the manner in which this distinction is made continues to evolve.

5.83 Looking back to the regulatory system put in place under the Financial Services Act 1986 (FSA 1986), the wholesale cash and OTC derivative markets included business in large-scale bank deposits, foreign exchange, short-term debt instruments, and OTC derivatives. These wholesale markets were exclusively OTC. The Bank of England used to supervise the wholesale markets by applying its paper 'The regulation of the wholesale cash and OTC derivatives markets' (which was known as the Grey Paper) and The London Code of Conduct and the Gilt Repo Code of Best Practice. Under section 43 of the FSA 1986, the Bank of England maintained a list of listed money market institutions (LMMIs). The Bank of England would determine whether or not to admit a particular organization to the list in accordance with the policies and criteria set out in the Grey Paper. Transactions between an LMMI and its counterparties, whether other LMMIs or certain wholesale counterparties that the LMMI was permitted to adopt under a prescribed procedure (including the despatch of a letter warning of the fewer protections afforded to adopted wholesale counterparties), would then be governed by the London Code of Conduct and, if relevant, the Gilt Repo Code of Best Practice. The supervision of the wholesale financial markets was said to be a carve-out from the onerous and prescriptive regime applied under the FSA 1986 and the self-regulating organizations established within that regime (see paragraph 5.05). Soon after its establishment, the FSA assumed the Bank of England's responsibilities for supervising the wholesale financial markets, and the Bank of England itself assumed the principal responsibility of applying monetary policy to control inflation within the targets set by the government.[93] As an interim measure, the FSA continued to maintain a list of LMMIs under section 43 of the FSA 1986 and continued to apply the Grey Paper, the London Code of Conduct, and The Gilt Repo Code of Best Practice until the effective date of the FSMA 2000 on 30 November 2002 and the introduction of the FSA Handbook.

5.84 More recently, following the coming into force of the FSMA 2000, the FSA applied a system of regulation based on the concept of the inter-professional market, as prescribed in Chapter 3 of the Market Conduct sourcebook ('Inter-professional conduct'). The scope of the inter-professional market was inter-professional business, which was defined as business undertaken by an authorized firm in respect of an inter-professional investment with or for a market counterparty from an establishment maintained by a firm in the United Kingdom. Crucially, and marking a departure from the demarcation between wholesale and other business under the FSA 1986, inter-professional business included both exchange-based and OTC derivatives. However, MAR 3 followed the same general principles that the London Code of Conduct contained, and the overall convention was very much caveat emptor (literally buyer beware). Accordingly, a firm was not required to ensure the suitability of a transaction or financial product for its market counterparty, and it was not obliged to ensure that its market counterparty fully understood the risks arising, and instead, the firm was required only to observe the fundamental standards of avoiding making misleading communications and, under the Principles, which were already in place at that time, of making communications which are clear, fair, and not misleading.

5.85 MAR 3 has now been deleted[94] following the transposing into the United Kingdom's regulatory system of the requirements of MiFID, and with this deletion, the rigid distinctions between inter-professional and other investment business have been removed. Instead, all authorized persons are required to comply with the same substantial set of rules and guidance, subject to modifications, such as those discussed in paragraph 5.27 in respect of COBS 9, and in paragraph 5.28 in respect of COBS 10. There is no longer any carve-out from a prescriptive regime (as was the case under the FSA 1986) or the establishment of a distinct and discrete set of rules governing business dealt exclusively between investment professionals (as was the case under MAR 3 before the transposing of the requirements of MiFID).

---

[93] Bank of England Act 1998. Section 11(1) provides that the Bank of England's objectives in relation to monetary policy are to maintain price stability and, subject to that, to support the economic policy of Her Majesty's Government, including its objectives for growth and employment. Section 13(1) provides that the Monetary Policy Committee of the Bank of England has responsibility for formulating monetary policy. Part III provides for the transfer of supervisory functions to the FSA.
[94] The last day in force of MAR 3 was 31 October 2007.

Further, with its inclusion of chapter 5 (Multilateral trading facilities) and chapter 6 (Systematic Internalisers), the latest iteration of MAR indicates that the regulatory system is now addressing the evolution of the financial markets in a process characterized by entrepreneurial segmentation of the financial markets. For example, the established investment exchanges, which are broadly the seat of regulated markets, are run like businesses, and investment firms themselves now readily establish new forums for trading various financial instruments, and these new forums constitute a new generation of organized trading systems which function alongside existing regulated markets such as the established investment exchanges.[95] Hitherto, the principal segmentation of the financial markets was observed in the dichotomy between wholesale institutional OTC business and other business, and more recently in the dichotomy between business dealt exclusively between investment professionals and business dealt between investment professionals and their lay clients. However, through its evolution, the regulatory system as set out in the FSA Handbook is converging closer with the basic tenet of the FSMA 2000, which under section 2(2) charges the FSA with the protection of consumers, irrespective of the experience, expertise, or resources of those consumers. **5.86**

5.6 EU Legislation

The various directives of the EU provide the foundation for much of the national legislation and regulation made in respect of the financial markets within the EEA, and not just the EU. Therefore, at a fundamental level, EU directives define common standards and thereby contribute to the definition of a single market across the EEA. Extensive legislation and regulation is made in different Member states under various EU directives, including in the United Kingdom under English law the FSMA 2000. **5.87**

Through its membership of the EU,[96] the United Kingdom is a part of the creation of a single European market for goods, services, and capital. The political and economic dimension to European integration remains a separate and ongoing debate outside the scope of this book. The European Economic Area (EEA) is a **5.88**

---

[95] This echoes paragraph 4 of the preamble to MiFID.
[96] Membership of the EU comprises the following member states (the date in parentheses is the date of joining): Austria (1 January 1995), Belgium (25 March 1957), Bulgaria (1 January 2007), Cyprus (1 May 2004), Czech Republic (1 May 2004), Denmark (1 January 1973), Estonia (1 May 2004), Finland (1 January 1995), France (25 March 1957), Germany (25 March 1957), Greece (1 January 1981), Hungary (1 May 2004), Italy (25 March 1957), Latvia (1 May 2004), Lithuania (1 May 2004), Luxembourg (25 March 1957), Malta (1 May 2004), The Netherlands (25 March 1957), Poland (1 May 2004), Portugal (1 January 1986), Republic of Ireland (1 January 1973), Romania (1 January 2007), Slovakia (1 May 2004), Slovenia (1 May 2004), Spain (1 January 1986), Sweden (1 January 1995), and the United Kingdom (1 January 1973).

free trade area generally comprising the EU and the European Free Trade Area (EFTA). The overall principle underpinning the establishment of the EEA is the creation of a free trade area throughout the EEA in goods, services, and capital.

The European Union

5.89 By way of brief background, the EU is a political framework built up from the European Communities. The term 'European Community' was the designation originally and widely used to refer to the political entity which comprised different legal entities with separate international legal personalities. The European Community was made up of the European Coal and Steel Community (ECSC), which was formed by the Treaty of Paris (which came into force on 25 June 1957), the European Atomic Energy Community (Euratom), which was formed by the first Treaty of Rome (which came into force on 1 January 1958), and the European Economic Community (EEC), which was formed by a second Treaty of Rome (which also came into force on 1 January 1958). The ECSC was established for a duration of 50 years, whereas Euratom and the EEC were established for an indefinite duration. The Treaty on European Union (the Treaty of Maastricht) designated the EEC as the 'European Community' (EC). Therefore the term 'European Communities', and note that this is plural, is now sometimes used to describe these entities, one of which is the European Community (that is, the entity which formerly was the European Economic Community, or EEC). The EC, ECSC, and Euratom remained distinct, although the Merger Treaty (which came into force on 1 July 1967) is sometimes described as fusing together these three European Communities. The United Kingdom joined the EEC on 1 January 1973, and is thereby a member state of the EU.

The European Free Trade Area

5.90 EFTA[97] was established on 3 May 1960, following the signing of the Stockholm Convention on 4 January 1960. It is important to note that although Switzerland is a member of EFTA, Switzerland has so far declined to participate in the EEA (see the following paragraph), although its domestic legislation rarely varies from the principles underpinning EU legislation.

The European Economic Area

5.91 The EEA Agreement was concluded on 13 December 1993 and came into force on 1 January 1994, and was originally intended to establish a free trade area, the European Economic Area, between the EU and EFTA. The overall principle of

---

[97] Membership of EFTA comprises the following: Iceland, Liechtenstein, Norway, and Switzerland.

the EEA Agreement is to establish a free trade area, characterized by the free movement of goods, persons, services, and capital. Each state ratifies and implements international treaties and agreements in accordance with its own individual timetable. The complex issue of whether or not a particular state has given effect to a treaty or an international agreement is outside the scope of this book.

Harmonization

Harmonization of standards is further facilitated through the activities of organizations outside the immediate infrastructure of the European Communities, such as CESR (the Committee of European Securities Regulators), CEBS (the Committee of European Banking Supervisors), and CEIOPS (the Committee of European Insurance and Occupational Pensions Supervisors). The work of CESR and CEBS are of greater relevance to this book. These two organizations share broadly similar objectives, to advise the EU Commission, including in connection with the preparation of draft measures to implement EU directives, to work towards ensuring more consistent and timely implementation of EU directives, and to improve generally coordination and the exchange of information amongst the relevant groups of regulators (securities regulators in the case of CESR, and banking regulators in the case of CEBS). **5.92**

Most EU directives made in respect of financial markets are intended to be implemented at national level, because they are not directly effective or applicable at national level. Individual member states are achieving different rates of progress in implementing various EU directives. However, an EU directive can give rise to rights that nationals of member states can enforce, notwithstanding that the EU directive has not been implemented. An individual can seek to enforce against a member state or an organ of a member state an identifiable right conferred by an EU directive that the member state has failed to implement. **5.93**

The European passport

One of the most important characteristics of the financial markets within the EEA, to which of course the United Kingdom belongs through its membership of the EU, is the concept usually referred to as the 'European passport'. Under the European passport, an EEA person authorized or licensed to carry on investment business in its home member state of the EEA (that is, a person with EEA legal personality) is also authorized to carry on that business outwards into another host member state of the EEA, either through a local branch or on a cross-border services basis without a local presence in the host state. The European passport operates so that the person is permitted to carry on business in host states subject in those host states only to the conduct of business rules or the equivalent that are applicable in the public good in those host states. Therefore the principle underpinning the European passport becomes discernible: member states mutually **5.94** recognize each other's legislation, and they are able to do so because national legislation conforms to the common standards defined by the various EU directives that they variously implement. To place EU legislation in context, the threshold conditions defined in COND[98] reflect the standards prescribed by various EU directives. From a broader perspective, the Financial Services Action Plan, which has been drafted by a committee chaired by Alexandre Lamfalussy, will give rise to further EU legislation, all of which must be implemented at the national level. The purpose of the Financial Services Action Plan is to harmonize further European financial services regulation.

5.95 Generally, a person, such as a credit institution or an investment firm, wishing to offer services outwards into the EEA from a member state notifies its home state regulator of its intention. The home state regulator then considers whether or not the applicant's systems and controls are sufficient for the conduct of investment business in other member states. If the applicant's systems and controls are sufficient, then the home state regulator liaises with the relevant host state regulator and notifies the relevant host state regulator that the application has been approved. The essence of the European passport is that the host state regulator is comfortable that the applicant is fit and proper to offer services in its territory on the strength of the home state regulator's authorization of and supervision of the applicant. A similar process is applied in respect of investment funds,[99] or to use the argot of the regulation, undertakings for collective investment in transferable securities (UCITS). The European passport in the context of a UCITS operates so that a UCITS which is approved by the regulator in one member state is permitted to market its units in other member states. Again, the essence of the European passport is that the host state regulator is comfortable that the UCITS should be able to market its units in its territory on the strength of the home state regulator's authorization of the UCITS. In this book, the regulation of UCITS is discussed in Chapter 9 in the context of the investment powers that a UCITS has to use derivatives.

---

[98] See paragraph 5.17.
[99] See 2001/107/EC Directive of the European Parliament and of the Council amending Council Directive 85/611/EEC on the coordination of laws, regulations and administrative provisions relating to undertakings for collective investment in transferable securities (UCITS) with a view to regulating management companies and simplified prospectuses, and 2001/108/EC Directive of the European Parliament and of the Council amending Council Directive 85/611/EEC on the coordination of laws, regulations and administrative provisions relating to undertakings for collective investment in transferable securities (UCITS) with regard to investments of UCITS. The term 'UCITS 1' refers to the original UCITS directive 85/611/EEC. The term 'UCITS 3' refers to the two new UCITS directives 2001/107/EC and 2001/108/EC. No 'UCITS 2' directive was adopted; it remained in draft.

Credit institutions

The European passport in the context of credit institutions is defined in the second Banking Consolidation Directive.[100] The first Banking Consolidation Directive[101] was repealed and replaced by the second Banking Consolidation Directive owing to the large number of amendments that had been made to it, and the first Banking Consolidation Directive was built on several earlier EU directives, including notably the First Banking Coordination Directive,[102] the Own Funds Directive,[103] the Second Banking Coordination Directive,[104] the Solvency Ratio Directive,[105] the Consolidated Supervision Directive,[106] the Large Exposures Directive,[107] the Capital Adequacy Directive,[108] the second Capital Adequacy Directive,[109] and the Banking, Solvency Ratio and Capital Adequacy Directive.[110]

5.96

Investment firms

The European passport in the context of investment firms is defined by MiFID. MiFID represents a significant evolution in the pan-European regulation of investment businesses, and it both repeals its immediate predecessor, the Investment Services Directive[111] (ISD), and amends the original UCITS 1 directive. Although MiFID was adopted 21 April 2004, it was only implemented by

5.97

---

[100] 2006/48/EC Directive of the European Parliament and of the Council relating to the taking up and pursuit of the business of credit institutions (recast).

[101] 2000/12/EC Directive of the European Parliament and of the Council on the taking up and pursuit of the business of credit institutions.

[102] 77/780/EEC Council Directive on the coordination of laws, regulations and administrative provisions relating to the taking up and pursuit of the business of credit institutions.

[103] 89/299/EEC Council Directive on the own funds of credit institutions.

[104] 89/646/EEC Council Directive on the coordination of laws, regulations and administrative provisions relating to the taking up and pursuit of the business of credit institutions and amending Directive 77/780/EEC.

[105] 89/647/EEC Council Directive on a solvency ratio for credit institutions.

[106] 92/30/EEC Council Directive on the supervision of credit institutions on a consolidated basis.

[107] 92/121/EEC Council Directive on the monitoring and control of large exposures of credit institutions.

[108] 93/6/EEC Council Directive on the capital adequacy of investment firms and credit institutions.

[109] 98/31/EC Directive of the European Parliament and of the Council amending Council Directive 93/6/EEC on the capital adequacy of investment firms and credit institutions.

[110] 98/33/EC Directive of the European Parliament and of the Council amending Article 12 of Council Directive 77/780/EEC on the taking up and pursuit of the business of credit institutions, Articles 2, 5, 6, 7, 8 of and Annexes II and III to Council Directive 89/647/EEC on a solvency ratio for credit institutions and Article 2 of and Annex II to Council Directive 93/6/EEC on the capital adequacy of investment firms and credit institutions.

[111] 93/22/EEC Council Directive on investment services in the securities field.

the MiFID Implementing Directive[112] some two years later, and the requirements set out in MiFID have only recently been transposed into national legislation. In the United Kingdom, the requirements set out in MiFID have been given effect by the various amendments to the Regulated Activities Order made by the Treasury and the various amendments made to the FSA Handbook by the FSA. MiFID came into force on 1 November 2007.

5.98 MiFID makes the following important changes to the regulation of financial services in the EEA. First, whereas the scope of the ISD did not include business relating to commodities, the scope of MiFID includes business relating to commodities. Accordingly, futures, options and contracts for differences written over commodities are now treated as investments under the regulatory system and therefore a person can now be authorized by the FSA to carry on investment business in respect of such investments, and moreover, the European passport is available in respect of such investment business. Second, the definition of investment services under MiFID now includes certain advisory services. Third, MiFID imposes more detailed requirements for the regulation of the conduct of investment business. In particular, the standards set out in MiFID address the governance and internal systems and controls; the concept of outsourcing (and thereby the extent to which an authorized person remains responsible for activities that have been outsourced to contractors); conflicts of interest; the categorization of clients; the content of communications made to clients; the innovation of MTFs and Systematic Internalizers; trade reporting (which is the continuous real time reporting of trades); transaction reporting (which is the reporting of relevant trades to the relevant trades at the end of the day following the day on which the trade is dealt); the obligation to provide best execution; the standards to be achieved in providing investment advice, and the requirement to assess the suitability and appropriateness of any advice or recommendation that is made; the safekeeping of client assets; and the training and competence of staff.

5.99 In particular, Annex 1 of MiFID sets out the list of services and activities (in Section A and Section B) and financial instruments (in Section C). The investment services set out in Section A comprise the reception and transmission of orders in relation to one or more financial instruments; the execution of orders on behalf of clients; dealing on own account; portfolio management; giving investment advice; underwriting financial instruments; placing financial instruments without a firm commitment basis; and the operation of MTFs.

---

[112] 2006/73/EC Directive of the Commission implementing Directive 2004/39/EC of the European Parliament and of the Council as regards organisational requirements and operating conditions for investment firms and defined terms for the purpose of that Directive. This Commission Directive is one of the technical implementing directives.

5.100 The ancillary services set out in Section B comprise the safekeeping and administration of financial instruments for the account of clients; lending to an investor to enable him to carry out a transaction in one or more financial instruments; giving corporate finance advice; providing foreign exchange services; providing investment research and financial analysis; providing certain services related to underwriting; and providing certain investment services and carrying out certain activities related to the underlying of derivatives.

5.101 The financial instruments set out in Section C comprise transferable securities; money-market instruments; units in collective investment undertakings; derivatives relating to securities, currencies, interest rates or yields, other derivatives, financial indices, or financial measures that are settled in cash or physically; derivatives relating to commodities that can be physically settled; derivatives relating to commodities which are not for commercial purposes and which have the characteristics of other financial instruments; credit derivatives; financial contracts for differences; and derivatives on other types of underlying such as climatic variables, freight rates, emission allowances, or inflation rates or other economic statistics.

5.102 Annex II of MiFID defines a professional client as a client who possesses the experience, knowledge, and expertise to make its own investment decisions and properly assess the risks that it incurs. Certain categories of professional client are set out in Annex II of MiFID; these categories are defined with reference to the nature of the client's business and the extent of the client's financial resources. A professional client is deemed to require fewer protections than a client who is not a professional client, and interestingly, the onus is on the client to request a higher level of protection when it deems it is unable to properly assess or manage the risks involved in its use of the financial system. Further, certain clients can request to be treated as professional clients and thereby waive certain of the protections afforded by the various conduct of business rules, provided that the firm makes an assessment of the expertise, experience, and knowledge of the client.

6

RISK, DOCUMENTS, AND THE EXCHANGE-BASED MARKET

6.1 Introduction	6.01
6.2 Recognized Investment Exchanges and Recognized Clearing Houses	6.02
6.3 Companies Act 1989	6.10
6.4 Give-up Agreements and Clearing Agreements	6.28

6.1 Introduction

Participants in the derivative markets, whether the exchange-based markets or the OTC markets, are exposed to the same basic counterparty risk, which is the risk that a counterparty fails to perform its obligations, whether to make a payment or to make a delivery. A key difference between the exchange-based market and the OTC market is the manner in which counterparty risk is controlled. The exchange-based market is supported by the clearing and margining system, which is introduced in Chapter 2 and Chapter 3. One aspect of counterparty risk is the risk that the counterparty might become insolvent and thereby become incapable of making a payment or delivery. As Chapter 7 explains, insolvency risk in the OTC market is controlled through the use of collateral, and as this chapter explains, insolvency risk in the exchange-based market that is subject to English law is in part neutralized by the legislative foundation underpinning that market.[1] These legislative provisions have a fairly powerful and wide-reaching effect on the usual and familiar processes of the English law of insolvency, albeit tempered by certain exceptions to preserve the overall balance of relative interests.[2]

6.01

---

[1] A significant control against counterparty risk is the maintenance of adequate capital to act as a cushion. See Chapter 10.

[2] See paragraph 6.12.

6.2 Recognized Investment Exchanges and Recognized Clearing Houses

Recognition and the effects of recognition

6.02 The concept of recognition is important, whether in the context of a recognized investment exchange (RIE) or a recognized clearing house (RCH). The legislative foundation underpinning the exchange-based market operates with reference to whether or not the relevant exchange or clearing house has been recognized within the meaning of the FSMA 2000.

6.03 The principal effect of recognition is that an RIE or an RCH is exempt from the general prohibition established by section 19 of the FSMA 2000, which is discussed in Chapter 5. Certain activities undertaken by an exchange or a clearing house might amount to regulated activities were it not for the recognition of that exchange or clearing house. For example, as Chapter 2 explains,[3] a key element of the clearing process is the clearing house becoming the seller to every buyer on the exchange and the buyer to every seller on the exchange through the transfer to it of all transactions that are dealt on the exchange. The clearing house might therefore be deemed to be dealing in those investments,[4] and therefore carrying on an activity for which permission is required, were it not for the effect of recognition.

6.04 Section 285(1) of the FSMA 2000 provides that a recognized investment exchange is an investment exchange in relation to which a recognition order is in force, and a recognized clearing house is a clearing house in relation to which a recognition order is in force. Section 285(2) of the FSMA 2000 provides that a recognized investment exchange is exempt from the general prohibition in respect of any regulated activity which is carried on as a part of the exchange's business as an investment exchange or which is carried on for the purposes of, or in connection with, the provision of clearing services by the exchange. Section 285(3) of the FSMA 2000 provides that a recognized clearing house is exempt from the general prohibition in respect of any regulated activity which is carried on for the purposes of, or in connection with, the provision of clearing services by the clearing house.

6.05 As an RIE or an RCH is exempt from the general prohibition, the RIE or RCH is not required to become authorized. Instead, consumer protection, which is one of the FSA's four statutory regulatory objectives under section 2(2) of the FSMA 2000, is achieved by the FSA recognizing an exchange or clearing house only if the

---

[3] See paragraph 2.13.
[4] See paragraph 5.69.

exchange or clearing house meets certain requirements, and therefore meets a certain standard of quality. The method of supervision applied to an exchange or clearing house differs from the method of supervision applied to a firm.

Obtaining a recognition order

6.06 An investment exchange may make an application under section 287 of the FSMA 2000 for an order to be made by the FSA under section 290(1) that it is an RIE for the purposes of the FSMA 2000. An overseas investment exchange may also make an application under section 287 of the FSMA 2000 for a recognition order, provided that the additional requirements imposed by section 292 of the FSMA 2000 are met. Section 287(2) provides that an application for a recognition order must be made in such manner as the FSA may direct and must be accompanied by a copy of the applicant investment exchange's rules, a copy of any guidance issued by the applicant, the required particulars, and such other information as the FSA may reasonably require for the purposes of determining the application. The required particulars include details of any arrangements which the applicant has made or proposes to make for the provision of clearing services; details of how the applicant will determine to whom it will provide clearing services, if it proposes to offer clearing services in respect of transactions dealt on other investment exchanges; a programme of the applicant's operations, including the applicant's organizational structure; details of the persons who effectively direct the applicant's business; and details of the ownership of the applicant. The last three items are not provided by an applicant which is an overseas investment exchange.

6.07 A clearing house may make an application under section 288 of the FSMA 2000 for an order to be made by the FSA under section 290(1) that it is an RCH for the purposes of the FSMA 2000. An overseas clearing house may also make an application under section 288 of the FSMA 2000 for a recognition order, provided that the additional requirements imposed by section 292 of the FSMA 2000 are met. Again, Section 288(2) provides that an application for a recognition order must be made in such manner as the FSA may direct and must be accompanied by a copy of the applicant clearing house's rules, a copy of any guidance issued by the applicant, the required particulars, and such other information as the FSA may reasonably require for the purposes of determining the application. The required particulars include details of any arrangements which the applicant has made or proposes to make with a recognized investment exchange, and details of how the applicant will determine to whom it will provide clearing services if it proposes to offer clearing services for persons other than recognized investment exchanges.

6.08 In determining an application made by an investment exchange or a clearing house for a recognition order, the FSA applies the rules and guidance set out in the specialist sourcebook in the Handbook of Recognised Investment Exchanges and Recognised Clearing Houses (REC). REC 2 sets out the recognition requirements for UK recognized bodies and sets out guidance on those requirements. The same standards apply both on initial recognition and at all times after initial recognition. Many of the requirements set out in RCS 2 apply to both investment exchanges and clearing houses. These requirements include: maintaining adequate financial resources; being a fit and proper person to perform the functions of an RIE or an RCH; the maintenance of adequate systems and controls; ensuring that business is conducted in an orderly manner and so as to afford proper protection to investors; ensuring that access to facilities is subject to criteria designed to protect the orderly functioning of the market and the interests of investors; ensuring that satisfactory arrangements are made for securing the timely discharge of settlement and clearing; ensuring that satisfactory arrangements are made for recording transactions; ensuring that appropriate measures are adopted to reduce the extent to which facilities can be used for a purpose connected with market abuse or financial crime; ensuring that satisfactory arrangements are made for the safeguarding and administration of assets belonging to users of facilities, if relevant; being able and willing to promote and maintain high standards of integrity and fair dealing; ensuring that appropriate procedures are adopted for making, amending and keeping under review rules; having effective arrangements for monitoring and enforcing compliance with its rules; and having effective arrangements for investigating and resolving complaints. Certain requirements apply just to investment exchanges, such as ensuring that appropriate arrangements are made for the provision of relevant information and admission to trading, and other requirements apply just to clearing houses.

Exchange contracts

6.09 The derivative contracts that are dealt on an exchange do not generally contain the detailed default and termination provisions that OTC derivative contracts contain.[5] Instead, the procedures of the exchanges themselves make the necessary provisions.[6] By way of example, a derivative contract dealt on LIFFE is an exchange contract under the rules of LIFFE. A default in respect of an exchange contract is defined with reference to the terms of the exchange contract itself, the rules of LIFFE, the administrative provisions that have been implemented under the rules of LIFFE, and the general regulations and default rules of the appointed clearing house, which is the London Clearing House. The default rules of the LCH are very detailed and have generally been developed to enable the market to withstand a default by an exchange member.

---

[5] See Chapter 7.
[6] As the following paragraphs explain, the default procedures of exchanges and clearing houses are given priority by the legislative foundation underpinning the exchange-based market.

6.3 Companies Act 1989

6.10 A key risk is the insolvency of an exchange member. Under English law, the assets of an insolvent company are distributed amongst the company's creditors in accordance with general insolvency law.[7] Schedule 6 to the Insolvency Act 1986, as amended (IA 1986) sets out the categories of preferential debts, and also sets out the ranking of creditors in the order in which they are to be satisfied out of the assets of the insolvent estate. IA 1986 is supplemented by the Insolvency Rules 1986, as amended, which combine rules of procedure with a number of provisions of substantive law, such as the priority of debts and the rules of insolvency set-off. The effect of these various provisions is that a particular creditor may not receive the entire amount that he is owed by the insolvent estate; instead, the amount that he actually receives will depend on the value of the assets of the insolvent estate which are available for distribution to creditors, the ranking of all of the creditors of the insolvent estate, and the security that has been taken by all or some of the creditors. The purpose of security is to protect the creditor in whose favour it is created from the competing claims of other creditors. Generally, the analysis of security rests on one, the attachment of the security to a particular asset or class of assets, which must be of sufficient value to offset the debt that is secured; two, perfection of the security, which connotes the procedural actions that must be taken to render the security valid against competing interests, including registration in the relevant register, such as the register kept by the registrar of companies; and three, the relevant rules of priority, which determine the ranking of creditors relative to competing claims against the debtor's assets. The Law of Property Act 1925 contains detailed rules which govern the ranking of the different types of security that might be taken, such as legal mortgages, equitable mortgages, fixed charges, and floating charges. The Enterprise Act 2002 (EA 2002) further modifies the English law of security by introducing the concept of the qualified floating charge.

6.11 The risk in the context of the exchange-based market is therefore that the clearing house might not receive all of the losses that an insolvent member is liable to pay to it. If there is a shortfall in the amount that the clearing house should receive, then the solvency of the clearing house is jeopardized, and the clearing house might not be able to make all of the payments due in respect of profitable positions on the exchange. This further shortfall would in turn threaten the solvency of other participants in the market dealt on the exchange. This is the essence of systemic risk: crystallization of risk in one area of the financial markets, or indeed the economy more widely, spreads into other areas of the markets and the broader economy.

---

[7] See Miles, *Principles of Corporate Insolvency Law* (Sweet & Maxwell, 2005).

From a practical perspective, the system of clearing should avoid the accumulation of losses, and the system of margining should ensure that the clearing house has available to it sufficient collateral to meet the losses that might be incurred during trading over the course of one session, effectively stopping the fall of the dominoes. However, reliance cannot be placed on the practical effects of the cash flows inherent in the clearing and settlement process, and therefore Part VII of the Companies Act 1989 (CA 1989) (Financial markets and insolvency) was enacted effectively to disconnect the usual insolvency procedures and distribution of assets, in order that the clearing house receives as much as possible of the amounts that the insolvent exchange member is liable to pay. Part VII of the CA 1989 broadly has the effect that on the insolvency of a member of an RIE or an RCH, certain relevant contracts and arrangements entered into by that member are excluded from the distribution of assets under the general law of insolvency and are instead applied in accordance with the rules of the RIE and the relevant RCH. The overall purpose of Part VII of the CA 1989 is therefore to make provision for safeguarding the operation of certain financial markets, by preserving to the greatest extent possible the assets of an insolvent member, and thereby control the potential systemic risk which might otherwise arise. However, a balance must be made between safeguarding the wider financial markets and preserving the rights and remedies that should be available to commercial actors who have taken valid, binding, and enforceable security.

6.12 The overall scheme of Part VII of the CA 1989 is set out in section 154, which describes how that Part of the CA 1989 contains provisions to safeguard the operation of certain financial markets with respect to the insolvency, winding up, or default by a person who is a party to transactions in those financial markets, the effectiveness or enforcement of certain charges given to secure obligations in connection with those transactions, and the rights and remedies in relation to certain property provided as cover for margin in relation to such transactions or subject to such a charge. It is relevant to note that Part VII of the CA 1989 applies to insolvency under both English law and Scottish law, which is consistent with the territorial scope of the FSMA 2000, which provides for recognition of investment exchanges and clearing houses.

Market contract

6.13 Part VII of the CA 1989 operates with reference to market contracts. Section 155 of the CA 1989 sets out the definition of a market contract, which is a contract entered into by a member of an RIE or a designated non-member of the RIE with a person other than that RIE, and which either is made on the RIE or (if it is not made on the RIE) is made subject to the rules of the RIE. The definition of a market contract also includes a contract which is made by the RIE with its members for the purpose of enabling the rights and liabilities of members under transactions in investments to be settled. The term 'designated non-member' means a person in respect of whom action may be taken under the default rules[8] of the RIE but who is not a member of the RIE. Section 155(2A) of the CA 1989 provides that Part VII of the CA 1989 does not apply to contracts and arrangements in respect of recognized overseas investment exchanges. Section 155(3) of the CA 1989 provides that Part VII of the CA 1989 applies to contracts entered into by the clearing house with a member of the clearing house for the purpose of enabling the rights and liabilities of that member under transactions in investments to be settled. By definition, a contract made on an RIE or made subject to the rules of an RIE is a contract in an investment. However, section 155(2)(b) and section 155(3) of the CA 1989 refer to contracts made for the purpose of enabling transactions in investments to be settled, in order to distinguish these types of contract from other contracts that might be made by an RIE or an RCH with its members (such contracts may, for example, govern the provision of data feeds), a default under which would not threaten the stability of the relevant financial market.

Modifications of the law of insolvency

6.14 Section 158(1) of the CA 1989 provides that the application of the general law of insolvency in relation to market contracts and action taken under the rules of an RIE or an RCH with respect to such market contracts is subject to sections 159 to 165 of the CA 1989. Section 158(2) of the CA 1989 limits the modifications to the law of insolvency to proceedings in respect of a member or designated non-member of an RIE or an RCH, and to proceedings in respect of a party to a market contract which began after the relevant RIE or RCH took action under its own default rules in relation to a person who is party to a market contract as principal. Specifically, the modifications to the law of insolvency do not extend to any other insolvency proceedings, notwithstanding that rights or liabilities arising under market contracts fall to be dealt with under those proceedings. Section 158(3) defines the scope of proceedings. Proceedings include one, the presentation of a bankruptcy petition or a petition for the sequestration of a person's estate; two, the application for an administration order (which includes the filing with the court of a copy of a notice of an intention to appoint an administrator by a floating charge holder[9]) or the presentation of a winding-up petition or the passing of a resolution for a voluntary winding up; and three, the appointment of an administrative receiver.

---

[8] The definition of default rules is set out in s 188(1) of the CA 1989.
[9] This provision was inserted into the CA 1989 by the EA 2002.

Precedence over insolvency procedures

6.15 Section 159(1) of the CA 1989 has the effect that a market contract, and the default rules of an RIE or an RCH, and the rules of an RIE or an RCH, other than its default rules, as to the settlement of market contracts shall not be regarded as invalid at law on the ground of inconsistency with the law relating to the distribution of the assets of a person on bankruptcy, winding up or sequestration, or in the administration of an insolvent estate. The purpose of section 159(1) of the CA 1989 is to ensure that a market contract and the relevant rules of an RIE or an RCH remain valid, and therefore enforceable, notwithstanding that under certain circumstances the application of the general law of insolvency would, in the absence of Part VII of the CA 1989, operate to nullify those market contracts and rules.

6.16 Section 159(2) of the CA 1989 has the effect that a relevant office-holder cannot exercise its power in such a way as to prevent or to interfere with settlement in accordance with the rules of an RIE or an RCH of a market contract, or any action taken under the default rules of such RIE or RCH. The purpose of section 159(2) of the CA 1989 is to prevent a relevant office-holder, such as the liquidator of the insolvent member of the RIE or RCH, or the court from preventing or interfering with the orderly unwinding of the insolvent member's transactions and trading positions. This orderly unwinding of positions is accomplished using the relevant procedures of the RIE or the RCH.

Net sums

6.17 Section 163(1) of the CA 1989 has the effect that the net sum that an RIE or an RCH certifies to be payable under its default rules by or to a defaulting member is then dealt with in the usual manner under general insolvency law. That net sum might be either provable in the bankruptcy or the winding up of the defaulting member, or payable to the relevant office-holder appointed in respect of the defaulting member's estate. That net sum might also be taken into account, where appropriate, under section 323 of the IA 1986 (mutual dealings and set-off) or under the corresponding provision applicable in the case of a winding up.

6.18 The effect of section 163(1) of the CA 1989 is important, as it demonstrates the tension inherent in the scheme of Part VII of the CA 1989. The need to control the risk of systemic risk in the financial markets must be balanced against established general insolvency law, which seeks to distribute the insolvent estate amongst creditors in accordance with certain principles that have already been set out.[10] The scheme of Part VII of the CA 1989 is that the defaulting member's assets are first applied in the process of an orderly unwinding of that defaulting

---

[10] See paragraph 6.10.

member's trading positions, and then applied in the usual distribution of assets under general insolvency law.

Disclaiming onerous property, the rescission of contracts, and avoiding transfers

6.19 Section 164(1) of the CA 1989 has the effect that sections 178, 186, 315, and 345 of the IA 1986, which provide for matters such as the power to disclaim onerous property and the court's power to order the rescission of contracts, do not apply in relation to a market contract or to a contract effected by the RIE or the RCH for the purpose of realizing property provided as margin in relation to market contracts. Section 164(3) of the CA 1989 has the effect that sections 127 and 284 of the IA 1986, which provide for the avoidance of dispositions of property made after the commencement of the winding up or the presentation of the bankruptcy petition, do not apply in relation to a market contract, to the provision in relation to market contracts, to a contract effected by the RIE or the RCH for the purpose of realizing property provided as margin in relation to market contracts, or to any disposition of property in accordance with the rules of the RIE or the RCH as to the application of property provided as margin. Section 164 of the CA 1989 is one of the principal statutory provisions underpinning the exchange-based market, giving effect to the important principle that contracts or arrangements entered into during the course of trading in an exchange-based market are excluded from the usual insolvency procedures and rules, which allow certain contracts and arrangements to be set aside for the purpose of making available as many assets as possible to satisfy the creditors of the insolvent estate.

Market charges

6.20 Section 174 of the CA 1989 provides for the modifications of the law of insolvency in respect of market charges, which are defined in section 173 of the CA 1989. Section 173(1) of the CA 1989 provides that a market charge is a fixed or floating charge which is granted in favour of either an RIE or an RCH for the purpose of securing debts or liabilities arising in connection with the settlement of market contracts, or in favour of an RCH for the purpose of securing debts or liabilities arising in connection with ensuring the performance of market contracts, or in favour of a person who agrees to make payments as a result of the transfer or the allotment of specified securities made through the medium of certain computer-based systems for the purpose of securing debts or liabilities of the recipient of those securities.

6.21 Section 174(1) of the CA 1989 provides that the general law of insolvency has effect in relation to market charges and any action taken to enforce market charges subject to the provisions of section 175 of the CA 1989.

6.22 Section 175(1) of the CA 1989 has the effect that certain provisions of Schedule B1 to the IA 1986 do not apply in relation to a market charge, subject to certain exceptions. The provisions of Schedule B1 which do not apply are paragraphs 43(2) and (3), which place restrictions on the enforcement of security or the repossession of goods, and paragraphs 70, 71, and 72, which give the administrator the power to deal with charged or hire-purchase property. Section 175(1A) of the CA 1989, which is inserted into the CA 1989 by the EA 2002, has the effect that paragraph 41(2) of Schedule B1 to the IA 1986 also does not apply to a market charge. That paragraph provides that a receiver is to vacate office at the request of an administrator.

6.23 Section 175(3) of the CA 1989 has the effect that section 43 of the IA 1986 also does not apply in relation to a market charge. Section 43 of the IA 1986 gives the administrative receiver the power to dispose of charged property.

6.24 Section 175(4) of the CA 1989 has the effect that sections 127 and 284 of the IA 1986 also do not apply in relation to a market charge. Sections 127 and 284 of the IA 1986 permit the setting aside of dispositions of property made after the commencement of a winding up or the presentation of a bankruptcy petition, and the effect of section 175(4) of the CA 1989 is that these sections of the IA 1986 cannot displace a transfer of property as a result of which that property becomes subject to a market charge.

Market property

6.25 Section 177 of the CA 1989 preserves property for use as margin in relation to market contracts dealt on an RIE or cleared through an RCH, notwithstanding that the property in question may be subject to any prior equitable interest or right, or any right or remedy arising from a breach of fiduciary duty. However, the property in question would not be available if the RIE or the RCH had notice of the interest, right, or breach of fiduciary duty at the time when the property was provided as margin. Section 177(3) of the CA 1989 further provides that no right or remedy which arises after the property in question is provided as margin may be enforced in such a manner which prevents or interferes with the application of the property by the RIE or the RCH in accordance with its rules. Section 177(4) of the CA 1989 further has the effect that any property provided as margin to the RIE or the RCH under section 177 of the CA 1989 can subsequently be transferred by the RIE or the RCH to a person under the rules of the RIE or the RCH free of any interest, right, or remedy that is effectively overridden by the operation of section 177(3) of the CA 1989. To place sections 177(3) and (4) of the CA 1989 in context, the flow of payments through the clearing house from the losers to the winners on the exchange at the end of each trading session is recollected.[11]

---

[11] See paragraph 3.06.

Priority of floating charges

One of the main principles of the English law of security is that a fixed charge prevails over a floating charge, including a floating charge that is created before the fixed charge is created, unless the fixed charge is created in favour of a person who has notice of a negative pledge supporting that earlier floating charge.[12] Section 178 of the CA 1989 empowers the Secretary of State to make regulations to provide that a market charge which is a floating charge has priority over a fixed charge which is created after it. **6.26**

Section 179 of the CA 1989 provides that where property subject to an unpaid vendor's lien becomes subject to a market charge, the market charge has priority over the lien unless the person in whose favour the market charge is created had actual notice of the lien at the time when the property became subject to the charge. **6.27**

6.4 Give-up Agreements and Clearing Agreements

The give-up agreement is the practical mechanism which enables every transaction entered into on an exchange to be cleared[13] by the clearing house which supports that exchange. **6.28**

Standard terms and conditions of a model give-up agreement, which is more formally known as the 'International Uniform Give-up Agreement', have been published by the Futures and Options Association (FOA), which is the trade association for the derivative industry in the United Kingdom. The FOA has agreed the provisions of the model give-up agreement with the Futures Industry Association (FIA) of the United States and with LIFFE. The intention is that the model give-up agreement should become more widely accepted in the global financial markets, and not just in the London financial markets. Many participants in the exchange-based market use the model give-up agreement with either little or no amendment. **6.29**

It is recollected that all payments of profits and losses, and all payments of margin, on an exchange flow through the accounts held by clearing members with the clearing house,[14] and therefore a non-clearing member (NCM) of an exchange **6.30**

---

[12] A substantial body of litigation as to the distinction between fixed charges and floating charges has been observed, culminating with the decision on 30 June 2005 of the House of Lords in *National Westminster Bank plc v Spectrum Plus Limited and others* [2005] UKHL 41. Creditors prefer to hold fixed charges and purport where possible to take fixed charges, because of the inherent advantages of fixed charges over floating charges, including the priority enjoyed by fixed charge holders over other categories of creditor. However, if a purported fixed charge does not demonstrate the characteristics of a fixed charge, it is susceptible to recharacterization as a floating charge and therefore demotion.

[13] See paragraphs 2.14 and 2.15.

[14] See paragraph 3.06.

must hold an account with a clearing member of an exchange in order to be able to access the clearing system. There are two types of clearing member. An individual clearing member (ICM) clears transactions for itself and for its customers. A general clearing member (GCM) clears transactions for itself, its customers, each NCM which holds an account with it, and the customers of each such NCM. Therefore an NCM gains access to the clearing system only indirectly through the account it holds with a GCM. A give-up agreement is used to document the different relationships between the various links of what is referred to as the clearing chain. Figure 6.1 illustrates the different relationships which may be documented under a give-up agreement.

6.31 By way of illustration, an end-user which is not an exchange member wishes to trade derivative contracts dealt on an exchange. The end-user is the customer of a broker which is an NCM. The end-user wishes to buy five futures contracts. The broker might fill the end-user's order by buying on-exchange five futures contracts from a counterparty and selling off-exchange five futures contracts to the end-user, so the economic effect of both transactions is that the end-user effectively buys five futures contracts from the counterparty. The on-exchange transaction between the broker and the counterparty is matched and cleared. As Chapter 2 explains, clearing involves the novation of the transaction to the clearing house, as the clearing house is the seller to every buyer on the exchange, and the buyer to every seller on the exchange.

6.32 It is a key principle that the clearing house only sells to and buys from clearing members. Therefore the transaction must be cleared through a GCM with which the broker as an NCM has an account.

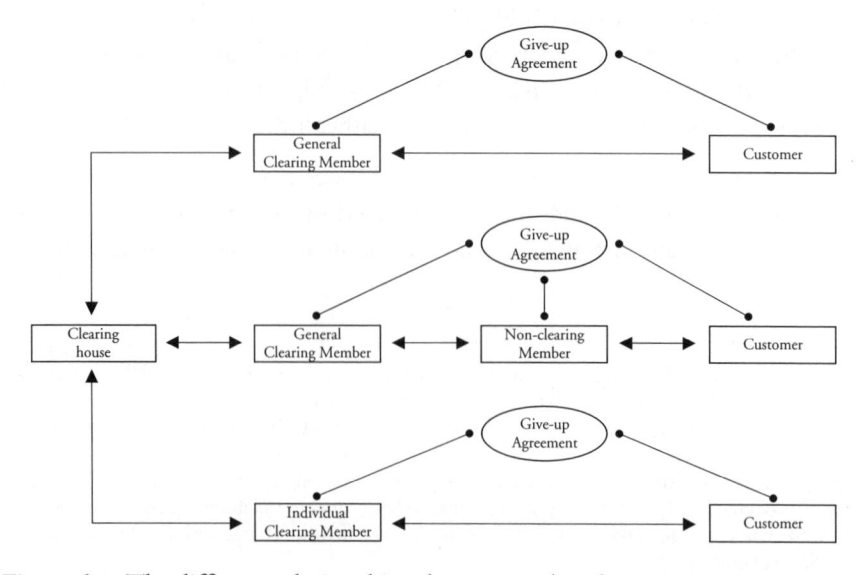

Figure 6.1 The different relationships documented under a give-up agreement

6.4 Give-up Agreements

6.33 Through the novation of transactions, the original on-exchange purchase by the broker of five futures contracts from the counterparty is cancelled. However, the broker does not buy five futures contracts from the clearing house, as the clearing house only sells to and buys from clearing members. Accordingly, the broker buys five futures contracts from the GCM, and the GCM in turn buys five futures contracts from the clearing house. The economic effect of these transactions is that the end-user buys five futures contracts from the clearing house. There is therefore a clearing chain, with the the end-user at one end and the clearing house at the other end. On the other side of the transaction, the counterparty (from whom the broker buys five futures contracts) sells five futures contracts to the clearing house, whether directly (if the counterparty is a GCM) or indirectly through another clearing chain (if the counterparty is an NCM).

6.34 The broker, the GCM providing clearing services to the broker, and perhaps the end-user enter into a give-up agreement to govern their relationships and their various inter-dependencies. A give-up agreement effectively contains the necessary consents to the cancellation of the original on-exchange purchase of the five futures contracts by the broker from the counterparty, the purchase by the broker from the GCM of five futures contracts, and the purchase by the GCM from the clearing house of five futures contracts. The give-up agreement contains the framework for the relationship between the broker, the GCM, and perhaps the end-user. Participants in the exchange-based market understand what is meant by clearing and therefore give-up agreements tend to be expressed in fairly general terms.

6.35 Different types of give-up agreement are used, depending on the number of parties involved. As Figure 6.1 illustrates, a give-up agreement can be bipartite, that is, entered into by two parties, or tripartite, that is, entered into by three parties.

6.36 To return to the illustration, the payments of profits, losses, initial margin, and variation margin in respect of the long position opened by the end-user are effected through the account held by the GCM with the clearing house. The GCM must pay initial margin to the clearing house. The broker pays the amount of the initial margin to the GCM, and the end-user pays the amount of the initial margin to the broker. Any variation margin to support losses in respect of the long futures position are paid to the clearing house by the GCM. The broker pays the amount of any variation margin to the GCM, and in turn the end-user pays the amount of any such variation margin to the broker. Similarly, the clearing house credits the account that the GCM holds with it with profits in respect of the long futures position, and the GCM in turn credits the account that the broker holds with it with the amount of such profits, and the broker in turn credits the account that the end-user holds with it with the amount of such profits. There is a flow of cash up and down the clearing chain.

6.37 The GCM is responsible to the clearing house for payments of margin in respect of the end-user's position. The clearing house therefore has the right, under the give-up agreement, to refuse to accept for clearing any transaction in order that it can control the risks to which it is exposed. Indeed, the model give-up agreement referred to in paragraph 6.29 permits the GCM to place limits and conditions on the positions that it will accept for clearing.

6.38 The broker and the GCM might also enter into a clearing agreement alongside their give-up agreement, which governs the payments that each makes to the other in respect of transactions that the broker has given up to the GCM for clearing. The clearing agreement allows the GCM to control the risk to which it is exposed, that the broker might fail to make a payment to the GCM. The GCM should not be exposed to any potential loss arising from the provision by it of clearing services. Although the payment of margin is implicit in the clearing relationship contemplated by the give-up agreement, market participants prefer the additional certainty and robustness that the clearing agreement confers. Indeed, the model give-up agreement warns that it is a basic document and that persons using it may elect to enter into a more detailed agreement to govern their relationship and control their risks more fully.

6.39 The customer documentation between the broker and the end-user should govern the payments that each makes to the other in respect of transactions that the broker effects for the end-user. Generally, the broker will require the end-user to provide more margin to it than the margin that it is required to provide to the GCM, in order to put in place additional protection against the credit risk of the end-user.

6.40 The observation might be made that the essence of the exchange-based market is cash flow, that is, the daily flow of profits from the losers on a day to the winners on that day through the clearing house, and the daily flow of any necessary supporting collateral to the clearing house. It is therefore important to ensure the traction of this cash flow, and traction is ensured by the clearing agreements and give-up agreements. The GCM provides clearing services to both the broker and to the end-user, and the GCM charges a fee for doing so. As the illustration developed in this chapter shows, a considerable amount of administration is involved in the clearing and margining process, and the GCM must invest significantly in systems and procedures to enable it to offer clearing services.

7

RISK, DOCUMENTS, AND THE OTC MARKET

7.1 Introduction	7.01	7.8	2002 ISDA Equity Derivatives Definitions	7.97
7.2 OTC Derivative Documentation Generally	7.02	7.9	2003 ISDA Credit Derivatives Definitions	7.127
7.3 ISDA	7.11	7.10	2005 ISDA Commodity Definitions	7.159
7.4 The ISDA 2002 Master Agreement and its Schedule	7.19	7.11	2006 ISDA Definitions	7.175
7.5 ISDA Credit Support Documents	7.69	7.12	2006 ISDA Fund Derivatives Definitions	7.204
7.6 ISDA Confirmation	7.88			
7.7 ISDA Definitions Generally	7.91			

7.1 Introduction

The OTC derivative market lacks the legislative foundation which underpins the exchange-based derivative market; under English law, the relevant legislative foundation is provided by Part VII of the CA 1989, which the previous chapter explores. The OTC market also generally lacks the involvement of a clearing and margining system.[1] Therefore, a participant in the OTC market must rely on two measures to control its risks. One, it carries out its own extensive counterparty due diligence checks, under which it verifies the risk generally of doing business with a prospective counterparty. These checks include establishing that the counterparty has the legal power to transact the relevant business contemplated and establishing that the counterparty has sufficient creditworthiness to be able to make the payments contemplated. Two, it executes various agreements to document the entire trading relationship. These documents set out how risk is controlled, including through obtaining appropriate representations and warranties, the right to terminate early transactions in response to certain events and circumstances, the computation of a net amount payable by one party to the other

7.01

---

[1] However, participants in the OTC market and the London Clearing House (as it then was) have collaborated to develop SwapClear, which is introduced in paragraph 2.21, and various initiatives emerge to facilitate the flow of trade information between market participants.

following the termination of transactions, and perhaps, looking at the wider relationship between the parties, a right of set-off as against other debts between them. In addition, the various agreements may also legislate for both the provision of collateral, and the maintenance of collateral during the course of the trading relationship at acceptable levels. Finally, legal opinion letters might also be obtained to provide assurance that certain agreements constitute the valid, binding, and enforceable obligations of the parties to them under the relevant laws, and to provide assurance that certain legal devices such as netting are effective under the relevant laws.

7.2 OTC Derivative Documentation Generally

7.02 Succinctly, as this chapter demonstrates, the purpose of OTC derivative documentation is to control risk and to ensure liquidity between the parties during the course of a dynamic trading relationship, with reference to both the values of transactions which are outstanding and to each party's tolerance of counterparty risk.

The basic architecture of OTC derivative documentation

7.03 OTC derivative documentation tends to conform to a generic blueprint. A master agreement governs the overall trading relationship between the parties, and each transaction within the framework of the trading relationship is described in a separate confirmation. Each confirmation is linked to the master agreement, thus an individual confirmation can be fairly brief, as the master agreement contains much of the contractual terms of the relationship, leaving the confirmation to record the economic terms of the relevant transaction. This generic blueprint is found elsewhere in commerce, such as the maritime shipping industry; the concept of the master agreement is not unique to the OTC derivative industry.

7.04 A master agreement generally provides for the following principal matters: (1) the basic obligation of each party to make payments or deliveries to the other as required in respect of individual transactions; (2) the netting of payments scheduled to be made on the same day, to simplify cash flows and to further mitigate credit risk; (3) the representations and warranties made by each party to the other, whether once or on an ongoing basis; (4) the events and circumstances which give either party the right to terminate early one or more outstanding transactions; (5) the procedure by which a transaction is terminated early, including the notice that is served and the timetable in accordance with which notice is served and becomes effective, and the calculation of the amount that is payable in respect of such early termination; (6) the process by which such early termination is settled; and (7) the basis on which the trading relationship in its entirety might be brought

7.2 OTC Derivative Documentation Generally

to an end. Other more 'boilerplate' matters such as governing law and jurisdiction are also dealt with.

7.05 Each individual transaction is described in a confirmation, which is governed by the framework master agreement. A confirmation can be very concise as it does not provide for the matters for which the master agreement makes provision, although of course the confirmations for more exotic transactions can be extremely intricate. The master agreement and each confirmation form a single agreement. The concept of the single agreement is extremely important, as the following paragraphs illustrate.

7.06 Other documents supporting the trading relationship might include credit enhancement or credit support agreements, under which collateral is provided for or on behalf of a party in order to support that party's obligations under outstanding transactions, and sets of standard definitions, the purpose of which is to introduce uniformity and therefore certainty to trading relationships and transaction structures. Standard definitions also render more efficient the documentation of individual transactions. In addition, the obligations of parties may be further reinforced by the provision of guarantees by parent companies with stronger balance sheets and credit ratings.

7.07 A number of master agreements have been developed over the last two decades or so, including the following principal examples in the English language: the various master agreements published by ISDA (which are considered in greater detail in the following pages of this chapter); the International Currency Options Market (ICOM) Master Agreement, which was published in 1992 by the British Bankers' Association (BBA) and the US Foreign Exchange Committee (FXC), which is independent of but sponsored by the Federal Reserve Bank of New York; the International Foreign Exchange Master Agreement (IFEMA), which was published in 1993 by the BBA and the FXC; the ICOM Master Agreement, which was published in 1997 by the BBA, the Canadian Foreign Exchange Committee (CFXC), the FXC, and the Tokyo Foreign Exchange Market Practices Committee (TFXMPC); the IFEMA, which was published in 1997 by the BBA; the Foreign Exchange and Options Master Agreement (FEOMA), which was published in 1997 by the BBA, the CFXC, the FXC, and the TFXMPC; agreements in the form of the 'BBAIRS terms', which are terms for interest rate swap agreements published by the BBA; agreements in the form of the 'FRABBA terms', which are terms for forward rate agreements published by the BBA; and the Global Master Repurchase Agreement, which was published by The Bond Market Association and the International Securities Market Association. Other forms of master agreement have been published in other languages, including notably in the French language, the German language, and the Japanese language, and work is under way in the People's Republic of China and Russia to develop master agreements for use in those jurisdictions.

Advantages and disadvantages of standard-form documentation

7.08 Using standard-form documents offers significant advantages. The use of standard contractual terms aids liquidity and contributes to certainty. Counterparties deal on terms that become familiar. By way of illustration, a dealer in swaps would prefer to buy swaps on the same contractual terms as it sells swaps, in order to avoid the risk of a mismatch in documents. Any mismatch in documents might have repercussions, especially in the context of defaults and the rights arising on an early termination of transactions. The dealer would generally want to be able to enforce the same rights against one of its counterparties as its other counterparty might seek to enforce against it. This risk of an asymmetry in the rights and obligations under documents is commonly referred to as a 'basis risk'. The use of standard contractual terms also reduces costs, and reduces delay, and therefore contractual uncertainty, between the striking of a commercial agreement and the execution of a binding legal agreement. The latter point is significant. Although the documentation for a particular transaction may not be complete and therefore not legally binding, counterparties are nonetheless required to observe the commercial terms of the transaction once those terms have been agreed. Aside from certain exceptions, a contract is not required to be in writing.[2] However, in the absence of a document in which the terms of a contract are recorded, there is uncertainty as one party's perception of what has been agreed may well differ from its counterparty's perception. A technical development which promises to ease the difficulties experienced with agreeing transaction documentation is the development of various extensible markup language (XML) message formats,[3] which are standardized formats for the electronic transmission of packets of data. Agreement of XML protocols should enable the large amounts of information required to describe a transaction accurately and fully to be exchanged using meta-data, which

---

[2] The principle that a contract is generally not required to be in writing or signed in order to be enforceable is firmly established under English law, although of course if an agreement is struck orally, there is scope for dispute as to whether the parties can show that they formed a sufficient intention to form a contract at all, and as to whether the terms of the purported contract demonstrate sufficient certainty to be enforceable. See for example *Bear Stearns Bank Plc v Forum Global Equity Limited* [2007] EWHC 1576 (Comm). Of course, standard practice in the financial markets is to agree transactions orally, perhaps during the course of a telephone conversation, with written confirmations constituting written contractual terms being subsequently executed; however, the more structured transactions are discussed on the basis of a term sheet, which records the intentions of the parties. Although it is superseded by the final contractual terms, the term sheet remains the record of the transaction until the execution of those final contractual terms. Further, a number of statutory rules require contracts to be made in writing; for example, a number of consumer contracts are required to be made in writing in order to be enforceable, as the imposition of formalities is deemed by the legislature to be an effective means of promoting consumer protection.

[3] For example, see the Financial products Markup Language (FpML) which is being developed under the auspices of ISDA.

effectively comprise the principal information to be communicated, and the additional information identifying the context and use of that principal information.

7.09 An important benefit of using one master agreement, and documenting individual transactions by a short confirmation, is that market participants are able to reduce substantially the credit exposures that they have to each other. For example, a common right under master agreements is the right to terminate early all transactions within the framework of that master agreement in response to the occurrence of certain events, and following early termination, the condensing of all terminated transactions into one obligation to pay a single net close-out amount.

7.10 However, there are limitations to the use of standard documents. A standard document contains terms which are intended to be balanced between the interests of the parties, and therefore consideration must be given to whether or not it is appropriate to use this approach in the context of a particular relationship or indeed transaction. For example, a standard document assumes that the two parties project an identical credit risk, and therefore some adaptation of the standard document will be necessary where the parties project substantially different credit risks. Other matters such as discrepancies in regional insolvency laws and the potential problems induced by operational risks, such as errors in payment processing, must also be considered. Nonetheless, it is to be remembered that standard documents can easily be adapted to accommodate the detail of an intended trading relationship, and the argument remains compelling to use standard documents wherever possible.

7.3 ISDA[4]

7.11 The materials published by the International Swaps and Derivatives Association, Inc. (ISDA) are now more or less the standard form of documentation that is used in the international derivative markets, having achieved prominence in the last 15 years or so.

7.12 ISDA was formed in May 1985 by a small group of participants in the nascent international swap markets, including investment banks and commercial banks. ISDA was originally established as the International Swap Dealers Association, Inc., and this name indicates ISDA's origins as a trade association for one particular segment of the global financial markets. The first co-chairmen of ISDA were Tom Jasper of Salomon Brothers and Artur Walter of Goldman Sachs.

---

[4] Materials published by ISDA are the copyright of the International Swaps and Derivatives Association, Inc., of 360 Madison Avenue, 16th Floor, New York, NY 10017.

ISDA changed its name to the International Swaps and Derivatives Association, Inc. in 1993 to reflect its growing influence.

7.13 ISDA has stated clearly its objectives in general terms in a mission statement, which is as follows. 'The Association's primary purpose is to encourage the prudent and efficient development of the privately negotiated derivatives business by: • Promoting practices conducive to the efficient conduct of the business, including the development and maintenance of derivatives documentation. • Promoting the development of sound risk management practices. • Fostering high standards of commercial conduct. • Advancing international public understanding of the business. • Educating members and others on legislative, regulatory, legal, documentation, accounting, tax, operational, technological and other issues affecting them. • Creating a forum for the analysis and discussion of, and the representing the common interest of its members on, these issues and developments.'

7.14 It is through the standard documents that it publishes that ISDA is known to many in the financial and commodity markets, although ISDA undertakes a significant variety of other activities, including lobbying with both governments, regulators, and other trade bodies, consulting, and educational activities, such as convening training conferences. In addition to publishing a broad range of documents, ISDA promotes various initiatives which are vital to the development of the derivative markets, including commissioning surveys investigating different aspects of legal systems, accounting practices, and trends in the market, including its very important series of opinions as to the enforceability of netting in various legal systems, developing models for the implementation of optimal laws to assist liquidity in the market,[5] and running various committees of market participants and other interested parties to build consensus and improve standards, for example in the field of risk management and operations.

7.15 In 1985, ISDA published the Swaps Code for US dollar interest rate swaps. This represented an early move by participants in the emerging swap market to standardize documentation. The transactions that had been concluded in the early 1980s had been individually negotiated and documented, and consequently the legal fees were predictably exceptionally high. In 1987, ISDA published two standard forms of agreement, entitled 'Interest Rate Swap Agreement' and 'Interest Rate and Currency Exchange Agreement', accompanied by the 1987 Interest Rate and Currency Exchange Definitions. After 1987, ISDA published various addenda in order that other financial instruments could be documented using the

---

[5] This work is undertaken by ISDA's Collateral & Financial Law Reform Group, which monitors developments in law on a global level.

1987 agreements, including options, caps, floors, and collars.[6] In June 1992, ISDA published two forms of master agreement: the 1992 Master Agreement (Multicurrency—Cross Border) and the 1992 Master Agreement (Single Currency—Single Jurisdiction). The 1992 multicurrency master agreement is much more widely used than the more limited 1992 single currency master agreement. The 1992 multicurrency master agreement is one of the most widely used master agreements in the global OTC derivative markets, and it became firmly established in the first decade or so after its initial publication as the standard master agreement to govern trading relationships and transactions.

7.16 However, events in the global OTC derivative markets over the course of that first decade highlighted certain aspects of the 1992 generation of master agreements that could be improved on. The global financial markets experienced high levels of volatility during Q4 1997, which continued throughout 1998, and which tested the robustness of the 1992 generation of master agreements. From a broad perspective, volatility in one market can spread quickly to other markets, and although a degree of volatility is generally conducive to the derivative markets, too much volatility might result in systemic stresses, such as potential defaults and actual defaults, and even failures of market participants. During periods of acute volatility and the deterioration of the quality of credit (which both increases funding costs and causes further uncertainty), market participants tend to look more closely at their trading relationships and consider how best to preserve the value they are owed. Therefore ISDA initiated a project in November 2001 to draft a replacement for the 1992 generation of master agreements, and this project reached fruition on schedule with the publication on Wednesday 8 January 2003 of the ISDA 2002 Master Agreement, which is the latest generation of ISDA's flagship document.

7.17 The 2002 Master Agreement is a significantly more complex document than either of the 1992 generation of master agreements, and more voluminous. Whereas the 1992 multicurrency master agreement and its schedule occupy 24 sides of US size paper, the 2002 Master Agreement and its schedule occupy some 36 sides of US size paper. However, despite its increased complexity, the 2002 Master Agreement legislates for the relationship between the two parties to a privately negotiated OTC derivative trading relationship in a flexible and reasonable manner, and serves the global OTC derivative market well. The framework of the 2002 Master Agreement can accommodate derivative transactions of any type. Although the materials published by ISDA were originally conceived for the burgeoning interest rate swap market in the mid-1980s, ISDA documentation now accommodates financial derivative transactions, commodity derivative transactions, and credit derivative transactions.

---

[6] See Chapter 4.

7.18 The main relevant ISDA materials at the time of writing comprise the 2002 Master Agreement,[7] the Schedule to the 2002 Master Agreement, various credit support documents, various sets of standard definitions, and various template confirmations. ISDA also from time to time publishes other documents, usually in response to events or circumstances that the financial markets as a whole must address, such as the introduction of the euro currency.

7.4 The ISDA 2002 Master Agreement and its Schedule

7.19 The architecture of the 2002 Master Agreement is substantially the same as that of the preceding generations of ISDA's relationship and transaction master agreements. The 2002 Master Agreement contains the framework terms which govern the trading relationship between the parties. The parties negotiate the Schedule. The Schedule contains the various elections that the parties make to apply or to not apply certain provisions of the 2002 Master Agreement. The parties also quantify in the Schedule particular numerical variables that are required to operate the 2002 Master Agreement. The 2002 Master Agreement is a standard document that should never be marked up or otherwise amended. Instead, the Schedule allows the parties to tailor the operation of the 2002 Master Agreement to reflect their particular circumstances and requirements. The 2002 Master Agreement is extremely complex, and to tamper with one element of it may have an adverse and unforeseeable effect. The form of the 2002 Master Agreement is suitable for either English law or the laws of the State of New York, and the parties specify in the Schedule which of these two laws governs their agreement and their trading relationship. The following paragraphs discuss certain of the more important provisions of the 2002 Master Agreement and give an indication of its operation. This book does not purport to give a detailed explanation of every provision of the 2002 Master Agreement. Unless otherwise indicated, as the context requires, in the following paragraphs discussing the 2002 Master Agreement, capitalized terms are terms that are defined in the 2002 Master Agreement, and references to Sections are references to the Sections of the 2002 Master Agreement.

Section 1(c)

7.20 Section 1(c) provides as follows. 'All Transactions are entered into in reliance on the fact that this Master Agreement and all Confirmations form a single agreement between the parties (collectively referred to as this "Agreement"), and the parties would not otherwise enter into any Transaction.'

---

[7] As mentioned in paragraph 4.158, ISDA is developing a Shari'a-compliant master agreement, working together with the International Islamic Financial Market.

7.21 Section 1(c) gives effect to what is commonly referred to as the single agreement approach highlighted above.[8] The purpose of the single agreement approach is generally to prevent cherry-picking. The term 'cherry-picking' describes the right of a liquidator of an insolvent company under section 178(3)(a) of the IA 1986 to disclaim any unprofitable contract and by extension to affirm, or to cherry-pick, only profitable contracts. In the context of a derivative trading relationship, the consequence for a solvent party of the right by the liquidator of its insolvent counterparty to disclaim any unprofitable contract would be that the solvent party would only recover a percentage, if anything, in respect of those Transactions which are in-the-money from its perspective (that is, those Transactions under which it is owed amounts), but by contrast it would be required to pay the full amount of the Transactions which are out-of-the-money from its perspective (that is, those Transactions under which it owes amounts). The single agreement approach lays the foundation for the calculation of a single net close-out amount in respect of all Transactions which remain outstanding,[9] and hopefully overriding any attempt by a liquidator of an insolvent counterparty to cherry-pick Transactions.

7.22 The single agreement approach should also reflect and reinforce the application of Rule 4.90 of the Insolvency Rules 1986, as amended[10] ('Rule 4.90') which provides for mutual credits and set-off. Rule 4.90(1) has the effect that Rule 4.90 applies to the liquidation of a company where, before the company goes into liquidation, there have been mutual credits, mutual debts, or other mutual dealings between the company and any creditor of the company proving or claiming to prove for a debt in the liquidation. Rule 4.90(3) requires that an account shall be taken of what is due from each party to the other in respect of the mutual dealings, and the sums due from one party shall be set off against the sums due from the other.

7.23 However, some academic doubt has been raised as to whether the single agreement approach is robust. The theory generally runs as follows. If the two parties to a trading relationship have entered into various Transactions in respect of different classes of underlying, with different economic terms and different start dates and different end dates, then there is a strong argument that each Transaction forms one agreement which is separate from the agreement formed by every other Transaction, and that each Transaction merely shares certain common terms with the other Transactions, these common terms being of course the terms contained

---

[8] See paragraph 7.05.
[9] The provisions of s 163 of the CA 1989, which provides for a net sum payable on completion of default proceedings, in the context of the exchange-based derivative market, is recollected. See Chapter 6.
[10] SI 1986/1925. The Insolvency (Amendment) Rules 2005, SI 2005/527, amend the Insolvency Rules 1986. The Insolvency Rules 1986 had of course been amended several times prior to the making of SI 2005/527.

in the master agreement. Nonetheless, even if such an argument is mustered, this argument might be countered by both Rule 4.90 and of course the basis of the parties' dealings; it is recollected that under Section 1(c) of the 2002 Master Agreement, each party contracts in reliance on the fact that a single agreement is formed between the parties and it would not have otherwise entered into any Transaction.

7.24 The reinforcement of a trading relationship by credit support, which is governed by a Credit Support Document,[11] of course neutralizes counterparty risk by providing for the transfer of collateral from each party to the other. It is useful to note in passing that the legislation of Part VII of the CA 1989[12] was in part a response to the risks posed by section 178(3)(a) of the IA 1986, and the ability that Act gives to the liquidator of a company to disclaim onerous contracts, to the integrity of the exchange-based derivative and other financial markets. Of course, Part VII of the CA 1989 does not apply to the OTC derivative markets, and therefore reliance must be placed on Rule 4.90 and Section 1(c) of the 2002 Master Agreement.

7.25 It is important to note that the Financial Collateral Arrangements (No. 2) Regulations 2003[13] (the 'Collateral Regulations'), which fully came into effect on 26 December 2003, effectively reinforce the operation of a Credit Support Document and thereby further strengthen Rule 4.90. Paragraph 12(1) of the Collateral Regulations has the effect that a close-out netting provision shall take effect in accordance with its terms, notwithstanding that the collateral-provider or the collateral-taker under the arrangement is subject to winding-up proceedings or reorganization measures. The term 'close-out netting provision' is defined in paragraph 3 of the Collateral Regulations as a provision under which, on the occurrence of an enforcement event, whether through the operation of netting or set-off or otherwise, either (1) the obligations of the parties are accelerated to become immediately due and expressed as an obligation to pay an amount representing the original obligation's estimated current value or replacement cost, or such obligations are terminated and replaced by an obligation to pay such an amount, or (2) an account is taken of what is due from each party to the other in respect of such obligations and a net sum equal to the balance of the account is payable by the party from whom the larger amount is due to the other party. The definition set out in paragraph 3 is wide, and its scope includes a term of a financial collateral arrangement, or an arrangement of which a financial collateral arrangement forms a part, or any legislative provision. Paragraph 12(2) of the

---

[11] See paragraphs 7.69 ff.
[12] See Chapter 6.
[13] SI 2003/3226. The Collateral Regulations implement in the United Kingdom 2002/47/EC Directive of the European Parliament and of the Council on financial collateral arrangements.

Collateral Regulations has the effect that paragraph 12(1) of the Collateral Regulations is not available to a party if that party was aware or should have been aware that winding-up proceedings or reorganization measures had commenced in relation to the other party at the time when the financial collateral arrangements were entered into or when the relevant financial obligations, which are secured by the financial collateral arrangements, came into existence. Altogether, therefore, it seems that Rule 4.90 continues to be of use in the context of a trading relationship that is not reinforced by credit support. A trading relationship that is not reinforced by credit support lacks the concept of a collateral-provider and a collateral-taker with reference to which the Collateral Regulations operate. By contrast, a trading relationship that is reinforced by credit support is further bolstered by the Collateral Regulations, which explicitly give primacy to the close-out netting provisions contained in the documents of that credit support, and which should put beyond doubt the enforceability of those close-out netting provisions. The effect of the Collateral Regulations on industry-standard credit support documents is explored below.

Section 2(a)(i)

7.26 Section 2(a)(i) provides as follows. 'Each party will make each payment or delivery specified in each Confirmation to be made by it, subject to the other provisions of this Agreement.' Section 2(a)(i) defines the principal obligation of each party under each Transaction, and this obligation lies at the very centre of the trading relationship.

Section 2(c)

7.27 Section 2(c) legislates for netting during the trading relationship. The parties elect in the Schedule whether or not netting is to be applied to their trading relationship. Netting is applied to amounts that are payable on a particular date in the same currency, whether in respect of one Transaction or in respect of more than one Transaction. Netting that is applied in respect of more than one Transaction is referred to as Multiple Transaction Payment Netting. The 2002 Master Agreement incorporates a more robust netting provision than the 1992 multicurrency master agreement.

7.28 Netting is the replacement of two existing obligations to make payments by a third obligation to pay the difference. To illustrate, A has the obligation to pay 100 to B, and B has the obligation to pay 70 to A. Under a netting arrangement, A's obligation to pay 100 to B and B's obligation to pay 70 to A are both automatically satisfied and discharged, and replaced by a third obligation on A to pay the difference 30 to B. The automatic satisfaction and discharge of two existing obligations is the important element of a netting arrangement. Any legal opinion as to the operation and enforceability of a netting arrangement considers whether or not there is an automatic satisfaction and discharge of the existing obligations. The netting arrangement contained in the 2002 Master Agreement is a form of netting by novation. The netting by novation has immediate contractual force, and gives rise to a single new indebtedness which does not fall due for payment until a later date, on which there is a single obligation on only one party to make one payment. Netting by novation assists with avoiding the risk that the liquidator of an insolvent counterparty might challenge a right of set-off and cherry-pick only profitable Transactions which are in-the-money from the perspective of the insolvent counterparty, leaving the solvent party to attempt to prove in liquidation for sums that are payable by the insolvent counterparty in respect of unprofitable Transactions that are out-of-the-money for the insolvent counterparty.

7.29 Netting also reduces counterparty risk on an ongoing basis by reducing the amount of the cash flows between the parties. Netting is therefore an important risk control mechanism and parties should seek to net their payment obligations wherever possible, although of course some participants in the OTC derivative markets are unable to net for operational reasons, such as the inability of their payment systems to calculate net amounts.

7.30 Although netting is recognized under English law, this is not the case in every jurisdiction. Accordingly, ISDA has obtained legal opinions, which are available to its members, as to the enforceability in various jurisdictions of the netting provisions of the 2002 Master Agreement. The risk that netting provisions are not enforceable would in particular crystallize on the insolvency of one of the parties.

Section 3

7.31 Section 3 contains the representations that each party makes to the other. These representations are deemed to be repeated on each date that a Transaction is entered into. The representations contained in Section 3 address the usual issues pertinent to a financial relationship. The representations contained in Section 3(a) are described as 'Basic Representations'. Under Section 3(a)(i), each party represents that it is duly organized and validly existing under the laws of the jurisdiction of its organization or incorporation, and if relevant under such laws, that it is in good standing. Under Section 3(a)(ii), each party represents (1) that it has the power to execute the Agreement and any other relevant documentation, to deliver the Agreement and any other relevant documentation, and to perform its obligations under the Agreement and any other relevant documentation; and (2) that it has taken all necessary action to authorize such execution, delivery, and performance. Under Section 3(a)(iii), each party represents that such execution, delivery, and performance do not violate or conflict with any applicable law, any of its constitutional documents, any order or judgment of any applicable court or other agency of government, or any contractual restriction. Under Section 3(a)(iv), each party represents that it has obtained all governmental and other consents that it is required to have, and that each such consent is in full force and effect, and all conditions of such consent have been complied with. Under Section 3(a)(v), each party represents that its obligations under the Agreement and any Credit Support Document constitute its legal, valid, and binding obligations enforceable in accordance with their respective terms, subject to applicable laws affecting creditors' rights generally, and subject to general equitable principles. The basic representations set out in Section 3(a) address the issues in respect of which opinion letters are often obtained. Of course, an opinion letter provided by independent counsel carries more weight in the analysis of potential counterparty risk than a representation made by the counterparty itself; nonetheless, the presence of a list of relevant representations guides the preparation of the opinion letter. Under Section 3(b), each party represents that no Event of Default or Potential Event of Default or, to its knowledge, Termination Event has occurred and is continuing with respect to it, and no such event will occur as a result of it entering into or performing its obligations under the Agreement and any Credit Support Document. Under Section 3(c), each party represents that there is no pending or threatened litigation against it or any of its Credit Support Provider or Specified Entities, that is likely to affect the legality, validity, or enforceability of the Agreement or any Credit Support Document, or its ability to perform its obligations under those documents. It is important to note the second element of the representation, the purpose of which is to confine the disclosure of pending or threatened litigation to only relevant litigation (for example, there is no requirement to disclose an employment law dispute with a former employee). Under Section 3(d), each party represents that information it provides is true, accurate, and complete in every material respect. Under Sections 3(e) and 3(f), each party makes tax representations. These are examined in Chapter 11. Under Section 3(g), each party represents that it is entering into the Agreement and each Transaction as principal, and not as agent for any other person or entity.

Section 5

Section 5 defines the Events of Default and Termination Events which give a party the right to terminate early Transactions, whether only some or all of the Transactions that are outstanding between the parties. The definition of this right, and the procedures which follow the exercise of this right, are the key elements of the Master Agreement. The rationale of the drafting is that a party must have the ability to reduce or to eliminate altogether its exposure to its counterparty, by terminating early one or more Transactions, if that counterparty begins to project a different shape of counterparty risk than that at the outset of the trading relationship.

7.32

7.33 Generally, an Event of Default might be said to go to the essence of a party's ability to continue in the trading relationship, and therefore to jeopardize the entire trading relationship. Therefore the response to the occurrence of an Event of Default is the early termination of all outstanding Transactions. By contrast, the occurrence of a Termination Event might be said to be caused by an event outside the influence or control of the parties, and to jeopardize only Affected Transactions. Not necessarily every Transaction is an Affected Transaction. Therefore the response to the occurrence of a Termination Event is the termination of only Affected Transactions, leaving in place any outstanding Transaction that is not an Affected Transaction.

7.34 Section 5(a) defines the various Events of Default. An Event of Default occurs through the fault of a Defaulting Party, for example, a failure by the Defaulting Party to make a payment or delivery. The occurrence of an Event of Default gives the Non-defaulting Party the right to terminate early all outstanding Transactions.

7.35 Section 5(a)(i) defines a Failure to Pay or Deliver. This Event of Default is the most obvious, and it is linked to Section 2(a)(i), which describes the obligation of each party to make each payment or delivery specified in each Confirmation to be made by it, and Section 9(h)(i)(2) and Section 9(h)(i)(4), which generally provide for the payment of interest or compensation under certain circumstances. Crucially, a Failure to Pay or Deliver occurs only after notice of the relevant failure is given and the failure is not remedied on or before the first Local Business Day after notice is effective. It is therefore important to consider the interaction between Section 5(a)(i) and Section 12, which sets out the manner in which notices are given and when they become effective. Contractual notice provisions are often overlooked in the course of negotiating agreements, yet they assume significance during a default scenario.

7.36 Section 5(a)(ii) defines a Breach of Agreement and a Repudiation of Agreement. The 2002 Master Agreement introduces the second element, the Repudiation of Agreement, as an Event of Default, which was not included in the 1992 generation of master agreements. Under Section 5(a)(ii)(2), an Event of Default occurs with respect to a party if it disaffirms, disclaims, repudiates or rejects, in whole or in part, or challenges the validity of the Master Agreement, any Confirmation, or any Transaction evidenced by any Confirmation. The definition is wide, and includes analogous action taken by any person or entity appointed or empowered to act on behalf of a party.

7.37 Section 5(a)(iii) defines a Credit Support Default. A Credit Support Default occurs with respect to a party if (1) it or any Credit Support Provider of it fails to comply with or to perform its obligations under a Credit Support Document and such failure continues after any applicable grace period has elapsed; or (2) following the premature termination or expiration of a Credit Support Document; or

7.4 The ISDA 2002 Master Agreement

(3) any security interest granted under a Credit Support Document fails or ceases to be in full force and effect, or it or any Credit Support Provider of it repudiates a Credit Support Document.

7.38 Section 5(a)(iv) defines a Misrepresentation. The test for whether or not such an Event of Default occurs is that the relevant statement proves to have been incorrect or misleading in any material respect when made or repeated or deemed to have been made or repeated.

7.39 Section 5(a)(v) defines a Default Under Specified Transaction. A Default Under Specified Transaction occurs with respect to a party if it or any Credit Support Provider of it or any Specified Entity of it defaults under a Specified Transaction. A Specified Transaction is an OTC derivative transaction which is not a part of the Agreement, and therefore which is outside the trading relationship documented under the Master Agreement, but which should nonetheless be monitored for the purposes of controlling risk. The definition of Specified Transaction in the 1992 generation of master agreements has been extended to include the new types of OTC derivative contract that have been developed since the publication of the 1992 generation of master agreements, such as credit derivatives, repurchase transactions, and weather derivatives. Whether or not a Default Under Specified Transaction occurs is monitored because even if a default does not occur within the confines of the trading relationship documented under the Master Agreement, the occurrence of a Default Under Specified Transaction should provide warning that a counterparty is beginning to experience difficulties.

7.40 Section 5(a)(vi) defines a Cross-Default. A Cross-Default occurs with respect to a party if it or any Credit Support Provider of it or any Specified Entity of it defaults in respect of an obligation owed to a third party outside the trading relationship under an Instrument of Specified Indebtedness. Specified Indebtedness is essentially a borrowing. A Cross-Default occurs if the amount of the default exceeds the Threshold Amount that is specified. Again, whether or not a Cross-Default occurs is monitored because even if a default does not occur within the confines of the trading relationship documented under the Master Agreement, the occurrence of a Cross-Default should provide warning that a counterparty is beginning to experience difficulties.

7.41 Section 5(a)(vii) defines a Bankruptcy. The term 'Bankruptcy' is given a comprehensive definition, and the term is arguably trans-Atlantic, so to speak, because of the elision of English law and New York law concepts. Under English law, for example, a bankruptcy occurs in respect of an individual and not a corporate entity. However, the definition set out in Section 5(a)(vii) makes clear that corporate insolvency is included.

7.42 Section 5(a)(viii) defines Merger Without Assumption. A Merger Without Assumption occurs with respect to a party if it or any Credit Support Provider of it or any Specified Entity of it merges and the resulting entity fails to assume the relevant obligations that are owed before the merger takes place. The scope of what is meant by a merger under Section 5(a)(viii) is wide, and an entity undergoes a merger if it consolidates or amalgamates with another entity, or merges with or into another entity, or transfers all or substantially all its assets to another entity, or reorganizes, reincorporates, or reconstitutes into or as another entity.

7.43 Section 5(b) defines the various Termination Events. The occurrence of a Termination Event affects either one party or both parties. Either party or each party might be an Affected Party. Depending on the type of Termination Event which occurs, either one or both parties has the right to terminate early the Affected Transactions.

7.44 Section 5(b)(i) defines an Illegality. The definition contained in the 2002 Master Agreement is more detailed than the definition contained in the 1992 generation of master agreements.

7.45 Section 5(b)(ii) defines a Force Majeure Event. The 1992 generation of master agreements did not contain such a Termination Event. The occurrence of a Force Majeure Event is generally that one, a party is prevented from either performing any absolute or contingent obligation or complying with any other material provision of the Agreement; or two, it is impossible or impracticable for a party to perform or to comply with its obligations; three, a Credit Support Provider is prevented from either performing any absolute or contingent obligation or complying with any other material provision of the Agreement; or four, it is impossible or impracticable for a Credit Support Provider to perform or to comply with its obligations. The Force Majeure Event is defined with reference to the concept of force majeure[14] and to acts of state, and therefore the definition would include events such as acts of terrorism or war, which may well disrupt the financial markets.

7.46 Section 5(b)(iii) defines a Tax Event. A Tax Event occurs in respect of one or more Transactions that have already been entered into; any such Transaction in respect of which a Tax Event occurs is an Affected Transaction. The party which suffers a

---

[14] There is no formal concept under English law of force majeure. Under English law, a draconian principle was laid down in *Paradine v Jane* (1647) Aleyn 26, Sty 47, [1558–1774] All ER Rep 172. The principle laid down in this case is that a party to a contract, if he assumes an obligation under that contract, remains liable to his counterparty for his failure to perform that obligation, even if such failure is caused by events which render performance of that obligation impossible. The occurrence of these events is sometimes referred to as a 'hardship'. The reasoning behind this principle is that contractual counterparties should be able to include in their contracts provisions to deal with such events. Accordingly, contractual counterparties tend to include in their contracts force majeure or hardship clauses if they believe that such events might occur, but they cannot predict the specifics of such events. On their face, force majeure or hardship clauses are useful, but they can give rise to difficulties of construction and application, although of course they are an established part of mercantile dealings, and the court would have regard to that.

7.4 The ISDA 2002 Master Agreement

detriment through the occurrence of a Tax Event is the Burdened Party. A Tax Event occurs as a consequence of action taken by a taxing authority or proceedings brought in a court of competent jurisdiction, or as a consequence of a Change in Tax Law. In broad terms, a Tax Event occurs if the Burdened Party is required to pay a gross-up to offset the effect of tax on a payment that it is due to make, or if the Burdened Party receives less than the full amount of a payment that it is due to receive because of the effect of tax.

Section 5(b)(iv) defines a Tax Event Upon Merger. Again, a Tax Event Upon Merger occurs in respect of one or more Transactions that have already been entered into; any such Transaction in respect of which a Tax Event Upon Merger occurs is an Affected Transaction. The party which suffers a detriment through the occurrence of a Tax Event Upon Merger is the Burdened Party. A merger within the meaning of the definition occurs if either party consolidates or amalgamates with another entity, or merges with or into another entity, or transfers all or substantially all its assets (or any substantial part of the assets comprising the business conducted by it as of the date of the Master Agreement) to another entity, or reorganizes, reincorporates, or reconstitutes into or as another entity, where such action does not constitute a Merger Without Assumption. In broad terms, a Tax Event Upon Merger occurs if, as a consequence of a merger of either party within the scope of the definition, the Burdened Party is required to pay a gross-up to offset the effect of tax on a payment that it is due to make, or if the Burdened Party receives less than the full amount of a payment that it is due to receive because of the effect of tax. Two observations become apparent. One, the concept of a merger is defined more widely under Section 5(b)(iv) than under Section 5(a)(viii) (Merger Without Assumption). Two, if the same event or circumstance could give rise to either a Merger Without Assumption or a Tax Event Upon Merger, then the Master Agreement operates on the basis that a Merger Without Assumption has taken place, thereby giving the right to terminate early all outstanding Transactions. **7.47**

Section 5(b)(v) defines a Credit Event Upon Merger. The definition of a Credit Event Upon Merger is complex. Whether or not a Credit Event Upon Merger occurs with respect to a party is determined by whether or not a Designated Event occurs with respect to that party or to a Credit Support Provider of it or a Specified Entity of it, each referred to as 'X'. Three Designated Events are defined in some detail: the first refers to a merger of X, the second refers to a change in the control of X, and the third refers to a change in the capital structure of X. A Credit Event Upon Merger takes place with respect to X if following the occurrence of a Designated Event the creditworthiness of X, or, if applicable, the successor, surviving or transferee entity of X, after taking into account any applicable Credit Support Document, is materially weaker. Again, if the same event or circumstance could give rise to either a Merger Without Assumption or a Credit Event Upon Merger, **7.48** then the Master Agreement operates on the basis that a Merger Without Assumption has taken place, thereby giving the right to terminate early all outstanding Transactions.

7.49 Section 5(b)(vi) refers to an Additional Termination Event, which the parties define in the Schedule to reflect the particular circumstances of their trading relationship. For example, a party may be a hedge fund managed by a key individual with a proven track record, and the fund's counterparty may require that an Additional Termination Event is the discontinuation of the involvement of that individual in the management of the fund, on the basis that the performance of the fund, and therefore the solvency of the fund, are very much determined by whether or not that individual is responsible for the management of the fund.

7.50 The right to terminate early one or more Transactions is particularly important in the context of a derivative trading relationship. Value can change very quickly, and value can be destroyed very quickly. It is therefore important to have the ability to preserve value. If difficulties arise in the trading relationship, the party which is in-the-money is exposed to the risk that its counterparty might default. Accordingly, the 2002 Master Agreement incorporates shorter cure periods than the 1992 generation of master agreements, to reflect the sometimes urgent need to preserve value.

Section 6

7.51 Section 6 contains the extremely complex terms which govern the early termination of one or more Transactions. Exercise of the right to terminate early a group of Transactions crystallizes all outstanding payment obligations and all outstanding delivery obligations under those Transactions included in the early termination into a single net close-out payment obligation. Obligations to make deliveries under Terminated Transactions are said to be monetized, that is, an obligation to make a delivery is replaced by an obligation to make a payment of an amount which reflects the economic equivalent of that delivery.

7.52 Section 6 contains provisions which govern the following matters. One, the party exercising the right to terminate early Transactions must follow the specified procedure, which includes giving notice and observing any Waiting Period; generally, a different procedure is used, depending on whether an Event of Default or a Termination Event has given rise to the early termination. Two, the single net close-out amount is calculated in respect of the relevant Early Termination Date. Three, the payment of the single net close-out amount is made. Crucially, more than one Early Termination Date can occur during the course of a trading relationship; the occurrence of a Termination Event does not necessarily result in the early termination of all outstanding Transactions, and therefore a subsequent further Early Termination Date may occur in respect of one or more of the remaining Transactions.

The calculations set out in Section 6 are complex, but from an overall perspective, the purpose of the payment of the single net close-out amount is to place, to the fullest extent possible, the parties in the economic position that they would have been in had the relevant Event of Default or Termination Event not taken place. **7.53**

Section 6(a) and Section 6(b) establish in some detail the right of a party to designate an Early Termination Date. Section 6(a) contains the right of the Non-defaulting Party to designate an Early Termination Date following the occurrence of an Event of Default with respect to the Defaulting Party. The Early Termination Date cannot be any earlier than 20 days following the date on which notice of the designation is effective. Again, it is important to have regard to the provisions of Section 12, which sets out the manner in which notices are given and when they become effective, and it is also important to note that the period of notice is measured with reference to just 'days', that is, ordinary calendar days, and not to Local Business Days. An Early Termination Date occurs immediately if the parties have specified that Automatic Early Termination applies in respect of certain of the events and circumstances comprising the definition of Bankruptcy in Section 5(a)(vii). The purpose of Automatic Early Termination is to ensure that termination of Transactions occurs as quickly as possible, with the purpose of defeating an attempt by a liquidator to disclaim onerous Transactions.[15] Whether or not Automatic Early Termination delivers any real benefit will depend on the jurisdictions involved and the treatment of insolvencies in those jurisdictions; the delay between the occurrence of an Event of Default and the Early Termination Date might afford a liquidator the opportunity to disclaim onerous Transactions. The disadvantage of Automatic Early Termination is that the solvent Non-defaulting Party might be unaware that Transactions have been terminated, and as a consequence of the Automatic Early Termination, it may have lost a hedge in respect of other positions it has with other contractual counterparties and thereby become unknowingly exposed to the risk of adverse market movements. **7.54**

The operation of Section 6(b) is rather more involved. First, notice is given of the occurrence of the Termination Event. In the case of a Termination Event other than a Force Majeure Event, an Affected Party is required to notify the other party of the occurrence of the Termination Event, and to provide such information about that occurrence as the other party may reasonably require. There may of course be more than one Affected Party. In the case of a Force Majeure Event, each party is required to use all reasonable efforts to notify the other party of the occurrence of the Force Majeure Event, and to provide such information about that occurrence as the other party may reasonably require. The subtle distinction between the two processes is that the obligation of a party following the occurrence **7.55**

---

[15] See paragraph 7.21.

of a Force Majeure Event is to use all reasonable efforts to make the required notification, whereas the analogous obligation following the occurrence of a Termination Event other than a Force Majeure Event is more prescriptive and to make the notification, using by implication any means necessary. Second, Section 6(b)(ii) operates so that the Affected Party under a Tax Event must use all reasonable efforts to transfer its rights and obligations under the Agreement in respect of the Affected Transactions to another of its Offices and Affiliates so that the Tax Event ceases to exist. The Affected Party only has the right to designate an Early Termination Date if it has tried to make such a transfer. Crucially, the Affected Party is not required to make such a transfer if it would incur a loss other than immaterial incidental expenses. Section 6(b)(ii) protects the party which is not affected by the Tax Event from losing the benefit of its Transactions as a consequence of a Tax Event that it does not suffer. In the same way, Section 6(b)(iii) operates so that if both parties are Affected Parties under a Tax Event, then each of them must use all reasonable efforts to reach agreement to avoid the Tax Event. Third, Section 6(b)(iv) sets out the right of either or both parties to designate an Early Termination Date. Again, the Early Termination Date cannot be any earlier than 20 days following the date on which notice of the designation is effective, and again, it is important to have regard to the provisions of Section 12, which sets out the manner in which notices are given and when they become effective, and again, the period of notice is measured with reference to just 'days' and not to Local Business Days. An additional Waiting Period is imposed in respect of an Illegality or a Force Majeure Event. Notice of the designation of an Early Termination Date can only be effective after the expiration of a Waiting Period (arguably, notice can be given before the expiration of the Waiting Period, such notice being timed so that it is effective immediately upon the expiration of the Waiting Period). Either or both parties is entitled to designate an Early Termination Date under Section 6(b)(iv), depending on the particular Termination Event involved.

7.56 Under Section 6(c)(ii), all Terminated Transactions effectively come to an end on the Early Termination Date, and more particularly, the obligations to make payments and to make deliveries come to an end.

7.57 An Early Termination Amount is calculated in respect of the Early Termination Date. The Early Termination Amount is the single net close-out amount that is payable, and it is determined by the Determining Party. Section 6(e) sets out which party is the Determining Party, depending on the relevant Event of Default or Termination Event. Under Section 6(d)(i), the specification of an Early Termination Amount must be supported by a statement showing in reasonable detail the calculation of the Early Termination Amount, including any quotations, market data or information from internal sources used in making such calculations. The statement that must be provided should also contain practical

7.4 The ISDA 2002 Master Agreement

information such as the mechanics of the payment of the Early Termination Amount. Under Section 6(d)(ii), the Early Termination Amount is payable on the day determined under that Section.

7.58 Section 6(e) sets out the overall methodology of how the Early Termination Amount is calculated. A different form of calculation is used, depending on whether early termination was precipitated by an Event of Default or by a Termination Event, and (in the case of an early termination precipitated by a Termination Event) depending on whether there is one Affected Party or two Affected Parties. Generally, the Early Termination Amount is calculated with reference to a Close-out Amount and Unpaid Amounts. The emphasis of the drafting of the 2002 Master Agreement is on flexibility; the 1992 generation of master agreements does not allow the same extent of flexibility.

7.59 Both the Close-out Amount and Unpaid Amounts are expressed as Termination Currency Equivalents. The parties select the Termination Currency in which the early Termination Amount is denominated. If the parties do not specify the Termination Currency, then the Termination Currency is the US dollar for an Agreement expressed to be governed by the laws of the State of New York or the euro for an Agreement expressed to be governed by English law. The Termination Currency Equivalent is the amount in the Termination Currency of an amount denominated in another currency and converted into the Termination Currency in accordance with the procedures built into the definition of Termination Currency Equivalent.

7.60 The definition of Close-out Amount is crucial and it occupies one and one-quarter sides of the 2002 Master Agreement, or almost 3.5% of the entire document. The Close-out Amount is determined with reference to each Terminated Transaction or each group of Terminated Transactions, and to the Determining Party. The Close-out Amount is either a positive number, in which case it expresses the amount of the losses and costs of the Determining Party, or it is a negative number, in which case it expresses the gains of the Determining Party. The Close-out Amount is either the losses and costs or the gains of the Determining Party 'in replacing, or in providing for the Determining Party the economic equivalent of, (a) the material terms of that Terminated Transaction or group of Terminated Transactions... and (b) the option rights of the parties in respect of that Terminated Transaction or group of Terminated Transactions'.[16] The key concept is that the Close-out Amount reflects the replacement value of each Terminated Transaction or each group of Terminated Transactions. By way of example, a swap dealer has sold an interest rate swap to its customer, and this swap has been terminated early. The dealer would have bought a second hedging interest rate swap from another

---

[16] The definition of 'Close-out Amount' in Section 14.

market participant in order to remain unexposed to movements in the relevant floating interest rate. From the dealer's perspective, the cash flow of the swap would have been largely offset by the cash flow under the hedging swap, and as paragraph 4.94 explains, the dealer earns a spread between the fixed rate of the swap that it has sold to its customer and the lower fixed rate of the hedging swap that it has bought from the other market participant. The early termination of the swap results in the dealer becoming exposed to movements in the relevant floating interest rate, as the hedging swap remains in place and there is no longer any transaction to offset the hedging swap. The dealer must therefore enter into a replacement transaction in order to hedge the exposure which has now emerged. The definition of Close-out Amount indicates that the dealer, which is for the purposes of this example the Determining Party, passes on to its customer any cost it incurs through entering into the replacement transaction. Although the 2002 Master Agreement provides significant detail as to how the information required to perform the relevant calculations might be obtained and used by the Determining Party, the overall stipulation remains more broad, that any replacement transaction replaces or provides the economic equivalent of the Terminated Transaction or group of Terminated Transactions. Pricing conventions in the market will therefore indicate how practically and mathematically the relevant costs or gains of the replacement transaction are computed. In calculating a Close-out Amount, a Determining Party 'will act in good faith and use commercially reasonable procedures in order to produce a commercially reasonable result'.[17]

7.61 The definition of Close-out Amount provides the Determining Party with considerable guidance and latitude in making the required calculations, in recognition of the complexity inherent in the business. The Determining Party is entitled to use the following types of information: '(i) quotations (either firm or indicative) for replacement transactions supplied by one or more third parties that may take into account the creditworthiness of the Determining Party at the time the quotation is provided and the terms of any relevant documentation, including credit support documentation, between the Determining Party and the party providing the quotation; (ii) information consisting of relevant market data in the relevant market supplied by one or more third parties including, without limitation, relevant rates, yields, yield curves, volatilities, spreads, correlations or other relevant market data in the relevant market; or (iii) information of the types described in clause (i) or (ii) above from internal sources (including any of the Determining Party's Affiliates) if that information is of the same type used by the Determining Party in the regular course of its business for the valuation of similar transactions.'[18]

---

[17] The definition of 'Close-out Amount' in Section 14.
[18] The definition of 'Close-out Amount' in Section 14.

7.62 Close-out Amount does not include Unpaid Amounts. Unpaid Amounts are generally the amounts that are owed to a party in respect of an Early Termination Date, and comprise the aggregate of the following: the amounts that became payable to that party but which remain unpaid, an amount equal to the fair market value of anything that was required to be delivered and has not been delivered, and any amount that became payable in respect of a prior Early Termination Date but which remains unpaid. The third element of the definition of Unpaid Amount recognizes that more than one Early Termination Date can occur during the course of a trading relationship, as indicated in paragraph 7.52.

7.63 By way of background and contrast, the early termination provisions of the 1992 generation of master agreements operate with reference to two payment measures, Market Quotation and Loss, and two payment methods, the First Method and the Second Method. Whereas Loss is a party's own assessment made in good faith of its total losses and costs, the calculation of Market Quotation is based on quotations provided by Reference Market-makers to enter into a Replacement Transaction which would preserve the economic equivalent of any payment or any delivery. Experience with the 1992 generation of master agreements has demonstrated that neither Loss nor Market Quotation is entirely satisfactory. The quantification of Loss by a party would be subject to challenge. The effectiveness of Market Quotation is threatened by the risk of a decrease in liquidity. Market Quotation relies on quotations provided by other market participants. The necessary quotations might not be available during periods of extreme market volatility, such as that experienced during Q1 1998, either because Reference Market-makers might not offer the quotations at all, because they are seeking to reduce their own exposures, or because Reference Market-makers effectively charge a premium to reflect the increased risk they would assume by opening new positions, which would render any quotation unrealistic and unworkable. The First Method operates effectively to penalize the Defaulting Party, whereas the Second Method operates effectively to place the parties in the economic position they would have been in had the relevant Event of Default or Termination Event not taken place. Parties would almost invariably select the Second Method, as many jurisdictions, including English law, generally do not recognize penalty clauses which go beyond the payment of compensation.[19]

---

[19] A good illustration of this principle is *Lordsvale Finance Plc v Bank of Zambia* [1996] QB 752. Under the loan facility in question, the interest rate payable was increased by 1% per annum from the date of the borrower's default. The increased interest rate was not held to be a penalty because the increase was modest and the dominant purpose of the increase was not to deter a breach but instead to reflect the greater credit risk projected by the borrower after its default. The decision in *Lordsvale* was applied by the Court of Appeal in *Jeancharm Ltd v Barnet Football Club Ltd* [2003] EWCA Civ 58. A default rate of interest which was not a genuine pre-estimate of loss was held to amount to a penalty and therefore it was not enforceable.

7.64 The potential difficulty that a penalty clause gives rise to under English law is addressed by Section 6(e)(v), which provides that the parties specifically agree that an amount recoverable under Section 6(e) is a reasonable pre-estimate of loss and not a penalty, and is payable for the loss of bargain and the loss of protection against future risks.

7.65 Section 6(f) contains a broad right of set-off, which purports to set off an Early Termination Amount payable to a Payee against Other Amounts payable by the Payee. The definition of Other Amounts includes any other amount, whether or not arising under the Agreement, and whether or not matured or contingent, and irrespective of the currency and the place of payment or booking of the relevant obligation.

Section 9(h)

7.66 The 2002 Master Agreement contains extensive provisions defining how interest is calculated under different circumstances. The calculation of interest and compensation under the 2002 Master Agreement is actually more straightforward than under the 1992 generation of master agreements, although reference must be made to extensive definitions.

7.67 Section 9(h)(i) provides for the calculation of interest and compensation prior to early termination. Interest is payable by a party at the Default Rate in respect of defaulted payments and at the Applicable Deferral Rate in respect of deferred payments that the party is required to make but does not make. Compensation at the Default Rate is payable by a party in respect of defaulted deliveries and at the Applicable Deferral Rate in respect of deferred deliveries that the party is required to make but does not make. The term 'compensation' reflects the conceptual difficulty of calculating interest in respect of an obligation to make a delivery. The compensation payable in respect of a defaulted delivery is calculated with reference to the fair market value of that which was required to be delivered.[20] The distinction between a default and a deferral is that a defaulted payment or delivery is not made at all, and might therefore constitute an Event of Default under Section 5(a)(i), whereas a deferred payment or delivery is actually eventually made before an Event of Default under Section 5(a)(i) occurs. This distinction is reflected in the application of a Default Rate and a separate Applicable Deferral Rate.

7.68 Section 9(h)(ii) provides for the calculation of the amount of interest on the occurrence or effective designation of an Early Termination Date. After the designation of an Early Termination Date, delivery obligations are monetized, as explained in paragraph 7.51, and therefore there is no conceptual difficulty in

---

[20] Section 9(h)(i)(2).

7.5 ISDA Credit Support Documents

calculating interest. A third interest rate, the Applicable Close-out Rate, is used to make the calculations under Section 9(h)(ii). Section 9(h)(iii) provides that the amount of interest calculated for the purposes of Section 9(h) is calculated on the basis of daily compounding and the actual number of days elapsed.

7.5 ISDA Credit Support Documents

7.69 As the OTC derivative market does not enjoy the infrastructure of the exchange-based market, whether in terms of legislation such as Part VII of the CA 1989, or systems such as a clearing house and a strict mechanism for the incremental payment of losses supported by collateral and for the incremental payment of profits, participants in the OTC market frequently use collateral or credit support to reinforce their trading relationships under bilateral contractual arrangements.

7.70 The application of credit support in the OTC derivative market tends to be complex, and therefore it is useful to develop an explanation of this issue, which is perhaps the most important aspect of a trading relationship. The overall objective of using credit support is to reduce counterparty risk in as certain a manner as possible.

7.71 In essence, each party is concerned that its counterparty might default in respect of a payment obligation or a delivery obligation. Therefore, each party requires its counterparty to transfer, or otherwise make available, credit support that the party is then able to use to make good any default by its counterparty. An additional complexity is that the payment and the delivery obligations under a derivative transaction often flow both ways, and therefore exposures are created both ways.

7.72 ISDA publishes Credit Support Documents that are governed by English law, the laws of the State of New York, and Japanese law. The two Credit Support Documents that are governed by English law, and which are discussed in this chapter,[21] are the 1995 Credit Support Annex (Bilateral Form—Transfer) and the 1995 Credit Support Deed (Bilateral Form—Security Interest). Unless otherwise indicated, as the context requires, in the following paragraphs discussing the ISDA Credit Support Documents, capitalized terms are terms that are defined in the relevant Credit Support Document, and references to Paragraphs are references to the Paragraphs of the relevant Credit Support Document.

The 1995 Credit Support Annex (Bilateral Form—Transfer)

7.73 The Annex is a part of the Schedule and forms one agreement with the Schedule and the Master Agreement. The Annex operates to transfer title to collateral, and it does not create a charge or other security interest. Paragraph 5(b) of the Annex

---

[21] See also the user's guide published by ISDA.

puts the matter beyond doubt. 'Nothing in this Annex is intended to create or does create in favour of either party any mortgage, charge, lien, pledge, encumbrance or other security interest in any cash or other property transferred by one party to the other party.' Whether or not a charge is created by a document depends on the operation of law, notwithstanding any statement made in a document. Therefore the risk remains that the Annex might be construed as creating a charge. However, the Annex should indeed normally operate to transfer title to collateral without creating a charge.

7.74 The preamble to the Annex provides that the credit support arrangements set out in the Annex constitute a Transaction for which the Annex constitutes a Confirmation. The purpose of defining the credit support arrangements set out in the Annex as a Transaction is to bring the various credit support obligations within the scope of the early termination processes of Section 5 and Section 6.

The 1995 Credit Support Deed (Bilateral Form—Security Interest)

7.75 By contrast, the Deed operates to require the transfer of collateral, and to create a security interest over elements of the Posted Collateral held by the Secured Party. The Deed forms a separate and distinct agreement, and therefore the Deed must be executed as a separate document. Paragraph 2 of the Deed describes the nature of the security interest that is created. The actual security provisions of Paragraph 2 are fairly complex and detailed, and distinguish between Posted Collateral that is held as cash, over which a first fixed charge is created, and Posted Collateral that is held other than as cash, for example as negotiable debt securities, over which a first fixed legal mortgage is created. Paragraph 2 also contains an assignment of all rights relating to the Posted Collateral that the Chargor has.

7.76 The Deed also gives rise to the additional complexity that the charge created by the Deed is potentially a charge which falls within the scope of the registration requirement imposed by section 395 of the Companies Act 1985, as amended (CA 1985).[22] By way of brief explanation, section 395 of the CA 1985 requires the registration of charges to which that section applies, and section 396(1) of the CA 1985 identifies the charges to which the registration requirement applies. Generally, the registration requirement applies to all floating charges[23] and to fixed charges on book debts.[24] A debt owed to a company is an asset of the company, and the company can therefore create a charge over that asset in favour of its creditor; that is, the company can create a charge in favour of its creditor over the

---

[22] The CA 1985 is being replaced in stages by the Companies Act 2006 (CA 2006). Section 395 of the CA 1985 will be replaced by s 860 of the CA 2006 with effect from 1 October 2008. Section 860 of the CA 2006 will operate in substantially the same way as s 396 of the CA 1985.

[23] Section 396(1)(f) of the CA 1985.

[24] Section 396(1)(e) of the CA 1985.

right it has to receive that debt. Whether or not a particular debt owed to the company is a book debt, and therefore whether or not a charge created by the company over its right to receive that debt is a charge to which the registration requirement applies by virtue of section 396(1)(e) of the CA 1985, broadly depends on the company and the business that it carries on. A debt is a book debt if it should be entered in the well-kept books of a company. Therefore the nature of the company's business will tend to indicate whether or not a particular debt owed to the company is indeed a book debt. The consequences of failing to register a charge to which the registration requirement applies are severe. Section 395(1) of the CA 1985 sets out the first consequence: the unregistered charge is void and therefore unenforceable. Section 395(2) of the CA 1985 sets out the second consequence: the money secured by the unregistered charge immediately becomes payable. This second consequence, which is often overlooked, might have serious implications for the liquidity and therefore the solvency of the affected company purportedly giving the charge.

7.77 The Collateral Regulations[25] now provide that under certain specified circumstances, the formalities required under certain pieces of legislation do not apply to 'financial collateral arrangements'. In particular, paragraph 4(4) of the Collateral Regulations provides as follows. 'Section 395 of the Companies Act 1985 (certain charges void if not registered) shall not apply (if it would otherwise do so) in relation to a security financial collateral arrangement or any charge created or otherwise arising under a security financial collateral arrangement.' Crucially, paragraph 4(4) of the Collateral Regulations applies to a security financial collateral arrangement, which is defined in paragraph 3 of the Collateral Regulations as 'an agreement or arrangement, evidenced in writing, where — (a) the purpose of the agreement or arrangement is to secure the relevant financial obligations owed to the collateral-taker; (b) the collateral-provider creates or there arises a security interest in financial collateral to secure those obligations; (c) the financial collateral is delivered, transferred, held, registered or otherwise designated so as to be in the possession or under the control of the collateral-taker or a person acting on its behalf; any right of the collateral-provider to substitute equivalent financial collateral or withdraw excess financial collateral shall not prevent the financial collateral being in the possession or under the control of the collateral-taker; and (d) the collateral-provider and the collateral-taker are both non-natural persons'. Therefore the charge created under the Deed appears to fall in many cases within the scope of the Collateral Regulations, obviating the need in such cases for registration under section 395 of the CA 1985. However, whether or not the Collateral Regulations actually apply to any particular trading relationship or transaction will depend on the relevant circumstances, which should be carefully

---

[25] See paragraph 7.25.

considered on an individual basis. Market participants can be expected to continue to register the charges created under the Deed if there is any doubt as to the availability of paragraph 4(4) of the Collateral Regulations, perhaps because the Deed has been amended for the purposes of a particular trading relationship or transaction in such a manner that it no longer fulfils the criteria set out in the definition contained in the Collateral Regulations of a security financial collateral regulation. Registration of the charge under these circumstances would certainly be prudent, given the potentially far-reaching consequences of a failure to register a relevant charge. Further, the scope of paragraph 4(4) of the Collateral Regulations is limited to financial collateral, which is defined in paragraph 3 as either cash or financial instruments. Therefore, paragraph 4(4) would not be available if other types of asset are used as collateral, such as gold or silver bullion or interests in real property.

The transfer of value under a Credit Support Document

7.78 Both the Annex and the Deed operate economically in the same manner. Both Credit Support Documents contain the same numerical procedures to determine the extent of a party's right to demand the transfer of collateral.[26] Only assets which fall within the scope of those specified to be Eligible Credit Support can be used as collateral. The scope of the assets that potentially can be used as Eligible Credit Support is wide. Cash, government debt securities, other debt securities which have a sufficient rating, and letters of credit are often used, although in theory other assets can also be used, such as gold and silver bullion. Under the Annex, the transferring party is the Transferor, the recipient is the Transferee, and the amount of the collateral that is transferred is the Delivery Amount. Under the Deed, the transferring party is the Chargor, the recipient is the Secured Party, and the amount of the collateral that is transferred is also the Delivery Amount.

7.79 The term 'Value' is intrinsic to the various calculations made under a Credit Support Document. The term 'Value' is used to compute the value of the collateral that has already been transferred, the Credit Support Balance, and the value of the collateral of which a party can demand the transfer. The definition of 'Value'[27] includes the requirement to convert if necessary amounts into the Base Currency of the Credit Support Document. The necessary calculations are performed by the Valuation Agent, which is usually one of the parties. The calculation of Value reflects both the market value of the relevant asset and any 'haircut' that is applied to that market value. The term 'Valuation Percentage' is used to give effect to a haircut. The parties specify the haircut that is applied to each type

---

[26] See paragraph 2 of the Annex and paragraph 3 of the Deed.
[27] See paragraph 10 of the Annex and paragraph 12 of the Deed.

7.5 ISDA Credit Support Documents

of asset which qualifies as Eligible Credit Support. The purpose of a haircut is to ensure that the recipient of the collateral, whether on an initial transfer or a subsequent transfer, is insulated from the effect of volatility in the market price of the relevant asset. For example, the parties specify that US Treasury bonds qualify as Eligible Credit Support, subject to a Valuation Percentage of 97%. This means that US Treasury bonds are accounted for at only 97% of their market value. A 3% haircut (which is 100% minus 97%) is therefore applied to them. For the purposes of this example, assume that the transferring party is required to transfer US Treasury bonds with a Value of 20. The amount that must be transferred is calculated as follows. At the relevant time, the market bid price of US Treasury bonds is 98%.[28] The purpose of the application of Value under the Credit Support Document is that the transferring party transfers enough US Treasury bonds so that the recipient would receive 20 if they are sold. Therefore the transferring party actually transfers 21.032 of US Treasury bonds. The Value of 21.032 of US Treasury bonds is 20. The amount 21.032 is calculated in the following manner. The actual amount to be transferred is the Value required multiplied by the inverse of the market bid price multiplied by the inverse of the Valuation Percentage. The actual amount to be transferred is therefore 20 * (1/98%) * (1/97%), which is 20 * 1.020 * 1.031, which is 21.032.

7.80 A Credit Support Document does not operate to require automatic transfers of assets. Instead, a Credit Support Document establishes a dynamic feedback mechanism. Generally, an equilibrium is established of the overall net exposure that each party has to its counterparty, and the disturbance of this equilibrium above a prescribed level against a party gives that party the right to demand that its counterparty makes a transfer which is sufficient to restore the equilibrium. The equilibrium is determined by the parties making various numerical elections of the Independent Amount, the Threshold, and the Minimum Transfer Amount which apply to each party. It is possible to calibrate the sensitivity of a Credit Support Document very precisely, and the cash flows generated by these numerical elections only become apparent when modelled using a spreadsheet. A Credit Support Document operates as a negative feedback loop, as Figure 7.1 illustrates. In cybernetics,[29] feedback is the flow of information about a process which is used to change the process. Feedback can be described as a circular causal process. Negative feedback reduces deviation from a required state,[30] and positive feedback

---

[28] The definition of 'Value' requires the Value of a security to be calculated using the market bid price obtained by the Valuation Agent.

[29] Cybernetics is the study of mechanical and electronic control systems.

[30] An important example of a negative feedback process is the 'centrifugal governor' developed by James Watt in 1788, which maintains the speed of a steam engine at a constant by increasing or decreasing the pressure within the engine. This invention was critical to the development of automated systems.

Chapter 7: Risk and the OTC Market

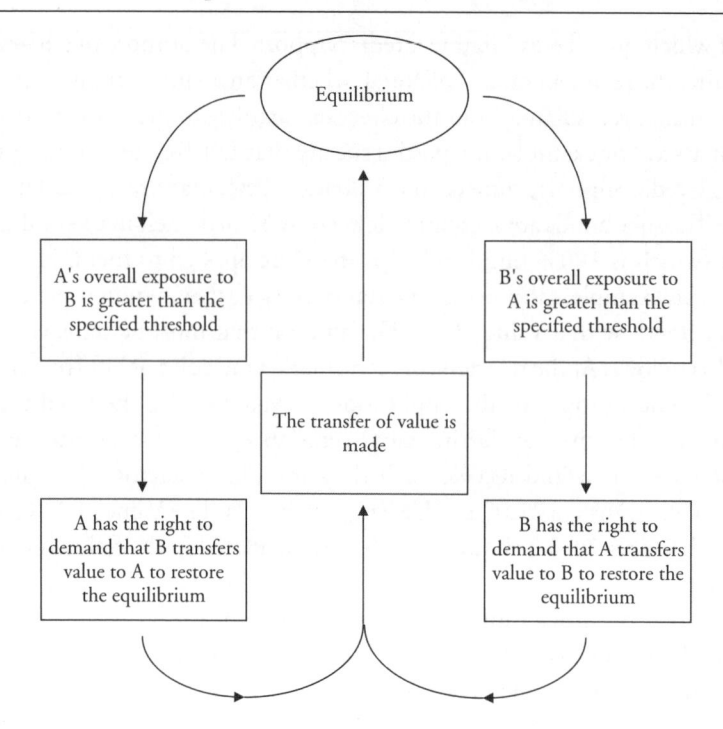

```
                    ┌─────────────┐
                    │ Equilibrium │
                    └─────────────┘
         ┌──────────────┐      ┌──────────────┐
         │ A's overall  │      │ B's overall  │
         │ exposure to  │      │ exposure to  │
         │ B is greater │      │ A is greater │
         │ than the     │      │ than the     │
         │ specified    │      │ specified    │
         │ threshold    │      │ threshold    │
         └──────────────┘      └──────────────┘
                    ┌──────────────┐
                    │The transfer  │
                    │of value is   │
                    │made          │
                    └──────────────┘
         ┌──────────────┐      ┌──────────────┐
         │ A has the    │      │ B has the    │
         │ right to     │      │ right to     │
         │ demand that  │      │ demand that  │
         │ B transfers  │      │ A transfers  │
         │ value to A   │      │ value to B   │
         │ to restore   │      │ to restore   │
         │ the          │      │ the          │
         │ equilibrium  │      │ equilibrium  │
         └──────────────┘      └──────────────┘
```

Figure 7.1 **The negative feedback loop established by a Credit Support Document**

increases deviation from a required state. Under a Credit Support Document, deviation from the equilibrium prompts action which is intended to restore the equilibrium, hence it establishes a negative feedback loop.

7.81 The overall exposure that each party has to its counterparty on a particular day is broadly calculated with reference to two factors. The first factor is the actual Exposure that the party has to its counterparty. The Exposure that a party has is the amount that its counterparty is required to pay to it under all outstanding Transactions. The term 'Exposure' bears a complex definition in the Annex and in the Deed.[31] The amount of Exposure is calculated with reference to the close-out netting provisions of the relevant master agreement. The definition is materially the same in both the Annex and in the Deed, and the definition stipulates how the calculation is performed. Exposure can either be a positive number or a negative number. If Exposure is a positive number, then the counterparty owes that amount to the party. If Exposure is a negative number, then the party owes that amount to the counterparty. The second factor is the amount of collateral that the party and its counterparty have already transferred to each other. Therefore, under some

---

[31] See paragraph 10 of the Annex and paragraph 12 of the Deed.

circumstances, a party may have an overall net exposure to its counterparty, even if it owes a net amount to its counterparty under all outstanding Transactions, because it has already transferred a greater amount of collateral to its counterparty. In very general terms, each party should hold only sufficient collateral in order to maintain the equilibrium that is established by the Credit Support Document, and if a party holds too little collateral, then it has the right to demand the transfer of further collateral to restore the equilibrium, and if it holds too much collateral, then its counterparty has the right, under the Annex, to demand the transfer of equivalent collateral to restore the equilibrium, or under the Deed, to demand the return of some or all of the collateral to restore the equilibrium.

7.82 The practical aspect to this necessarily brief introduction to the intricacies of credit support is that the numerical elections and variables of a Credit Support Document must be carefully considered. The sensitivity of a Credit Support Document is important, and reflects two factors. The first factor is the frequency with which whether or not there is an equilibrium is determined. The second factor is the extent to which there must be a deviation from the equilibrium in order for a party to have the right to demand a transfer to restore the equilibrium. The calibration of the sensitivity of a Credit Support Document must therefore reflect each party's tolerance of counterparty risk, and the ability of each party to effect the necessary transfers, deliveries, and receipts. From a practical perspective, if a Credit Support Document is too sensitive, then the parties will potentially be required to make transfers more frequently than the circumstances of their trading relationship actually merit or their payment systems can accommodate. A Credit Support Document should be negotiated with reference to a party's credit policy and operational capabilities.

Annex or deed?

7.83 Although the Annex and the Deed operate economically in the same manner, the key difference between them is that a charge is created under the Deed. In addition to this key difference, they also differ in one further important respect. Under the Annex, the party which has received collateral has the obligation, if there is a deviation from the equilibrium in its favour and its counterparty demands a transfer to restore the equilibrium, to transfer Equivalent Credit Support back to its counterparty. The Equivalent Credit Support subsequently transferred would not necessarily comprise the very same assets that the party had originally received as Eligible Credit Support. The concept of the fungibility of financial instruments[32] permits the transfer back of assets that are equivalent but not identical to the assets that had been originally transferred. For example, a party might

---

[32] See paragraphs 4.251 ff.

receive from its counterparty bond A as Eligible Credit Support, and transfer back, in response to a disturbance in its favour of the equilibrium, to its counterparty bond B as Equivalent Credit Support, provided that both bonds are parts of the same issue and confer the same rights. The transfer of ownership of the Eligible Credit Support and the obligation to transfer back Equivalent Credit Support enable the party which has received collateral to use that collateral in the course of its business. For example, a party may receive as Eligible Credit Support certain government bonds, which it then lends out under securities lending transactions. This lending enables the party holding the Eligible Credit Support to leverage its use of collateral.[33] Indeed, collateral management is now an integral element of a financial institution's business. The party which receives Eligible Credit Support, the Transferee, accounts to the Transferor for receipts of any Distributions or any Interest Amount in respect of the Eligible Credit Support that it holds.[34] The Transferor retains the economic risk or benefit flowing from the assets that have been transferred. This mechanism is consistent with the overall concept that collateral is returned when it is no longer needed, and the party which has supplied the collateral should retain economic exposure to the collateral if there is no recourse to the collateral as that collateral is ultimately returned to it.

7.84 By contrast, under the Deed, the party which has received the Eligible Credit Support, the Secured Party, does not have the benefit of ownership. A party also receives Eligible Credit Support under the Deed, but there is no transfer of the ownership of the assets comprising that Eligible Credit Support. Instead, the Secured Party holds the Eligible Credit Support that it receives as Posted Collateral, subject to a security interest in its favour, and subject to the duties imposed by paragraph 6 of the Deed. As ownership over the Posted Collateral remains with the Chargor, under paragraph 6(a) of the Deed, the Secured Party is required to exercise reasonable care to assure the safe custody of all the Posted Collateral. Paragraph 6(b) of the Deed allows the Secured Party to appoint a custodian to hold the Posted Collateral. Paragraph 6(c) of the Deed requires the Posted Collateral to be held in segregated accounts, whether by the Secured Party or by a custodian acting for the Secured Party, in order to ensure that it remains the property of the Chargor and would not therefore be distributed to the creditors of the Secured Party or the custodian acting for the Secured Party in the event of a winding up of the Secured Party or any such custodian. Paragraph 6(d) of the Deed prohibits the Secured Party from selling, pledging, rehypothecating, assigning, investing, using, commingling, or otherwise disposing of or otherwise using the Posted Collateral in its business. Under the Deed, the Secured Party has the obligation, if there is now a deviation from the equilibrium in its favour and the

---

[33] In this context, the term 'leverage' means to make greater use of.
[34] Paragraph 5(c) of the Annex.

7.5 ISDA Credit Support Documents

Chargor demands a transfer to restore the equilibrium, to return to the Chargor exactly the same assets that it originally received as Eligible Credit Support. Again, the Chargor retains economic exposure to the Posted Collateral, and has all the rights and obligations concomitant with its continued ownership of the Posted Collateral. Under paragraph 6(e) of the Deed, the Chargor is entitled to all Distributions and to exercise any voting rights attached to the Posted Collateral. Under paragraph 6(f) of the Deed, the Chargor is required to pay all calls or other payments which may become due in respect of the Posted Collateral. Under paragraph 6(f)(iii) of the Deed, the Chargor remains liable to observe and to perform all of the conditions and obligations assumed by it in respect of the Posted Collateral, and under paragraph 6(f)(iv) of the Deed, the Secured Party has no such obligation. Paragraph 6(g) of the Deed provides for the transfer by the Secured Party to the Chargor of any Distributions and any Interest Amount.

7.85 Market participants tend to favour the Annex, because the Annex permits greater flexibility and does not involve the potential complexity of perfecting security. The ISDA Collateral Survey 2000 indicates that the overwhelming majority of respondents to the survey favour the use of the Annex. Nonetheless, the Deed is available if the circumstances of the trading relationship merit its use. The following factors may be relevant to a decision whether to use the Annex or the Deed. One, the Annex operates to transfer title to the Eligible Credit Support being moved from one party to another. This transfer of title might generally give rise to a liability to capital gains tax. If a party has owned the asset that it proposes to use for a significant period, then tax issues will be expected to become more relevant. Two, the Annex is a part of the Schedule to the Master Agreement, and therefore it forms a part of the single agreement between the parties. Therefore, any amount outstanding under the Annex would potentially be included in the set-off of debts in the event that Transactions are terminated early and condensed into a single net close-out amount. If a party is concerned that it has exposure to a significant credit risk emanating from its counterparty, and yet wishes to trade with that counterparty, that party may well consider using a Deed. If Transactions are indeed terminated early, perhaps because a Bankruptcy has occurred with respect to the counterparty, and the party has the benefit of the charge created under the Deed, then the party's risk, of not recovering the full amount owed to it under the Transactions that have been terminated early, should be reduced, subject of course to the validity of the charge. This would be a significant benefit, outweighing the administrative burden of perfecting through registration, if this is indeed necessary, the charge created under the Deed at the time of execution of the Deed. Three, the circumstances of the trading relationship or even of a particular Transaction may necessitate the use of a particular asset, such as an interest in real property, as collateral. It is particularly important to ensure that security taken over certain types of asset, such as interests in real property, is both taken and perfected in the prescribed manner.

Summary of the principal differences between the Annex and the Deed

	Annex	Deed
	Transferor.	Chargor.
	Transferee.	Secured Party.
Initial transfer	There is an outright transfer of title to Eligible Credit Support.	There is a transfer of Eligible Credit Support and a charge is created over Posted Collateral.
Security	No security interest should be created.	A security interest is specifically and expressly created.
Subsequent transfer	There is an outright transfer of title to Equivalent Credit Support.	The Posted Collateral is released from the charge and returned.
Tax	Transfers may give rise to a liability to capital gains tax.	Transfers should be tax neutral.

Practical implementation

7.86 Both the Annex and the Deed contain references to the close-out netting provisions of the 1992 generations of master agreement, which is inevitable as the Annex and the Deed were both published in 1995 some three years after the publication of the 1992 generations of master agreement. Therefore users must consider how to adapt their existing Credit Support Documents to accommodate the algorithms for calculating the single net amount, the Early Termination Amount, with reference to which the 2002 Master Agreement operates. ISDA has published language[35] which modifies the Credit Support Documents to accommodate the procedure under which the Early Termination Amount is calculated using the Close-out Amount.

7.87 ISDA has also published the '2001 ISDA Margin Provisions', which comprise standard provisions that the parties can select to govern the collateralization of their trading relationship by the application of margin. The standard provisions, which have been drafted to conform with English law, the laws of the State of New York, and Japanese law, address certain operational issues and contain forms of notices.

---

[35] For example, see the 'Form of Amendment to 1995 ISDA Credit Support Annex (Transfer—English Law)', published by ISDA in May 2003, which replaces the definition of 'Exposure' in a Credit Support Document in order to reflect the calculation of an Early Termination Amount under Section 6 of the 2002 Master Agreement, and the '2002 Master Agreement Protocol', published by ISDA in July 2003, which sets out standard provisions migrating a trading relationship from an agreement in the form of one of the 1992 generation of master agreements to an agreement in the form of the 2002 Master Agreement.

7.6 ISDA Confirmation

7.88 A Confirmation describes a particular Transaction. The Confirmation contains the economic terms of the Transaction. The Confirmation is therefore crucial. ISDA publishes a variety of template Confirmations, but many market participants prefer to use their own form of Confirmation, which are largely adapted from those suggested by ISDA.

7.89 The economic terms of the Transaction represent the interface between the work of product developers, structuring staff, quantitative analysts, and marketing representatives on the one side, and the work of legal counsel and the documentation function on the other side. In the case of more complex transaction structures, which are bespoke and outside the scope of standard documented structures, intricate mathematical procedures must be described in contractual terms, and therefore the skill is required to express algorithmically in contractual terms the intended economic effect of the Transaction.

7.90 Care must be taken to draft the Confirmation to record the exact and precise terms of the Transaction, as the case *Deutsche Bank AG v ANZ Banking Group Ltd*[36] illustrates. The English courts will interpret the terms of a Confirmation strictly, and effect will not be given to a provision in a Confirmation which fails to record with certainty the intentions of the contractual parties. The complexity of drafting a Confirmation arises from the fact that the Confirmation records the financial and economic effect of the relevant Transaction.

7.7 ISDA Definitions Generally

7.91 ISDA publishes a wide variety of definitions in the form of books which are specific to different categories of derivative product.[37] ISDA also publishes from time to time various supplements and amendments to the definitions to reflect market developments. The broad categories of derivative product that are now accommodated by the various ISDA definitions are financial derivatives, commodity derivatives, and credit derivatives. Within the broad classification of financial derivatives are included all types of financial instrument, including rates, securities, and fund interests. Other more specialized classes of underlying are also covered by ISDA definitions, such as the property market, but these more specialized classes of underlying are not yet a mainstream component of the derivative market.

---

[36] Unreported. See Chapter 8.
[37] Various working groups of market participants convened by ISDA discuss the drafting and preparation of the definitions.

7.92 These definitions are extremely useful, in that standard terminology, transaction structures, and procedures for effecting determinations, calculations, payments, and deliveries are established. These structures and processes are invoked by the relevant Confirmation. A Confirmation should contain an introductory statement to the effect that one or more sets of definitions applies to the Transaction, and that these definitions form a part of a single agreement with the Confirmation, the Master Agreement, and the Schedule, which may include the Annex.

7.93 The benefit of using a set of definitions is that the Confirmation itself is thereby required to contain only a minimal amount of information. The risk of error is significantly reduced. The information contained in the Confirmation is used to operate the provisions of the relevant set of definitions. For example, the set of definitions relevant to a Transaction contains the procedure by which an amount that is payable by a party is calculated. The calculation is carried out using numerical data contained in the Confirmation, or obtained from a market price source. The Confirmation itself does not set out the calculation algorithm. Issues such as the actual date when a payment is made can quickly become intricate. For example, if the date when a payment falls due is not a Business Day,[38] when should the payment actually be made? The definitions set out the detailed rules by which certainty is achieved. It is interesting to note, as an aside, that the detailed drafting solutions published by ISDA are sometimes used outside the context of derivative documentation, and this underlines the prominence achieved by ISDA.

Matters covered by a set of definitions in more detail

7.94 A set of definitions addresses the following matters.[39] First, the payment and delivery obligations of standard transaction structures are established, which includes the settlement of these standard transaction structures, together with contractual terms to describe in sufficient detail and with sufficient certainty the underlying of a particular transaction. Further contractual terms are established for the exercise of any right in connection with a particular transaction; for example, the manner in which an option is exercised, and the limitations on the exercise of that option are set out. Second, the process is set out by which the price or level of the underlying is observed. The specification of this valuation process includes the source of the valuations; for example, the investment exchange on which the underlying is dealt, the dates on which valuations are made, the times at which valuations are made, and the consequences of any lack of availability of a valuation.

---

[38] The term 'Business Day' and the manner in which it is used is a key concept of the ISDA library of materials. It is discussed at paragraph 7.177 in the context of the 2006 ISDA Definitions; this is a purely arbitrary matter of the organization of this book, in recognition of the fact that most newcomers first encounter the 2006 ISDA Definitions.

[39] See paragraph 4.228 for a general introduction and context.

A valuation of an underlying might not be available because the source of the valuation is not scheduled to be open; for example, the investment exchange on which the underlying is dealt is closed for a scheduled holiday, or because the source of the valuation is somehow disrupted, for example, trading on the investment exchange on which the underlying is dealt is disrupted, with the consequence that prices of the underlying are not discovered. Third, the consequences of certain events which may affect the underlying and thereby change the economics of the transaction are set out. These are events are usually referred to as adjustment events and extraordinary events, and the occurrence of such an event usually precipitates either an adjustment to the terms of the transaction to offset the effect of the event, or the early termination of the transaction if no adjustment to the terms of the transaction would have a commercially reasonable result. Certain events are fairly standard across all derivative trading relationships, such as the loss of a party's ability to hedge its exposures, whereas other events are particular to the relevant class of underlying. Fourth, various miscellaneous matters are addressed, such as the representations and warranties given by the parties to each other, and any disclaimer as to liability made necessary by the nature of an underlying; for example, the disclaimer of each party to a transaction linked to an equity index that it is not the sponsor of that index.

7.95 The calculations and determinations made under a set of definitions are made by a Calculation Agent, which is usually one of the parties to the Transaction, although sometimes a third party is appointed. The Calculation Agent is required to make determinations and calculations in good faith and in a commercially reasonable manner, and the Calculation Agent does not act as a fiduciary for or as an advisor to any party.[40] Given that the standard of conduct required is open to a degree of interpretation and latitude, parties to OTC derivative contracts commonly include provisions which allow a party that is not a Calculation Agent to challenge the calculations and determinations made by the Calculation Agent, and any unresolved dispute is referred to an independent third party, such as an established dealer in the relevant derivative product. The broad discretions of the Calculation Agent can cause some difficulty in the context of the securitization of the cash flows of an OTC derivative contract, for example, the issue of equity-linked debt securities.[41] Rating agencies rating such issues tend to look carefully at the extent of the discretions of the Calculation Agent under the derivative transaction backing the issue of securities in order to be satisfied as to the impact on the securities of the exercise of its discretion by the Calculation Agent. Similar difficulties arise in the regulatory treatment of such issues of securities. It is interesting to note that if a difficulty arises within the confines of a particular Transaction,

---

[40] See for example Section 1.40 of the 2002 ISDA Equity Derivatives Definitions.
[41] See paragraphs 4.230 ff.

which is then terminated early, the Calculation Agent usually calculates the close-out termination amount of that Transaction. By contrast, where that Transaction is terminated early as a consequence of an Event of Default or a Termination Event, the Close-out Amount of that Transaction, as defined in the ISDA 2002 Master Agreement, is calculated by the Determining Party, which is potentially either party.[42]

7.96 The following paragraphs consider in more detail the salient provisions[43] of the 2002 ISDA Equity Derivatives Definitions, the 2003 ISDA Credit Derivatives Definitions, the 2005 ISDA Commodity Definitions, the 2006 ISDA Definitions, and the 2006 ISDA Fund Derivatives Definitions. These definitions provide a balanced overview of the diverse types of underlying for which ISDA's materials cater,[44] and a common approach is discerned in the treatment of certain fundamental concepts. The purpose of the following paragraphs is to set out a clear and workmanlike overview of the overall effect of the definitions and the transaction structures they create, and inevitably some simplification is required in the confines of this introductory book. Nonetheless, the overall scheme of the definitions, which can make for quite formidable technical reading, should be made clear. Unless otherwise indicated, as the context requires, in the following paragraphs discussing the various sets of ISDA definitions, capitalized terms are terms that are defined in the relevant set of definitions, references to Sections are references to the Sections of the relevant set of definitions, and references to Articles are references to the Articles of the relevant set of definitions.

7.8 2002 ISDA Equity Derivatives Definitions[45]

7.97 Article 1 contains certain general definitions, and establishes that the Equity Definitions contain standard structures for transactions linked to shares or other securities, whether singly or in baskets, and for structures linked to share indices, again whether singly or in baskets. The standard groups of transaction structures are the Option Transaction, the Forward Transaction, and the Equity Swap Transaction, either of which might be a Share Transaction, a Share Basket Transaction, an Index Transaction, or an Index Basket Transaction.

---

[42] See paragraph 7.60.
[43] ISDA publishes extremely detailed user's guides to accompany the sets of definitions that it publishes.
[44] Other sets of definitions outside the scope of this chapter include the ISDA Government Bond Option Definitions, the ISDA Inflation Derivatives Definitions, the ISDA Property Index Derivatives Definitions, and the FX and Currency Option Definitions.
[45] Herein, the 'Equity Definitions'. The Equity Definitions replaced the 1996 ISDA Equity Derivatives Definitions.

7.8 2002 ISDA Equity Derivatives Definitions

7.98 Article 1 also contains definitions for Transactions which operate with reference to Knock-in Events and Knock-out Events; these are usually referred to as 'barrier' Transactions. If a Transaction operates with reference to a Knock-in Event, then rights under the Transaction, for example, the right to exercise an option, are only exercisable if the relevant Knock-in Event occurs. For example, a Knock-in Event might be specified to be the price of the Knock-in Reference Security (which curiously might be an index, share, other security, or basket) moving through a barrier on a Knock-in Determination Day. A Knock-in Event can only take place on a Knock-in Determination Day. Conversely, if a Transaction operates with reference to a Knock-out Event, then rights under the Transaction, for example, the right to exercise an option, are only exercisable if the relevant Knock-out Event does not occur. Again, a Knock-out Event might be specified to be the price of the Knock-out Reference Security (which again might be an index, share, other security, or basket) moving through a barrier on a Knock-out Determination Day, and again, a Knock-out Event can only take place on a Knock-out Determination Day. Knock-in Determination Days and Knock-out Determination Days are subject to the same rules setting out the consequences of holidays and disruptions as other scheduled dates; these rules are examined in more depth in the following paragraphs. The inclusion of barrier Transactions is an innovation of the Equity Definitions; barrier Transactions are proving to be an increasingly popular type of derivative product.

Option Transaction

7.99 Article 2 contains general terms relating to Option Transactions. Section 2.2 defines the three option styles: under an American Option, rights are exercisable on any Scheduled Trading Day during the Exercise Period, under a Bermuda Option, rights are exercisable only on the specified Potential Exercise Dates during the Exercise Period and on the Expiration Date, and under a European Option, rights are exercisable only on the Expiration Date. Section 2.3 defines the two option types: call and put. If 'Cash Settlement' is applicable to an Option Transaction, then an Option Cash Settlement Amount is payable by the Seller (of the Option) to the Buyer (of the Option) if the Option is In-the-Money, and if 'Physical Settlement' is applicable to an Option Transaction, then the Buyer (of the Option) is entitled to buy from the Seller (of the Option, where the Option is a call) or to sell to the Seller (of the Option, where the Option is a put) the Shares or Basket of Shares. It is important to note that Physical Settlement does not apply to Index Option Transactions; delivery of the correct amount of each component security of an Index would prove to be a disproportionately complex and administratively burdensome task.

7.100 Article 3 provides for the exercise of options. The rights under an Option Transaction are generally extinguished at the Expiration Time on the Expiration Date. The Exercise Date is the actual date on which an Option is exercised.

American Options and Bermuda Options operate with reference to an Exercise Period, which starts on the Commencement Date and ends on the Expiration Date. The difference between an American Option and a Bermuda Option is that an American Option can be exercised on each Scheduled Trading Day during the Exercise Period and a Bermuda Option can be exercised only on each Scheduled Trading Day during the Exercise Period which is also a Potential Exercise Date. To exercise an Option, the Buyer must give irrevocable notice, which can be given by telephone. If Automatic Exercise applies, then an Option which has not been exercised is deemed to be exercised without the giving of any notice if it is In-the-Money on its Expiration Date. A subtlety to be considered is that any such Automatic Exercise can only occur on the Expiration Date of the Option, and not before. The purpose of Automatic Exercise is administrative convenience, and effectively clears a portfolio of outstanding Option Transactions to which it applies. A further subtlety to be considered is that an Option Transaction can comprise more than one Option, each of which can be exercised independently of the others. Accordingly, Section 3.3 provides for the Multiple Exercise of such Transactions. The provisions of the Equity Definitions which provide for Options therefore follow very closely the familiar concepts underpinning the analysis of options.[46]

Forward Transaction

7.101 Article 4 contains general terms relating to Forward Transactions. The inclusion of Forward Transactions is an innovation of the Equity Definitions. Forward Transactions are most usefully discussed by considering the applicable settlement processes in tandem with their overall scheme, as a reading of just one aspect of the relevant provisions would not suffice. Under a Forward Transaction for which 'Physical Settlement' is applicable, on the Settlement Date, the Buyer takes delivery of the relevant number of underlying Shares and pays the Forward Price, which is agreed in advance, thereby effectively locking the price paid for those Shares.[47] The Forward Transaction generates a profit for the Buyer if the Forward Price is less than the prevailing market price of the Shares on the Settlement Date (on the basis that the Buyer is buying the Shares under the Forward Transaction and is able to sell them on into the market at a higher price), and a loss for the Buyer if the Forward Price is more than the prevailing market price of the Shares on the Settlement Date (on the basis that the Buyer is buying the Shares under the Forward Transaction and can only sell them on into the market at a loss). Thus if 'Cash Settlement' is applicable, instead of an actual delivery of the underlying Shares taking place, just the difference between the Forward Price and the prevailing

---

[46] See part 4.4 of Chapter 4.
[47] The description of the forward contract in part 4.2 of Chapter 4 is recollected.

market price of the Shares (the Settlement Price) is paid. The Buyer receives the difference if the Settlement Price is more than the Forward Price, and the Seller receives the difference if the Forward Price is more than the Settlement Price.

7.102 Three subtleties should be considered. One, if 'Prepayment' applies to a Forward Transaction, then the Buyer pays the Prepayment Amount to the Seller, and the Prepayment Amount is effectively an upfront payment for the underlying. Assume 'Prepayment' does not apply to a Forward Transaction in respect of 1,000 Shares. The Forward Price is £10 per Share, and the subsequent Settlement Price is £12 per Share. The Forward Cash Settlement Amount is the difference £2 multiplied by 1,000 Shares, which is £2,000, payable by the Seller to the Buyer (the Buyer receives the profit generated by the Settlement Price being more than the Forward Price). Assume that 'Prepayment' applies to the same Transaction, and that a Prepayment Amount of £10,000 is paid by the Buyer. Again, the Settlement Price is £12 per Share. The Forward Cash Settlement Amount is the Settlement Price £12 per Share multiplied by 1,000 Shares, which is £12,000, payable by the Seller to the Buyer. Whether or not 'Prepayment' applies, the Buyer makes a £2,000 gain. If 'Prepayment' does not apply, then the £2,000 gain is made through the £2 difference between the Forward Price and the Settlement Price. If 'Prepayment' applies, then the £2,000 gain is made through the difference between the £10,000 upfront payment made by the Buyer and the subsequent £12,000 payment made by the Seller. As the Buyer is making an upfront payment if 'Prepayment' applies, the Forward Cash Settlement Amount paid by the Seller includes an amount to reflect the dividends paid in respect of the Shares during the tenor of the Transaction, in order that the Buyer is able to enjoy the benefit of ownership from the time when the Prepayment Amount is paid. Again, if 'Physical Settlement' is applicable, the Seller delivers the relevant number of Shares (again, the Equity Definitions do not provide for the physical settlement of a Forward Transaction linked to Indices).

7.103 Two, if 'Variable Obligation' applies to a Forward Transaction, the settlement of the Forward Transaction reflects the Settlement Price relative to the Forward Floor Price and the Forward Cap Price that are specified. The Forward Floor Price effectively sets a level below which the prevailing market price of the Shares is deemed not to fall, and the Forward Cap Price effectively sets a level above which the prevailing market price of the Shares is deemed not to rise. The concept of 'Variable Obligation' does not apply to Forward Transactions linked to Indices.

7.104 Three, if 'Physical Settlement' is applicable, as well as delivering the Number of Shares to be Delivered, the Seller also makes a payment of a Fractional Share Amount, which reflects that only a whole number of Shares can be delivered. The Fractional Share Amount is the amount remaining after there has been a rounding-down to the nearest whole number of Shares.

Equity Swap Transaction

7.105 Article 5 contains general terms relating to Equity Swap Transactions. As with the discussion set out above of the mechanics of the Forward Transaction, Equity Swap Transactions are most usefully discussed by considering the applicable settlement processes in tandem with their overall scheme. Under an Equity Swap Transaction, one party receives a payment if the price or level of the underlying Share, Index, Basket of Shares, or Basket of Indices increases, and the other party receives a payment if that price or level decreases. These payments are made periodically during the life of the Equity Swap Transaction, and therefore the payment made in respect of a particular period must only capture the performance of the underlying during that period, and accordingly an Equity Swap Transaction is reset at the end of each period. How this reset is achieved, and the reason why it is used, is discussed in the following paragraphs.

7.106 Under an Equity Swap Transaction, one party is specified to be the Equity Amount Payer, and the other party is specified to be the Equity Amount Receiver. Crucially, despite the labels they are given, either of them either makes a payment or receives a payment, depending on the performance of the underlying. The Equity Amount Receiver receives a payment if the price or level of the underlying increases, and the Equity Amount Payer receives a payment if the price or level of the underlying decreases. The Equity Amount Receiver is said to be 'long' the swap as the Equity Amount Receiver receives a payment if the price or level of the underlying increases, which of course is the same long exposure that the Equity Amount Receiver would acquire through actually buying the underlying. Generally, by using a long Equity Swap Transaction, the Equity Amount Receiver can express an investment view that the price or level of the underlying will increase without actually buying the underlying, and therefore without incurring brokerage costs or the administrative burdens of arranging safe custody of the underlying. The Equity Amount Receiver is also said to buy the underlying 'on swap'. Further, individual Shares can be packaged together in Baskets, and Equity Swap Transactions offer a more diversified approach to gaining investment exposure to Indices, which again can be packaged together in Baskets, and which can be difficult to access without resorting to listed futures contracts.[48] Conversely, the Equity Amount Payer is said to be 'short' the swap as the Equity Amount Payer receives a payment if the price or level of the underlying decreases, which of course is the same short exposure that the Equity Amount Payer would acquire through actually selling short the underlying. Again, the Equity Swap Transaction offers a flexible solution.

---

[48] It should be noted that the innovation of single-stock futures contracts should make the use of exchange-based solutions more flexible. Single-stock futures contracts were an innovation in the financial markets in the autumn of 2002.

7.8 2002 ISDA Equity Derivatives Definitions

7.107 The performance of the underlying is captured through the concept of the Equity Amount, which is the key concept of an Equity Swap Transaction. The Equity Amount is the amount that is paid and received by the parties, and it is calculated using the Rate of Return. The Rate is defined in Section 5.7 as the Final Price minus the Initial Price, divided by the Initial Price. If the price or level of the underlying has increased, then the Rate of Return is a positive number, and if the price or level of the underlying has decreased, then the Rate of Return is a negative number. The Equity Amount in respect of a particular period is the Rate of Return for that period multiplied by the Equity Notional Amount for that period. If the Equity Amount is a positive number, then the Equity Amount Payer pays it, and if the Equity Amount is a negative number, because the Rate of Return is a negative number signifying that the price or level of the underlying has decreased, then the Equity Amount Receiver pays the absolute value[49] of it. Again, the label 'Receiver' is potentially misleading, as the 'Receiver' on occasion makes a payment.

7.108 The documentation for an Equity Swap Transaction has been developed from the perspective of the sell side of the market, and the requirement that a participant in the sell side of the market, referred to in this discussion for convenience as a dealer, has to hedge the exposures it assumes by selling the opportunity to enter into an Equity Swap Transaction to an end-user. The adjustment of the Equity Notional Amount reflects the hedging operations that a dealer employs, and the dealer's ability to manage its hedging is extremely important, which is why the Equity Definitions allow for the early termination of the Transaction under certain circumstances.[50]

7.109 In providing a long Equity Swap Transaction, as Equity Amount Payer, the dealer is exposed to the price risk that it will have an obligation to make a payment if the price or level of the underlying increases. The dealer might choose to hedge itself, perhaps by buying the underlying Shares or taking a long position in the underlying Index through a listed futures contract. The value of the dealer's long position in the underlying matches the dealer's obligations under the swap. Amounts that the dealer is required to pay under the swap are met by increases in the value of the dealer's hedge position. The dealer might borrow to finance its purchase of the underlying. The dealer pays interest on its borrowing, and the end-user is charged this cost by making periodic payments to the dealer of Floating Amounts.[51] These periodic payments are consistent with the concept that the purchase of the swap

---

[49] The absolute value of a negative number is the positive of that number, and the absolute value of a positive number is also the positive of that number. For example, the absolute value of −2 is 2, and the absolute value of 3 is 3.
[50] See paragraphs 7.115 ff.
[51] The Equity Definitions do not legislate for the Floating Amounts, so market participants build in the ISDA 2006 Definitions which contain provisions for transactions linked to interest rates.

by the end-user is equivalent to the purchase of the underlying by the end-user, who presumably must finance this purchase of the underlying. In providing the long swap, the dealer remains neutral to movements in the price or level of the underlying, and locks in the spread between (1) in respect of its hedge position, the interest it pays on its borrowing to buy the underlying, and (2) under the swap, the Floating Amounts it receives from the end-user.

7.110 In providing a short Equity Swap Transaction, as Equity Amount Receiver, the dealer is exposed to the price risk that it will have an obligation to make a payment if the price or level of the underlying decreases. The dealer might choose to hedge itself by opening a short position in the underlying; the dealer opens the hedge by selling the underlying Shares or taking a short position in the underlying Index through a listed futures contract. The value of the dealer's short position in the underlying matches the dealer's obligations under the swap. Again, amounts that the dealer is required to pay under the swap are met by increases in the value of the dealer's hedge position. If the price or level of the underlying decreases, then the dealer is required to make a payment under the swap. However, the decrease in the price or level of the underlying means that the dealer's own short position in the underlying has increased in value. The dealer sells the underlying high to open the hedge, and later buys it back low to close the hedge and crystallize the gain that it uses to meet the payment that it makes under the swap. In order to sell the underlying to open its hedge position, the dealer might first borrow the underlying under a lending transaction. The dealer places on deposit the cash sale proceeds it receives by selling the underlying, and the dealer earns interest on this cash deposit. The dealer also makes periodic payments of Floating Amounts to the end-user. Essentially, market forces dictate that the dealer makes these periodic payments. If the dealer did not make these periodic payments, it would realize a windfall gain by receiving interest on its cash deposit, and the dealer therefore passes on to the end-user this interest, less any cost incurred by the dealer in opening and maintaining its hedge position. Again, in providing the short swap, the dealer remains neutral to movements in the price or level of the underlying, and locks in the spread between (1) under the swap, the Floating Amounts it pays to the end-user, and (2) in respect of its hedge position, the interest it receives on its cash deposit less any cost incurred in opening and maintaining the hedge position. At the end of the swap, the dealer buys back the underlying in order to close the hedge position and to enable it to return the underlying to the stock lender.

7.111 To return to the concept of the reset of an Equity Swap Transaction, the Equity Notional Amount of the swap is set at the outset. On each Cash Settlement Payment Date, the Equity Amount for that date is added to the Equity Notional Amount. Therefore the Equity Notional Amount is increased by any positive Equity Amount, and it is decreased by any negative Equity Amount. The purpose of this resetting is to ensure that each Cash Settlement Payment Date captures the

Valuations

Article 6 provides for valuation. Valuations are specified to be made at the Valuation Time on a Valuation Date or on an Averaging Date. The concept of the Averaging Date is used to allow the valuation of the underlying for the purposes of a particular Valuation Date to be calculated as the average of the price or level of the underlying across a series of dates linked to that Valuation Date. Any date on which a valuation is expected to be made, whether a Valuation Date or an Averaging Date, must be made on a Scheduled Trading Day. The definition of a Scheduled Trading Day is therefore very important; the effect of the definition[53] is that a Scheduled Trading Day in respect of an underlying is a day on which both the exchange on which that underlying is listed (the Exchange in respect of the underlying) is scheduled to be open for its regular trading session and every exchange on which listed derivative contracts written on that underlying (the Related Exchanges in respect of the underlying) is scheduled to be open for its regular trading session. The concept of the Scheduled Trading Day therefore anticipates the ability of parties to Transactions to hedge their exposures under Transactions by entering into the appropriate offsetting positions in exchange-based transactions. The necessary liquidity is only available if those underlying markets are open. Article 6 also provides for the consequences of a disruption to the valuation process. Section 6.4 provides that a Disrupted Day is a Scheduled Trading Day on which an Exchange or a Related Exchange fails to open for trading during its regular trading session or on which a Market Disruption Event has occurred. Section 6.3 defines a Market Disruption Event as the occurrence or existence of a Trading Disruption, an Exchange Disruption, or an Early Closure. The occurrence of a Market Disruption Event in respect of one or more securities included in an Index can result in a Market Disruption Event taking place in respect of that Index if the affected securities comprise 20% or more of the level of that Index. Section 6.6 sets out the consequences of Disrupted Days. Under Section 6.6(a), generally if a Valuation Date is a Disrupted Day, then the relevant valuation is postponed to the first succeeding Scheduled Trading Day which is not a Disrupted Day, and if each

7.112

---

[52] To maintain clarity, this discussion omits any corporate action which might increase or decrease the quantity of the underlying.
[53] Section 1.31.

of the eight Scheduled Trading Days following that original affected Valuation Date is a Disrupted Day, then the relevant valuation is made on the eighth Scheduled Trading Day following that original affected Valuation Date, effectively using the best information and methodology that is available. This process is sometimes colloquially referred to as the 'eight-day roll'. A similar process is followed in respect of an Index Basket Transaction under Section 6.6(b) and in respect of a Share Basket Transaction under Section 6.6(c), with the refinement that any component of the Basket that is not affected by the occurrence of the Disrupted Day is valued on the original affected Valuation Date, and each component affected by that occurrence is valued in accordance with the roll process described above. This approach is usually referred to as 'value what you can'. The alternative approach that is sometimes used, and for which the Equity Definitions do not supply language, is 'move in block'. Under this alternative approach, the valuation of every component in the Basket is subject to the eight-day roll described above. The 'move in block' approach is appropriate if the economics of the Transaction are predicated on the correlation, or otherwise, between the components of the basket. Section 6.7 provides for Averaging. Section 6.7(c) provides for disruptions to an Averaging Date. The parties specify the approach that is to apply. Under 'Omission', the affected Averaging Date is disregarded, unless as a consequence no Averaging Date is available, whereupon the provisions of Section 6.6 and the eight-day roll apply. Under 'Postponement', Section 6.6 and the eight-day roll apply. Under 'Modified Postponement', a process similar to the eight-day roll applies, but using the concept of a Valid Date. Section 6.8 provides for Futures Price Valuation, which is available for Index Transactions for the purposes of which the level of the Index is determined using the Official Settlement Price of an exchange-based futures or option contract written on that Index, an Exchange-traded Contract, instead of the actual level of that Index as calculated and published by the Index Sponsor.[54] Section 6.8 also anticipates the particular difficulties that might arise in respect of an Exchange-traded Contract and sets out the response to any such difficulty. The responses set out in Section 6.8 do not include the early termination of the Transaction, which is generally considered to be suitable only in extremis, as parties tend to attempt to preserve Transactions to the fullest extent possible. The difficulties that Section 6.8 anticipates are (1) the relevant exchange on which the Exchange-traded Contract is dealt changes or modifies the terms of the Exchange-traded Contract, the response to which is an

---

[54] By way of example, if 'Futures Price Valuation' applies to an Index Transaction in respect of the FTSE 100 index, then the level of the FTSE 100 index for the purposes of the calculations under that Index Transaction might be the price of a particular FTSE 100 index futures contract dealt on LIFFE and not the actual level of the FTSE 100 index as calculated and published by FTSE International Limited and its group of companies, the organization which owns the intellectual property in that index and which calculates and publishes its levels.

adjustment, if necessary, made by the Calculation Agent to the terms of the index Transaction;[55] (2) trading in the Exchange-based Contract never starts or is permanently discontinued, the response to which is that valuation of the Index is made with reference to the level of the Index itself and not to the Official Settlement Price of the Exchange-based Contract;[56] and (3) the exchange on which the Exchange-based Contract is dealt corrects the Official Settlement Price of the Exchange-traded Contract, the response to which is that one party may make a payment to the other if appropriate or an adjustment, if necessary, is made by the Calculation Agent to the terms of the index Transaction.[57]

Settlement

Article 7 contains brief general terms relating to settlement, and Article 8 provides for the settlement of Transactions by the making of a payment, and Article 9 provides for the settlement of Transactions by the making of a delivery of Shares and the making of a payment. Article 9 recognizes that where a Number of Shares to be Delivered or a Number of Baskets to Be Delivered is determined, only whole Shares can be delivered, although the result of the calculations might be a fractional number of Shares;[58] where a fractional number of Shares is computed, the party required to make the delivery delivers that fractional number of Shares rounded down to the nearest whole, and pays the Fractional Share Amount.[59] Article 9 recognizes that Shares might be held in a dematerialized form in a clearing system. Under Section 9.9, the expenses relating to the transfer of the Shares to be delivered, such as any stamp duty or fees, are paid by the party which would customarily pay such expenses in accordance with market practice. Under Section 9.11, the party required to deliver Shares makes a representation that it is able to transfer those Shares with good marketable title free from any security or other encumbrance. However, the lien routinely imposed on securities held in a clearing system is outside the scope of the representation. The transferring party also represents that it transfers the Shares free from any restrictions and limitations, and that the Shares are in proper form for transfer under the procedures of the relevant clearing system.[60] Under Section 9.12, a party which fails to perform any obligation required to be settled by delivery pays an indemnity to the other party. The scope of the indemnity is wide, and explicitly includes the cost incurred by

7.113

---

[55] Section 6.8(d).
[56] Section 6.8(e).
[57] Section 6.8(f).
[58] As observed in paragraph 7.104.
[59] Fractional Share Amount is an innovation of the Equity Definitions.
[60] Transfers of securities held in dematerialized form in a clearing system are effected by adjusting the balances of accounts held in the clearing system; this process offers the advantages of efficiency, cost-effectiveness, and reliability. The documents evidencing those securities are held by a custodian.

the party expecting to receive the Shares of borrowing those Shares if it needs those Shares to meet its own delivery obligations elsewhere.

Dividends

7.114 Article 10 provides for dividends. However, Article 10 can only provide a framework, as the treatment of dividends is very much dependent on the relevant jurisdiction and the specific circumstances of a Transaction. In broad terms, the parties decide which of them receives the benefit of dividends paid in respect of the Shares underlying a Transaction. A telling indication of the difficulty of preparing language which would be compatible with the various potential circumstances in which it would be invoked is that the parties must specify for themselves the Dividend Amount that is applied to their Transaction; no definition of Dividend Amount could be found to cover every possibility. A further election that the parties must make[61] is whether a particular amount by way of dividend forms a part of the Dividend Amount on the record date, which is the date when the shareholders who are eligible to receive the dividend are identified, or when the relevant Shares in respect of which it is to be paid start trading on an 'ex-dividend' basis,[62] or when it is actually paid. Under Section 10.4, if 'Re-investment of Dividends' applies to an Equity Swap Transaction, the Notional Equity Amount is increased by the Dividend Amount which is determined in respect of the relevant period. A particular complication which might arise is the scenario where the Issuer (the company which issues the Shares underlying a Transaction) declares a dividend, the amounts and values of a Transaction are then changed accordingly, and yet subsequently the Issuer fails to pay the full amount of that dividend. The terms of the Transaction should set out the response to such a shortfall in actual dividends received, including the repayment or re-crediting of an appropriate amount.[63]

Adjustments and modifications

7.115 Article 11 provides for adjustments and modifications affecting Indices, Shares and Transactions. Certain events and circumstances may arise which affect the Shares or Indices underlying a Transaction, and Article 11 sets out the responses to such events and circumstances that the parties wish to adopt. Section 11.1 provides for adjustments to Indices. Where an Index is calculated by a successor

---

[61] Section 10.1.
[62] When a share starts trading on an 'ex-dividend' basis, it is bought and sold without the right to receive the forthcoming dividend, which is paid to the owner of the share on the relevant record date preceding the date when ex-dividend trading started. The share resumes trading on a 'cum dividend' basis after the dividend has been paid, being bought and sold with the right to receive the next payment of any dividend that is declared.
[63] See the sample provision in the User's Guide to the 2002 ISDA Equity Derivatives Definitions (2003 Edition).

sponsor, that Index continues to underlie the Transaction if the successor sponsor is acceptable to the Calculation Agent, and where an Index is replaced by a successor index, that successor index becomes the Index for the purposes of the Transaction, if the Calculation Agent is satisfied that the successor index is suitably similar to the original Index.[64] An Index Adjustment Event is one of three events: an Index Modification, an Index Cancellation, and an Index Disruption; the title of each is sufficiently descriptive. Section 11.1(b) sets out three consequences of an Index Adjustment Event; the parties select in the Confirmation which applies to their Transaction. If 'Calculation Agent Adjustment' is the specified consequence, then the Transaction continues, and if the Calculation Agent considers that the Index Adjustment Event has a material effect on the Transaction, then the relevant calculations under the Transaction are made by the Calculation Agent using the most recent data and calculation methodology. It is evident that despite the label given to this consequence, the range of the Calculation Agent's discretion is limited to making the initial determination as to whether there has been a material effect on the Transaction, and there is potential for uncertainty as to what constitutes a material effect, and to substituting recent data and methodology. If 'Negotiated Close-out' applies, then the parties may decide to terminate the Transaction 'on mutually acceptable terms', and if the parties do not decide to terminate the Transaction, then it continues without amendment. This particular consequence is arguably almost meaningless, as irrespective of whether this consequence is specified, the parties are at liberty to amend the terms of their Transaction in any case; this consequence does not amount to an agreement to agree, as the operative word is 'may' and not 'shall', and therefore the analysis as to whether or not this consequence is enforceable should not enter consideration.[65] By contrast, 'Cancellation and Payment' is the consequence which results in the early termination of the Transaction, subject to the timetable established in Section 11.1(b)(C). The amount of the cancellation payment is calculated in accordance with Section 12.7(c), and not in accordance with the provisions of the framework master agreement. As the following paragraphs make clear, there is an overlap between the treatment of Indices under Article 11 and Article 12.

7.116 Section 11.2 provides for adjustments to Share Transactions and Share Basket Transactions. Under Section 11.2(b), if an Options Exchange, on which option

---

[64] Section 11.1(a).
[65] Although as a general principle of English law, an agreement to agree is unenforceable, a number of cases illustrate that the English courts are increasingly willing to uphold provisions which amount to an agreement to agree, provided that the agreement to agree forms a part of a contract that is otherwise enforceable. A close reading of the relevant provision is required. For example, in *Petromec Inc v Petroleo Brasileiro SA* [2005] EWCA Civ 891, an agreement to negotiate in good faith certain costs was upheld as enforceable by the Court of Appeal, as the relevant obligation was an obligation to negotiate those costs, and the obligation formed a part of an otherwise enforceable agreement.

contracts relating to the relevant Shares are traded, makes an adjustment to the terms of such options contracts, then the Calculation Agent determines whether or not such an adjustment has 'a diluting or concentrative effect on the theoretical value of the relevant Shares',[66] and if the Calculation Agent so determines, then the Calculation Agent makes an adjustment to the terms of the Transaction which corresponds with the adjustment that is made on the Options Exchange to account for the diluting or concentrative effect of that Options Exchange adjustment. Under Section 11.2(c), if a Potential Adjustment Event occurs, then again the Calculation Agent determines whether or not such an adjustment has 'a diluting or concentrative effect on the theoretical value of the relevant Shares',[67] and if the Calculation Agent so determines, then the Calculation Agent makes an adjustment to the terms of the Transaction as the Calculation Agent considers appropriate to account for that diluting or concentrative effect. Section 11.2(e) sets out the Potential Adjustment Events, which include a subdivision, consolidation, or reclassification of the relevant Shares, corporate actions, an Extraordinary Dividend, a call by the Issuer in respect of the relevant Shares that are not fully paid, a repurchase of the relevant Shares, any separation of shareholder rights, and any other event which may have a diluting or concentrative effect. Under both Options Exchange Adjustment and Calculation Agent Adjustment, no adjustment to the Transaction is made to account solely for changes in volatility, expected dividends, stock loan rate, or liquidity of the relevant Shares. Instead, the determination as to whether or not the particular consequence is triggered rests with an analysis as to whether or not there has been a diluting or concentrative effect on the theoretical value of the relevant Shares.

Extraordinary Events

7.117 Article 12 provides for Extraordinary Events; these are events which affect Shares or Indices.[68] Article 12 contains some of the more complex drafting of the Equity Definitions. An Extraordinary Event in respect of Shares occurs if one of the following occurs in respect of those Shares: a Merger Event,[69] a Tender Offer,[70]

---

[66] Section 11.2(a).
[67] Section 11.2(a).
[68] From a broad perspective, the contractual response to an Extraordinary Event which changes the nature or quality of the underlying is determined by market practice. In the European market, the preference is to attempt to preserve the Transaction to the fullest extent possible, and therefore an adjustment to the terms of the Transaction to offset the effect of the Extraordinary Event is sought. By contrast, in the Asiapac market, the more favoured response is to terminate early the Transaction.
[69] Section 12.1(b).
[70] Section 12.1(d).

a Nationalization,[71] an Insolvency,[72] a Delisting,[73] or any applicable Additional Disruption Event.

7.118 An Extraordinary Event occurs in respect of an Index if an Index Adjustment Event occurs in respect of that Index. There is therefore an overlap between the provisions of Article 11 and Article 12 in respect of the treatment of Indices. Two of the three consequences specified for an Index Adjustment Event in Article 11, Calculation Agent Adjustment and Negotiated Close-out, are arguably weak, and the third, Cancellation and Payment, invokes the calculation methodology set out in Section 12.7(a); Section 12.7 itself provides for payment upon certain Extraordinary Events.

7.119 Extremely detailed consequences are specified for each such Extraordinary Event.[74] The definitions of the Extraordinary Events are grouped according to their type, and the analysis that they require. Mergers and acquisitions activity gives rise to the difficulty of identifying the underlying Shares of the Transaction if the Shares originally underlying the Transaction are issued by an Issuer which has undergone a merger or other manoeuvre. There can be no prescriptive response to Mergers and Tender Offers, and the parties therefore select which approach they wish to apply. Broadly, if a Merger Event occurs, the consequence might be that the shares of the resulting entity are the underlying Shares of the Transaction, in which case 'Alternative Obligation' is the appropriate consequence,[75] although an adjustment would be needed to the terms of the Transaction to reflect the changes in the number of Shares and their values; a direct one-for-one replacement of the underlying Shares is unlikely to be sufficient. The parties may decide that such a replacement is inappropriate, and therefore other consequences are available, such as cancellation and payment, or an adjustment to the terms of the Transaction. The making of a Tender Offer, which by definition has not yet resulted in a change to the relevant Shares or their Issuer, is sufficient to amount to an Extraordinary Event, but a takeover offer, tender offer, exchange offer, solicitation or other proposal only qualifies as a Tender Offer if it is made in respect of more than 10% of the relevant outstanding shares of the Issuer. The consequence of a Tender Offer is either broadly cancellation and payment, or an adjustment to the terms of the Transaction. The consequence of a Nationalization, Insolvency, or Delisting is

---

[71] Section 12.6(a)(i).
[72] Section 12.6(a)(ii).
[73] Section 12.6(a)(iii).
[74] See Section 12.2 for the consequences of Merger Events, Section 12.3 for the consequences of Tender Offers, and Section 12.4 for settlement following a Merger Event or Tender Offer.
[75] Section 12.2(a).

either broadly the right to close-out the Transaction,[76] cancellation and payment, or an adjustment to the terms of the Transaction.

7.120 Section 12.9 sets out a wide selection of Additional Disruption Events that the parties can select to apply to the Transaction. The parties are of course able to specify any further Additional Disruption Event that is not defined in Section 12.9(a). Whether or not certain of these Additional Disruption Events should apply to a particular Transaction can cause some difficulty in the final agreement of the terms of a Transaction. The definitions of certain Additional Disruption Events are clear-cut, and there should be no difficulty in discerning their import and therefore deciding whether or not they should apply. However, there is a degree of overlap between certain other Additional Disruption Events, with subtle distinctions between them, and these distinctions should be borne in mind when negotiating the Additional Disruption Events which should apply to a Transaction. There are two effects of a Change in Law:[77] first, a party becomes unable to hold, acquire, or dispose of Shares relating to the Transaction, and second, a party incurs a materially increased cost in performing its obligations. Following the occurrence of a Hedging Disruption,[78] a party is unable, after using commercially reasonable efforts, to enter into or to realize the benefit of a hedging transaction. It is important to note that the scope of Hedging Disruption is a hedging transaction that the party enters into for the purposes of mitigating the equity price risk of its obligations under the Transaction. Following the occurrence of an Increased Cost of Hedging,[79] the cost to a party of entering into or of realizing the benefit of a hedging transaction is materially increased, as compared with the circumstances existing when the Transaction starts. Again, the scope of Increased Cost of Hedging is a hedging transaction that the party enters into for the purposes of mitigating the equity price risk of its obligations under the Transaction. An inability to hedge caused by a change in any applicable law or regulation can fall within the scope of Change in Law if that hedging involves buying, holding, or selling the relevant Shares, although the threshold is that such buying, holding, or selling is rendered illegal by that change in applicable law or regulation. Moreover, that inability to hedge can also fall within the scope of Hedging Disruption, which is cast wider than Change in Law, in that the activity which constitutes hedging is more widely defined, but the threshold is that such inability to hedge is experienced after commercially reasonable efforts to hedge have failed. Some difficulty may arise as to the meaning of 'commercially reasonable efforts'. Generally, to expend commercially reasonable efforts involves expending effort which does

---

[76] 'Negotiated Close-out', which bears substantially the same definition as that found in Section 11.1(b)(B) as a consequence to an Index Adjustment Event.
[77] Section 12.9(a)(ii).
[78] Section 12.9(a)(v).
[79] Section 12.9(a)(vi).

not give rise to additional cost or delay, although some latitude will clearly apply. An increase in the cost of hedging will not fall within the scope of Change in Law, as the second limb of Change in Law captures only materially increased costs of performing obligations, and no party is under an obligation to hedge its obligations. An increase in the cost of hedging will not fall within the scope of Hedging Disruption, as a Hedging Disruption is defined with reference to a party's actual ability to hedge, and not the cost it incurs in doing so. Accordingly, if a party is concerned to be able to respond to an increase in its cost of hedging, it must argue for the inclusion of Increased Cost of Hedging as an Additional Disruption Event.

7.121 Section 12.7 provides in some detail for the payments that are made as a consequence of certain Extraordinary Events. Section 12.7(b) sets out the methodology for the calculation of an amount that is paid in respect of an Option Transaction, and Section 12.7(c) sets out the methodology for the calculation of an amount that is paid in respect of either a Forward Transaction or an Equity Swap Transaction.

7.122 The provisions of Section 12.7(b) are extensive as a result of the difficulties of option valuation.[80] As a first step, the parties seek to agree the amount to be paid, and if the parties are not able to agree the amount, then one of two fallbacks applies. The particular fallback which should apply is specified in the Confirmation.

7.123 If the 'Agreed Model' fallback applies, then the amount payable as a consequence of the Extraordinary Event is the Unadjusted Value plus the Adjusted Value. The Unadjusted Value is the value of the Option Transaction for the period from the date of the occurrence of the Extraordinary Event (the Closing Date) to the Expiration Date of the Option Transaction. The Unadjusted Value is calculated on the basis of certain assumptions[81] as to the volatility exhibited by the price of the relevant underlying Shares, dividends, the value of the relevant underlying Shares, interest and stock loan rates, and that period. The Adjusted Value is the difference between the value of the Option Transaction for the period from the Announcement Date of the Extraordinary Event to the Expiration Date of the Option Transaction based on different measurements of volatility. One measurement of volatility is derived from a period of 15 Business Days ending on but excluding the Announcement Date, and the other measurement of volatility is derived from a period of 15 Business Days starting on the Announcement Date.

---

[80] See paragraph 4.44; the provisions of Section 12.7(b) are predicated on the established pattern of most standard option pricing models, as discussed in Chapter 4. It is recollected from paragraph 4.46 that volatility is the most important variable in the calculation of the price of an option; accordingly the provisions of Section 12.7(b) operate with reference to the changes in volatility experienced.

[81] See Section 12.7(b)(i)(A)(1) to (5).

The Adjustment Value therefore captures the effect of the announcement or of other publicity surrounding the Extraordinary Event on the volatility of the relevant underlying Shares. The broad scheme of the Agreed Model methodology is to assess the value of the Option Transaction on the date of the occurrence of the Extraordinary Event, and then adjust that value to reflect any change in the value of the Option Transaction caused by a change in the volatility of the underlying Shares on the Announcement Date.

7.124 If 'Calculation Agent Determination' fallback applies, then the Calculation Agent determines the relevant amount payable. The Calculation Agent may have regard to the 'Agreed Model' methodology, but is not bound to do so.

7.125 The provisions of Section 12.7(c) require the calculation of a Cancellation Amount. The overall methodology of the calculation of a Cancellation Amount echoes the provisions under the ISDA 2002 Master Agreement for the calculation of a Close-out Amount in respect of a Transaction.[82] The calculation is undertaken by the party specified in the Confirmation to the Determining Party, and therefore it is important that the Confirmation includes this specification.

Agreements and representations

7.126 Article 13 provides for various agreements and representations that the parties make to each other, the overall purpose of which is to reinforce the basis of their trading relationship, which is essentially that each transacts with the other at arm's length with no provision of any advice or other fiduciary duty, and with no reliance being placed by either on the other. The parties specify which of the four sets of agreements and representations applies to their Transaction. If Section 13.1 applies, then the parties agree and represent that neither acts as a fiduciary for the other and that neither relies on any representation of the other apart from those set out in the Master Agreement. If Section 13.2 applies, then the parties agree and represent that neither of them is obliged to hedge its obligations under the Transaction, and that any hedging undertaken by a party is a matter solely for that party, and is not undertaken for the benefit of the other party. This latter agreement is necessary in the context of a Transaction under which one party is selling to the other a synthetic exposure to the underlying Shares or Indices. If Section 13.3 applies, then the parties agree and represent that any Index Sponsor of any Index with reference to which the Transaction operates does not sponsor, endorse, sell, or promote the Transaction and is not liable for any result obtained through entering into the Transaction, and that neither party is liable for any error or omission on the part of the Index Sponsor. The application of Section 13.3 would be inappropriate if the Transaction is linked to an Index published by one of the

---

[82] See paragraph 7.60.

parties to the Transaction, whether that Index is more widely published and recognized or is tailored to the specific Transaction.[83] If Section 13.4 applies, then the parties agree and represent that neither provides any form of specialized advice to the other in respect of the Transaction, that each party has been given the opportunity to obtain sufficient information on the terms of the Transaction in order to be able to evaluate the merits and risks of the Transaction, and that each party and its Affiliates may engage in trading of the relevant Shares.

7.9 2003 ISDA Credit Derivatives Definitions[84]

7.127 The observation is made[85] that the documentation of credit derivative transactions requires significantly more contractual analysis than the documentation of derivative transactions in respect of other classes of underlying. In particular, the risk transferred under credit derivative transactions is defined with reference to a complex set of contractual terms, whereas under other classes of derivative transaction, the transfer of risk is achieved through significantly more straightforward processes such as obtaining the relevant valuations from agreed sources of market data, and applying those valuations within the transaction structure; the movement of a price or a rate results in a payment. Although the Credit Definitions set out the fundamental provisions for the documentation of Credit Derivative Transactions, including principally the definition of the credit risk that is transferred and the means by which Credit Derivative Transactions are settled, numerous conventions have emerged in the credit derivative market, prompting the publication of various supplements. These supplements will be introduced after a discussion of the overall scheme of the Credit Definitions. Inevitably, this book can only provide an overview of the Credit Definitions, given the dense and complex detail they embody and the non-linear manner in which various provisions located in different parts of the Credit Definitions must be read together for particular purposes, and rather than setting out commentary on each Article in sequence, this chapter instead considers, in a more intuitive fashion, the definition of the credit protection that is written, the declaration of a Credit Event, and the subsequent settlement of the Credit Derivative Transaction. A brief survey then follows of the various supplements and ancillary documents that have been published to accompany the Credit Definitions, and the various initiatives

---

[83] Investment banks in particular increasingly publish a variety of proprietary indices, the levels of which they publish on websites or through electronic news services.
[84] Herein, the 'Credit Definitions'. The Credit Definitions replaced the 1999 ISDA Credit Derivatives Definitions. See Parker, *Credit Derivatives: Documenting and Understanding Credit Derivative Products* (Globe Law and Business, 2007) for a useful and comprehensive survey of the credit derivative market and its documentation.
[85] Paragraph 4.168.

7.128 Article I sets out certain general definitions, and establishes that the Credit Definitions contain standard provisions in respect of Credit Derivative Transactions. By way of introduction, under the Credit Definitions, the Buyer of credit protection is the Fixed Rate Payer,[86] and the Seller of credit protection is the Floating Rate Payer. The Buyer makes payments of premium to buy the credit protection; these payments of premium are Fixed Amounts. The credit protection is written for a period referred to as the Term, which starts on the Effective Date and ends on the Termination Date.[87] Whereas the Effective Date is not generally subject to adjustment, unless the parties specify that the Effective Date can be moved, the Termination Date is the Scheduled Termination Date specified in the Confirmation, subject to adjustment in accordance with a number of provisions. The Term of the Credit Derivative Transaction is extended under certain circumstances, and these circumstances are examined in greater detail in the following paragraphs where relevant.

The credit protection that is written: Reference Entities and Obligations

7.129 Under a Credit Derivative Transaction, credit protection is written in respect of the credit risk projected by a Reference Entity,[88] and under the Credit Definitions a separate Credit Derivative Transaction is entered into in respect of each reference Entity. A Transaction may therefore comprise one or more Credit Derivative Transactions.[89] The credit risk projected by a Reference Entity is defined with reference to a Credit Event, and depending on the particular Credit Event specified in respect of a Credit Derivative Transaction, that credit risk is also defined with reference to one or more Obligations[90] of the Reference Entity for that Credit Derivative Transaction. Settlement of a Credit Derivative Transaction is effected either, if 'Cash Settlement' is specified, by the payment by the Seller to the Buyer

---

[86] Section 1.19.
[87] Section 1.3.
[88] A clear moral hazard emerges if the Buyer or the Seller under a Credit Derivative Transaction is also the Reference Entity of that Credit Derivative Transaction; such a Credit Derivative Transaction is referred to as a 'self-referencing' transaction. A range of difficulties arise, including clear conflicts of interest and the interposition of insolvency analysis. Indeed, Section 2.31 has the effect of bringing to an end a Credit Derivative Transaction the Reference Entity of which merges with the Seller under that Credit Derivative Transaction.
[89] Practitioners therefore find it necessary to provide in the Confirmation of a Transaction which transfers the credit risk projected by a portfolio of names that a separate Credit Derivative Transaction is deemed to be entered into in respect of each Reference Entity for certain purposes of the Credit Definitions, although other provisions function at the level of the overarching Transaction as a whole.
[90] Obligation is defined widely in Section 2.14 as any obligation of a Reference Entity, whether that Reference Entity owes that obligation as a debtor or as a guarantor.

of a Cash Settlement Amount, or, if 'Physical Settlement' is specified, by the payment by the Seller to the Buyer of a Physical Settlement Amount and the delivery by the Buyer to the Seller of Deliverable Obligations. Settlement is considered in greater detail in the following paragraphs.

Article II sets out the definitions which identify the Reference Entity underlying a Credit Derivative Transaction. A Reference Entity is[91] each entity specified as such in the Confirmation. Any Successor to a Reference Entity becomes and is treated as a Reference Entity, and therefore the scope of the credit protection that is written includes Successors. A broad variety of obligor qualify as Reference Entities, including sovereign obligors, such as states, political subdivisions, and governments, and agencies and other authorities variously described thereof,[92] including central banks, and non-sovereign obligors, such as trading companies in all commercial sectors, including the financial sector, and structured finance vehicles issuing structured debt. The occurrence of a Succession Event may result in one or more Successors of an original Reference Entity becoming a Reference Entity, whether replacing the original Reference Entity or becoming an additional Reference Entity alongside the original Reference Entity. The definition of Succession Event includes[93] a merger, consolidation, amalgamation, transfer of assets or liabilities, demerger, spin-off or other similar event in which one entity succeeds to the obligations of another, and clearly includes mergers and acquisitions activity, although such activity is strictly not relevant to a Sovereign. 7.130

The process for determining the Successor[94] of a Reference Entity which is not a Sovereign is formulaic, and follows a strict timetable which requires the collation of Best Available Information and an assessment of that information. The entities which succeed directly or indirectly to the original Reference Entity, and therefore which are Successors, are determined with reference to the percentage of the Relevant Obligations of the original Reference Entity succeeded to by these entities.[95] Generally, if one entity succeeds directly or indirectly to a sufficient percentage of the Relevant Obligations of the original Reference Entity, that entity is the sole Successor for the entire original Credit Derivative Transaction, which continues. If more than one entity each succeeds directly or indirectly to a sufficient percentage of the Relevant Obligations of the original Reference Entity, then each such entity is a Successor for a New Credit Derivative Transaction, and the original Credit Derivative Transaction ceases. If more than one entity each succeeds 7.131

---

[91] Section 2.1.
[92] Section 2.26.
[93] Section 2.2(b).
[94] See part 8.6 of Chapter 8 for a discussion of the development of the provisions for determining the Successor of a Reference Entity.
[95] Section 2.2(a).

directly or indirectly to a sufficient percentage of the Relevant Obligations of the original Reference Entity, and a sufficient percentage of the Relevant Obligations remains with the original Reference Entity, then each such entity and the original Reference Entity is each a Successor for a New Credit Derivative Transaction, and the original Credit Derivative Transaction ceases. No change is made to the original Credit Derivative Transaction if following a Succession Event the entity or entities succeeding to the Relevant Obligations of the original Reference Entity succeed to less than the stipulated percentage. The Relevant Obligations of a Reference Entity are the Obligations of that Reference Entity constituting Bonds[96] and Loans[97] and which are outstanding immediately prior to the effective date of the Succession Event.[98] The Calculation Agent determines each entity which succeeds to the relevant Obligations of the original Reference Entity on the basis of Best Available Information, and Section 2.2(g) sets out the type and quality of information which might amount to Best Available Information.

7.132 Considerably more latitude is allowed in the process for determining the Successor of a Reference Entity which is a Sovereign. Under Section 2.2(h), the Successor of a Reference Entity which is a Sovereign is 'any direct or indirect successor(s) to that Reference Entity irrespective of whether such successor(s) assumes any of the obligations of such Reference Entity'. The contemporary geopolitical landscape offers examples of a Sovereign being succeeded by other states, for example, the division of Yugoslavia into no less than seven new states, and this phenomenon therefore is a real possibility.

7.133 Article II also sets out the definitions which identify the Obligations of a Reference Entity in respect of which credit protection is written. Obligations are either Reference Obligations that are actually named or otherwise identified in the Confirmation,[99] or alternatively a set of criteria is specified in the Confirmation, and any obligation of the Reference Entity which fulfils the specified criteria is an Obligation.

7.134 Section 2.19 sets out the method for determining Obligations. The term 'Obligation' is generic within the Credit Definitions, and it is used to describe the obligations of the Reference Entity for various purposes within the Credit Definitions, including the definition of the credit risk that is transferred and the Deliverable Obligations which are relevant in the physical settlement of a Credit Derivative Transaction.[100] An obligation constitutes an Obligation under

---

[96] Bond is defined in Section 2.19(a)(iv).
[97] Loan is defined in Section 2.19(a)(v).
[98] Section 2.2(f).
[99] For example, an issue of debt securities which is to be treated as a Reference Obligation would be identified using its ISIN.
[100] See paragraphs 7.153 ff.

Section 2.19 if that obligation both falls within the Obligation Category that is specified in the Confirmation and exhibits the Obligation Characteristics that are specified in the Confirmation. Section 2.19(a) sets out the six Obligation Categories, only one of which is selected. Section 2.19(b) sets out the eight Obligation Characteristics, more than one of which may be selected, provided that the selections are conceptually consistent with each other. Conventions have emerged in the credit derivative markets as to the standards for writing credit protection, and the appropriate combination of Obligation Category and Obligation Characteristics for a particular Reference Entity is determined by that Reference Entity's geographical location in accordance with these conventions.

7.135 The Obligation Categories are: Payment, Borrowed Money, Reference Obligations Only, Bond, Loan, and Bond or Loan. The sensitivity of the Credit Derivative Transaction can be calibrated by selecting a wide or a narrow Obligation Category. For example, Payment is wide and includes any present, future, or contingent obligation to repay money. Payment is wider than Borrowed Money, because Payment includes debts that are incurred in any type of transaction or relationship, and not just under borrowings. Selection of the Reference Obligations Only category means that the Obligations under the Credit Derivative Transaction are only the obligations that are identified as Reference Obligations in the Confirmation. This is the most narrow category, as the list of Reference Obligations is definite with no scope for including any further obligations.

7.136 The Obligation Characteristics are: Not Subordinated, Specified Currency, Not Sovereign Lender, Not Domestic Currency, Not Domestic Law, Listed, and Not Domestic Issuance. In order to qualify as Not Subordinated, broadly a particular obligation must not be subordinated to the most senior obligation specified for this purpose in respect of the relevant Reference Entity, or if no such benchmark obligation is specified, then in order to qualify, that obligation must not be subordinated to any borrowed money obligation of the relevant Reference Entity. The actual definition of Not Subordinated is quite involved, and considers in detail the concept of Subordination. In order to qualify under Specified Currency, an obligation must be denominated in the currency or currencies specified for this purpose, although if no currency is specified, then that obligation must be denominated in the lawful currency of one of Canada, Japan, Switzerland, the United Kingdom, and the United States, and the euro, and any successor currency to any of them. In order to qualify under Not Sovereign Lender, an obligation must be owed to a creditor which is not a Sovereign or a Supranational Organization.[101] In order to qualify as Not Domestic Currency, an obligation must be denominated

---

[101] Supranational Organizations include the International Monetary Fund, the European Central Bank, the International Bank for Reconstruction and Development, and the European Bank for Reconstruction and Development.

in a currency other than the relevant Domestic Currency, which is either the currency specified for this purpose or, if no such currency is specified, the lawful currency of the Reference Entity (if the Reference Entity is a Sovereign) or the jurisdiction in which the Reference Entity is organized (if the Reference Entity is not a Sovereign). In order to qualify as Not Domestic Law, an obligation must be governed by laws other than the laws of the Reference Entity (if the Reference Entity is a Sovereign) or the jurisdiction in which the Reference Entity is organized (if the Reference Entity is not a Sovereign). In order to qualify as Listed, an obligation must be quoted, listed, or ordinarily purchased and sold on an exchange. In order to qualify as Not Domestic Issuance, an obligation must be issued, incurred, or intended to be offered for sale in a market other than the domestic market of the Reference Entity.

The credit protection that is written: Credit Events

7.137 Article IV sets out the Credit Events, one or more of which apply to a Credit Derivative Transaction. Six Credit Events are defined in Article IV, and these are: Bankruptcy, Failure to Pay, Obligation Acceleration, Obligation Default, Repudiation/Moratorium, and Restructuring. Section 4.1, in addition to identifying each event which constitutes a Credit Event, has the effect that these events will not be prevented from constituting a Credit Event even if particular circumstances exist; the effect of this qualification is that a party is less able to argue that a particular Credit Event did not occur, and therefore the analysis of whether or not an event constitutes a Credit Event should be rendered more predictable and therefore more certain. An event can still qualify as a Credit Event in respect of a Reference Entity and an Obligation of that Reference Entity notwithstanding any of the following: (1) the Reference Entity actually or allegedly lacks the authority or capacity to enter into the Obligation; (2) the Obligation is actually or allegedly unenforceable, illegal, impossible, or invalid; (3) that event amounts to a Credit Event as a result of any applicable law, order, regulation, decree or notice, or any judicial or administrative interpretation of the same; and (4) that event amounts to a Credit Event as a result of the imposition of any exchange control or capital restriction by any monetary authority or other authority.

7.138 Bankruptcy only applies to the Reference Entity and not to any Obligation of the Reference Entity. The definition of Bankruptcy in Section 4.2 is substantially similar to the definition of Bankruptcy in Section 5(a)(vii) of the ISDA 2002 Master Agreement.[102] The definition of Bankruptcy is drafted in broad terms in order to be able to capture the variations in insolvency laws in different jurisdictions, and yet the definition also seeks to filter out certain insolvency actions and proceedings

---

[102] See paragraph 7.41.

which do not culminate in an actual insolvency. A petition or proceeding for insolvency relief or the winding up or liquidation of the Reference Entity will only constitute a Credit Event if generally that petition or proceeding results in the actual judgment or order sought, or that petition or proceeding is not dismissed, discharged, stayed, or restrained within 30 calendar days of being made.

7.139 An Obligation Acceleration[103] occurs if an event of default occurs in respect of an Obligation, and consequently that Obligation is declared to be immediately due and payable. An Obligation Acceleration only occurs if the amount of the relevant Obligation subject to the acceleration is no less than the specified threshold, which is the Default Requirement. If no amount is specified as the Default Requirement, then the Default Requirement is US$10 million.[104]

7.140 An Obligation Default[105] occurs if an Obligation has become capable of being declared to be immediately due and payable. Again, an Obligation Default only occurs if the amount of the relevant Obligation subject to the default is no less than the Default Requirement. The test for an Obligation Default is more easily satisfied than the test for an Obligation Acceleration, and arguably Obligation Acceleration is the better indication of whether or not the credit risk projected by the relevant Reference Entity has crystallized, as an Obligation Default can be waived or cured, and therefore does not necessarily represent the actual quality or otherwise of the credit of the Reference Entity.

7.141 A Failure to Pay[106] occurs if the Reference Entity fails to make a payment under an Obligation. A Failure to Pay only occurs if the amount of the Obligation that the Reference Entity fails to pay is no less than the specified threshold, which is the Payment Requirement. If no amount is specified as the Payment Requirement, then the Payment Requirement is US$1 million.[107] A Failure to Pay only occurs if the Grace Period applicable to the Obligation has expired, and the applicable Grace Period is ascertained by working through Section 1.12. The applicable Grace Period is found in the documents of the Obligation. The effect of Section 1.12(a)(iii) is that a Grace Period lasts for at least three Grace Period Business Days.

7.142 A Repudiation/Moratorium[108] occurs if both a repudiation or a moratorium of an Obligation of the Reference Entity is declared by an authorized officer of the Reference Entity, and a Failure to Pay then occurs in respect of that Obligation. A repudiation of an Obligation is a statement that the Reference Entity no longer intends to meet that Obligation, and the declaration of a moratorium of an

---

[103] Section 4.3.
[104] Section 4.8(a).
[105] Section 4.4.
[106] Section 4.5.
[107] Section 4.8(d).
[108] Section 4.6.

Obligation is a statement that the Reference Entity intends to delay meeting that Obligation.

7.143 Some considerable, and almost impenetrable, detail is provided in Section 4.6 governing the circumstances in which the occurrence of a Potential Repudiation/Moratorium before the Scheduled Termination Date of a Credit Derivative Transaction has the effect of extending the duration of the Credit Derivative Transaction, provided that certain conditions have been satisfied. A Potential Repudiation/Moratorium is the initial declaration by the authorized officer on behalf of the Reference Entity of the intention to not pay under an Obligation or to delay making a payment under an Obligation. The sequence of events anticipated by Section 4.6 is as follows. First, the relevant initial declaration amounting to a potential event is made, before the Scheduled Termination Date of the relevant Credit Derivative Transaction. Second, a valid Repudiation/Moratorium Extension Notice, accompanied, if required under the relevant Confirmation, by a Notice of Publicly Available Information,[109] is served. Third, the determination is made whether an additional period of 14 calendar days following the Scheduled Termination Date is allowed; a Credit Event then occurs if the relevant Failure to Pay completing the potential event occurs during this additional period of 14 calendar days. This period of 14 calendar days is the Notice Delivery Period. The additional period is allowed if the Repudiation/Moratorium Evaluation Date that is determined in respect of the potential event occurs after the Scheduled Termination Date. The evaluation date is broadly the later of (1) 60 days following the date of the potential event; or (2) the first date on which a payment is due under the relevant Obligation, after reflecting any Grace Period. It is important to appreciate that this process extends by 14 days only the period for which credit protection is written, and only if the potential event which might develop into a Credit Event occurs sufficiently near to, but before, the Scheduled Termination Date. The date of the initial declaration of a repudiation or moratorium signifies that the credit risk projected by the Reference Entity seems likely to be worsening, and therefore it is appropriate that an additional 14 days after the Scheduled Termination Date is allowed in order to assess whether that potential event unfolds into the full Credit Event against which credit protection is written.

7.144 A Restructuring[110] occurs if the Reference Entity agrees with its relevant creditors to amend the terms of its Obligation, whether a reduction in the rate or amount of interest payable, a reduction in the amount of principal payable, a postponement of amounts payable, a change in the ranking in priority of payment obligations, or a change in the currency or composition of a payment. A Restructuring

---

[109] See paragraph 7.147.
[110] Section 4.7.

only occurs if the amount of the relevant Obligation subject to the Restructuring is no less than the specified threshold, which is the Default Requirement. The Default Requirement for Restructuring is the same as that for Obligation Acceleration. A Restructuring does not occur if one of three possible exceptions applies: (1) payment in euros is made in satisfaction of an Obligation denominated in the currency of a member state of the European Union that has adopted the single currency; (2) the relevant agreement reached with creditors is due to an administrative adjustment, accounting adjustment, tax adjustment, or other technical adjustment, made in the ordinary course of business; or (3) the relevant agreement does not arise directly or indirectly from a deterioration in the creditworthiness or financial condition of the Reference Entity.

7.145 Whether or not an agreement to amend the terms of an Obligation should amount to a Credit Event has proved to be controversial, as the purpose of a restructuring or a rescheduling of debt is to enable the debtor to overcome a short-term inability to pay its debts, on the basis that it should be able to pay its debts in the longer term, that is, the debtor's long-term prospects are good. The question therefore arises, does a restructuring properly constitute the credit risk in respect of which protection is written under the Credit Derivative Transaction? Conceptually, there is a strong argument that it should not, as the creditors who allow and agree to the restructuring are demonstrating their belief that the debtor is fundamentally sound. Indeed, given the third of the exceptions to the occurrence of a Restructuring noted above, the intention of the definition is to capture deteriorations in the Reference Entity's creditworthiness. The credit derivative market itself is uncertain as to the treatment of restructurings, and therefore variations of the Restructuring event have been developed: the basic Restructuring under Section 4.7, the 'modified Restructuring' under Section 4.7 and Section 2.32, and the 'modified modified Restructuring' under Section 2.33. Unfortunately, the Credit Definitions do not actually use these labels, which are applied in the credit derivative market as shorthand.[111] The different approaches to Restructuring have emerged in response to the conceptual difficulties that the credit derivative market experienced with Restructuring.

7.146 Article V provides for Fixed Amounts, which are the payments made by way of premium to pay for the credit protection written under the Credit Derivative Transaction. The price of credit protection is generally expressed as a percentage of the notional amount of credit risk underlying the Credit Derivative Transaction. Accordingly, the provisions governing the calculation and payment of Fixed Amounts resemble those for the calculation and payment of interest,[112] hence

---

[111] See paragraph 7.154. The evolution of credit derivative documentation is also considered in greater depth in part 8.6 of Chapter 8.
[112] See paragraphs 7.183 ff.

concepts such as the Day Count Fraction become important; the price of the credit protection, or the Fixed Rate, is substituted for the interest rate.

Observing Credit Events

7.147 Leaving aside the intricate contractual definition of each Credit Event, the actual observation of the events or circumstances which might fall within the definition of a Credit Event are of intrinsic importance. The observations for the purposes of a derivative transaction that is linked to a rate or a price are easily made; the contractual counterparties often have access to market data supplying the minute-by-minute changes in the relevant data population underlying the transaction, and payments under the transaction are calculated from that data population. Potential difficulties only arise in the interpretation of the events or circumstances which change the nature or quality of the underlying asset or rate. By contrast, the very observation of the events or circumstances that are claimed to constitute a Credit Event under a Credit Derivative Transaction can give rise to difficulties. These difficulties are compounded by the fact that credit risk can be priced and traded through the use of credit derivatives by parties which have no connection with the actual obligors and their obligations which project that risk. Accordingly, the Credit Definitions use the concept of Publicly Available Information[113] to reinforce the process by which the occurrence of a Credit Event is declared by one party and that declaration is accepted by the other party. Publicly Available Information is information 'that reasonably confirms any of the facts relevant to the determination that the Credit Event or Potential Repudiation/Moratorium, as applicable ... has occurred'. In order to qualify as Publicly Available Information, information must be published in no less than the particular number of Public Sources of information specified in the Confirmation. A Public Source of information is defined broadly[114] as any internationally recognized published or electronically displayed news source, and the definition sets out a number of examples (this list is not exhaustive). The Confirmation of a Credit Derivative Transaction will specify whether or not a party wishing to claim that a Credit Event or a Potential Repudiation/Moratorium has occurred is required to provide a Notice of Publicly Available Information in support of that claim; given that the information is available to the public, a citation or reference to the information in the notice is sufficient. The Confirmation will also specify the number of Public Sources of information that is required. If no number is specified, then the number is two.

---

[113] Section 3.5.
[114] Section 3.7.

Settlement

7.148 Article III provides for the Conditions to Settlement. The effect of Section 3.1 is that the settlement of a Credit Derivative Transaction occurs upon the occurrence of a Credit Event and the satisfaction in full of all of the Conditions to Settlement with respect to such Credit Derivative Transaction. The Conditions to Settlement comprise delivery of the required notices within the required timetable. A party wishing to declare that a Credit Event has occurred serves a valid Credit Event Notice on the other party. Either party or both parties may have the right to serve a Credit Event Notice. The Credit Event Notice[115] is irrevocable but it may be made by telephone (although clearly a written notice is preferable), and it must be served within the specified times. The party declaring that a Credit Event has occurred may also be required to serve a Notice of Publicly Available Information, citing the required number of Public Sources. If Physical Settlement applies to the Credit Derivative Transaction, then the Buyer of the credit protection is required to deliver to the Seller a Notice of Physical Settlement. The main purpose of the Notice of Physical Settlement[116] is the notification by the Buyer to the Seller of the Deliverable Obligations that the Buyer proposes to Deliver to the Seller as part of the settlement of the Credit Derivative Transaction. Physical settlement is discussed at paragraph 7.153.

Cash settlement

7.149 Article VII provides for cash settlement. The cash settlement[117] of a Credit Derivative Transaction is effected by the payment by the Seller to the Buyer of a Cash Settlement Amount on the Cash Settlement Date. The Cash Settlement Amount[118] is either an amount that is specified as such in the Confirmation, or it is the Floating Rate Payer Calculation Amount multiplied by the result of the Reference Price minus the Final Price. In general terms, the Seller is the Floating Rate Payer, and the Floating Rate Payer Calculation Amount is the notional amount of credit risk underlying the Credit Derivative Transaction. The Reference Price is effectively the initial price of the Reference Obligation on the Effective Date of the Credit Derivative Transaction, and the Final Price is effectively the price of the Reference Obligation after the occurrence of the relevant Credit Event. The decrease in the price of the Reference Obligation from the Reference Price to the Final Price is assumed to be attributed to the occurrence of the Credit Event, and multiplying the amount of this decrease by the notional amount of the underlying credit risk derives the quantification of the loss against which

---

[115] Section 3.3.
[116] Section 3.4.
[117] Section 7.1.
[118] Section 7.3.

protection is written under the Credit Derivative Transaction. This calculation meshes with the calculation of the premium paid by the Buyer to acquire the credit protection that is written.[119]

7.150   One subtlety to be aware of is that although the test for whether or not a Credit Event occurs is assessed with reference to an Obligation of the Reference Entity, the calculation of the Cash Settlement Amount is made with reference to the change in the price of a Reference Obligation of the Reference Entity.

7.151   Article VII sets out a variety of methods[120] by which the Final Price of the Reference Obligation is discovered by the Calculation Agent; these are too numerous to discuss fully, but each method of calculation is predicated on the Calculation Agent obtaining the required number of quotations for the Reference Obligation from independent dealers which customarily buy and sell obligations of the relevant type, in order that the valuation process is as objective as possible. Crucially, quotations are not obtained from either party or an Affiliate of a party. Depending on the method of calculation that is used, the Final Price might be the highest of the quotations obtained or an unweighted arithmetic mean of the quotations obtained. Further, the quotations sought might be bids, offers, or mid-market quotations. Further, the Calculation Agent solicits quotations for an appropriate amount of the Reference Obligation; this is the Minimum Quotation Amount. The parties either specify the amount of the Reference Obligation in respect of which quotations should be sought, or the amount is generally the lower of US$1 million and the notional amount of underlying credit risk. It is therefore evident that a method of calculation which yields a higher Final Price will generate a lower Cash Settlement Amount, and this should be in the contemplation of a party negotiating the method of calculation which will apply; a Buyer will favour a method which yields a lower Final Price, and the Seller will favour a method which yields a higher Final Price.

7.152   The Reference Obligation is valued on one or more Valuation Dates. Either a single Valuation Date is used to obtain the required quotations, or a series of consecutive Valuation Dates is used. The Valuation Date is the date which occurs a specified number of Business Days following the date when all the Conditions to Settlement have been satisfied. Satisfaction of the applicable Conditions to Settlement connotes that both a Credit Event has occurred and sufficient supporting evidence has been provided. The purpose of the delay between the satisfaction of the applicable Conditions to Settlement and the start of the valuation of the Reference Obligation is to allow the market for the Reference Obligation to settle in the aftermath of the occurrence of the events or circumstances which gave

---

[119] See paragraph 7.146.
[120] Section 7.5.

rise to the Credit Event; in the immediate aftermath, the market for the Reference Obligation would be operating with imperfect information, and any valuation obtained would therefore be considered to be extremely unreliable. Indeed, rating agencies which rate synthetic CDO issues[121] generally require a considerable delay between satisfaction of the applicable Conditions to Settlement and the start of the valuation process.

Physical settlement

7.153 Article VIII provides for physical settlement. The physical settlement[122] of a Credit Derivative Transaction is effected by the payment by the Seller to the Buyer of a Physical Settlement Amount on the Cash Settlement Date, and the delivery by the Buyer to the Seller of the Deliverable Obligations specified in the Notice of Physical Settlement previously served by the Buyer on the Seller as a part of the Conditions to Settlement. Delivery of the Deliverable Obligations is made on or before the Physical Settlement Date. The Physical Settlement Amount[123] is the Floating Rate Payer Calculation Amount multiplied by the Reference Price; again, the Floating Rate Payer Calculation Amount is the notional amount of credit risk underlying the Credit Derivative Transaction, and the Reference Price is effectively the initial price of the Deliverable Obligation on the Effective Date of the Credit Derivative Transaction. Receipt of the Physical Settlement Amount therefore puts the Buyer in the financial position it would have been in had the events or circumstances which gave rise to the Credit Event not occurred. Receipt of the Deliverable Obligations puts the Seller in the position of being able to retrieve some value from those Deliverable Obligations, whether through a sale or through ranking as a creditor. The Deliverable Obligations that the Buyer delivers to the Seller are Obligations of the Reference Entity that are determined in accordance with the provisions of Section 2.20. The basic scheme of Section 2.20 is the same as that of Section 2.19[124], differing in that an obligation constitutes a Deliverable Obligation under Section 2.20 if that obligation both falls within the particular Deliverable Obligation Category that is specified in the Confirmation and exhibits one or more of the Deliverable Obligation Characteristics specified in the Confirmation. Although the definitions of the six Deliverable Obligation Categories are materially the same as the definitions of the six Obligation Categories, there are 15 categories of Deliverable Obligation Characteristics.[125]

---

[121] See paragraphs 4.183 ff.
[122] Section 8.1.
[123] Section 8.5.
[124] See paragraph 7.134.
[125] Not Subordinated, Specified Currency, Not Sovereign Lender, Not Domestic Currency, Not Domestic Law, Listed, Not Contingent, Not Domestic Issuance, Assignable Loan, Consent Required Loan, Direct Loan Participation, Transferable, Maximum Maturity, Accelerated or Matured, and Not Bearer.

7.154 Section 2.32 and Section 2.33 further qualify the obligations that are eligible to be Deliverable Obligations. These two sections reflect the divergent responses to the Restructuring Credit Event.[126] Broadly, under Section 2.32, selection of 'Restructuring Maturity Limitation and Fully Transferable Obligation Applicable' has the result that an obligation only qualifies as a Deliverable Obligation for the purposes of physically settling a Credit Derivative Transaction, the only Credit Event of which is a Restructuring, if it exhibits the characteristic of being capable of being transferred without any contractual, statutory, or regulatory restriction and has a final maturity date not later than the latest final maturity date of the restructured obligation, subject to a longstop of 30 months following the date on which the restructuring is legally effective. Broadly, under Section 2.33, selection of 'Modified Restructuring Maturity Limitation and Conditionally Transferable Obligation Applicable' has the result that an obligation only qualifies as a Deliverable Obligation for the purposes of physically settling a Credit Derivative Transaction, the only Credit Event of which is a Restructuring, if it exhibits the characteristic of generally being capable of being transferred without the consent of any person and has a final maturity date not later than the final maturity date of the restructured obligation, again subject to a longstop of 30 months following the date on which the restructuring is legally effective. An obligation will qualify as a Deliverable Obligation for these purposes even if the consent of the Reference Entity or a guarantor is required for its transfer, provided that the obligation is not a bond and provided that its terms stipulate that the required consent may not be unreasonably withheld or delayed.

7.155 Other provisions of Article IX, the Partial Cash Settlement Terms, anticipate that the Buyer may experience difficulties in delivering the Deliverable Obligations to the Seller, or that the Seller may experience difficulties in taking delivery from the Buyer, under which circumstances the Credit Derivative Transaction is settled only partially through a delivery and partially through the payment of a Cash Settlement Amount.

Novation

7.156 Article X contains novation provisions. These provisions constitute a framework for the transfer of a Credit Derivative Transaction through a novation of the rights and the obligations under that Credit Derivative Transaction, by one of the original parties to a person wishing to assume the position of the transferring party. As the foregoing paragraphs intimate, credit derivative transactions are so heavily reliant on a complex of interlocking and highly technical contractual terms, and

---

[126] See paragraph 7.145.

many elections and variables, that in order to safely transfer a credit derivative position a contractual novation is required, under which the transferring party is replaced entirely in the contract by the person wishing to buy that credit derivative position. The novation agreement used is based on the 2002 ISDA Novation Agreement.

2005 Matrix Supplement

Although the following paragraph identifies in broad terms the many additions that have been made to the standard ISDA credit derivatives documentation, one such addition in particular merits individual discussion as it adds a new Article to the Credit Definitions. The 2005 Matrix Supplement adds a new Article XI to the Credit Definitions, which sets out the elections that should apply in respect of certain Reference Entities under Credit Derivative Transactions for which Physical Settlement applies as the relevant Settlement Method. The 2005 Matrix Supplement is effectively a contractual means of bringing within the scope of a Credit Derivative Transaction the applicable physical settlement matrix. Article XI, as inserted into the Credit Definitions by the 2005 Matrix Supplement, imports into a Confirmation the most recent version of the applicable physical settlement matrix. Physical settlement matrices are tables of the elections that should apply in respect of the physical settlement of Credit Derivative Transactions written on Reference Entities incorporated or otherwise organized in various jurisdictions, and represents the standards that have emerged in respect of those Reference Entities and their geographical locations. The physical settlement matrices are published on ISDA's website. Article XI also contains a 60 business day cap on physical settlement, with the effect that the physical settlement of a Credit Derivative Transaction is aborted if it is not successful 60 Business Days following the applicable Physical Settlement Date, whereupon an alternative process based on cash settlement is substituted.

7.157

Closing remarks

As a postscript to this necessarily brief introduction to the Credit Definitions, the observation is made that the heavy reliance on contractual construction and the ongoing development of the credit derivative market has prompted the publication of several supplements and addenda to the Credit Definitions, the details of which are outside the scope of this treatment. Certain supplements and addenda are published to provide more certainty as to the various transaction processes,[127]

7.158

---

[127] For example, see the May 2003 Supplement to the 2003 ISDA Credit Derivatives Definitions, and the various supplements which provide for certain obligors, such as the Russian Federation (13 August 2004) and the Republic of Hungary (14 February 2005).

whereas other supplements and addenda are published in response to the development of new products.[128] The objective of other market initiatives is to standardize the definition and transfer of the credit risk projected by certain categories of name. This process of standardization is achieved through the publication of the standard specifications to be made in a Confirmation[129] and the assembly of databases[130] to ensure that market participants include correct information in their contracts. The purpose of all of these innovations is to promote contractual certainty, which arguably is often compromised by the sheer complexity and therefore unpredictability of the contracts themselves, and by the practicalities of the asset class underlying the market, and the need for accurate and consistent information. The countervailing argument might be mustered that the crystallization of credit risk represents an interface between contractual construction, which inevitably entails a degree of subjectivity, and the observation of objective market data, as contrasted with the crystallization of the market or price risk that underlies other types of derivative contract, which depends purely on movements in numerical data which are capable of purely objective observation. Accordingly, it is inevitable that the contractual transfer of credit risk is both intricate and susceptible to nuance and development, and the innovation of databases to record and track market developments and standards, as well as growing experience with the operation of the relevant contractual provisions themselves, should enable the credit derivative market to mature into an ever more commoditized pool of investment opportunities. It is to be remembered that credit risk as a discrete asset class has, as at 2008, been available for but 15 years or so, and has demonstrated remarkable and resilient growth in that short period.

---

[128] For example, see the various supplements which provide for new types of underlying obligation, such as loan participation notes (21 December 2005), asset-backed securities (8 December 2006), US municipal debt issuers, leveraged loans (12 March 2008), and the various supplements which amend the physical settlement process in order to accommodate the practicalities of sourcing and delivering the relevant Deliverable Obligations, such as the template letter agreement relating to a 60 business day cap on settlement. This latter template letter agreement is particularly important, as it permits market counterparties to bring to an end an abortive physical settlement exercise; the 2005 Matrix Supplement (see paragraph 7.157) also contains a 60 business day cap on settlement. Other supplements provide for new structures of credit derivative transaction, such as constant maturity credit default swaps (21 November 2005).

[129] For example, see the 2005 Matrix Supplement (which is introduced at paragraph 7.157).

[130] For example, the Markit organization provides data and various services to the credit derivative industry, and the data it provides includes data on reference names and lists of their obligations; Markit's databases are accessed by investment banks, hedge funds, and asset managers, amongst others, and introduce a bedrock of certainty.

7.10 2005 ISDA Commodity Definitions[131]

Although the term 'commodity' connotes a physical asset, such as agricultural produce, a chemical, or base and precious metals, the term in the context of the derivative markets has increasingly been held to include intangibles such as generated energy, freight prices, and now emission rights. Part 4.14 of Chapter 4 introduces freight derivatives[132] and carbon trading.[133] Whether derivative contracts written on these classes of underlying should be categorized as commodity derivatives or as something else remains a conceptual moot point. Nonetheless, the practice of market participants is that derivative contracts written on such classes of underlying fall within the broad taxonomy of commodity derivatives, perhaps because these and other classes of commodity are all manifestations of the physical world and human interaction with it and exploitation of it. Indeed, the internal organization of the trading and sales departments of investment banks currently tends to be predicated on this broad definition of a commodity. Accordingly, Section 1.1 contains a broad definition of Transaction, which includes familiar derivative structures written on diverse classes of underlying including weather statistics, various forms of energy, emissions allowances, and freight prices.

7.159

Article I also sets out other general definitions, including making provision for barrier transactions. The definitions for Knock-in Event and Knock-out Event in Section 1.9 and Section 1.10 respectively echo the analogous provisions found in the Equity Definitions,[134] and these features operate in the same manner, in that a particular advantageous payout only becomes available if a specified Knock-in Event occurs, and conversely, a particular advantageous payout only remains available if a specified Knock-out Event does not occur.

7.160

Article II identifies the parties to a Transaction. The Fixed Price Payer[135] is the party which makes payments from time to time that are either of amounts that are calculated with reference to a fixed price or are specified to be Fixed Amounts, and the Floating Price Payer[136] is the party which makes payments from time to time that are either of amounts that are calculated with reference to a floating price or are specified to be Floating Amounts.

7.161

---

[131] Herein, the 'Commodity Definitions'. The Commodity Definitions replaced the 1993 ISDA Commodity Derivatives Definitions, as supplemented by the 2000 Supplement to the 1993 Definitions. The 1997 ISDA Bullion Definitions have also been consolidated into the Commodity Definitions.
[132] See paragraphs 4.205 ff.
[133] See paragraphs 4.219 ff.
[134] See paragraph 7.98.
[135] Section 2.1.
[136] Section 2.2.

7.162 Article III provides for the term and dates of a Transaction. Familiar concepts are used. The Effective Date[137] is the date when exposures created under the Transaction start, and when the rights conferred under the Transaction are available, subject to the interaction of any Knock-in Event or Knock-out Event. Exposures and rights generally come to an end on the Termination Date,[138] and the Expiration Date[139] is the last day on which rights conferred under an Option can be exercised. If the Termination Date or the Expiration Date is specified to occur on a day which is not a Commodity Business Day, then it is adjusted so that it does occur on a Commodity Business Day, which is broadly[140] a day on which the relevant underlying market is scheduled to be open for trading during its regular trading session. The Expiration Date is also capable of being adjusted so that it does not occur on a day on which the relevant underlying market is disrupted. Again, in common with the Equity Definitions, the general scheme of the Commodity Definitions is that prices and values discovered in the relevant underlying market are the prices and values that are used to determine whether or not any threshold has been reached and to calculate the amounts payable under the Transaction. The underlying markets tend to be markets on which the relevant commodity is traded either on a spot basis for immediate delivery or under an exchange-based futures or options contract. The contractual terms which achieve the link between the relevant underlying market and the Transaction are fairly intricate, as the following paragraphs indicate.

7.163 Article IV sets out certain definitions relating to payments. The amounts of the payments are determined in accordance with Article V, for Fixed Amounts, and with Article VI, for Floating Amounts. However, both Fixed Amounts and Floating Amounts are calculated with reference to a Calculation Period and a Notional Quantity of the underlying. Under Article V, the Fixed Amount for a particular Calculation Period is the Notional Quantity for that Calculation Period multiplied by the Fixed Price, and under Article VI, the Floating Amount for a particular Calculation Period is the Notional Quantity for that Calculation Period multiplied by the Floating Price. Article VI also gives effect to cap and floor structures[141] by providing[142] that the Floating Price is the excess of the price discovered in the relevant underlying market over the specified cap price, and that the Floating Price is the excess of the specified floor price over the price discovered in the relevant underlying market. In this respect, the Commodity Definitions operate in the same manner as the Rates Definitions, which are discussed below.

---

[137] Section 3.2.
[138] Section 3.4.
[139] Section 3.6.
[140] Section 1.4.
[141] See part 4.8 of Chapter 4.
[142] Section 6.2(a).

Although the Commodity Definitions can be used to document a variety of Commodity-based structures, such as forwards and swaps, the Commodity Definitions represent a departure from the approach of the Equity Definitions in that the Commodity Definitions do not contain rigid definitions giving effect to such structures; instead, broad concepts are provided.

Commodity Reference Price

7.164 Article VII provides for the calculation of prices for Commodity Reference Prices. The purpose of Article VII is to import into a Transaction the prices that are discovered in the relevant underlying market, and to ensure certainty in the event that the underlying market suffers a disruption which prevents the discovery of reliable data. The actual price discovered in the relevant underlying market, that is, the price that is used in the calculation of the Fixed Amount or the Floating Amount payable under a Transaction, is the Relevant Price. Broadly any published price can be used to determine the Relevant Price of a Commodity, including in many instances the price of exchange-based futures contracts on that Commodity. The Commodity Definitions provide a detailed framework within which the Relevant Price of a particular Commodity is determined, with reference to factors such as (1) the identity of the Commodity itself; (2) the Unit by which quantities of the Commodity are measured, and therefore by which prices are quoted; (3) the Price Source, which is the organization, whether or not an exchange or a publisher of news or other market information, which disseminates prices; (4) the Relevant Currency in which prices are quoted; (5) the Specified Price, which is the type of price that is used to determine the Relevant Price, such as the spot price of the Commodity or the settlement price of an exchange-based Futures Contract; and (6) other relevant information such as the Delivery Date of a Futures Contract that is used. Of course, more or less information might be required for a particular Transaction. For example, the Commodity Reference Price for a Transaction linked to the price of copper might be the price of a particular copper Futures Contract traded on a specified exchange. The Price Source might be the exchange on which that Futures Contract is dealt, such as the London Metal Exchange. The Relevant Currency might be US dollars. The Specified Price for the purposes of the Transaction might then be the daily Settlement Price of that Futures Contract. The Delivery Date might be specified to be 'first Nearby Month'.[143]

---

[143] Section 7.2, which is located in the Annex to the Commodity Definitions, sets out rules to determine which particular Futures Contract is used. If 'first Nearby Month' is specified, then under the definitions set out in Section 7.2(c), the Relevant Price on a particular Pricing Date is the price of the particular futures contract the Delivery Date of which is the first to occur following that Pricing Date.

Chapter 7: Risk and the OTC Market

7.165 Section 7.2(c)(v), which is located in the Annex to the Commodity Definitions, sets out the Commodity Reference Price Framework, which is a format for the specification of the information required, and the parties select whether or not they use it.

7.166 The conventions of the relevant market determine the information that is required, and these conventions have in turn informed the relevant specifications that are made in the Annex. The Annex comprises a substantial volume of information detailing the various Commodities, the relevant sources of market data applicable to them, and the manner in which prices are quoted and therefore imported into a Transaction. The Commodity Definitions also allow for a more flexible description of the relevant underlying market data to be set out in a Confirmation, by recognizing that the documentation for a Transaction may not necessarily use the terms 'Commodity Reference Price', 'Relevant Price', or any of the many terms used in the Annex to the Commodity Definitions; for example, a Confirmation may simply state that the Floating Price is the price quoted for a particular commodity by a particular Price Source.

7.167 Section 7.1 links the body of the Commodity Definitions with the Annex to the Commodity Definitions, and together Section 7.1 and the Annex identify the Commodity Reference Price of a substantial number of underlying Commodities. The Annex is therefore expected to be updated from time to time. Section 7.2 also links the body of the Commodity Definitions with the Annex, and sets out certain definitions relating to Commodity Reference Prices. The Annex is divided into Sub-Annexes, each of which forms an integral part of the Commodity Definitions and identifies the Commodity Reference Prices.[144]

7.168 Section 7.3 anticipates that the person who publishes the Relevant Price of a Commodity may correct that price. If a Relevant Price is corrected within 30 calendar days of its original publication, or 90 days in the case of a Weather Index Derivative Transaction, then either party may notify the other of the correction and require payment of any additional amount payable as a result of the correction, together with interest.

7.169 Section 7.4 sets out the process by which a Relevant Price is obtained in the event of the occurrence of a Market Disruption Event or an Additional Market Disruption Event. The parties specify which Market Disruption Events apply to their Transaction, out of a list of six defined in Section 7.4(c): a Price Source

---

[144] Sub-Annex A provides for agricultural products, energy, freight, metals, papers, and composite commodity indices, Sub-Annex B provides for Bullion Transactions, Sub-Annex C provides for various structures of weather index derivatives transactions, Sub-Annex D provides for physical gas transactions in Europe, Sub-Annex E provides for physical gas transactions in North America, Sub-Annex F provides for electricity and other energy products in North America, Sub-Annex G provides for electricity and other energy products in England, Sub-Annex H provides for emissions allowance trading, and Sub-Annex I provides for Freight Transactions.

Disruption, a Trading Disruption, a Disappearance of Commodity Reference Price, a Material Change in Formula, a Material Change in Content, and a Tax Disruption. Section 7.4(d) sets out the Market Disruption Events that are deemed to apply to a Transaction if the parties do not specify any. The parties may find that the choices of Market Disruption Event set out in Section 7.4 are inadequate to address the particular risks or concerns that they have in respect of their Transaction, and therefore they are able to define an Additional Market Disruption Event. The Market Disruption Events address the potential difficulties that may arise in respect of any derivative transaction, including the risk that the provision of underlying market data by the Price Source is temporarily or permanently discontinued, the risk that a party to the Transaction is no longer able to hedge the exposures it assumes by entering into the Transaction, and the risk that the underlying of the Transaction undergoes a change or modification of sufficient magnitude that the economic basis of the Transaction changes. There is some overlap in the Market Disruption Events defined in Section 4.7(c). For example, the price of a particular exchange-based Futures Contract in respect of the relevant Commodity of a Transaction might be used to determine the Floating Amounts payable under the Transaction, and the Floating Price Payer might also trade in that Futures Contract to hedge the exposures it assumes by entering into the Transaction. A suspension in the trading in that Futures Contract would have two distinct effects on the Transaction: the calculation of Floating Amounts would no longer be possible, and the Floating Price Payer would lose its ability to hedge its exposures.

7.170 Section 7.5 sets out the consequences which follow the occurrence of a Market Disruption Event. In general terms, the particular Disruption Fallback that the parties specify will apply to the occurrence of a Market Disruption Event either indicates an alternative basis for determining the Relevant Price or results in the termination of the Transaction. The parties specify which Disruption Fallbacks apply to their Transaction, out of a list of seven defined in Section 7.5(d): Fallback Reference Dealers, Fallback Reference Price, Negotiated Fallback, No Fault Termination, Postponement, Calculation Agent Determination, and Delayed Publication or Announcement. Section 7.5(d) sets out the Disruption Fallbacks that are deemed to apply to a Transaction, and the order in which they are to be applied, if the parties do not specify any. Two of the Disruption Fallbacks, Fallback Reference Price and Calculation Agent Determination, rely on the discretion of the Calculation Agent to determine the Relevant Price. Of the two Disruption Fallbacks, the former allows the Calculation Agent less of a discretion, in that any determination the Calculation Agent makes should be based on an alternative Commodity Reference Price that is specified for that purpose in the Confirmation, and therefore this particular Disruption Fallback might be more appropriate if there is some sensitivity as to the extent of the discretion that a Calculation Agent should be permitted. Under Postponement, the relevant Pricing Date that is affected by the occurrence of the Market Disruption Event is delayed to the first succeeding day which is not affected by that occurrence, subject to a longstop number of days specified for that purpose in the Confirmation. The purpose of such a longstop is to promote certainty, and if the longstop is reached and no Relevant Price has been determined, then the next Disruption Fallback applies, curtailing an abortive attempt to obtain the Relevant Price. Crucially, postponement of a Pricing Date results in the postponement of other dates in the Transaction's timetable, including the Settlement Date or the Payment Date. By contrast, under Delayed Publication or Announcement, the Pricing Date affected by the Market Disruption Event, and therefore the other dates in the Transaction's timetable, remain as originally specified, but the Relevant Price that is applied in respect of that Pricing Date is the price or level that is published by the relevant Price Source retrospectively. Again, this process is subject to a longstop number of days specified for that purpose in the Confirmation, and if the longstop is reached, and no Relevant Price has been determined, then the next Disruption Fallback applies. Whether Postponement or Delayed Publication or Announcement is suitable for a particular Transaction depends on purely practical matters; Postponement would not be appropriate where the parties wish to adhere to the timetable they originally set for their Transaction, whereas Delayed Publication or Announcement would not be appropriate where the practice of the relevant Price Source is to not publish prices or levels retrospectively for the particular Pricing Date that has been affected.

7.171 As a general observation, although the overall processes embedded in the Commodity Definitions are substantially the same as those embedded in the Equity Definitions,[145] the Commodity Definitions permit greater flexibility than the Equity Definitions, and allow the parties to specify a series of fallbacks to disruptions, which operate concurrently.[146] Again, whether the parties favour making an attempt to preserve their Transaction, or bringing their Transaction to an end, with the payment of an appropriate close-out amount, is a matter for commercial negotiation and imperative.

---

[145] See paragraphs 7.112 ff.

[146] The Commodity Definitions differ in one subtle way from other sets of definitions. Although the Commodity Definitions address contingencies which may affect how a valuation is obtained, including disruptions to the various markets in which commodities and commodity futures are traded, there is no concept in the Commodity Definitions of a disruption to a commodity itself. Unlike financial assests, which can disappear or be altered through special events such as corporate actions or mergers and acquisitions activity, requiring a response under the derivative contract, commodities themselves are generally not expected to disappear or change, other than, of course, the eventual depletion of non-renewable natural resources such as fossil fuels.

Commodity Option

Article VIII provides for Commodity Options. Familiar concepts are used, such as Commodity Option Buyer, Commodity Option Seller, and the basic transaction structures distinguishing options by style; hence Section 8.3 defines the manner in which rights under American Options, Asian Options, Bermuda Options, and European Options can be exercised, and distinguishes between a Call Option and a Put Option.[147] However, two important aspects of Article XIII should be noted. One, Article VIII introduces the Swaption, which is an option contract written on an underlying swap contract.[148] Exercise of the right conferred by the option piece causes the rights conferred by the swap piece to become effective, and therefore exercise of a Swaption by the buyer is said to put the buyer into a swap contract with the seller. Two, Article VIII does not generally anticipate the physical settlement of Commodity Options; instead, following exercise, Commodity Options are settled by the payment of a difference determined with reference to the Strike Price Differential. However, a Swaption can be settled physically; in the context of a Swaption, physical settlement of the option piece connotes that the rights and obligations under the swap piece become effective, and does not connote any delivery of the Commodity underlying the structure. Section 8.5 contains the terms relating to exercise, and Section 8.6 contains the terms relating to the premium that is paid by the Commodity Option Buyer; the amount of the premium that is paid is expressed either as one amount that is payable or as an amount per Unit of the Notional Quantity. Section 8.7 provides for the calculation of the Cash Settlement Amount, which as mentioned incorporates the concept of the Strike Price Differential, and the manner of the calculation of the Strike Price Differential depends on whether the Commodity Option is a Call or a Put. **7.172**

Article IX sets out a convention for the rounding of numbers expressing monetary amounts, for Fixed Amounts, Floating Amounts, and Cash Settlement Amounts only. Monetary amounts are rounded to the nearest 'unit' of the relevant currency, and halves are rounded up. A 'unit' is the lowest amount of the relevant currency which is available as legal tender in the country of such currency. **7.173**

Articles X, XI, XII, XIII, XIV, XV, XVI, and XVII provide links to the various relevant Sub-Annexes of the Commodity Definitions for the purposes of, respectively, Bullion Transactions, Weather Index Derivative Transactions, physically-settled European Gas Transactions, physically-settled North American Gas Transactions, physically-settled GTMA Transactions, EU Emissions Allowance Transactions, and Freight Transactions. **7.174**

---

[147] See paragraph 7.100 for a description of these variations of option in the context of the Equity Definitions. The operation of these variations of option remains the same notwithstanding the underlying.
[148] Section 8.1(b).

7.11 2006 ISDA Definitions[149]

7.175 The Rates Definitions represent the latest iteration of the basic set of definitions which provide the basic framework for interest rate and currency derivative transactions. The Rates Definitions can be used for other types of transaction; for example, the structure of an equity derivative transaction or a commodity derivative transaction might include the payment of interest, and therefore the Rates Definitions would be used alongside the Equity Definitions or the Commodity Definitions to provide the necessary definitions for those interest payments.[150] The Rates Definitions are voluminous, and much of their extent is taken up by identifying the conventions specific to the various interest rate and currency markets, such as the abbreviations that are used to denote particular currencies, the financial centres that are linked with particular currencies, and the pages on electronic data vendor systems on which particular interest rates and currency rates are published.

7.176 Article 1 sets out certain general definitions. The Rates Definitions cover a spectrum of transaction structures, comprising the Swap Transaction, the Mark-to-market Currency Swap, the Option Transaction, the Swaption, and the Swaption Straddle. As the following paragraphs demonstrate, these structures represent permutations on the basic swap structure, hence the Rates Definitions are also referred to as the 'Swap Definitions' by some market participants. These structures have been traded in the OTC rates and currencies derivative markets for a number of years, and the Rates Definitions represent a certain formalizing of these structures. These structures rely on a set of core concepts and definitions, which are examined first, and then some detail is provided of how these structures operate. Many of the core concepts are found throughout the universe of finance documents, and a brief reminder should prove useful to those who are already familiar with the basic terms of swap documentation as well as providing an explanation to newcomers. Again, it is necessary to consider the Rates Definitions in a non-linear fashion; the terms and concepts that are built up for the various transaction structures are not found in strict order within the Rates Definitions. Accordingly, the survey set out in the following paragraphs should be of some assistance.

7.177 The concept of a Business Day[151] is fundamental to the operation of the entire range of ISDA materials, and it is appropriate to consider it in the context of the

---

[149] Herein, the 'Rates Definitions'. The Rates Definitions replaced the 2000 ISDA Definitions, and represent a continuation of the principles first established in the 1987 Interest Rate and Currency Exchange Definitions.

[150] See paragraph 7.109.

[151] Section 1.4. The concept of the Business Day is of course found throughout the universe of finance documents; it is by no means peculiar to the derivative markets.

Rates Definitions, as these definitions might be said to constitute the foundation of ISDA's definitions. A Business Day is 'a day on which banks and foreign exchange markets settle payments and are open for general business (including dealings in foreign exchange and foreign currency deposits) in the place(s) and on the days specified for that purpose in the related Confirmation'. The concept of the Business Day is used to determine whether or not a particular obligation can be performed on a particular day in a particular place (and this is the common application), or whether or not a particular event can occur on a particular day in a particular place. The date on which the obligation is specified to be fulfilled is then adjusted if it is not a Business Day. Thus if a payment is specified to be made on a particular date, and the places specified for the purposes of determining Business Days are London and New York, then that date only qualifies as a Business Day if on that date banks and foreign exchange markets are open in both London and New York. As a matter of practicality, the greater the number of locations that are used to specify the Business Day, the fewer calendar days will satisfy the complete specification. A Business Day Convention[152] is used to adjust the original date in response to it not qualifying as a Business Day, whether, to continue the illustration, by moving the obligation to make the payment to the first following day[153] which is a Business Day or to the first preceding day[154] which is a Business Day; one subtlety is that the obligation might be moved to the next following day which is a Business Day, unless that day falls in the next calendar month, in which case the obligation is moved to the first preceding Business Day.[155]

7.178 The Rates Definitions make use of familiar terminology, such as the Effective Date of a Transaction, the Termination Date of a Transaction, the Term of a Transaction, and the Trade Date of a Transaction, which are defined in Article 3. The parties agree to enter into the Transaction on the Trade Date, and the exposures created under the Transaction start on the Effective Date and end on the Termination Date, and both the Effective Date and the Termination Date are adjusted if necessary so as to fall on Business Days. The Term of the Transaction starts on, and includes, the Effective Date, and ends on, and includes, the Termination Date.

7.179 Article 8 contains detailed provisions which govern the rounding, interpolation, and discounting of amounts. Section 8.1 sets out the detailed rules governing the rounding of percentages and currency amounts, and Section 8.2 sets out the rules governing the rounding of currency amounts denominated in particular currencies.[156]

---

[152] Section 4.12.
[153] 'Following'.
[154] 'Preceding'.
[155] 'Modified Following'.
[156] The Chilean Peso, the Hungarian Forint, the Japanese Yen, and the Korean Won.

Section 8.3 provides for interpolation, which is a computational method to determine the interest rate that is to applied in respect of a particular 'odd' period for which no market rate is published. By way of background, interest rates tend to be quoted for particular currencies and particular 'round' periods, such as three month sterling LIBOR,[157] which is the LIBOR interest rate for an amount denominated in pounds sterling for a period of three months. Therefore say an interest rate for four-and-a-quarter months is required, and the only rates available are for four months and five months. The Linear Interpolation technique described in Section 8.3 would be used to determine the four-and-a-quarter month interest rate by using the rate for the next shorter period, that is, four months, and the next longer period, that is, five months. A line is then drawn on an imaginary graph, the vertical axis of which represents the values of rates, and the horizontal axis of which represents periods. The line runs diagonally between the two rates, and a third vertical line is drawn at the particular period for which the 'odd' rate is required. This 'odd' rate is the rate found at the point where the third vertical line bisects the diagonal line. The term 'linear' connotes that the diagonal line is straight, and therefore no statistical subtleties that may otherwise be observed in the relevant market are captured in this technique. Section 8.4 provides for discounting. Discounting, as paragraphs 4.68 and 4.135 explain, is the calculation of the present value of a future amount assuming a rate of interest, hence £100 in three years is worth £87.63 now, assuming an interest rate of 4.5% per annum.

Swap Transaction

7.180 The term 'Swap Transaction'[158] embraces a range of transactions built on the fundamental swap structure under which each party makes periodic payments to the other, the amount of each payment made by a party being calculated broadly as the underlying notional amount of the Transaction multiplied by the interest rate or the currency rate specified to be paid by that party.[159] Under Article 2, the parties to a Swap Transaction are identified as the Fixed Rate Payer, or the Fixed Amount Payer, and the Floating Rate Payer, or the Floating Amount Payer. Under the Swap Transaction, therefore, the Fixed Rate Payer pays a stream of interest on the underlying notional amount at a fixed rate, and the Floating Rate Payer pays a stratum of interest on the underlying notional amount at a

---

[157] The London Interbank Offered Rate, which is the acronym given to any one of a family of widely used benchmark interest rates published by the British Bankers' Association, in different currencies and different durations.

[158] Section 1.1. The term 'Swap Transaction' includes a rate swap transaction, a basis swap, a forward rate transaction, an interest rate cap transaction, an interest rate floor transaction, an interest rate collar transaction, a currency swap transaction, and a cross-currency rate swap transaction. Chapter 4 introduces many of these from an economic standpoint.

[159] See part 4.7 of Chapter 4.

floating rate. Under Article 3 and Article 4, provisions are made for certain payments to be made at the outset of the Swap Transaction or at the end of the Swap Transaction. It is entirely appropriate that much detail is specified for the calculation of the payments of interest and amounts under a Swap Transaction. Therefore, in addition to the more generic concepts already mentioned, Section 4.16 sets out the different permutations of Day Count Fraction, which add more precision to the calculation of amounts of interest for particular periods. Interest rates are quoted as percentages per annum, and the Day Count Fraction is the fraction by which the amount of interest calculated for one year is multiplied in order to derive the amount of interest applicable to a particular period. Different conventions have developed based on the number of days that one year is deemed to comprise. For example, 'Actual/Actual' uses the actual number of days in the relevant period and the actual number of days in a calendar year, reflecting leap years, whereas 'Actual/360' assumes that one year comprises just 360 days.

7.181 The term of a Swap Transaction is divided into Calculation Periods, and each Calculation Period has its own Payment Date. On each Payment Date, each party has the obligation to make a payment to the other, whether at a fixed rate of interest or at a floating rate of interest. The payment that is made by each party on a Payment Date is calculated with reference to the Calculation Amount which applies to the relevant Calculation Period. The Calculation Amount is the underlying notional amount that is used for the purposes of the relevant Calculation Period, and by enabling a different Calculation Amount to be applied for the purposes of each Calculation Period, the Swap Transaction can be used in a flexible manner. The Calculation Amount is generally the amount specified as the Notional Amount. However, a Swap Transaction can be structured so that each party makes a stream of payments denominated in a different currency, and under such a currency swap transaction, the Calculation Amount that is used to determine the payments made by a party is the Currency Amount specified in respect of that party.

7.182 The general operation of a swap is recollected from part 4.7 of Chapter 4. The example is provided of a swap used by a borrower to hedge exposures to the fluctuating interest rate paid on a lending, and in order that the borrower remains perfectly hedged, the underlying notional amount of the swap tracks the principal outstanding on the loan; thus any decrease in the principal outstanding on the loan is matched by a corresponding decrease in the underlying notional amount of the swap.[160] Crucially, the two payment obligations which arise on a Payment Date are usually netted, so that both payment obligations are discharged and replaced by a single obligation on the party which owes the greater amount to pay

---

[160] See paragraph 4.75.

7.183 Article 5 provides for the calculation of Fixed Amounts. A Fixed Amount is the Calculation Amount multiplied by the Fixed Rate multiplied by the Fixed Rate Day Count Fraction. Article 6 provides for the Calculation for Floating Amounts. A Floating Amount is the Calculation Amount multiplied by the Floating Rate multiplied by the Floating Rate Day Count Fraction. The Floating Rate may have a Spread added to it. The Rates Definitions also allow for the compounding of amounts. Section 6.2(a) allows for a Cap Rate or a Floor Rate to be applied, which modifies the Floating Rate to give effect to cap structures or floor structures,[161] under which the effective rate that is applied is not greater than a specified 'cap' or is not less than a specified 'floor'. A Floating Rate is, by definition, expected to fluctuate, and fluctuations are captured on Reset Dates. The timetable of Reset Dates should synchronize with the timetable of Payment Dates. For example, under a Swap Transaction, the Floating Rate of which is a three month interest rate, the Payment Dates and the Reset Dates should occur at intervals of three months. The Floating Rate that is applied may be identified in two different ways; it may be actually specified in the Confirmation, or it may be determined using information specified for that purpose in the Confirmation. The latter approach is by far the more common. The basic scheme of the Rates Definitions is that the Floating Rate for a particular Reset Date is the Relevant Rate that is determined for that Reset Date. Article 7 contains an extensive library of provisions for identifying the Relevant Rate for particular currencies and particular durations, covering a significant number of currencies and the sources on which the relevant data may be read, such as the electronic pages of information vendors. The term 'Rate Option'[162] is used to refer to the various terms set out in Section 7.1. Indeed, Article 7 accounts for the bulk of the Rates Definitions, whereas the previous edition of the Rates Definitions set this data out in a separate Annex. Changes to this library of provisions are made from time to time in various supplements to the Rates Definitions.

7.184 One curiosity that should be mentioned is the possibility of a negative interest rate.[163] Section 6.4 anticipates the possibility that a Floating Amount is a negative

---

[161] See part 4.8 of Chapter 4.
[162] The term 'Rate Option' does not of course mean a type of transaction; it is a somewhat misleading label.
[163] Negative interest rates are a rare economic phenomenon. For example, in late 1998, negative interest rates were applied to yen deposits in the inter-bank market; Japanese banks seeking to place yen on deposit did not receive interest on their deposits, and instead paid what amounted to a fee to the deposit-takers. Economic conditions in Japan at that time prompted Japanese banks to seek to place their money outside the Japanese financial system, resulting in a surplus in the supply of yen outside Japan, and a severe weakening in the interest rate paid on deposits denominated in yen, as deposit-takers had no use for the yen they accepted as deposits.

number, whether because the relevant Floating Rate that is quoted in the market is itself a negative number, or whether as a consequence of the application of a negative Spread to a quoted Floating Rate which is already low. Under Section 6.4, if the 'Negative Interest Rate Method' is applicable to a Swap Transaction, and the Floating Amount payable by a party on a particular Payment Date is a negative number, then the Floating Amount to be paid by that party on that Payment Date is deemed to be zero, and the absolute value of that negative Floating Amount is instead added to the amount specified to be paid by the other party, in the same currency as the original Floating Amount.

Mark-to-market Currency Swap

A Mark-to-market Currency Swap is a Swap Transaction which operates to give an exposure to the rate of exchange between two currencies, the Constant Currency and the Variable Currency. The amounts of the payments made by one of the parties are calculated with reference to this rate of exchange. Article 10 contains the additional provisions which are required to give effect to a Mark-to-market Currency Swap; the basic operative provisions of a Mark-to-market Currency Swap are the same as those of the more straightforward Swap Transaction from which it is derived, such as the concepts of a Calculation Period, a Payment Date, and the Calculation Amount. **7.185**

Under a Mark-to-market Currency Swap, one party is the Variable Currency Payer and the other party is the Constant Currency Payer.[164] On each Payment Date, the Variable Currency Payer makes a payment the amount of which is calculated with reference to the Variable Currency Amount, and the Constant Currency Payer makes a payment the amount of which is calculated with reference to the Constant Currency Amount. The Variable Currency Amount for a particular Calculation Period is an amount equal to the Constant Currency Amount expressed in the Variable Currency. The conversion of the Constant Currency Amount into the Variable Currency Amount for a particular Calculation Period is achieved using the Currency Exchange Rate which is determined for that Calculation Period. The parties to a Mark-to-market Currency Swap can either specify in the Confirmation the method for determining the Currency Exchange Rate, or they can elect to use the ISDA MTM Matrix,[165] which specifies the electronic page, or Source Page, on which the relevant exchange rate is published as at a specified Fixing Time, with a fallback if no rate is so published. The purpose of the ISDA MTM Matrix is to enable the parties to merely allow their Transaction to be deemed to incorporate certain elections that they would otherwise be required to specify in the Confirmation. **7.186**

---

[164] Section 10.2.
[165] The 2006 ISDA Definitions MTM Matrix for Mark-to-market Currency Swaps, which is published on ISDA's website.

7.187 Further, an MTM Amount also becomes payable between the parties. Under Section 10.5, the MTM Amount in respect of a Calculation Period is the Variable Currency Amount for such Calculation Period minus the Variable Currency Amount for the immediately preceding Calculation Period. If the MTM Amount is positive, the Constant Currency Payer pays it to the Variable Currency Payer, and if it is negative, the Variable Currency Payer pays the absolute value of it to the Constant Currency Payer. The purpose of the MTM Amount is therefore to offset the effect of the increase or decrease in the underlying notional amount caused by the shift in the Currency Exchange Rate, as a shift in the Currency Exchange Rate results in a lower or a higher underlying notional amount with reference to which payments are calculated.

7.188 By way of general illustration, under a Mark-to-market Currency Swap, the amounts paid by the Variable Currency Payer decrease if the Variable Currency strengthens against the Constant Currency, and conversely the amounts paid by the Variable Currency Payer increase if the Variable Currency weakens against the Constant Currency. Say the Constant Currency is US dollars, the Constant Currency Amount is US$1 million, the Variable Currency is euros, and the Currency Exchange Rate is 1.2 euros to 1 dollar. The Variable Currency Amount for the first Calculation Period is therefore euros 1.2 million. The Currency Exchange Rate then shifts to 1.3 euros to 1 dollar for the second Calculation Period. This shift represents a weakening of the euro, as more of it can be bought with dollars, and more of it is required to buy dollars. The Variable Currency Amount for the second Calculation Period is therefore euros 1.3 million, and accordingly the amount of the payment made by the Variable Currency Payer, which is of course calculated as a percentage of the Variable Currency Amount, will increase as the Variable Currency weakens. In addition, an MTM Amount of euros 100,000 is calculated; this is the Variable Currency Amount determined for the second Calculation Period (euros 1.3 million) minus the Variable Currency Amount determined for the first Calculation Period (euros 1.2 million). As the MTM Amount is a positive number, the Constant Currency Payer pays it to the Variable Currency Payer. In very crude terms, there is a form of offset between the payment by the Constant Currency Payer of the MTM Amount and the receipt by it of an increased amount as a result of the shift in the Currency Exchange Rate.

Option Transaction

7.189 The term 'Option Transaction'[166] includes both a Swap Transaction which is a Swaption, and a Swap Transaction under which a party has the right to terminate

---

[166] Section 11.1. It is important to remember that an Option Transaction under the Rates Definitions does not function in strictly the same manner as an option written over other classes of underlying; an Option Transaction is merely a Swap Transaction that can be brought to an end before its scheduled Termination Date through the exercise of a right by a party.

the Swap Transaction early at will, on giving notice (this latter category is said to be a Swap Transaction to which Optional Early Termination is specified to be applicable). The term can also include any other transaction which features the defining characteristic of the option, that is, the choice available to the buyer of the contract as to whether or not to exercise the rights conferred under the contract. The parties to an Option Transaction[167] are the Seller and the Buyer, in keeping with the established pattern of the option structure. The Seller is the party which grants the rights under the Option Transaction, and the Buyer is the party which can exercise those rights. Again, in keeping with the established pattern of the option structure, there are three styles of Option Transaction: American, Bermuda, and European, which are distinguished by when the Buyer is entitled to exercise the rights conferred, whether, respectively, at any time during the Exercise Period, only at specified times during the Exercise Period, or only on the Expiration Date. Article 13 sets out the detail of the manner in which Option Transactions are exercised, including the procedure by which exercise is effected and the rules governing when notices of exercise are deemed to become effective; again, it is worth emphasizing that seemingly mundane details such as the rules governing the validity and effectiveness of notices are often disregarded, with consequences which are at best inconvenient.

7.190 Exercise of a basic Option Transaction, that is, a Swap Transaction in respect of which Optional Early Termination is specified to be applicable, results in the early termination of that Swap Transaction, whether in whole or in part. Under Article 16, which legislates for Optional Early Termination, exercise of the right to terminate early a Swap Transaction results in either (1) if 'Cash Settlement' is specified to be applicable, the payment on the Cash Settlement Payment of the Cash Settlement Amount, and the reduction of the Notional Amount of the Swap Transaction by the amount that is subject to the optional early termination; or (2) if 'Cash Settlement' is specified to be not applicable, just the reduction of the Notional Amount of the Swap Transaction by the amount that is subject to the optional early termination. Two observations are made. First, exercise of the right to terminate early a Swap Transaction does not necessarily result in the payment of a Cash Settlement Amount; and second, the party terminating early a Swap Transaction pursuant to an option right can select the extent to which that Swap Transaction is terminated early, that is, the party can leave a proportion of the Swap Transaction in place. It therefore follows that an Option Transaction can be exercised more than once, and the parties therefore specify whether or not 'Multiple Exercise' is applicable. Article 18 provides for cash settlement. The considerable detail of the computation of the Cash Settlement Amount is set out in Section 18.2, but the principle is straightforward; the Cash Settlement Amount is the amount by which

---

[167] Section 12.1.

the Swap Transaction is in-the-money and therefore it is the amount that is paid to the party from whose perspective the Swap Transaction is in-the-money to offset the loss of the economic effect of the Swap Transaction. Section 18.4 sets out the test for whether or not the Swap Transaction is in-the-money for a party. A different test is applied depending on whether the party in question is the Fixed Rate Payer or the Floating Rate Payer. From a broad perspective, a Swap Transaction is in-the-money for a Fixed Rate Payer if the Settlement Rate is greater than the Fixed Rate, which implies that the amounts that the Fixed Rate Payer is required to pay are less than the amounts that prevailing market conditions imply the Fixed Rate Payer should be paying. Further, a Swap Transaction is in-the-money for a Floating Rate Payer if the Fixed Rate is greater than the Settlement Rate, which implies that the amounts that the Floating Rate Payer is entitled to receive are greater than the amounts that prevailing market conditions imply the Floating Rate Payer should be receiving. The Settlement Rate is essentially the market rate for Swap Transactions that are equivalent to the relevant Swap Transaction in respect of which a determination is made.[168]

7.191 Under Section 18.2, the parties first attempt to agree the Cash Settlement Amount, and if the parties are unable to reach agreement, then the intricate provisions of Section 18.2 are used to provide an objective framework for the computation of the relevant amount. The parties should specify in the Confirmation the relevant Cash Settlement Method which should be followed, out of five choices:[169] (1) Cash Price, (2) Cash Price—Alternative Method, (3) Par Yield Curve—Adjusted, (4) Zero Coupon Yield — Adjusted, and (5) Par Yield Curve — Unadjusted. Both Cash Price and Cash Price — Alternative Method invoke the methodology set out in the master agreement for the determination of the amount payable in respect of the early termination of a transaction, subject to certain assumptions to link that methodology with the requirements of the early termination of the Swap Transaction. A different technique altogether is described for Par Yield Curve — Adjusted. The Cash Settlement Amount is the present value of an annuity equal to the difference between the actual Fixed Amounts payable and the Fixed Amounts that would be payable if the Fixed Rate were the Settlement Rate. The terms 'annuity' and 'present value' together capture the concept that the valuation of the Swap Transaction carried out now in the present must look forward over the remaining tenor of the Swap Transaction and the valuation itself is based on the cash flow that the Swap Transaction would have given rise to if it had not been terminated early. The discounting rate used to calculate the present value is equal to the Settlement Rate. Zero Coupon Yield — Adjusted is similar to Par Yield Curve — Adjusted, but the discounting rate that is used is derived from a zero coupon bond.

---

[168] Section 18.2(f).
[169] Section 18.3(a) to (e).

Par Yield Curve — Unadjusted is similar to Zero Coupon Yield — Adjusted, but without the adjustment for the applicable Business Day Convention that the latter incorporates. Of course, the foregoing can only provide a summary of the distinctions between the five Cash Settlement Methods; the actual provisions in the Rates Definitions are quite voluminous.

Mention should also be made of Article 17, which allows the parties to configure a Swap Transaction to terminate early automatically if certain conditions are met, whereupon the Swap Transaction is cash settled in accordance with the provisions of Article 18.

7.192

Swaption

Paragraph 7.172 introduces the swaption in the context of the Commodity Definitions as an option contract written on an underlying swap contract; exercise of the option results in a payment being made in respect of the underlying swap contract or delivery being made of the underlying swap contract. A Swaption under the Rates Definitions has as its underlying an Underlying Swap Transaction. Therefore the Confirmation for a Swaption is required to lay out the terms of both the Swaption and the Underlying Swap Transaction. A Swaption is either cash settled or physically settled, and settlement is triggered either automatically or upon exercise of its rights by the Buyer.

7.193

Unlike a basic Option Transaction, a Swaption is capable of being exercised automatically if the parties specify that 'Automatic Exercise' is applicable. A Swaption is exercised automatically[170] if the Buyer of the Swaption is in-the-money. The parties may specify that a Threshold applies, and a Swaption is not exercised automatically if the difference between the Settlement Rate and the Fixed Rate remains less than the Threshold, notwithstanding that the Swaption has actually moved in-the-money for the Buyer. Again, Section 18.4 sets out the test for whether or not the Swap Transaction is in-the-money.

7.194

If the Swaption is cash settled, the Buyer then has the right[171] to require the Seller to pay to the Buyer on the relevant Cash Settlement Payment Date the Cash Settlement Amount, if the Swaption is in-the-money for the Buyer. However, if the Swaption is in-the-money for the Seller, no amount is payable. That the Seller does not receive a payment even if the Swaption is in-the-money for the Seller is entirely consistent with the general principles of option theory, under which the seller of an option only receives the premium paid by the buyer; the premium thus paid represents the total 'upside' enjoyed by the seller of an option. The Cash Settlement Amount that is payable on the exercise of a Swaption is calculated in

7.195

---

[170] Section 13.7.
[171] Section 18.1(a).

substantially the same manner as the Cash Settlement Amount that is payable on the exercise of a basic Option Transaction,[172] although with reference to the Underlying Swap Transaction and not to the 'top level' transaction.

7.196 If the Swaption is physically settled, the Buyer then has the right to cause the Underlying Swap Transaction to become effective (this is what is meant by 'delivery' of the underlying contract in more colloquial language). Article 15 provides for the physical settlement of Swaptions.

Swaption Straddle

7.197 A Swaption Straddle[173] comprises two Swaptions, each of which has an Underlying Swap Transaction. 'Straddle' is the term given to an option derivative structure under which both a call option and a put option are simultaneously written on the same underlying, with the same exercise price. A straddle, under general option theory, can be either a long straddle, which is profitable if the underlying price remains away from the exercise price, whether above or below, or a short straddle, which is profitable if the underlying price remains near to or the same as the exercise price.[174] A long straddle is made up of a combination of a long call position and a long put position, each having the same exercise price, and a short straddle is made up of a combination of a short call position and a short put position, again each having the same exercise price. The interaction of the two options which in combination constitute the straddle determines the overall profile of the profit or loss made under the straddle depending on the price of the underlying.

7.198 Under Section 11.3, the Underlying Swap Transaction of one of the Swaptions constituting a Straddle is an Underlying Payer Swap, and the Underlying Swap Transaction of the other Swaption constituting that Straddle is an Underlying Receiver Swap. An Underlying Payer Swap[175] is an Underlying Swap Transaction in respect of which the Buyer of the Straddle is the Fixed Rate Payer, and an Underlying Receiver Swap[176] is an Underlying Swap Transaction in respect of which the Buyer of the Straddle is the Floating Rate Payer. The conventions of the swap market as to terminology are recollected from paragraph 4.94, and this

---

[172] See paragraph 7.191.
[173] Section 11.3. A Swaption Straddle is also referred to as a Straddle for convenience.
[174] The phenomenon that the price of a long option position decreases over time is disregarded to preserve clarity in this illustration. Paragraph 4.50 explains that the Option Greek Theta indicates the sensitivity of the price of an option to the passage of time to the expiry date, and 'theta decay' is the term used to describe the decrease in the price of an option during the term of the option, even if all of the other factors are held constant. Straddle strategies can be used to express an investment view as to the volatility exhibited by the price or level of the underlying.
[175] Section 14.1(d).
[176] Section 14.1(e).

	Swaption 1 **Underlying Payer Swap**	**Swaption 2** **Underlying Receiver Swap**
Buyer of the Straddle	Fixed Rate Payer 'long' the fixed rate	Floating Rate Payer 'short' the fixed rate
Seller of the Straddle	Floating Rate Payer 'short' the fixed rate	Fixed Rate Payer 'long' the fixed rate

analysis also ties in with the basic premise of the straddle set out in the foregoing paragraph. Accordingly, it can be demonstrated that a Straddle is a long straddle for the Buyer and a short straddle for the Seller. The table set out above indicates how the Buyer and the Seller of a Straddle assume different positions in respect of the Underlying Swap Transaction of each of the two Swaptions constituting the Straddle.

7.199 Following the conventions of the swap market, the Buyer of the Straddle effectively 'buys' the fixed rate of the Underlying Payer Swap of Swaption 1, under which it is the Fixed Rate Payer, and effectively 'sells' the fixed rate of the Underlying Receiver Swap of Swaption 2, under which it is the Floating Rate Payer. Conversely, the Seller of the Straddle effectively 'sells' the fixed rate of the Underlying Payer Swap of Swaption 1, under which it is the Floating Rate Payer, and effectively 'buys' the fixed rate of the Underlying Receiver Swap of Swaption 2, under which it is the Fixed Rate Payer. For the Buyer of the Straddle, Swaption 1 is effectively a long call option on the fixed rate, and Swaption 2 is effectively a long put option on the fixed rate, which corresponds with the principle that a long straddle comprises a long call position plus a long put position. For the Seller of the Straddle, Swaption 1 is effectively a short call option on the fixed rate, and Swaption 2 is effectively a short put option on the fixed rate, which corresponds with the principle that a short straddle comprises a short call position plus a short put position.

7.200 Section 13.10 provides for the exercise of Straddles. Under Section 13.10(a), the Buyer may exercise either Swaption constituting a European-style Straddle on the Expiration Date, and upon exercise of one such Swaption, the other of the pair is deemed to expire unexercised. Under Section 13.10(b), the Buyer may exercise either Swaption constituting an American-style Straddle or a Bermuda-style Straddle during the relevant Exercise Period, and the Buyer may also subsequently exercise, if the relevant underlying rates move advantageously, the other Swaption constituting that Straddle later during the Exercise Period.

7.201 Either cash settlement or physical settlement can apply to a Swaption Straddle, and each Swaption constituting a Straddle is settled in the same manner as a single Swaption, as discussed in the foregoing paragraphs.

7.202 Article 19 provides for the ISDA Settlement Matrix.[177] Under Section 19.1, the elections set out from time to time in the ISDA Settlement Matrix will apply to the exercise and settlement of Swap Transactions, unless the parties specifically exclude the applicability of the ISDA Settlement Matrix. The parties must therefore opt out of the applicability of the ISDA Settlement Matrix. Again, the purpose of the ISDA Settlement Matrix is to enable the parties to merely allow their Transaction to be deemed to incorporate certain elections that they would otherwise be required to specify in the Confirmation.

Closing remarks

7.203 In summary, therefore, the focus of the Rates Definitions is on defining the various permutations of the basic swap structure and on the methodology for determining the market rates that are used for calculations, as opposed to providing for disruptions to the market for the underlying. In this regard the Rates Definitions differ from the Equity Definitions and the Commodity Definitions, the focus of which is on the preservation of the terms of a transaction and the ability of a party to hedge its obligations by accommodating the risks of a disruption to the market for the underlying.

7.12 2006 ISDA Fund Derivatives Definitions[178]

7.204 The Fund Definitions represent a significant addition to the library of ISDA's materials, and they were developed using the Equity Definitions as a foundation, on the basis that there are strong similarities between the treatment of shares issued by companies, as covered by the Equity Definitions, and certain types of interest in funds. Indeed, prior to the publication of the Fund Definitions, the Equity Definitions were used for the purposes of documenting fund-linked derivative transactions, albeit in an amended form in certain respects. However, the Fund Definitions do of course cater for other types of fund interest other than shares, and they also provide for the two different broad categories of fund: the mutual fund and the hedge fund. There are significant differences between how these two types of fund operate, and therefore between the parcel of risks that they pose. The risks posed by the different types of fund inform the manner in which a party to a fund-linked transaction choosing to hedge itself by holding interests in a fund would need to protect itself and the integrity of its hedging operations by specifying certain events which would allow it to make adjustments to the

---

[177] The 2006 ISDA Definitions Settlement Matrix for Early Termination and Swaptions, which is published on ISDA's website.
[178] Herein, the 'Fund Definitions'.

terms of the transaction or to terminate early the transaction. In this regard, the Fund Definitions are no different from the definitions already discussed in the foregoing paragraphs, notably the Equity Definitions.

7.205 However, as a general introductory remark, although both the Fund Definitions and the Equity Definitions set out processes for valuing the underlying assets of transactions, the Equity Definitions also contain extensive provisions detailing the consequences of disruptions to valuations precipitated by disruptions in the secondary market. The Fund Definitions do not use the concept of a secondary market, and instead must lay out other methodologies for achieving the necessary valuations, using language which makes for formidable technical reading. The Fund Definitions also contain a more extensive list of risks which might have an effect on the underlying assets of transactions: crystallization of these risks might have an impact on the fund interests, the funds, and the various managers and other providers of various services to the funds.

7.206 Article 1 contains certain general definitions, and under Section 1.8, a Fund Interest is 'an interest issued to or held by an investor in a fund, pooled investment vehicle or any other interest identified as such in the related Confirmation'. This is a necessarily wide definition, as it must include both hedge funds and mutual funds,[179] which have proved to be the most common type of underlying fund. Of course, other types of fund can be accommodated under the Fund Definitions, although it is arguable that a listed investment trust company, for example, might be more usefully covered by a combination of the Equity Definitions, which already contain the necessary provisions for valuations observed in a liquid exchange-based secondary market and disruptions to those valuations, and the Fund Definitions, which include certain risks peculiar to the fund universe. This definition does capture the key principle, however, of a pooled investment vehicle, which is the characteristic of any fund, irrespective of its more detailed categorization. Curiously, the word 'fund' itself is not defined, although 'Reference Fund' is defined[180] as 'in respect of a Fund Interest, unless otherwise specified in the related Confirmation, the issuer of, or other legal arrangement giving rise to, the relevant Fund Interest'. This definition anticipates that a Fund Interest might take the form of a share issued by a fund established as a company, or that a Fund Interest might take the form of a unit in a fund organized as a unit

---

[179] The distinctions between different types of fund is explored in more detail in Chapter 9. For immediate purposes, it is sufficient to note that a distinction is drawn between funds that are regulated, such as unit trusts and mutual funds, and those that are not, such as hedge funds, although of course the various persons providing services to hedge funds, including investment managers, are themselves usually regulated.
[180] Section 1.11.

trust, or that a Fund Interest might take the form of an interest in a partnership.[181] Other possibilities include a Fund Interest taking the form of a beneficial entitlement under a trust structure, without the infrastructure of a unit trust 'wrapper'. A Reference Fund might also constitute a fund of funds, which is a fund established to invest in other funds, whether those other funds themselves are regulated or unregulated. Finally, a Fund Interest Unit[182] is effectively each relevant individual unit that an investor in the Reference Fund holds or which represents the investor's ownership. A Fund Interest Unit might therefore be a share, or a unit in a unit trust. The Fund Interest Unit is often, but not always, a convenient means of expressing a price.

7.207 Article 1 also establishes that the Fund Definitions contain standard structures for transactions linked to funds and Fund Interests, whether singly or in baskets. The standard groups of transaction structures are the Fund Option Transaction, the Fund Forward Transaction, and the Fund Swap Transaction. The operation of these types of Fund Derivative Transaction is substantially similar to the operation of their equivalents under the Equity Definitions: the Option Transaction, the Forward Transaction, and the Equity Swap Transaction, respectively.[183] The Fund Definitions also include provisions for barrier transactions. The definitions for Knock-in Event and Knock-out Event in Section 1.57 and Section 1.58 respectively echo the analogous provisions found in the Equity Definitions,[184] and these features operate in the same manner, in that a particular advantageous payout only becomes available if a specified Knock-in Event occurs, and conversely, a particular advantageous payout only remains available if a specified Knock-out Event does not occur.

7.208 Given the essential similarity between the transaction structures established under the Fund Definitions and under the Equity Definitions, which have already been considered in the context of the Equity Definitions, this introduction to the Fund Definitions instead focuses on the key themes which emerge from a consideration of their terms. First, the two methods of valuing a Fund Interest under the Fund Definitions are examined: these two methods are the Deemed Payout Method and the Reported Value Method. These two methods involve several different definitions whose interaction is complex. The use of the Hypothetical Investor concept is considered as a proxy for the more overtly objective standards imposed by an exchange-based secondary market, and this concept is of particular relevance to the

---

[181] Such an interest is sometimes referred to as a 'partnership share', although the word 'share' can be misleading as it suggests a share in the capital of a company, which is a different form of legal entity.
[182] Section 1.9.
[183] See paragraphs 7.97 ff.
[184] See paragraph 7.98.

Deemed Payout Method. Second, the special risks to which an investment in Fund Interests is susceptible, and the measures contained in the Fund Definitions to ameliorate those risks, are examined. Third, certain pertinent similarities between the Fund Definitions and the Equity Definitions are identified, and the subtle differences highlighted, in the context of the treatment of dividends and the miscellaneous representations and agreements that each party makes to the other.

Valuing fund interests

7.209 As mentioned in the foregoing paragraph, the Fund Definitions permit two different mechanisms for valuing Fund Interests for the purposes of a Fund Derivative Transaction to be used. Valuation of a Fund Interest under the Deemed Payout Method is predicated on the amounts that a Hypothetical Investor[185] would receive in respect of that Fund Interest in all the relevant circumstances, and valuation of a Fund Interest under the Reported Value Method is predicated on the valuations that are reported by or published on behalf of the relevant Reference Fund. Immediately it is noticeable that the Reported Value Method offers a more objective basis for valuation, but herein lies a significant practical difficulty. The prices of Fund Interest Units in certain types of fund, such as hedge funds, are not available publicly, and are only released to investors, and this practical difficulty therefore compels the use of the Deemed Payout Method. Yet under the Deemed Payout Method, account must be taken of the amounts received by a Hypothetical Investor, and ascertaining the amounts received by a Hypothetical Investor in the absence of any publicly available information again will prove difficult. Often the practical solution is that one of the parties to the Fund Derivative Transaction is effectively selling an exposure to the underlying Reference Fund to the other party, and in doing so the party selling the exposure hedges its obligations under the Fund Derivative Transaction by subscribing for the appropriate value of Fund Interests, and obtains the required information in its capacity as an 'investor' in the underlying Reference Fund. The word 'investor' is used loosely; the party selling the exposure would generally seek to maintain a neutral stance towards movements in the valuation of the Fund Interests by remaining hedged. However, the extent of the information that is acquired can itself pose further difficulties, particularly from a regulatory perspective. A regulatory principle has emerged that there should be no preferential or asymmetrical treatment of investors without disclosure of that treatment being made to all investors in the fund, and therefore the receipt of more detailed information or the enjoyment of more advantageous liquidity by a party to a Fund Derivative Transaction

---

[185] See paragraph 7.211.

in respect of its holding in the underlying Reference Fund should be considered carefully.[186]

7.210 Both the Deemed Payout Method and the Reported Value Method feed valuations into the principal operative provisions of the Fund Definitions, including the Relevant Price,[187] the Final Price,[188] and the Settlement Price.[189] These three prices are determined in respect of a particular Fund Interest, and they are expressed as an amount per Fund Interest Unit related to that Fund Interest. The definition of each price is divided into a treatment of the two valuation methods.

Deemed Payout Method

7.211 The Deemed Payout Method is defined at Section 1.36, in a somewhat circular fashion, and its true import becomes discernible in a group of related definitions. Before considering the relevant group of definitions, it is useful to note that a Hypothetical Investor[190] is generally a hypothetical investor which exhibits certain characteristics. One, the Hypothetical Investor is subject to the laws and the tax treatment of a particular jurisdiction that is specified for this purpose. Two, the Hypothetical Investor holds the relevant amount of the relevant Reference Fund. Three, the Hypothetical Investor has the rights and obligations set out in the Fund Documents of the relevant Reference Fund. Four, the timing of the Hypothetical Investor's investment in the relevant Reference Fund is compatible with the schedule of dates for the purposes of the particular Fund Derivative Transaction. The timing of the Hypothetical Investor's investment is important; making a subscription in a fund is not necessarily simultaneous with making payment for that subscription, and ownership of the Fund Interest does not necessarily start when payment for that subscription is made, and placing an order for a redemption is not necessarily simultaneous with receipt of the redemption proceeds, and ownership of the Fund Interest (and therefore exposure to the performance and strategy of the fund) does not necessarily end when the redemption order is placed. These are matters that are dealt with under the Fund Documents.

---

[186] The underlying Reference Fund's motivation for supplying more detailed information or allowing more advantageous liquidity to a party to a Fund Derivative Transaction subscribing for Fund Interests in that Reference Fund is that the Reference Fund's assets under management are increased by the business being written through the Fund Derivative Transaction and by that hedging subscription. Therefore the Reference Fund endeavours to encourage such a subscription. These arrangements are usually documented in a side-letter.
[187] Section 1.18.
[188] Section 5.9.
[189] Section 7.3.
[190] Section 1.33.

7.212 The price of a Fund Interest Unit on a particular valuation date is an amount equal to the Redemption Proceeds relating to that Fund Interest Unit that a Hypothetical Investor would receive on the basis that the Hypothetical Investor effected a redemption of all of the Fund Interest Units that are being valued as at that valuation date. The Redemption Proceeds[191] are the amount of the proceeds that the Calculation Agent determines that the relevant Reference Fund would pay to the Hypothetical Investor on the basis that this amount is determined on the relevant Redemption Valuation Date. A further group of definitions must be considered for the purposes of the Redemption Valuation Date.

7.213 The Redemption Valuation Date[192] is the date on which the relevant Reference Fund determines the net asset value of the Fund Interest for the purposes of calculating the redemption proceeds that are to be paid to a Hypothetical Investor that had submitted a valid notice for redemption on or before the Redemption Notice Date which is linked to that Redemption Valuation Date. It is interesting to note that this definition refers to the net asset value of the relevant Fund Interest, which is effectively the price per Fund Interest Unit being determined.

7.214 The Redemption Notice Date[193] is the last date on which the Hypothetical Investor is able to submit a redemption notice which would be valid to achieve a redemption on the Scheduled Redemption Payment Date which occurs on or immediately prior to the valuation date.

7.215 The Scheduled Redemption Payment Date[194] is the date on which the relevant Reference Fund pays the redemption proceeds to an investor that has submitted a timely and valid notice requesting redemption as of the Scheduled Redemption Valuation Date. Alternatively, the Scheduled Redemption Payment Date might be specified in the Confirmation.

7.216 The definition of Scheduled Redemption Payment Date is the critical link in the chain, and it is predicated on the usual operation of a fund, which is to permit subscriptions and redemptions, that is, to give investors liquidity, only on particular days in accordance with a timetable contained in the relevant Fund Documents. This timetable would also prescribe the last date on which a notice requesting a redemption should be submitted, which is usually some time before the date on which the redemption is actually effected. The price of the Fund Interest Unit is equal to redemption proceeds, and the price of the Fund Interest Unit on a particular valuation date must therefore be the proceeds that are paid by the relevant Reference Fund on the particular liquidity day, or Scheduled Redemption

---

[191] Section 1.43.
[192] Section 1.45.
[193] Section 1.48.
[194] Section 1.46.

Payment Date, which occurs either on that valuation date or immediately before it. Having established when the relevant Scheduled Redemption Payment Date occurs, it is necessary to work back to determine the particular Redemption Notice Date by which the redemption notice must be served in order that redemption is effected on that particular Scheduled Redemption Payment Date. It is also necessary to work back from that particular Scheduled Redemption Payment Date to determine the relevant Redemption Valuation Date on which the net asset value underpinning the calculation of the redemption proceeds is determined.

7.217 The purpose of this elaborate chain of definitions is to ensure that the price of the Fund Interest Unit on a particular valuation date is determined using the data and information that are available at particular times leading up to that valuation date. It is to be remembered that the determination of the net asset value of a fund is based on a valuation of the assets of that fund, and these assets must therefore be valued at the correct times.

7.218 One final subtlety is the concept of the Initial Observation Date[195] and the Final Observation Date.[196] The purposes of these two dates is to define a period which is linked to the relevant valuation date; unless otherwise specified in the Confirmation, the Final Observation Date is the relevant valuation date. Only redemption proceeds that are paid during this period are used to determine the price of the Fund Interest Unit; redemption proceeds that are paid outside this period are not used. This subtlety recognizes that a fund does not always pay its redemption proceeds in one amount; redemption proceeds may be paid in instalments, particularly if the valuations of the underlying assets of the fund are being refined to greater degrees of accuracy, and the fund may hold back redemption proceeds, or even seek to recover redemption proceeds that have already been paid, as the relevant valuations and accounting are finalized.

7.219 The Deemed Payout Method is therefore more appropriate for the purposes of funds which have well-defined timetables and rules for subscriptions, redemptions, and the delivery of notices requesting liquidity, and for the purposes of funds which do not readily or publicly report their net asset values. The Deemed Payout Method is therefore particularly appropriate for the purposes of determining the value of interests in hedge funds.

Reported value method

7.220 The alternative to the Deemed Payout Method is the Reported Value Method, which is defined at Section 1.35, again in a somewhat circular fashion, and again its true import becomes discernible in a group of related definitions. The price of

---

[195] Section 1.49.
[196] Section 1.50.

a Fund Interest Unit on a particular valuation date is an amount equal to the Reported Fund Interest Value of that Fund Interest Unit as at that valuation date. The Reported Fund Interest Value is determined using the Reported Value Convention that is specified in the Confirmation to be applicable. In very general terms, on the basis that funds offer liquidity and valuations on specified scheduled liquidity days only, the purpose of the Reported Value Convention is to identify the appropriate scheduled liquidity day on which a valuation can be obtained if the valuation is required on a day which is not itself such a scheduled liquidity day. Thus the Reported Value Convention is analogous with the Business Day Convention that is applied to identify the days which satisfy the criteria for a Business Day.[197]

7.221 The actual terms that are used are the Scheduled Fund Valuation Date[198] and its corollary the Fund Valuation Date,[199] and the Scheduled Redemption Valuation Date[200] and its corollary the Redemption Valuation Date.[201] The Scheduled Fund Valuation Date and the Scheduled Redemption Valuation Date are both dates on which the relevant Reference Fund is scheduled, according to its Fund Documents, to determine valuations; the difference between them is that the Scheduled Redemption Valuation Date is the date on which valuations are determined for the purposes of calculating the redemption proceeds to be paid to an investor that has submitted a valid and timely notice for redemptions based on valuations as of that particular date. In both definitions, no account is taken of any right that the relevant Reference Fund might have to apply any gating, deferral, suspension, or other amendment to the scheduled liquidity and valuation timetable. The Reported Valuation Convention that is used determines whether the Scheduled Fund Valuation Date and its group of definitions, or the Scheduled Redemption Valuation Date and its group of definitions, is used.

7.222 The Reported Fund Interest Value[202] is the value of the relevant number of Fund Interest Units, or the value of the relevant amount of Fund Interest,[203] on the relevant Fund Valuation Date. The Reported Fund Interest Value on a particular Fund Valuation Date is reported on the Fund Reporting Date linked to that

---

[197] See paragraph 7.177.
[198] Section 1.38.
[199] Section 1.39.
[200] Section 1.44.
[201] Section 1.45.
[202] Section 1.41.
[203] The contractual link between the definitions of 'Relevant Price', Final Price', and 'Settlement Price', and the definition of 'Reported Fund Interest Value' is not strong. Reported Fund Interest Value is expressed as the value of a number of Fund Interest Units or the value of a Fund Interest, whereas the three definitions in which this value is used anticipate that Reported Fund Interest Value is expressed as an amount per Fund Interest Unit. Nonetheless, it should be remembered that the overall intention underpinning the drafting is clear and that the drafting provides a framework.

particular Fund Valuation Date. The definition also anticipates that the Reported Fund Interest Value might be calculated on the basis of a net asset value and that it might be reported on behalf of the relevant Reference Fund by an agent or by a publishing service.

7.223 The Fund Valuation Date is the date on which the relevant Reference Fund (or an agent on its behalf) determines the value of Fund Interests or its net asset value. The Fund Reporting Date[204] in respect of a particular Fund Valuation Date is the date on which the value that is determined on that Fund Valuation Date is actually published. The particular Fund Valuation Date that is used will be the particular Scheduled Fund Valuation Date identified by the application of the Reported Valuation Convention.

7.224 There is some overlap between the two pricing methods. The two concepts of Scheduled Redemption Valuation Date and Redemption Valuation Date are used under both the Deemed Payout Method[205] and the Reported Value Method. Under the Reported Value Method, these two concepts are used if the relevant Reported Valuation Convention prescribes the use of a valuation date that is used for the specific purpose of calculating the amount of the redemption proceeds to be paid to an exiting investor.

7.225 The five different Reported Valuation Conventions set out in Section 1.42(a) to Section 1.42(e) are: (1) Prior Redemption Valuation Date, (2) Prior Fund Valuation Date, (3) Last Reported Value, (4) Following Fund Valuation Date, and (5) Following Redemption Valuation Date. The Prior Redemption Valuation Date convention requires the valuation to be made as at the immediately preceding Scheduled Redemption Valuation Date. The Prior Fund Valuation Date convention requires the valuation to be made as at the immediately preceding Scheduled Fund Valuation Date. The Following Fund Valuation Date convention requires the valuation to be made as at the next following Scheduled Fund Valuation Date. The Following Redemption Valuation Date convention requires the valuation to be made as at the next following Scheduled Redemption Valuation Date. Unlike the four conventions already described, the Last Reported Value convention does not specify the date as at which the valuation is to be made. Instead, it stipulates that the relevant valuation is the most recently available Reported Fund Interest Value for the relevant number of Fund Interest Units or amount of the relevant Fund Interest, which implies that the valuation is made at the most recent to occur of either the immediately preceding Scheduled Fund Valuation Date or the immediately preceding Scheduled Redemption Valuation Date.

---

[204] Section 1.40.
[205] See paragraphs 7.211 ff.

The Reported Value Method is therefore more appropriate for the purposes of **7.226**
funds which report their net asset values on a fairly frequent basis, and for the purposes of funds which tend to pay redemption proceeds at the corresponding reported value. This latter characteristic suggests that the Reported Value Method would not be suitable for hedge funds, which offer less liquidity and which effect redemptions at values which are not necessarily the same as those prevailing when the redemption orders are placed. Instead, the Reported Value Method would be more appropriate for unit trusts and mutual funds, which tend to be characterized by regular liquidity and regular publication of prices and values.

Valuation date and disruptions to valuations

Both the Deemed Payout Method and the Reported Value Method require a valuation to be made on a particular date specified for that purpose; this is the Valuation Date.[206] Article 6 legislates for the fallbacks that are followed in the event that the valuation process is disrupted, and Article 6 operates in a substantially similar fashion to the equivalent provisions of the Equity Definitions. The broad scheme of Article 6 is that a Scheduled Valuation Date[207] is any original date which is scheduled to be a Valuation Date, and a Disrupted Day[208] is a Scheduled Valuation Date on which a Fund Disruption Event has occurred and is continuing. The term 'Fund Disruption Event'[209] achieves the necessary conceptual distinction between the Deemed Payout Method and the Reported Value Method. If the Deemed Payout Method is used, then a Fund Disruption Event occurs if the relevant Reference Fund fails to pay in full the Redemption Proceeds that it was scheduled to pay. This failure is described as constituting a disruption to settlement, on the basis that a valuation obtained using the Deemed Payout Method is based on the amount of redemption proceeds that a Hypothetical Investor receives. If the Reported Value Method is used, then a Fund Disruption Event occurs if, in general terms, the relevant Reference Fund fails to publish the relevant price or net asset value, which is entirely consistent with the basis on which valuations are obtained using that method. The term 'Fund Disruption Event' therefore has the useful function of converging the two different strands represented by the two methods into one common treatment of valuation disruptions. **7.227**

Section 6.6 sets out the consequences of Disrupted Days. Section 6.6(a) provides **7.228**
for a Fund Interest Transaction, the underlying of which is one Fund Interest, and Section 6.6(b) provides for a Fund Interest Basket Transaction, the underlying of which is two or more Fund Interests. The process set out is that if a Valuation Date is a Disrupted Day, then the valuation is instead made on the first calendar day

---

[206] Section 6.2.
[207] Section 6.5.
[208] Section 6.4.
[209] Section 6.3(a).

following that original date which is not disrupted, subject to a longstop. If no valuation has been achieved on the cut-off date, then the cut-off date is used as the Valuation Date, even if it is a Disrupted Day, and the valuation is the determination made by the Calculation Agent of its good faith estimate of the relevant value on that cut-off date. The cut-off date is the date which is the last day of the Cut-off Period,[210] which is the period specified as such in the Confirmation. The Cut-off Period starts on the original date on which the valuation was expected to be made. If no period is specified in the Confirmation, then the Cut-off Period is one year. This marks a significant difference with the Equity Definitions, under which the longstop to the valuation fallback process is measured in days. The length of the Cut-off Period reflects the delays and difficulties that can be experienced in valuing interests in funds, which is a theme running through this introduction to the Fund Definitions. Similar provisions are also set out in Section 6.7 for averaging; the fallbacks operate with reference to the various dates comprising the timetable of dates for which valuations are obtained for the purposes of determining the average valuation.

Adjustments and modifications, and Extraordinary Events

7.229 Turning to the second topic of discussion, the Fund Definitions contain provisions to offset the effect on the Fund Derivative Transaction of certain events and circumstances. In this regard, the Fund Definitions operate in the same fashion as the other sets of definitions published by ISDA, with the exception of the Credit Definitions.[211] Article 11 provides for adjustments and modifications affecting Fund Interests and transactions. Article 12 provides for Extraordinary Events.

7.230 Under Section 11.1, in general terms, the occurrence of a Potential Adjustment Event which has a diluting or concentrative effect on the theoretical value of the relevant Fund Interest Units or amount of Fund Interest results in an adjustment being made to the terms of the Fund Derivative Transaction. As in the Equity Definitions, a Potential Adjustment Event[212] is an event which amounts to a corporate action in respect of the relevant Fund Interest Units or Fund Interest. The definition of 'Potential Adjustment Event' therefore includes a subdivision, consolidation or reclassification of the relevant number of Fund Interest Units or amount of Fund Interest, corporate actions, an Extraordinary Dividend, a repurchase of the relevant Fund Interest Units or amount of Fund Interest, and any other event which may have a diluting or concentrative effect. Under Section 11.1(b), the consequence of the occurrence of a Potential Adjustment Event which has the requisite diluting or concentrative effect is Calculation Agent Adjustment,

---

[210] Section 1.51.
[211] A different type of risk is transferred under the Credit Definitions.
[212] Section 11.1(c).

unless an alternative is specified in the Confirmation. Under the Calculation Agent Adjustment consequence, the Calculation Agent makes adjustments which correspond to the diluting or concentrative effect; that is, the adjustment should offset the diluting or concentrative effect. Again, as with the analogous provisions of the Equity Definitions, no adjustment is made to account solely for changes in volatility, expected dividends, or liquidity, as these are deemed to be risks that are external to the relevant Reference Fund, and the purpose of Article 11 is to capture the risks which arise internally to the relevant Reference Fund. Although Section 11.1(a) anticipates that the parties may specify an alternative process to Calculation Agent Adjustment, any alternative that the parties do specify must be 'appropriate'.

7.231 The Extraordinary Events and their consequences set out in Article 12 again echo the equivalent provisions of the Equity Definitions. The familiar concepts of Nationalization[213] and Insolvency[214] are therefore found, with a choice of three consequences: Negotiated Close-out,[215] Cancellation and Payment,[216] and Partial Cancellation and Payment.[217] The operation of these consequences is similar to their equivalents under the Equity Definitions. However, the difficult nature of the fund as an asset class has prompted the development of an additional set of Extraordinary Fund Events in Section 12.2, which reflects the special risks which arise through investing in funds. The parties select which of these apply to their Fund Derivative Transaction. Crystallization of one of these special risks might impair the valuation process or it might affect the ability of a party to the Fund Derivative Transaction to hedge the exposures it assumes through entering into the transaction and performing its obligations. The extensive library of Extraordinary Fund Events set out in Section 12.2 might be divided into events and circumstances which might occur in respect of the relevant Reference Fund itself or the manner in which it operates,[218] in respect of one of the persons or organizations performing functions on behalf of the Reference Fund, such as investment management services or administrative services,[219] and in respect of the ability of one of the parties to the Fund Derivative Transaction to hedge its obligations or otherwise perform its obligations under the Fund Derivative Transaction.[220]

---

[213] Section 12.1(b).
[214] Section 12.1(c).
[215] Section 12.1(e)(i).
[216] Section 12.1(e)(ii).
[217] Section 12.1(e)(iii).
[218] Fund Insolvency Event, NAV Trigger Event, Fund Modification, Strategy Breach, Regulatory Action, and Reporting Disruption.
[219] Adviser Resignation Event and Regulatory Action.
[220] Fund Hedging Disruption, Change in Law, and Increased Cost of Hedging.

7.232 It is important to appreciate that the discovery of traded share prices on an exchange and the determination of the price of a Fund Interest Unit or the net asset value of a fund differ in a further important respect. The net asset value of the fund is calculated on the basis of the valuation of the assets in which the fund has invested, less its liabilities. Determination of the net asset value therefore depends on the timely and accurate completion of the relevant valuation and accounting processes, and this process is susceptible to the risk of error or even fraud. Further, if the fund is a fund of funds, the risk of error or fraud is also apparent at the level of the funds in which the fund of funds has invested. None of the menu of Extraordinary Fund Events refers to this additional risk, and therefore this is a risk that market participants should consider including. This additional risk might fall within the scope of the third limb of the definition of Regulatory Action,[221] but that merely connotes that the relevant Reference Fund, its Fund Administrator, or its Fund Adviser become subject to any investigation, proceeding or litigation.

7.233 The six possible consequences of an Extraordinary Fund Event are set out in Section 12.3. Two of these, Cancellation and Payment[222] and Partial Cancellation and Payment,[223] generally operate in the same manner as their equivalents under the Equity Definitions. Under Fund Interest Replacement,[224] the Fund Interest which is affected by the Extraordinary Fund Event is replaced by another Fund Interest. A comprehensive set of rules governs the replacement. The Successor Fund Interest must demonstrate the same characteristics, investment objectives, and policies as the Affected Fund Interest being replaced, and if the Confirmation does not specify how the replacement is to be carried out, the replacement is carried out on the basis that the value of the Successor Fund Interest being placed into the Fund Derivative Transaction is equal to the value of the outgoing Affected Fund Interest. The term 'Removal Value' is used to capture this concept, and it is used elsewhere in the Fund Definitions.[225] If no Successor Fund Interest is identified within five Currency Business Days, then Partial Cancellation and Payment apply. Under Negotiated Replacement,[226] the parties use 'reasonable efforts to agree upon mutually acceptable Successor Fund Interests and the manner in and time at which such Successor Fund Interests shall replace the relevant Affected Fund Interests'. This fourth consequence is arguably weak, and poses the risk of being rendered unenforceable as it amounts to an agreement to agree.[227]

---

[221] Section 12.2(g).
[222] Section 12.3(e)(i).
[223] Section 12.3(e)(ii).
[224] Section 12.3(e)(iii).
[225] See paragraph 7.237.
[226] Section 12.3(e)(iv).
[227] See paragraph 7.115.

Under Calculation Agent Adjustment,[228] the Calculation Agent makes the adjustments to the terms of the Fund Derivative Transaction as it considers appropriate to account for the economic effect of the Extraordinary Fund Event. Under Delayed Settlement,[229] the parties settle their obligations under the Fund Derivative Transaction and the amount of the payment that is made is calculated in the same manner as the Removal Value that is calculated for Fund Interest Replacement. Settlement can be delayed to the last day of the Cut-off Period.[230]

7.234 The parties specify whether or not Increased Cost of Hedging is included as an Extraordinary Fund Event, and Section 12.2(e)(vii) sets out the consequences of an Increased Cost of Hedging. The Hedging Party, and therefore the party which suffers the Increased Cost of Hedging, notifies the other party that the relevant increased costs have occurred and suggests a Price Adjustment to offset that increase in costs. The other party then decides within two Currency Days whether or not it agrees to the suggested Price Adjustment, whereupon it pays the Price Adjustment. If the other party does not agree to the suggested Price Adjustment, then the Fund Derivative Transaction is terminated and a close-out payment is made. A Price Adjustment[231] is an adjustment to a price, value, or other variable with reference to which the Fund Derivative Transaction operates.

7.235 The parties specify whether or not Change in Law is included as an Extraordinary Fund Event, and Section 12.2(e)(viii) sets out the consequence of a Change in Law. Either party has the right on the occurrence of a Change in Law to terminate the Fund Derivative Transaction on notice of at least two Currency Business Days, although a shorter period of notice will be applicable if that is necessary to comply with the Change in Law. The Determining Party, which is the party specified as such in the Confirmation, then calculates the Cancellation Amount that is payable.

7.236 Under Section 12.4, a Cancellation Amount is paid as a consequence of the occurrence of certain Extraordinary Events if either Cancellation and Payment or Partial Cancellation and Payment is applicable. Section 12.4(b) applies to a payment made in respect of a Fund Option Transaction. The amount of the payment that is made is agreed by the parties, but if no agreement is reached, the calculation is based on the factors described in Section 12.7(b)(i) of the Equity Definitions, which is specifically imported into the Fund Definitions.[232] Section 12.4(c) applies to a payment made in respect of a Fund Forward Transaction or a Fund Swap Transaction. If one of the parties is specified to be the Determining Party,

---

[228] Section 12.3(e)(v).
[229] Section 12.3(e)(vi).
[230] See paragraph 7.228.
[231] Section 12.2(f)(v).
[232] See paragraph 7.122.

then that Determining Party calculates the Cancellation Amount, and if both parties are specified to be Determining Parties, then each of them calculates a Cancellation Amount, and an amount equal to one half of the difference between the two Cancellation Amounts is paid by the party with the lower Cancellation Amount.

7.237 The method for the calculation of the Cancellation Amount is set out in Section 12.5. A Cancellation Amount is calculated in respect of a Determining Party, and it is the amount of the losses or costs or the gains of the Determining Party under the circumstances prevailing at the time of calculation in replacing or providing for the Determining Party the economic equivalent of the material terms of the Fund Derivative Transaction and any option rights under the Fund Derivative Transaction. Losses and costs are recorded as a positive number and gains are recorded as a negative number. From this it broadly follows that the other party pays to the Determining Party a Cancellation Amount which has a positive value, and the Determining Party pays to the other party the absolute value of a Cancellation Amount which has a negative value. The general principles of the calculation of the Cancellation Amount are therefore consistent with the general principles established in Section 6 of the ISDA 2002 Master Agreement, and it is based on the equivalent calculation contained in Section 12.8 of the Equity Definitions. Section 12.5(b) sets out the factors that are reflected in the calculation of a Cancellation Amount. The Determining Party is required to act in good faith and to use commercially reasonable procedures, and within these broad parameters, the Determining Party is free to use any relevant information, including any Removal Value that might be calculated. Again, the basic principles of the close-out calculations of the ISDA 2002 Master Agreement are discernible.

Miscellaneous matters

7.238 Turning to the third topic of discussion, Article 10 anticipates the payments of dividends by a fund. The treatment of dividends under the Fund Definitions is essentially similar to that under the Equity Definitions, in that the Dividend Amount that is calculated for a Dividend Period is made up of amounts that are paid and calculated as dividends during that period. However, the Fund Definitions, in recognition of the reality that public information in respect of certain types of fund is limited, introduce the concept of the Hypothetical Investor Paid Amount[233] as a third type of dividend that can qualify for inclusion in the Dividend Amount. The Hypothetical Investor Paid Amount is the amount of a dividend that would have been paid to a Hypothetical Investor during the relevant

---

[233] Section 10.1(c).

Dividend Period. Again, the parties determine how the benefit of a dividend is allocated under the Fund Derivative Transaction.

Article 13 contains certain miscellaneous agreements and representations. The parties specify whether or not each of them applies to the Fund Derivative Transaction. The overall purpose of the agreements and representations is to reinforce the basis of the relationship between the parties, that they transact with each other on an arm's length basis. The agreements and representations contained in Sections 13.1, 13.2, and 13.3 are similar to their equivalents in the Equity Definitions. Section 13.4 sets out Additional Fund Representations and Agreements of the Parties. If Section 13.4 applies, each party represents to the other that it has been given the opportunity to obtain and consider the Fund Documents and other information pertaining to the Reference Fund and the Fund Interests, that it has read these materials, and that it is fully aware of all the material details relating to the Reference Fund and the Fund Interests, including matters such as investment objectives, investment process, investment guidelines, risk factors, conflicts of interest, tax considerations, and sales restrictions. Section 13.4(ii) anticipates that either party may actually hold interests in the Reference Fund and provide services to it, such as prime brokerage services, and Section 13.4(iii) anticipates that either party may be in possession of information that is not publicly available or known to the other party, and the party in possession of that information is under no obligation to disclose that information. Such information might easily become known to a party if it acts as prime broker to the Reference Fund, and would thus be subject to internal conflicts management and the strict compartmentalization of information that investment institutions are required to maintain.

7.239

Concluding remarks

As a final observation, it is important to appreciate that despite its innovative provisions, reliance cannot be placed on the Fund Definitions. It is extremely important to investigate fully the basis on which an investment is made in the relevant Fund Interests, both under the relevant Fund Documents and other ancillary agreements which are read alongside those Fund Documents, and on the strength of that investigation to tailor the terms of the Fund Derivative Transaction accordingly, as the Fund Definitions themselves can only legislate for the more commonly encountered funds. This investigatory exercise is particularly important in the context of hedge funds, which tend to be bespoke and therefore atypical in approach.

7.240

8

LEGAL ISSUES

8.1 Introduction	8.01	8.5 The Doctrine of Ultra Vires	8.49
8.2 Unregulated Forwards and Regulated Futures	8.11	8.6 The Duty of Care: Selling and Misselling	8.94
8.3 The Construction of the Terms of a Derivative Contract	8.28	8.7 Retail Offer of Derivatives and Issues Arising	8.142
8.4 Derivative Contracts Recharacterized as Other Contracts	8.33	8.8 The Swap Analysed as a Contract	8.182
		8.9 Credit Derivatives Documentation	8.192

8.1 Introduction

A number of diverse legal issues arise in respect of either or both the exchange-based and the OTC derivative markets. The purpose of this chapter is to introduce these issues, and to illustrate how the broad concepts underpinning derivatives as financial products, as laid out in Chapter 4, the legal and regulatory foundation of the derivative markets, as identified in Chapter 5, and the contractual basis on which the derivative markets operate, as explained in Chapters 6 and 7, can be seen to form a cohesive whole. The general observation is made that OTC derivative contracts give rise to more challenging legal questions than listed derivative contracts that are traded on exchanges. Accordingly, aside from part 8.2 of this chapter, which discusses the regulatory perimeter against the background of business in listed sugar futures dealt on-exchange, the focus of this chapter remains firmly on the OTC market. **8.01**

As the following pages show, judicial attention has tended to be less focused on the actual terms of a derivative contract, that is, how those terms operate to create certain rights and obligations, which is essentially a straightforward matter of interpretation of the contractual terms before the court.[1] As with any other type **8.02**

---

[1] For example, see the judgment handed down on 18 May 2000 by Moore-Bick J in *Peregrine Fixed Income Limited (In Liquidation) v Robinson Department Store Public Company Limited* [2000] All ER (D) 1177 which concerned the settlement terms of the ISDA 1992 Master Agreement (Multicurrency—Cross Border) and the ability of a party to challenge the use of the Market Quotation payment measure.

of contract, a derivative contract must satisfy the requirements for a binding and enforceable contract, and therefore the well-established principles of law are applied.[2] However, given the complexity that derivative structures occasionally demonstrate, it is appropriate to observe that one of the key requirements for contractual certainty is a lack of ambiguity, and within the complexity of certain structures lies the risk that the contract might at best operate in an 'odd' manner if it lacks a conceptual coherence, and at worst give rise to litigation if the parties are unable to harmonize their differing views as to the transaction they have entered into.

8.03 Instead, judicial attention has tended to address rather more familiar problems, including the capacity of one of the parties to enter into the contract, the effect of any misrepresentation, misstatement, or other misselling or malpractice that might have induced the formation of the contract, the recharacterization of the contract, the recovery of property if the contract is not properly made or performed, and the rectification of the contract if this is an appropriate response to a dispute.

8.04 Part 8.3 therefore considers the manner in which the construction of a derivative contract is effected, and offers the warning that the court expects financial institutions to be able to record accurately and with precision the terms of their transaction. Rectification by the court of the written agreement, although available in theory, should not be relied on.

8.05 Part 8.4 sets out the considerable risk that a derivative contract under certain circumstances is susceptible to recharacterization as another type of contract. The various risks of recharacterization have arisen on a regular basis during the development of the various classes of modern derivative contract.

8.06 Part 8.5 discusses the local authority swaps cases and the doctrine of ultra vires. The consequences of the judgment in *Hazell v Hammersmith & Fulham London Borough Council*[3] reverberated through the 1990s and indeed into the 21st century. From the initial finding that local government authorities in the United Kingdom lacked the statutory power to enter into OTC derivative contracts, a series of litigation commenced which precipitated the development of the equitable remedy of restitution in English law and an important discussion at high judicial level of the availability of equitable trusts,[4] and more recently the legacy

---

[2] The usual basic principles apply, that a contract validly exists if the following conditions are satisfied: there is an offer and unqualified acceptance, the parties are in agreement, the parties intend to create a legal relationship, the parties genuinely consent to enter into the contract, the parties have the capacity to enter into the contract, the purpose of the contract is legal, performance of the contract is possible, the terms of contract are certain, and the contract involves the exchange of value, which is the concept of consideration.
[3] [1992] 2 AC 1.
[4] *Westdeutsche Landesbank Girozentrale v Islington London Borough Council* [1996] AC 669.

8.1 Introduction

of the local authority swaps cases has resulted in the increased availability of an award of compound interest, accompanied by a broad survey of the award of both simple interest and compound interest.[5]

8.07 The duty of care owed by a dealer in OTC derivatives to its customer, the ramifications of misselling, and the response of the courts is discussed in part 8.6. It is established that a dealer in derivatives is under no obligation to furnish its professional customer with an explanation of their transaction, but if it does offer an explanation, then that explanation must be given with due care and attention.[6] Further litigation shows that the written terms of a structured product can override the erroneous statements made during the process of sale and negotiation of that structured product, effectively defeating a claim based on misrepresentation, but it is emphasized that much depends on the particular circumstances of the case.[7] In particular, an experienced and sophisticated investor who chooses not to read transaction documents before signing them cannot subsequently rely on a claim that the terms of the transaction were misrepresented to him, although of course a misrepresentation of the terms of an investment remains a formidable difficulty for the financial institution against which the allegation of misrepresentation is made. The scope of the duty owed by a financial institution generally should not include a duty to advise an experienced and sophisticated investor, although again much depends on the particular circumstances of the case,[8] and therefore a consistent and hardening strand of authority becomes discernible.

8.08 The impetus continues to grow within the derivative industry to offer increasingly complex derivative products to a more broad base of consumers; this is the drive towards retail distribution that is widely seen as the next phase in the evolution of the derivative industry. Of course, private customers[9] have long been able to access derivative products in the guise of exchange-based listed contracts dealt through a broker, but use of these products invariably does not require a detailed consideration of legal terms as their contractual effect and dealing procedures are standardized. By contrast, more structured, and by definition more complex, products are being mooted for inclusion in the portfolios of private customers. Part 8.7 surveys the issues which arise in offering structured derivative products to private customers.

---

[5] *Sempra Metals Limited (formerly Metallgesellschaft Limited) v Her Majesty's Commissioners of Inland Revenue and another* [2007] UKHL 34.
[6] *Bankers Trust International PLC v PT Dharmala Sakti Sejahtera; PT Dharmala Sakti Sejahtera v Bankers Trust International PLC and another* [1996] CLC 518.
[7] *Peekay Intermark Limited (1) Harish Pawani (2) v Australia and New Zealand Banking Group Limited* [2006] EWCA Civ 386.
[8] *JP Morgan Chase Bank v Springwell Navigation Corporation* [2008] EWHC 1186 (Comm).
[9] The use of the term 'private customer' here connotes a retail consumer of financial services as opposed to a professional consumer of financial services or a financial institution acting as a consumer.

Observance of familiar regulatory standards is required, in terms of treating the customer fairly and ensuring the suitability of the particular product in the hands of the customer, but the practical means of ensuring that these standards are met prompts a careful review of these standards. Regulators and market participants alike must try to establish an appropriate balance between protecting the customer and allowing the derivative industry to innovate and to develop. Nonetheless, as part 8.7 shows, from a broad perspective the norms of regulation, bolstered by the court's approach to misselling as indicated in part 8.6, are not incompatible with the offer of structured or derivative products to retail consumers.

8.09 Leaving aside the questions of how a derivative contract is formed, interpreted, and ultimately enforced, part 8.8 offers an analysis of the swap as a contract, bringing together the economic concepts first considered in part 4.7 of Chapter 4, the established documentary standards explored throughout Chapter 7, and the narrative of the judicial treatment of swaps in this chapter. As such, part 8.8 offers a pleasing bookend to the theoretical and empirical treatment of swaps contained in this book.

8.10 Finally, part 8.9 considers the development of credit derivatives documentation, and serves as a useful reminder that the preparation and publication of market-standard documentation for OTC derivative relationships and transactions very much reflects the pace and change of the markets themselves. Part 8.9 also serves as a useful summary of the development of the documentation for this sector of the derivative markets.

8.2 Unregulated Forwards and Regulated Futures

8.11 The definition of the perimeter established by the FSMA 2000 and its secondary legislation[10] is the foundation of the regulatory system applied under English law to the majority of the United Kingdom's financial markets, including its derivative markets. As Chapter 5 explains, the scheme of the FSMA 2000 and its secondary legislation is to differentiate between investment activities which fall within the perimeter and commercial activities which fall outside the perimeter. Paragraph 5.06 refers to the regulatory, criminal, and civil sanctions which apply to persons who contravene the basic requirement to be authorized to carry on certain activities within the perimeter.

8.12 The civil sanction for breaching the general prohibition established by the FSMA 2000 for carrying on regulated activities without authorization or an exemption from the requirement to be authorized is broadly twofold. Section 26

---

[10] See Chapter 5.

8.2 Unregulated Forwards and Regulated Futures

of the FSMA 2000 sets out the civil sanction. One, a person who enters into a contract in breach of the general prohibition cannot enforce that contract against the counterparty. Two, the counterparty can recover from that person any money paid or other property transferred under that contract, together with compensation for any loss sustained as a result of having parted with that money or other property.

8.13 The civil sanction was illustrated in very stark terms by the judgment handed down on 31 January 2003 in the Commercial Court by David Steel J in *CR Sugar Trading Ltd (in administration) v China National Sugar & Alcohol Group Corporation*.[11] Although the *CR Sugar* case involved the FSA 1986 and the secondary legislation made under the FSA 1986, the case remains relevant because the general scheme and policy of the FSMA 2000 is the same as that of the FSA 1986.

8.14 In the *CR Sugar* case, CR Sugar Trading Ltd (CR) and China National Sugar & Alcohol Group Corporation (China National) entered into various derivative contracts. CR could not enforce those contracts because it had entered into them in breach of the requirement under the FSA 1986 to be authorized, or exempt from the requirement to be authorized, to carry on investment business in the United Kingdom, to use the general phraseology of section 3 of the FSA 1986. The case generated considerable comments and analysis: a headline figure of some US$20 million was involved.

8.15 CR had bought put options from China National. As the holder of the put options, CR had the right to sell, or to put, sugar to China National. However, if CR exercised its right to sell the underlying sugar to China National, China National could then choose how it would take delivery of the sugar. China National could choose between either taking delivery of the specified quantity of sugar or taking over from CR long futures positions. The long futures positions that China National would take over, if it decided to do so, were exchange-based positions held by CR's affiliate in New York in the 'Sugar 11' contract traded on the New York Coffee, Sugar and Cocoa Exchange (the NYCSCE).

8.16 By trading the Sugar 11 contract, the New York affiliate crucially paid losses on an incremental basis in respect of loss-making futures positions, and received profits on an incremental basis in respect of profit-making futures positions.[12] The exercise price of the put options that CR bought were below the spot price of sugar. Therefore, from CR's perspective, the put options were out-of-the-money because exercise of the options would have been unprofitable. Nonetheless, CR paid a high premium for the options. The high premium paid by CR for the options must be considered in the context of the overall trading strategy developed by

---

[11] [2003] EWHC 79 (Comm).
[12] See part 4.3 of Chapter 4.

CR and its affiliate. The affiliate bought futures and received a reasonably constant cash flow of incremental profits as the spot price of sugar increased, and of course, if the spot price of sugar declined to below the exercise price of the options, then CR would exercise the options and sell the sugar to China National, either (depending on China National's choice) as physical sugar or as a transfer of the affiliate's long futures positions. The long futures positions would have been transferred by back-to-back transactions, although this aspect of the arrangements put in place by CR and China National was never made clear. The put options therefore appeared to operate as a form of stop-loss for the affiliate's trading of the Sugar 11 contract. The premium that CR paid to China National for the put options was effectively payment to China National for providing the stop-loss.

8.17 The arrangements put in place by CR and China National were designed to generate a profit for both parties in a rising market for sugar. However, the spot price of sugar had decreased substantially by the second half of February 1998. The New York affiliate made large losses on its long futures positions. CR therefore asked China National to enter into further arrangements, under which CR would sell sugar to China National, and China National would pay for the sugar using letters of credit. CR planned to use the letters of credit to arrange the financing of the incremental losses and margin calls that the affiliate was required to pay in respect of the long futures positions. CR and China National signed a memorandum of agreement on 15 July 1998, under which China National stated that it fully recognized the put options, and under which CR and China National agreed that CR would sell sugar to China National if CR exercised the put options, that China National was entitled to request the postponement of the sale of the sugar, and that CR was not entitled to force China National to take delivery of the sugar. China National's activities of importing and exporting sugar were subject to quotas imposed by the Chinese Government.

8.18 CR tried to exercise the put options on 11 February 1999. China National rejected the attempted exercise of the put options, and refused to establish the letters of credit. CR claimed damages of US$19,653,085. CR's claim was referred to a tribunal of arbitrators of the Sugar Association of London.

8.19 China National argued that the put options were unenforceable because they were investments within the meaning of the FSA 1986, and under the FSA 1986, a person who enters into an investment agreement without authorization or exemption from the requirement to be authorized cannot enforce that agreement. CR was not authorized.

8.20 The initial question was whether the put options were regulated investments within the meaning of the FSA 1986 or unregulated contracts. The differentiation between a regulated option and an unregulated option is the underlying. For example, an option to acquire or to dispose of an interest in real property is

8.2 Unregulated Forwards and Regulated Futures

not an investment within the meaning of the FSA 1986. The definition of an option contained in paragraph 7 of Part I of Schedule 1 to the FSA 1986 is that options consist of 'options to acquire or dispose of — (a) any investment falling within any other paragraph of this part of the schedule'. The definition of an option therefore includes an option to acquire or dispose of any other investment within the meaning of the 1986 Act. Therefore, in order to consider whether the put options bought by CR were investments, the tribunal had to consider whether the long futures positions disposed of under the put options constituted futures contracts. A futures contract is another investment within the meaning of the FSA 1986.

8.21 The definition of a futures contract is contained in paragraph 8 of Part I of Schedule 1 to the FSA 1986. A futures contract consists of 'rights under a contract for the sale of a commodity or property of any other description under which delivery is to be made at a future date and at a price agreed upon when the contract is made'. The definition of a futures contract is accompanied by fairly substantial notes which have statutory effect and which indicate whether a particular contract is a futures contract, and therefore a regulated investment, or a forward contract, and therefore an unregulated contract. It is important to appreciate that both a regulated futures contract and an unregulated forward contract operate in the same manner. The buyer and the seller effectively agree both the delivery date and the price to be paid by the buyer when they enter into the contract. Delivery and payment do not take place when the buyer and the seller enter into the contract; instead delivery and payment take place later on the delivery date.

8.22 Paragraph 1(1) of the notes to the definitions of a futures contract provides that a particular contract does not amount to a futures contract if it is made for commercial and not for investment purposes. Subsequent paragraphs of the notes then set out the indications as to whether or not a particular contract is made for commercial purposes, and therefore does not constitute a regulated futures contract but instead constitutes an unregulated forward contract, or for investment purposes, and therefore constitutes a regulated futures contract.

8.23 Although the particular futures contracts discussed in the *CR Sugar* case were traded on an exchange, the tribunal did not consider paragraph (2) of the notes, which provides that a contract 'shall be regarded as made for investment purposes if it is made or traded on a recognised investment exchange or made otherwise than on a recognised investment exchange but expressed to be as traded on such an exchange or on the same terms as those on which an equivalent contract would be made on such an exchange'. Although the New York affiliate traded the Sugar 11 contract on an exchange, apparently the affiliate did not trade the Sugar 11 contract on a recognized investment exchange.[13]

---

[13] See Chapter 6 for an explanation of the concept of the recognition of investment exchanges.

8.24 Therefore the tribunal considered paragraph (4) of the notes, which suggests that a contract is an unregulated forward contract if either (1) either or each of the parties to the contract is a producer of the commodity or other property, or uses the commodity or other property in his business; or (2) the seller delivers or intends to deliver the commodity or other property, or the purchaser takes or intends to take delivery of it. The tribunal found on the facts that CR and China National did not intend that delivery should take place. A letter sent by facsimile by China National on 23 April 1997 was found to be significant. China National stated the following. 'We hope that this contract still be a tool to make profit for both of us in the future, not to commit between us to deliver the physicals. This is our basic thought about the contract by now.' The tribunal also found that a trader does not use the asset that he trades in his business within the meaning anticipated in the notes. The basis for the tribunal's finding is that to use an asset within the meaning anticipated in the notes connotes that either a process is applied to the asset, such as a step in a manufacturing process, or that the asset is consumed during a process. Therefore the tribunal found that the long futures positions were investments, and therefore the put options bought by CR were also investments, and therefore unenforceable by CR.

8.25 The Commercial Court upheld the tribunal's decision, considering that the parties' intentions, whether or not to deliver the underlying sugar, are properly assessed when the put options were entered into, and not when the put options were purportedly exercised. This analysis was in accordance with guidance release M3/88 issued by the Securities and Investment Board.[14] The Commercial Court also refused CR's appeal on procedural grounds. Section 67 of the Arbitration Act 1996 governs a party's right to appeal arbitral awards on the ground that the relevant tribunal has acted beyond its substantive jurisdiction. The Commercial Court noted that CR did not frame its appeal in the manner allowed by the Arbitration Act 1996, and such an appeal would in any event have been out of time and therefore barred by section 73 of that Act.

8.26 The *CR Sugar* case remains a useful illustration of the scheme of the FSMA 2000 and its secondary legislation, as the FSMA 2000 differentiates between regulated futures contracts and unregulated forward contracts in generally the same manner as the FSA 1986. The differentiation is achieved by article 84 of the Regulated Activities Order.[15] Article 84(2) provides that a contract is not a futures contract if it is made for commercial and not investment purposes. Subsequent paragraphs of article 84 then set out the indications as to whether or not a particular contract is made for commercial purposes or for investment purposes.

---

[14] See paragraph 5.05.
[15] See paragraphs 5.61 ff.

8.27 It is important to emphasize that the provisions of the various paragraphs of article 84 generally serve as indications, and also operate as contra-indications. For example, if a particular contract does not satisfy one of the requirements needed to demonstrate that it is made for commercial purposes, then the contract is apparently made for investment purposes. Further, the particular facts and circumstances surrounding a particular contract will determine whether or not that contract is a regulated futures contract or an unregulated forward contract, and the court will always look at the substance of the parties' dealings to determine their intentions, notwithstanding any contractual provision to the contrary. Thus much was made of the letter sent by China National on 23 April 1997, which was evidence of the discussions that had taken place between CR and China National, and which demonstrated that the parties did not contemplate that physical delivery of the sugar would actually take place. In this way, the *CR Sugar* case also demonstrates the common principle that judicial analysis will always include the parties' intentions, whatever the subject of the litigation, and therefore written contractual terms which clearly contradict the parties' course of dealings will be disregarded. This principle resonates more widely than the judicial consideration of derivative contracts.

8.3 The Construction of the Terms of a Derivative Contract

8.28 A key early case which established the very high standard of detail and accuracy expected of the documents used in the institutional OTC derivative markets was the unreported litigation *Deutsche Bank AG v ANZ Banking Group Ltd*. A brief judgment was handed down by Langley J in the High Court on 28 May 1999. The case involved a credit default swap, one of the class of credit derivative transactions which were becoming more mainstream in the late 1990s. Daiwa (Europe) Ltd (Daiwa) had lent US$50 million to the City of Moscow under a loan agreement. Daiwa and Deutsche Bank AG (Deutsche) entered into a credit default swap, under which Deutsche sold credit protection to Daiwa in respect of the credit risk projected by the loan and to which Daiwa was exposed. Deutsche in turn entered into a second credit default swap with ANZ Banking Group Ltd ('ANZ'), under which Deutsche bought credit protection to offset its exposure under the first credit default swap it had with Daiwa. Presumably, and this is not indicated by Langley J's judgment, Deutsche sold credit protection to Daiwa for a higher premium than the premium paid by Deutsche to buy the hedging protection from ANZ, and so Deutsche was trading the credit risk projected by the City of Moscow's repayment obligations.

8.29 The second credit default swap was described in a confirmation letter dated 19 September 1997. Under the second credit default swap, on the occurrence of the specified credit event, Deutsche would deliver to ANZ bonds issued by the

City of Moscow, and ANZ would pay Deutsche US$25 million. The definition of credit event set out in the second credit default swap contract incorporated three requirements, all of which had to be fulfilled to trigger the obligations of ANZ and Deutsche. One, the City of Moscow fails to pay, after an applicable grace period, an amount equal to or exceeding a threshold amount of US$10 million. Two, Deutsche delivers to ANZ a credit event notice and a notice of publicly available information. Three, the bonds to be delivered decrease in value to 85% of their face value for a period lasting 14 days or longer after the delivery of the required notices. A notice of publicly available information was defined as a notice which confirmed the occurrence of the credit event, and publicly available information was defined as information which reasonably confirmed any assertion made in the credit event notice and which was published in one internationally recognized published or electronically displayed news source.

8.30 The City of Moscow was to have repaid to Daiwa its loan in full on 19 August 1998. However, the terms of the loan were amended on 19 August 1998 so that the City of Moscow could repay the loan by instalments, with the final instalment being scheduled to be made on 21 August 1998. In the event, the City of Moscow paid the final instalment on 24 August 1998, one working day late. Deutsche fulfilled its obligations under the first credit default swap, and on 28 September 1998 Deutsche sent a letter to ANZ, purporting to be both a credit event notice and a notice of publicly available information. Deutsche relied on an article which was published on 26 September 1998 in the 'International Financing Review' as the required publicly available information. However, ANZ resisted taking delivery of the bonds and making the payment to Deutsche of the US$25 million.

8.31 Deutsche therefore sought to enforce the second credit default swap. ANZ attempted to argue that the events which actually took place constituted a 'technical' credit event and not a 'substantial' credit event, and therefore the events which actually took place did not constitute a credit event within the definition contained in the documentation for the second credit default swap. Langley J disagreed with ANZ's assertion, stating '. . . I cannot conceive of any banker who would agree to matters of such imprecision'. Langley J therefore ordered that ANZ should fulfil its obligations under the second credit default swap, on the basis that in litigation ANZ was seeking to rewrite the contract that it had signed. Langley J was clear that '. . . the law is that rewriting the agreement they did make is not permissible'. Langley J therefore gave effect to the terms of the second credit default swap and did not permit any variation to those terms. Langley J drew attention to the fact that the litigants were 'two banks operating in the derivatives market' and therefore by implication they would be expected to enter into an agreement which sets out exactly the transaction they had negotiated.

8.32 Although rectification was not available to ANZ in its litigation against Deutsche, rectification is of course available as an equitable remedy to correct the written terms of a contract in order that the true intentions of the parties as to their agreement are accurately recorded. The actual availability of rectification is limited in that rectification corrects an error in the documentation of an agreement and does not modify the actual promises made in the agreement; the distinction can be subtle, and there are few grounds upon which the apparent agreement reached can be displaced. Cozens-Hardy MR expressed[16] the use to which rectification is put. 'The essence of rectification is to bring the document which was expressed and intended to be in pursuance of a prior agreement into harmony with that prior agreement.' The definition of the credit event in the documentation for the second credit default swap, whether in retrospect describing a 'technical' credit event or a 'substantial' credit event, was the definition by which ANZ expressed itself willing to be bound.

8.4 Derivative Contracts Recharacterized as Other Contracts

One of the principal risks of which commercial actors must be cognizant is the risk that their contract is recharacterized in a manner that they did not anticipate or desire. The recharacterization of a contract potentially gives rise to severe difficulties, whether in terms of regulatory consequences, the enforceability of the contract, which may include the priority and therefore effectiveness of a security device, the risk of an unexpected effect following the insolvency of one of the parties, or a treatment of the contract for tax purposes which threatens to undermine the economic benefits of entering into the contract in the first place. This risk of a recharacterization of a contract is not confined to derivative contracts; this risk is indeed found in the wider commercial arena.[17] However, derivative contracts do bear witness to significant examples of the risk of a recharacterization. **8.33**

As a general comment, the recharacterization of a contract appears to contradict the foundation of certainty which underpins commercial dealings under English law. The need for certainty has long been understood, as Lord Mansfield declared in *Vallejo v Wheeler*.[18] 'In all mercantile transactions the great object should be certainty: and, therefore, it is of more consequence that a rule be certain, then whether the rule is established one way or other. Because speculators in trade then know what ground to go upon.' This well-established principle has informed the court's view that it should where possible give effect to what contracting **8.34**

---

[16] *Lovell and Christmas Ltd v Wall* (1911) 104 LT 85.
[17] See *WT Ramsay Ltd v Inland Revenue Commissioners* [1982] AC 300, which is discussed in Chapter 11, and *National Westminster Bank plc v Spectrum Plus and others* [2005] UKHL 41, which is discussed at paragraph 6.26.
[18] (1774) 1 Cowp 143 at 153.

parties intend,[19] but under certain circumstances, a contract should be recharacterized. A contract which does not set out the true intentions and agreement of the parties is generally referred to as a 'sham', and such a contract is usually treated as void.[20] A contract which does set out the true intentions and agreement of the parties, and which therefore is not a sham, but to which the parties have applied a particular legal label which does not accord with its proper categorization as a matter of law, is susceptible to the risk of recharacterization. The risk of a recharacterization arises if there is some inconsistency between the rights and obligations set out in the contract and the intended effect of the contract.

8.35 The contemporary stance of the courts to recharacterization of contracts is found in the decision of the Court of Appeal in *Welsh Development Agency v Export Finance Co Ltd*,[21] which is generally referred to as the '*Exfinco* case'. If the parties had entered into a sham contract which creates rights and obligations that are different to their intentions, then the court will disregard the description applied to the contract by the parties. By contrast, if the contract is not a sham, then the court will only disregard the description applied to the contract by the parties if the rights and obligations contained in the contract are inconsistent with that description. Following the *Exfinco* case, the Privy Council developed a more detailed test for determining whether or not a contract, or indeed any other type of legal instrument, should be recharacterized in *Agnew and another v The Commissioner of Inland Revenue*,[22] as described by Lord Millett.[23] First, the court will attempt to determine the rights and obligations that the parties intended to create through the language that they used to draw up the contract. Second, the court will categorize the contract, and in doing so, the court will disregard the intentions of the parties as expressed in the language of the contract if those rights and obligations are clearly inconsistent with the actual arrangement that the parties intended to put in place, as demonstrated perhaps by the course of dealings between the parties.

Gaming contracts

8.36 One of the key issues that the nascent organized derivative markets faced was whether or not a derivative contract amounted to a gaming contract. Given that a

---

[19] See for example *Bank of Credit and Commerce International SA* (In Liquidation) *v Ali (No.1)* [2001] UKHL 8.

[20] A sham contract may remain in force in favour of an innocent third party.

[21] [1992] BCLC 148.

[22] [2001] 2 AC 710. The *Agnew* case is one of a series of litigation in respect of the proper characterization of charges, involving a charge over uncollected book debts that had been described as a fixed charge but was held to be a floating charge.

[23] A decision of the Privy Council is not binding, but persuasive. Lord Millett's approach was followed by Lord Hoffmann in *Smith v Bridgend County Borough Council* [2001] UKHL 58.

derivative can be used for both hedging purposes and for speculative purposes, the argument was put forward that a derivative contract used for speculative purposes is a gaming contract, or a wager. The key risk of a derivative contract being characterized as a gaming contract under the Gaming Act 1845 was that the derivative contract would therefore be unenforceable under the Gaming Act 1892. Provisions in the FSA 1986[24] and the FSMA 2000[25] should serve to put the matter beyond doubt, but this remains an issue that market participants and their legal advisers continued to remain wary of. However, the Gambling Act 2005, which has been enacted as a part of the reorganization and regulation of the gaming industry in the United Kingdom, has the important effect that gambling contracts are enforceable,[26] repealing certain pieces of legislation which hitherto prevented the enforcement of gambling contracts. These repeals do not permit enforcement of a gambling contract which was made before the repeals took effect.[27]

Insurance contracts

8.37 In recent years, the derivative markets have been required to address another issue of recharacterization of contract, no less important. The argument may be made that a derivative contract entered into for hedging purposes might be held to be an insurance contract. This argument particularly gained currency during the late 1990s as the credit derivative markets first began to evolve. Indeed, from an economic perspective, a credit default swap resembles very closely an insurance contract,[28] and the terms 'protection buyer' and 'protection seller', whilst serving to provide a useful framework for the comprehension of such contracts, also highlight the jeopardy of a recharacterization of such contracts.

8.38 The suggestion that a derivative contract is an insurance contract is important because entering into contracts of insurance is another regulated activity within the perimeter created by the FSMA 2000 and its secondary legislation. By way of necessary background, before the effective date of the FSMA 2000 (N2), the Insurance Companies Act 1982 governed the writing of insurance contracts. As paragraph 5.20 explains, a firm can only carry on the particular regulated activities for which it has a Part IV permission under the FSMA 2000, and civil, regulatory, and criminal sanctions are applied if the general prohibition is breached.

8.39 The principal risk to which market participants on the sell side are therefore exposed is the risk that a derivative is unenforceable because it has been recharacterized as

---

[24] Section 63.
[25] Section 412.
[26] Section 335(1) of the Gambling Act 2005 provides that the fact that a contract relates to gambling shall not prevent its enforcement.
[27] Section 334(2) of the Gambling Act 2005.
[28] See paragraph 4.173.

an insurance contract. The risk is that a counterparty on the buy side, from whose perspective a derivative contract has moved out-of-the-money, may attempt to claim that the contract is an insurance contract and that the seller of the contract therefore should not be able to claim payment. Certain parallels may therefore be drawn between the risk of adverse contractual characterization and the local authority swaps cases which were litigated throughout the 1990s. However, a number of arguments might be put forward that a derivative contract is after all not an insurance contract, and certain practicalities may also be of some assistance.

8.40 First, the intention of the parties is that their contract is a derivative contract. They do not intend to enter into an insurance contract, even though the economic effect of the derivative contract is to insulate the buyer of the derivative from an adverse economic effect. This argument might be developed by considering the difference between the operation of a derivative transaction and the operation of an insurance contract. An insurance contract is generally entered into to provide protection from financial loss caused by the occurrence of a low probability high impact event. By contrast, a derivative contract such as a swap might be entered into to provide protection from financial loss caused by the occurrence of a high probability low impact event, such as an adverse movement in the underlying rate. Indeed, as part 4.7 of Chapter 4 explains, from the broadest perspective, a swap can be expected occasionally to move in-the-money and occasionally to move out-of-the-money, as the swap smoothes out fluctuations in the underlying rate to a straight line. Of course, other derivative contracts tend to resemble insurance contracts in that they also provide protection from financial loss caused by the occurrence of a low probability high impact event. For example, the payment by a protection seller to the protection buyer under a credit default swap might only be triggered by the insolvency of the reference entity which owes a payment obligation to the protection buyer. Such a credit derivative contract conforms with the informal definition of an insurance contract as a contract which provides protection from financial loss caused by a low probability high impact event. Therefore, heavy reliance cannot be placed on an analysis of the economic effect of the contract. Nonetheless, the intention of the parties as indicated by the intended economic effect of the contract is a significant factor. In particular, participants in the credit derivative market tend to state that their intention is that they enter into derivative contracts and not insurance contracts.

8.41 Second, a strict legal analysis of derivative contracts and insurance contracts indicates that there are differences between them, and a number of settled legal principles support the conclusion that a derivative contract is not an insurance contract. One, as stated in the foregoing paragraphs, the purpose of an insurance contract is to provide protection against the risk of a loss. This purpose is the only purpose of an insurance contract. An indemnifying payment is made under an

8.4 Derivative Contracts Recharacterized

insurance contract only if the insured party has suffered the specified loss. By contrast, a payment is made under a derivative contract irrespective of whether or not the payee has suffered a loss. Of course, the payee may have a suffered a loss that the payment that is made under the derivative contract offsets, but crucially for the purpose of this analysis, the payment that is made under the derivative contract is not triggered by the payee suffering any loss; the payment is instead triggered by the specified market movement, or, in the case of a credit derivative, the occurrence of the specified credit event. The distinction is admittedly fine. Two, under an insurance contract, the insured party must have an insurable interest. Blackburn J stated the following in *Wilson v Jones*.[29] 'A policy [of insurance] is, properly operating, a contract to indemnify the insured in respect of some interest which he has against the perils which he contemplates it will be liable to; and I know of no better definition of an interest in an event than that indicated by Laurence J in *Barclay v Cousins*[30] and more fully stated by him in *Lucena v Craufurd*[31] that if the event happens the party will gain an advantage. If it is frustrated he will suffer a loss.' By contrast, a party to a derivative contract is not required to have an interest in the underlying. Indeed, for example, no payment or delivery is made of the underlying of a swap. Three, and building on points one and two, although the economic effect of certain derivatives, in particular credit derivatives, can be similar to the economic effect of insurance contracts, the appropriate analysis of whether a particular contract is a derivative contract or an insurance contract rests on the rights and obligations set out in the contract. Crucially, if the parties genuinely intend to operate their contract in accordance with the specified rights and obligations, then the contract is characterized in accordance with those rights and obligations, However, if the parties are found by the court not to have operated their contract in accordance with the rights and obligations set out in the agreement, then the court can characterize the contract, whether as a derivative contract or as an insurance contract, with reference to the actual conduct of the parties.

8.42 The correct characterization and drafting of contracts, as either derivative contracts or as insurance contracts, can be particularly important in the context of 'insurance transformer' transaction structures, which involve the transfer of risk between banks and insurance companies. Generally a bank buys credit protection from a special purpose vehicle (SPV) under a credit derivative transaction, and the SPV in turn buys insurance from an insurance company, which might then be able to buy reinsurance. The transfer of risk across the sectors of the financial markets is complex, and one of the key issues is the correct drafting of the relevant contracts.

---

[29] (1867) 2 Ex 150.
[30] (1802) 2 East 544.
[31] (1806) 127 ER 630.

8.43 Third, as paragraph 8.36 indicates, an authorized person is not precluded by section 20 of the FSMA 2000 from enforcing an agreement if he enters into the agreement during the course of carrying on a regulated activity in respect of which he does not have a Part IV permission. The civil sanction contained in section 26 of the FSMA 2000, that an agreement made in contravention of the general prohibition is unenforceable, is applied only to unauthorized persons.

8.44 Fourth, the attempt by the party buying the derivative contract effectively to claim that the contract is unenforceable should constitute an event of default under section 5(a)(ii) of the ISDA 2002 Master Agreement. Of course, if the master agreement itself is found to be void and unenforceable, then whether or not the early termination close-out provisions would be applied, which broadly require the party which is out-of-the-money to make a single net payment to the other party, remains an uncertain issue. The local authority swaps cases suggest that there is growing jurisprudence under English law which would seek to enforce contractual terms under certain circumstances. Lord Woolf speaking in the House of Lords in the *Islington* case suggested that a commercial commonsense approach might be applied by the courts to give effect to the provisions of derivative contracts which allocate risk; in this context, the relevant provisions which allocate risk are the provisions which stipulate how transactions are unwound and a net sum becomes payable.

8.45 It is worth noting that ISDA has obtained a legal opinion that a credit derivative contract is not an insurance contract; this legal opinion is available to ISDA's members.

8.46 As a final observation, mortality rates constitute one of the new classes of underlying in respect of which derivative products are being developed. Derivative contracts written on mortality rates represent a means of transferring into the financial markets a category of risk that has hitherto remained within the boundaries of the life insurance sector and its accompanying reinsurance market. However, the transfer of such risks into the financial markets is not without precedent, as witnessed by the issue of 'catastrophe bonds' in the 1990s[32] and of course the development more recently of 'insurance transformer' transactions and catastrophe swaps.

---

[32] Catastrophe bonds, which are also referred to as 'cat bonds', were first issued by insurance companies seeking to lay off the risks of natural disasters, such as hurricanes, that they had insured. The principal of the bonds is written down if the particular natural disaster specified for the purpose of the terms and conditions of the bonds occurs, thereby giving investors an exposure to an asset class other than financial assets and commodities.

8.5 The Doctrine of Ultra Vires

Loans

Two examples are shown in this book of a derivative transaction that can be used as **8.47** a means of raising finance: the accreting strike call option[33] and the discounted swap in the *Islington* case.[34] The economic effect of a derivative financing transaction is the same as the economic effect of a lending arrangement, and therefore a derivative financing transaction may, under certain circumstances, be recharacterized as a lending arrangement. Although the parties intend that they enter into a derivative contract, because the derivative contract is economically indistinguishable from a lending arrangement, the risk that the derivative contract is recharacterized as a lending arrangement arises if the derivative contract contains rights and obligations which have more the character of those found in a lending arrangement.

The consequences of such a recharacterization as a lending arrangement might **8.48** include the following. One, if the derivative contract is recharacterized as a secured lending transaction, then the court may find that a security interest has been created that should be registered under the regime established by companies legislation, and that security interest is found to be void and ineffective because it has not been registered.[35] The second, and potentially more damaging, consequence of a failure to register a charge to which the registration requirement applies is that money purportedly secured by it immediately becomes repayable. Two, if one of the parties to the purported derivative contract is holding assets in order to hedge its obligations under that contract, recharacterization of that contract may constrain that party from dealing freely with those assets, particularly if those assets were delivered to that party by the other as a part of the transaction. Three, the regulatory and accounting treatment of a loan may differ from that of a derivative contract, and therefore recharacterization of that contract may render inaccurate the records and accounts of the parties. The implications of inaccurate records and accounts being maintained could extend further than difficulties with obtaining a clean audit; the financial institution involved may hold less regulatory capital than it is required to, with potentially serious regulatory consequences. The particular circumstances of the recharacterized derivative transaction may give rise to other consequences.

8.5 The Doctrine of Ultra Vires

A critical risk that participants in the derivative markets, and indeed commercial **8.49** actors more widely, must recognize and control is the risk that a counterparty is

---

[33] See part 4.10 of Chapter 4.
[34] See paragraphs 8.56 ff.
[35] The registration requirement under successive enactments of the Companies Act is discussed at paragraph 7.76.

acting ultra vires, or literally 'beyond the powers'.[36] A party is said to be acting ultra vires if it enters into a transaction which is outside the scope of its legal power. A party's legal power to act might be described in the documents of its establishment, such as a company's memorandum or articles of association, or it might be contained in applicable legislation, such as the statutes governing the function of local government authorities in the United Kingdom.

8.50 An ultra vires contract is treated in law as never having been entered into, and it is therefore void ab initio, that is, from the very outset of the purported agreement. The risk is therefore that the rights and remedies that are set out in the ultra vires contract are not available because through the operation of law the contract has never been entered into. An ultra vires contract is not enforced by the courts, and therefore recovery of any money that has already been paid out under the contract might become difficult, as any payment that has been made under the ultra vires contract has been made for consideration that has failed. A claimant seeking recovery of money that has been paid under the contract must therefore look outside the contract for a remedy. This is the very crux of the difficulty that an ultra vires contract poses; a party may be denied repayment of money that has been paid under the contract, and this might result in the unjust enrichment of the counterparty, unless equitable relief is given.

8.51 Capacity risk is therefore the risk that a counterparty is acting outside the scope of its legal powers. Capacity risk is less significant in the exchange-based market, as almost by definition a member of an investment exchange is not exposed to any capacity risk in respect of any other member of the exchange, and of course the clearing house assumes the role of central counterparty. However, a member of an exchange may be exposed to capacity risk in respect of a counterparty which is not a member of the exchange and to which that member provides services such as access to the exchange-based market or clearing services. Capacity risk is therefore more significant in the bilateral privately negotiated OTC market, which generally lacks the protective framework afforded by the exchange and its associated infrastructure.

The local authority swaps cases

8.52 A series of litigation which was fought during the 1990s arose from the crystallization of capacity risk in respect of OTC derivative transactions. These cases are

---

[36] Successive enactments of the Companies Act contain provisions which purport to minimize the risk that a company might act ultra vires. Section 31(1) of the Companies Act 2006 provides that unless a company's articles specifically restrict its objects, its objects are unrestricted, and s 39(1) of the Companies Act 2006 provides that the validity of an act done by a company shall not be called into question on the ground of lack of capacity by reason of anything in the company's constitution.

8.5 The Doctrine of Ultra Vires

sometimes referred to as the local authority swaps cases, because they all involve the use of swaps by United Kingdom local government authorities. The local authority swaps cases represent an important phase in the evolution of the English law of trusts and the equitable remedy of restitution. The relevance of these cases therefore resonates considerably wider than the derivative markets.

The *Hammersmith* case

8.53 The risk that ultra vires transactions are unenforceable came to light in the headline decision in *Hazell v Hammersmith & Fulham London Borough Council*.[37] During the fiscal years 1987/88 and 1988/89, the London Borough of Hammersmith & Fulham entered into a significant number of interest rate swap transactions with a number of financial institutions. As well as hedging its exposures to adverse movements in interest rates, Hammersmith was also taking speculative positions, seeking to profit from interest rate movements. As interest rates moved against it, Hammersmith began to lose increasing amounts of money in respect of certain of its transactions, and Hammersmith's auditor Anthony John Hazell, acting through the Audit Commission for local authorities, took proceedings to have the transactions declared void, on the grounds that Hammersmith was acting ultra vires. Hammersmith's powers were contained in part in the Local Government Act 1972, and judicial consideration of the case involved an analysis of whether or not a local government authority had the legal capacity under that Act to enter into derivative transactions, both for hedging purposes and for speculative purposes.

8.54 The High Court ruled on 1 November 1989 that all of the transactions were ultra vires and therefore void. The Court of Appeal ruled on 22 February 1990 that the hedging transactions were valid, but not the speculative transactions. However, the Judicial Committee of the House of Lords ruled on 24 January 1991 that all of the transactions, both the hedging transactions and the speculative transactions, were ultra vires and therefore void, upholding the decision of the High Court.

8.55 The effect of the decision in the *Hammersmith* case was far-reaching. Many other transactions entered into between local authorities and financial institutions were effectively invalidated by the decision, and consequently further local authority swaps cases were litigated. The decision in *Hammersmith* precipitated a rush of litigation as financial institutions commenced proceedings to recover money they had paid under swap transactions that were now being held to be ultra vires and therefore unenforceable.

---

[37] [1992] 2 AC 1.

Chapter 8: Legal Issues

The *Islington* case

8.56 The next significant local authority swaps case to be decided after the *Hammersmith* case was *Westdeutsche Landesbank Girozentrale v Islington London Borough Council*.[38] The *Islington* case is extremely important as it provides a clear expression of the English law of trusts and it represents a distinct step in the development of the remedy of restitution. Indeed, the *Islington* case has attracted significant academic attention, including Alastair Hudson's excellent book *Swaps, Restitutions & Trusts*.

8.57 Islington London Borough Council had entered into a discounted swap with Westdeutsche Landesbank Girozentrale. Aside from constituting an important element in the extensive swaps litigation of the 1990s, the *Islington* case is also a useful example of the flexibility and adaptability of swaps techniques. The discounted swap was effectively a loan wrapped in a swap. At the relevant time during the mid-1980s, local government authorities in the United Kingdom were subject to limits on the amount of financing they were permitted to raise. This was the practice of rate-capping, which was a major political issue at the time. Islington therefore borrowed money from WestLB under a discounted swap to make up the shortfall between its projected income, the rates it levied, and its projected expenditure. The discounted swap was a ten year swap of interest payments calculated in respect of an underlying notional amount of £25 million. Under the discounted swap, WestLB made an initial payment of £2,500,000, Islington was scheduled to pay to WestLB a floating rate of interest on the underlying notional £25 million, and WestLB was scheduled to pay to Islington a fixed rate of interest on the underlying notional £25 million. Crucially, the appropriate fixed rate in the prevailing interest rate environment for the ten year term of the £25 million was 9.43%. However, the actual fixed rate that WestLB was scheduled to pay to Islington was set lower at 7.5%. Therefore, by receiving a lower fixed rate under the swap, Islington was effectively repaying the £2,500,000 that it received at the outset of the transaction from WestLB. The swap was described as a discounted swap because the fixed rate that was actually applied was 1.93% less than the appropriate fixed rate that the prevailing interest rate environment implied.

8.58 Interest rates were raised during the late 1980s as monetary policy in the United Kingdom was tightened. From Islington's perspective, this was an adverse movement in interest rates. Islington was paying a floating rate of interest under the discounted swap it had on with WestLB, and therefore Islington began to owe to WestLB more than it originally anticipated it would have to pay. However, the decision of the High Court on 1 November 1989, that swaps entered into by local authorities are ultra vires and unenforceable, provided Islington with the

---

[38] [1996] AC 669.

opportunity to avoid further losses. Islington therefore disclaimed its obligations under the discounted swap. WestLB then commenced proceedings to recover the amount of the initial payment that had not been repaid, which amounted to £1,145,525.93.

The appeal to the House of Lords in the *Islington* case was on the issue as to whether or not WestLB could recover compound interest. Under English law, compound interest is only awarded against a trustee or another person in a fiduciary position or similar position of trust who has made an improper profit. An award of compound interest is made by the court exercising its equitable jurisdiction, whereas simple interest is awarded by the court under the jurisdiction conferred on it by section 35A of the Supreme Court Act 1981.[39] It was therefore necessary for the House of Lords to consider the nature of WestLB's remedy in order to be able to determine whether or not WestLB was entitled to recover compound interest from Islington. **8.59**

A key element of the decision in the House of Lords was the determination of whether or not WestLB's remedy was a common law remedy or an equitable remedy. By way of brief background, equity is a jurisprudence based on equality and fair-dealing, and the origins of equity can be traced back to the 13th century. A person who remained aggrieved because a common law court had failed to settle a matter in a just manner could petition the King and the King's court for an equitable, or fair, dispensation of justice. The Chancellor, and not the King, would actually consider the petition and gradually the Chancellor's office, the Chancery, began to assume the characteristics of a court, and hence the Court of Chancery became established. Certain equitable principles have emerged from the jurisprudence of the court: the twelve maxims of equity, providing guidance as to what is just and how to achieve justice. During the 19th century, courts other than the Court of Chancery were given jurisdiction to apply equity by the Supreme Court of Judicature Acts 1873 and 1875. Today, equity remains woven into the fabric of English law. A court determines the appropriate equitable response to a set of facts by exercising a discretion, but this discretion is exercised within an established boundary. **8.60**

The High Court ruled on 12 February 1993 for WestLB. Hobhouse J gave judgment that the initial payment received by Islington was held on a resulting trust for WestLB. Accordingly, WestLB was entitled to the return of the initial payment and an award of compound interest. Another case, *Kleinwort Benson Ltd v Sandwell Borough Council*[40] came on for hearing before Hobhouse J, but only the *Islington* case proceeded to the House of Lords. **8.61**

---

[39] Section 35A of the Supreme Court Act 1981 applies generally to proceedings for recovery of a debt or damages.
[40] [1994] 4 All ER 890.

8.62 The Court of Appeal, Dillon, Kennedy, and Leggatt LJJ, ruled on 17 December 1993 for WestLB, also giving judgment that the initial payment received by Islington was held on a resulting trust for WestLB and that WestLB was entitled to the return of the initial payment and an award of compound interest. Islington appealed to the House of Lords on the question of whether or not it should pay compound interest.

8.63 The Judicial Committee of the House of Lords (Lord Browne-Wilkinson, Lord Goff, Lord Slynn, and Lord Woolf) ruled on 22 May 1996. The decision of the House of Lords is extremely complex. The House of Lords reached its conclusion that WestLB should not recover compound interest by working through the nature of constructive trusts, the nature of resulting trusts, and the remedy of restitution. In summary, the House of Lords held that Islington did not hold the initial payment for WestLB on a constructive trust or on a resulting trust, and therefore WestLB did not have an equitable claim against WestLB. Instead, WestLB was entitled to a common law remedy of restitution under a personal claim for money had and received. WestLB's claim was personal because WestLB lacked any proprietary right to the money that it had paid to Islington; WestLB had no proprietary right to the money because Islington did not hold the money on trust.

8.64 Restitution is granted generally if three conditions are satisfied. One, a person A has been enriched by a benefit. Two, A has gained the benefit at the expense of another person B. Three, the circumstances of A's enrichment to the detriment of B are such that it would be unjust for A to retain the benefit.

8.65 Three divergent views were formed by the House of Lords. One, the majority view of the House of Lords was expressed by Lord Browne-Wilkinson. Lord Lloyd and Lord Slynn agreed with Lord Browne-Wilkinson. Lord Browne-Wilkinson's approach has been characterized as the equity approach, because his Lordship considered the availability of equitable trusts, which are trusts that are imposed by a court exercising its equitable jurisdiction, such as resulting trusts, and trusts which arise automatically through the operation of law, with no element of discretion. Two, Lord Goff expressed the classical restitution approach. His Lordship sought to analyse precedent to award restitution of a payment that had been made by mistake, recognizing the need to achieve a just result by reversing an unjust enrichment. Three, Lord Woolf expressed the commercial commonsense approach, by anticipating the enforcement by the courts of the expectations which arise in the course of commercial dealings. The divergence of the views expressed in the House of Lords has prompted the observation made by Alastair Hudson that 'the commercial context of financial derivatives became the battleground for an ideological conflict between the rules of equity and the emerging principles of restitution'.[41]

---

[41] *Swaps, Restitution & Trusts*, paragraph 1-04.

8.5 The Doctrine of Ultra Vires

8.66 The House of Lords analysed the nature of WestLB's remedy in order to determine whether or not WestLB should be entitled to an award of compound interest. Islington did not hold the initial payment of any of the other payments made by WestLB on a resulting trust because the parties intended that the money should be transferred outright to Islington. Islington did not hold the initial payment or any of the other payments made by WestLB on a constructive trust, because its conscience was not affected: Islington did not know that it had received the payments under a void transaction at the time when it received the payments. Islington did not owe a fiduciary duty to WestLB. Therefore, WestLB was entitled to restitution of the amount of the money that it had paid to Islington, and, allowing Islington's appeal on the issue of whether or not it should pay compound interest, WestLB was entitled only to an award of simple interest.

8.67 Lord Browne-Wilkinson's speech contains an elegant exposition of the English law of trusts. The trust is an important element of English law, essentially dividing ownership of property into a legal title and an equitable (or beneficial) title. The owner of the legal title to the trust property, the trustee, has control over the trust property, and the trustee's ownership should be perfected by fulfilling any relevant registration requirements. The owner of the equitable title to the trust property, the beneficiary, has certain rights over the trust property. These rights arise because the trustee holds the trust property on behalf of, and for the benefit of, the beneficiary. Some trusts are established using a formal document, and the division of the title to the trust property is achieved for administrative purposes; for example, a pension fund is almost invariably constituted as a trust. Other trusts are not created by a formal document, but instead arise through the operation of law, for example to remedy the unconscionable act of the person identified as the trustee, or they are imposed by the court as an equitable remedy. English law recognizes four broad categories of trust: the express trust, the implied trust, the constructive trust (or properly the institutional constructive trust), and the resulting trust. It is important to appreciate that there is no authoritative classification of trusts, which makes judicial consideration of this subject, such as that undertaken by Lord Browne-Wilkinson in the *Islington* case, especially important.

8.68 Briefly, a constructive trust arises through the operation of law. The function of the court is merely to declare that a constructive trust has arisen, and then to give effect to the constructive trust by making the appropriate order. A constructive trust arises automatically in response to four principles. The court has no discretion as to whether or not a constructive trust has arisen. Lord Browne-Wilkinson identified[42] the four principles. One, 'required dealing': the conscience of the legal owner of the property requires the legal owner to deal with the property in a

---

[42] [1996] AC 669 at 705 C.

manner which is consistent with the beneficial title to the property of the beneficial owner. Two, 'affected conscience': the equitable jurisdiction to enforce a constructive trust depends on the conscience being affected of the legal owner of the property. The legal owner cannot be a trustee if he is ignorant of the facts that are alleged to affect his conscience. Three, 'identifiable property': in order to establish a trust, the property that is alleged to be held under the trust must be identifiable. The only apparent exception to this principle is that a constructive trust might be imposed on a person who dishonestly assists with the breach of a trust even if that person does not actually hold the property in respect of which the constructive trust arises. Four, 'divided ownership': there is a division of the ownership of the property. From the date of the establishment of the trust, the beneficial owner holds the beneficial title to the property. The beneficial owner's interest in the property will be enforced against any subsequent holder of the property, or any substitute property that can be traced as being substitute property, other than a person who buys the legal title to the property with no notice of the existence of the beneficial title to the property.

8.69 In the *Islington* case, there was no affected conscience and therefore no constructive trust arose. The initial payment was made before the judgment was handed down by the High Court in the *Hammersmith* case that swaps are ultra vires and therefore void in the hands of local authorities. At the time when WestLB made the initial payment, both WestLB and Islington intended to give effect to a transaction that they both believed was within the capacity of each of them. There was no divided ownership and therefore no constructive trust arose. WestLB and Islington did not intend at the time when WestLB made the initial payment to divide the ownership of the money into a legal title, which Islington had, and a beneficial title, which WestLB would have had.

8.70 By contrast, a resulting trust is imposed as an equitable remedy by the court exercising its discretion. The court will only impose a resulting trust if the court is satisfied that either of two presumptions is raised by the circumstances of the case. The first presumption is 'presumed purpose': a voluntary payment is made by a person A to another person B for the purpose of purchasing property that is to be vested in B alone or in the joint names of A and B. There is a presumption that A did not intend to make a gift of the money to B. That is, there is a presumption that A made the payment for the purchase of the property to be held on trust, and therefore B holds the money or property on a resulting trust for A. The presumption can of course be rebutted if it can be demonstrated that A did after all intend to make a gift or outright transfer to B. The second presumption is 'presumed retention': a person A transfers property to another person B on an express trust, but the express trust does not provide for, or exhaust, the entire beneficial interest in the property. The circumstances of the transfer might be such that there is

8.5 The Doctrine of Ultra Vires

a presumption that A intends to retain the beneficial title to the property. Therefore B holds the property on a resulting trust for A.

8.71 In the *Islington* case, there was presumed purpose and therefore no resulting trust was imposed. WestLB and Islington intended at the time when WestLB made the initial payment that the initial payment was to be made outright to Islington. There was no presumed retention and therefore no resulting trust was imposed. WestLB and Islington did not intend at the time when WestLB made the initial payment to divide the ownership of the money into a legal title, which Islington had, and a beneficial title, which WestLB would have had.

8.72 Lord Browne-Wilkinson also suggested that the remedial constructive trust might become a part of English law.[43] 'Although the resulting trust is an unsuitable basis for developing proprietary restitutionary remedies, the remedial constructive trust, if introduced into English law, may provide a more satisfactory road forward. The court by way of remedy might impose a constructive trust on a defendant who knowingly retains property of which the plaintiff has been unjustly deprived.' The remedial constructive trust would combine the principal requirement for the subsistence of a constructive trust, that the conscience of the alleged trustee has been affected, with the discretionary quality of the resulting trust, that the trust is awarded by the court in its discretion, and the extent to which the trust operates is also in the court's discretion. Goulding J had suggested in *Chase Manhattan Bank NA v Israel-British Bank (London) Ltd*[44] that there was no distinction between English law and the laws of the State of New York as to the availability of a remedial constructive trust. Although New York law does allow the imposition of a constructive remedial trust, English law does not.

8.73 Lord Goff delivered a conservative speech setting out the classical principles of restitution. Lord Goff's view was that restitution should be achieved to return the parties to the position they had originally occupied. Lord Goff therefore propounded restitution by way of rescission. The overall approach was that each party should pay back the money it had received, but more sensibly, that the party which had received the most should pay the difference to the other party, together with an appropriate award of interest. Lord Goff considered[45] that WestLB should be awarded a 'complete remedy', which would be effected through full rescission. Therefore Lord Goff considered that WestLB should recover compound interest, having regard to 'the commercial realities of the case'. Lord Goff analysed the commercial realities in a very succinct manner. 'The council has had the use of the bank's money over a period of years. It is plain on the evidence that, if it had not

---

[43] [1996] AC 669 at 716.
[44] [1981] Ch 105.
[45] [1996] AC 669 at 691.

had the use of the bank's money, it would (if free to do so) have borrowed the money elsewhere at compound interest. It has to that extent profited from the use of the bank's money. Moreover, if the bank had not advanced the money to the council, it would itself have employed the money on similar terms in its business.'

8.74 Lord Goff did not consider that a resulting trust would be available to effect restitution, on the ground that the imposition of a resulting trust would be inconsistent with the traditional principles of trust law. Lord Goff drew attention to the perceived difficulty with establishing the role of the trustee, whose obligations to deal with trust property would not be clear. Therefore Lord Goff agreed with Lord Browne-Wilkinson that a resulting trust should not be imposed, but whereas Lord Goff's reasoning was drawn from a consideration of principle, Lord Browne-Wilkinson instead focused on the conditions necessary for the subsistence of a trust.

8.75 Lord Woolf considered the development of a commercial commonsense approach, which is discussed in the following paragraphs.

8.76 The principal implication of the decision in the *Islington* case is that the availability of a particular equitable remedy, the imposition and enforcement of a resulting trust, is limited. A potential consequence of the *Islington* case is therefore that the mutual intentions of the parties to a commercial contract might not be enforced. Therefore, commentators assert that further legal risk has been introduced into the financial markets, although this risk must be considered in the light of the willingness of the judiciary to promote commercial certainty. The *Islington* case also represents an important step in the evolution of the English law of restitution.

The *Lincoln* case

8.77 The effect of the decision in the *Islington* case has been confirmed and in part qualified by the decision of the House of Lords on 29 October 1998 in *Kleinwort Benson Ltd v Lincoln City Council and others*.[46] The *Lincoln* case represents the evolution of the remedy of restitution, building on the foundation laid in the *Islington* case. Kleinwort Benson sought to recover money that it had paid to various local government authorities, including Lincoln City Council, under various swap transactions that were found to be void and unenforceable following the decision in the *Hammersmith* case.

8.78 The decision in the *Lincoln* case principally addressed the application of the Limitation Acts, principally the Limitation Act 1980, to claims for restitution. The Limitation Acts generally operate to bar a claim that is brought after a specified period, which is referred to as the period of limitation. However, certain

---

[46] [1998] 3 WLR 1095.

8.5 *The Doctrine of Ultra Vires*

provisions of the Limitation Acts delay the start of the period of limitation in certain circumstances, allowing more time for a claim to be brought. In order to bring its claims against the local authorities, Kleinwort Benson needed to demonstrate that its claim was for money paid under a mistake; that is, its claim was for restitution, in order that the Limitation Act 1980 would operate with the effect that Kleinwort Benson's claim would not be time-barred. However, the complexity in the *Lincoln* case was that the mistake that had been made was a mistake of law and not of fact. Kleinwort Benson and the local authorities had entered into their swap transactions on the basis of a mistake as to the law governing the capacity of local authorities to enter into swap transactions. Before the *Lincoln* case, restitution had only been available to recover money that had been paid under a mistake of fact and not under a mistake of law. This was what the Law Commission described in its report *Restitution: Mistakes of Law and Ultra Vires Public Authority Receipts and Payments*[47] as a 'perceived unfairness' of the law of restitution before the *Lincoln* case.

8.79 The *Lincoln* case established that the English law recognizes a general right to recover money that had been paid under a mistake, on the ground that the recipient has been unjustly enriched, whether that mistake is a mistake of fact or of law. Lord Goff stated that[48] 'the mistake of law rule should no longer be maintained as part of English law, and . . . English law should now recognise that there is a general right to recover money paid under a mistake, whether of fact or law, subject to the defences available in the law of restitution . . .'.

8.80 From Lord Goff's exposition of the development of the remedy of restitution, the second principle flows that restitution should be available to recover money that has been paid under a settled understanding of the law, which was subsequently changed by a judicial decision. The context of this principle is of course the decision in the *Hammersmith* case which was handed down after the payments had been made.

8.81 A further three principles, no less important than the first two, emerge in the *Lincoln* case. One, it is no defence to a claim for restitution of money paid under a mistake that the recipient believed that he was entitled to retain the money, either at the time when the payment was made or when he became aware of the mistake. Two, whether or not an ultra vires contract has been fully performed is irrelevant to the issue whether or not money that has been paid under that contract should be recovered. Three, restitution is not based on the profitability or otherwise of the contract.

---

[47] Law Com No 227 Cm 2731.
[48] [1998] 4 All ER 513 at 533a.

The legacy of the local authority swaps cases

8.82 The decision in the *Lincoln* case was followed by Neuberger J presiding over the High Court in *Nurdin & Peacock PLC v DB Ramsden & Co Ltd*.[49] This case was unrelated to the financial markets, and concerned an action for the repayment of an overpayment of rent; this case illustrates the broader significance of the local authority swaps cases.

8.83 The local authority swaps cases represent a certain tension between, on one hand, the system of the financial markets, and on the other hand, the traditional elements of English law. Many commentators believe that the remedies available under English law are insufficient to give effect to the intentions of the parties to modern derivative contracts. These commentators argue that the artifice of the local authority swaps cases illustrates the imprecise link between the principles of equity and the risk control processes that a derivative contract seeks to establish.

8.84 To develop this observation, the financial institutions and the local authorities in both the *Islington* case and the *Lincoln* case had made a mistake as to law; they had entered into the swap transactions on the basis of a mistake as to the law governing the local authorities' capacity to enter into those transactions. The remedy in both the *Islington* case and the *Lincoln* case was restitution, but it was the decision in the *Lincoln* case, some two years after the decision in the *Islington* case, which formally broadened the availability of the remedy of restitution to include the repayment of money that had been paid under a mistake of law. Of course, from a practical perspective, the decision in the *Islington* case could not have been challenged by a lower court, and the decision in the *Islington* case should therefore be seen as an initial stage in the development of the remedy of restitution.

8.85 The extensive risk control provisions of a derivative contract, such as the ISDA 2002 Master Agreement, which is discussed in Chapter 7, already allocates the risks inherent in the overall trading relationship between the parties. These contractual provisions constitute the standard that is applied in the derivative markets. However, until more recent years, there has been little judicial consideration of the relevant derivative contracts. The local authority swaps cases involved contracts which had in the eyes of the law never been entered into, and therefore the terms of these contracts had not been analysed.

8.86 Lord Woolf speaking in the *Islington* case espoused the commercial commonsense approach, which would have regard to the allocation of risks by the contractual counterparties in their documentation. Lord Woolf remarked[50] 'it is no secret that the decision at first instance in [the *Hammersmith* case], which was approved by

---

[49] [1999] 1 WLR 1249.
[50] [1996] AC 669 at 720.

this House, caused dismay among some of those concerned with the standing abroad of the commercial law of this country'.

8.87 Lord Woolf's approach in the *Islington* case therefore suggests that a jurisprudence should develop which gives effect to the provisions in derivative contracts which allocate risk and put in place arrangements for credit support. Such a jurisprudence would minimize the difficulties witnessed to date, which have arisen in the context of the English law of equitable remedies such as restitution.

8.88 Measures to avoid capacity risk include performing an adequate and diligent investigation of the prospective counterparty. Of course, counterparty 'due diligence' procedures should be designed to control additional risks such as credit risk, and to establish that the prospective counterparty is not engaged in a money laundering scheme. A more efficient administration of the trading relationship is an additional benefit offered by well-designed processes. A legal opinion letter might also be obtained from independent legal advisers, confirming that the counterparty has the capacity to enter into the transaction and to execute any required document, and that the obligations assumed by the counterparty are its legal, valid, and enforceable obligations. Opinions are still sought despite the availability of companies legislation which erodes the ultra vires principle in the commercial context. Although omissions from a company's memorandum of association are explicitly addressed by companies legislation, reliance is generally not placed on this. Of course, opinion letters are often heavily negotiated and contain robust caveats, and therefore it is important to determine the matters on which an opinion is being obtained and to exercise a degree of practicality as to the matters in respect of which the independent legal advisers can actually provide an opinion; they work from publicly available documents, such as records held by company registrars.

8.89 Notwithstanding the apparent tension which is said to exist between the system of the financial markets and the traditional elements of English law, the local authority swaps cases demonstrate the willingness of the English judiciary to develop certain equitable principles, such as the remedy of restitution, to prevent the unjust enrichment of a party to a derivative contract that is subsequently found to be ultra vires in the hands of the counterparty. However, whether or not an equitable remedy is available will be determined in part by the claimant's own conduct. The very basis of equity is fair-dealing, and a claim for an equitable remedy will generally only succeed if the claimant's own conduct is beyond reproach. In the context of a claim for restitution following the crystallization of capacity risk, the claimant must be able to demonstrate that it had investigated its counterparty's capacity to enter into the trading relationship and the relevant transactions. It would not be enough to claim restitution on the strength of any particular representation or warranty contained in any documentation. The claimant must generally be able to demonstrate the implementation and use of counterparty 'due diligence' procedures, and to demonstrate that any adverse information that those procedures indicated has been acted upon.

8.90 The commercial commonsense approach that Lord Woolf favoured in the *Islington* case continues to become apparent, through the application of the provisions of OTC derivative documentation which allocate risk to ascertain the liability that each party owes to the other on what would be an early termination of outstanding transactions. The importance of these documents will grow if the commercial commonsense approach is adopted. An indication of the growing awareness of the legislature of the commercial realities of derivative trading relationships is the innovation of the Financial Collateral Arrangements (No. 2) regulations 2003.[51]

8.91 Certain of the speeches constituting the decision of the House of Lords in *Sempra Metals Limited (formerly Metallgesellschaft Limited) v Her Majesty's Commissioners of Inland Revenue and another*[52] in part reflect the desire of the judiciary to give greater effect to the realities of contemporary commercial relationships and conventions. Sempra Metals Limited (Sempra) dealt in metals listed on the London Metal Exchange, both as a trader and as a broker for clients. Sempra was resident for tax purposes in the United Kingdom, and it was a subsidiary of a parent company that was resident for tax purposes in Germany. Sempra paid dividends to the German parent company, and Sempra also paid advanced corporation tax (ACT) on those dividends. The amounts of ACT paid were later set off against Sempra's liability for mainstream corporation tax. Sempra made the payments of ACT in reliance on a statutory scheme that was not compliant with European Union law, and therefore Sempra made payments of tax before that tax was properly incurred. The decision of the House of Lords was that Sempra should recover compound interest.

8.92 Lord Nicholls made the observation that the 19th-century treatment of interest is not compatible with the 21st-century evaluation of money and the time-value of money, exploring the background to how interest came to be awarded.[53] In the first half of the 19th century, loans and debts did not carry interest, as illustrated by the judgment of Lord Tenterden CJ in *Page v Newman*.[54] Despite judicial concern at the inability of the courts to award interest, such as that expressed by Lord Herschell LC in *London, Chatham and Dover Railway Co v South Eastern Railway Co*,[55] who observed that a person wrongfully withholding money ought not in justice to benefit by enjoying the use of that money, this area of law was not revised until some 40 years later with the enactment of section 3 of the Law Reform

---

[51] See paragraphs 7.25 and 7.77.
[52] [2007] UKHL 34.
[53] [2007] UKHL 34 at paragraphs 76 ff.
[54] (1829) 9 B & C 378.
[55] [1893] AC 429 at 437.

(Miscellaneous Provisions) Act 1934. Under section 3, courts were empowered to award simple interest on the amount for which judgment was given, in proceedings to recover any debts or damages, for the period from when the cause of action arose to the date of judgment. Litigation which followed in the years after the enactment of section 3[56] explored the distinction between general damages, which are losses that must be pleaded and proved, but the amount of which is determined by the court, and special damages, which are losses that are pleaded and proved purely in monetary terms.

The decision in *Sempra* was arguably presaged by the *Lincoln* case. Lord Hope referred to the 'Kleinwort Benson principle'[57] that a cause of action at common law is available for money paid under a mistake of law, and referred to a recent judgment which followed the principle, *Deutsche Morgan Grenfell plc v Inland Revenue Commissioners*.[58] Having established that restitution is available under common law as well as equity, an award of compound interest becomes available under common law. In the *Islington* case, which was decided some 11 years prior to the *Sempra* case, compound interest was not awarded because WestLB's remedy was found in common law, and not equity, and the court had the power to award only simple interest. The principle established in the *Lincoln* case, that restitution is available as a common law remedy as well as an equitable remedy, together with the premise that compound interest is required to achieve full restitution, as suggested by Lord Goff in the *Islington* case,[59] has resulted in the position now reached in the *Sempra* case and the availability of compound interest. Lord Hope concluded[60] that the opportunity to turn the money to account during the period of enrichment had passed from Sempra to the Revenue, and that restitution requires the entirety of the time value of the money that was paid prematurely to be transferred back to Sempra. In determining the correct time value of the money, simple interest is not enough, because it is an imperfect way of measuring the time value of the money. Several important principles of English law have developed as a result of the local authority swaps cases, the importance of which cannot be overestimated.

8.93

8.6 The Duty of Care: Selling and Misselling

One of the tensions within the derivative markets, particularly the OTC derivative markets, arises in the context of the duties and obligations that a dealer owes to its customer. In general terms, a dealer wishes to insulate itself from liability,

8.94

---

[56] See in particular *President of India v La Pintada Compania Navigacion SA* [1985] AC 104.
[57] Paragraph 22.
[58] [2006] UKHL 49.
[59] See paragraph 8.73.
[60] Paragraph 33.

and accordingly the dealer would seek to execute documentation which purports to achieve this limitation of liability. By contrast, the customer might on occasion be expected to seek, sometimes in court, to rely on the skills and care of the dealer. The extent of the duties and obligations that a dealer owes generally arise from its regulatory arrangements, the documentation that it negotiates and executes with its customer, and the duties that the courts have established are owed to the customer under general law. A further refinement of this broad expression of the duties that the dealer owes is the requirement to categorize the customer; the recent trend to develop and offer derivative exposures to retail consumers is discussed in part 8.7 of this chapter.

8.95 As Chapter 5 indicates, the convention of the institutional OTC derivative market might be summarized as caveat emptor, and various regulatory provisions and judicial commentary have reinforced this convention. However, the principle of caveat emptor is very much tempered by the framework within which these markets operate, and a participant in the markets cannot evade certain fundamental regulatory duties and obligations, such as the duty to not mislead customers and the duty to treat customers fairly, by arguing caveat emptor. Of course, as the following paragraphs show, the law in any event imposes a broad duty, which is independent of any regulatory rule, to not misrepresent facts and not to commit fraud. Further, in some circumstances, consumer protection legislation applies, and the offer of derivative exposures to retail consumers requires a modification of the standards imposed because of the different relationship between the financial institution and the retail consumer.

The *Bankers Trust* case

8.96 Leaving aside the regulatory standards that are applied, which are discussed in some detail in Chapter 5, the judicial consideration of the duties that a dealer owes to its customer should be noted. A key decision is the extensive judgment handed down on 1 December 1995 by Mance J in *Bankers Trust International PLC v PT Dharmala Sakti Sejahtera; PT Dharmala Sakti Sejahtera v Bankers Trust International PLC and another*.[61]

8.97 The facts of the *Bankers Trust* case are complex, but a number of clear principles have emerged from the litigation. These principles are entirely consistent with the manner in which the OTC derivative market operates. During the spring of 1994, Bankers Trust International PLC (BTI) entered into two swap transactions with the Indonesian company PT Dharmala Sakti Sejahtera (DSS). BTI acted through the Singapore branch of another company within the same group, Bankers Trust

---

[61] [1996] CLC 518.

8.6 Selling and Misselling

Company (BTCo), whose representatives marketed the participation of BTI in the two swap transactions.

8.98 BTI and DSS entered into the first swap on 27 January 1994. The first swap was a two year swap of interest payments in respect of an underlying notional amount of US$50 million. The structure of the first swap was complex, but it was designed to achieve a straightforward purpose. The first swap comprised two parts, and the amount payable by each party to the other in respect of each part was calculated separately. The combined effect of both parts was that if during each reference period of the first swap the reference interest rate, six month US dollar LIBOR, remained below a certain level, or barrier, then DSS would receive a payment from BTI, and if during that reference period the reference interest rate exceeded the barrier, then DSS would make a payment to BTI.

8.99 The US Federal Reserve Board raised its key Federal Funds rate by 0.25% from 3% to 3.25% on 4 February 1994. The reference interest rate of the first swap increased as a consequence of this tightening of US monetary policy. The first swap became unprofitable for DSS, and therefore following negotiation, BTI and DSS entered into a second swap, which was described as a 'LIBOR Barrier Swap'. The second swap was intended to replace the first swap, which was cancelled. Again, the second swap was a two year swap of interest payments in respect of an underlying notional amount of US$50 million, and the overall scheme of the second swap was the same as that of the first swap. Again, the second swap comprised two parts, and the amount payable by each party in respect of each part was calculated separately. Again, if during each reference period of the second swap the reference interest rate remained below the barrier, then DSS would receive a payment from BTI, and if during that reference period the reference interest rate exceeded the barrier, then DSS would make a payment to BTI. However, the structure of the second swap was more complex than the first, notwithstanding that they achieved the same effect. The second swap contained a more intricate formula than the first swap, and the second swap was more 'leveraged' than the first swap, which meant that movements in the reference interest rate resulted in more magnified profits or losses under the second swap.

8.100 The US Federal Reserve Board again raised the Federal Funds rate on 22 March 1994 and on 18 April 1994, and again the reference interest rate of the second swap increased in response to the further tightening of US monetary policy. The second swap moved out-of-the-money from DSS's perspective. DSS requested a valuation of the second swap. On 10 May 1994, BTCo valued the second swap at just over US$45 million in favour of BTI. On 13 May 1994, DSS wrote to Bankers Trust that it did not wish to proceed with the second swap, asserting that the 'gross misrepresentation' of BTCo had the effect of 'highlighting the rewards but not the high risks associated with the LIBOR Barrier Swap' and asserting that

BTCo had provided 'wrongful advice on the economic outlook'. Through BTCo, BTI had provided an analysis of the US interest rate environment.

8.101 In December 1994, BTI served a notice of default on DSS under the terms of the ISDA master agreement which governed the relationship between DSS and BTI, specifying that the amount of US$64,702,981 had become payable by DSS to BTI. BTI then brought proceedings on 20 December 1994 claiming that amount. DSS counterclaimed.

8.102 In summary, Mance J's judgment was that BTI's claim against DSS in respect of the second swap succeeded, and DSS's defence and counterclaim against BTCo and BTI failed. From a broad perspective, the judgment in the *Bankers Trust* case involved a close analysis of the relationship between BTCo, BTI, and DSS. Mance J made the following observation. 'The relationship under examination is not the conventional banker-customer relationship, although that too may on occasions be affected by representations, undertakings or the assumption of an advisory role. The bank here was marketing to existing or prospective purchasers derivative products of its own devising which were both novel and complex. The analysis of the relationship is in the circumstances one of some delicacy.'

8.103 The scope of the duty owed by a dealer to its customer depends very much on the particular circumstances of the relationship between them and the particular transaction. Although the *Bankers Trust* case involved esoteric commercial contracts, the scope of the duty of care owed by BTCo and BTI was defined with reference to well-established principles of law. In order to succeed, DSS generally had to prove '. . . the well-recognised, overlapping criteria of (a) foreseeability; (b) proximity; and (c) fairness, justice and reasonableness in the context of the particular relationship and situation and in the light of the type of harm (here financial loss) against which protection is sought. The ultimate decision whether to recognise a duty of care, and if so of what scope, is pragmatic.'

8.104 There was an imbalance between the expertise of the representatives of BTCo marketing the first swap and the second swap, and the officers of DSS who negotiated with them. However, Mance J found that the imbalance was sufficiently small that the officers of DSS who negotiated the purchase of the swaps possessed the necessary expertise to appreciate the nature of the transactions. Mance J commented that 'DSS was . . . to all appearances a company with considerable relevant skill, experience and diligence, which would be expected to analyse and assess [the second swap] in the same thorough way which it had demonstrated in relation to the previous proposals'. As DSS possessed the relevant skill and experience and demonstrated the appropriate degree of diligence, Mance J concluded elsewhere in his judgment that BTCo and BTI '. . . did not occupy a general advisory role'.

8.105 Although BTCo and BTI did not occupy a general advisory role, BTCo's representatives did set out in a letter dated 14 February 1994, and during a presentation

8.6 Selling and Misselling

which was given on 16 February 1994, an explanation of the operation of the second swap. In providing this explanation, BTI, through BTCo which was representing BTI, assumed a degree of responsibility. Mance J explored the degree of responsibility that BTI assumed, that is, the scope of the duty of care that BTI owed. 'BTI owed to DSS a duty not carelessly to misstate facts... this duty would oblige BTI and BTCo to present the financial implications of the proposal by a properly constructed graph and letter. The downside and upside of the proposal should have been presented in a balanced fashion.'

Mance J in particular criticized the manner in which BTCo's representatives explained the operation of the second swap, considering that the presentation 'fell below best standards'. However, Mance J felt that the deficiencies of the presentation came about because of 'lack of sufficient thought and over-enthusiastic salesmanship rather than deliberate misrepresentation or misconduct'. DSS could only succeed in its claim if there was a sufficiently close link between the actions of BTI acting through BTCo and the losses made by DSS. Mance J drew the following significant conclusion. 'The key factors are ultimately that DSS was, at the very least, aware that [the two parts of the second swap] involved a sharply escalating straight-line progression which could lead to large losses, even if DSS did not focus on their full extent before agreeing the swap, and that, when DSS did identify their full extent, it did not act in a manner which suggests that DSS felt that the presentation had been seriously misleading or that DSS would have acted any differently had it appreciated the full extent of the potential losses from the outset.' 8.106

Mance J's conclusion demonstrates that the extent of the duty of care owed by a dealer to its customer very much depends on the particular circumstances, and whether or not a dealer is liable for the losses made by its customer depends on all of the relevant circumstances taken together, and the assessment of the liability of the dealer is not made just by considering one circumstance in isolation from the others. The key elements of the decision in the *Bankers Trust* case might therefore be distilled as follows. One, BTCo and BTI did not owe a duty to DSS to explain the operation of the second swap. Two, nonetheless, BTCo and BTI did provide an explanation of the operation of the second swap, in a letter dated 14 February 1994 and a presentation made on 16 February 1994. Three, in providing the explanation, BTCo and BTI owed a duty to DSS 'not carelessly to misstate facts' and 'to present the financial implications of the proposal by properly constructed graph and letter'. Four, BTCo and BTI did not entirely fulfil their duty, but neither did they engage in some deliberate misrepresentation or misconduct. Five, although BTCo and BTI did not entirely fulfil their duty, DSS's decision to enter into the second swap was not influenced by the explanation given to its officers by BTCo's representatives. Although BTCo's representatives did not explain adequately the risks that DSS might make significant losses under the second swap, DSS was nonetheless aware of those risks, and significantly entered into the 8.107

second swap knowing about those risks. Hypothetically, the decision in the *Bankers Trust* case may well have been different had the court's finding been that DSS had been influenced by the explanation given to its officers by BTCo's representatives or that BTCo's representatives had engaged in some deliberate misrepresentation or misconduct.

8.108 The decision in the *Bankers Trust* case, although in favour of a financial institution acting as a dealer in derivatives and confirming the standards and conventions of the market, caused some considerable comment in the industry in 1996. The convention of the OTC derivative market might well have been caveat emptor, as reinforced by the various regulatory provisions which apply to this market, but the involved negotiation and sale of complex structured products might result in the assumption of responsibility by the dealer, and in assuming this responsibility, the dealer becomes exposed to the risk of a greater degree of liability.

8.109 In response to the concern expressed by market participants, in 1996 ISDA published its standard Representation Regarding Relationship Between Parties. The standard representation is intended to be incorporated into a master agreement and reflects the expectations of participants in the OTC derivative market that parties transact on an arm's length basis. In summary, each party makes the following representations to the other. One, the party does not rely on its counterparty. The party is acting for its own account and has made its own independent decisions, both whether or not to enter into the relevant transaction and whether or not the transaction is suitable for it, based on its own judgment. The party is not relying on any communication made by its counterparty, whether written or oral, as investment advice or as a recommendation. Two, the party is capable of assessing for itself the merits of a transaction, of understanding the transaction, and of accepting the terms, conditions, and risks of the transaction. Three, the party acknowledges that its counterparty does not act as a fiduciary or as an adviser to it. Parties would incorporate the standard representation in the schedule to their master agreement. The standard representation is now included as Part 4(m) of the Schedule to the 2002 ISDA Master Agreement.

8.110 As a consequence of the relationship risks which arise under scenarios such as that found in the *Bankers Trust* case and the local authority swaps cases, financial institutions began to incorporate into their terms of business agreements that generally the financial institution is not acting as its customer's investment adviser, and representations and warranties made by the financial institution and its customer that generally each of them has full capacity and authority to enter into and to perform its obligations under the derivative contract. Also, financial institutions began to express term sheets which set out the financial implications of a transaction or trading strategy such that the customer determines its own market view, reinforcing the limitations of the reliance that the customer is placing on the

8.6 Selling and Misselling

financial institution. Again, the term sheets categorically state that the financial institution is not acting as the customer's investment adviser.

8.111 Of course, the financial institution's reliance on such disclaimers might well be eroded in the particular circumstances of the case, such as the payment by the customer to the financial institution of a fee for devising trading strategies, the degree of reliance placed by the customer on the representatives of the financial institution, and the conduct or misconduct of any of the financial institution's representatives.

8.112 As mentioned, Part 4(m) of the Schedule to the ISDA 2002 Master Agreement now incorporates a representation made by each party to the other in the form of the standard representation. Inclusion of this standard representation in the usual form of agreement that is struck emphasizes that this is the norm that is applied in the OTC derivative market. The parties can of course amend the Schedule so that Part 4(m) does not apply to their relationship, and whether or not this is done is a matter of commercial balance and negotiation. It would however be very rare.

8.113 The standards required under MiFID and the refinement of the regulatory standards imposed by the FSA, which is focusing on the requirement that customers are treated fairly under the general legislative imperative of consumer protection, have qualified the application of caveat emptor. Although the protection given to eligible counterparties and professional clients is lighter than that given to retail clients,[62] all customers must be treated fairly and moreover, the financial institution is under an obligation to consider whether or not the particular transaction is suitable for its customer, in terms of the nature of the risks and the disclosure of those risks.

The *Peekay* case

8.114 Peekay Intermark Limited (Peekay) was a company controlled by its director and shareholder, Mr Harish Pawani. Peekay bought from the Australia and New Zealand Banking Group Limited (ANZ) a derivative product linked to a GKO[63] bond, which was a zero-coupon bond issued by the Russian Treasury and denominated in roubles. The derivative product was formulated by ANZ's structured products group, and marketed by ANZ's private bank. Pawani discussed Peekay's forthcoming investment with a sales representative of ANZ, who told him that ANZ would hold the GKO bond on behalf of Peekay. This description of the structure implied that ANZ would hold the GKO bond on behalf of Peekay under a trust; such a description gave rise to the expectation that Peekay would have recourse to the GKO bond in the event of a default by the Russian government.

---

[62] See paragraphs 5.24 ff.
[63] GKO is an acronym for Gosudarstvenniye Kratkosrochniye Beskuponniye Obligatsio.

Further, Pawani received a term sheet from ANZ which was consistent with the oral description given of the structure.

8.115 Peekay invested US$250,000 in the derivative product, and the Russian government subsequently defaulted in making payments on the GKO bonds it had issued. Following the cash settlement of the derivative product Peekay had bought, Peekay received back about 2.5% of its investment, which amounted to some US$5,000.

8.116 Contrary to the conversations which preceded Peekay's investment, and the term sheet that had been sent by ANZ's sales representative, the derivative product bought by Peekay was purely synthetic, in that although payments under the product were linked to the performance of the GKO bond, Peekay in fact had no beneficial interest in the GKO bond. That is, ANZ did not hold the GKO bond on trust for Peekay. In practical terms, the lack of any beneficial interest in the GKO bond denied Peekay any opportunity to attempt to retrieve some value from the GKO bond. Crucially, the actual transaction documents correctly described the structure of the derivative product that Peekay had bought, and included a statement that no reliance can be placed on any antecedent communication, whether written or oral, including the conversations with ANZ's sales representative.

8.117 Peekay and Pawani brought an action against ANZ.[64] The fundamental argument put forward by Peekay and Pawani was that Pawani had decided to invest in the derivative product on the basis of a misrepresentation made by ANZ's sales representative, and that Pawani would not have invested in the derivative product had he been aware of its terms. Further, Pawani argued that ANZ should have notified him of the difference between the description of the derivative product made by ANZ's sales representative and the actual written terms of that product. ANZ drew attention to the correct description of the structure of the derivative product contained in the final terms and conditions of the product, and the risk warning statement which accompanied the final terms and conditions, that any potential investor should ensure that he fully understands the nature of the transaction and the contractual relationship involved. Peekay and Pawani's case was weakened by the fact that Pawani had initialled every page of the final terms and conditions of the derivative product despite not having read the document.

8.118 The Commercial Court considered the description given by ANZ's sales representative as to the terms of the derivative product, considering what an investor could be expected to understand on the basis of the statements made to him, and

---

[64] *Peekay Intermark Limited (1) Harish Pawani (2) v Australia and New Zealand Banking Group Limited* [2005] EWHC 830 (Comm).

8.6 Selling and Misselling

the case turned on the extent to which any misrepresentation made by ANZ's sales representative was superseded by the documents. Richard Siberry QC sitting as judge in the Commercial Court concluded on 25 May 2005 that ANZ's sales representative did misrepresent the nature of the derivative product, in that Pawani was entitled to believe that Peekay would acquire a beneficial interest in the GKO bond under the structure described by the sales representative. ANZ's sales representative did not attempt to mislead Pawani; instead, the sales representative did not understand the product. However, the judge found that Pawani did not read any of the documents, and that he was 'unwise' to have not read the documents, but the judge nonetheless found that Pawani had placed a significant amount of trust and confidence in ANZ's private bankers and had no reason to believe that the derivative product would be anything other than that described by the sales representative. Accordingly, the judge awarded Peekay damages equal to the difference between the amount invested and the amount subsequently paid out. The judge was careful to warn that nothing in his judgment should be taken as encouragement to potential investors to ignore written terms and conditions applicable to their investments. The decision of the judge in the first instance in the *Peekay* litigation immediately generated concern in the financial services industry, and ANZ promptly appealed.

8.119 The Court of Appeal found for ANZ in a judgment delivered on 6 April 2006,[65] reversing the first instance ruling. The Court of Appeal's analysis was that the case turned on whether or not the derivative product was described sufficiently clearly so that Pawani was able to understand its structure and terms, and whether or not Pawani was induced to commit Peekay to buying the derivative product by the statements made by ANZ's sales representative. The Court of Appeal concluded that the written final terms and conditions of the derivative product were sufficiently clear, and that Pawani would have understood the nature of the derivative product had he actually read them. The Court of Appeal also concluded that Pawani was not induced to commit Peekay to the investment by the statements made by the ANZ sales representative, but by his own assumptions that the statements made correctly described the structure of the derivative product.

8.120 The judgment of the Court of Appeal tempered the concerns of the financial services industry. Investors are less able to allege misrepresentation if they do not read the terms and conditions applicable to their investments. The *Peekay* case nonetheless illustrates the considerable risks to which a financial institution is exposed, that an erroneous description of an investment given by a sales representative may not in all circumstances be superseded by the written contractual terms. In the *Peekay* case, it was significant that ANZ's sales representative did not tell Pawani

---

[65] [2006] EWCA Civ 386.

that Pawani did not need to read the documents; Pawani had decided for himself that he did not need to read them. The outcome could well have been different had Pawani decided to not read the documents as a consequence of deliberate misselling. The *Peekay* case makes clear there must be a consistent and accurate description of a transaction throughout the entire marketing, negotiation, and documentation process. Pawani was described as a sophisticated investor, who had acted unwisely in failing to read the documents that he signed. Therefore he failed to exercise the due care that he could have been expected to exercise. As part 8.7 of this Chapter 8 shows, the due care that a less experienced and knowledgeable investor, that is, a retail consumer, can be expected to exercise is considerably less, and this of course means that the marketing and delivery of derivative products to retail consumers will depend more critically on the consistency and accuracy of the entire marketing and documentation process. The risk that a misrepresentation is made to a retail consumer by a financial institution is more acute because of the greater reliance the retail consumer would reasonably place on the sales representatives of the financial institution.

The *Springwell* case[66]

8.121 Springwell Navigation Corporation (Springwell) was one of a group of companies through which the Polemis family owned and operated a Greek shipping fleet. The Polemis family used Springwell as an investment vehicle. During the 1990s, Springwell made a number of investments through certain companies in the JP Morgan Chase group of companies (collectively 'Chase'), building up a substantial portfolio of some US$700 million containing both Russian debt, or GKOs,[67] and other structured debt which generated a payout linked to the performance of underlying GKOs (this structured debt of course having derivative characteristics, passing through to investors the risks as well as the returns of the underlying GKOs). As a consequence of the Russian financial crisis in 1998, the Russian Federation defaulted on certain of its financial obligations, including the GKOs underlying the structured debt that Springwell had acquired. Springwell made a number of wide-ranging claims and counterclaims against Chase,[68] including, of relevance to this discussion, that Chase had breached a duty to advise Springwell as to the acquisition of its investments (the general advisory claims) and that Chase's sales representative had made specific misrepresentations and negligent misstatements (the specific misrepresentation claims). The essence of the general advisory claims was that Chase was under a duty to advise Springwell as to its

---

[66] *JP Morgan Chase Bank v Springwell Navigation Corporation* [2008] EWHC 1186 (Comm).
[67] See paragraph 8.114.
[68] The categories of claim brought by Springwell were: the investment claims (comprising general advisory claims and specific misrepresentation claims), the excess profit claims, the shipping losses claims, the post-default claims, and the custody fees claims.

8.6 Selling and Misselling

investments, both under contract and as a matter of tort, having regard to Springwell's investment objectives and its tolerance for risk. The specific misrepresentation claims were framed with reference to the various conversations between Chase's sales representatives and Adamandios Polemis, who exercised day-to-day control over Springwell's investment activities.

8.122 A detailed judgment of 27 May 2008 was handed down by Mrs Justice Gloster, DBE. Gloster J found[69] that Chase did not owe a duty, whether founded in contract or in tort, to advise Springwell as to its portfolio, and that the statements made by Chase's sales representative were subject to the relevant contractual documentation put in place between Springwell and Chase, the effect of which was that Springwell should not place reliance on those statements.

8.123 The *Springwell* case reinforces the position of the English courts as expressed in the *Bankers Trust* case and the *Peekay* case. Gloster J considers[70] the judgment of Mance J in the *Bankers Trust* case that no general duty to advise arose, finding instructive Mance J's approach of analysing the actual representations that were made, the skill and knowledge of the financial institution relative to the investor, the particular circumstances of the presentations made by the financial institution to the investor, and the perception of the financial institution's sales representative as to his role and responsibilities. Gloster J also considers[71] the *Peekay* case and the academic commentary it attracted[72] that the English courts are reluctant to impose a general advisory duty of the type asserted by Springwell.

8.124 In some more detail, Gloster J adopted a two-stage approach, comprising as a starting point three basic tests for the existence of a duty of care in tort giving rise to a liability for economic loss, and then a set of 'lower level' factors which indicate the existence or otherwise of a contractual or tortious duty of care. The three basic tests[73] are (1) whether or not responsibility had been assumed; (2) whether or not the loss was reasonably foreseeable, whether or not the relationship between the parties was of sufficient proximity, and whether or not in all the circumstances it would be fair, just, and reasonable to impose a duty of care; and (3) the incremental test of extending existing categories of duty. The 'lower level' factors[74] are the contractual context, the statements made at the outset of the relationship, the

---

[69] By way of interesting aside, and looking beyond the legal argument and patterns of fact, Gloster J's judgment also illustrates the importance of the impression made by witnesses giving evidence in person; Gloster J draws attention at paragraphs 64 ff. to the credibility of the various witnesses before her in the trial.

[70] Paragraphs 487 and 488.

[71] Paragraph 489.

[72] Wood, *Regulation of International Finance* (Sweet & Maxwell, 2007) at paragraphs 14–16.

[73] Paragraph 48. Reference is made to the speeches of the House of Lords in *Commissioners of Customs & Excise v Barclays Bank PLC* (see paragraph 8.152).

[74] Paragraph 53.

actual role of Chase's sales representative, the actual role of other members of Chase's staff, the extent of Adamandios Polemis's financial experience or sophistication, the extent of the reliance placed by Adamandios Polemis on various members of Chase's staff, and the regulatory background.

8.125 Applying the various tests, Gloster J found that although advice was given by various members of Chase's staff, Chase did not owe any duty to advise Springwell. Springwell was a highly sophisticated investor[75] and the contractual documentation succeeded in establishing that Springwell was to be treated as a sophisticated investor to whom no duty to advise was owed.[76]

8.126 Springwell's voluminous claim for misrepresentation included misrepresentation as to the content and effect of the documents, as well as general misrepresentation and more specific misrepresentation as to Russia, the state of the Russian economy, the structured debt sold, and about Russian banks. Gloster J's analysis[77] is that the general misrepresentation claim was indistinguishable from the general advisory claim, as both turned on whether or not Chase owed a duty of care, and the general claim was correctly one made at common law on the basis of negligent misrepresentation and not under the Misrepresentation Act 1967. The law of misrepresentation, as far as it is relevant to this book, is introduced in the paragraphs below. Gloster J found highly persuasive[78] the description in their contract of the relationship between Chase and Springwell. Significantly, Chase had obtained signed agreements from Springwell the effect of which was that Chase did not take responsibility for the 'fairness, accuracy or completeness' of any written or oral information, that Chase did not take 'independent steps' to verify the information, that Chase and its officers made 'no representation or warranty express or implied' as to the information, and that Springwell expressly represented that it was a 'sophisticated investor' and that it did not rely on Chase. Finally, the more specific misrepresentation claims were disposed of through a careful and lengthy analysis of the statements actually made by Chase's sales representative, which involved reviewing transcripts of telephone conversations, and considering whether those statements were false, had been relied on, and had been made negligently (in the case of the common law claims) or in the belief that they were true (in the case of the claims made under the Misrepresentation Act 1967).

---

[75] Paragraph 432.
[76] Paragraph 479. At paragraph 480, Gloster J refers to the judgment of Toulson J in *IFE Fund SA v Goldman Sachs International* [2006] EWHC 2887 (Comm) that 'contractual documentation can define the relationship between the parties, so as to exclude any parallel or free-standing common law duties of care'.
[77] Paragraphs 661 and 662.
[78] Paragraph 670.

8.6 Selling and Misselling

8.127 Finally, of relevance to this discussion, a part of Springwell's case sought to avoid certain contractual provisions on the ground of the principle in *Interfoto v Stiletto*,[79] as formulated by Dillon LJ and Bingham LJ. Dillon LJ's formulation of the principle was that an unusual or onerous clause should not be effective if it had not been brought to the relevant party's attention, and Bingham LJ's formulation was that an unusual or onerous clause should not be effective if the party seeking to rely on it had not done what was necessary to draw it to the attention of the other party. Subsequent authorities have demonstrated that application of the principle is very restricted, in the interests of preserving commercial certainty, not least because there is no general duty under English law to negotiate in good faith, and Gloster J found that the principle should not apply in the *Springwell* case. Nonetheless, notwithstanding its restricted application, it is not inconceivable that the principle may yet apply in the context of the retail offer of derivatives.[80]

8.128 The judgment in the *Springwell* case, consistent as it is with the hardening line demonstrated by the English courts, and therefore reassuring to the investment banking industry, offers the warning that much depends on the circumstances of the case, and the importance of appropriately worded documents disclaiming any advisory duty or responsibility and the importance of a properly focused approach to selling are emphasized.

Misrepresentation

8.129 Neither the *Bankers Trust* case, nor the *Peekay* case, nor the *Springwell* case erodes the requirement incumbent on a financial institution selling derivatives that it makes no misrepresentation as to the terms of the derivative contracts that it sells. Whether or not a misrepresentation is made is a matter of law, and the standard imposed by common law and statute is reinforced by both the basic standard imposed by applicable regulations, essentially that communications are clear, fair, and not misleading, and the more detailed communication and disclosure requirements found in the body of those regulations. Any inconsistency in communications and documentation would of course be at the very least misleading, and of course potentially problematic.

8.130 The law of misrepresentation concerns the effect of statements made before a contract is entered into, such as those made by the sales representatives of the financial institutions in the *Bankers Trust* case, the *Peekay* case, and the *Springwell* case. The common law principle, that statements should not be given effect unless they form part of the contract, does not address situations where false pre-contractual statements, whether made innocently or otherwise, have induced a party to enter

---

[79] [1989] 1 QB 433, at 439 et seq.
[80] See part 8.7 of this chapter.

into the contract to his detriment. The position under the common law was that the remedy to fraudulent misrepresentation was the right to rescind the contract and an award of damages, but the damages would only be awarded for deceit, which is an action based on a tort[81] and not breach of contract. Further, the common law did not address misrepresentations that were made other than fraudulently but which nonetheless induced formation of the contract to the detriment of the party acting on the misrepresentation. Hence the equitable position developed during the 19th century to allow rescission in response to all misrepresentations. Thus it is seen that the circumstances of a misrepresentation include both a contract between the parties and the pre-contractual dealings of the parties, and therefore cases involving misrepresentation look at the law of contract, the principles of equity, and the tortious actions which can be brought, such as the tort of deceit. The law of misrepresentation therefore represents a complex and difficult interface between these different aspects of law.

8.131 Turning to a more technical definition, a misrepresentation arises where prior to entering into a contract a false statement is made, which induces the party claiming misrepresentation to enter into the contract, and that party enters into the contract in reliance on the false statement. The statement is a statement of fact, and not mere opinion, and this distinction is particularly important in the context of derivative transactions. There are three categories of misrepresentation: innocent misrepresentation, which does not involve any element of wrongdoing; negligent misrepresentation, which is a false statement that is made carelessly without any reasonable grounds for believing that it is true; and fraudulent misrepresentation, which is a false statement that is made knowingly, or without belief in the truth of the statement, or carelessly as to whether the statement is true or false.[82] The remedy for an innocent misrepresentation is that the contract becomes voidable and a payment is made of an indemnity in respect of any obligation created by the contract. A contract that is voidable is not immediately set aside and made null and void; instead, the party which has successfully claimed misrepresentation is free to decide whether to bring the contract to an end, that is, to rescind the contract, or to affirm the contract, in which case the contract continues. A voidable contract can be affirmed by both statement or an action which is consistent with affirmation of the contract. If the contract is brought to an end, then the contract is treated as though it had never been made, and the parties are restored as much as possible to the condition they were in before they entered into the contract (this restoration is referred to as 'restitutio in integrum'). Under certain

---

[81] A tort is an action for a wrongdoing, such as negligence or deceit.
[82] This is the classical formulation of fraudulent misrepresentation expressed by Lord Herschell in *Derry v Peek* (1889) 14 App Cas 337 at 374.

8.6 Selling and Misselling

circumstances, a contract cannot be rescinded.[83] The remedy for both negligent misrepresentation and fraudulent misrepresentation is that the contract becomes voidable and damages are paid. The amount of damages awarded for fraudulent misrepresentation is potentially higher than the damages awarded for negligent misrepresentation; whereas the damages awarded for negligent misrepresentation are assessed with reference to all the direct consequences of the negligence that are reasonably foreseeable, the damages awarded for fraudulent misrepresentation are assessed to include items such as the difference between a price paid and a value received, expenditure wasted in reliance on the contract, and opportunities foregone as a consequence of relying on the contract.

8.132 Before the decision of the House of Lords in *Hedley Byrne & Co Ltd v Heller & Partners Ltd*,[84] damages were awarded for a false statement only if that statement was a part of the contract, or where that statement was made outside the contract, only if that statement was made fraudulently. In *Hedley Byrne*, damages were awarded for economic loss caused by a negligent misrepresentation, that is for a false statement which was made outside a contract and not made fraudulently. Negligence under the principle established in *Hedley Byrne*, like other instances of negligence, occurs if a duty of care that is owed is breached, and the duty of care arises if the relationship between the claimant and the defendant is sufficiently close, if the loss or damage that the claimant suffers is reasonably foreseeable, and if it is reasonable to impose liability on the defendant. Although *Hedley Byrne* was based on a tort, it had an effect on the law of contract. As Gloster J observes in the *Springwell* case,[85] 'quasi-contract' cases are those which involve a consideration as to whether or not a party owes a duty of care in tort giving rise to a liability in economic loss. The special relationship required for there to be a duty of care that is breached might well arise in the context of the sale by a financial institution of a derivative.

8.133 Further development in the law of misrepresentation quickly followed the judgment in *Hedley Byrne* with the passing of the Misrepresentation Act 1967. In particular, section 2(1) of the Misrepresentation Act 1967 should be noted. 'Where a person has entered into a contract after a misrepresentation has been made to him by another party thereto and as a result thereof he has suffered loss, then, if the person making the misrepresentation would be liable to damages in respect thereof had the misrepresentation been made fraudulently, that person shall be so liable notwithstanding that the misrepresentation was not made fraudulently, unless he proves that he had reasonable ground to believe and did believe up to the

---

[83] These circumstances are: the contract has already been affirmed, whether by statement or by action; in certain circumstances, the lapse of time; if restitutio in integrum is not possible; or if rescission would deprive a third party of a right that he has acquired in good faith and for value.
[84] [1964] AC 465.
[85] Paragraph 48.

time the contract was made that the facts represented were true.' Liability for negligent misrepresentation under this subsection arises if the party to whom the false statement has been made suffers a loss and the party who has made the false statement would have been liable to damages if the false statement had been made fraudulently. The party who has made the false statement then has the burden of proving that he had reasonable grounds to believe that the statement in question was true and that he did believe that the statement was true; if he cannot do so, then he is liable for negligent misrepresentation under statute. Therefore the actions available to a claimant potentially include negligent misrepresentation under both common law and statute. Whereas a claim for negligent misrepresentation under common law would require the breach of a duty of care to succeed, liability for negligent misrepresentation under statute can be imposed without finding that any duty of care has been breached.

8.134 The modern formulation of the imposition of the duty of care in allegations of negligence is found in the speech of Lord Bridge of Harwich in *Caparo Industries Plc v Dickman*,[86] which is discussed in part 8.7 of this chapter.

8.135 The foregoing paragraph illustrates the risks to which a financial institution is exposed if its sales representatives commit it to making a misrepresentation. The customer of the financial institution who relies on a false statement would have grounds for alleging misrepresentation. However, the false statement which is fundamental to an allegation of misrepresentation must be a statement of fact, and not of opinion or forecast. Therefore, an action for misrepresentation based on a statement that a particular derivative product should be used because of an expectation that a particular market movement or event will take place would not be likely to succeed. By contrast, a statement that a particular derivative product has a particular structure, as in the *Peekay* case, or behaves in a particular manner, whether in terms of how it responds to the underlying or the rights and obligations that it creates, as in the *Bankers Trust* case, would be grounds for bringing an action for misrepresentation if that statement is false. Both these cases, and the law of misrepresentation generally, compel the realization that as much attention must be applied to the sales practices at financial institutions as is applied to the documentation processes, as the greatest risks arguably arise during the marketing and sales conversations which precede the structuring of a transaction and the preparation of the documents. Of course, more complex structured products are often heavily negotiated, and this in part mitigates the risk of a misrepresentation, as the customer should be fully aware of the effect of the provisions being discussed and agreed, sometimes over a considerable period. However, a misrepresentation can still made if the relevant statement is made in respect of a matter that is not

---

[86] [1990] 2 AC 605 at 618.

dealt with in the negotiation. A substantial amount of business, even structured business, is still dealt without protracted negotiation, and therefore the need to be cognizant of the risks of misrepresentation remains real.

As the introduction to the law of misrepresentation set out in the preceding paragraphs indicates, the consequences of a successful action alleging misrepresentation might include the rescission of the contract, and the restoration of the parties to the condition they were in prior to the contract being made. Rescission would therefore involve repayment of any amount that had been paid under the contract, together with an award of interest, instead of the calculation and payment of a single net close-out amount under the derivative contract, such as that contemplated by section 8.6 of the ISDA 2002 Master Agreement.[87] The ISDA 2002 Master Agreement, including the standard form of its Schedule, therefore purports to establish a relationship between the parties under which they transact at arm's length: neither party relies on the other for advice, and neither party acts as fiduciary for the other. The standard form of representation establishing the relationship between the parties was developed as a consequence of the *Bankers Trust* case, as explained in the foregoing paragraphs, with the purpose of reducing the potential for an action being brought for misrepresentation. Certain fundamental representations are set out in section 3 of the ISDA 2002 Master Agreement, and additional representations can be made in the Schedule, and breach of one of these would give rise to early termination of outstanding transactions under the processes contained in the master agreement. Payment of a single net close-out amount would reflect the prevailing valuation of the transactions being terminated, and would therefore also reflect the costs or gains in lifting any hedge position that a party may have entered into; inclusion of a hedge position in the accounting of the profit or loss for the corresponding transaction is vital. The exercise of calculating the single net close-out amount should give the same result as adjusting the flow of payments that are made to restore the parties to the condition they were in prior to the contract being made to reflect the costs and gains in lifting any hedge position, but the computation of the single net close-out amount would be a contractual obligation, and not the result of litigation and judgment. **8.136**

Suitability

The requirement that a financial institution sells a derivative product which is suitable in the hands of the customer recurs in litigation involving derivatives.[88] **8.137**

---

[87] See paragraphs 7.51 ff.
[88] The counterclaim of DSS in the *Bankers Trust* case included an allegation that BTCo and BTI had sold an unsuitable product to DSS, and judgments in *Morgan Stanley UK Group v Puglisi Cosentino* [1998] CLC 481 and *Valse Holdings SA v Merrill Lynch International Bank Ltd* [2004] EWHC 2471 (Comm) refer to the suitability or otherwise of the various investments and transactions in the hands of the claimants.

Allegations of the misselling of derivatives in other jurisdictions have also been framed with reference to the concept of suitability.[89] The concept of suitability has long been a part of the policy and regulation of the financial services industry, and the FSA has now enshrined suitability in its Principles for Businesses.[90] The requirement that a financial institution considers whether or not a derivative product or transaction is suitable in the hands of its customer is imposed in MiFID, as transposed into the United Kingdom's regulatory system through the FSA Handbook. The financial services industry more widely internationally has become attuned to the need that only suitable products and services are marketed to and sold to investors.[91]

8.138 The concept of suitability connotes that the processes by which a financial institution interacts with its customer are suitable and that any product or service sold to that customer is suitable, and this concept seems to be a natural part of the overall imperative in regulation that customers are treated fairly. This is the theme which resonates through the FSA's approach to regulation.

8.139 Looking at the concept of suitability in some more detail, the requirement has been succinctly described in the report *Customer suitability in the retail sale of financial products and services*;[92] although the report discusses the retail offer of financial products, a more general concept of suitability and appropriateness can be discerned. The suitability and appropriateness of a particular financial product or service for any consumer is the degree to which the product or service matches the consumer's financial situation, investment objectives, level of risk tolerance, financial need, knowledge, and experience. Although at first glance the concepts of suitability and appropriateness appear to be the same, there is a distinction which is more easily examined in the context of the retail offer of derivatives in part 8.7 of this chapter.[93]

8.140 The standard that must be achieved in both the interaction with the customer, including marketing and sales promotions, the provision of information and the nature, style, and content of documentation that is used, and in the actual

---

[89] Examples include the high profile filings made in the United States of America during the mid-1990s such as *Gibson Greetings v Bankers Trust Co*, *Orange County Investment Pool v Merrill Lynch & Co*, and *Proctor and Gamble v Bankers Trust Co*.

[90] Principle 9 requires a firm to take reasonable care to ensure the suitability of its advice and discretionary decisions for any customer who is entitled to rely upon its judgment, and less directly, Principle 6 requires a firm to pay due regard to the interests of its customers and to treat them fairly.

[91] See *Customer suitability in the retail sale of financial products and services*, Basel Committee on Banking Supervision, April 2008; this is a report of the Joint Forum comprising the Basel Committee on Banking Supervision, the International Organization of Securities Commissions, and the International Association of Insurance Supervisors.

[92] *Customer suitability in the retail sale of financial products and services*, p. 4.

[93] See paragraph 8.157.

8.6 Selling and Misselling

product or service itself, in order to ensure that the service or the product is suitable, will depend very much on the particular customer. Accordingly, the correct categorization of the customer and the customer's requirements become important; clearly a high risk investment product is not suitable for a customer, no matter how expert or experienced, who requires a low risk investment. Particular care should be taken with a customer of limited expertise or experience. As a part of the wider responsibilities owed by the financial institution, the management of conflicts of interest is important. Conflicts of interest may arise where the customer's requirements are subordinated to those of the financial institution or another customer. Given that conflicts of interest are inevitable in a complex large-scale financial institution, the emphasis is on the correct identification and categorization of the various types of conflicts of interest which may arise, and the development of processes which minimize their occurrence, and which resolve them fairly.[94] At a minimum, disclosure of potential conflicts of interest must be made to customers, and conflicts of interest which do develop should be resolved by a suitably senior tier of management, who have sufficient independence from the day-to-day running of the business unit in which the conflict arose, to be able to weigh the appropriate considerations.

Product design

Closely related to the concepts of suitability and appropriateness is the requirement that customers are treated fairly in the actual design of a product. A variety of factors are at play in the design of a financial product, but fundamentally the financial institution structuring the product must have a good understanding of how the product behaves in different market conditions, in order that it can both control the risks to which it is exposed in delivering the product, including any hedging and structural risks, and market and sell the product in terms that are clear, fair, and not misleading. Developing a comprehensive understanding of the risks will contribute to an understanding of the potential conflicts of interest which might arise; in some structures, action taken by the financial institution writing the product in response to a relationship it has may have a material and adverse effect on the consumer of the product. The full effect of the mathematical link between the performance of the underlying market and the performance of the derivative product should be explored, by 'stress-testing' the product in a variety of scenarios. The financial institution designing the product should follow a clear and consistent internal process for the development, test, and approval of the product; necessarily, risk controllers independent of the structuring and sales staff should be involved in the approval exercise. Consideration should also be given to the withdrawal of the product, as consumers who have bought the product should

8.141

---

[94] See Principle 8 of the FSA's Principles for Businesses.

not be treated unfairly in the unwinding or purchase back of the product; ideally, the mechanisms for addressing this process should be developed in tandem with the origination of the product.

8.7 Retail Offer of Derivatives and Issues Arising[95]

Regulation

8.142 Issues arising in the context of the offer of derivative exposures to retail consumers must be considered in the light of the stance adopted by the FSA; this sets the scene for what follows. The fundamental difficulties which the industry and its regulators must address are by now well rehearsed: many financial products, and this clearly includes derivative products, are complex, are bought infrequently, and have a long duration, which implies that whether or not the product has been satisfactory may not be known for a considerable period after the product has been bought; the risks and rewards of complex products can be difficult to assess; and the buyer of a complex product often knows very much less about it than the seller, a phenomenon that is usually referred to as an information asymmetry.[96] The FSA's strategy is built on four 'pillars' which reflect what the FSA considers to be the four main features of an effective and efficient retail market: capable and confident consumers; clear, simple, and understandable information provided to and used by consumers; soundly managed and well-resourced firms which treat their customers fairly; and finally proportionate, risk-based, and principles-based regulation.[97] In practical terms, the FSA proposes to implement its strategy through three measures. The first is the prudential supervision of firms. The second is the refinement of the rules governing the conduct of business, which includes the initiative that customers are treated fairly. The third is promoting the development of a customer base which is more capable and confident. On closer examination, the third measure seems to require (1) the general education of the retail customer base, the importance of which cannot be overestimated given the long-term trend that individuals are becoming increasingly responsible for their own financial affairs, whether investments, pensions, or insurance; (2) a regulatory regime which requires the use of financial promotions which clearly, concisely, and accurately describe the product in question, including the risks arising from the use of the product; and (3) the use of documents which are easily

---

[95] It is important to appreciate that the issues of suitability and treating the customer fairly, and the proper design of financial products, apply to all customer relationships. The emerging trend to offer derivative exposures to retail consumers has prompted a renewed focus on these concepts.
[96] Speech delivered on 9 February 2006 by Callum McCarthy, Chairman, FSA.
[97] Speech delivered on 27 February 2008 by Clive Briault, Managing Director, Retail Markets, FSA.

8.7 *Retail Offer of Derivatives*

understood and which set out the respective rights and obligations of the parties. Although much of what the FSA is debating involves financial products such as casualty insurance, life insurance, and packaged investments, the general approach and the standards described apply equally to the offer of derivative exposures to retail consumers.

In proposing the style of the regulation that it will apply to the offer of derivatives to retail consumers, that regulation will be appropriate, the FSA has reflected the requirement imposed on it by section 2(1)(b) of the FSMA 2000. Guidance as to what constitutes an appropriate degree of regulation is found in this context in section 5 of the FSMA 2000, which requires an appropriate degree of protection for consumers, as indicated by the factors specified in section 5(2), namely the risks inherent in the products or transactions in question, the experience and expertise of the consumers in question, the need that consumers have for advice and accurate information, and the general principle that consumers should take responsibility for their decisions. Further, the FSA must balance against the imperative of consumer protection its obligation to have regard to the desirability of facilitating innovation in connection with regulated activities, and to have regard to the international character of financial services and markets and the desirability of maintaining the competitive position of the United Kingdom, both as required under section 3(d) and section 3(e) respectively of the FSMA 2000. **8.143**

The last factor specified in section 5(2), that consumers should take responsibility for their decisions, is the key principle underpinning the FSA's approach, which may be summarized as helping retail consumers to help themselves.[98] The FSA is therefore seeking to ensure that a regulatory framework is in place in which derivative products are made available to retail consumers in a manner which allows them to make properly informed decisions for themselves whether or not to invest. **8.144**

Responsibility: providers and distributors

Financial products may be manufactured and delivered to the consumer by two or more firms, which either provide the product, that is, structure and issue the product, or which distribute the product, that is, market and sell the product. Hence the terms 'provider' and 'distributor' have entered the regulatory argot. **8.145**

---

[98] See the paper 'Structured Products: Principles for Managing the Distributor-Individual Investor Relationship' published jointly by the European Securitisation Forum, the International Capital Markets Association, ISDA, the London Investment Banking Association, and the Financial Markets Association. This paper echoes the principle that individual investors need to take responsibility for their investment goals and to stay informed about the risks and rewards of their investments, but firms must help them to do so by observing certain standards.

By way of example, structured debt securities and equity securities[99] are becoming more widely used as a means of packaging a derivative exposure to a variety of underlying classes of asset in a convenient investment that is easily transferred to, held by, and potentially subsequently sold on by investors. Typically, the securities are structured by a financial institution such as an investment bank, which may also issue the securities itself, or it may arrange the issue of the securities by another entity, perhaps a special purpose vehicle, or SPV. Structuring, that is designing, the securities and issuing the securities constitute providing the securities for the purposes of this discussion. The securities are marketed to the consumers who will ultimately buy the investments.[100] The marketing may be undertaken by another financial institution such as a commercial bank and by a network of financial advisers. The investment bank which designs the securities does not market them to the consumers; instead, its sales representatives market them to the commercial bank and the financial advisers, and in this way the analogy is drawn with the design and production of goods that are sold by a manufacturer on a wholesale basis to a retailer, and the marketing and sale of the goods to the consumer by the retailer. Where the securities are issued by an SPV, the securities are bought by the investment bank, which effectively acts as a warehouse, and from the warehouse the securities are delivered to the retailers; again, this is a process that is analogous with the manufacturing and distribution of tangible goods. The relationship between the investment bank and the commercial bank is a B2B[101] relationship, and the relationship between the commercial bank and various financial advisers is also a B2B relationship. The relationship between the commercial bank and a consumer, or between a financial adviser and a consumer, is a B2C relationship.[102] Questions of liability arise in the manufacturing and supply chain of tangible goods, and the same questions arise in the similar manufacturing and supply chain of intangible products such as the structured securities giving a derivative exposure in this example. As a fundamental principle, the FSA requires that a consumer's experience of buying a financial product should not be affected by the number of firms involved in delivering that product, and that each firm involved in delivering that product, whether as a provider or as a distributor, bears a measure of responsibility.[103] The regulatory position that is developing might be seen as a reaction to the *Ockwell* case discussed in the following paragraphs.

---

[99] See part 4.16 of Chapter 4.

[100] Technically, a distinction should be drawn between the beneficial title of investors in securities and the legal title to the securities held by the common depositary. See paragraph 4.247 for a brief discussion of the clearing system.

[101] Business to business.

[102] Business to customer.

[103] See the regulatory guide *Responsibilities of Providers and Distributors for the Fair Treatment of Customers*, which is appended to Policy Statement 07/11 released in July 2007 by the FSA.

The *Ockwell* case

8.146 The judgment handed down on 13 May 2005 by Havelock-Allan J in *Seymour v Caroline Ockwell & Co; Zurich IFA Limited*[104] explored three relationships. The first was between the claimants, Edward Arthur Seymour and Pauline Mary Seymour, and the first defendant, the independent financial adviser Caroline Ockwell trading as a sole practitioner under the name 'Caroline Ockwell & Co.'. The second was between the claimants and the second defendant, Zurich IFA Limited (ZIFA), which was a holding company at the head of a group of companies which offered various insurance and investment products, including companies operating under the 'Eagle Star' name and the 'Allied Dunbar' name. The third was between Ockwell and ZIFA. The basic facts of the *Ockwell* case were that the Seymours realized a considerable sum on the sale of their farming business, and wished to minimize their liability to capital gains tax (CGT) on that sale through the use of various reliefs, and to invest a proportion of their capital in a low risk investment product. Ockwell, having liaised with a sales representative of ZIFA, recommended that the Seymours invest in the Allied Dunbar International Managed Portfolio Bond (the ADIMP Bond). The ADIMP Bond was effectively a 'wrapper' through which the Seymours acquired an investment exposure to the Imperial Consolidated Alpha + Fixed Income Fund (the Alpha Fund). The Alpha Fund was managed by the Imperial Consolidated Group. The Seymours invested £500,000 in the ADIMP Bond, having discussed the protections available for their money in the structure of the ADIMP Bond and the underlying Alpha Fund. After the investment was made, concern was expressed within ZIFA, as demonstrated by internal communications, as to the soundness of the Alpha Fund. Crucially, these ZIFA internal communications were not forwarded to the particular ZIFA representative who had liaised with Ockwell. Eventually, the Alpha Fund was liquidated, and the Serious Fraud Office began to investigate the activities of the Imperial Consolidated Group. The Seymours lost all their money.

8.147 The Seymours' main claim against Ockwell succeeded; this was the claim for the capital they had lost, and the income they had lost through the loss of that capital. Turning to the secondary claims brought, Ockwell was partially liable for the charge to CGT that the Seymours had incurred, and Ockwell was required to account for a proportion of the commissions that she earned through the sale of the ADIMP Bond. However, Ockwell was not liable for any stress or anxiety suffered by the Seymours. The Seymours' claim against ZIFA failed. Ockwell brought a claim against ZIFA as a part of the proceedings, and Havelock-Allan J found that ZIFA were liable for two-thirds of Ockwell's liability to the Seymours.

---

[104] [2005] EWHC 1137 (QB).

8.148 A key element of the *Ockwell* case was the question of the negligence of both Ockwell and ZIFA, and the scope of the duty of care that each of them owed. The *Ockwell* case therefore illustrates a further category of claim that might be brought against a financial institution, and indicates the standard of care that the law requires. Havelock-Allan J found that the Alpha Fund was not a low risk investment, and Ockwell's undoing was that she failed to appreciate that the Alpha Fund was not a low risk investment, having become too immersed in the detail; it was beyond her retainer to recommend the Alpha Fund, or anything remotely like it, to the Seymours. Professional negligence is generally assessed with reference to the standard expected of a reasonably competent professional, but the extent of competence which acts as the yardstick by which negligence is assessed is determined by the nature of the business or the field of practice. Thus in *Matrix Securities Ltd v Theodore Goddard*[105] a solicitor practising in the specialist tax department of a law firm was judged by the standard of a specialist tax department and not that of a high street solicitor. However, crucially, Ockwell was found not to have been asked to act beyond her expertise. Further, although the defence raised by Ockwell was that she had received negligent advice from ZIFA, Havelock-Allan J found that she could not delegate her basic duty to advise the Seymours; she had undertaken to advise the Seymours on suitable investments which carried very little risk, and it was for her to form her own opinion, and she was required to exercise independent judgment, effectively sifting the advice received from ZIFA.

8.149 Ockwell was also found to have failed to comply with the regulatory rules which applied to her business at the relevant time.[106] One of the regulatory rules governed the Client's Understanding of Risk. Havelock-Allan J made the following important observation at paragraph 106 of his judgment. 'Miss Ockwell agreed that the structure of the Alpha Fund was "phenomenally complicated". She thought that she understood the basic mechanism, but not perhaps the finer details. It is therefore hardly surprising that the Seymours did not understand it at all. Their lack of understanding was in large part a concomitant of the complexity of the product. It was too sophisticated for investors such as the claimants and was therefore an investment the risks of which Miss Ockwell was not likely to be able to express in terms which the Seymours would be likely to understand.' This observation has obvious implications for any attempt to distribute derivative exposures to retail consumers, and this discussion will therefore return to this particular issue.

8.150 The Seymours' claim against ZIFA was not as straightforward to analyse as their claim against Ockwell. The Seymours' claim against ZIFA was for negligent

---

[105] [1998] PNLR 290.
[106] The rules of the Financial Intermediaries Managers and Brokers Regulatory Association (FIMBRA) which had been adopted by the FSA at the relevant time.

8.7 Retail Offer of Derivatives

misstatement at common law and breach of statutory duty under section 62 of the FSA 1986, because ZIFA had breached either section 76(1)(a) of the FSA 1986 or section 76(1)(b) of the FSA 1986.[107]

8.151 The general formulation of the duty of care was stated by Lord Bridge of Harwich in *Caparo Industries Plc v Dickman*.[108] Generally, a duty of care is held to exist if the damage suffered by the claimant is foreseeable, if the relationship between the parties is a relationship that is characterized by the law as one of 'proximity' or 'neighbourhood', and if it is fair, just, and reasonable to impose a duty of care.

8.152 Havelock-Allan J considered, in a very useful survey of the English law of negligence, the various methods by which the courts have endeavoured to analyse whether or not a duty of care should be imposed. The first method is the threefold test first stated by Lord Griffiths in *Smith v Eric Bush*,[109] as reformulated by Sir Brian Neill in *Bank of Credit and Commerce International (Overseas) Ltd (In Liquidation) v Price Waterhouse (No. 2)*,[110] highlighting five factors to be taken into account. Generally, a duty of care is held to exist if it was reasonably foreseeable that the claimant would suffer the kind of damage which occurred, if there was sufficient proximity between the parties, and if it was just and reasonable that the defendant should owe a duty of the scope asserted by the claimant. The second method is to determine whether or not the party alleged to owe the duty of care can be said to have assumed responsibility for the task in question. This method was applied by Lord Goff of Chievely in *Henderson v Merrett Syndicates*,[111] and Lord Browne-Wilkinson speaking in *White v Jones*[112] suggested that the assumption of responsibility for the relevant task in itself created the special relationship between the parties. The third method, which has been referred to as an 'incremental' approach, is to permit the extension of a duty of care to new categories of case by analogy with established existing principles, as favoured by Lord Bridge in *Caparo Industries Plc v Dickman*.[113] The Court of Appeal concluded in *Commissioners of Customs and Excise v Barclays Bank PLC*[114] that it is helpful to apply all three methods, but against the background that the courts have taken a more cautious approach to imposing a duty of care where economic loss is claimed without physical damage, and that considerations of legal policy should predominate.

---

[107] By way of brief background, section 76(1) of the FSA 1986 restricted promotions by authorized persons of collective investment schemes other than authorized unit trust schemes, investment companies with variable capital, and schemes recognized under the FSA 1986.
[108] [1990] 2 AC 605 at 618.
[109] [1990] 1 AC 831 at 864H.
[110] [1998] Ch 84.
[111] [1995] 2 AC 145.
[112] [1995] 2 AC 207 at 273.
[113] [1990] 2 AC 605 at 618.
[114] [2004] EWCA Civ 1555.

Chapter 8: Legal Issues

8.153 Havelock-Allan J considered that ZIFA did not owe the Seymours a duty of care, finding that there was not a sufficiently close relationship between the Seymours and ZIFA. 'It is not an essential prerequisite of a duty of care that the party alleged to owe the duty should have had direct dealings with the party to whom the duty was owed; but it is an important factor. In [these] circumstances, where the Seymours were not aware of the involvement of ZIFA, I do not think that there was a sufficiently close relationship to justify the imposition of a direct duty.' Havelock-Allan J found that ZIFA had not assumed any duty to the Seymours. ZIFA gave advice to Ockwell and not to the Seymours, and it was Ockwell who sold the investment to the Seymours. Again, this judgment has obvious implications for any attempt to distribute derivative exposures to retail consumers, and this judgment must be viewed in the light of the stance taken by the FSA, and this discussion will therefore return to this particular issue.

8.154 Havelock-Allan J found that although Ockwell was responsible for advising the Seymours, elements of ZIFA's conduct were found wanting. In particular, ZIFA had failed to bring to Ockwell's attention the concerns that ZIFA had in respect of the management and administration of the Alpha Fund. Havelock-Allan J balanced[115] the implications of imposing a duty to provide updated information against the logical and well-recognized principle that a duty to speak arises where an original statement, if not corrected or qualified in the light of subsequent information or events, may appear false or misleading; in particular, if the original statement could be said to constitute a continuing representation, because continuing reliance was being placed on it, then a duty to correct the original statement would arise if silence would result in that original statement becoming false or misleading. The principle applies equally to actions as well as to statements. Accordingly, Havelock-Allan J found that the *Ockwell* case represented an exemplar of circumstances which gave rise to a duty to speak, and ZIFA was found to have contributed to Ockwell's liability. ZIFA was not liable for the whole of Ockwell's liability to the Seymours, but two-thirds of it. The greater proportion of the liability that Ockwell owed to the Seymours arose through the actions and failures to act by ZIFA, because ZIFA's failure to communicate the contents of an important internal memorandum to Ockwell caused the Seymours to maintain the investment exposure to the Alpha Fund rather than to cancel it.

After the *Ockwell* case

8.155 Aside from providing a useful rehearsal of the principle of professional negligence, and showing that these principles apply to the provision of financial services as well as other arenas, the *Ockwell* case suggests that the provider or manufacturer

---

[115] Paragraph 155 of the judgment.

of a financial product involved in a supply chain might in certain circumstances raise the defence to a claim of negligence that it does not owe a duty to the consumer. However, ZIFA was still found to be responsible for two-thirds of the loss suffered by the Seymours, and through the judgment awarded against ZIFA in Ockwell's favour, ZIFA was effectively ordered to pay two-thirds of the damages ultimately awarded to the Seymours.

8.156 Nonetheless, although the 'right' result was obtained for the claimants in the *Ockwell* case, from a regulatory perspective a perceived gap had emerged in the coverage of regulation, as highlighted by the *Ockwell* case. Regulators had become concerned at the absence of any regulatory responsibility owed directly by the provider of a financial product to the ultimate consumer. This gap has emerged because a provider of a financial product would owe a regulatory duty to its own customer, the distributor of the product, and not to the ultimate consumer of the product. The ultimate consumer of the product would be treated as the customer of the distributor.

8.157 The regulatory response to the *Ockwell* case therefore appears to be a tightening of the responsibilities owed by the various firms in the supply chain. In particular, the FSA has published its Regulatory Guide, *The Responsibilities of Providers and Distributors for the Fair Treatment of Customers*.[116] The Regulatory Guide offers the FSA's guidance as to how the combination of the Principles for Business and the detailed rules require both providers and distributors to achieve the fair treatment of customers. The concept of fair treatment seems to embrace conveniently both appropriateness and suitability. The Regulatory Guide identifies the Principles which are of particular relevance,[117] although of course the other Principles remain applicable, and the Regulatory Guide considers in turn the links in the supply chain: the design of the financial product by the provider,[118] the sale and marketing of the financial product by the provider to the distributor, and the marketing and sale of the financial product by the distributor to the ultimate consumer. Both providers and distributors have a responsibility to consider, at each link in the supply chain, the effect of any action or failure to act on the ultimate consumer. The distributor has the relationship with the ultimate consumer, and therefore the distributor has the responsibility to ensure that the financial product is suitable for that particular consumer, taking into account the relevant factors. By contrast, the provider has a more general responsibility to develop and offer a financial product which is appropriate for a particular class of ultimate consumer. A subtlety emerges: a particular product can be appropriate for a particular class of ultimate consumer but unsuitable for a particular individual

---

[116] ibid.
[117] Principle 2, Principle 3, Principle 6, and Principle 7. See paragraph 5.14.
[118] See paragraph 8.145.

ultimate consumer, and only the distributor is capable of making the assessment as to suitability. It therefore follows that a provider should conduct an appropriate 'due diligence' exercise prior to establishing a relationship with a distributor, and then to monitor its relationship with that distributor. The following paragraphs discuss the three main issues which emerge: the fundamental question as to whether or not derivative exposures are inherently inappropriate for distribution to retail consumers, the design of the product, and achieving the right balance between clarity and detail in disclosure and documentation.

Are derivative exposures inherently inappropriate for distribution to retail consumers?

8.158 Derivatives do not seem at first glance to constitute appropriate products for distribution to retail consumers. The particular product in the *Ockwell* case, although not a derivative, was described[119] as being too sophisticated for investors such as the claimants, and because of that sophistication, Havelock-Allan J suggested that the financial adviser discussing the product with the claimants was unlikely to be able to express the risks of it in terms that the claimants would be able to understand.[120] The inference that is drawn from this statement is that because the claimants would not have appreciated the risks of the product, they would not have been equipped with the understanding that they would have needed to be able to make a properly informed decision to invest. Given the structural and mathematical complexity that some derivatives demonstrate, the application of this principle to derivatives is easy to make.

8.159 However, on a closer examination of the issue, the potential problem lies not with the complexity of the product, but rather with the disclosure of the risks of the product. The bold statement may be made, that a complex product is not necessarily an inappropriate or unsuitable product. The observation is made in paragraph 8.138 that the concept of suitability connotes that both the product is suitable for the consumer and the process by which the financial institution interacts with the consumer is suitable. Certain complex derivative products expose the investor to less risk than other investment products. For example, derivative structures can be formulated such that the investor's principal is protected, and therefore the value of the investment does not decline below the amount originally invested.[121] Usually, the investor pays for the protection of principal

---

[119] Paragraph 106 of the judgment.
[120] A basic truism might be that a financial product should not be sold if it cannot be explained.
[121] A distinction is drawn between full principal protection and partial principal protection (as to which, see paragraph 4.234), and under certain structures, the investor remains exposed to the consequences of an extraordinary event (as to which, see Chapter 7 generally), following the occurrence of which the investor may not receive back the full amount invested.

8.7 Retail Offer of Derivatives

by receiving less of the upside potential, and therefore certain principal-protected structures perform less well than other structures. However, leaving aside the loss of some of the upside performance, principal-protected structures would be more suitable for an investor with a lesser appetite for risk. All things being equal, in the hands of a more conservative investor, the principal-protected structure is more suitable and less risky than other forms of investment which lack the protection of principal, yet the structure is more complex than these other forms of investment precisely because it is required to have the additional features which enable it to deliver the protection of principal.

Care must still be taken in the marketing and sale of the principal-protected structure in order that the extent of the protection of principal is not misrepresented and the circumstances, if any, in which the investor may receive back less than the amount originally invested are made clear (for example, if the investor is exposed through the structure to the occurrence of an extraordinary event in respect of the underlying, or at a more fundamental level, the investor is exposed to the risk of a default). **8.160**

It is emphasized that although it is contended that certain derivatives are not inherently inappropriate for certain categories of investor, the regulatory and broader legal requirements of suitability remain in full force. A high risk investment product will be unsuitable for a customer who states a requirement for a low risk investment product. Further, the regulatory and broader legal requirements of course apply to business dealt with all categories of consumer, although the focus of this discussion has been distribution to retail consumers. **8.161**

Design of the product

The imperative that financial institutions must treat customers fairly extends to the design of financial products, which is discussed at paragraph 8.141. The fair treatment of retail consumers in the context of the design of financial products connotes that products to be distributed to them operate in as straightforward a manner as possible, with no gratuitous complexity. Where complexity is necessary, for example the complexity that is an inevitable feature of a principal-protected product, then the potential difficulty that the retail consumers may encounter in understanding the product should be tempered by the manner in which the contractual terms are cast and the pre-contract selling process, which should be accompanied by clear and complete illustrations of how the product performs, such as scenarios and graphs showing the different payouts that are made depending on movements in the underlying market, and a clear description of the risks arising. In particular, the conditions under which the investor may lose any of the amount invested should be made explicit. **8.162**

Disclosure and documents

8.163 A balance must be struck in the preparation of marketing and advertising materials, including documents making certain disclosures of the features and risks of products, between providing sufficient information that the potential investor is able to make a properly informed decision whether or not to invest, and providing too much information, which would have the effect of overwhelming the potential investor. Matters that should certainly be disclosed in respect of a derivative investment include the link between the performance of the underlying and the performance of the derivative investment, and of course risk. The risks that might arise include, one, the market risk that the return on the derivative investment will be affected by adverse movements in the underlying, and the mathematical link between movements in the underlying and the amount returned by the derivative investment, and two, other structural risks, such as the creditworthiness of the entity which issued or otherwise has payment obligations under the derivative contract. To return to the example of the structured securities described in paragraph 8.145, a key structural risk is that the issuer of the securities may become unable to pay the amounts that it is scheduled to pay, and this particular risk is more realistic if the issuer is not a bankruptcy-remote SPV, which is established and run so that its liabilities match its assets, but instead a fully-fledged financial institution that is itself exposed to the volatilities and dangers of the markets. Under other structures, the issuer of the structured securities may rely on payments received from a swap counterparty to fund the payments it is scheduled to make, and therefore the investor is exposed, indirectly, to the credit risk projected by that swap counterparty.

8.164 Aside from the mathematical link between the performance of the derivative investment and the performance of the underlying, disclosure must be made of the attributes of the underlying. After all, the investor is buying an investment exposure to the underlying, and the investor must therefore be provided with sufficient information about the underlying to be able to make a properly informed decision whether or not to invest. Further, a distinction should be drawn between making an investment in the underlying and making an investment in the derivative product, as an investment in the derivative product does not confer the same rights as an investment in the underlying. This distinction was not apparent to the investor in the *Peekay* case, who thought that an investment in the particular structured product involved would confer rights over the underlying GKO bond and therefore permit some retrieval of value.

8.165 Information should be provided as to whether or not the investor will have the right to redeem or otherwise sell into a secondary market the derivative investment before its maturity. If the investor will have the right to redeem or sell back the derivative investment, then full disclosure must be made of any restriction or other constraint which may prevent the investor from exercising such a right.

8.7 Retail Offer of Derivatives

If the derivative investment is in a form which is in theory transferable, such as an issue of structured securities, then a warning should be given if there is any risk that the secondary market for the investment may be illiquid. Illiquidity in the secondary market may have two consequences: either no buyer for the investment can be found, or the only prices bid are less than the fair value of the investment.

8.166 Full and transparent disclosure should also be made of the various fees, costs, commissions, and discounts paid to any distributor, whether these payments are made once or several times over the life of the product. Further, the scale of fees and other payments should be appropriate, and the appropriate controls should be implemented to ensure that this is the case.

8.167 The actual contractual terms of an investment to be bought by a retail consumer should also be expressed as clearly and in as straightforward a manner as possible (of course, the observation is made that any contract should be expressed as clearly and in as straightforward a manner as possible, irrespective of who the counterparty is).[122] Aside from strengthening the contract as a matter of certainty and therefore enforceability, documents that are expressed clearly can also become a perceived benefit of doing business with the particular financial institution, and this effect is more apparent in the retail market. For example, insurance companies and commercial banks whose activities include significant volumes of business dealt with retail customers often apply for the Crystal Mark of the Plain English Campaign,[123] award of which indicates that their documents have been prepared to a high standard of clarity and comprehensibility; the Crystal Mark is not awarded unless the relevant document can be read, understood, and acted upon by the intended audience.

8.168 Again, it is important to emphasize that the principles explained in the preceding paragraphs apply to business that is dealt with all categories of consumer. However, the quality and completeness of the disclosure and the documents offered to retail consumers will be judged in the context of the resources available to retail customers for reviewing the material that is offered to them. Retail consumers almost invariably have no access to research or independent legal advice in connection with their investments, and in order to treat them fairly, the financial institution will therefore be required to factor into its dealings with them the apparent asymmetry of the availability of information and resources. Moreover, to treat a retail consumer fairly requires a standard of behaviour wider than the presentation of

---

[122] The principle articulated in *Interfoto v Stiletto* [1989] 1 QB 433 should be borne in mind; see paragraph 8.127.
[123] The Plain English Campaign, which officially began in 1979, has worked with both public and private organizations, including high street banks, insurance companies, and investment management firms. See <http://www.plainenglish.co.uk>

appropriate documents which reflects not only the consumer's stated investment objectives and tolerance of risk, but also other factors which may be relevant, such as the liquid net worth of the consumer, the consumer's experience and expertise, and the consumer's general circumstances such as age and commitments.

Further regulatory protections

8.169 Retail consumers have recourse to the ombudsman[124] scheme established under Part XVI of the FSMA 2000, the Financial Ombudsman Service. A consumer who has a complaint about a particular product or service can apply to the ombudsman for quick resolution of the dispute with minimum formality. The ombudsman does not act as a regulator, trade association, or consumer champion, but instead as an impartial expert to adjudicate disputes. The ombudsman scheme applies to complaints made against a respondent who was an authorized person at the time of the act or omission to which the complaint relates.

8.170 Under section 229 of the FSMA 2000, the ombudsman has wide powers to make an award against the respondent of such amount that the ombudsman considers fair compensation for loss or damage, or to make a direction that the respondent take such steps in relation to the complainant as the ombudsman considers just and appropriate, whether or not a court could order those steps to be taken. The money award that the ombudsman can make may compensate for financial loss or any other loss or damage of a specified kind. Although the discretion the ombudsman has is wide, the FSA is empowered to limit the amount of compensation that can be awarded.[125] Interestingly, in the light of the extensive litigation that has concerned whether an award of simple interest or compound interest should be made in common law or in equity, the ombudsman has statutory power under section 229(8)(a) to include in a money award interest at a rate and from a date in its discretion, subject to the overarching requirement that the money award is fair compensation. This might be described as a manifestation of a more realistic treatment of money and the time value of money as foreshadowed in the *Sempra* case.[126] The ombudsman also has the power under section 231 of the FSMA 2000 to require the production of specified information or specified documents that the ombudsman considers necessary for the determination of a complaint, and the ombudsman has the specific power to take copies or extracts from a document that is produced. Under section 232 of the FSMA 2000, the

---

[124] An 'ombudsman' is an official appointed to investigate complaints brought by individuals, usually against malpractice by public bodies, but in other contexts also (the word 'ombudsman' derives from the Swedish for 'legal representative').

[125] Section 229(4) of the FSMA 2000.

[126] [2007] UKHL 34.

ombudsman has recourse to the High Court if a person fails to comply with a demand made under section 231 to produce information or documents.

Ancillary matters such as orders for costs[127] and funding of the ombudsman scheme by the financial services industry[128] are dealt with elsewhere in Part XVI.

8.171

Wider legal protections for consumers[129]

Mention should be made of two separate but complementary statutory regimes which might provide further protections for the retail consumer of derivatives; these are the Unfair Contract Terms Act 1977 (UCTA 1977) and the Unfair Terms in Consumer Contracts Regulations 1999 (Unfair Terms Regulations).[130]

8.172

The purpose of the UCTA 1977 is to strike out from the standard-form contractual terms used by a business a term which purports to exclude or to limit the liability of that business. Whereas some categories of contractual term are struck out directly through the operation of the UCTA 1977, other categories of contractual term remain in effect if they are found to be reasonable. The latter category of contractual term is of potential relevance to derivatives.[131]

8.173

The UCTA 1977 applies to many, but not all, contracts. Schedule 1 to the UCTA 1977 sets out the contracts to which the operative provisions of the Act do not apply, and interestingly includes 'any contract so far as it relates to the creation or transfer of securities or of any right or interest in securities',[132] apparently excluding from the scope of the Act derivative contracts linked to debt securities or equity securities. However, the context in which the UCTA 1977 is most likely to be relevant is the terms of business with which a financial institution might attempt to regulate its relationship with a retail consumer. These terms of business may well purport to limit the liability of the financial institution, and therefore become subject to the scheme of the Act. Although the claimant relying on the UCTA 1977 may be either a natural person or a body corporate,[133] the claimant must deal as a consumer, as defined in section 12(1) of the UCTA 1977.[134] A person deals as a consumer if he neither makes the contract in the course of a business nor holds himself out as doing so; and the other party makes the contract in the course

8.174

---

[127] Section 230 of the FSMA 2000.
[128] Section 234 of the FSMA 2000.
[129] See Cheshire, Fifoot and Furmston, *Law of Contract* (Oxford University Press, 2007).
[130] SI 1999/2083.
[131] Under section 2(1) of the UCTA 1977, a contractual term which purports to exclude or to restrict liability in negligence for personal injury or death is totally ineffective; clearly such a term should not apply to the sale of derivatives.
[132] Paragraph 1(e) of Schedule 1 to the UCTA 1977.
[133] See *R & B Customs Brokers Co Ltd v United Dominions Trust Ltd (Saunders Abbott (1980) Ltd, third party)* [1988] 1 WLR 321.
[134] However, see paragraph 8.175.

of a business.[135] The term 'business' is not defined in the UCTA 1977, but a wide definition is accepted to apply.

8.175 Certain provisions of the UCTA 1977 have the effect that particular contract terms in particular circumstances remain effective only if they satisfy the requirement of reasonableness. Section 2(2) applies to a contract term purporting to exclude or to restrict liability for loss or damage (other than death or personal injury) resulting from negligence. Section 3(2) applies to a contract term, where one of the parties deals as consumer or deals on the other's written standard terms of business, purporting to exclude or to restrict the liability of the other for breach of contract, or purporting to entitle the other to render contractual performance substantially different from that which was reasonably expected, or to render no performance at all. Section 4(1) applies to a contract term purporting to require a person dealing as consumer to indemnify another person, whether a party to the contract or not, for loss or damage that the other may incur through negligence or breach of contract. Curiously, section 3(2) is expressed to apply to a contract under which one of the parties either deals as consumer or on the other's written standard terms of business: the crucial word is 'or', which suggests that a party dealing on the other's written standard terms of business need not deal as consumer in order to be able to bring a claim, and therefore this subsection appears to be inconsistent with the rest of the UCTA 1977.

8.176 Under section 11(1), a contract term is reasonable if inclusion of it in the contract is fair and reasonable, having regard to the circumstances which were, or which ought reasonably to have been, in the contemplation of the parties when the contract was made.

8.177 From a more broad perspective, the UCTA 1977 does not address contractual terms which are unfair; instead, it addresses contractual terms which purport to exclude or limit liability, and in doing so, it uses the concept of reasonableness and not unfairness.

8.178 By contrast with the UCTA 1977, the implementation of the directive on unfair terms in consumer contracts[136] (the Unfair Terms Directive) does address contractual terms which are unfair. The Unfair Terms Regulations apply to consumer contracts which are in a standard form. The purpose of the Unfair Terms Regulations is to render contractual terms which are 'unfair' unenforceable against a consumer. The Unfair Terms Regulations define a consumer as 'a natural person who in making a contract to which these Regulations apply, is acting for purposes

---

[135] A third limb of the definition of dealing as a consumer is applied only in contracts for the sale or supply of goods, and is that the goods passing under or in pursuance of the contract are of a type ordinarily supplied for private use or consumption.

[136] 93/13/EEC Council Directive on unfair terms in consumer contracts.

which are outside his business'. Although a company can avail itself of the UCTA 1977, the Unfair Terms Regulations are explicitly only for the benefit of natural persons who are not acting for the purpose of a business.

The Unfair Terms Regulations apply to contracts which are in a standard form, such as the terms of business that financial institutions seek to rely on, although the Unfair Terms Regulations do recognize that even if a contract is in a standard form, some detail or aspect of it may have been negotiated; accordingly, the Unfair Terms Regulations will continue to apply to such contract if on an overall assessment its basis is a standard form. **8.179**

The effect of the Unfair Terms Regulations is that contractual terms which are unfair are struck out,[137] and the remainder of the contract remains in place and continues to bind the parties, unless the remainder of the contract is rendered incomprehensible by the deletion of the struck-out unfair terms.[138] The concept of unfairness is defined in Clause 5(1). An unfair term is 'any term which, contrary to the requirement of good faith, causes significant imbalance in the parties' rights and obligations arising under the contract to the detriment of the consumer'. Although this drafting seems wide, it is in fact tempered by Clause 6(2), which excludes from the assessment of unfairness the definition of the main subject matter of the contract or the adequacy of the price or remuneration paid as against the goods or services sold or supplied. Recital 16 of the Unfair Terms Directive refers to the relative strength of the parties' bargaining positions, and therefore although this concept is not included in the Unfair Terms Regulations, a consideration of unfairness would prompt a consideration of whether or not the consumer has been treated fairly and equitably. Interestingly, Clause 7 of the Unfair Terms Regulations requires that a seller or supplier 'shall ensure that any written term of a contract is expressed in plain intelligible language'; award of the Crystal Mark to the standard-form documents used by certain financial institutions bears testament to the efforts being made in the field of consumer financial services.[139] Clause 7 also provides that if there is doubt as to the meaning of a term, the interpretation most favourable to the consumer shall prevail. **8.180**

Closing remarks

Paragraph 8.143 refers to the need for consumers to take a degree of responsibility for their own decisions. This is a distillation of the treatment that the FSA envisages is appropriate for retail consumers.[140] If a firm fulfils all obligations and treats a customer fairly, then the firm should not be blamed for a transaction which **8.181**

---

[137] Clause 8(1) of the Unfair Terms Regulations.
[138] Clause 8(2) of the Unfair Terms Regulations.
[139] Paragraph 8.167.
[140] Speech delivered on 9 February 2006 by Callum McCarthy, Chairman, FSA.

disappoints the consumer, as the consumer should exercise a degree of judgment. Following from this, a relevant factor in determining the culpability of the firm would be any failure by the consumer to exercise reasonable care. However, the actions that consumers should or should not take are not prescribed or codified, and therefore consumers do not owe responsibilities in the strict sense of the word. The ombudsman, like the courts, must take into account all the circumstances of the case, which would include the complexity of the materials and contract, and how the consumer has been treated, and whether or not the consumer had read the materials and contract.

8.8 The Swap Analysed as a Contract

8.182 Although part 4.7 of chapter 4 illustrates that both the purpose of a swap and how a swap actually operates are conceptually easy, a swap nonetheless presents a legal practitioner with a number of conceptual challenges which arise from an analysis of the swap as a contract. One of the themes running through this book is the need to bring closer together the lawyer's understanding of a derivative and the financial engineer's understanding of a derivative, and thus a swap can be analysed as both a contract and a cash flow. Although from an economic perspective, a swap is a series or 'strip' of forward payments,[141] the analysis of a swap as a contract is less easy to explain, and significant judicial and academic consideration has been directed at this topic.

8.183 Woolf LJ speaking in the Court of Appeal in the landmark case *Hazell v Hammersmith & Fulham London Borough Council*[142] defined a swap in the following manner at 739. '[An interest rate swap] is an agreement between two parties by which each agrees to pay the other on a specified date or dates an amount calculated by reference to the interest which would have accrued over a given period on the same notional principal sum assuming different rates of interest are payable in each case. For example, one rate may be fixed at 10% and the other rate may be equivalent to the six-month London Interbank Offered Rate (LIBOR). If the LIBOR rate over the period of the swap is higher than 10%, then the party agreeing to receive "interest" in accordance with LIBOR will receive more than the party entitled to receive the 10%. Normally neither party will in fact pay the sums which it has agreed to pay over the period of the swap but instead will make a settlement on a "net payment basis" under which the party owing the greater amount on any day simply pays the difference between the two amounts due to the other.'

---

[141] See paragraph 4.97.
[142] [1990] 2 QB 697.

8.184 His Lordship's judicial analysis of a swap emphasizes the importance of netting, and provides a useful fundamental description of the cash flow created by a swap. However, this analysis does not consider the superimposition of the swap over the underlying transaction, and the analysis which logically follows of the combined effect of the swap and the underlying transaction, which demonstrates how a party's exposure to movements in the reference interest rates is changed. As the following paragraphs demonstrate, the contractual analysis of a swap should include a consideration of the combined effect of the swap and its underlying transaction if the swap is used for hedging purposes.

8.185 There are two broad analyses of a swap as a contract. Alastair Hudson identifies these two analyses,[143] which contradict each other and thereby underscore the difficulty that swaps present at a theoretical level.

8.186 The first analysis is referred to as the mutual debts analysis. A swap is a series of forward payments, each of which is performed separately. The second analysis is referred to as the executory contract analysis. A swap is a single executory contract that is only considered to be performed when the last payment has been made.

8.187 Hudson links each legal analysis to a different method for pricing swaps. The mutual debts analysis is consistent with the method of pricing a swap with reference to a series of forward contracts, as described in paragraph 4.97, and the executory contract analysis is consistent with the method of pricing a swap with reference to competing yields, as described in paragraph 4.98.

8.188 Hudson identifies a further four subsidiary legal analyses, each of which approximates to one or the other of the two broad analyses identified in the foregoing paragraphs. The first subsidiary analysis is built on Hobhouse J's statement in his judgment in the High Court in *Westdeutsche Landesbank Girozentrale v Islington London Borough Council*.[144] 'Where there have been cross-payments in respect of the same swap, reverse payments pro tanto reduce or reverse the pre-existing equity. Since the payments were made pursuant to the same void transaction, they fall to be looked at together and there is no equity in respect of one payment independent of the equity in respect of the others.' On the basis of Hobhouse J's statement, the repayment analysis would tend to conform with the executory contract analysis. The second subsidiary analysis is a refinement of the mutual debt analysis which considers the imposition of conditions precedent. The requirement to make a particular payment under a swap is conditional on two factors. The first factor is that the relevant rate has moved in the specified manner. The second factor is that there is no mathematically exact offset of the two payments that are

---

[143] *Swaps, Restitution & Trusts* (Sweet & Maxwell, 1999), and latterly in *The Law on Financial Derivatives* (Sweet & Maxwell, 2006).
[144] [1994] 4 All ER 890 at 937.

subject to netting, so a difference becomes payable. The third subsidiary analysis develops the mutual debts analysis by focusing on the financial forwards that make up a swap. However, the financial forwards analysis connotes that a swap is a series of reciprocal debts that are linked by the relevant master agreement itself. The significance of the financial forwards analysis is that the term 'swap' does not refer to a single contract or indeed a single transaction, but instead refers to a group of discrete transactions which have been assembled to create a particular economic effect. An element of confusion might arise, as the concept of assembling different cash flows, that is, forward contracts, to create a particular economic effect might also support the executory contract analysis. The economic effect of the swap would only be discerned after the entire swap has been performed. For example, the purpose of buying a two year interest rate swap, as the fixed rate payer, to hedge an exposure to an obligation to make payments at a floating rate of interest under a two year borrowing is arguably only fully fulfilled at the end of the two year term of that borrowing. Termination of the swap before the end of the two year term of the borrowing would suggest that the intended economic effect of the swap, to change an exposure to an obligation to make floating rate payments over the term of the borrowing, has not been achieved. The fourth subsidiary analysis, which is referred to as the disjointed option analysis, is included for the sake of completeness and considers the link between the exercise of rights under an option and the rights which arise or are extinguished in the underlying property of that option.

8.189 There is no definite view as to whether the mutual debts analysis or the executory contract analysis prevails. The pragmatic approach suggested by Hudson, that the commercial intentions of the parties indicate the appropriate legal analysis of their transaction, seems to be the sensible approach to adopt, and is consistent with the approach of the courts generally in determining how to give effect to the written terms of contracts. To continue the example of the two year interest rate swap bought to hedge a floating rate exposure, the appropriate legal analysis would appear to be the executory contract analysis. By contrast, the mutual debts analysis might arguably conform with an equity swap entered into to smooth out the fluctuations in the return of a holding of shares. The intended economic effect of the equity swap might be described as indeterminate, because the equity swap is only useful for as long as the underlying shares are held. Each payment date of the equity swap refers only to a particular period during which the underlying shares are held. The amounts of the payments that both parties are required to make on a payment date are calculated with reference to the relevant period only, and it would be appropriate to analyse the equity swap as a series of discrete transactions.

8.190 The issue as to whether or not a swap constitutes a series of discrete contracts or a single executory contract might become relevant in the context of determining whether or not a swap has been performed. One of the local authority swaps cases,

Guinness Mahon & Co Ltd v Kensington & Chelsea Royal London Borough Council,[145] however, is judicial authority that there is no principle to justify distinguishing between a swap which is open, and therefore which remains to be performed, and a swap which is closed, and which has therefore been performed, for the purpose of determining the appropriate judicial remedy to a swap that has been found to be ultra vires one of the parties. The principle that this case established is that a party's remedy is not affected by whether or not the apparent contract has been completely performed. This principle is consistent with the overall body of law developed by the local authority swaps cases, which involved ultra vires derivative contracts which were devoid of any legal effect because they had been entered into by various local government treasuries operating outside the scope of their statutory powers. From a conceptual perspective, it is impossible to perform a contract that has not been entered into, and therefore it is impossible to determine whether or not that contract has been performed.

8.191 However, from a practical perspective, whether or not a swap has been performed is not relevant if effect is given to the close-out netting provisions of a transaction master agreement. For example, section 6 of the ISDA 2002 Master Agreement[146] legislates for the calculation of the single net close-out amount payable in respect of one or more transactions that have been terminated early. The calculation is based on the computation of a close-out amount, which reflects either the losses and costs or the gains realized in replacing or providing the economic equivalent of the terminated transactions included in the computation. Although references to the economic equivalent of the terminated transactions suggest that the executory contract analysis is the more appropriate, the reference does not preclude the application of the mutual debts analysis. The operation of the practical language of section 6 of the ISDA 2002 Master Agreement does not depend on the legal analysis of the relevant terminated transactions, but on the proper construction of the master agreement as a contract. Therefore the key risk is that, under certain circumstances, the practical language of section 6 is not given proper effect because the contract itself is devoid of any legal effect because it is ultra vires one of the parties. This key legal risk is the source of the controversy generated by the local authority swaps cases.

8.9 Credit Derivatives Documentation

8.192 The observation is made in Chapter 7 that credit derivative contracts rely more heavily on a set of highly technical definitions than derivative contracts written on other classes of underlying. In essence, the underlying of a credit derivative

---

[145] [1998] 2 All ER 272.
[146] See paragraphs 7.51 ff.

transaction may well be credit risk, but the actual substance of that credit risk is the relationship between the reference entity and the party to which the reference entity owes obligations, which might be, but is not necessarily, the protection buyer. The documentation of this relationship, whether a loan agreement, a guarantee, or the documentation of an issue of debt securities, defines what constitutes a default by the reference entity, and therefore what constitutes a credit event for the purposes of the credit derivative transaction.

8.193 The development of the credit derivative market has been characterized by two issues: the successor issue and the restructuring issue. Both issues must be considered in the context of the development by ISDA of its market-standard credit derivative documentation, which has achieved almost universal acceptance. The relevant steps in the development of the documentation are: publication in 1992 of the 1992 Master Agreement (Multicurrency—Cross Border); publication in 1998 of the long form confirmation for credit default swaps; publication in 1999 of the 1999 ISDA Credit Derivatives Definitions; publication in 2003 of the ISDA 2002 Master Agreement; and publication in 2003 of the 2003 ISDA Credit Derivatives Definitions. In this part of this chapter, capitalized terms are terms that are defined in the relevant ISDA document.

8.194 Both the successor issue and the restructuring issue actually illustrate the same principal issue, which is, what is the scope of the credit risk in respect of which the protection Seller sells protection to the protection Buyer? Credit risk is defined with reference to a Reference Entity and one or more Obligations, and the benefit of a credit derivative contract is triggered by the occurrence of a Credit Event. Although it is often evident whether or not a Credit Event has occurred, sometimes there is uncertainty, and this uncertainty can cause tension between the protection Seller, who would argue that the Credit Event has not occurred, and the protection Buyer, who would argue that the Credit Event has occurred.

The successor issue

8.195 The successor issue arose because of the uncertainty caused by a Reference Entity transferring its assets and liabilities to a new entity. Generally, the credit protection conferred by a Credit Derivative Transaction only continues if the new entity is the Successor of the original Reference Entity. The 1999 credit definitions define a Successor in the following manner: '(a) in relation to a Reference Entity that is not a Sovereign, a direct or indirect successor to a Reference Entity that assumes all or substantially all of the obligations thereof by way of merger, consolidation, amalgamation, transfer or otherwise, whether by operation of law or pursuant to any agreement, as determined by the Calculation Agent (after consultation with the parties), and (b) in relation to a Sovereign Reference Entity, any direct or indirect successor to that Reference Entity irrespective of whether such successor assumes any of the obligations of the Reference Entity.'

8.9 Credit Derivatives Documentation

8.196 The demerger of National Power plc illustrates the potential difficulty. In 2000, National Power plc underwent a demerger to create two new entities, International Power plc and Innogy plc. Approximately two-thirds of the assets and certain obligations denominated in pounds sterling of National Power plc were transferred to Innogy plc. After the demerger, Innogy plc was expected to have a high credit rating, and International Power plc was expected to have a lower credit rating than that of National Power plc. A protection Seller would tend to argue that the Successor was the highly rated Innogy plc, and its motivation for doing so would be the perceived decreased probability that a Credit Event might take place in respect of the stronger credit, whereas a protection Buyer would tend to argue that the Successor was the weaker-rated International Power plc, and its motivation for doing so would be the perceived increased probability that a Credit Event might take place in respect of the weaker credit. The phrase used in the 1999 credit definitions, 'all or substantially all of the obligations', is not quantified, and therefore provided scope for the disagreement which ensued in the market. Eventually, the market reached the consensus that the phrase 'all or substantially all of the obligations' refers to over 90% of the obligations.

8.197 On 28 November 2001, ISDA published its Supplement relating to Successor and Credit Event to the 1999 ISDA Credit Derivatives Definitions. The successor supplement contains a more objective and therefore a more quantifiable test as to what is a Successor. Generally, an entity is the sole Successor if it succeeds to 75% or more of the Relevant Obligations of the Reference Entity. The successor supplement also legislates in some considerable detail for circumstances when an entity succeeds to, or in the case of the original Reference Entity retains, more than 25% but less than 75% of the Relevant Obligations.

8.198 The 2003 credit definitions build on the successor supplement, and contain detailed rules which determine whether or not an entity, or indeed the original Reference Entity, is a Successor. Section 2.2 of Article II of the 2003 credit definitions[147] sets out six circumstances, each of which is defined with reference to one or more entities succeeding to various percentages of the Relevant Obligations. Section 2.2(c) of Article II contains a very wide definition of a Succession Event.

The restructuring issue

8.199 The restructuring issue arose from two potential causes of uncertainty: one, whether or not a Restructuring of the Reference Obligations has occurred; and two, if there has been a Restructuring of the Reference Obligations, the manner in which Physical Settlement of the Credit Derivative Transaction should be effected.

---

[147] See paragraphs 7.130 ff.

Chapter 8: Legal Issues

8.200 By way of necessary reminder, the parties elect whether their Credit Derivative Transaction incorporates Physical Settlement or Cash Settlement. Settlement of a Credit Derivative Transaction takes place after the occurrence of a Credit Event has been verified. Generally, under Physical Settlement, the protection Seller makes a payment to the protection Buyer, and the protection Buyer in turn transfers to the protection Seller certain Obligations which satisfy the definition of Deliverable Obligation, in order that the Seller might attempt to extract some value from those Deliverable Obligations, by effectively becoming a creditor to the Reference Entity, to offset to the extent possible the payment it makes to the protection Buyer.

8.201 The lengthy definition of a Restructuring in the 1999 credit definitions was a response to the criticism that the definition contained in the 1998 long form confirmation was too subjective and therefore too uncertain. The 1998 long form confirmation provides that a Restructuring occurs in respect of an Obligation if 'the terms of the Obligation are, overall, materially less favourable from an economic, credit or risk perspective to any holder of such Obligation'.

8.202 On 11 May 2001, ISDA published the Restructuring Supplement to the 1999 ISDA Credit Derivatives Definitions, the effect of which generally is that a Restructuring only takes place in respect of an Obligation which is a Multiple Holder Obligation. A Multiple Holder Obligation is held by more than three holders, and the consent of at least two-thirds of the holders is required to initiate a Restructuring of that obligation.

8.203 The restructuring supplement also modifies the operation of Physical Settlement under the 1999 credit definitions. If the parties elect that the Restructuring Maturity Limitation applies to the Physical Settlement of their Credit Derivative Transaction, then the protection Buyer is entitled to deliver to the protection Seller only a Deliverable Obligation which is a Fully Transferable Obligation and which has a final maturity date no later than 30 months after the Scheduled Termination Date of the relevant Credit Derivative Transaction. The purpose of the Restructuring Maturity Limitation is to prevent the protection Buyer from delivering inferior assets to the protection Seller.

8.204 The global credit derivative market was fragmented by the publication of the restructuring supplement. Participants in the US and Asian markets have tended to use the restructuring supplement; that is, they have used 'modified R', which incorporates the Restructuring Maturity Limitation. By contrast, participants in the European market have tended to use 'modified modified R', which incorporates a modified form of the Restructuring Maturity Limitation. This modified form of Restructuring Maturity Limitation permits the protection Buyer to deliver to the protection Seller a Deliverable Obligation which can be transferred with consent and which has a final maturity date no later than 60 months after the

8.9 Credit Derivatives Documentation

Scheduled Termination Date of the relevant Credit Derivative Transaction. Under 'modified R', the Deliverable Obligation must be capable of being transferred without the requirement to obtain the consent, whether of the Reference Entity or another party; that is, the Deliverable Obligation must qualify as a Fully Transferable Obligation. Under 'modified modified R', the Deliverable Obligation can be an obligation which can only be transferred with the consent of the Reference Entity or another party, provided that the consent is not unreasonably withheld. The 'modified modified R' process is therefore more liberal than the 'modified R' process, in respect of both the maturity of the Deliverable Obligation and the ease with which the Deliverable Obligation is capable of being transferred. The 'modified modified R' process permits a more broad range of Deliverable Obligation than the 'modified R' process. The difference between the two processes generally arose from the difference between the emphasis of the two credit derivative markets which have diverged in their treatment of this issue. The emphasis of the US credit derivative markets tended to be on liquid traded debt securities, whereas the emphasis of the European credit derivative market tended to be on loan obligations, which are generally less easily transferred, and therefore which required the more liberal transfer regime of the 'modified modified R' process that the European credit derivative market adopted.

Section 4.7 of Article IV of the 2003 credit definitions contains a new and somewhat complex two-part test for whether or not a Restructuring has occurred.[148] Article VIII of the 2003 credit definitions contains 'Terms relating to Physical Settlement'.[149] The 2003 credit definitions contain three mechanisms to effect Physical Delivery. One, under the usual method, the protection Buyer is entitled to Deliver (this term has a precise meaning) to the protection Seller any Deliverable Obligation. Two, Restructuring Maturity Limitation and Fully Transferable Obligation is broadly the same as the 'modified R' process which has evolved through market convention, particularly in the US and Asian markets. Three, Modified Restructuring Maturity Limitation and Conditionally Transferable Obligation are broadly the same as the 'modified modified R' process which has evolved through market convention, particularly in the European market. Parties to a Credit Derivative Transaction can therefore choose how to effect Physical Settlement, and the 2003 credit definitions should accommodate the three different strands which have emerged.

8.205

---

[148] See paragraph 7.144.
[149] See paragraphs 7.153 ff.

Looking wider

8.206 The 2003 credit definitions were prepared very much as a response to the conventions and practices that emerged in the markets themselves. The ongoing development and refinement of the suite of credit derivative documentation continues to reflect the evolutionary pressure of this segment of the derivative markets, and the weight of work in this field bears testimony to the emphasis in the credit derivative market on the complex contractual terms which define the risk being transferred.

9

END-USERS

9.1 The Investment Management Industry	9.01
9.2 Hedge Funds	9.25
9.3 Prime Brokerage	9.40
9.4 Corporate Treasuries	9.52

9.1 The Investment Management Industry

9.01 In considering the investment management industry, difficult questions often arise as to the classification of investment vehicles in terms of their structure and the regulation to which they are subject, and regulation in part determines whether or not derivatives can be used, and the extent to which and the manner in which derivatives can be used. A crude distinction can be drawn between an arrangement for the management of a portfolio of investments carried out under a mandate, and a pooled investment arrangement. The management of a portfolio of investments under a mandate is usually undertaken either for individuals who enjoy substantial wealth[1] or for institutions including pension schemes and charities. The management of a portfolio under a mandate is undertaken either by investment professionals who are employed for that purpose, such as the staff of a family office, or by an investment management firm. Many stockbrokers and private banks offer investment management services, often in conjunction with more general wealth management and estate planning services. An investment management firm accepting a mandate to manage a portfolio generally enters into an investment management agreement with the client, which specifies the methodology by which the client's portfolio is to be managed. The investment management agreement should address matters such as the different types of asset which qualify for inclusion in the portfolio, the extent to which the portfolio is to be diversified, the degree of risk to which the portfolio is to be exposed, the use of derivatives and borrowing,[2] any benchmark by which the performance of the

---

[1] Investors such as these are usually referred to as high net worth individuals.
[2] Borrowing in a portfolio is sometimes referred to as gearing or leverage.

portfolio is to be measured, and the remuneration of the investment management firm. The investment management agreement should also address 'boilerplate' matters including the circumstances in which either the client or the investment manager is entitled to terminate the appointment of the investment manager and the period of notice to be given, and general administrative matters. Leaving aside the requirement that the investment management firm is authorized to carry on the relevant activity of managing investments,[3] and the regulatory obligations which arise from authorization, the performance of the investment management firm will be assessed with reference to the requirements and standards of the investment management agreement it has entered into and the standards imposed by the law generally. For example, investing the client's portfolio in high risk assets whereas the mandate stipulates low risk assets would expose the investment management firm to regulatory sanction as well as potentially to claims for breach of contract and negligence. Generally, there is no restriction on the type of asset in which the client's portfolio can be invested, and accordingly there are no constraints on the use of derivatives or borrowing. However, the investment management firm will nonetheless owe a duty to ensure that any strategy it suggests is suitable for the client's resources and of course investment objectives.

9.02 By contrast, the investment management industry also offers pooled investment arrangements, under which different individual investors contribute capital to an investment vehicle. The capital of the investment vehicle is then invested by the investment manager in various assets and property. The principal advantage of a pooled investment arrangement is that the aggregate of each investor's contribution to the capital of the investment vehicle achieves greater economies of scale than would be achieved by the investors investing independently of each other. Additionally, the establishment of a pooled investment arrangement facilitates the appointment of a professional investment manager, and the payment of the manager's fees is less of a burden through the economies of scale that are achieved. There are many different forms of pooled investment arrangements; at one end of the spectrum lie private arrangements such as hedge funds, which are discussed in part 9.2 of this chapter, and at the other end of the spectrum is found the industry which creates and markets to the public pooled investment arrangements such as unit trusts and investment trust companies. One final introductory comment is that the differentiation between the different segments of the investment management industry can be indistinct; for example, although some hedge funds constitute purely private arrangements, others are promoted and offered to a limited number of investors, albeit investors of high net worth, giving rise to the label 'alternative investment industry' that is occasionally applied to the hedge fund sector.

---

[3] See paragraph 5.71.

9.1 The Investment Management Industry

Collective investment undertaking

The term 'collective investment undertaking' is used here to refer to a pooled investment arrangement. Although proper meaning[4] is given to the term in the UCITS 3 Directives,[5] and the UCITS 3 Directives have a particular application which is discussed in the following paragraphs, it remains a useful descriptor of an arrangement for raising capital from the public and investing that capital for investors in accordance with the principles of spreading risk, without connoting a particular structure. Structure and the classification which flows from structure are examined in the following paragraphs. **9.03**

A distinction may conveniently be drawn between a collective investment undertaking which has a closed-ended structure and a collective investment undertaking which has an open-ended structure. Depending on the structure, different rules apply for promoting and offering the collective investment undertaking to the public, and different rules apply for the investments that can be made, including the use of derivatives and borrowing. In general terms, a particular regulatory regime applies to collective investment undertakings which are funds, and this funds regime does not apply to other collective investment undertakings which are not funds; instead, different legal standards are applied to these collective investment undertakings which are not funds. **9.04**

Closed-ended structure

A collective investment undertaking which has a closed-ended structure usually takes the form of a company. The term 'closed-ended' connotes that the company is able to issue shares up to its authorized share capital. In the United Kingdom, the Companies Acts regulate the establishment and governance of companies. Investors subscribe for shares in the company, and the company in turn invests the capital raised through the issuance of the shares in the portfolio of investments. Broadly, the value of the shares should correspond with the portfolio of investments held by the company. The shares issued by the company can be listed or unlisted. **9.05**

---

[4] The term 'collective investment undertaking' connotes that investors contribute capital to the undertaking, and the capital raised is invested by the undertaking to acquire investment assets, and each investor's investment is represented by units which are, at the request of the investor, repurchased or redeemed out of the investment assets.

[5] The UCITS 3 Directives are 2001/107/EC Directive of the European Parliament and of the Council amending Council Directive 85/611/EEC on the coordination of laws, regulations and administrative provisions relating to undertakings for collective investment in transferable securities (UCITS) with a view to regulating management companies and simplified prospectuses, and 2001/108/EC Directive of the European Parliament and of the Council amending Council Directive 85/611/EEC on the coordination of laws, regulations and administrative provisions relating to undertakings for collective investment in transferable securities (UCITS) with regard to investments of UCITS.

An offer of the shares in the company to the public,[6] or an application for admission of the shares to trading, must be made in accordance with the usual rules which follow the standards laid down in the Prospectus Directive.[7] One of the principal requirements for an offer of securities to the public or a listing of securities is the publication of a prospectus which contains the required information in the required format, including details of the assets and property that the proceeds of the issue of shares will be used to acquire. The relevant listing rules are also relevant. Other forms of closed-ended structure exist, such as some trusts and limited partnerships. Collective investment undertakings which are closed-ended are not regulated within the funds regime referred to above, and therefore the rules contained within the funds regime which govern investment methodology do not apply to them. However, certain bodies corporate qualify as funds, as the following paragraphs indicate, and the funds regime applies to them; these types of body corporate are not the usual types of company incorporated under the Companies Acts.

Open-ended structure

9.06 A collective investment undertaking which has an open-ended structure is typically referred to as a 'fund'. One of the most important characteristics of a fund that falls within the funds regime is that investors in the fund have the right to redeem their investments at net asset value within a reasonable time, that is, the fund makes available reasonably frequent liquidity. The key legal and regulatory concept underpinning the fund is the collective investment scheme. A detailed definition of collective investment scheme is contained in section 235 of the FSMA 2000; the term applies to 'any arrangements with respect to property of any description, including money, the purpose or effect of which is to enable persons taking part in the arrangements (whether by becoming owners of the property or any part of it or otherwise) to participate in or receive profits or income arising from the acquisition, holding, management or disposal of the property or sums paid out of such profits or income'. Particular arrangements must have certain attributes in order to constitute a collective investment scheme, including the main attribute that investors in the scheme do not exercise day-to-day control over the scheme, although they may have the right to be consulted or to give directions.[8] In addition, the arrangements must have either or both of the attributes that the contributions made by participants

---

[6] An 'offer of transferable securities to the public' is defined in section 102B of the FSMA 2000 as generally a communication to any person which presents sufficient information on the transferable securities to be offered and the terms on which they are offered to enable an investor to decide to buy or subscribe for the securities in question.

[7] 2003/71/EC Directive of the European Parliament and of the Council on the prospectus to be published when securities are offered to the public or admitted to trading and amending Directive 2001/34/EEC.

[8] Section 235(2) of the FSMA 2000.

and the profits and income are pooled, or that the property is managed by or on behalf of the operator of the scheme.[9] Further detail is added by the Financial Services and Markets Act 2000 (Collective Investment Schemes) Order 2001,[10] as amended ('Collective Investment Schemes Order'). The Schedule to the Collective Investment Schemes Order specifies arrangements which do not amount to a collective investment scheme, and include individual investment management arrangements, of the type discussed at paragraph 9.01,[11] and bodies corporate generally.[12] However, some potential for confusion arises, because certain bodies corporate specifically fall within the classification of collective investment schemes: these are open-ended investment companies, which are discussed in the following paragraphs. The classification of a fund as a collective investment scheme is crucial, as regulatory consequences flow from such classification, including the requirement to be authorized and restrictions on promotion. This is the funds regime. It is useful first to consider the different types of collective investment scheme which are encountered, and then to describe the effect of regulation; the applicable regulations include provisions which govern the use of derivatives, and it is on this aspect of the regulation that this chapter focuses.

9.07 Collective investment schemes may be classified according to their structure and the strand of regulation to which they are subject. The broad classification of collective investment schemes includes unit trust schemes and open-ended investment companies. A unit trust scheme is constituted under a trust deed, and as a basic matter of prudent governance, the trustee of the scheme must be independent of the investment manager of the scheme. An authorized unit trust (AUT) is a unit trust scheme that has been authorized by the FSA.

Open-ended investment company (OEIC)

9.08 An open-ended investment company (OEIC) is a collective investment scheme which satisfies the definition contained in section 236 of the FSMA 2000. An OEIC is a collective investment scheme which satisfies both the property condition, which is fulfilled if the property of the fund belongs beneficially to and is managed by or on behalf of a body corporate,[13] and the investment condition, which is fulfilled if a reasonable investor in the fund can expect to be able to withdraw his investment reasonably quickly and on a basis calculated wholly or mainly by reference to the value of the property held by the fund.[14] The property condition establishes that an

---

[9] Section 235(3) of the FSMA 2000.
[10] SI 2001/1062 (as amended).
[11] Paragraph 1.
[12] Paragraph 21. However, the effect of paragraph 21(2) is that a limited liability partnership can constitute a collective investment scheme.
[13] Section 236(2) of the FSMA 2000.
[14] Section 236(3) of the FSMA 2000.

OEIC is a body corporate, and the investment condition establishes that a principal requirement is that investors have sufficient liquidity, which means that they are able to subscribe for and redeem their investments without suffering undue delay.

Investment company with variable capital (ICVC)

9.09 An investment company with variable capital (ICVC)[15] is a type of OEIC which is based in the United Kingdom. HM Treasury has exercised its power under section 262 of the FSMA 2000 to make the Open-Ended Investment Companies Regulations 2001,[16] as amended (OEIC Regulations), which govern the establishment of an ICVC as an OEIC. The OEIC Regulations address matters such as the formation, supervision, and control of an OEIC, the governance of an OEIC, and the registration of the OEIC by the FSA. The investment methodology that an OEIC must follow is instead contained in the FSA Handbook, and this is considered in more detail in the following paragraphs.

9.10 At a more conceptual level, an OEIC (including an ICVC) is a company, albeit a company the structure of which is open-ended. Being open-ended, the OEIC is able to create and to issue new shares to investors, without the ceiling of an authorized share capital which characterizes a closed-ended structure. Of course, a closed-ended company is able to increase its authorized share capital, but to effect such an increase requires the passing of the required resolutions. Further, one of the prerequisites of a company satisfying the definition of an OEIC is that the reasonable investor enjoys reasonably frequent liquidity, and this reinforces the concept that the OEIC is open-ended.[17] By contrast, a company established under the Companies Acts and which does not constitute an OEIC cannot deal in its own shares sufficiently frequently to qualify as open-ended. The rule in *Trevor v Whitworth*[18] generally prevents such a company from offering to buy back its own shares.

Authorization and regulation

9.11 A unit trust scheme can be either authorized and regulated as a UCITS or authorized and regulated other than as a UCITS; a unit trust scheme that is authorized is an AUT. Similarly, an OEIC (including an ICVC) can be either authorized and

---

[15] Neither the term 'investment company with variable capital' nor the acronym 'ICVC' is used in the OEIC Regulations. Instead, these are concepts that are found in the FSA Handbook.
[16] SI 2001/1228. The OEIC Regulations replaced the Open-ended Investment Companies (Investment Companies with Variable Capital) Regulations 1996, SI 1996/2827.
[17] Section 236(3)(a) of the FSMA 2000.
[18] (1887) 12 App Cas 409. The basic rule established by *Trevor v Whitworth*, that a company cannot buy the shares that it issues, has been modified by successive Companies Acts, which do allow a company to buy the shares that it issues under certain circumstances, for example, shares that are specifically created as redeemable. However, the issue of such shares is subject to other rules and principles.

regulated as a UCITS or authorized and regulated other than as a UCITS. The acronym 'UCITS' refers to an undertaking for collective investment in transferable securities, and it is the key concept of the UCITS 3 Directives. In broad terms, a UCITS that is authorized in one member state of the EEA can be offered to the public in both that member state and elsewhere in the EEA, making use of the freedoms conferred by the UCITS 3 Directives. Section 264 of the FSMA 2000 provides that a collective investment scheme constituted in another EEA member state is a recognized scheme if the prescribed administrative steps have been taken. By contrast, a unit trust scheme or an OEIC which is authorized, but not as a UCITS, can only be offered to the public in the jurisdiction in which it is authorized and regulated. Some, but not all, member states of the EEA have put in place legislation and regulation which allows for the authorization and regulation of funds purely for their domestic markets; the United Kingdom has done so, and such a domestic fund is referred to in the United Kingdom as a non-UCITS regulated scheme (NURS).

9.12 Section 270 of the FSMA 2000 allows collective investment schemes that are managed and authorized outside the United Kingdom, but that are not recognized under section 264 of the FSMA 2000, and therefore which are not UCITS, to become recognized under an order made by HM Treasury.[19] Section 272 of the FSMA 2000 empowers the FSA to recognize upon application a collective investment scheme that is managed and authorized outside the United Kingdom and to which neither section 264 of the FSMA 2000 nor section 272 of the FSMA 2000 applies, provided that such a collective investment scheme demonstrates the required standard of investor protection.

9.13 The UCITS 3 Directives constrain the investment methodology that a fund which constitutes a UCITS can adopt, including the use of derivatives. The standards of the UCITS 3 Directives in respect of investment methodology[20] have been transposed into the Collective Investment Schemes specialist sourcebook of the FSA Handbook (COLL). COLL 5 sets out the investment and borrowing powers of funds which are both UCITS funds and non-UCITS funds, that is, funds which are within the funds regime.

---

[19] Jersey, Guernsey, and the Isle of Man have been designated for the purposes of s 270 of the FSMA 2000 by the Financial Services and Markets Act 2000 (Collective Investment Schemes) (Designated Countries and Territories) Order 2003, SI 2003/1181. Further, Bermuda remains designated for the purposes of s 270 of the FSMA 2000 by the continuation in force and effect of the Financial Services (Designated Countries and Territories) (Overseas Collective Investment Schemes) (Bermuda) Order 1988, SI 1988/2284.

[20] The more general regulatory requirements underpinning the establishment and authorization of a UCITS, such as the prudential supervision of a UCITS firm set out in UPRU, are outside the scope of this book.

Chapter 9: End-Users

Unauthorized and unregulated

9.14 Before turning to the detail of the investment and borrowing powers of funds within the funds regime, it should be noted for the sake of completeness that both closed-ended and open-ended collective investment undertakings can fall outside the scope of authorization and regulation, and therefore the rules of the funds regime which control the use of derivatives do not apply to them. These unauthorized collective investment undertakings cannot be offered to the public, and they include hedge funds and private investment clubs. Hedge funds are considered in part 9.2 of this chapter.

Regulation of Collective Investment Schemes

9.15 The principle underlying the approach to regulation set out in COLL 5 is that[21] securing the regulatory objective of protecting consumers is helped by laying down minimum standards for the assets that may be held by an authorized fund. The purpose of the extremely detailed technical rules contained in COLL 5 is primarily to restrict a fund, whether a UCITS fund[22] or a non-UCITS fund,[23] to investing in certain classes of asset which are dealt in markets which allow for the ready valuation of those assets and the ready disposal of those assets, and to limit investment in assets that are not dealt in such liquid markets to specified percentages of the fund's value. Other technical rules prescribe the extent to which risk is spread through the diversification of the assets in which the fund invests, and the use that can be made of techniques such as stock lending and borrowing. The purpose of these restrictions is to ensure that a fund amounts to as diverse and as stable a pool of investments as can be achieved without stifling unduly its potential; it must be remembered that such a fund is intended for offer and distribution to retail consumers. A UCITS fund is subject to more restriction that a non-UCITS fund. Generally, a UCITS fund can only invest[24] in transferable securities,[25] units in collective investment schemes, approved money-market instruments, derivatives and forward transactions, and deposits, subject to the parameters specified in COLL 5.2. Generally, a non-UCITS fund can only invest[26] in the same classes of assets as a UCITS fund, and also in interests in real property (these interests are termed

---

[21] COLL 5.1.2G.
[22] COLL 5.2.
[23] COLL 5.6.
[24] COLL 5.2.8R.
[25] The definition of 'transferable security' contained in COLL 5.2.7R includes a share, a debenture, a government or public security, a warrant, and a certificate representing certain securities, and an investment is not a transferable security if the title to it cannot be transferred, or can be transferred only with the consent of a third party. The concept of the 'transferable security' is central to the concept of the UCITS and the pooling of investment in equity and debt securities for retail consumers.
[26] COLL 5.6.4R.

9.1 The Investment Management Industry

'immovables') and in gold, subject to the parameters specified in COLL 5.6. Whereas a UCITS fund is only permitted to borrow to cover temporary shortfalls in its cash flow,[27] a non-UCITS fund is permitted to borrow up to 10% of the value of its assets.[28]

Use of derivatives (UCITS fund)

9.16 The rules which govern the use that a UCITS fund can make of derivatives govern the following matters: (1) the type of derivative that can be used, in terms of whether the derivative is exchange-based or OTC, and in terms of the underlying; (2) the concentrations of derivative exposure that the fund can assume; and (3) the risk management process that must accompany any use of derivatives. As the following paragraphs indicate, the rules are surprisingly accommodating in respect of the use of derivatives.

9.17 As intimated in the preceding paragraph, a UCITS fund can make use of both exchange-based derivatives and OTC derivatives.[29] A transaction in an exchange-based derivative must be effected on or under the rules of an eligible derivatives market;[30] the purpose of this requirement is to ensure that the UCITS fund only accesses a derivatives market which confers an appropriate degree of protection, and a market confers an appropriate degree of protection if it is regulated, operates regularly, is recognized as a market or an exchange or a self-regulating organization, is open to the public, is adequately liquid, and has adequate arrangements for the movement of funds.[31] A transaction in an OTC derivative must be entered into with an approved counterparty,[32] which is either an eligible institution or an approved bank, on approved terms. Approved terms are terms which comprise the approved counterparty's agreement to provide reliable and verifiable valuations of the derivative at least daily, and to provide liquidity. Again, the purpose of this requirement is to ensure that the UCITS fund is able to account easily for the derivative and to close readily its derivative exposure; these standards are analogous with those achieved in respect of exchange-based trading, which is by its nature transparent and liquid.

9.18 A derivative can only be used by a UCITS fund if the underlying of the derivative is an asset to which the UCITS fund is dedicated, and in any event, the underlying of the derivative must be drawn from a list.[33] Further controls are that use of

---

[27] COLL 5.5.4R.
[28] COLL 5.6.22R, which applies certain rules contained in COLL 5.5.
[29] COLL 5.2.20(1)R.
[30] COLL 5.2.20(3)R.
[31] COLL 5.2.10(3)R.
[32] COLL 5.2.23R.
[33] This list is set out in COLL 5.2.20(2)R.

the derivative must not cause the UCITS fund to diverge from its investment objectives,[34] and that the derivative cannot be used to create the potential for an uncovered sale of securities,[35] although a sale effected using a derivative is not deemed to be uncovered if certain conditions are satisfied.[36] Further, use of a derivative or a forward transaction which will result in, or which may result in, the delivery of property to or for the account of the UCITS fund is only permitted if the UCITS fund is permitted to hold that property, and any relevant limits must be observed.[37]

9.19 Quantitative rules[38] specify the concentration of exposure to derivatives that a UCITS fund is permitted to assume. The exposure to any one counterparty in an OTC derivative transaction must not exceed 5% in value of the assets of a UCITS fund, although this ceiling is raised to 10% if the counterparty is an approved bank, on the basis that an approved bank should, all things being equal, project less credit risk. The specified percentage ceilings are reduced if adequate collateral and netting arrangements are in place, on the basis that, again, such arrangements should result in a reduction in the credit risk to which the UCITS fund is exposed. However, the rules are relaxed if the derivative is exchange-based, as the mechanisms supporting an exchange are deemed to confer adequate protection. These protections include the clearing and settlement function, which tend to prevent daily losses and profits accumulating.[39]

9.20 However, surprisingly, there appears to be no specified limit on the proportion of the UCITS fund's assets that are permitted to be invested in derivatives generally. This is an innovation of the rules contained in the UCITS 3 Directives, which are more liberal in this regard than previous iterations of the rules. In theory, therefore, the entirety of a UCITS fund can be invested synthetically, using derivatives, subject of course to the rules which control concentrations.

9.21 The risk management process that must accompany the use of derivatives should enable the relevant investment manager of the UCITS fund to monitor and to measure as frequently as appropriate the risk of the derivatives used by the UCITS fund, and the effect of those derivatives on the overall risk profile of the UCITS fund; details of the risk management process must be notified to the FSA prior to any use of that process.[40]

---

[34] COLL 5.2.20(4)R.
[35] COLL 5.2.20(5)R.
[36] The conditions that must be satisfied are set out in detail in COLL 5.2.22R.
[37] COLL 5.2.21R.
[38] COLL 5.2.11R.
[39] See part 2.2 of Chapter 2 and part 3.4 of Chapter 3.
[40] COLL 5.2.24R.

Use of derivatives (non-UCITS fund)

9.22 The rules governing the use of derivatives by a non-UCITS fund are substantially the same as the rules governing the use of derivatives by a UCITS fund.

Closing remarks

9.23 The liberalization of the use of derivatives under the UCITS 3 Directives and consequently COLL 5 reflects the emerging reality that regulators are growing more familiar with derivatives, focusing less on trying to curtail the use of derivatives and instead requiring the implementation of the framework of methodology and controls which will promote the safer use of derivatives. It is submitted that this approach is entirely correct. Derivatives can be used to calibrate very precisely the risk profile of a fund, and provided that the fund is marketed and promoted in terms which are clear, fair, and not misleading, which implies that full disclosure is made of the strategy and style of the fund, and the extent to which derivatives will affect the performance of the fund, then the use of derivatives should not of itself be a matter of controversy. This is not to say, however, that a fund which makes extensive use of derivatives will necessarily be suitable for every investor. More than ever, requirements remain in place to ensure that investors are sold products that are suitable in the context of their expertise, experience, and needs, but a necessary part of that process is the ability of investors to make properly informed decisions for themselves. Derivatives offer greater choice for the consumer.

9.24 The investment management industry itself has been slow to make use of the wider powers it now has to use derivatives. Although sophisticated funds can now be assembled using advanced derivative techniques, the investment management industry has for the most part remained reluctant to do so, particularly those managers which have traditionally offered 'long-only' funds.[41] Thus the position has arisen that regulators have ushered in a more liberal regime and the regulated industry has been slow to avail itself of the new possibilities, particularly in the context of the offer of funds to retail consumers.

9.2 Hedge Funds

9.25 There is no definition of the term 'hedge fund' in law or regulation. As the previous paragraphs demonstrate, the legal and regulatory treatment of a collective investment undertaking is determined by its structure and by whether or not it is

---

[41] See 'Fund managers still wary of using new powers', *Financial Times*, 24 November/25 November 2007.

to be offered to the public; an open-ended collective investment undertaking can only be offered to the public in a manner permitted by the funds regime, and a closed-ended collective investment undertaking can only be offered to the public in a manner permitted by the legislation governing the public offer of securities. The term 'hedge fund' tends more to connote a particular style of investment management and tends less to connote a particular structure. As the previous paragraphs indicate, and as the 2006 ISDA Fund Definitions illustrate,[42] hedge funds can be established in any one of a number of different formats.

9.26 The hedge fund investment model makes use of both long and short exposures, whereas the traditional investment model makes use only of long exposures. Accordingly, the mainstream investment management industry is sometimes referred to as the 'long-only' investment management industry.

9.27 However, despite the recent debate that hedge funds have attracted, the first hedge fund was apparently established over half a century ago in 1949 by Alfred Winslow Jones (1900–88). Jones, the author of the social commentary *Life, Liberty and Prosperity*, which was published in 1941, earned a bachelor's degree at Harvard University, and after service with the US foreign service, read for a Ph.D. at Columbia University. Jones was the editor of *Fortune* magazine during the Second World War, and he then established the private investment partnership A W Jones and Company in the late 1940s.

9.28 Jones set out to devise a new model for building an investment portfolio. Jones determined to build a portfolio which was insulated from the effects of systemic risk, and instead was only exposed to non-systemic risk. In this context, systemic risk is the risk of an adverse movement in the markets generally. Therefore, Jones's objective was to build a portfolio the value of which would only be affected by movements in the prices of actual individual shares or debt held in that portfolio. More general movements in the markets would not affect the value of the portfolio, and therefore the investment manager's selection of individual shares or debt would determine the success or failure of that portfolio. Jones's fundamental insight was that a portfolio's capital is fixed, but its exposure to the markets generally is variable. Jones developed the following expression of market exposure.

Market exposure = (long exposure – short exposure) / capital

9.29 The classical hedge fund investment model is based on this simple formula. Derivatives are used by hedge funds because derivatives allow short exposures to be created and gearing to be achieved.

9.30 By way of illustration, there are two competing funds. Each fund has seed capital of US$15 million and each invests in shares issued by the same companies which

---

[42] See part 7.12 of Chapter 7.

are constituents of the S&P 500 index, although of course it would not be possible to replicate precisely the composition and value of the index at any given time through a shareholding. Movements in the S&P 500 index enable movements in the markets generally to be quantified, and exchange-based futures contracts on the S&P 500 index provide hedging opportunities. Crucially, whereas one fund is a traditional fund which only takes long positions, the other is a hedge fund which uses derivatives to create both short exposures and long exposures.

9.31 The long-only fund buys US$15 million of shares. The hedge fund's strategy is more complex. One, the hedge fund borrows US$30 million, which gives it a working capital of US$45 million, including its seed capital. Two, the hedge fund buys US$45 million of shares. Three, the hedge fund establishes a short position to the market by selling S&P 500 index futures for US$37.5 million. The number of S&P 500 index futures sold by the hedge fund must generally be calculated to achieve a balance between hedging the systemic risk to which the hedge fund is exposed, and retaining an element of 'upside potential'. It is worthwhile to note that it is difficult to establish a perfect hedge using standardized exchange-based derivative contracts, and this difficulty has contributed to the growth in the OTC derivative markets. Significantly, the entire amount of the investment that the hedge fund has financed through borrowing, US$30 million, has been protected by the hedging sale of S&P 500 index futures, and half of the investment that the hedge fund has financed from its seed capital, US$7.5 million, has been protected by the hedging sale of S&P 500 index futures. Therefore, only half of the hedge fund's seed capital of US$15 million has been exposed to systemic risk, although the hedge fund has actually gained exposure to shares worth US$45 million. The hedge fund has geared its seed capital by 300%. Turning back to the formula to calculate market exposure, the hedge fund's market exposure, as a percentage of its seed capital, is (US$45 million − US$37.5 million) / US$15 million, which is 50%.

9.32 Assume that the shares in the companies rise by 5% and the S&P 500 index as a whole remains static. The return of the long-only fund is US$0.75 million. The return of the hedge fund is 5% of the exposure US$45 million, which is US$2.25 million. The long-only fund is exposed to twice as much systemic risk as the hedge fund. Only half of the hedge fund's seed capital is exposed to systemic risk, but all of the long-only fund's seed capital is exposed to systemic risk. Yet the long-only fund earns only one-third of the return that the hedge fund earns.

9.33 Assume that the shares in the companies fall by 5% and the S&P 500 index as a whole falls by 10%. The long-only fund's loss is US$0.75 million. The hedge fund is protected by its short S&P 500 index futures position. The hedge fund opened the position by selling futures for US$37.5 million. The position is now closed by buying futures for US$33.75 million, which is the original US$37.5 million less 10%. The hedge fund now makes a net gain of US$1.5 million. This net gain is the loss on the shares plus the gain on the futures, which equals

(US$45 million * 0.05) + (US$37.5 million * 0.10), which is US$2.25 million loss + US$3.75 million gain, which is a US$1.5 million gain.

9.34 Assume that the shares in the companies rise by 8% and the S&P 500 index as a whole rises by 5%. The return of the long-only fund is US$1.2 million. The hedge fund's short S&P 500 index futures position makes a loss, which erodes, but does not cancel, the return of the hedge fund. The hedge fund makes a net gain of US$1.725 million. This net gain is the gain on the shares less the loss on the futures, which equals (US$45 million * 0.08) – (US$37.5 million * 0.05), which is US$3.6 million gain – US$1.875 million loss, which is a US$1.725 million gain.

9.35 The key observation is made that the hedge fund makes an absolute return. Crucially, the long-only fund makes a relative return. The return of the long-only fund is assessed with reference to the performance of the market as a whole, and the performance of the S&P 500 index serves as a proxy for the performance of the market as a whole. The long-only fund succeeds in outperforming the market. When the market declines, the long-only fund also declines, but by less, and when the market rises, the long-only fund also rises, but by more. The extent to which the long-only fund outperforms the market demonstrates the investment manager's skill, in terms of the selection of the particular shares and the timing of the various purchases and sales that are made. By contrast, the hedge fund consistently makes an absolute return, irrespective of the performance of the market.

9.36 Of course, the illustration developed over the preceding paragraphs omits for the sake of clarity the cost incurred by the hedge fund in borrowing US$30 million and the costs generally of dealing, that is, paying brokerage fees and a bid and offer spread. Also, any loss made in respect of short futures positions must be financed on an incremental basis.[43] Further, the key assumption is made that the futures contracts move broadly in line with the cash market, hence a 10% decline in the cash market, as represented by the S&P 500 index, is matched by a 10% decrease in the futures price. As part 4.3 of Chapter 4 explains, this synchrony of movement does not always occur. Nonetheless, the advantages of using derivatives are apparent. The hedge fund gains increased exposure, or gearing, whilst maintaining 'downside' protection.

9.37 Hedge funds were originally structured to make absolute returns throughout a variety of market conditions at all times. This objective can be met more easily through the use of derivatives to complement the selection of winning assets. Derivatives allow a hedge fund's exposure to be engineered much more flexibly through the use of both long positions and short positions than can be achieved through relying just on short-selling.

---

[43] See Chapters 2 and 3 for an explanation of the exchange-based clearing and margining system.

However, the term 'hedge fund' is now used to describe a wide range of investment vehicles which vary in scale and scope from the global macro funds to the more narrow specialist funds that have been set up to exploit investment opportunities in specific markets.[44] Some modern hedge funds have moved away from the original concept of seeking to make absolute returns despite prevailing market conditions to adopting the more aggressive strategy of leveraging exposure through borrowing.

9.38

Given the intrinsic appeal of hedge funds, and their objective of securing absolute returns as opposed to relative returns, some investment managers have started to develop hedge fund products for mainstream investors. Hedge funds are therefore starting to lose their cachet of being available only to the wealthy. As part 9.1 of this chapter has shown, regulators have facilitated the development of retail hedge funds by making available to the investment management industry the necessary financial tools, but both the regulators and the investment management industry themselves are proceeding cautiously. Indeed, the view prevails within the investment management industry that certain of their products remain suitable only for institutional investors and sophisticated investors.

9.39

9.3 Prime Brokerage

'Prime brokerage'[45] is the term used to describe a package of services that certain financial institutions, such as investment banks, have begun to offer to investment managers. Managers of hedge funds are significant users of prime brokerage services. A prime broker is often described quite informally as a trading partner to the investment manager, and this succinctly describes the purpose of prime brokerage accounts. There are many different models of prime brokerage, which is a service offered in respect of not just derivatives, but also cash market investments (including equity and debt) and foreign exchange. In essence, a prime brokerage account offers cost-effective and easy access to the markets through one 'gateway', and confers several significant benefits on the investment manager.

9.40

The first benefit is achieving better prices and rates. A counterparty, such as an investment bank or other dealer with which the investment manager wishes to trade, is exposed to the credit risk emanating from the fund vehicle under management. The dealer may charge higher prices or rates to that fund in order to reflect the credit risk it assumes by entering into transactions with the fund.

9.41

---

[44] Hedge funds invest in all classes of asset, including financial instruments, commodities, and interests in real property, in all geographical and economic sectors. Hedge funds employ a wide range of strategies.
[45] Also 'prime finance'.

The prime broker effectively lends its balance sheet to the fund. The investment manager decides to commit the fund to a transaction with the dealer, and negotiates the transaction with the dealer. The dealer then enters into the transaction with the prime broker. The dealer is exposed to the credit risk emanating from the prime broker, and as the prime broker is a significant financial institution which projects a lower credit risk than the fund, an improved price or rate is achieved for the transaction. The prime broker then enters into an equivalent transaction with the fund, earning a spread between the two transactions that it enters into. For example, the investment manager decides to commit the fund to buying a swap. The investment manager negotiates the terms of the swap with the dealer, and agrees the purchase of the swap by the fund through its prime brokerage account. The prime broker then buys the swap from the dealer, paying the fixed rate. The prime broker sells an equivalent swap to the fund. The fund pays a slightly higher fixed rate. The prime broker earns a spread between the two fixed rates. The prime broker is exposed to the credit risks projected by both the dealer and the fund, and the spread it charges compensates it for its assumption of two strands of credit risk. Of course, the prime broker will have collateral arrangements in place with both the dealer and the fund, ameliorating considerably its credit risk.

9.42 The second benefit is the provision of ongoing financing and liquidity. The hedge fund in the example set out in part 9.2 of this chapter opens a short futures position, and as Chapters 2 and 3 explain, initial margin must be provided to the clearing house when the position is opened, and variation margin might be required at the end of any trading session during which the position has generated a loss and insufficient collateral has already been lodged. Although the fund might make an overall net gain, the fund must nonetheless meet its margin calls in respect of its futures losses, as and when these calls are made. The prime broker might therefore provide liquidity to the fund, as the fund might not have the necessary funds immediately available despite its overall profitability. The fund might also make use of short-term borrowing to meet other demands, such as financing redemptions.

9.43 The third benefit is that the hedge fund is required to provide less collateral. The third benefit is potentially the most valuable to the fund. The prime broker is able to calculate the net exposure it has to the fund across all products, whether exchange-based or OTC derivative positions, or cash market positions. Generally, for example, the fund's exchange-based losses can be offset by its OTC gains, and vice versa, thereby reducing the overall exposure that the prime broker has to the fund for the purpose of calculating the collateral that the prime broker requires the fund to provide. Without such an offset, the fund would be required to provide collateral to the prime broker in respect of exchange-based losses, and the prime broker would transfer the collateral to the relevant clearing house under the margining system applied by the clearing house, with no allowance for the lack of exposure that the prime broker has to the fund in respect of the open OTC business. The netting of exposures in this manner can be undertaken frequently in order to prevent any accumulation of losses.

The fourth benefit is that the prime broker can offer securities lending facilities to the hedge fund. The fund may have equity or debt securities that the fund can lend to the prime broker, and thereby earn an enhanced return on its portfolio. Similarly, the prime broker may have in its inventory equity or debt securities that it can lend to the fund, in order that the fund can meet its delivery obligations. **9.44**

The fifth benefit is that the prime broker can offer clearing, settlement, and custody services. The prime broker can clear exchange-based transactions that the fund enters into, whether or not the fund transacts through the prime broker. The fund has one account with the prime broker, and all exchange-based and OTC derivative business and cash business is settled against that account. The fund deposits its securities with the prime broker, and the prime broker makes the arrangements for the safe custody of those securities, whether by acting as custodian itself or by appointing other custodians. Further, the prime broker will be a member of various clearing and settlement systems to further facilitate the fund's business. **9.45**

The sixth benefit is administrative convenience and efficiency of documentation. The fund generally only enters into transaction documentation with the prime broker, and not with every dealer with which it wishes to transact business, although a give-up agreement may be entered into between the prime broker, the fund, and each dealer with which the investment manager requires the fund to trade. In any event, the give-up agreement that the fund enters into with each dealer would be considerably less voluminous than a complete set of trading documentation, such as that based on the materials published by ISDA. **9.46**

The seventh benefit might be general support. For example, some prime brokers offer start-up services to hedge funds, which include, in addition to the services and features described in the preceding paragraphs, the lending of seed capital, whether or not at preferential rates, in the expectation of a long-term prime brokerage relationship, and assistance with marketing. Indeed, some larger financial institutions complement the prime brokerage services that they offer with facilitating introductions between the fund and potential investors; this is termed capital introduction. **9.47**

The documentation describing a prime brokerage relationship tends to be somewhat lengthy, but nonetheless less voluminous than the documentation that the hedge fund would otherwise be required to enter into in order to access the same markets and products without a prime brokerage account. Although the actual documentation used by individual prime brokers varies, reflecting the different businesses and different prime brokerage models, the following paragraphs **9.48** indicate the usual form of documentation. The documentation tends to comprise the prime broker's general terms of business, an agreement for exchange-based transaction execution and clearing, an OTC transaction master agreement and credit support document, for example the ISDA 2002 Master Agreement and an ISDA Credit Support Annex, an OTC transaction give-up agreement, a stock lending master agreement, a global netting agreement, and an agreement containing the relevant security package. Generally, the prime broker takes security over the fund's cash and securities.

9.49 A give-up agreement is tripartite. The prime broker and the hedge fund enter into a give-up agreement with each dealer that the prime broker and the investment manager agree that the fund can trade with. Under the give-up agreement, each OTC transaction that the investment manager commits the fund to entering into with a dealer is given up to the prime broker: the rights that the fund would have acquired become the prime broker's rights, and the obligations that the fund would have assumed become the prime broker's obligations. The give-up agreement defines the parameters within which the investment manager is permitted to trade, by specifying trading limits and the tenor of individual transactions that are allowed.

9.50 The global netting agreement links the collateral management provisions of the three types of business: cash and derivative exchange-based trading, cash and derivative OTC trading, and securities lending. The net exposure that either the prime broker or the hedge fund has to the other in respect of all three types of business is calculated. If necessary, collateral is then transferred to reduce the net exposure that either the prime broker or the fund has to the other to a specified threshold.

9.51 Prime brokerage services are often accompanied by administrative services, sometimes provided by a specialist administrator such as a financial IT company. The administration services tend to comprise middle office functions such as valuing positions and calculating various risk metrics, which smaller investment managers may not be capable of performing themselves. Also, various data and price feeds may be packaged together and tailored to the particular requirements of the investment manager. Confirmations of transactions are also produced by the administrator.

9.4 Corporate Treasuries

9.52 Any business is exposed to financial risk, and the globalization of commerce has magnified and broadened the categories of the financial risks that must be controlled. Such risks include exposures to adverse movements in foreign exchange rates, the prices of commodities and financial instruments, and interest rates.

9.53 For example, an airline might be exposed to many different risks. One, it may receive receipts, the fares it earns from passengers, denominated in different currencies, but its principal outgoings are almost certainly denominated in US dollars: aircraft purchasing and leasing, and the price of aviation fuel, all tend to be denominated in US dollars. The airline may therefore have an exposure to the change in the value of US dollars relative to other currencies. Two, the airline will have an exposure to fluctuations in the price of aviation fuel. Three, the airline may have an exposure arising from any borrowing that it undertakes, for example to buy or to lease aircraft, to increases in floating rates of interest. These various exposures to variable prices and variable rates will affect the airline's cash flow, and therefore potentially affect its profitability. Accordingly, the airline may use a variety of derivatives, such as foreign exchange products, commodity products, and interest rate products, to neutralize its exposures to the underlying foreign exchange, oil, and interest rate markets. Consistency in cash flow is very important for planning a company's financial strategy, and reassures both existing and potential lenders that the company represents a good credit risk. A company which is able to demonstrate stable earnings will generally, all things being equal, be able to borrow at better rates than a company which has volatile earnings.

9.54 The treasury function of a company monitors and controls the company's exposure to a variety of financial risks. The treasury department hedges against these risks by entering into the appropriate derivative transactions with financial institutions. More sophisticated treasury departments also hold assets, such as government debt or bullion, which are used to provide collateral from time to time. The value of these holdings is also exposed to price risk, which might be hedged.

10

CAPITAL

10.1 Introduction	10.01
10.2 Sources of Regulation	10.03
10.3 FSA Handbook	10.09
10.4 The Basel Committee	10.20
10.5 Basel 2	10.23
10.6 Credit Rating	10.33

10.1 Introduction

The regulations governing capital are voluminous and complex, containing intricate calculations, and this chapter can only indicate in general terms the various sources of these regulations and how these regulations are implemented in practice. Regulatory authorities around the world emphasize the importance of the maintenance by financial institutions, whether banks, investment firms, building societies and other types of savings institutions, or insurance companies, of adequate financial resources, that is, both adequate capital and adequate liquidity. No discussion of the derivative industry, or indeed any other facet of the financial services industry more widely, would be complete without some mention of this important and fascinating topic. **10.01**

Adequate financial resources enable a financial institution to absorb losses, which might arise from a variety of different risks, without jeopardizing the business itself, the assets of depositors or other persons for whom assets are being held, or indeed at a more intrinsic level the interests of investors in the business. Regulatory capital is the capital that a financial institution is required, by the regulations which apply to it, to hold in order to cushion it against certain risks. Although regulatory capital[1] is most often associated with the system to mitigate credit risk, regulatory capital is now also used to mitigate other forms of risk, arising both **10.02**

---

[1] The term 'risk capital' is also used, which usefully captures the concept that capital is set aside to cushion against the crystallization of the relevant risks.

from adverse movements in the markets themselves and from operational processes. As the regulations defining the requirement to hold regulatory capital have evolved, to ever-increasing levels of sophistication, opportunities to exploit, using derivative products, a new asset class, credit risk, have emerged.[2] A financial institution has the opportunity either to sell credit protection, and earn a return for doing so, or to buy credit protection, and thereby become able to recycle its own capital for regulatory purposes in order to generate a higher return on its capital by writing additional business. Other financial institutions of course trade credit risk.

10.2 Sources of Regulation

FSA Handbook

10.03 The provisions of the FSA Handbook distinguish between banks and investment firms, which are the types of financial institution most relevant to this book, although the same methodology is generally applied to both.[3] One of the threshold conditions for authorization under the FSMA 2000[4] is that the applicant, whether a bank or an investment firm, must have adequate financial resources. The generic term 'firm' is used to refer to either type of financial institution. Then, once the relevant Part IV permission has been granted, the firm must maintain its financial resources above the stipulated amount as a condition for retaining its authorization. The requirement that an authorized firm maintains adequate financial resources is a key element of the regulatory system, and it is enshrined in the Principles for Businesses.[5] The FSA has made clear that adequate financial resources means both adequate capital and adequate liquidity.[6] The requirements for the adequacy of financial resources and regulatory capital generally are set out in the General Prudential sourcebook of the FSA Handbook (GENPRU)[7] and the core rule is that a firm must at all times maintain overall financial resources, including capital resources and liquidity resources, which are adequate, both as to

---

[2] See part 4.12 of Chapter 4.
[3] The methodology is based on the approach traditionally taken to define and allocate a bank's capital base.
[4] See Chapter 5.
[5] Principle 4 requires a firm to maintain adequate financial resources.
[6] GENPRU 1.2.13G.
[7] GENPRU applies generally to insurers, banks, building societies, investment firms, and groups containing such firms. Prior to the introduction of GENPRU, the standards applied to the regulation of banks and investment firms were set out in the Interim Prudential Sourcebook for Banks and the Interim Prudential Sourcebook for Investment Businesses, respectively, as the FSA assumed regulatory responsibility for banks for the first time (this supervisory responsibility had been a part of the duties of the Bank of England until the reorganization of the supervision and regulation of the financial markets in the United Kingdom which took place in 1997).

amount and quality, to ensure that there is no significant risk that its liabilities cannot be met as they fall due.[8]

The general scheme of GENPRU is to set out the detailed calculations to determine the amount of capital resources that a firm is required to hold and the amount of capital resources that a firm actually has, to specify how the firm's capital resources of varying types should be allocated to cover its capital resources requirement, and to specify the objectives and standards of the systems and controls that the firm must maintain in order to be able to manage effectively the risks to which it is exposed. **10.04**

The Prudential sourcebooks for Banks, Building Societies and Investment Firms of the FSA Handbook (BIPRU) complement GENPRU. BIPRU contains certain important elements of the regulations governing the maintenance of adequate financial resources, and contains much of the detail. **10.05**

Banking (Special Provisions) Act 2008

Brief mention should be made of the Banking (Special Provisions) Act 2008 (BSPA 2008). The BSPA 2008 facilitates the giving of financial assistance by HM Treasury, whether or not acting with the Bank of England, to an authorized UK deposit-taker. The BSPA 2008 enables the Treasury to make various orders amounting to a nationalization of the deposit-taker. The scope of the financial assistance that may be given is wide, and can include guarantee arrangements protecting some or all of the depositors or other creditors of the deposit-taker.[9] The Treasury can exercise the powers given to it under the BSPA 2008 for the specified purposes of maintaining the stability of the UK financial system[10] and protecting the public interest where financial assistance is given.[11] Among the orders that the Treasury can make is an order for the transfer into public ownership of securities, including shares, issued by the deposit-taker.[12] Crucially, the BSPA 2008 does not actually change the methodology for calculating the amount of regulatory capital that must be held. Instead, the BSPA 2008 forms the legislative foundation for the UK government to assume the obligations of a stricken financial institution to prevent damage to the financial system, and to nationalize that financial institution. Action taken under the BSPA 2008 becomes necessary presumably because that **10.06**

---

[8] GENPRU 1.2.26R.
[9] Section 2(6) of the BSPA 2008.
[10] Section 2(2)(a) of the BSPA 2008.
[11] Section 2(2)(b) of the BSPA 2008.
[12] Section 3(1) of the BSPA 2008 specifies the parties to whom the securities can be transferred: the Bank of England, a nominee of the Treasury, a company wholly owned by the Bank of England or the Treasury, or any other body corporate.

financial institution has failed to maintain adequate financial resources, including liquidity.[13]

EU directives

10.07 In common with other elements of the regulatory system created within the framework of the FSMA 2000, the various provisions of the FSA Handbook which govern regulatory capital, both for banks and for investment firms, conform to international standards. These international standards are defined most immediately by various EU directives. The principal relevant EU directives are now the Banking Consolidation Directive[14] and the Capital Adequacy Directive.[15]

The Capital Accord and Basel 2

10.08 The EU directives themselves reflect the higher-level principles set out in the Capital Accord and its successor Basel 2, which were formulated by the Basel Committee of banking supervisors. As part 10.5 of this chapter shows, Basel 2 is built up on three conceptual pillars, which are referred to in GENPRU; the source of the extremely detailed rules of GENPRU and BIPRU is clearly discernible in the text of Basel 2. The following paragraphs set out a brief discussion of the general scheme of GENPRU as it applies to banks and investment firms, and then background to the work of the Basel Committee and the development of the Basel 2 statement is provided, in order to set in context the rules promulgated by the FSA. It is emphasized that the standards and regulations governing the maintenance of adequate financial resources continue to evolve, and already there is

---

[13] The background to the legislation of the BSPA 2008 is the nationalization in February 2008 of the Northern Rock bank, whose funding model failed during the credit crisis which emerged in the summer of 2007. The Northern Rock had borrowed heavily from the government and suffered a run on deposits, being the first bank in a little over 140 years to experience a run (before Northern Rock, the last British bank to fail was Overend, Gurney & Co in 1866, the failure of which had a consequential effect on other banks and companies), before the controversial decision was made to nationalize it. One of the consequences of the nationalization of Northern Rock was a close scrutiny of the model of regulation applied in the United Kingdom, and following on from this, the FSA, the Bank of England, and the Treasury have now proposed (as this edition of *Derivatives: The Key Principles* is going to print) a 'special resolution regime'. This regime as formulated will include processes for minimizing the impact of the failure of a bank, including the attempted rescue of a failing bank, and (if a rescue is not effected) special insolvency procedures. Moreover, as the credit crisis continues and further financial institutions are nationalized (such as Bradford & Bingley) or merge, or are recapitalized with public funding, attention will undoubtedly turn to whether or not the regulations governing capital have been properly followed, or indeed are at all adequate in the context of contemporary banking techniques and practice. Commentators have observed that these measures may affect the rights of various stakeholders, as presaged by the various controversies of the Northen Rock experience.

[14] 2006/48/EC Directive of the European Parliament and of the Council relating to the taking up and pursuit of the business of credit institutions (recast).

[15] 2006/49/EC Directive of the European Parliament and of the Council on the capital adequacy of investment firms and credit institutions (recast).

talk of a Basel 3.[16] It is also emphasized that the Capital Accord and Basel 2 focus on banks, whereas of course the EU directives and the materials of the FSA Handbook encompass both banks and other types of financial institution.

10.3 FSA Handbook

Capital resources requirement

10.09 The capital resources requirement for a firm are set out in section 1 of chapter 2 of GENPRU. The generic term 'BIPRU firm' is used in the FSA Handbook to denote a bank, building society, or investment firm; however, as mentioned above, this book is concerned with banks and investment firms. Two main requirements are imposed: a bank or investment firm must maintain capital resources which are equal to or in excess of each of (1) the relevant amount determined in GENPRU 2 as a variable capital requirement,[17] and (2) the relevant amount determined in GENPRU 2 as a base capital resources requirement.[18] Guidance[19] explains that the purpose of the base capital resources requirement is to act as a minimum capital requirement or floor, and a distinction is made between the two requirements because certain types of capital can be used to meet the base capital resources requirement but cannot be used to meet the variable capital requirement. The base capital resources requirement and the variable capital requirement together are the firm's capital resources requirement (which is abbreviated to 'CRR').

10.10 The base capital resources requirement[20] of a bank is the currency equivalent of euros 5 million, and of an investment firm the currency equivalent of the relevant amount that is specified in respect of the scale of the investment firm's business: either euros 50,000, euros 125,000, or euros 730,000 (broadly a higher requirement is imposed on investment firms which undertake more extensive business, and which are therefore exposed to the greater risks). In contrast to the variable capital requirement, the base capital resources requirement remains static.

10.11 The variable capital requirement[21] of a bank or investment firm is the sum of its credit risk capital requirement, its market risk capital requirement, and its operational risk requirement.[22] Each of these three main categories of risk is considered in turn.

---

[16] See paragraph 10.32.
[17] GENPRU 2.1.40R.
[18] GENPRU 2.1.41R.
[19] GENPRU 2.1.43G.
[20] GENPRU 2.1.48R.
[21] GENPRU 2.1.45R.
[22] A different calculation applies to firms which are limited in terms of the business that they write or the scope of their regulatory licence.

10.12 The term 'variable' connotes that the variable capital requirement, built up from its three main components of credit risk, market risk, and operational risk, is expected to fluctuate, depending on the nature and extent of the business that the firm is writing and the circumstances in which that business is written.

10.13 The calculation of the credit risk capital requirement[23] reflects the amount of the obligations that are owed to the bank or investment firm, and the counterparties which owe those obligations. The calculation also reflects the number of counterparties which owe those obligations, that is, the calculation reflects the extent to which the credit risk is concentrated; a default by one counterparty which owes a disproportionate amount of the obligations owed to the firm would have a disproportionate effect on the stability of the firm. BIPRU 3 contains the detailed rules under which the credit risk capital component is calculated. The credit risk capital component of a firm is 8% of the total of its risk-weighted exposure amounts for relevant exposures,[24] which are broadly exposures in the firm's non-trading book. A distinction is made between the non-trading book and the trading book. Generally, assets that are held for a longer term are held in the non-trading book, which for a bank equates to what was previously referred to as the banking book.[25] The risks projected by assets that are held in the trading book are addressed by the market risk capital requirement, which is considered in the following paragraph. Section 4 of BIPRU 3 sets out the risk weights that are applied to the various exposures, in order to derive the risk-weighted exposures. Five broad classes of risk weight are used: 0%, 20%, 50%, 100%, and 150%. These classes of risk weight are found in both the Capital Accord and its successor Basel 2 (Basel 2 introduced the 150% class). First, a credit quality step is determined for the particular exposure that the firm has. Second, depending on the credit quality step that is determined for a particular exposure, the appropriate risk weight is read from the relevant table. A low risk weight is applied to a high-quality exposure, which implies in broad terms that the firm is required to use less capital to cushion itself against the credit risk projected by such an exposure. The key rule is that the exposure value of an asset must be its balance-sheet value, subject to any adjustment that might be required,[26] and off-balance sheet items are assigned a risk weight under a table set out in section 4 of BIPRU 3. Putting these two concepts together in an example, a bank has lent £100 to a particular borrower, and the loan therefore comprises both an asset of the bank and an exposure of the bank. The bank is exposed to the risk that the borrower may fail to repay the loan. On the

---

[23] GENPRU 2.1.51R.
[24] BIPRU 3.1.5R.
[25] The term 'banking book' is no longer used following the convergence of the treatment under the FSA Handbook of the capital requirements of different types of financial institution; hence the somewhat clumsy label 'non-trading book' is used.
[26] BIPRU 3.2.1R.

basis of the credit quality step applied to the borrower, reading from the relevant table set out in section 4 of BIPRU 3, say a risk weight of 50% is applied to the exposure. Therefore, the credit risk capital requirement to which the exposure gives rise is £100 * 50% * 8%, which is £4. This simple example illustrates that higher risk weights are applied to higher risks in order that more regulatory capital is set aside to cushion against those risks. This simple example also illustrates the basic concept: the bank's asset consists of a debt that is owed to the bank, and the bank is exposed to the risk that the debtor may default on the loan. The bank is therefore required to ensure that it has available to it a cushion of at least 8% of the risk-weighted value of that asset. This cushion would be available to the bank as capital. It is also worth mentioning that 8% continues to be considered as the basic ratio that should be maintained of capital to risk-weighted assets. This percentage is sometimes referred to as the Cooke ratio (Cooke was the chairman of the Basel Committee (see below) at the relevant time).

10.14 The calculation of the market risk capital requirement[27] reflects the different sources of market risk: equity price risk, commodity price risk, foreign currency price risk, option risk, and fund price risk. Market risk is the risk of an adverse movement in a particular market price or rate, and particular rules govern how these risks are quantified for the purposes of calculating the market risk capital requirement. BIPRU 7 sets out these rules, the scope of which are assets held in the trading book of the firm, together with certain positions whether or not held in the trading book (foreign exchange positions and commodities, including physical holdings).

10.15 The calculation of the operational risk requirement is a quantification of the operational risks to which the firm is exposed. Operational risk has been introduced by Basel 2 as a factor in allocating risk capital, and this has led to its introduction in the calculation under the FSA Handbook of the amount of risk capital that a firm is required to hold. The categories of operational risk are broad, but operational risk specifically does not include either credit risk or market risk. Operational risk is the risk of a loss caused by internal processes which are inadequate or which have failed, by the criminal or negligent activities of employees, or by events which are external to the financial institution.[28] Many of the sensationalistic headlines which have accompanied the significant losses sustained by financial institutions in connection with their derivative businesses were distracting; these losses were in fact caused by operational failures, whether unauthorized trading or other activity, fraudulent transaction booking, or incorrect and even fraudulent pricing of derivatives. Basel 2 offers three methods for quantifying the amount of capital

---

[27] GENPRU 2.1.52R.
[28] See Chapter 12.

that should be held to mitigate operational risk: the basic approach, the standardized approach, and the advanced measurement approach. These approaches have been adopted by the FSA, and under BIPRU 6, the operational risk requirement is calculated in accordance with either the basic indicator approach, the standardized approach, or (if the FSA permits) the advanced measurement approach. Under the basic indicator approach,[29] the operational risk requirement is equal to 15% of the various indicators that are defined, such as the three year average of the firm's net interest income and net non-interest income. The basic indicator approach is therefore suitable only for more straightforward businesses. Under the standardized approach,[30] a specified percentage is assigned to each business line of the firm, and the operational risk requirement is equal to the weighted three year average of these percentages. Section 4 of BIPRU 6 contains tables which specify the percentage that is applied to the various business lines.[31] The standardized approach offers a more tailored calculation of a firm's operational risk requirement. By contrast, under the advanced measurement approach,[32] the firm is able to quantify its own operational risk, and to allocate capital depending on the expected incidence of various categories of loss event types.[33] The advanced measurement approach offers a firm the opportunity to hold less regulatory capital than the other two methods, but it requires the mathematical modelling of potential losses with a high level of confidence, which entails an extensive and systematic statistical analysis of a considerable amount of data pertaining to losses and their causes. The FSA therefore imposes stringent criteria that a firm must satisfy in order to be permitted to use the advanced measurement approach, including[34] that the firm calculates its capital requirement as comprising both expected loss and unexpected loss, and that 'potentially severe tail events' are captured, achieving 'a soundness standard comparable to a 99.9% confidence interval over a one year period'. This language illustrates the importance of collating and analysing the relevant data with a high degree of accuracy and applying statistical analysis to anticipate the effect of a low-probability but high-impact event (hence the reference to the 'tail' of the bell-shaped curve obtained through the statistical analysis of a data population[35]).

---

[29] Section 3 of BIPRU 6.
[30] Section 4 of BIPRU 6.
[31] Corporate finance, trading and sales, retail brokerage, commercial banking, retail banking, payment and settlement activities, agency services, and asset management.
[32] Section 5 of BIPRU 6.
[33] The categories of loss event types specified in BIPRU 6.5.25R are: internal fraud; external fraud; employee practices and workplace safety; clients, products, and business practices; damage to physical assets; business disruption and system failures; and execution, delivery, and process management.
[34] BIPRU 6.5.12R.
[35] See Chapter 12.

10.16 Finally, BIPRU 13 contains provisions for the 'calculation of counterparty risk exposure values for financial derivatives, securities financing transactions and long settlement transactions'. The scheme of BIPRU 13 is that a firm is entitled to net its exposures with a particular counterparty, and to apply one number to the relevant positions it has with that counterparty, if certain conditions are satisfied. In this way, BIPRU 13 allows netting to be recognized as a means of reducing risk and therefore as a means of reducing the amount of regulatory capital that the firm should set aside in respect of the business that it transacts with that counterparty. BIPRU 13 contains calculations and rules that are relevant to assets and positions that are recorded in both the non-trading book and the trading book of the firm. BIPRU 13 applies to transactions in financial derivatives,[36] securities financing transactions, and long settlement transactions.[37] Crucially, BIPRU 13.7 sets out the types of netting that are recognized for the purposes of BIPRU 13. Generally, the firm is entitled to treat a contractual netting arrangement as reducing risk only if the arrangement creates a single legal obligation covering all included transactions, such that the firm (in the event of the counterparty's failure to perform owing to default, bankruptcy, liquidation, or any other similar circumstance) would have a claim to receive or an obligation to pay only the net sum of the positive and negative mark-to-market values of included individual transactions, and the firm must obtain written and reasoned legal opinions to support its reliance on that arrangement.[38] Broadly, the mark-to-market value of a transaction reflects the cost of replacing that transaction.[39] BIPRU 13 is extremely sophisticated and prescriptive as to the processes that the firm must use and the standards that the firm must attain in order to be able to derive the required mark-to-market values: broadly, valuations should be made by a unit in the firm which is independent from the business unit which originated the relevant transaction and which has adequate resources, and the valuations themselves should be made with reference to the appropriate data, including more broad factors such as the economic environment. BIPRU 13 is therefore an adjunct to the fundamental rules set out in BIPRU, and offers the opportunity to hold less regulatory capital.

---

[36] Under BIPRU 13.3.3R, financial derivative instruments comprise interest rate contracts, foreign currency contracts, and certain other types of contract.
[37] Under BIPRU 13.3.4R, a long settlement transaction is a transaction under which settlement is specified to occur after the earlier of the market standard for the relevant type of transaction or five days following the date on which the transaction is entered into.
[38] BIPRU Rule 13.7.6R.
[39] The methodology for determining the Close-out Amount under the ISDA 2002 Master Agreement is recalled; see paragraph 7.60.

Capital resources

10.17 Section 2 of chapter 2 of GENPRU sets out how the capital resources of a firm are defined and measured. In broad terms, once the capital resources requirement has been calculated, the firm's capital is allocated in order that the firm holds sufficient capital of sufficient quality to meet that requirement. Guidance[40] explains that a firm's capital is divided into tiers[41] which broadly reflect the quality of that capital; the different types of capital differ in the degree of protection that they offer to the firm and to other relevant stakeholders, and therefore restrictions are placed on the extent to which certain types of capital can be included in the calculation of a firm's capital resources. Only specified amounts of each different tier of capital can be used to satisfy the different components of the variable capital requirement and the base capital resources requirement, lending further complexity to the calculations. Section 2 of chapter 2 of GENPRU contains several examples of the relevant calculations.

10.18 Further detailed rules govern the assets that may be included in each tier of capital, and the tables set out in the annexes of section 2 of chapter 2 of GENPRU contain the algorithms for the calculation of the amount of each tier of capital. Clearly the valuation of the different assets constituting each tier of capital is important, and therefore section 3 of chapter 1 of GENPRU sets out the rules and guidance as to how a firm should recognize and value assets, liabilities, exposures, and financial statements, including the application of the relevant accounting standards and practices, and legislation. The general requirement[42] is that the appropriate valuation methodology[43] is used and that the firm establishes and maintains systems and controls which are sufficient to provide prudent and reliable valuation estimates; these systems and controls should be clearly documented and valuations should be made independently of the business unit of the firm which originally wrote the relevant business.

Systems and controls

10.19 The main requirement[44] is that a firm must have in place sound, effective, and complete processes, strategies, and systems to assess the risks to which it is exposed, to determine the amount of regulatory capital that it must hold, and the value of its capital. For the most part, the architecture of these systems and controls reflects

---

[40] GENPRU 2.2.8G and GENPRU 2.2.24G.
[41] Tier one capital, tier two capital, and tier three capital. Tier one capital is the core capital of the firm. Tier two capital comprises upper tier two capital and lower tier two capital.
[42] GENPRU 1.3.13R.
[43] Marking to market, marking to model, independent price verification, and adjustments or reserves.
[44] GENPRU 1.2.30R.

the task of collecting data and using that data, which involves a largely quantitative analysis. However, as indicated previously, the measurement and control of operational risk is a more subtle and qualitative process, and BIPRU 6 accordingly contains further rules which impose the key requirement that a firm maintains appropriate systems and controls to manage operational risk.[45]

10.4 The Basel Committee

10.20 The banking supervisors of the major global economies meet on a regular basis at the Bank for International Settlements (BIS) at its offices in Basel, Switzerland, to discuss issues of common interest. The Basel Committee on Banking Supervision,[46] which is usually referred to just as the Basel Committee, is a committee of banking supervisory authorities which was established at the end of 1974 by the governors of the central banks of the Group of Ten (G10) countries. The Basel Committee was established in response to serious disturbances in the financial markets,[47] and first met in February 1975. The Basel Committee has devoted more of its time to the topic of capital adequacy; its work in this field began in the early 1980s, when it became concerned that the capital ratios of major banks were deteriorating against a backdrop of increasing risks, and it determined to develop greater convergence in the international measurement of capital adequacy.

The Capital Accord

10.21 In July 1998, the Basel Committee issued the Capital Accord, the full title of which is *International Convergence of Capital Measurement and Capital Standards*. The Capital Accord was drafted 'to secure international coverage of supervisory regulations governing the capital adequacy of international banks'.[48] The Basel Committee had worked with IOSCO (the International Organization for Governmental Securities Commissions) and IAIS (the International Association of Insurance Supervisors) to develop the Capital Accord.

---

[45] BIPRU 6.1.3G.
[46] The Basel Committee was originally established as the Committee on Banking Regulations and Supervisory Practices.
[47] Aside from the volatility in the oil markets which precipitated a decline in the global equity markets and persistent economic stagflation, the early 1970s witnessed the failure in 1974 of the West German bank Bankhaus Herstatt. The collapse of Bankhaus Herstatt illustrates a broad category of settlement risk which crystallizes when a party pays funds to a financial institution which then fails before it can pay that party obligations that it owes to that party (Bankhaus Herstatt's banking licence was withdrawn after the close of the German payments system but before the close of business in New York; accordingly, certain of Bankhaus Herstatt's counterparties in foreign exchange transactions had made payments to it and it then ceased operations before it could make the corresponding payments to them).
[48] Capital Accord, p. 1.

10.22 The Capital Accord established minimum levels of capital that a bank with international operations must hold in order to cushion itself against certain risks. The focus of the Capital Accord as originally issued was on credit risk, although the Capital Accord was amended in 1996 to include market risk and certain operational risks. The Capital Accord defined the required minimum levels of capital that a bank must hold, with reference to a risk weighting system and a trigger ratio. The preceding paragraphs which examine the FSA Handbook illustrate the resonance within the FSA Handbook of these concepts.

10.5 Basel 2

10.23 Although the Capital Accord was refined in 1996, the principal development at the international level in the definition of capital adequacy was indicated in June 1999, when the Basel Committee issued its consultative paper entitled *A New Capital Adequacy Framework*. This discussion paper set out a proposed reform of the Capital Accord. The Basel Committee had identified certain perceived weaknesses in the Capital Accord and therefore started to develop a new methodology which now forms the foundation of a new capital accord, which has become known as 'Basel 2'. The Basel Committee's overall objective in formulating Basel 2, which is also referred to as the 'New Accord', is broadly to maintain the existing aggregate level of regulatory capital in the banking system. Basel 2 however provides more flexibility in how this amount of regulatory capital is allocated. Although Basel 2 contains reasonably simple provisions equivalent to the provisions of the Capital Accord, Basel 2 also creates a framework for certain more advanced methodologies for calculating the amount of regulatory capital that a bank is required to hold, to reflect evolving practice in risk measurement and management.

10.24 The overall criticism of the Capital Accord was that it was rudimentary and therefore inadequate for certain applications. The underlying concept of the Capital Accord is that the risk to which a bank is exposed is quantified with reference to the type of entity to which the bank has an exposure, and very broad bands of counterparty weight are specified. The Capital Accord then applied a uniform percentage, the trigger ratio, for all types of asset in order to establish the amount of regulatory capital that must be held. There was no distinction within any band between the risk profiles of different individual entities. By contrast, Basel 2 permits the quantification of the risk to which the bank is exposed with reference to the probability that the entity to which the bank has an exposure might default in respect of an obligation owed to the bank. Under Basel 2, a bank is entitled to calculate its exposure to a particular transaction very precisely. Therefore the term 'granularity' has gained currency as a way of describing a methodology, for setting regulatory capital, which reflects more accurately the particular features of the relevant asset in respect of which regulatory capital is being held. Provided that the bank's systems are sufficiently sophisticated, individual exposures may be treated on an individual basis.

10.25 One more specific criticism of the Capital Accord was that a bank's capital, as calculated under the Capital Accord, was not always an accurate indication of the bank's financial condition. Certain risks, such as the risk of a loss caused by a failure of the bank's systems, were not included within the calculations under the Capital Accord. A second more specific criticism of the Capital Accord was that a bank may be able to exploit a divergence between the true economic risk to which it is exposed and its risk as measured under the Capital Accord. Such exploitation is sometimes referred to as regulatory arbitrage. A third more specific criticism of the Capital Accord was that it did not provide a proper incentive for the management of risk in respect of certain transactions.

10.26 Following an involved and protracted process of consultation, the Basel Committee published Basel 2, the full title of which is *International Convergence of Capital Measurements and Capital Standards: a Revised Framework* on 26 June 2004. The overall philosophy of Basel 2 was expressed by Jean-Claude Trichet, Chairman of the G10 group of central bank governors and heads of supervisory authorities, and President of the European Central Bank. 'It will enhance banks' safety and soundness, strengthen the stability of the financial system as a whole, and improve the financial sector's ability to serve as a source for sustainable growth for the broader economy. I am pleased to offer this revised framework to the international community.'

10.27 Basel 2 comprises three pillars. The first pillar comprises the imposition of minimum capital requirements. The Basel Committee continues to recognize the importance of defining minimum capital requirements, and Basel 2 offers three methods for determining the risk weighting that should be applied to a particular counterparty. One, the standardized approach is actually based on the methodology of the original Capital Accord, including the use of broad categories of risk weighting.[49] However, a refinement of Basel 2 is the addition of 150% as a further category of risk weighting. Two, the foundation internal ratings-based approach involves the use of the financial institution's own assessment of the probability of its counterparty defaulting in a model prescribed by its prudential regulator. Three, the advanced internal ratings-based approach also involves the use of the financial institution's own assessment of the probability of its counterparty defaulting, but in a model developed by the financial institution itself and approved by its prudential regulator. In other words, under Basel 2, sophisticated banks are

---

[49] The broad categories of risk weighting are 0%, 10%, 20%, 50%, and 150%. See paragraph 10.13.

permitted to use an approach based on credit ratings that are assessed by these banks themselves. Banks are exposed to three broad categories of risk: credit risk, market risk, and a variety of other risks, including interest rate risk, operational risk, liquidity risk, legal risk, and reputational risk. Many sophisticated banks already employ risk management systems which quantify certain of these risks, but clearly a uniform approach is required in order that all banks are subject to the same standards, and therefore are able to compete fairly with each other for business.

10.28 The second pillar comprises a supervisory review of capital adequacy. A supervisory review of capital adequacy will seek to ensure that a bank's capital structure is consistent with its overall risk profile and operational strategy. The supervisory review will include a mechanism for early supervisory intervention. The Basel Committee has identified[50] four basic and complementary principles. One, 'supervisors expect banks to operate above minimum regulatory capital ratios, and should have the ability to require banks to hold capital in excess of the minimum'. Two, 'a bank should have a process for assessing its overall capital adequacy in relation to its risk profile, as well as a strategy for maintaining its capital levels'. Three, 'supervisors should review and evaluate a bank's internal capital adequacy assessment and strategy, as well as its compliance with regulatory capital ratios'. Four, 'supervisors should seek to intervene at an early stage to prevent capital from falling below prudent levels'. The second pillar contains a more formal expression of these principles.

10.29 The third pillar comprises market discipline. The third pillar comprises the requirement that a bank makes significant disclosures about its risk management and its maintenance of adequate capital. These disclosures should impart market discipline, as investors, depositors, and counterparties in the market will determine the extent of the exposure that they are willing to assume to the bank, on the basis of the information that is made available. In simple terms, if the bank's risk management techniques and capital policies are considered to be deficient by investors, depositors, and counterparties, then the bank will lose investment and business. The Basel Committee observed[51] that effective market discipline 'imposes strong incentives on banks to conduct their business in a safe, sound and efficient manner. It can also provide a bank with an incentive to maintain a strong capital base as a cushion against potential future losses arising from its risk exposures.'

10.30 Given that the Capital Accord is retained as the standardized approach, albeit in a modified form, the Basel Committee set out to develop a more flexible framework

---

[50] *A New Capital Adequacy Framework*, 1999, paragraph 32.
[51] Ibid, paragraph 38.

for the Capital Accord, so that the Capital Accord can evolve to reflect more accurately the risks which arise through financial innovation and developments in risk management methodology.

The scope of Basel 2 is international; it is not confined to the EEA. International banking regulators generally have regard to Basel 2 in the drafting of their own detailed regulations governing capital adequacy. Basel 2, like the Capital Accord before it, represents a standard that is generally accepted at an international level, particularly by the G10 countries. In particular, and of relevance to this book, the various EU directives have been prepared to reflect the standards defined by Basel 2. **10.31**

The financial services industry is already looking ahead to Basel 3, as certain shortcomings in Basel 2 have already been identified. The calculations under the Basel 2 methodology are sensitive to creditworthiness, and therefore the effect of the peaks and troughs of the economic cycle may be magnified in those calculations. As creditworthiness deteriorates, more regulatory capital will be required. Of course, the countervailing argument is easily made, that deteriorating creditworthiness increases risk, and the capital adequacy framework is designed to neutralize that risk by ensuring that a sufficient cushion is in place. A second potential criticism is that implementation of Basel 2 may not succeed in removing distortions in the competitiveness of the financial services industry, because Basel 2 permits different approaches to be taken within an overall framework. A third potential criticism is that the greater need for rating agencies, to supply the increased number of ratings that the Basel 2 methodology requires, may result in a decrease in the quality of the rating analyses that are carried out, giving rise to both disparities in the treatment of risk, and even a failure to control adequately risk. Whether or not the experience of Basel 2 confirms any of these concerns will of course shape the development of Basel 3 in the years to come. **10.32**

10.6 Credit Rating

The importance of the work of the credit rating agencies is growing. Credit rating agencies assess the creditworthiness of a broad variety of participants in the financial markets, on both the buy side and the sell side. If a particular entity has a strong credit rating, then that entity is viewed as a 'good' or low risk because the probability that it might default in respect of its obligations is low. **10.33**

Weak or deteriorating creditworthiness has serious implications. Under circumstances of weak or deteriorating creditworthiness, a financial institution on the sell side is required to pay higher costs to acquire funding, and downward pressure is applied to the price of any derivative product that it sells, to compensate the buyer for the higher risk to which the buyer is exposed by entering into a transaction. It is to be remembered that while financial institutions on the sell side make their **10.34** own assessment of the credit risk projected by their customers as part of the process by which they open accounts for those customers, those same customers are of course increasingly performing their own 'due diligence' investigations into the financial institutions from which they propose to buy derivative exposures. Thus, notwithstanding its legal and regulatory obligations to maintain adequate financial resources, a financial institution on the sell side requires sufficient capital to satisfy the increasingly sophisticated investigations undertaken by its customers, to reassure them that it will be able to meet any payment obligation it may assume. The natural selection of financial institutions on the sell side through the external scrutiny of their creditworthiness, which is already a reality that every financial institution now faces, illustrates the objectives of the third pillar of Basel 2.

10.35 Given that an assessment of the creditworthiness of a proposed counterparty or customer is an intrinsic part of the processes by which a financial institution on the sell side puts in place a new sales and trading relationship, it is evident that such a process makes reference to the credit assessment made of that proposed counterparty or customer by a credit rating agency, as well as a 'due diligence' analysis of the proposed counterparty or customer's financial statements. Once the sales and trading relationship is in place, the regulatory requirement that adequate financial resources are maintained imposes the discipline of monitoring exposures to the counterparty or customer. The credit assessments made and published by rating agencies can now be used in the calculation of capital adequacy,[52] subject to the requirement that the credit assessments that are used are published by a rating agency which is recognized by the FSA for these purposes, and that the credit assessments are used consistently and in accordance with the provisions of the FSA Handbook.

---

[52] See Section 3 of BIPRU 3 ('The use of credit assessments of ratings agencies') and Section 6 of BIPRU 3 ('Use of rating agencies' credit assessments for the determination of risk weights under the standardised approach to credit risk'). A rating agency is referred to as an external credit assessment institution (ECAI) and the FSA recognizes an ECAI under the Capital Requirements Regulations 2006, SI 2006/3221.

11

ACCOUNTING AND TAX[1]

11.1 Financial Reporting	11.01
11.2 The Taxation of Transactions: Hedging or Trading	11.19
11.3 The Taxation of Transactions: Income or Capital Gains	11.23
11.4 The Taxation of Transactions: Withholding Tax	11.41
11.5 The Substance of Transactions	11.46
11.6 'Accounting-driven' Transactions	11.50

11.1 Financial Reporting

11.01 Financial services industry regulators already require authorized firms to make reports as to their exposure to the markets and to a variety of risks. This reporting is needed in order to monitor metrics such as whether or not compliance is being achieved with the requirement that adequate financial resources are maintained, and for other purposes such as the prevention of market abuse. Chapter 10 shows that compliance with the requirement that adequate financial resources are maintained is especially important in the context of the derivative markets, given the inherently greater risks that derivatives give rise to if they are not used properly. Financial institutions active in the derivative markets on both the sell side, such as investment banks, and the buy side, such as investment managers, should therefore already be familiar with the methodology required to monitor and to account for derivative transactions. However, other participants in the market such as corporate treasuries might not be so readily acquainted with the particular subtleties that derivatives can give rise to.

---

[1] It is emphasized that the topics discussed in this chapter are extremely broad and detailed, and therefore only the key principles are introduced.

11.02 Nonetheless, broad company law imposes on a company a significant requirement to prepare meaningful financial statements. A corporate user should already be familiar with this basic requirement. However, as the following paragraphs show, putting into practice this basic requirement is not straightforward. In summary, under English law, the overall requirement is that the accounts of a company must give a true and fair view of the financial status of that company[2] and that the company prepares individual accounts.[3]

11.03 The practical application of the requirement that a company's accounts provide a clear and fair view is found in the definition of the accounting standards[4] that are drawn up to reflect and to keep pace with evolving business practice. Unsurprisingly, this is a complex field of accountancy. Further, in the context of the globalization of business and investment opportunities, accounting standards that are drawn up at a national level must be compatible with the accounting standards being developed at an international level. The broad perspective is that the international application of uniform accounting standards would promote a more liquid pool of international investment, obviating the requirement for adjustments to be made to an analysis of a company's accounts in order merely to compensate for the nuances of the particular financial reporting regime to which that company is subject.

11.04 The principal challenge in formulating accounting standards is the need to ensure that a set of financial statements reflects clearly, accurately, and appropriately the realities of the use of derivatives. How this challenge is met is seen in the development of the requirements that are prescribed for reporting derivative positions

---

[2] Section 393(1) of the Companies Act 2006 (CA 2006) provides that the directors of a company must not approve accounts unless they are satisfied that they give a true and fair view of the assets, liabilities, financial position, and profit or loss of the company.

[3] Section 394 of the CA 2006 provides that the directors of every company must prepare accounts for the company for each of its financial years. Under s 395(1) of the CA 2006, these so-called individual accounts may be prepared either as Companies Act individual accounts or as IAS individual accounts; IAS individual accounts are prepared in accordance with international accounting standards (which are discussed in paragraphs 11.15 ff). Section 396(1) of the CA 2006 provides that the Companies Act individual accounts of a company must comprise a balance sheet as at the last day of the financial year, and a profit and loss account. Section 397 of the CA 2006 provides that IAS individual accounts must be identified in the notes to the accounts, having been prepared in accordance with international accounting standards. International accounting standards are considered at paragraphs 11.15 ff.

[4] Accounting standards are rules in accordance with which accounts must be drawn up. Accounting standards define the key principles of accounting, including definitions and the calculations of relevant amounts, and prescribe the minimum standards of disclosure that must be met. Accounts for different entities that have been drawn up under a common accounting standard can easily be compared, thus like can be compared with like. Accounting standards are also referred to in legislation, as this chapter shows in connection with the derivative contracts rules at paragraphs 11.29 ff. GAAP are generally accepted accounting principles, which are the standards used in a particular jurisdiction or region, and include UK GAAP (which is set by the UK Accounting Standards Board) and US GAAP (which is set by the US Financial Accounting Standards Board).

in accounts. Previously, certain types of derivative, such as interest rate swaps, were occasionally described as off-balance sheet instruments because a company's participation in such a contract was not indicated on its balance sheet. The rationale for omitting from a company's balance sheet its participation in an interest rate swap was that the balance sheet does not record cash flows. An interest rate swap, it is recollected from part 4.7 of Chapter 4, merely requires the payment or receipt of a cash flow of interest, and not the payment or receipt of the underlying notional amount. Therefore omission of the swap from the balance sheet was considered appropriate. Accordingly, there has been, and continues to be, some scope for omitting certain derivative positions from a set of accounts, with arguably a loss from those accounts of clarity, accuracy, and completeness. Nonetheless, the potential for certain types of derivative contract to give rise to ultimate liabilities far in excess of the original liabilities that are apparent when those contracts are first entered into is a powerful argument for the inclusion in a set of accounts of the potential and actual liabilities arising. Accounting standards must therefore capture the effect of these derivative contracts and prescribe an accurate and consistent rubric for reporting the flows of cash and capital under these contracts. The importance of accounting standards is not to be underestimated; the general principle is that tax follows accounts, that is, liability to tax is computed on the basis of the flows of cash and capital reported in a set of financial statements, and accounting standards prescribe how those flows are to be recognized and recorded.

UK accounting

11.05 The United Kingdom's Accounting Standards Board (ASB) published Financial Reporting Standard 13, *Derivatives and Other Financial Instruments: Disclosures* (FRS 13), in September 1998. Although now largely superseded, FRS 13 continues to have conceptual relevance, as it indicates the basic objective that a reporting standard is established under which an entity is required to disclose, in a timely and relevant manner, the significance and effect on that entity of its transactions and positions in all manner of financial instruments, including derivatives.

11.06 The scope of FRS 13 includes a contract which falls within the definition of a derivative financial instrument, which is 'a financial instrument that derives its value from the price or rate of some underlying item'. Whether or not a particular contract amounts to a derivative financial instrument depends on the economic effect of that contract. FRS 13 sets out the reporting standards in respect of open derivative positions, and defines both the narrative disclosures and the numerical disclosures that are required. Although the narrative disclosures are mandatory, FRS 13 does permit some flexibility in how those narrative disclosures are made. The numerical disclosures required by FRS 13 include disclosures as to interest rate risk, currency risk, liquidity risk, fair values, financial instruments used for trading, financial instruments used for hedging, and certain commodity contracts. The extent of the disclosure required depends on whether the reporting company is a bank, a financial institution other than a bank, or neither.

11.07 The ASB published Financial Reporting Standard 25, *Financial Instruments: Disclosure and Presentation* (FRS 25) and Financial Reporting Standard 26, *Financial Instruments: Measurement* (FRS 26), in December 2004. Broadly, both FRS 25 and FRS 26 have the effect of withdrawing and replacing elements of FRS 13 for certain entities.

11.08 The overall objective of FRS 25 is to enhance the understanding of users of financial statements of the significance of financial instruments to an entity's position, performance, and cash flows. In general terms, the presentation requirements of FRS 25 require an entity's financial statements (1) to classify financial instruments as liabilities or as equity; (2) to identify related interest, dividends, losses, and gains; and (3) to identify offsets of financial assets and financial liabilities. In general terms, the disclosure requirements of FRS 25 require an entity's financial statements primarily to disclose the entity's risk management policies and hedging activities, accounting policies, interest rate risk, credit risk, and the fair value of its assets. The definition of a derivative for the purposes of FRS 25 is set out in FRS 26, and broadly a contract is a derivative if (1) its value changes in response to a change in the specified underlying; and (2) it requires no initial net investment or an initial net investment which is smaller than would be required for other types of contract that would be expected to have a similar response to changes in market factors; and (3) it is settled at a future date. FRS 25 brings the definition of a financial instrument into alignment with the definition contained in International Accounting Standard IAS 32, published by the International Accounting Standards Board.[5]

11.09 FRS 26 implements the requirements of International Accounting Standard IAS 39, published by the International Accounting Standards Board,[6] in respect of the recognition and measurement of financial assets, including derivatives. FRS 26 requires, amongst other things, that all financial assets, including derivatives, that are held for trading are recognized and measured at their fair value, and changes in value are recognized immediately in the profit and loss account.

11.10 The ASB published Financial Reporting Standard 29, *Financial Instruments: Disclosure* (FRS 29), in December 2005. FRS 29 implements International Financial Reporting Standard IFRS 7, published by the International Accounting Standards Board.[7] FRS 29, which applies to entities which prepare statements in

---

[5] See paragraphs 11.15 ff.
[6] See paragraphs 11.15 ff. IAS 39 underwent a lengthy process of development and evolution.
[7] See paragraphs 11.15 ff.

accordance with FRS 26, further refines the standard of disclosure that should be made to include information on the significance of financial instruments for an entity's financial position, on the exposure to risks projected by financial instruments, and on the entity's objectives and policies for managing capital. Successive amendments to the Disregard Regulations make provision for various types of relationship and contract.

11.11 The various accounting standards mentioned in the preceding paragraphs give rise to an interesting difficulty. In requiring derivative transactions to be accounted for at fair value and separately from other items, application of these accounting standards may in certain circumstances result in a derivative that is held to hedge the risks projected by a particular corresponding balance sheet item being brought into account in a way which does not link it sufficiently with that balance sheet item being hedged. The fair value of the derivative may fluctuate, and if its fair value is recognized immediately, then potentially the treatment of it for tax purposes may not accurately reflect the purpose for which it is held and the manner in which it delivers the required hedging effect. Short-term volatility in the value of the derivative may trigger profits or losses for tax purposes which would then be taken into account prematurely relative to the period over which the corrsponding item being hedged is held. Movements in the value of a hedge and the corresponding item being hedged should be equal and opposite and therefore cancel each other out,[8] and it therefore follows as a matter of intuition that the value of the hedge should be brought into account in synchrony with the value of the item being hedged. Hedge accounting is a type of accounting which generally allows gains and losses to be deferred, with the purpose of avoiding distortions of the type discussed in the preceding sentences. Under hedge accounting, the offset of changes in the value of the hedge and the corresponding item being hedged are recognized. For example, FRS 26 permits the use of hedge accounting for financial instruments, but only if (1) the hedging relationship was designated as such at the outset and certain prescribed criteria are satisfied, including that the hedge and the corresponding item being hedged are specifically recognized and that the hedging relationship is formally documented; and (2) the particular specified hedge accounting techniques are used. Hedge accounting models include fair value hedges, cash flow hedges, and hedges of net investments in foreign operations. From a more practical perspective, the use of hedge accounting requires the establishment of adequate valuation and accounting systems, as the effectiveness of the hedging arrangements must be verified for the duration of the relevant positions. The Disregard Regulations,[9] which have been amended several times,

---

[8] See paragraph 4.80.
[9] The Loan Relationships and Derivative Contracts (Disregard and Bringing into Account of Profits and Losses) Regulations 2004, SI 2004/3256.

were put in place to ameliorate further this potential difficulty. The Disregard Regulations allow certain profits and losses from loan relationships and derivative contracts to be left out of account, to be brought into account in a different way, or to be brought into account at a later date.[10]

11.12 Listed companies in the EU are now required to prepare accounts in accordance with International Financial Reporting Standards, which are set by the International Accounting Standards Board,[11] and therefore the role of the ASB is now limited to private companies and unincorporated entities. However, the ASB remains responsible for the enforcement of standards, including the IFRS, on companies incorporated within UK jurisdictions.

US accounting

11.13 The US Financial Accounting Standards Board (FASB) issued Statement 133 *Accounting for Derivative Instruments and Hedging Activities* (FAS 133) on 16 July 1998, and FAS 133 continues to be applicable to companies subject to US accounting regulations. FAS 133 is complex,[12] and it has been amended periodically. In summary, FAS 133 requires a company to include on its balance sheet all derivative contracts[13] at fair market value, including contracts which have embedded derivative components, other than transactions which fall within a limited exemption (which is available generally for positions the fair value of which cannot be easily calculated). A company is also required to report fully the methodology it uses to calculate the fair value of a contract, and to monitor the performance of hedging contracts, disclosing its risk management policy and explaining how a hedging contract is used as a part of that policy. Crucially, a company must disclose why it is holding a contract for speculative purposes.

11.14 Companies subject to US accounting regulations have experienced different levels of difficulty in implementing FAS 133, which imposes a significant burden. Some companies such as energy traders have been able easily to adapt existing management and information systems and controls to achieve compliance with FAS 133, whereas other companies have discovered that they must develop and build new systems and controls at considerable expense.

---

[10] The explanatory note to SI 2004/3256.
[11] See paragraphs 11.15 ff.
[12] The FASB has established the Derivatives Implementation Group to assist with the many questions arising as to the implementation and interpretation of FAS 133.
[13] Crucially, the definition of a derivative under FAS 133 is purposely extremely broad so as to capture both present and future types of contract.

The international perspective

The International Accounting Standards Board (IASB)[14] is an independent private sector body which was established in 1973 to promote convergence between the different accounting principles applied in different jurisdictions. The IASB issues International Financial Reporting Standards (IFRS).[15]   **11.15**

The IASB issued IAS 39, 'Financial Instruments: Recognition and Measurement', in December 1998. In summary, IAS 39 requires that all financial assets and all financial liabilities, including derivatives, are included on a company's balance sheet. IAS 39 has been amended since its original publication.   **11.16**

Both IAS 39, and FAS 133 share the same underlying concept, although they differ in detail. Whereas FAS 133 has been published by a national accounting regulator, the US Financial Accounting Standards Board, which has enforcement powers, IAS 39 has instead been published by a body whose objective is to achieve consensus between different national accounting regulators, and therefore IAS 39 lacks directly the mandatory quality of FAS 133.   **11.17**

Nonetheless, IAS 39 has considerable importance as an international accounting standard. International financial reporting standards prompt the unification and convergence of national accounting standards, facilitating comparisons between companies in different countries, and thereby facilitating meaningful relative investment analysis, and the simplification and easing of the burden on some companies either to prepare different accounts to different standards or to formulate reconciliations between their accounts and the different applicable standards. The national accounting standards of many countries are being brought into line with the international financial reporting standards, including, as indicated by the preceding paragraphs, the standards applied in the United Kingdom, although the process is expected to take many years and promises to be anything but smooth.   **11.18**

11.2 The Taxation of Transactions: Hedging or Trading

The accounting treatment of a derivative transaction is inevitably determined by the particular circumstances of the transaction, and the tax status of each party to the transaction, including most importantly the particular tax legislation and regulation to which that party is subject. One of the fundamental issues that must be considered is the distinction between the tax treatment of a derivative transaction that is entered into for hedging purposes and one that is entered into for   **11.19**

---

[14] Formerly, until 2001, the International Accounting Standards Committee.
[15] The various IAS issued by the International Accounting Standards Board are now referred to as IFRS.

Chapter 11: Accounting and Tax

trading purposes. The purposes for which a transaction is entered into determine the tax treatment of that transaction.

11.20 The two broad principles that may be observed are that one, the premium paid by a party to buy a hedging derivative is an operating cost of that party and is therefore deductible from that party's taxable income, and two, any profit earned by a party from a speculative derivative is an element of the taxable income of that party.

11.21 The treatment of a derivative transaction in a set of accounts should reflect whether or not that transaction was entered into for hedging or speculative purposes. However, the Revenue,[16] in enacting tax legislation for derivative transactions, has recognized that under certain circumstances identifying a hedging transaction might be difficult. A particular difficulty arises in the context of a partial hedge, or a hedge the shape of which does not match the underlying exposure. The Revenue therefore generally tends to restrict the population of derivative transactions which qualify for advantageous treatment under tax legislation to interest rate products, currency products, and debt products, as these are the types of derivative which are usually used to hedge exposures.

11.22 Whether or not a derivative transaction is entered into to hedge an exposure might be assessed with reference to three criteria: intent, correlation, and certainty. The intention to establish a hedge is disclosed in the transaction documentation in the case of OTC contracts. The movement in the price of the derivative must demonstrate a high degree of correlation with the movement in the price of the underlying. In the case of an anticipatory hedge, there must be a reasonable expectation that the transaction to be hedged will be entered into, and that therefore the hedge will be required. Generally, a derivative transaction that is entered into to establish a hedge must be treated consistently with the underlying transaction under which the exposure being hedged arises.

11.3 The Taxation of Transactions: Income or Capital Gains[17]

11.23 Income and capital gains are treated differently, in that different reliefs, exemptions, and allowances are available in respect of either. It is therefore important to identify whether or not a particular cash flow generated by a derivative transaction should be treated as income or as a capital gain, in order that the correct amount

---

[16] HM Revenue & Customs, which was established as the amalgamation of the Inland Revenue and HM Customs & Excise.

[17] By way of general observation, the tax system that is applied in the United Kingdom comprises both the enactment of successive pieces of legislation, regulation, and rules, and the interpretation of law by both the courts and the Revenue, all of which have a cumulative effect.

of tax is computed.[18] The appropriate categorization of a cash flow as income or as a capital gain is under some circumstances unclear, although legislation should generally assist. The nature of the different reliefs, exemptions, and allowances is outside the scope of this book. Instead, this chapter focuses on the fundamental underlying concept: should a particular cash flow be treated on an income basis or on a capital gains basis?

11.24 Generally the Income and Corporation Taxes Act 1988 (ICTA 1988), as amended establishes the framework for the taxation of the chargeable profits of companies.[19] The term 'chargeable profits' includes both the income and the chargeable gains made by a company, and the company pays tax at the relevant rate of corporation tax.[20] The capital gains realized by a company form a part of its chargeable profits. The Taxation of Chargeable Gains Act 1992 (TCGA 1992) specifies how capital gains are taxed; the capital gains earned by a person are treated as part of the income of that person, and one amount of tax is paid on both the income element and the capital gains element of that person's overall income. Although individuals, and not companies, are liable to capital gains tax, the method of calculating capital gains is the same for both individuals and companies, with certain exceptions.[21]

11.25 A company pays UK corporation tax if it is resident in the United Kingdom. Broadly, a company is resident in the United Kingdom for tax purposes if either it was incorporated in the United Kingdom on or after 15 March 1988[22] or if it is centrally managed and controlled in the United Kingdom in accordance with the test established in *De Beers Consolidated Mines Ltd v Howe*.[23] Further guidelines[24] are used to determine the residence in the United Kingdom of a company which is not incorporated in the United Kingdom. A company also pays UK corporation tax if it carries on a trade in the United Kingdom through a branch or an agency; such a company pays corporation tax on chargeable gains which are attributable to its UK branch or agency. There are five steps to calculating a company's liability to corporation tax for a given accounting period.

---

[18] Paragraph 4.238 introduces the choice that investors can make as to whether the delivery of a derivative exposure should generate income or a capital gain.

[19] Individuals pay income tax, and companies pay corporation tax. This chapter only considers the taxation of a company.

[20] The rate of corporation tax payable is fixed for each financial year, which for the purposes of companies starts on 1 April of one year and ends on 31 March of the next following year. Successive Finance Acts set out the rates that apply.

[21] For example, an individual enjoys an annual exemption, but a company does not, and an individual's tax liability is calculated with reference to an income tax year of assessment, but a company's tax liability is calculated with reference to an accounting period.

[22] Section 66 of the Finance Act 1988.

[23] [1906] AC 455.

[24] Statement of Practice SP1/90, 9 January 1990.

11.26 One, the company's income profit is calculated, which is broadly its income less any loss that is available. A loss, if it is available for the purpose of this calculation, reduces the amount on which the company is taxed. Two, the company's capital profit is calculated. Sales or gifts of chargeable assets give rise to a potential capital gain or loss[25] and therefore relevant disposals are identified which trigger a liability. The company's capital profit is the aggregate of all relevant gains less the aggregate of all relevant losses; a part of the calculation of a relevant gain is an indexation allowance which is designed to neutralize the effect of inflation. Three, the company's total profit is calculated, which is its income profit plus its capital profit. Four, any charge on income is deducted from the company's total profit. The amount of the company's total profit is reduced by various payments that the company must make in order to earn its profits, such as certain annuities and annual payments, and items such as royalties on patents or rents paid to use property. Certain charitable donations made by the company also reduce the amount on which it pays tax. Five, the amount of corporation tax paid by the company on its total profit in respect of the relevant accounting period is calculated. Corporation tax is payable at different rates, which are varied in accordance with the fiscal policy of the government; these rates are fixed for a financial year.

The principal difficulty

11.27 If a cash flow generated by a derivative transaction is treated on an income basis, then it is reflected in the first step of the process described above in paragraph 11.26, whereas if it is treated on a capital gains basis, then it is reflected in the second step of that process. The characterization of a cash flow, as income or as a capital gain, should be fairly straightforward in many circumstances; a particular cash flow can be treated as income if the asset is not disposed of in whole or in part, or if the asset is disposed of in whole or in part and the taxpayer carries on a trade which involves buying and selling assets, and as a capital gain if the asset is disposed of in whole or in part and it was held by the taxpayer as an investment.

11.28 However, a person is treated as disposing of an asset if that person receives a capital sum derived from that asset, notwithstanding that the asset is not actually disposed of whether in whole or in part.[26] The principle which emerges is that occasionally statutory codes operate to cause payments that appear to be income to be treated as capital gains, and vice versa, with the practical effect that there might well be a lack of coherence and clarity in the computation of a tax liability. Various pieces of tax legislation create so-called gateways into self-contained statutory codes governing the cash flows arising in respect of particular types of transaction

---

[25] Section 15(2) of the TCGA 1992.
[26] Section 22 of the TCGA 1992. In particular, s 22(1)(d) has the effect that capital sums received as consideration for use or exploitation of assets are treated on a capital gains basis.

or particular types of relationship between the payer and the recipient of the cash flow in question. A transaction which passes through a gateway is taxed in accordance with the rules set out in the statutory code beyond that gateway, and whether or not the transaction can pass through that gateway is determined by the particular criteria defining that gateway. The gateway criteria may include factors such as whether or not a particular legal relationship has been created or the circumstances of the particular transaction. The derivative contracts rules comprise the statutory code of most relevance to this chapter.

Derivative contracts rules

11.29 The derivative contracts rules were established by the Finance Act 2002 (FA 2002)[27] with effect from 1 October 2002, and have been frequently amended. The derivative contracts rules are contained in Schedule 26 to the FA 2002, and the overall policy of the derivative contracts rules is that all profits, whether income or capital in nature, arising from a company's derivative contracts should be taxed and relieved on an income basis,[28] with a few limited exceptions.

11.30 A particular contract entered into by a company passes through the gateway into the derivative contracts rules if it is a relevant contract. A relevant contract is an option, a future, or a contract for differences.[29] It is important to appreciate that the emphasis of the definitions contained in the derivative contracts rules[30] is not entirely the same as the emphasis of the definitions set out in financial markets legislation and regulation more generally,[31] although they are of course broadly the same.

11.31 In order to be treated as a derivative contract under the derivative contracts rules, a relevant contract must satisfy an accounting test and not be excluded from the derivative contracts rules because of its underlying subject matter.[32] A relevant contract satisfies the accounting test if either it is treated for accounting purposes (that is, in accordance with the applicable accounting standard) as a derivative, or alternatively (if it is not treated for accounting purposes as a derivative) it is not treated as a derivative for a reason other than failing to be treated for accounting purposes as, or forming part of, a financial asset or liability. A relevant contract is excluded from the derivative contracts rules if its underlying subject matter falls within one of numerous categories specified in the derivative contracts rules.[33]

---

[27] The derivative contracts rules replaced the earlier financial instruments rules. The financial instruments rules had been established by the Finance Act 1994.
[28] Paragraph 1 of Part 1 of Schedule 26 to the FA 2002.
[29] Paragraph 2(2) of the derivative contracts rules.
[30] Paragraph 12 of the derivative contracts rules.
[31] See Chapter 5.
[32] Paragraph 2(1) of the derivative contracts rules.
[33] Paragraph 4 of the derivative contracts rules.

11.32 Certain types of contract which appear to satisfy the definition of a derivative contract are excluded, such as life assurance contracts and insurance contracts. The scope of the derivative contracts rules is therefore consistent with the general principle that derivatives do not constitute contracts of insurance.[34]

11.33 It is apparent that the policy of the derivative contracts rules is to align the tax treatment of derivatives more closely with the accounting treatment of derivatives, as indicated by the accounting test which forms a part of the derivative contracts rules. Part 3 of the derivative contracts rules provides for the method of taxation, which as mentioned above is to tax as income the profits earned by a company from its derivative contracts.[35] However, circumstances may arise when the profits earned by a company from its derivative contracts are capital in nature, and the company wishes to be taxed on those profits on a capital basis. The application of the derivative contract rules would not be advantageous, and therefore the impetus for the continuing development of these rules becomes clear. It is stressed that this is a complex field of law and accountancy, which is subject to frequent and subtle change, and therefore this chapter can only show the broad direction of the relevant provisions and the principles lying behind them.

Complex series of transactions

11.34 Structured finance occasionally involves aggregating two or more derivative transactions, whether or not these transactions are documented separately, to create a complex, or composite, overall transaction. Such composite transactions may be designed for any number of reasons, including the avoidance of tax, and the tax treatment of such transactions can be challenged in the courts by the Revenue, with the result, if the challenge is successful, that the anticipated tax treatment is lost. These revenue cases have given rise to a strand of case law which considers the appropriate interpretation of legislation.

11.35 The 'Ramsay principle' is the phrase given to the formulation set out by the House of Lords in *WT Ramsay Ltd v Inland Revenue Commissioners*[36] of the approach that the court should follow in determining the legal nature of a new and sophisticated tax avoidance device and in relating that device to the relevant fiscal legislation. In essence, under the Ramsay principle, for the purpose of identifying the correct tax treatment of a series of transactions that have been structured in advance, any intermediate transaction in the series which has no commercial purpose other than the avoidance of tax should be disregarded and the overall cash flow of the series should be taxed accordingly. The court is entitled to look at a pre-arranged

---

[34] See part 8.4 of Chapter 8.
[35] Paragraphs 14 and 15 of the derivative contracts rules.
[36] [1982] AC 300.

11.3 The Taxation of Transactions: Income or Capital Gains

series of transactions as a whole, and it is irrelevant that the intention of the parties to proceed with the entire series is a binding contractual obligation or a mere expectation without contractual force. Since the *Ramsay* case, the principles of statutory construction have been discussed at length in litigation concerning revenue statutes. The modern approach to statutory construction was explained by Lord Steyn in *Inland Revenue Commissioners v McGuckian*:[37] the language of a statute is interpreted, so far as possible, in a way which best gives effect to the purpose of that statute. The court should have regard to the underlying purpose that the statute in question is seeking to achieve when considering the meaning with which Parliament has used the statutory language in question.

11.36 Lord Hoffman speaking in *MacNiven (Her Majesty's Inspector of Taxes) v Westmoreland Investments Ltd*[38] qualified the Ramsay principle. A court considering whether or not a piece of tax legislation applies to a transaction, and if so, how it applies to that transaction, should examine the relevant statute to determine whether the statute refers to a legal concept or to a different commercial concept. If the statute refers to a commercial concept, then if the transaction is anticipated by that commercial concept, the statute applies to the transaction, irrespective of whether or not the transaction is anticipated by the legal concept. This qualification of the Ramsay principle in the *Westmoreland* case appears to allow the court some latitude in applying statutory provisions, by allowing the court to look beyond just the letter of the statute.

11.37 However, the decision of the House of Lords in *Barclays Mercantile Business Finance Limited v Mawson (Her Majesty's Inspector of Taxes)*[39] confirmed that the Ramsay principle is based on statutory construction. The *Mawson* case involved a sale and leaseback of certain items of plant connected with a gas pipeline under the Irish Sea. The claim for capital allowances made by Barclays Mercantile Business Finance Limited (Barclays) under section 24(1) of the Capital Allowances Act 1990 was challenged by the Inland Revenue on the grounds that the chain of deposits made of the proceeds of the sale were artificial and contrived for the purpose of obtaining the relevant capital allowances. The House of Lords found, applying the Ramsay principle, that the statutory requirements for obtaining the capital allowances depended on the acts and purposes of the lessor Barclays, and how the person making the sale to the lessor used the proceeds of the sale was not relevant. Accordingly, as Barclays had acquired the relevant asset, it was entitled to the capital allowances.

---

[37] [1997] 1 WLR 991 at 999.
[38] [2001] UKHL 6.
[39] [2004] UKHL 51.

11.38 The Inland Revenue succeeded in a second decision of the House of Lords, *Her Majesty's Commissioners of Inland Revenue v Scottish Provident Institution*,[40] which was handed down on the same day as the decision in the *Mawson* case. The facts of the *Scottish Provident* case are difficult and concern a prospective change from one statutory regime for taxing gains to another statutory regime, but the case does very usefully demonstrate an application of more general option analysis. Under the old statutory regime, Scottish Provident Institution ('Scottish Provident') as a mutual life office was not liable to corporation tax on any premium it received on selling an option to buy or to sell debt securities, including government debt securities. A bank devised a scheme under which Scottish Provident sold a call option which was substantially in-the-money[41] to the bank, giving the bank the right to buy underlying UK government debt, or gilts, from Scottish Provident at an exercise price which was significantly less than the prevailing spot price of the gilts. Crucially, Scottish Provident received the premium for selling the option during the old statutory regime, and was not taxed on the premium. Under the scheme, the bank would subsequently exercise its option during the new statutory regime, and Scottish Provident would deliver the gilts to the bank and receive the low exercise price. Scottish Provident would thereby sustain a tax loss of some £20 million, which would be available to it to offset taxable income elsewhere in its business to reduce its overall tax burden. Of course, each of Scottish Provident and the bank was exposed to the risk of making a real loss on the option, depending on movements in the spot price of the underlying gilts, and given that the purpose of the scheme was to deliver a particular tax effect to Scottish Provident, and not to enable either party to express an investment view and thereby become exposed to the risk of sustaining a real loss, the bank sold a second offsetting call option on the same quantity of underlying gilts to Scottish Provident. The two options had to be carefully engineered, so that (1) they would both be in-the-money and therefore be exercised after the commencement of the new statutory regime; (2) the obligations owed by Scottish Provident and the bank to each other to deliver the underlying gilts would be cancelled out; and (3) the obligations owed by Scottish Provident and the bank to each other to pay premium would be netted to the payment of the difference by Scottish Provident to the bank.

11.39 Crucially, Scottish Provident and the bank had to maintain the characterization of the two options as genuine transactions; if the two options were not treated as genuine transactions, they could be ignored for tax purposes and Scottish Provident would lose the tax effect that the scheme had been designed to create. If the two options were held to cancel each other out (as opposed to merely giving

---

[40] [2004] UKHL 52.
[41] See paragraph 4.44.

rise to obligations that could be netted) and comprise a composite transaction, then they could be ignored for tax purposes.

In its factual investigation, the special commissioners found that it was possible, albeit improbable given the dynamics of the market in gilts, that just one option would be exercised. Each of Scottish Provident and the bank was at liberty to choose whether or not to exercise the particular option it held, and whether or not either of them would choose to exercise the option it held would depend on movements in the spot price of the underlying gilts relative to the exercise price of the option it held. However, although each party was free to choose whether or not to exercise the option it held, the scheme would only work if both options were exercised. The special commissioners determined that the two options did not form a composite transaction because of the uncertainty as to whether or not they would be exercised, although this finding was described as being 'near the limit'.[42] Although it upheld the finding of fact that there was an outside but commercially real possibility that circumstances may occur in which the two options would not be exercised so as to cancel each other out, and that they did not comprise a composite transaction, the House of Lords determined that they should nonetheless be taxed as a composite transaction, considering that the low level of market risk was introduced into the structure solely in order to maintain the characterization of the two options as genuine transactions to be treated separately. The opinion of the Appellate Committee was that 'it would destroy the value of the Ramsay principle of construing [statutory] provisions ... as referring to the effect of composite transactions if their composite effect had to be disregarded simply because the parties had deliberately included a commercially irrelevant contingency, creating an acceptable risk that the scheme might not work as planned ... The composite effect of such a scheme should be considered as it was intended to operate and without regard to the possibility that, contrary to the intention and expectations of the parties, it might not work as planned.'[43]

11.40

11.4 The Taxation of Transactions: Withholding Tax

Withholding tax is generally a tax which is deducted or withheld from a payment and paid by the payer to the relevant taxing authority, with the result that the payee receives a net amount and is not required to pay the tax to the taxing authority. The withholding tax regime applied in the United Kingdom is based on a variety of different enactments, adding to the complexity of establishing the correct tax treatment of a transaction. Generally, the UK withholding tax regime includes

11.41

---

[42] [2002] STC (SCD) 252.
[43] [2004] UKHL 52, paragraph 23.

payments of interest which have a UK source, and a payment of interest has a UK source if there is a sufficiently close nexus between the interest payment and the United Kingdom. The decision in *Westminster Bank Executor & Trustee Co (Channel Islands) Ltd v National Bank of Greece SA*[44] established a basket test for determining whether or not a payment of interest has a nexus with the United Kingdom. The relevant factors include the place of the enforcement of the debt, the source from which interest is paid, how the debt is secured, the place where interest is paid, and other relevant factors, which might include the governing law of the agreement and the currency in which the debt is denominated.

11.42 The UK withholding tax regime generally does not include payments of interest to a bank or from a bank, provided that these payments are made during the course of the bank's ordinary business. As with other regimes for tax, the UK withholding tax regime is subject to ongoing development.

The ISDA 2002 Master Agreement[45]

11.43 Section 2(d)(i) of the ISDA 2002 Master Agreement has the effect that all payments made under it are made without any deduction or withholding for or on account of any tax unless such deduction or withholding is required by any applicable law, as modified by the practice of any relevant governmental revenue authority. The effect of Section 2(d)(i) is that the payer makes a payment gross with no deduction or withholding for tax, unless a deduction or withholding is required. The scope of Section 2(d)(i) is wide, and includes[46] any present or future tax, levy, impost, duty, charge, assessment or fee of any nature (including interest, penalties, and additions) imposed by any government or other taxing authority, but does not include stamp, registration, or documentation taxes. Each party as a payer usually represents[47] to the other that it will make payments gross with no deduction or withholding for Tax. Each party as a recipient usually represents[48] to the other to confirm its business and the jurisdiction in which that business is carried on. Whether or not a deduction or withholding for Tax should be made from a payment depends on the jurisdiction and the nature of the business of the recipient. Under the laws of some jurisdictions, the payer becomes liable for tax that should have been deducted or withheld from a payment. Under such circumstances, the payer should be able to rely on the representation made by the recipient as to the appropriate tax treatment of payments received by the recipient. The purpose of the payer tax representation and the payee tax representation is to

---

[44] [1970] 46 TC 472.
[45] See part 7.4 of Chapter 7.
[46] The definition of Tax is set out in Section 14 of the ISDA 2002 Master Agreement.
[47] The payer tax representation.
[48] The payee tax representation.

11.4 The Taxation of Transactions: Withholding Tax

ensure that each party remains responsible for the determination of its own tax affairs and the settlement of its own tax liability. Of course, it is to be emphasized that actual representations made by a party to a particular trading relationship or transaction depend very much on the status of that party and the circumstances of that trading relationship or transaction.

11.44 Section 2(d)(i) also contains the procedure that is followed in the event that a party 'X' is required to deduct or withhold for Tax from a payment made to the other party 'Y'. Generally X pays the Tax to the relevant taxing authorities, and if the Tax falls within the definition of an Indemnifiable Tax, X also pays to Y a gross-up amount such that Y receives the full amount of the payment as though no deduction or withholding had been made. The definition of Indemnifiable Tax[49] is not easy, operating as it does with a double negative.[50] Broadly, an Indemnifiable Tax is any Tax but it is not a Tax that is imposed on Y where Y has a present or future connection with the relevant jurisdiction, government, or taxing authority imposing the Tax. The intention underlying the drafting is that Y should only be entitled to receive a gross-up payment if Y does not have any connection with the relevant jurisdiction, government, or taxing authority; if Y does have such a connection, then presumably Y should be able to settle its own tax liabilities. Under Section 2(d)(ii), if X fails to make a deduction or withholding that is required, and the relevant Tax is not an Indemnifiable Tax, and X becomes liable for the amount of the Tax, then Y is required to pay to X the amount of the Tax.

Jurisdiction and double tax treaties

11.45 Double taxation occurs when a recipient of a payment made across a border bears the burden of tax in two jurisdictions. The payer makes a deduction or withholding for tax in one jurisdiction, and the recipient pays further tax on the net payment received in the other jurisdiction. If there is a double tax treaty between the jurisdictions, then whether or not there is any deduction or withholding for tax from a payment depends on the terms of that double tax treaty. Some double tax treaties have the effect that there is no deduction or withholding, and the recipient receives the full amount of the payment and pays tax from that full amount. Other treaties have the effect that there is a deduction or withholding, and the recipient receives the net amount of the payment but does not pay tax from that net amount. Other treaties have the effect that there is a deduction or withholding, but at a lower rate. A double tax treaty might also provide for any tax credit if there is some

---

[49] Section 14 of the ISDA 2002 Master Agreement.
[50] The language of the definition of Indemnifiable Tax is '... any Tax other than a Tax that would not be imposed in respect of a payment under this Agreement but for a present or former connection between the jurisdiction or government or taxing authority imposing such Tax and the recipient of such payment or a person related to such recipient...'.

deduction or withholding. It is clear that a careful review of any relevant double tax treaty is essential; the United Kingdom has entered into double tax treaties with a number of jurisdictions.

11.5 The Substance of Transactions

11.46 Derivatives have the ability to move assets and liabilities, including cash flows, in such a manner as to achieve an economic effect which is different from the economic effect that is reported in a company's financial statements.

11.47 The Accounting Standards Board in the United Kingdom published in April 1994 Financial Reporting Standard 5, 'Reporting the Substance of Transactions' (FRS 5). The objective of FRS 5[51] is to ensure that the substance of an entity's transactions is reported in its financial statements, and the commercial effect of the entity's transactions, and any resulting assets, liabilities, gains, or losses should be faithfully represented in its financial statements. Therefore, FRS 5 requires[52] that a reporting entity's financial statements report the substance of transactions, and in determining the substance of a transaction, all its aspects and implications should be identified and greater weight given to those more likely to have a commercial effect; in addition, a series of transactions which is designed to achieve a particular commercial effect should be viewed as a whole. FRS 5 was therefore formulated to address the problems posed by an 'off balance sheet financing' arrangement, under which a company's business is financed in such a way that the financing is not shown on its balance sheet as a liability, and consequently the asset being financed is also not shown on its balance sheet, with the effect that the balance sheet understates both liabilities and assets of the company.

11.48 FRS 5 develops certain principles for identifying assets and liabilities and for recognizing assets and liabilities for the purposes of preparing financial statements. The overall principle[53] is that the manner in which a transaction is disclosed in a set of financial statements should be sufficient to enable a user of those financial statements to understand the commercial effect of that transaction. FRS 5 contains Application Notes which specify how the requirements of FRS 5 are applied to transactions which have certain prescribed features.

11.49 Other financial reporting standards have superseded and amended FRS 5 for certain applications, including FRS 25 and FRS 26 which are discussed in

---

[51] Paragraph 1 of FRS 5.
[52] Paragraph 14 of FRS 5.
[53] Paragraph 30 of FRS 5.

11.6 'Accounting-driven' Transactions

this chapter. Nonetheless, the general principles expressed in FRS 5 have informed the preparation of these other financial reporting standards.

11.6 'Accounting-driven' Transactions

Derivatives offer the potential to move assets and liabilities, including cash flows, from one accounting period to another, and some derivative transactions have been deliberately structured to achieve this effect.[54] Indeed, such transactions have been marketed as being suitable for this application. However, the practice of marketing and entering into 'accounting-driven' transactions raises serious issues. **11.50**

The *Financial Times* reported[55] that the Tokyo Financial Supervisory Agency had revoked the licence held by the local operating company of one financial institution and publicly reprimanded another after the Agency had discovered that these financial institutions had entered into accounting-driven transactions with various customers, and the purpose of these transactions was to assist the customers to conceal losses, by moving those losses from one accounting period to another. The Agency's lengthy investigations into the records and communications of the financial institutions revealed that they had to a greater or lesser extent marketed these structures during the mid to late 1990s with that particular purpose given some prominence. **11.51**

Accounting-driven transactions therefore pose considerable risks to a financial institution; at the very least, its reputation can be tarnished by a regulatory investigation, and the revocation of its licence, or authorization, has obvious and serious ramifications for its business. **11.52**

In the context of derivatives, the principal risk to a financial institution would therefore appear to be that it assists its customer to distort the customer's cash flows and thereby enable the customer to prepare financial statements which do not accurately describe the customer's financial health. The implications for investors in the customer's business are serious; inaccurate financial statements might well prevent investors from being able to gauge accurately the risk of their investment, and it is to be remembered that the foundation of investment is the ratio between risk and reward. **11.53**

---

[54] See the *Scottish Provident* case.
[55] 2 March 2000.

12

DEFINING THE RISK MAP

12.1 Introduction	12.01
12.2 The Framework for Risk Control	12.02
12.3 The Risk Taxonomy	12.07

12.1 Introduction

12.01 One of the themes which resonates through this book is risk. Risk may be considered from two perspectives with respect to derivatives. From one point of view, derivatives have emerged as a means of either neutralizing risk, that is, hedging against the crystallization of risk, or exploiting risk, that is, speculating on risk and the price attached to it. Any consideration of the purpose generally of derivatives, and how they function, must be undertaken with reference to the risks underlying the particular transactions and being transferred under those transactions. Hopefully this book shows how this is achieved. However, derivatives must be used in an appropriate and controlled fashion if the considerable benefits and potential that they offer are to be realized, and the considerable damage that they are capable of inflicting, often accompanied by sensationalistic media headlines, is to be avoided. Therefore derivatives must be used within an appropriate framework which promotes the control of risk, by ensuring that only suitable transactions are entered into which achieve the required economic effect, the performance of those transactions is monitored, and remedial action is taken if necessary. The maintenance of adequate financial resources is an important part of controlling risk, as Chapter 10 explains, more so now that the discipline embraces not only credit risk but also market risk and operational risk. This chapter shows how that overall framework for risk control might be established.

12.2 The Framework for Risk Control

12.02 Investment banks are significant participants in the sell side of the derivative markets, and the control of risk is of paramount importance to an investment bank.

Chapter 12: Defining the Risk Map

Therefore a brief consideration of the different departments of a model of the trading and sales business of an investment bank, and the links and interdependencies of those departments, should serve as a guide to how risk is identified and controlled. Of course, every investment bank is organized in a unique manner, but the functions and interdependencies of the different departments are broadly the same across the industry.

12.03 The sales and marketing desks solicit business for the bank, and manage the bank's relationships with its customers. The sales and marketing desks work with the structuring desks to develop transaction structures which meet the demands of customers, and transactions and structures are priced by the trading desks. The hedging of risk is undertaken by the trading desks, either on the basis of individual transactions, or on an aggregate or 'book' basis. Quantitative analysts prepare the mathematical models that are used by the structuring and trading desks. Some trading is undertaken on a proprietary basis, and not to hedge a customer-facing transaction; the term 'proprietary' means that the bank is committing its own capital to expressing an investment view, and the proportion of proprietary trading undertaken by different banks differs significantly. The business model of some banks emphasizes customer-driven business, whereas other banks engage in such a high volume of proprietary business that they attract the quite unofficial (and of course erroneous) description of being quasi-funds. The bank may also make a market in certain instruments, offering customers the facility to buy or to sell those instruments. Research analysts[1] prepare forecasts and commentaries of market movements, which are used by the sales and marketing desks to write the investment stories that are used to solicit business. The sales and marketing desks, structuring desks, and trading desks collectively comprise the front office of the bank.

12.04 The middle office of the bank monitors and controls risk. The middle office also values trading positions, whether these are customer-facing or proprietary. The middle office is independent of the front office, and this independence is a crucial element of the management of potential conflicts of interest which might otherwise arise.

12.05 The back office of the bank is responsible for the operational aspects of the bank's business, including ensuring that all transactions are documented properly and settle successfully in accordance with their terms. Transactions must be entered

---

[1] A distinction is made between the public side and the private side of a barrier to the flow of information (or 'Chinese wall', to use more common terminology) to manage conflicts of interest which may from time to time emerge. Information obtained about the issuer of securities which is material and not made public must remain in the private side. By way of interesting aside, a derivative transaction the underlying of which comprises shares issued by a counterparty to the transaction, that is, a self-referencing derivative, can be problematic because one of the parties to the transaction is inevitably privy to price-sensitive non-public information in respect of the underlying.

into the bank's payment systems in order that the relevant payments are made automatically at the correct time. Moreover, the receipt of amounts owed to the bank is also monitored, and defaults are escalated. The back office also prepares the various notifications that are made during the life of the more complex transactions that the bank enters into. Specific departments, which may reside outside the back office, undertake specific and specialized documentation roles, such as the negotiation of ISDA master agreements and ancillary documents, including credit support documents, and transaction management.

Certain risks are monitored by specific control functions within the bank. Depending on how the bank is organized, these control functions may or may not reside in the middle office. Notwithstanding the work of the specific risk control functions, each department takes responsibility for being cognizant of, monitoring, and controlling the particular risks within its ambit. The risk committee of the bank's senior management considers reports from the various department of the bank, and determines the overall strategy to control, and to exploit, these risks. The compliance department assists with the development of the various procedures to control the bank's businesses and operations, and monitors adherence throughout the bank with these procedures. The internal audit function certifies the integrity of the bank's procedures, and works with the compliance department to monitor adherence throughout the bank with the procedures. The internal audit function also monitors the work of the compliance department. **12.06**

12.3 The Risk Taxonomy

Market risk

Market risk, or price risk, is the risk that the relevant market might move unfavourably. Market risk is one of the key risks that a bank must address, whether it is hedging customer-facing transactions, taking proprietary positions, or making a market. If the bank is making a market, then it must maintain a position through which it is neutral to movements in the market, by balancing sales against purchases, and by entering into hedging transactions if the internal hedge cannot be maintained. However, the risk remains that the market might move unfavourably and disrupt the bank's hedging operations. The market risk to which the bank is exposed also has implications for the maintenance by the bank of adequate financial resources, as Chapter 10 discusses, and some element of regulatory capital covers potential losses from the crystallization of market risk. **12.07**

Traders monitor their positions on an ongoing basis, by considering all the relevant information; in the context of derivatives, it is particularly important that the rights and obligations created under the derivative contracts are properly understood, and the legal department contributes the necessary analysis. Option traders **12.08** monitor not only the changes in the prices of the options that they have bought or sold, but also the sensitivity of those prices to various factors, including movements in the price or level of the underlying and movements in prevailing interest rates, in order to assess the risk that their positions may move out-of-the-money. Once a position has been opened, it is important to establish the conditions under which that position will then be closed; this is the 'exit strategy'.

12.09 The usual statistic that is prepared by the risk managers is Value-at-Risk (VaR). In general terms, VaR is the measure of the maximum potential loss in the market value of a portfolio under normal circumstances during a specified period, given a specified level of confidence. The term 'normal' is key and it refers to the statistical analysis that is undertaken. VaR is generally calculated on the assumption that movements in the market are distributed normally, and that the pattern of the losses which occur in the portfolio is also distributed normally, following the observation that many natural phenomena exhibit variety, and these variations in natural phenomena follow a distinct pattern. A normal distribution of a particular data population suggests that there is an even distribution of specimens on either side of the mean value calculated for that data population, and the most number of specimens have that mean value. Intuitively the shape of the familiar bell curve, which is discussed in the following paragraphs, is glimpsed.

12.10 However, in some more detail, the key statistical tool that is used is the standard deviation.[2] The mean of a data population represents the average of the specimens of that data population, and the standard deviation of that data population represents the extent to which the specimens vary, or deviate, around the mean. Hence standard deviation is sometimes referred to as the root-mean-square. A more widely distributed data population has a higher standard deviation that does a less widely distributed data population. In a data population which exhibits a normal distribution, 68% of the specimens occur within one standard deviation above and below the mean, and 95% of the specimens occur within two standard deviations above and below the mean.

---

[2] Standard deviation is usually denoted as σ and is generally calculated using the following equation:

$$\sigma = \sqrt{\frac{\sum_{n=1}^{number}(X_n - \text{average})^2}{(\text{number} - 1)}}$$

where 'number' is the number of specimens comprising the data population, 'X_n' is the current value of the variable 'X' representing the data population, and 'average' is the mean of the data population. The denominator is usually the number minus 1 if the specimens for which σ is calculated constitute only a sample of the entire data population. The denominator is usually just the number if σ is calculated for the entire data population.

12.3 The Risk Taxonomy

A variable representing a data population is standardized when it is adjusted so that its mean is equal to zero and its standard deviation is equal to one. Standardization is required because classification of a data population depends on a subjective assessment of the most appropriate size of class to be used. Standardization introduces objectivity by adjusting all variables to exhibit a mean of zero. The standardized value of a particular value 'X' occurring within the data population is called the z-score. The familiar bell curve is obtained by plotting z-score against the horizontal axis, and probability against the vertical axis. The scale of the vertical axis ranges from zero (which indicates that an event, such as the occurrence of X in the data population, is impossible) to one (which indicates that an event, such as the occurrence of X in the data population, is certain). Figure 12.1 illustrates the bell curve. In accordance with probability theory, the area under the bell curve is equal to one, because the sum of the probability of an event occurring and the probability of that event not occurring must equal one. The calculation of the z-score of X occurring in the data population is achieved by expressing the difference between X and the mean in relation to the standard deviation of the data population. Calculation of the z-score expresses the gradations of the x-axis, so that 68% of the area beneath the curve occurs within one standard deviation above and below the mean, 95% of the area beneath the curve occurs within two standard deviations above and below the mean, and 99% of the

12.11

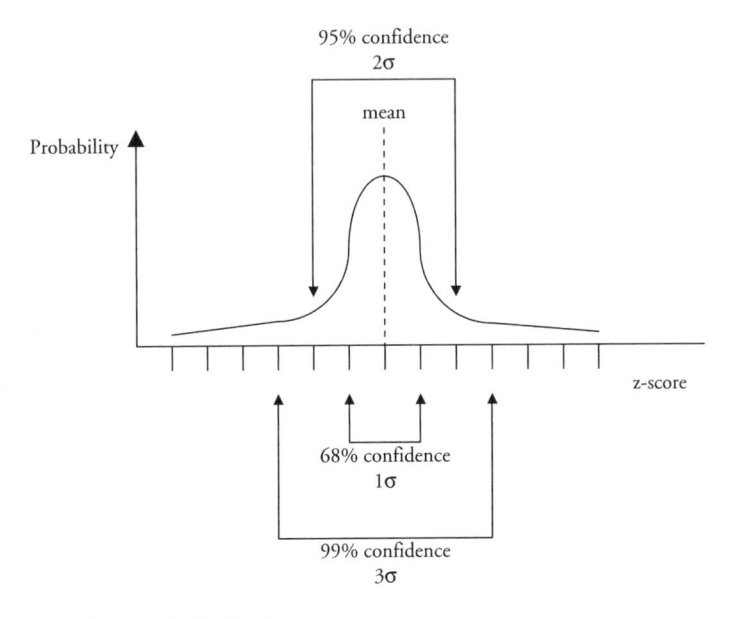

Figure 12.1 The statistical bell curve

area beneath the curve occurs within three standard deviations above and below the mean, as predicted by the work of Gauss.[3]

12.12 If the data population sampled for these purposes is sufficiently representative of the particular phenomenon, and crucially if that phenomenon actually exhibits a normal distribution, then future occurrences of that phenomenon can be predicted with accuracy. These predictions can be made with varying degrees of confidence, usually expressed as 99% confidence (three standard deviations), 95% confidence (two standard deviations), and 68% confidence (one standard deviation).

12.13 The application of statistical analysis to the calculation of VaR connotes the prediction of the maximum potential loss in the market value of the portfolio. If the VaR of a portfolio is determined to be a particular amount with 95% confidence, then this quantification of VaR suggests that the maximum loss that the portfolio will suffer over a 20 day period is that amount, and the risk is accepted that on one day in the 20 day period the loss that the portfolio may suffer may exceed that amount. Nineteen days out of 20 is 95%, hence the VaR in this illustration is calculated with 95% confidence.

12.14 The quantification of market risk is usually achieved through analysing the volatility exhibited by the underlying market, using a suitable model. However, use of and reliance on a model gives rise to the risk that the model might itself be flawed or based on assumptions which are inappropriate, or that incorrect variables are used to operate the model.

12.15 One of the shortcomings of VaR, other than that it looks back in time and not forwards and that it does not offer any quantification or analysis of the loss by which it is exceeded, is that it does not accommodate extreme market movements. To return to the bell curve, the risk is that the data population does not exhibit a normal distribution, that is, the shape of the bell curve does not fit the actual distribution of specimens within that data population.[4] Therefore extreme value theory has been suggested as an attempt to model the probability of exceptional market movements taking place. Extreme value theory is a statistical discipline which examines extreme variations from the mean of a data population, and aside from the financial markets, it has found an application in other fields requiring statistical analysis, including notably meteorology. The idea that events the occurrence of which is predicted to be extremely unlikely nonetheless do occur more frequently than statistical analysis suggests, and with considerable impact, is an

---

[3] Johann Carl Friedrich Gauss (1777–1855).
[4] The term 'leptokurtosis' describes the distortion of the 'tail-ends' of the bell curve caused by statistical outliers.

12.3 The Risk Taxonomy

argument which is gaining momentum.[5] Nonetheless, VaR remains an important tool for risk management, providing a common and widely accepted basis for the evaluation of a variety of risks.

Basel 2 and the legislation and regulation which flow from it[6] define a standard approach for the calculation of the capital required to accommodate market risk. Some banks prefer to use their own proprietary models to calculate market risk for the purposes of determining the amount of regulatory capital that they are required to hold. The FSA in the United Kingdom recognizes a bank's proprietary model on the basis of whether or not it is adequate and appropriate in the context of the particular risks to which the bank is exposed. The model is assessed by the FSA with reference to the algorithms it uses, including the assumptions underpinning the mathematics, and the systems and controls associated with its use, including the collation and analysis of raw data. The FSA also requires that the model is stress-tested. **12.16**

Complex trading operations involve simultaneous exposures to different markets, and the aggregate exposure must be determined. Correlation risk is the risk that the aggregation of the bank's exposure is incorrectly calculated, and consequently an incorrect hedge is established. Stress-testing a complex derivative structure is undertaken to evaluate how the value of the structure changes under different adverse market conditions, and under changes in the conditions of some of the relevant markets and not others underlying the structure. **12.17**

Liquidity risk

Liquidity risk is the risk that a position cannot be closed, either in a reasonable time or at a reasonable price. Liquidity risk arises if there are too few buyers and sellers in a market, and becomes more acute during times of market stress. However, the real difficulty that liquidity risk gives rise to is more subtle. Certain of the key risk metrics that are analysed are determined using mathematical models, and these mathematical models assume that the relevant market has unlimited liquidity, that is, assets can always be bought and sold at the prices indicated. Reality is of course very different, and transactions of any significant volume will move prices. Accordingly, mathematical pricing techniques are being developed **12.18**

---

[5] See Taleb, *The Black Swan: The Impact of the Highly Improbable* (Random House Inc., 2007). The title of this book refers to the dangers of trying to predict future events on the basis of the empirical evidence to hand: prior to the discovery of swans with black plumage in Australia, all swans were believed to have white plumage, and from this follows the observation that one statistical outlier has the potential to unravel, sometimes with considerable impact, theories and rules which have been established on the basis of the empirical evidence that has hitherto remained without contradiction.

[6] See Chapter 10.

which capture the effect of different depths of liquidity in the market, and these more subtle quantifications are used in the various pricing models.

Counterparty risk

12.19   Counterparty risk is the risk that a counterparty might default in respect of its obligations, and there are different aspects of counterparty risk. Credit risk is the risk that a counterparty might fail to make a payment when it is due to make that payment or become insolvent and therefore unable to make payments. Capacity risk is the risk that an obligation cannot be enforced against the counterparty because the counterparty lacks the legal power to enter into the relevant agreement and to perform its obligations under that agreement.[7] Strong processes must be established to verify at the outset of a trading relationship that the prospective counterparty has been properly established in the relevant jurisdiction, that it has the legal capacity to enter into the proposed trading relationship and each individual transaction within that relationship, that it has sufficient resources to be able to meet its payment and delivery obligations, and that it is not engaging in any form of money laundering scheme.

Legal risk

12.20   Legal risk is the risk that contractual provisions are unenforceable or operate in an unexpected manner, for example, through a failure to understand fully those provisions. Legal risk also includes the risk that a security device is unenforceable, perhaps because it has not been perfected, or recharacterized such that it loses its priority relative to the competing claims of other creditors and therefore its value.

12.21   The risk that a transaction or structure that has been sold has been misrepresented to a customer, or that sales communications have taken on the characteristics of advice which is wrong, or that a transaction or structure is unsuitable in the hands of the customer, constitutes a significant legal and regulatory risk.[8] The only effective method of controlling this risk is to ensure that the entire process of delivering the product to the customer is undertaken in a rigorous fashion. The prospective transaction or structure should be clearly and accurately described during all phases of sales and negotiation, and term sheets and the executed contracts themselves should be consistent with each other and with any marketing material that has been produced and any oral descriptions given of the prospective transaction or structure. The correct categorization of the customer and adherence to clear policies as to the types of product that are offered, and the manner in which products are delivered, including the clear disclosure of risk, form the

---

[7] See the discussion of the local authority swaps cases in part 8.5 of Chapter 8.
[8] See part 8.6 of Chapter 8.

bedrock of controlling this risk. Above all else, a culture must exist which promotes the control of risk.

The risk that a transaction or structure that has been sold is being used for an inappropriate or even criminal purpose by the customer also constitutes a significant legal and regulatory risk. Part 11.6 of Chapter 11 discusses the risk of becoming involved in an 'accounting-driven' transaction, which might be used by the customer to conceal a loss or to inflate a profit. The bank must therefore understand the rationale for the transaction, and the different steps comprising a complex transaction. A proposed structure which appears to contain circular cash flows or steps which economically cancel each other out should be examined very carefully. If a proposed transaction or structure that has given cause for concern is allowed to proceed, an opinion letter giving the necessary unqualified assurances from independent accounting and tax advisers should be obtained. **12.22**

Settlement risk

Settlement risk is the risk that payments are not made in the manner specified in the relevant contract. A crystallization of settlement risk might trigger a default under the relevant contract, although now certain contracts provide that a failure to make a payment for a technical reason, as opposed to a more substantive reason such as a reason connected with solvency, will not amount to a default, provided that payment is effected within a specified period of the original scheduled date;[9] this is a pragmatic reflection of the reality that temporary difficulties are experienced from time to time. **12.23**

Operational risk

The concept of operational risk is introduced in Chapter 10, and may be summarized as the risk of a loss caused by internal processes which are inadequate or which have failed, by the criminal or negligent activities of employees or clients, or by events which are external to the financial institution. The definition set out in the preceding sentence is extremely wide, and it encompasses several of the risks already discussed in this chapter, with the exception of market or price risk. The term 'operational risk' is therefore a generic description of elements of the risk map other than market or price risk, and excluded from the working definition are losses caused by the exercise of poor judgment as to any market movement or condition (including the level of interest rates and availability of liquidity), or credit exposures. Operational risk might be described as the risk arising from executing business as opposed to the risk arising from the business itself. Operational risk **12.24**

---

[9] See for example Section 5(a)(i) of the ISDA 2002 Master Agreement.

can be divided into three main categories: risks related to processes,[10] risks related to conduct,[11] and external risks.[12]

12.25 The measurement and control of operational risk are becoming more sophisticated, and with the implementation of the standards imposed by Basel 2,[13] the identification and measurement of operational risk has become a more quantitative discipline. The advanced measurement approach[14] to the analysis of operational risk requires (1) the collation of statistics as to losses caused by internal operational risks, and an assessment as to the frequency of the occurrence of such losses; (2) the collation of statistics as to losses caused by external operational losses, and an assessment as to the relevance and severity of such losses; (3) the analysis of the different scenarios which may arise, with a view to identifying trends as to the severity and the frequency of the losses which may occur; and (4) the implementation of the appropriate processes to better protect against those risks, and to capture useful data from any loss which does occur.

Reputation risk

12.26 Reputation risk, or franchise risk, is perhaps the most important and yet the most nebulous element of the risk map. The derivative industry, like the financial services industry as a whole, is built on trust, and the reputation of a bank, or indeed of any financial institution, for probity, fair-dealing, and stability is arguably its most important asset. Reputation can be eroded all too easily, with damaging consequences for both the marketing of the bank's products and the cost to the bank of acquiring funding. The risk of becoming involved in a money laundering scheme, financial fraud, insider dealing, or market abuse must be identified, managed, and neutralized. A clear understanding must be developed of a proposed counterparty and its business; this principle is referred to as 'know your counterparty' or 'know your customer', as applicable, or 'KYC', and it lies at the heart of contemporary compliance theory and practice.[15] Of course, a detailed knowledge of a customer's business will enable the bank to market more effectively to that customer, and therefore robust and effective compliance procedures should be

---

[10] For example, the risk of a failure to follow the appropriate process or procedure, and the risk of a disruption to systems.

[11] For example, the risk of negligent or fraudulent practices by an employee, including misrepresentation of a transaction or structure.

[12] For example, the risk of negligent or fraudulent practices by an employee of a customer or trading counterparty, and the risk to infrastructure, such as fire, flood, or deliberate damage.

[13] See Chapter 10 generally.

[14] See paragraph 10.15.

[15] The judgment of Gloster J in *JP Morgan Chase Bank v Springwell Navigation Corporation* [2008] EWHC 1186 (Comm) recalls at paragraph 205 how the concept of KYC became established during the early 1990s.

12.3 The Risk Taxonomy

seen as an opportunity to generate business and profitability through establishing detailed and useful databases.

Closing remarks

It is clear that the different categories of risk are related, and that no one risk can be addressed in isolation. Accordingly, banks have established committees of the various internal risk managers to review new lines of business, in order to identify the relevant risks and to formulate a way of mitigating those risks, and individual transactions are managed so that appropriate documentation is negotiated and signed, and the bank's payment systems are correctly programmed to make and to receive the relevant amounts. New lines of business are only approved if the appropriate risk controllers have either indicated that the risks are minimal or prescribed the measures that must be put in place to address particular concerns; approval is contingent on those prescribed measures being implemented. **12.27**

Generally it is recognized that not all risk can be eliminated, and indeed, from the broadest perspective, the ratio between risk and reward determines profitability. Whereas there must be a zero tolerance for certain risks,[16] other risks[17] can be accepted in the expectation that acceptance of those risks will enable profits potentially to be earned in such amount to justify acceptance of those risks. This book shows that the use and misuse of derivatives offer ample opportunity for both gain and loss. To come full circle, it is fitting to close this book with the observation made at the outset, that derivatives are merely a piece of technology, and as such everything depends on how they are used, whether foolishly or wisely. **12.28**

---

[16] For example, the risk of the commission of a criminal offence should never be accepted; the potential downside far outweighs any potential upside.

[17] For example, the risk of the unenforceability of a contract in a particular jurisdiction may be a risk that is justifiable if the potential upside is sufficient to outweigh the potential downside, which can be quantified in monetary terms.

SELECTED GLOSSARY

American option An American-style option is an option that can be exercised at any time before its expiry date (cf. European option).

Arbitrage Arbitrage is the exploitation of the differences in the prices in different markets. Arbitrage may involve the exploitation of the differences between two cash markets, between a cash market and its related derivative market, or between two derivative markets.

ASB The ASB is the UK Accounting Standards Board. The ASB issues accounting standards, which are contained in Financial Reporting Standards (FRS).

Asian option (also average rate option) An Asian option is an option, the exercise price of which is the average of the price, level, or rate of the underlying over a specified period. The parties must agree, in addition to the usual variables, the interval at which the price, level, or rate of the underlying is observed.

Automatic exercise Some options are exercised automatically if they are in-the-money on their expiry date.

Backwardation Backwardation is a market condition under which the underlying spot price is more than the futures price. Backwardation occurs when the underlying is scarce in the short term, and this scarcity applies upward pressure on the underlying spot price (cf. contango).

Barrier option The rights under a barrier option are only available if the price, level, or rate of the underlying reaches (in the case of a knock-in barrier option) or fails to reach (in the case of a knock-out barrier option) a prescribed threshold or 'barrier'.

Basis point A basis point is $\frac{1}{100}$ of 1%, or 0.01%.

Basis risk Basis risk arises when an underlying exposure is not perfectly hedged by a derivative transaction. Basis risk is the difference between the underlying exposure and the hedge. Basis risk also describes the risk of a mismatch between the documents governing the underlying exposure and the corresponding hedging derivative transaction.

Basis swap A basis swap is a transaction under which an exposure to an obligation to make payments at one floating rate is converted into an exposure to an obligation to make payments at another floating rate.

BBA The BBA is the British Bankers' Association, which is the trade association for the United Kingdom's banking market. The BBA was established in 1919, and worked closely with the Committee of London Clearing Bankers. In 1972, the BBA's membership expanded to include overseas banks and British merchant banks, and in 1975 the BBA and the Committee of London Clearing Bankers separated; however, in 1991 the Committee of London Clearing Bankers was wound up, and the BBA assumed its responsibilities. The BBA represents its members in various forums and publishes the Banking Code, which is a voluntary code indicating best practice in the industry. Of particular relevance to this book, the BBA also publishes benchmark interest rates such as the LIBOR rates.

Selected Glossary

Bermudan option A Bermudan option is an option which can be exercised only on one of a series of specified dates before its expiry date.

BIS The BIS is the Bank for International Settlements, which was established on the basis of a proposal put forward by the Young Committee in 1930. The Young Committee was more formally the Committee of Experts, and it was convened in Geneva in 1928 under the chairmanship of Owen D. Young to draw up proposals for a complete and final settlement of the reparation issues arising from the First World War. The initial purpose of the BIS was to coordinate the flow of funds between the various national banks arising from German reparations after the First World War. Since the Second World War, the BIS has acted as banker to various national central banks, accepting deposits and making short-term loans, although this function has been more recently assumed by the International Monetary Fund (IMF). The BIS has executed financial transactions for various international organizations such as the Organization for Economic Cooperation and Development (OECD) and the IMF. The BIS now serves as a forum for international and monetary cooperation, hosting various meetings of central bankers and providing facilities for various committees, with a view to promoting international financial stability. The BIS also continues to act as banker to national central banks, assisting them to manage their external reserves. The BIS serves as a centre for monetary and economic research, and facilitates the implementation of various international financial agreements.

Black Scholes Equation The Black Scholes Equation (after Fischer Black and Myron Scholes) is a mathematical model for pricing options. The Black Scholes Equation was originally formulated to calculate the theoretical fair price of a European option written over a share which does not pay a dividend. Other formulae have been developed for pricing other types of option, but the Black Scholes Equation and its variants remain the foundation of option pricing theory and the most well-known example of an option pricing model.

Bond A bond is a debt security, usually of longer maturity, which is negotiable and therefore which can be traded.

Call option A call option is an option which gives the holder the right, but not the obligation, to buy the underlying against payment of the exercise price (cf. put option).

Cap contract A cap contract is a derivative which generally confers protection against increases in the price, level, or rate of the underlying above a specified threshold (cf. floor contract).

Capital markets The capital markets are generally the markets in which longer-term financial instruments are issued to raise funds. The capital markets comprise the debt capital markets and the equity capital markets. The capital markets are separate from the traditional bank markets for raising funds through taking up loans, whether from one bank or from a syndicate of banks.

Cash market (also spot market) The cash market is the market for immediate delivery, as contrasted with the derivative market, in which delivery takes place at some future time under the terms of a derivative contract. The cash market is also the underlying market of a derivative market. Movements in the cash market affect the prices and rates at which trading in the derivative market takes place.

Cash-settled An obligation which is cash-settled is settled through making a payment (cf. physically-settled).

CEBS CEBS is the Committee of European Banking Supervisors.

Selected Glossary

CEIOPS   CEIOPS is the Committee of European Insurance and Occupational Pensions Supervisors.

CESR   CESR is the Committee of European Securities Regulators.

CFD   A CFD is a contract for differences. Generally a CFD generates a payment the amount of which is calculated with reference to fluctuations in a specified data population, such as interest rates, share prices, or commodity prices. The definition of a CFD is set out in the Financial Services and Markets Act 2000 and its secondary legislation. All swaps are CFDs. A cash-settled option is a CFD.

Clearing   Clearing, the context of exchange-based derivative trading, is the payment of losses at the end of a trading session by market participants whose positions have lost value during the trading session to market participants whose positions have gained value during the trading session. The payment of losses from the losers to the winners is made through the clearing house. The payment of losses by the losers may be supported by the payment of collateral, or margin, to the clearing house, as the clearing house guarantees the payments to the winners and must ensure that it has available to it sufficient funds. The clearing process therefore involves the registration of matched transactions (a sale by one market participant is matched with the corresponding purchase by another market participant), the administration of the payments, and the settlement of transactions on a net basis. The purpose of clearing is the reduction of risk and the simplification of the cash flows involved in trading in a market.

Clearing house   The clearing house of an exchange is an institution which guarantees the performance of every transaction that is dealt on that exchange and which administers payments on a net basis. The clearing house is either a part of the exchange's organization or it is separate.

Cliquet option (also ratchet option)   A cliquet option is an option the exercise price of which is reset at predetermined dates during the life of the option.

Collar contract   A collar contract is a derivative which generally confers protection against increases in the price, level, or rate of the underlying above a specified upper threshold, but under which a payment is made if the price, level, or rate of the underlying decreases to below a specified lower threshold.

Collateral   'Collateral' is the term used to describe property that is provided to a creditor to whom an obligation is owed and is therefore available to that creditor to make up any shortfall in the performance of that obligation. Strictly, the term 'collateral' was used to refer to such property provided by a third party and not by the debtor; however, the term is now used to describe property that is provided by either the debtor or by a third party to support the obligations of the debtor.

Compound option   A compound option is an option written on an underlying option.

Contango   Contango is a market condition under which the underlying spot price is less than the futures price. Contango is the usual market condition (cf. backwardation), and broadly reflects the principle of futures pricing, that the futures price includes the cost-of-carry, or the cost of holding or carrying the underlying asset from one point in time to the next.

Convertible   A convertible debt security entitles the holder to convert the debt into the equity of either the issuer or a company related to the issuer (cf. exchangeable).

Correlation   Correlation is the measure of the extent to which the price, level, or rate of one asset moves in the same direction as the price, level, or rate of another asset (cf. dispersion).

CPPI   CPPI is constant proportion portfolio insurance, which is a technique for creating an investment exposure to an asset which is commonly referred to as the 'risky

Selected Glossary

asset' (it is referred to as such because the investor assumes exposure to the price risk of that asset). The proportion of the total invested amount that is allocated to the risky asset increases if the risky asset performs favourably, but decreases if the risky asset performs badly. The proportion of the total invested amount that is not allocated to the risky asset is allocated to a so-called 'reserve asset' which generally offers low-risk stable returns. Allocations between the risky asset and the risk-free asset are made regularly and the overall purpose of the CPPI technique is to protect a proportion of the invested amount; the proportion of the invested amount that is protected can be calibrated. Under certain CPPI structures, a leveraged exposure to the risky asset is created if the risky asset continues to perform favourably; under such circumstances, the amount that is allocated to the risky asset is greater than the total invested amount.

Credit default swap (also CDS) A credit default swap is a credit derivative, under which the protection buyer pays a premium to buy the credit protection, and if the specified credit event occurs, then the protection seller makes a payment to the protection buyer. If the CDS is physically-settled, then the protection buyer also transfers debt or loan obligations which satisfy a prescribed specification to the protection seller. CDS are the most common credit derivative contracts.

Credit derivative A credit derivative is a derivative contract which transfers credit risk from a protection buyer, who wishes to lay off its exposure to the credit risk projected by a reference entity, to a protection seller, who wishes to assume that credit risk for reward. A credit derivative can be used to isolate the credit risk generated by a transaction, asset, or relationship, and that risk can then be traded for profit.

Credit risk Credit risk is the risk that a person who owes an obligation to make a payment fails to make that payment or becomes insolvent and therefore incapable of making that payment in full. Credit risk now forms a distinct class of asset that can be isolated and transferred by a credit derivative.

Credit spread option A credit spread option is a credit derivative under which the payment made by the protection seller to the protection buyer is triggered if the yield of the reference debt security over a specified benchmark increases; the increase in yield indicates that the perception in the market is that creditworthiness of the issuer of the reference debt security has worsened.

Derivative contracts rules These rules are a self-contained statutory code established by the Finance Act 2002, as amended, for the taxation of derivative contracts. Broadly, under the rules, the cash flows generated by a derivative transaction to which they apply are taxed on an income basis and not on a capital gains basis. The rules replaced the earlier codification, the Financial Instruments Rules, which were contained in the Finance Act 1994.

Digital option (also binary option) A digital option is an option which pays out a specified fixed amount in the event that the price, level, or rate of the underlying reaches a specified threshold, but does not pay out if that specified threshold is not reached.

Dispersion Dispersion is the measure of the extent to which the volatility exhibited by the price, level, or rate of one asset moves in the same direction as the volatility exhibited by the price, level, or rate of another asset (cf. correlation).

Embedded option An embedded option is a right contained in the terms and conditions of a debt security. An issuer call option gives the issuer the right to require the early repayment (or redemption) of the debt, and an investor put option gives the holder of the debt the right to require the early repayment (or redemption) of the debt.

Emissions trading (also carbon trading)   Emissions trading is the sale and purchase of regulatory permits to emit greenhouse gases into the atmosphere. Emissions trading is based on units of carbon dioxide and on units of the carbon dioxide equivalent of other greenhouse gases (carbon dioxide is the principal greenhouse gas).

European Economic Area (EEA)   The EEA was established by the EEA Agreement, which came into force on 1 January 1994. The EEA Agreement was originally intended to create a free trade area between the European Communities (now known as the European Union) and the European Free Trade Area (with the notable exception of Switzerland). The overall principle of the EEA Agreement is to establish the freedom of movement of goods, services, persons, and capital within the region; these freedoms are usually referred to as the 'four freedoms'. The various EU directives that have been made apply within the EEA.

European option   A European-style option is an option that can only be exercised on its expiry date (cf. American option).

European Passport   The general principle of the European Passport is that (subject to due process) authorization and prudential supervision in one 'home' member state of the EEA allow the conduct of business or the offer of funds in another 'host' member state of the EEA. It is important to appreciate that the home state regulator must be notified that an applicant wishes to use the European Passport. In the context of banking and investment business generally, a financial institution which is authorized, or licensed, and supervised in one home member state of the EEA is generally entitled to carry on its business in another host member state of the EEA, whether through a branch or on a cross-border basis, subject to the rules of the host member state governing the conduct of business. In the context of funds, the European Passport allows the offer to the public within the EEA of a fund that has been authorized as a UCITS in one member state of the EEA. The harmonization of legislation throughout the EEA to conform to certain standards defined under the various EU directives enables the European Passport to operate and regulators throughout the EEA to rely on the regulatory systems in place in the various individual EEA jurisdictions.

Exchangeable   An exchangeable debt security entitles the holder to convert the debt into the equity of a company unrelated to the issuer (cf. convertible).

Exercise   The holder of an option exercises it by using the right conferred by it to buy or to sell the underlying.

Exercise price (also strike price)   The exercise price of an option is the price, level, or rate at which, in the event that the option is exercised, the underlying is bought or sold, or with reference to which the amount of a cash settlement payment is calculated.

Expiry date   The expiry date of an option is the last day on which the option can be exercised. The right to exercise the option ceases to exist after the expiry date.

Exposure   Exposure is the amount of risk that a person assumes in respect of a counterparty, transaction, or asset. The term 'risk' in this context is not necessarily a negative: properly quantified and controlled exposure to risk gives rise to the opportunity to make profit.

FASB   The FASB is the US Financial Accounting Standards Board. The FASB issues Financial Accounting Standards (FAS).

Floor contract   A floor contract is a derivative which generally confers protection against decreases in the price, level, or rate of the underlying below a specified threshold (cf. cap contract).

Selected Glossary

FOA The FOA is the Futures and Options Association, which is the trade association of the derivative industry in the United Kingdom.

Forward contract A forward contract is a derivative contract under which the underlying is bought or sold, with payment of an agreed price and delivery of an agreed amount of the underlying being made at a specified future time.

Forward rate agreement A forward rate agreement is a derivative contract under which the rate of interest that is applied to a notional underlying loan or a notional underlying deposit is specified, and under which a payment is made of an amount calculated with reference to the difference between the specified rate and the actual rate that is applied to an actual loan or an actual deposit.

FRN An FRN is a floating rate note, which is a debt security which pays a rate of interest that is periodically reset with reference to a benchmark such as a LIBOR rate in order to reflect the prevailing interest rate environment.

FSA (also the Authority) The FSA is the Financial Services Authority, which is the unified regulator of much of the United Kingdom's financial services industry.

FSAP The FSAP is the Financial Services Action Plan, which was drafted by a committee chaired by Alexandre Lamfalussy, with the objective of securing further harmonization of European financial services regulation.

FSF The FSF is the Financial Stability Forum, which is a discussion forum for various national authorities, including central banks and supervisory authorities, responsible for financial stability. The FSF was convened in April 1999 following the near-collapse of the Long-Term Capital Management hedge fund, an event which was perceived to pose a significant systemic risk to the financial markets. The FSF has established a Working Group on Capital Flows and a Compendium of Standards which identifies various economic and financial standards necessary for sound, stable, and well-functioning financial systems.

Fungible Two financial instruments are described as being fungible if ownership of one creates the same economic exposure and the same legal rights and obligations as ownership of the other. Both fungible instruments are interchangeable. The term is usually used in the context of debt securities of the same issue.

Futures contract A futures contract is a standardized forward contract that is dealt on an exchange; standard terms specify the delivery date and the quantity of the underlying being bought or sold, and the parties agree only the price. Futures contracts are supported by the clearing and margining system supporting the exchange.

GAAP GAAP are generally accepted accounting principles, which are the accounting rules and standards that are commonly used in a particular jurisdiction or region, such as UK GAAP (which is set by the UK Accounting Standards Board) and US GAAP (which is set by the US Financial Accounting Standards Board).

Gearing The term 'gearing' has two meanings. (1) Gearing in the context of the derivative markets describes the property of a derivative to generate an exposure to varying quantities of the underlying. (2) Gearing also describes the level of debt that a person has assumed (the term 'leverage' is also used in this context).

General prohibition The general prohibition is the prohibition contained in the Financial Services and Markets Act 2000 against carrying on a regulated investment activity in the United Kingdom without authorization or an exemption from the requirement to be authorized.

Selected Glossary

Hedge A hedge is a transaction which reduces or mitigates the price risk, market risk, or credit risk arising under another transaction.

Hedge accounting Hedge accounting is a system of accounting under which an offset is recognized in a set of financial statements of (1) the change in the value of a hedge and (2) the change in the value of the corresponding asset being hedged. Hedge accounting is generally achieved through deferring bringing into account the profits and losses triggered by short-term volatility in the value of the hedge.

Hedge fund A hedge fund is a collective investment arrangement which makes use of investment techniques not usually employed in the traditional (or 'long-only') investment management industry. Owing to the diversity of hedge fund structures and strategies, there is no succinct definition of the term 'hedge fund', and indeed the term is not defined in English law. Hedge funds tend to be unregulated, but this is not a defining characteristic as some occupational pension schemes in the United Kingdom are unregulated; hedge funds tend to make extensive use of derivatives, but again this is not a defining characteristic as many financial institutions also make use of derivatives; and hedge funds tend to use techniques to short the markets and to leverage the exposures that they take, but again these techniques are not peculiar to them. Although hedge funds themselves tend to be unregulated, the investment managers and other service providers to them tend to be regulated. Owing to their unregulated status, hedge funds tend not to be marketed to the investing public. Hedge funds of funds are funds which invest in hedge funds, offering greater diversity of investment style. Various indices are also published, offering the ability to track the performance of the hedge fund sector generally.

IASB The IASB is the International Accounting Standards Board, which was formerly until 2001 the International Accounting Standards Committee, and which was first established in 1973 to promote convergence between the different accounting principles that are applied in different jurisdictions. The IASB issues International Financial Reporting Standards (which were formerly referred to as International Accounting Standards).

ICVC An ICVC is an investment company with variable capital, and it is an OEIC established in the United Kingdom.

In-the-money The term 'in-the-money' indicates that an option, from the perspective of its holder at a particular time, can be exercised profitably at that time (cf. out-of-the-money).

Initial margin Initial margin is the collateral lodged when a position is opened. The amount of initial margin is generally the amount which is sufficient to cover the maximum loss that the position might sustain during one trading session. The initial margin is returned when the position is closed. If the position makes a loss while it is open, further variation margin must also be lodged in order that after the payment of incremental losses the amount of collateral lodged is never less than the amount of initial margin.

IOSCO IOSCO is the International Organization for Governmental Securities Commissions. IOSCO is an association of global securities regulators, who work together to promote just, efficient, and sound financial markets through establishing standards of regulation and exchanging information.

ISDA ISDA is the International Swaps and Derivatives Association, Inc. ISDA was previously known as the International Swaps Dealers' Association. ISDA was formed in 1985 by a small group of participants in the nascent swap market, and the association's membership has now grown to include participants on both the sell side and the buy side, including investment banks, commercial banks, corporate treasuries, and other commercial organizations, and advisers to the industry such as law firms. ISDA's principal objective is to promote practices which are conducive to an efficient derivative market and to encourage high standards of business and commercial conduct. ISDA innovated the use of standard documentation for swap transactions, and ISDA now publishes a range of agreements and ancillary documents to legislate for different transaction structures (forwards, options, swaps, and their exotic permutations) and different classes of underlying (broadly financial assets, commodities, credit, and interests in real property). ISDA also acts as a forum for debate and lobbies governments, regulatory authorities, and other organizations on behalf of its membership.

ISMA ISMA is the International Securities Markets Association. ISMA, which was formerly the Association of International Bond Dealers, was formed on 7 February 1969, with the objective of standardizing the payment and settlement of transactions entered into in the Euromarket for debt securities. ISMA's role has since expanded, and ISMA issues rules and regulations governing both trading and settlement, as well as market conduct, disciplinary proceedings, and dispute resolution.

ISO ISO is the International Organization for Standardization, which is a federation of national bodies which develops and promotes standards for communications systems, including the numbering systems used in international commerce and finance.

LIBID LIBID is the London Interbank Bid Rate. See LIBOR.

LIBOR LIBOR is the London Interbank Offered Rate. Although the term 'LIBOR' is frequently used generically to refer to a floating rate of interest, different LIBOR rates are published by the British Bankers' Association (BBA). Each LIBOR rate reflects the cost to a bank of borrowing funds in 'marketable size' from another bank in the Interbank lending market in a particular currency for a particular term. For example, three month sterling LIBOR is the interest paid by a bank to borrow funds in pounds sterling for three months. The different LIBOR rates are calculated and published on each business day, at approximately 11:00 a.m. The BBA publishes a detailed definition of LIBOR and the definition explains the procedure that the BBA uses to calculate the different rates. Generally, banks which contribute to the process pass instructions to the BBA which indicate the rates at which they are prepared to borrow funds in 'marketable size', and the BBA calculates the average of these rates in accordance with the mathematical model that the BBA publishes. The rate at which banks are willing to lend to their customers is generally the relevant LIBOR rate plus a margin, or spread. The London Interbank Bid Rate (LIBID) is the rate at which banks are willing to lend to other banks, making up a bid and offer spread. A bank expects to pay LIBOR for funds that it borrows from another bank and to receive LIBID for funds that it lends to another bank. The LIBID-LIBOR spread is the spread that a particular bank sees from another bank; it receives the lower LIBID rate from the other bank and it pays the higher LIBOR rate to the other bank.

Liquidity Liquidity is an indication of how easy it is to buy or to sell in a particular market at prices which are commercially reasonable.

Long A long position is opened by buying, and the position is subsequently closed by making an offsetting sale. The term 'long' is also used to describe the party to a transaction who has bought or who owns the relevant asset or right (cf. short).

Selected Glossary

Lookback option A lookback option is an option under which the holder has the right to exercise at the most favourable price, level, or rate that the underlying has achieved during a specified period.

Margin Margin is collateral that is lodged by a party to cover, to the extent required, its obligations under an open position. See initial margin and variation margin.

Marking to market Marking to market is the process under which an open position is valued, usually at the end of a trading session or a trading day, in order to determine whether a profit or a loss has been made during that trading session. Valuation is determined by market prices, levels, or rates, and therefore marking to market inherently imposes the discipline of objective valuation.

MiFID MiFID[1] is the Market in Financial Instruments Directive.

Money market The money market is the market for all short-term financial instruments which are generally based on interest rates. The interest rate is either paid under the terms of the instrument or implicit in the pricing of the instrument (for example, a zero-coupon bond is issued at a discount and the difference between the discounted amount paid to buy it and the amount it repays is equivalent to interest). The money market generally includes both debt instruments and derivative products.

Multiplicative binomial model The multiplicative binomial model is a mathematical model for pricing American options.

Negotiable The term 'negotiable' connotes the ease with which an instrument is bought and sold. The capital markets are generally liquid because securities are easily transferred from sellers to buyers. The basic requisites for an instrument to be negotiable are that it is transferable by delivery or by endorsement and that transfer of it must be in such form that the holder of it from time to time can sue on it.[2]

Note A note is a debt security usually of longer maturity which is negotiable and therefore which can be traded.

NPV NPV is net present value, which is the value in the present of an amount to be paid in the future, which is calculated by discounting the amount to be paid in the future by an appropriate rate of interest. For example, assuming an interest rate of 4.5% per annum, £100 in three years is worth £87.63 now.

OEIC An OEIC is an open-ended investment company. As new investors contribute capital to the company, new shares are created and issued to them, and as existing investors redeem their investments, their shares are bought back by the company and cancelled. In this way, the capital of the company is variable, and increases or decreases, and the company is therefore described as being open-ended.

Option contract An option contract is a derivative contract under which the holder has the right, but not the obligation, to buy (in the case of a call option) or to sell (in the case of a put option) the underlying against payment of the exercise price. Although the holder of an option chooses whether or not to exercise it,[3] the holder assumes

---

[1] 2004/39/EC Directive of the European Parliament and of the Council on markets in financial instruments amending Council Directives 85/611/EEC and 93/6/EC of the European Parliament and of the Council and repealing Council Directive 93/22/EEC.

[2] See *Halsbury's Laws of England*, volume 4(1), paragraphs 306 ff, and the Bills of Exchange Act 1882.

[3] Some options are exercised automatically.

Selected Glossary

obligations if the option is exercised, for example whether to pay the exercise price (in the case of a call option) or to deliver the underlying (in the case of a put option). Options can be purely cash-settled.

Option Greeks The Option Greeks are a set of sensitivities which demonstrate how changes in the various determinants of the price of an option affect other variables, including the price of the option. The principal Option Greeks comprise delta, gamma, theta, vega, and rho.

OTC The acronym 'OTC' refers to over-the-counter, and describes sales and trading activity which takes place between market participants, whether directly or through intermediaries, and which does not involve an exchange or clearing house, or the rules of an exchange or clearing house.

Out-of-the-money The term 'out-of-the-money' indicates that an option, from the perspective of its holder at a particular time, cannot be exercised profitably at that time (cf. in-the-money).

P&L P&L is the profit and loss of a transaction or a trading book.

Part IV permission A firm that is authorized by the Financial Services Authority to carry on one or more regulated activities under the Financial Services and Markets Act 2000 is said to have a 'Part IV permission' because Part IV of that Act governs authorization.

Perimeter The Financial Services and Markets Act 2000 establishes a perimeter; regulated activities are undertaken within the perimeter, and authorization or exemption from the requirement to be authorized is needed to carry on such regulated activities, and unregulated commercial activities are undertaken outside the perimeter, and no authorization is needed to carry on such unregulated commercial activities

Physically-settled An obligation which is physically-settled is settled through making a delivery (cf. cash-settled).

Plain vanilla The term 'plain vanilla' is an adjective that is used to describe a financial instrument or structure which is uncomplicated.

Premium The premium is the price paid by a buyer to a seller to acquire an asset or a right.

Price risk (also market risk) Price risk is the risk of an adverse movement in prices, rates, or levels in a particular market.

Prime brokerage Prime brokerage is a bundle of services offered by financial institutions, usually investment banks, to funds, with the general purpose of facilitating access to a diverse range of markets (both exchange-based and OTC), reducing costs, and simplifying administration.

Put option A put option is an option which gives the holder the right, but not the obligation, to sell the underlying against receipt of the exercise price (cf. call option).

Rainbow option A rainbow option is an option under which the holder has the right to choose which underlying asset to buy (in the case of a call rainbow option) or to sell (in the case of a put rainbow option) out of a specified selection.

Random walk The random walk is a mathematical system for predicting movements in a market by using random values, generated by an application of probability theory. The key principle of the random walk is that any movement in a data population is independent of all past movements.

RCH An RCH is a recognized clearing house.

Regulatory capital Regulatory capital is the capital that a bank or other financial institution is required to hold, and not to expose to business or risk generally, in order to absorb losses which might arise from a variety of risks, including credit risk, market risk, and operational risk.

Repurchase agreement (also repo agreement) A repurchase agreement is more fully a sale and repurchase agreement, and is usually entered into in respect of underlying debt securities. A repurchase transaction takes place in two stages: an initial sale of underlying securities, and a subsequent repurchase of fungible, or equivalent, securities. Crucially, the subsequent repurchase is a forward transaction, as the price paid is agreed when the initial sale is made.

RIE An RIE is a recognized investment exchange.

Securitization Securitization is the structuring and issue into a primary market of debt securities by an issuer. The issuer uses the principal it receives on issuing the securities to develop or to acquire an asset which generates a cash flow, and the issuer uses that cash flow to finance its obligations under the securities to pay interest and to repay the principal.[4] The cash flow is said to be 'securitized'. The securities are negotiable, which means that they can be bought and sold, and transferred, easily in a secondary market, and the issuer's obligations to pay interest and to repay capital are owed to the holders of the securities from time to time. The interests of the holders of the securities are often protected by a trustee, which takes security over the assets of the issuer, including those generating the cash flow that has been securitized, and the trustee enforces that security in the event that the issuer defaults under its obligations.

Settlement Settlement of a transaction is generally completion of all of the obligations under that transaction.

Settlement price The settlement price of an exchange-based derivative is the price at which all positions which remain open at the end of a trading session are marked to market for the purposes of calculating the profit or loss of those positions and the extent to which any margin is required. The settlement price is generally calculated with reference to the closing bid and offer prices, the last actual price traded, and a weighted average of the prices traded during a specified period before the end of the trading session. The rules of the exchange specify the actual manner in which the calculation is performed.

Shari'a The Shari'a is the Islamic legal system, under which certain principles, with respect to which the conventional financial system operates, are not permitted. Accordingly, a number of financial products which do not contravene the Shari'a have been developed.

Short A short position is opened by selling, and the position is subsequently closed by making an offsetting purchase. The term 'short' is also used to describe the party to a transaction who has sold or who has the obligation to deliver the relevant asset or to perform the relevant obligation (cf. long).

Spot price (also cash price) The spot price of an asset is the price of that asset in the market for immediate delivery.

Structured finance Structured finance usually involves incorporating a derivative structure into an issue of debt securities or equity securities, in order to modify the

---

[4] For example, the well-known issue by Autostrade, the Italian motorway operator and subsidiary of the Istituto per la Ricostruzione Industriale, of the first eurobonds in 1963 was a securitization of the receivables received by Autostrade from motorway tolls.

payout of the securities, although broadly a structured product is any single product which is made up of two or more separate components.

Swap A swap is a derivative contract under which the parties make payments to each other on a series of payment dates. The amount of a payment made by a party is calculated with reference to the underlying notional amount of the swap (whether an amount of money, a commodity, shares, or another asset) and the price or rate specified to be paid by that party. The underlying is generally not delivered.

Swaption A swaption is an option written on an underlying swap.

SWIFT SWIFT is the Society for Worldwide Interbank Financial Telecommunications. SWIFT was established in 1973, to introduce a system of standard electronic messaging between banks to facilitate payments. In 1987, SWIFT expanded to provide communication links with investment exchanges, brokers, and depositaries.

Synthetic The term 'synthetic' is an adjective that is used to describe a replication of the economic effect of holding an asset. For example, a synthetic debt security might be created using one or more derivatives and the synthetic debt security replicates the cash flows and the risks of actually holding the corresponding 'real' debt security.

Synthetic Collateralized Debt Obligation (also CDO or synthetic CDO or CSO) A CDO is a securitization of the cash flow of a credit default swap.

Systemic risk The term 'systemic risk' has two meanings. (1) Systemic risk is the risk that the failure by one market participant will cause the failure of other market participants who rely on the performance by the first market participant of obligations that it owes. The crystallization of systemic risk has therefore been described as having a 'domino effect'. (2) In the context of hedge fund analysis, systemic risk is the risk of an adverse movement in the financial markets generally as opposed to the risk of an adverse movement in the price, level, or rate of particular individual assets.

Tick A tick is the minimum movement in the price of an exchange-based derivative. Each tick is represented by a monetary amount.

Total return swap A total return swap is a credit derivative under which the protection seller pays to the protection buyer the total amount that should be paid under a reference obligation, and the protection buyer pays to the protection seller the actual amount that is paid under that reference obligation. The risk of a default under that reference obligation therefore passes from the protection buyer to the protection seller.

UCITS A UCITS is an undertaking for collective investment in transferable securities, and it is therefore a type of fund vehicle. The acronym 'UCITS' is found in the UCITS 3 directives,[5] the scheme of which is to establish a European Passport for funds. A fund that is authorized as a UCITS by the regulator in one member state of the EEA can then be offered to the public in other member states of the EEA. The UCITS 3 directives define the scope of the assets that a UCITS can hold, the prudential standards that are applied to the investment management firm managing a UCITS, and the information that must be published in connection with an offering of a UCITS. The UCITS 3 directives have significantly expanded the use that a UCITS can make of derivatives.

---

[5] The original UCITS directive was Council Directive 85/611/EEC. The UCITS 3 directives are 2001/107/EC and 2001/108/EC. There was no UCITS 2 directive, as the proposed directive remained in draft.

Selected Glossary

VaR   VaR is Value-at-Risk, which is the measure of the maximum potential loss that can be expected in the market value of a portfolio under 'normal' circumstances over a specified period, given a specified level of confidence. The assumption is made that movements in the market value of the portfolio, and therefore losses, exhibit a normal distribution.

Variation margin   Variation margin is the collateral lodged to support an open position which has made a loss during a trading session. The amount of variation margin that is required is determined by marking to market the position and the amount of collateral that has already been lodged to support that position.

Volatility   Volatility is the measurement of the extent of the variability, but not the direction, of movements in a data population. It is usually calculated as the annualized standard deviation of the daily returns of the data population.

Volatility swap   A volatility swap is a swap under which payments are made to reflect the change in the volatility of the reference asset. The change in volatility is given a monetary value, and the amount of a payment is calculated with reference to the notional amount of the reference asset to which exposure is required.

Warrant (also call warrant)   A warrant is a security that is traded on an exchange under the terms of which the holder has the right, but not the obligation, to buy the underlying debt or equity securities at the specified price. Put warrants are also issued, but these are more rare than call warrants.

Yield   Yield is a measure of the return on an investment, reflecting the amount that is paid to buy the investment and any interest or distribution made under the investment. Yield is usually calculated on an annual basis. Yield is not the same as the actual return that an investment makes; for example, the yield of holding a tranche of debt securities is different from the interest paid under those debt securities.

Yield curve   The yield curve is a graphical representation comparing the yields of different issues of debt (issued by issuers of similar creditworthiness) with different maturities. The vertical axis of the graph represents the yields of the various issues of debt, and the horizontal axis represents the maturity of them. The yield curve is usually positive, indicating that long-term yields are higher than short-term yields. A negative yield curve indicates that long-term yields are lower than short-term yields.

Zero-sum game   In game theory, a zero-sum game is a scenario in which the gain made by the winner is equal to the loss made by the loser. From one perspective, futures trading is a zero-sum game.

BIBLIOGRAPHY

Furmston, M P, *Cheshire, Fifoot and Furmston's Law of Contract* (Oxford University Press, 2007)
Das, S, *Swaps/Financial Derivatives* (John Wiley & Sons Inc., 2005)
Firth, S, *Derivatives Law and Practice* (Sweet & Maxwell, 2003)
Fuller, G, *The Law and Practice of International Capital Markets* (Lexis Nexis Butterworths, 2007)
Henderson, S K, *Henderson on Derivatives* (Lexis Nexis, 2003)
Hudson, A, *The Law on Financial Derivatives* (Sweet & Maxwell, 2006)
────── *Swaps, Restitutions and Trusts* (Sweet & Maxwell, 1999)
Hull, J, *Options, Futures, and Other Derivatives* (Prentice Hall, 2007)
Parker, E, *Credit Derivatives: Documenting and Understanding Credit Derivative Products* (Globe Law and Business, 2007)
Taleb, N N, *The Black Swan: The Impact of the Highly Improbable* (Random House Inc., 2007)

Derivatives Week magazine, Institutional Investor Ltd
FOW magazine, Euromoney Institutional Investor PLC
Journal of Derivatives and Hedge Funds, Palgrave Macmillan Journals
Risk, Incisive Media Limited

INDEX

accounts
  accounting-driven transactions 11.50–11.53, 12.22
  accounting standards 11.03–11.05, 11.07–11.11
  Accounting Standards Board (ASB) 11.05, 11.07, 11.10, 11.12, 11.47
  accreting strike call options 4.156
  assets and liabilities, moving 11.46–11.53, 12.22
  balance sheets 11.04, 11.11, 11.13, 11.16, 11.47
  cash flows 11.04, 11.46
  convergence 11.15, 11.18
  definition of derivative financial instruments 11.06
  disclosure 11.05–11.08, 11.10
  Disregard Regulations 11.11
  Financial Accounting Standards Board (FASB) (United States) 11.13, 11.17
  financial accounting statements (FAS) (United States) 11.13–11.14, 11.17
  Financial Reporting Standards 11.05–11.10, 11.47–11.49
  give-up agreements 6.30, 6.36
  hedging 11.06, 11.11
  income or capital gains tax 11.33
  International Accounting Standards 11.08–11.10, 11.12, 11.15–11.18
  International Financial Reporting Board (IFRB) 11.12, 11.15–11.16
  International Financial Reporting Standards (IFRS) 11.12, 11.15–11.17
  legal risk 12.22
  loans 8.47
  margin 3.06, 3.14–3.16
  off-balance sheet instruments 11.04, 11.47
  omissions 11.04
  profit and loss accounts 11.09
  substance of transactions 11.46–11.49
  tax 11.04, 11.11, 11.21
  true and fair view 11.02–11.03
  UK accounting 11.05–11.12, 11.47
  United States accounting 11.13–11.14, 11.17
accreting strike call options 4.149–4.156, 8.47
Additional Disruption Events 7.120, 7.169
Additional Termination Event, definition of 7.49
adjustments and modifications
  Adjustment Events 7.94
  2002 ISDA Equity Derivatives Definitions 7.115–7.116
  2006 ISDA definitions 7.94
  2006 ISDA Fund Derivatives Definitions 7.229–7.237
  Potential Adjustment Event 7.230
  Price Adjustment 7.234
  shares 7.116
advisory duties 5.72, 8.110, 8.121, 8.123, 8.125–8.126
Affected Transactions 7.33
agents
  Calculation Agent 7.95, 7.151, 7.170, 7.212
  conduct of business 5.23
  hedge funds 4.200
  valuation 4.200
American-style options 4.33, 7.99–7.100
American-style Straddle 7.200
ancient world 1.18, 1.20
approved persons, definition of 5.13
arranging deals in investments 5.70
Asian (average rate) options 4.34
assumption of responsibility 8.124, 8.157, 8.158–8.161
at-the-money 4.44, 4.48, 4.78
audits 12.06
authorizations
  authorized persons 5.48–5.55, 8.43
  collective investment undertakings 9.12, 9.14
  Financial Services and Markets Act 2000 5.08
  general prohibition, civil sanctions for breach of 8.12–8.27
  open-ended investment companies (OEICs) 9.11, 9.14
  regulated activities 5.08
  UCITS 9.11
  unit trusts 9.07, 9.11
Automatic Early Termination 7.54
automatic exercise of options 4.52, 7.100, 7.194

Bachelier, Louis. *Théore de la Spéculation* 4.56–4.57
backwardation 4.30
balance sheets 4.92, 9.41, 11.04, 11.11, 11.13, 11.16, 11.47
Balancing and Settlement Code Company (ELEXON) 4.209
Baltic Exchange 2.29, 4.205

Index

Baltic International Freight Futures Exchange (BIFFEX) 2.29
Bank for International Settlements (BIS) 4.111, 10.20
Banking Consolidation Directive 5.96
bankruptcy
  credit events 7.138
  definition 7.41
  insolvency 7.41, 7.138
  ISDA 2002 Master Agreement 7.41
banks *see also* Basel Committee on Banking Supervision
  back office of banks 12.05
  Bank for International Settlements (BIS) 10.20
  Bank of England 5.83
  Banking (Special Provisions) Act 2008 10.06
  BIPRU firm 10.09
  capital 10.03, 10.09–10.10
  committees of risk managers 12.27
  credit derivatives 4.168
  documentation role of banks 12.05
  interest 11.42
  internal audits 12.06
  middle office of banks 12.04, 12.06
  risk committee of senior management of banks 12.06
  risk controllers of banks 12.27
  sales and marketing desks 12.03
barrier transactions 4.34, 4.52, 7.98, 7.207
Beckström, Rod 4.99
Basel 2 10.08, 10.13, 10.23–10.32
  Basel 3 10.08, 10.32
  Basel Capital Accord 10.23–10.25, 10.30–10.31
  Basel Committee on Banking Supervision 10.08, 10.23, 10.26–10.30
  capital adequacy 10.23-10.25, 10.28–10.32
  credit rating 10.27
  creditworthiness 10.32
  granularity 10.24
  international use 10.31
  market discipline 10.29
  market or price risk 12.16
  minimum capital requirements, defining 10.27
  operational risk 12.25
  regulatory arbitrage 10.25
  risk
    categories 10.27
    measurement and management 10.23, 10.25, 10.27–10.29
    operational 12.25
  scope 10.31
  supervisory review of capital adequacy 10.28
  three pillars 10.27–10.29

Basel Capital Accord 10.08, 10.21–10.25, 10.30–10.31, 10.10, 10.13
Basel Committee on Banking Supervision
  Bank for International Settlements (BIS) 10.20
  Basel 2 10.08, 10.23, 10.26–10.30
  Basel Capital Accord 10.08, 10.21–10.25, 10.30–10.31
  capital adequacy 10.08, 10.20–10.22
  credit risk 10.22
  FSA Handbook 10.22
  Group of Ten (G10) countries 10.20
  market risk 10.22
  operational risk 10.22
Beetroot Sugar Association 2.46
bei al-arboun (option contract) 4.162
Bermudan options 4.34, 7.99–7.100
Bermuda-style Straddle 7.200
bid and offer spread 3.03, 4.91
BIFFEX 2.29
Black Scholes equation 4.53, 4.57, 4.59
boilerplates 9.01
bonds 4.59, 4.135
Breach of Agreement, definition of 7.36
Bretton Woods System 4.113–4.119
brokers 2.09–2.12, 2.20, 9.40–9.51
Business Day 7.177
Business Day Convention 7.177
buy-side participants 2.05

Calculation Agent
  cash settlement 7.151
  2005 ISDA Commodity Definitions 7.170
  2006 ISDA definitions 7.95
  2006 ISDA Fund Derivatives Definitions 7.212, 7.230, 7.233
call options 4.149–4.156, 4.243
  accreting strike call options 4.149–4.156, 8.47
  definitions 4.32, 7.99
  development 4.55, 4.57
  embedded derivatives 4.240
  financial engineering 4.257
  long call position, analysis of 4.37–4.38
  put options 4.43
  rainbow option 4.34
  short call position, analysis of 4.39–4.40
  strategies 4.43
  Swaption Straddle 7.197
  underlying 4.33, 4.37, 4.43
  warrants 4.60
cancellation 7.233, 7.235–7.237
cap options 4.125–4.126, 4.129, 4.131, 4.257, 7.103
capable and confident customers, promoting the development of 8.142

Index

capacity risk
  counterparties 12.19
  local authority interest rate swaps cases, *ultra vires* and 8.52–8.54, 8.69, 8.88–8.89
  over-the-counter (OTC) market 8.52–8.54, 8.69, 8.88–8.89
  ultra vires 8.51

capital 10.01–10.35
  Banking (Special Provisions) Act 2008 10.06
  banks 10.03, 10.09–10.10
  Basel 2 10.08, 10.13, 10.23–10.32
  Basel Capital Accord 10.08, 10.10, 10.13
  Basel Committee 10.08, 10.20–10.22
  BIPRU 10.05, 10.08–10.09, 10.13–10.16
  BIPRU firm 10.09
  calculations 12.16
  capital resources
    capital resources requirements (CRR) 10.09–10.18
    definition 10.17–10.18
  counterparty risk, calculation of 10.16
  credit rating 10.33–10.35
  credit risk 10.02, 10.11–10.13
  directives 10.07–10.08
  financial assistance to UK deposit-taker, giving by HM Treasury of 10.06
  Financial Services and Markets Act 2000 10.03, 10.07
  Financial Services Authority (FSA)
    BIPRU 10.05, 10.08–10.09, 10.13–10.16
    GENPRU 10.03–10.04, 10.08–10.09, 10.17–10.18
    Handbook 10.03–10.04, 10.07, 10.09–10.19
    Principles for Business 10.03
    Prudential Sourcebooks 10.05
  GENPRU 10.03–10.04, 10.08–10.09, 10.17–10.18
  HM Treasury 10.06
  investment firms 10.03, 10.09–10.10
  market risk 10.11–10.12, 10.14, 12.16
  netting 10.16
  operational risk 10.11–10.12, 10.15
  Part IV permission 10.03
  Prudential Sourcebooks 10.05
  regulation 10.01–10.08
  risk 10.02
  sources of regulation 10.03–10.08
  supervisory review of capital adequacy 10.28
  systems and controls 10.18–10.19
  variable capital requirements 10.10–10.12

capital gains *see* **income or capital gains tax**

carbon trading 4.197, 4.219–4.227
  allowances 4.224–4.227
  Assigned Amount Units 4.221
  carbon dioxide 4.219
  Climate Change Convention 4.220
  definition 4.219
  ECX CFI 4.224–4.225
  EU Emissions Trading System 4.222–4.226
  European Climate Exchange 4.224
  exchanges 4.224, 4.227
  futures contracts 4.224–4.225
  greenhouse gases 4.219–4.222
  International Swaps and Derivatives Association, Inc. (ISDA) 4.227
  Joint Implementation (JI) 4.221
  Kyoto Protocol 4.220–4.222, 4.226
  Linking Directive 4.222
  Marrakesh Accords 4.221
  over-the-counter (OTC) market 4.226–4.227
  standard contracts 4.224, 4.227
  underlying 4.223, 4.226

cash flows
  accounts 11.04, 11.46
  characterization 11.27–11.28
  circular 12.22
  definition 4.255
  financial engineering 4.254–4.257
  forward cash flow 4.09
  give-up agreements 6.36
  income or capital gains tax 11.23, 11.27–11.28
  legal risk 12.22
  regulated activities 5.58
  securitization of derivative cash flows 4.07, 4.230–4.239
  wrappers 4.229–4.244

cash settlement
  Calculation Agent 7.151
  Cash Settlement Amount 7.149–7.150
  Cash Settlement Date 7.149
  contracts 1.08
  credit derivatives 4.167
  Final Price 7.149, 7.151
  forward transactions 7.101–7.102
  2002 ISDA Equity Derivatives Definitions 7.111
  2003 ISDA Credit Derivatives Definitions 7.129, 7.149–7.152
  no delivery made 1.08
  Option Transaction 7.99
  Partial Cash Settlement Terms 7.155
  Reference Obligation 7.149–7.152
  Reference Price 7.149
  restructuring 8.200
  Swaption Straddle 7.201
  swaptions 7.195, 7.201
  Valuation Date 7.152

Index

Castelli, Charles, *The Theory of Options in Stocks and Shares* 4.55
catastrophe swaps 8.46
caveat emptor 8.95, 8.108
certainty
  2003 ISDA Credit Derivatives Definitions 7.158
  commercial certainty 8.76, 8.127
  contractual certainty 1.21, 4.160, 8.02, 8.34
  duty of care 8.127
  Islamic compliant derivatives 4.160
  local authority swaps cases 1.21, 8.76
  recharacterization of derivative contracts 8.34
  standard forms 7.08
Change in Law 7.120, 7.235
CHAPS 2.45
charges
  fixed charges 4.230, 6.26–6.27
  floating charges 6.26–6.27
  insolvency risk 6.26–6.27
  priority 6.26–6.27
  securitization 4.230
cherry-picking transactions 7.21
Chiang and Okunev model 4.59
Chicago Board of Trade (CBOT) 4.18
Chicago Mercantile Exchange (CME) 4.18
Chicago Produce Exchange 4.18
civil sanctions for breach of general prohibition 8.12–8.27
  authorization, carrying on business without 8.12–8.27
  compensation 8.12
  enforcement of contracts 8.12–8.27
  exemptions, carrying on business without 8.12–8.27
  Financial Services and Markets Act 2000 5.49–5.53, 8.12–8.27
  futures contract
    commercial or investment purposes, made for 8.22–8.27
    definition of 8.21–8.27
  insurance contracts 8.43
  recovery of money paid 8.12
  regulated activities 8.12–8.27
  regulated option and unregulated option, differentiation between 8.20
clearing
  capacity risk 8.51
  ChangeAlley 2.45
  CHAPs 2.45
  Clearnet SA 2.48
  collateral to minimize risk, payment of 2.16
  dematerialized shares in clearing 7.113
  electricity and power trading 4.211, 4.218
  exchanges 2.08, 2.12–2.17, 2.44, 2.46–2.48
  general clearing member (GCM) 6.30, 6.32–6.34, 6.36–6.40
  give-up agreements 6.28–6.40
  guarantees for counterparties 2.12
  individual clearing member (ICM) 6.30
  insolvency risk 6.11
  International Air Transport Association (IATA) 2.45
  LCH.Clearnet 2.46–2.48
  legal market structures 5.78
  London Clearing House 6.09
  London Metal Exchange 2.39
  margining 2.08, 2.16, 3.05–3.18, 6.11
  novation 2.13–2.16
  overseas clearing houses 6.07
  over-the-counter (OTC) market 1.23, 7.01
  ownership by members of exchange 2.17
  prime brokerage 9.43, 9.45
  Railway Clearing House 2.45
  recognised clearing houses (RCHs) 6.02–6.09
  registration 2.13
  risk 2.12, 2.14, 2.16
  seller 2.13
  UCITS 9.19
  ultra vires 8.51
Climate Change Convention 4.220
cliquet (ratchet) option 4.34
close-out netting 7.25, 7.70–7.71, 8.191
collars 4.129–4.131
collateral
  clearing 2.16
  counterparties 2.21
  exchanges 2.08, 2.16
  ISDA 2002 Master Agreement 7.25
  margining 2.08, 2.16, 3.07–3.08
  over-the-counter (OTC) market 2.21
  prime brokerage 9.50
  UCITS 9.19
collateralized debt obligations (CDOs) 4.164, 4.183–4.184, 4.190, 4.192
collective investment undertakings *see also* UCITS (undertakings for collective investment in transferable securities)
  admission of shares to trading 9.05
  authorization 9.12, 9.14
  authorized unit trusts (AUTs) 9.07
  classification 9.06–9.07
  closed-ended structure 9.04–9.05, 9.25
  COLL 9.15
  definition 9.03, 9.06
  financial promotion 9.04

Index

Financial Services and Markets Act 2000 9.06, 9.12
hedge funds 9.25
independence 9.07
investment management 9.03–9.07, 9.12–9.15
open-ended structure 9.04, 9.06–9.11, 9.25
overseas, schemes that are authorized 9.12
Prospectus Directive 9.05
public offers of shares 9.05
regulation 9.14–9.15
unit trust schemes 9.07
variable capital, investment companies with (ICVC) 9.09–9.10
commercial activities and investment activities, differentiation between 5.74–5.76
commission 5.23, 8.166
Committee of European Banking Supervisors (CEBS) 5.93
Committee of European Securities Regulators (CESR) 5.93
commodity definitions *see* 2005 ISDA Commodity Definitions
commodity derivatives 2.29
commodity forward contracts 4.31
commodity swaps 4.102–4.109
  applications 4.103
  consumer swaps 4.106–4.109
  counterparties 4.103
  exchange of exposure to movements in underlying price 4.102–4.108
  fixed amounts 4.104–4.105, 4.107–4.109
  floating amounts 4.105, 4.107–4.108
  fluctuations 4.104–4.107
  freight, price of 4.103
  futures contracts, price of 4.103
  in-the-money 4.105, 4.108–4.109
  netting 4.102, 4.105
  out-of-the-money 4.108–4.109
  over-the-counter (OTC) market 4.103
  payment dates 4.102, 4.105–4.107
  price
    risk 4.106
    underlying 4.102–4.108
  producer swaps 4.104, 4.109
  purpose 4.102
  soft or hard commodity, price of 4.103
  spot price 4.103, 4.105, 4.108
  underlying price 4.102–4.108
communications failure, risk of 2.44
Companies Act 1989, risk of insolvency of exchange members and 6.10–6.27
  avoiding transfers 6.19
  charges 6.20–6.24
  clearing houses, risk to 6.11

disclaimer of onerous property 6.19
fiduciary duty, breach of 6.25
financial markets, safeguarding of 6.12
fixed charges 6.26–6.27
floating charges 6.26–6.27
Insolvency Rules 6.10
market charges 6.20–6.24, 6.27
market contracts 6.13–6.16, 6.19
market property 6.25
modifications of insolvency law 6.14, 6.20
net sums 6.17–6.18
preferential debts 6.10
priority 6.10, 6.26–6.27
property 6.25
qualified floating charges 6.10
recognized investment exchanges (RIEs) and recognized clearing houses (RCHs) 6.11, 6.13–6.20
rescission of contracts 6.19
security 6.10
set-off 6.10
settlement 6.16
systemic risk 6.11, 6.18
compensation *see also* **damages**
  early termination 7.66–7.67
  Financial Ombudsman Service (FOS) 8.170
  general prohibition, civil sanctions for breach of 5.52, 8.12
  retail offers 8.170
complex products 8.08, 8.158–8.159, 8.162
compound interest, awards of 8.06, 8.59–8.62, 8.66, 8.73, 8.93
computed data 4.207–4.208
conduct of business
  agents 5.23
  categorization of clients 5.24–5.28
  commission 5.23
  Conduct of Business Sourcebook (COBS) 5.22–5.29
  criminal offences 5.26
  EC law 5.98
  eligible counterparties 5.24
  false or misleading statements 5.26, 5.30
  fees 5.23
  financial promotion 5.24, 5.26
  Financial Services Authority (FSA) 5.12, 5.79, 5.85
  FSA Handbook 5.22, 5.26, 5.30
  information, provision of 5.23–5.24, 5.26, 5.29–5.30
  insider information 5.30
  legal market structures 5.79, 5.85
  market abuse 5.30
  Market Conduct sourcebook (MAR) 5.30–5.31

Index

conduct of business (*cont*):
  Market in Financial Instruments Directive
    (MiFiD) 5.24
  professional clients 5.28
  recommendations 5.27–5.28
  regulated activities 5.24
  regulation 5.22–5.30
  retail clients, protection of 5.25, 8.142
  risk warnings 5.26
confidentiality 4.92
confirmations
  2006 ISDA definitions 7.94
  credit events 7.147
  International Swaps and Derivatives Association,
    Inc. (ISDA) 7.12, 7.88–7.90
  master agreements 7.04, 7.05
  over-the-counter (OTC) market
    documentation 7.04, 7.05
  prime brokerage 9.50
  swaps 7.183
  swaptions 7.193
conflicts of interest 8.140, 8.141
constant proportion debt obligation
    (CPDO) 4.194
constant proportion portfolio insurance
    (CPPI) 4.02, 4.132–4.147
  advantages 4.147
  derivative structuring techniques 4.02
  exposure to the underlying 4.02
  formula 4.136–4.147
  index, calculation of value of 4.02, 4.132–4.147
  risk-free and risky assets 4.133–4.146
  synthetic CPPI structures 4.194
  underlying 4.02, 4.132–4.133
  use 4.132
  value, calculation of 4.132–4.147
  variations 4.147
  wrapper 4.132
  zero-coupon bonds 4.135
construction of contracts 8.04, 8.28–8.32
consumer protection 6.05, 8.95, 8.113, 8.143
contango 4.30
contract, swaps analysed as 8.182–8.191
  close-out netting 8.191
  conditions precedent, imposition of 8.188
  definition of a swap 8.183
  disjointed option analysis 8.188
  economic effect of swap, intended 8.188–8.189
  executor contract analysis 8.186–8.189, 8.191
  financial forwards analysis 8.188
  forward payments 8.186–8.188
  interest rates 8.183, 8.188–8.189
  ISDA 2002 Master Agreement 8.191
  local authority swaps cases, *ultra vires*
    and 8.190–8.191
  mutual debts analysis 8.186–8.189, 8.191
  netting 8.183–8.184, 8.188, 8.191
  pricing methods 8.187
  repayment analysis 8.188
  settlement 8.183
  single executory contract, swap as 8.186,
    8.188, 8.190
  subsidiary analyses 8.188
  underlying 8.184, 8.189
contracts *see also* **futures contracts; option contracts;**
    standard contracts; terms
  bid and offer spread 3.03
  capacity 8.03
  cash-settled contracts 1.08
  certainty 1.21, 4.160, 8.02, 8.34
  commercial purposes, contracts made for 5.64
  complexity 2.19–2.20
  construction of terms, of derivative contract 8.02,
    8.28–8.32
  definition of a derivative 1.01–1.03
  definition of derivative contracts 1.03
  development of new contracts 1.22
  differences, contracts for 5.65–5.66, 5.74–5.76
  duty of care 8.124
  electricity and power trading 4.210
  forward rate agreements (FRA) 4.63–4.68
  gaming contracts 8.36
  give-up agreements 6.28–6.40, 9.46, 9.48–9.49
  guaranteed investment contracts
    (GIC) 4.185–4.186
  income or capital gains tax 11.29–11.33
  insurance 8.37–8.46
  legal issues 8.01–8.05, 8.07–8.09, 8.182–8.191
  legal risk 12.20
  liquidity 2.20
  London Metal Exchange 2.39
  market contracts 6.13–6.16, 6.19
  misrepresentations 8.03, 8.07
  novation 2.15, 7.156
  off-exchange contracts 2.11
  on-exchange contracts 2.11
  over-the-counter (OTC) market 2.19–2.20,
    8.01–8.02
  recharacterization risk 8.05, 8.33–8.48
  records 8.04
  repurchase and reverse repurchase
    agreements 4.245–4.253
  swaps 4.169, 8.182–8.191
  tick and basis point 3.04
controlled activities 5.33, 5.35, 5.39–5.40,
    5.46, 5.77

Index

convertible and exchangeable debt, wrapper for 4.241–4.244
copper 2.36
corporate treasuries 9.52–9.54
corporate trustees 4.230
corporation tax 11.25
correlation risk 12.17
cost-of-carry concept 2.36
counterparties
  buyers of derivatives 1.17
  capacity risk 12.19
  checks 7.01
  collateral 2.21
  commodity swaps 4.103
  conduct of business 5.24
  creditworthiness 7.01
  exchanges 2.12, 2.14
  failure to fulfil obligations 2.12
  guarantees 2.12
  infrastructure 1.23
  ISDA 2002 Master Agreement 7.29, 7.32
  ISDA Credit Support Documents 7.70–7.71, 7.82
  legal market structures 5.78, 5.83
  list of types of 1.16
  listed money market institutions (LMMI) 5.83
  margin 3.07
  market service providers 2.23, 2.25
  netting 7.29
  over-the-counter (OTC) market 2.20 1.23, 2.20–2.21, 7.01
  reputation risk 12.26
  risk 2.12, 2.14, 6.01, 7.01, 7.29, 7.32, 7.70–7.71, 7.82, 10.16, 12.19, 12.26
  sellers of derivatives 1.17
Cox, Ingersoll and Ross model 4.59
CPPI *see* constant proportion portfolio insurance (CPPI)
credit default swaps
  collateralized debt obligations (CDOs) 4.185–4.190
  credit derivatives 4.172–4.174
  insurance contracts 8.37
  interpretation 8.28–8.32
  securitization 4.230
credit derivatives 4.03, 4.164–4.194, 4.228
    see also credit derivatives documentation; **2003 ISDA Credit Derivatives Definitions**
  cash settlement 4.167
  collateralized debt obligations 4.164, 4.183–4.190, 4.192
  commercial banks 4.168

constant proportion debt obligation (CPDO) 4.194
credit default swap contracts 4.172–4.174
credit event 4.166–4.167, 4.173, 4.177, 4.182, 4.191, 4.228
credit index 4.193
credit risk 4.03, 4.164–4.177
credit spread option contracts 4.172, 4.178–4.182
creditworthiness 4.171
debt securities 4.178–4.182, 4.191
delivery obligation 4.167
development of market 4.191–4.194
first transactions 4.191
guarantees 4.164
indices 4.193
insolvency 4.164
insurance contracts 8.37, 8.40, 8.42, 8.45
investment funds 4.170
OTC credit default swap contracts 4.172–4.174
OTC credit spread option contracts 4.172, 4.178–4.182
OTC total return swap contracts 4.172, 4.175–4.177
physical settlement 4.167
price 4.171
protection buyers and sellers 4.165, 4.175
securitization 4.172
settlements 4.166–4.167
standard contracts 4.193
swaps 4.124
synthetic collateralized debt obligations (CDOs) 4.183–4.190, 4.192
synthetic CPPI structures 4.194
total return swap contracts 4.172, 4.175–4.177
transactions 4.165–4.172
underlying 4.03
credit derivatives documentation 8.10, 8.192–8.206
  2003 ISDA Credit Derivatives Definitions 7.127–7.158, 8.197–8.198, 8.201–8.206
  credit event 8.192, 8.194, 8.196, 8.200
  credit risk 8.192–8.198, 8.200
  default 8.192
  definitions 8.192, 8.194–8.197
  development of 8.10, 8.192–8.206
  International Swaps and Derivatives Association, Inc. (ISDA) standard documentation 8.193, 8.197–8.198, 8.201–8.205
  National Power plc, demerger of 8.196
  Physical Settlement 8.199–8.200
  restructuring issue 8.193–8.194, 8.199–8.205

Index

credit derivatives documentation (*cont*):
  settlement 8.199–8.200, 8.203, 8.205
  successor issue 8.193–8.198
  underlying 8.192
credit events
  2003 ISDA Credit Derivatives
    Definitions 7.137–7.147
  collateralized debt obligations (CDOs) 4.187
  credit derivatives 4.166–4.168, 4.173, 4.177,
    4.182, 4.191, 8.192, 8.194, 8.196, 8.200
  Credit Event Upon Merger, definition of 7.48
  credit risk 8.194, 8.196, 8.197, 8.200
  definition 4.168, 8.29, 8.31
  notification 4.167
  restructuring 7.154, 8.200
  settlement 4.167
  types 4.166
credit events, 2003 ISDA Credit Derivatives
    Definitions and 7.137–7.147
  amendment of terms of Obligations 7.145
  Bankruptcy 7.137–7.138
  Confirmation 7.147
  Credit Event Notice 7.148
  credit protection 7.146
  Default Requirement 7.139, 7.144
  Failure to Pay 7.137, 7.141
  Fixed Amounts 7.146
  Obligation Acceleration 7.137, 7.139–7.140
  Obligation Default 7.137, 7.140
  observing credit events 7.147
  Publicly Available Information 7.147
  Reference Entity 7.137–7.144
  Repudiation/Moratorium 7.137,
    7.142–7.143, 7.147
  Restructuring 7.137, 7.144–7.145, 7.154
  settlement 7.148, 7.150, 7.152, 7.154
credit rating
  Basel 2 10.27
  buy-side 10.33
  capital adequacy 10.33–10.35
  credit risk 10.34
  creditworthiness 10.33–10.35
  due diligence 10.34–10.35
  FSA Handbook 10.35
  interest rate swaps 4.83, 4.85, 4.92
  rating agencies 7,95
  sell-side 10.33–10.35
credit risk
  2003 ISDA Credit Derivatives Definitions 7.158
  Basel Committee 10.22
  capital 10.02, 10.11–10.13
  calculation 10.13
  collateralized debt obligations (CDOs) 4.184,
    4.187–4.188

credit derivatives 4.03, 4.164–4.177
credit derivatives documentation
  credit events 8.194, 8.196, 8.197, 8.200
  Obligations 8.194, 8.197–8.198
  Reference Entity 8.194–8.198
  successor issue 8.193–8.198
credit event 4.166, 8.194, 8.196, 8.197, 8.200
credit rating 10.34
crystallization 4.165
give-up agreements 6.39
guarantees 4.164
insolvency 4.164
local authority interest rate swaps cases, *ultra vires*
  and 8.88
Obligations 8.194, 8.197–8.198
prime brokerage 9.41
protection buyers and sellers 4.165
purpose of derivatives 1.05
Reference Entity 8.194–8.198
settlements 4.166–4.167
standard forms 7.10
successor issue 8.193–8.198
UCITS 9.19
credit support *see* **ISDA Credit Support Documents**
creditworthiness 4.171, 7.01, 10.32–10.35
criminal offences
  conduct of business 5.26
  false or misleading statements 5.26
  financial promotion 5.33–5.34
  general prohibition 5.49, 5.54–5.55
  operational risk 12.24
Cross-Default, definition of 7.40
currency
  2003 ISDA Credit Derivatives Definitions 7.134
  2006 ISDA Definitions 7.175
  debt capital market, first currency swap to
    complement a 4.121
  deutschmark
    debt capital market, first currency swap to
      complement a 4.121
    undervaluing of 4.115–4.118
  devaluation 4.119
  first currency swap 4.120
  fixed currency exchange rates 4.113–4.120
  foreign exchange options 4.59
  interest rate swaps 4.101
  reserve currencies, designation of 4.114
  sterling as reserve currency 4.114
  swaps 4.121–4.122
  US dollar 4.113–4.119, 4.122
  World Bank and IBM, currency swap
    between 4.122
  yen, undervaluing of 4.115–4.118
custody services 9.44

Index

damages *see also* **compensation**
   general damages 8.92
   local authority interest rate swaps cases, *ultra vires* and 8.92
   misrepresentation 8.130, 8.131–8.133
   retail offers 8.155, 8.170
   simple interest 8.92
   special damages 8.92
Das, Satyajit 4.97
dealers, role of 4.89–4.93
dealing in investments 5.69–5.70
debt securities
   collateralized debt obligations (CDOs) 4.183
   convertible and exchangeable debt, wrapper for 4.241–4.244
   credit derivatives 4.178–4.182, 4.191
   embedded derivatives 4.240
   financial engineering 4.255
   hedging 4.239
   notes 4.234
   prime brokerage 9.44
   repayment amount 4.234–4.236
   retail offers 8.145
   securitization 4.230–4.236, 4.239
   sukuks (debt securities) 4.161
deceit 8.130
Default Under Specified Transaction, definition of 7.39
definition of a derivative 1.01–1.03
definitions *see* **2006 ISDA definitions**
Delisting 7.119
Deliverable Obligations 7.153–7.155, 8.200, 8.203–8.204
delivery date 4.17, 4.18, 4.30, 7.164
deposits 4.66–4.67
derivative contracts, definition of 1.03, 1.22
design of products 8.141, 8.162
Deutsche Bank 4.123
digital options 4.34
differences, contracts for 5.65–5.66, 5.74–5.76
disclaimers 6.19, 7.94, 8.111
disclosure
   accounts 11.05–11.08, 11.10
   commission 8.166
   discounts 8.166
   fees 8.166
   Financial Ombudsman Service (FOS) 8.170
   misrepresentation 8.129
   retail offers 8.163–8.168
discounts 4.68, 8.57–8.58, 8.166
Disrupted Days 7.112, 7.227–7.228
Disruption Fallback 7.170
distributors, responsibility of 8.145–8.157
dividends 7.114, 7.238

documentation *see also* **credit derivatives documentation; ISDA Credit Support Documents**
   2002 ISDA Equity Derivatives Definitions 7.108
   banks, duty of 12.05
   duty of care 8.94, 8.125–8.126, 8.128
   give-up agreements 6.39
   local authority interest rate swaps cases, *ultra vires* and 8.90
   misrepresentation 8.129
   multi-asset derivatives 4.196
   over-the-counter (OTC) market documentation 7.01–7.10
   prime brokerage 9.46, 9.48
   retail offers 8.142, 8.162–8.168, 8.170
   risk 12.05
   standards 8.09
double tax treaties
   definition 11.45
   jurisdiction 11.45
   treaties 11.45
due diligence
   credit rating 10.34–10.35
   financial promotion 5.34
   general prohibition 5.54
   local authority interest rate swaps cases, *ultra vires* and 8.88–8.89
   over-the-counter (OTC) market 7.01
   retail offers 8.157
duty of care 8.07, 8.94–8.141
   advisory duties 8.110, 8.121, 8.123, 8.125–8.126
   antecedent communications 8.117
   assumption of responsibility 8.124, 8.152–8.153
   Bankers Trust case 8.96–8.113, 8.123, 8.129
   categorization of customers 8.94
   caveat emptor 8.95, 8.108
   commercial certainty 8.127
   conflicts of interest 8.141
   consumer protection 8.95, 8.113
   contractual context 8.124
   descriptions 8.114–8.120
   disclaimers 8.111
   documentation 8.94, 8.125–8.126, 8.128
   economic loss 8.124
   explanations, duty to provide 8.07
   fair, just and reasonableness test 8.103, 8.124, 8.152–8.153
   foreseeability 8.103, 8.124, 8.151–8.152
   good faith 8.127
   incremental test 8.124, 8.152
   ISDA 2002 Master Agreement 8.109, 8.112
   limitation of liability 8.94

duty of care (*cont*):
  Market in Financial Instruments Directive (MiFiD) 8.113
  misrepresentation 8.100, 8.106–8.107, 8.117–8.136
  misselling 8.120, 8.137
  negligent misstatements 8.121, 8.126
  over-the-counter (OTC) market 8.07, 8.95, 8.97, 8.108, 8.112
  Peekay case 8.114–8.120, 8.123, 8.129, 8.164
  product design 8.141, 8.162
  proximity 8.103, 8.124, 8.151–8.152
  reliance, degree of 8.110–8.111, 8.122, 8.154
  retail customers 8.08, 8.120, 8.142–8.181
  risks
    disclosure of 8.113, 8.117
    warnings 8.117
  skill and care 8.94, 8.104
  sophisticated investors 8.125–8.126
  Springwell case 8.121–8.128, 8.129
  standard representations 8.112
  standards 8.113
  statements made at outset of relationship 8.124, 8.126
  suitability 8.137–8.140, 8.157, 8.159–8.160
  swaps 8.97–8.113
  terms of business agreements 8.110
  term sheets explaining financial implications of deals 8.110
  unusual or onerous clauses, bringing party's attention to 8.127

early termination
  2002 ISDA Equity Derivatives Definitions 7.108
  Affected Parties, number of 7.58
  Automatic Early Termination 7.54
  Close-Out Amount 7.58–7.62
  compensation 7.66–7.67
  crystallization of obligations 7.51
  Early Termination Amount 7.57–7.62, 7.65, 7.86
  Early Termination Date 7.52, 7.54–7.56, 7.68
  Events of Default 7.52–7.54, 7.57–7.62
  interest, calculation of 7.66–7.68
  ISDA 2002 Master Agreement
    Automatic Early Termination 7.54
    compensation, calculation of 7.66–7.67
    crystallization of obligations 7.51
    Early Termination Amount 7.57–7.62, 7.65
    Early Termination Date 7.52, 7.54–7.56, 7.68
    Events of Default 7.52–7.54, 7.57–7.62
    interest, calculation of 7.66–7.68
    Market Quotation and Loss 7.63
    penalty clauses 7.64
    set-off 7.65
    Tax Event 7.55
    Termination Event 7.50, 7.52–7.53, 7.55, 7.57–7.62
  ISDA Credit Support Documents 7.86
  Market Quotation and Loss 7.63
  penalty clauses 7.64
  set-off 7.65
  Tax Event 7.55
  Termination Event 7.50, 7.52–7.53, 7.55, 7.57–7.62

EC law 5.87–5.102 *see also* **Market in Financial Instruments Directive (MiFiD)**
  Banking Consolidation Directive 5.96
  Basel Capital Accord 10.08
  capital 10.07–10.08
  Committee of European Banking Supervisors (CEBS) 5.93
  Committee of European Securities Regulators (CESR) 5.93
  conduct of business 5.98
  credit institutions 5.96
  directives 4.222, 5.87, 5.93–5.94, 5.96, 10.07–10.08
  Emissions Trading System 4.222–4.226
  Euratom 5.89
  European Climate Exchange 4.224
  European Coal and Steel Community (ECSC) 5.89
  European Community 5.89
  European Economic Area (EEA) 5.88, 5.90, 5.91, 5.94–5.95, 5.98
  European Economic Community (EEC) 5.89
  European Free Trade Area (EFTA) 5.88, 5.90–5.91
  Financial Services Action Plan (FSAP) 5.94
  Financial Services and Markets Act 2000 5.87
  Financial Services Authority (FSA) 5.98
  fit and proper persons test 5.95
  futures contracts 4.224–4.225
  harmonization 5.92–5.93
  home state regulators 5.95
  International Financial Reporting Standards (IFRS) 11.12
  investment firms 5.97–5.102
  Investment Services Directive 5.97–5.98
  Lamfalussy Committee 5.94
  legislation 5.87
  Linking Directive 4.222
  Merger Treaty 5.89
  passport 5.94–5.95
  regulated activities 5.97
  single market 5.87–5.88
  Switzerland 5.90

Index

Treaty of Rome 5.89
Treaty on European Union 5.89
UCITS 5.95, 5.97, 9.11, 9.13, 9.20, 9.23
unfair contract terms 8.178, 8.180
economic loss 8.124, 8.132, 8.152
economic policies, coordination of 4.115
education of customers 8.142
Effective Date 7.128, 7.162
electricity and power trading 4.197, 4.209–4.218
   Balancing and Settlement Code Company (ELEXON) 4.209
   BSC Trading Parties 4.209, 4.211–4.217
   clearing 4.211, 4.218
   contracts 4.210
   ELEXON 4.209
   Energy Imbalance Prices 4.214–4.216
   forward sales 4.213–4.214, 4.218
   Gate Closure 4.213–4.216
   imbalances, system for payment of 4.210–4.211, 4.214–4.216
   National Grid 4.209, 4.212, 4.214–4.215
   over-the-counter (OTC) market 4.210
   power exchanges 4.210
   settlement 4.211, 4.218
   spot sales 4.213–4.214, 4.218
   System Buy Price 4.216
electronic trading
   exchanges 1.15, 2.18, 2.27, 2.44
   ICE Futures 2.43
   London Metal Exchange 2.39
   market service providers 2.22
   NYSE Euronext LIFFE 2.30–2.31
embedded derivatives 4.240
emission derivatives, definition of 1.22
end-users 9.01–9.54
   buy-side 2.05
   corporate treasuries 9.52–9.54
   exchanges 2.09–2.12
   failure to fulfil obligations 2.12
   hedge funds 9.25–9.39
   investment management industry 9.01–9.24
   price 2.10
   prime brokerage 9.40–9.51
   risk 2.12
enforcement
   Financial Services Authority (FSA) 5.11
   general prohibition, civil sanctions for breach of 8.12–8.27
   insurance contracts 8.39, 8.44
   legal risk 12.20
   local authority interest rate swaps cases, *ultra vires* and 8.55, 8.58
   securitization 4.230
   ultra vires 8.50, 8.55, 8.58

Equity Amount 7.105, 7.107–7.111
equity derivatives *see* equity swap transactions, 2002 ISDA Equity Derivatives Definitions
equitable remedies 8.60, 8.63, 8.65–8.80, 8.83, 8.87, 8.89, 8.93
equity swap transactions, 2002 ISDA Equity Derivatives Definitions and
   Cash Settlement Payment Date 7.111
   documentation 7.108
   early termination 7.108
   Equity Amount 7.105, 7.107–7.111
   Equity Amount Payer 7.105, 7.109
   Equity Amount Receiver 7.105, 7.110
   long Equity Swap Transactions 7.109
   payments 7.105–7.106
   price 7.105–7.106, 7.109–7.110
   Rate of Return 7.107
   reset 7.105
   sell side of market 7.108
   underlying 7.107, 7.109–7.110
error *see* mistake
Euratom 5.89
Euronext 2.32
European Coal and Steel Community (ECSC) 5.89
European Community 5.89
European Economic Area (EEA) 5.88, 5.90, 5.91, 5.94–5.95, 5.98
European Economic Community (EEC) 5.89
European Free Trade Area (EFTA) 5.88, 5.90–5.91
European-style options 4.33, 7.99
European-style Swaption Straddle 7.200
European Union 5.89 *see also* EC law
Events of Default, ISDA 2002 Master Agreement and 7.31–7.50, 7.52–7.54
   Bankruptcy, definition of 7.41
   Breach of Agreement, definition of 7.36
   Credit Default Support, definition of 7.37
   Cross-Default, definition of 7.40
   Default Under Specified Transaction, definition of 7.39
   definitions 7.34–7.42
   early termination 7.52–7.54, 7.57–7.63
   Failure to Pay or Deliver, definition of 7.35
   interest, calculation of 7.67
   Merger Without Assumption, definition of 7.42
   Misrepresentation, definition of 7.38
   Repudiation of Agreement, definition of 7.36
   Specified Transaction, definition of 7.39
   Termination Events 7.31–7.52
exchange-based market 2.07–2.18, 8.01
   brokers 2.09–2.12
   capacity risk 8.51

exchange-based market (cont):
  carbon trading 4.224, 4.227
  Chicago Mercantile Exchange (CME) 4.18
  Chicago Produce Exchange 4.18
  clearing 2.08, 2.12–2.17, 2.44, 2.46–2.48
  collateral to minimize risk, payment of 2.08, 2.16
  communications failure, risk of 2.44
  Companies Act 1989 6.10–6.27
  competition 2.07
  counterparties 2.12, 2.14, 5.78
  descriptions of exchanges 2.27–2.48
  electricity and power trading 4.210
  electronic trading 1.15, 2.18, 2.27, 2.44
  elements of markets 2.07
  Emissions Trading System 4.224
  end-users 2.09–2.12
  Exchange-traded Contract 7.112
  failure to fulfil obligations 2.12
  flow of payments in exchange-based markets 3.07
  freight derivatives 4.205
  futures contracts 4.18
  give-up agreements 6.28–6.40
  globalization 2.27
  guarantees 2.12
  hedge funds 9.30
  hedging 2.43
  historical background 1.18–1.19
  ICE Futures 2.41–2.43
  insolvency risk 6.01, 6.10–6.27
  IntercontinentalExchange (ICE) 2.43
  International Petroleum Exchange
    (IPE) 2.41–2.43
  LCH.Clearnet 2.46–2.48
  LIFFE 6.09
  liquidity 2.14
  London Commodities Exchange 2.29
  London Metal Exchange 2.33–2.40
  London Stock Exchange 2.28–2.29
  London Traded Options Market 2.29
  margining 2.08, 2.16, 3.05–3.07
  market-makers 2.09
  market service providers 2.22, 2.25–2.26
  members 2.09, 2.17
  novation 2.13–2.15
  New York Stock Exchange (NYSE) 2.32
  NYSE Euronext LIFFE 2.28–2.32
  off-exchange contracts 2.11
  on-exchange contracts 2.11
  open-outcry (physical trading) 2.18
  option contracts 4.35, 4.55
  over-the-counter (OTC) market 2.08, 5.78, 6.01
  participants 2.07
  price 2.08, 2.10, 2.44
  prime brokerage 9.43, 9.45

  recognized investment exchanges (RIEs) and
    recognized clearing houses (RCHs) 6.09
  registration 2.13
  regulated activities 5.64
  risk 2.12, 2.14, 2.16, 2.44
  sellers 2.13
  settlement 2.44
  standard contracts 1.15, 2.07–2.08, 4.18
  tick and basis point 3.04
  UCITS 9.16–9.17, 9.19
  ultra vires 8.51
  virtual exchanges 2.18, 2.27, 2.44
  warrants 4.61
exchange rates 4.113–4.120
**exchangeable debt and convertible debt, wrapper
  for** 4.241–5.244
exemptions
  financial promotion 5.40, 5.44–5.47
  general prohibition, civil sanctions for breach
    of 8.12–8.27
  income or capital gains tax 11.23
  recognized investment exchanges (RIEs) and
    recognized clearing houses (RCHs) 6.05
exercise price of options 4.36–4.39, 4.41–4.44
explanations, duty to provide 8.07
**extraordinary events, 2002 ISDA Equity
  Derivatives Definitions and** 7.117–7.125
  2006 ISDA definitions 7.94–7.96
  2006 ISDA Fund Derivatives
    Definitions 7.231–7.235
  Additional Disruption Events 7.120
  Change in Law 7.120
  consequences of events 7.119
  Delisting 7.119
  Hedging Disruption 7.120
  Increased Cost of Hedging 7.120
  indices, affecting 7.117–7.118
  Insolvency 7.119
  Merger Event 7.119
  Nationalization 7.119
  option valuation 7.121–7.125
  payments 7.121
  shares, affecting 7.117
  Tender Offer 7.119

Failure to Pay 7.35, 7.137, 7.141
fair, just and reasonableness test
  duty of care 8.103, 8.124, 8.151–8.152
  retail offers 8.151–8.152
fatwas 4.159, 4.163
fees 5.23, 8.166
fiduciaries 6.25, 8.59, 8.136
**Financial Accounting Standards Board (FASB)
  (United States)** 11.13, 11.17

Index

financial accounting statements (FAS) (United States) 11.13–11.14, 11.17
financial assistance to UK deposit-taker, giving by HM Treasury of 10.06
financial engineering
  building blocks 4.254, 4.256
  call options 4.257
  cap options 4.257
  cash flow 4.254–4.257
  characteristics 4.254
  debt securities 4.255
  definition 4.254
  floor options 4.257
  homogeneity 4.257
  interest rate swaps 4.259
  products 4.08, 4.254–4.259
  put options 4.257
  underlying 4.257–4.259
  value 4.259
Financial Ombudsman Service (FOS) 8.169–8.171
  ancillary matters 8.171
  compensation 8.170
  interest 8.170
  production of information and disclosure 8.170
financial promotion
  collective investment undertakings 9.04
  communications 5.38, 5.41–5.47
  conduct of business 5.24, 5.26
  controlled activities 5.33, 5.35, 5.39–5.40, 5.46
  controlled agreements, definition of 5.35
  criminal offences 5.33–5.34
  due diligence 5.34
  email 5.38
  exemptions 5.40, 5.44–5.47
  Financial Promotion Order 5.37–5.41, 5.45
  Financial Services and Markets Act 2000 5.32–5.37
  Financial Services Authority (FSA) 5.09, 5.12
  fines 5.34
  invitations or inducements 5.37, 5.43–5.44, 5.47
  overseas communications 5.42
  regulated activities 5.32, 5.77
  regulation 5.32–5.46
  retail offer 8.142, 8.145, 8.160, 8.163
  United Kingdom, within the 5.41
financial reporting 11.01–11.18 *see also* accounts
  buy-side 11.01
  company law 11.02
  Financial Reporting Standards 11.05–11.10, 11.47–11.49
  sell-side 11.01
Financial Services Action Plan (FSAP) 5.94
Financial Services and Markets Act 2000 5.02–5.08, 8.11–8.27
  authorization 5.08
  capital 10.03, 10.07
  civil sanctions 5.49–5.53
  collective investment undertakings 9.06, 9.12
  Crown dependencies 5.04
  debates 5.02
  EC law 5.87
  entry into force 5.02
  Financial Ombudsman Service (FOS) 8.169–8.171
  financial promotion 5.32–5.37
  Financial Services Act 1986 5.05, 5.83–5.84
  Financial Services Authority (FSA) 5.08
  framework, as 5.03
  general prohibition, breach of 5.48–5.55, 8.12–8.27
  legal market structures 5.84
  open-ended investment companies (OEICs) 9.08
  perimeter 5.06–5.07, 8.11
  permission 5.17–5.19
  recognized investment exchanges (RIEs) and recognized clearing houses (RCHs) 6.02–6.08
  regulated activities 5.07–5.08, 5.56–5.59, 5.62, 5.65, 5.67–5.77, 8.12–8.27
  retail offers 8.143–8.144, 8.169–8.171
  Royal Assent 5.02
  rules 5.03
  secondary legislation 5.03, 5.06, 8.11
  Select Committee on the Modernization of the House of Lords 5.02
  self-regulating organizations 5.05
  territorial scope 5.04
  UCITS 9.11
  variable capital, investment companies with (ICVC) 9.09
Financial Services Authority (FSA)
  approved persons 5.13
  BIPRU 10.05, 10.08–10.09, 10.13–10.16
  capital
    BIPRU 10.05, 10.08–10.09, 10.13–10.16
    GENPRU 10.03–10.04, 10.08–10.09, 10.17–10.18
    Handbook 10.03–10.04, 10.07, 10.09–10.19
    Principles for Business 10.03
    Prudential Sourcebooks 10.05
  COLL 9.13, 9.15, 9.23
  conduct of business 5.22–5.30, 5.79, 5.85, 8.142
  consumer, definition of 5.12
  controlled functions 5.13
  credit rating 10.35
  disciplinary sanctions 5.15
  dishonesty 5.12

Index

Financial Services Authority (FSA) (*cont*):
  EC law 5.98
  enforcement 5.11
  financial promotion 5.43–5.47
  Financial Services and Markets Act 2000 5.08, 5.09, 5.12
  fraud 5.12
  general prohibition 5.48–5.49
  GENPRU 10.03–10.04, 10.08–10.09, 10.17–10.18
  guidance 5.16
  Handbook of Rules and Guidance 5.09, 5.13, 5.16
    Basel Committee 10.22
    BIPRU 10.05, 10.08–10.09, 10.13–10.16
    capital 10.03–10.04, 10.07, 10.09–10.19
    conduct of business 5.22, 5.26, 5.30
    credit rating 10.35
    general prohibition 5.48–5.49
    GENPRU 10.03–10.04, 10.08–10.09, 10.17–10.18
    legal market structures 5.83, 5.86
    Market in Financial Instruments Directive (MiFiD) 5.97
    suitability 8.137
  legal market structures 5.79–5.80, 5.83, 5.86
  Market Conduct sourcebook (MAR) 5.30–5.31, 5.79–5.81, 5.84–5.86
  Market in Financial Instruments Directive (MiFiD) 5.98
  money laundering 5.12
  permission 5.17–5.21
  PRIN 5.16
  principles-based regulation 5.10–5.11, 5.16
  Principles for Businesses 5.14–5.15, 8.137, 8.157, 10.03
  Prudential Sourcebooks 10.05
  prudential supervision 8.142
  public awareness 5.12
  recognized investment exchanges (RIEs) and recognized clearing houses (RCHs) 6.05–6.08
  regulated activities 5.13
  regulation 5.10–5.47
    principles-based 5.10–5.11
    rules-based approach 5.10
    statutory objectives of regulation 5.12
    style of 5.10
  Responsibilities of Providers and Distributors for the Fair Treatment of Customers 8.157
  retail offers 8.142–8.145, 8.157, 8.181
  rules-based approach 5.10
  sophisticated users 5.12
  stability of financial system 5.12
  standards 5.14
  suitability 8.137–8.138
  terminology 5.13
  United States 5.11
  variable capital, investment companies with (ICVC) 9.09
financing tools, derivatives as 4.148–4.157
  accreting strike call options 4.149–4.156, 8.47
  hedging 4.153, 4.156
  insolvency 4.156
  shares, exposure to 4.149–4.156
  underlying, leveraged exposure to 4.148–4.156
fines 5.34, 5.49, 5.54–5.55
fit and proper persons test 5.95
fixed charges 4.230, 6.26–6.27
floating charges 4.230, 6.26–6.27
floor options 4.128–4.128, 4.257, 7.103
Force Majeure 7.45
forecasts, misrepresentation and 8.135
foreign exchange options 4.59
foreseeability
  duty of care 8.103, 8.124, 8.151–8.152
  misrepresentation 8.132
  retail offers 8.151–8.152
formats or wrappers *see* **wrappers**
forward cash flow 4.09
forward contracts 4.10–4.16
  agricultural markets 4.13–4.16
  binding obligation 4.11
  definition 4.10
  delivery date 4.10, 4.14
  electricity and power trading 4.213–4.214, 4.218
  freight 4.205
  guarantees 4.12
  London Metal Exchange 2.36
  payment profile 4.14
  price of underlying 4.10–4.16
  repurchase and reverse repurchase agreements 4.245–4.246
  spot market 4.11–4.16
  standard terms 4.18
  underlying, contract to buy and sell 4.10
  unregulated forwards 8.11–8.27
forward rate agreements (FRA) 4.63–4.68
  definition 4.63
  deposits, hedging in respect of 4.66–4.67
  discounting funds 4.68
  hedging 4.63–4.67
  interest rate 4.63–4.67
  interest rate swaps 4.97
  loans, hedging in respect of 4.64–4.65
  underlying 4.63
forward transaction, 2002 ISDA Equity Derivatives Definitions and 7.97, 7.101–7.104
  caps 7.103

Index

Cash Settlement 7.101–7.102
floors 7.103
Fractional Share Amount 7.104
general terms 7.101
Physical Settlement 7.101, 7.104
Prepayment Amount 7.102
price 7.101–7.103
settlement 7.101
Variable Obligations 7.103
FOS *see* **Financial Ombudsman Service (FOS)**
fraud 5.12, 8.130, 8.131–8.133
freight derivatives 4.103, 4.205–4.206
FTSE 100 2.28, 4.31
fund derivatives *see* **2006 ISDA Fund Derivatives Definitions**
fungibles 4.246, 4.251–4.252
futures contracts 4.17–4.31
  agricultural futures contracts 4.31
  backwardation 4.30
  bid and offer spread 3.03
  carbon trading 4.224–4.225
  Chicago Board of Trade (CBOT) 4.18
  Chicago Mercantile Exchange (CME) 4.18
  Chicago Produce Exchange 4.18
  commercial or investment purposes, made for 8.22–8.27
  commodity forward contracts 4.31
  commodity swaps 4.103
  definition 4.17–4.18, 5.61–5.62, 8.21–8.27
  delivery date 4.17, 4.18, 4.30
  discovery of prices 4.19
  Emissions Trading System 4.224–4.225
  equity indices 4.18
  example of use of contracts 4.20–4.26
  exchange, trading on an 4.18, 4.31
  financing rate 4.28–4.29
  forward contracts 4.18
  FTSE 100 4.31
  futures price 4.28–4.31
  general prohibition, civil sanctions for breach of 8.22–8.27
  hedging 4.20
  ICE Futures 2.42
  interest rates 4.18
  margining 3.12–3.18, 4.26
  open interest 4.19
  payment profile 4.22
  price 4.19–4.31
  regulated activities 5.61–5.64
  settlement 3.15
  soft commodities 4.18
  spot price 4.20–4.31
  standard terms 4.18
  underlying 4.17–4.30

gaming contracts
  Gambling Act 2005 8.36
  hedging 8.36
  speculation 8.36
Garman and Kohlhagen model 4.59
gearing, definition of 1.10
general prohibition 5.48–5.55 *see also* **civil sanctions for breach of general prohibition**
  authorized persons 5.48–5.55
  compensation 5.52
  criminal sanctions 5.49, 5.54–5.55
  deposit-taking 5.53
  due diligence 5.54
  exempt persons 5.48–5.55
  Financial Services and Markets Act 2000 5.48–5.55
  Financial Services Authority (FSA) 5.48–5.49
  fines 5.49, 5.54–5.55
  FSA Handbook 5.48–5.49
  perimeter 5.48
  precautions 5.55
  recognized investment exchanges (RIEs) and recognized clearing houses (RCHs) 6.03–6.04
  regulated activities 5.48–5.55, 5.68, 5.77, 8.12–8.27
  regulation 5.48–5.55
  sanctions 5.49
Gilt Repo Code of Best Practice 5.83
give-up agreements
  accounts 6.30, 6.36
  cash flow 6.36
  clearing 6.28–6.40
  clearing agreements 6.38–6.40
  credit risk 6.39
  definition 6.28
  documentation 6.39
  exchanges 6.28–6.40
  general clearing member (GCM) 6.30, 6.32–6.34, 6.36–6.40
  individual clearing member (ICM) 6.30
  International Uniform Give-Up Agreement of the Futures and Options Association (FOA) 6.29
  non-clearing members (NCM) 6.30–6.32
  novation 6.32–6.33
  prime brokerage 9.46, 9.48–9.49
  standard terms 6.29
  types 6.35
  variation margin 6.36
good faith 8.127
Grabbe model 4.59
Greek city states 1.18
Greek traders, options and 4.54

Index

greenhouse gases 4.219–4.222
Grey Paper 5.83
guarantees
  clearing 2.12
  counterparties 2.12
  credit derivatives 4.164
  credit risk 4.164
  exchanges 2.12
  forward contracts 4.12
  guaranteed investment contracts (GIC) 4.185–4.186

Handbook of Recognised Investment Exchanges and Recognised Clearing Houses (REC) 6.08
Heath, Jarrow and Morton model 4.59
hedge funds 4.197, 4.199–4.204 *see also* hedging
  agents 4.200
  classical fund, formula for 9.29–9.36
  closed-ended collective investment undertakings 9.25
  collective investment undertakings 9.25
  corporation, as 4.199
  costs 9.36
  definition 9.25, 9.38
  exchanges 9.30
  first funds 9.27
  formula 9.29–9.36
  gating 4.201
  hedge fund interest 4.199–4.200
  index 9.30–9.36
  investment management 4.202–4.203, 9.02
  liquidity 4.201
  long exposures 9.26, 9.31–9.37
  long-only fund 9.26, 9.31–9.35
  mutual funds 4.204
  open-ended collective investment undertakings 9.25
  over-the-counter (OTC) market 4.204, 9.31
  price 4.200
  prime brokerage 9.40–9.44, 9.47, 9.49–9.50
  redemption 4.201
  regulation 4.203–4.204, 9.25
  returns 9.29–9.39
  risk 4.201–4.204
  share prices 4.200
  short exposure 9.26, 9.37
  style drift 4.202
  systemic risk 9.28, 9.31–9.32
  underlying 4.199–4.201
  valuation 4.200, 9.28
hedging 1.13 *see also* hedge funds
  accounts 11.06, 11.11
  corporate treasuries 9.54
  currency swaps 4.101
  debt securities 4.239
  deposits 4.66–4.67
  disruption 7.120
  equity securities 4.239
  exchanges 2.43
  extraordinary events 7.120
  financing tools, derivatives as 4.153, 4.156
  forward rate agreements (FRA) 4.63–4.67
  futures contracts 4.20
  gaming contracts 8.36
  Increased Cost of Hedging 7.120, 7.234
  insurance contracts 8.37
  interest rate cap 4.125–4.126
  interest rate floor 4.127–4.128
  interest rate swaps 4.70–4.81, 4.95, 4.97–4.98, 4.101
  loans 4.64–4.65
  local authority interest rate swaps cases, *ultra vires* and 8.53–8.54
  market-makers 2.03
  market or price risk 1.05, 12.07
  misrepresentation 8.136
  option contracts 4.46
  price 2.44
  purpose of derivatives 1.05
  risk 12.01, 12.03
  securitization 4.239
  tax 11.19–11.23
historical background 1.18–1.20
  ancient world 1.18, 1.20
  exchanges, establishment of 1.18–1.19
  Greek city states 1.18
  Industrial Revolution 2.35
  legal market structures 5.82–5.86
  mathematical and computation techniques 1.20
  olive presses, options for 4.54
  option technique, origins of 4.54–4.59
  Phoenician traders 4.54
  Roman Empire 1.18
  Roman traders 4.54
  swaps 4.111–4.124
HM Treasury, financial assistance to UK deposit-takers from 10.06
how derivatives work 1.08–1.14
  cash-settled derivative contracts 1.08
  control of underlying, derivative contracts' disproportionate 1.10
  exposure to underlying 1.09
  gearing 1.10
  hedging, 1.13
  price or value of derivative 1.11–1.13
  price or value of underlying 1.12
  risk management tool, as 1.10
  speculation, as tool for 1.10, 1.13

Index

synthetic exposure to underlying 1.10
underlying, markets for 1.08
Hypothetical Investor concept 7.208–7.214, 7.238

2002 ISDA Equity Derivatives
  Definitions 7.97–7.126
  adjustments and modifications 7.115–7.116
  agreements and representations 7.126
  barrier transactions 7.98
  dividends 7.114
  Equity Swap Transaction 7.97, 7.105–7.111
  extraordinary events 7.117–7.125
  Forward Transaction 7.97, 7.101–7.104
  Fund Derivatives Definitions 7.204–7.208
  Index Basket Transaction 7.97
  Index Transaction 7.97
  Indices, adjustments and modifications affecting 7.115
  Knock-in Events 7.98
  Knock-out Events 7.98
  Option Transaction 7.97, 7.99–7.100
  representations 7.126
  Settlement 7.113
  Share Basket Transaction 7.97
  share indices, structures linked to 7.97
  Share Transaction 7.97
  Shares, adjustments and modifications affecting 7.116
  standard structures 7.97
  valuations 7.112
2003 ISDA Credit Derivatives Definitions
  7.127–7.158
  2005 matrix supplement 7.157
  Cash Settlement Amount 7.129
  certainty, promotion of 7.158
  credit events 7.137–7.147
  credit risk 7.158
  currency 7.134
  documentation 7.127–7.158, 8.197–8.198, 8.201–8.206
  Effective Date 7.128
  Fixed Rate Payer 7.128
  Floating Rate Payer 7.128
  matrix supplement 2005 7.157
  novation 7.156
  Obligations
    categories 7.134–7.135
    characteristics 7.136
    determination of 7.134–7.136
  Obligations of Reference Entities 7.133
  Physical Settlement Event 7.129
  reference entities and obligations 7.129–7.136, 7.157
  Relevant Obligations 7.131

settlement 7.148–7.155, 7.157
Specified Currency 7.134
standardisation 7.158
Subordination 7.136
Successors of Reference Entities 7.131–7.132
Termination Date 7.128
written credit protection 7.129–7.147
2005 ISDA Commodity Definitions 7.159–7.174
  Additional Market Disruption Event 7.169
  Calculation Agent 7.170
  Calculation Period 7.163
  classes of commodity 7.159
  Commodity Business Days 7.162
  Commodity Reference Prices 7.164–7.168
  credit derivatives documentation 8.197–8.198, 8.201–8.206
  Delivery Date 7.164
  Disruption Fallback 7.170
  Effective Date 7.162
  Expiration Date 7.162
  Fixed Amounts 7.163–7.164
  Fixed Price Payer 7.161
  Floating Amounts 7.160, 7.163–7.164
  Floating Price Payer 7.161, 7.163, 7.165, 7.169
  freight derivatives 4.206
  intangibles 7.159
  Knock-In Event 7.160, 7.162
  Knock-Out Event 7.160, 7.162
  Market Disruption Event 7.169–7.170
  Notional Quantity 7.163
  options 7.172–7.174
  parties 7.161
  payments 7.163
  price 7.164–7.169
  Relevant Price 7.167–7.170
  rounding of amounts 7.173
  Swaptions 7.172
  Termination Date 7.162
  underlying 7.159
  Weather Index Derivative Transaction 7.167–7.168
2006 ISDA definitions 7.91–7.240 *see also*
  2002 ISDA Equity Derivatives Definitions;
  2003 ISDA Credit Derivatives Definitions;
  2005 ISDA Commodity Definitions; 2006
  ISDA Fund Derivatives Definitions; 2006
  ISDA Rates Definitions
  adjustment events 7.94
  benefits 7.93
  Calculation Agent 7.95
  calculation of amounts payable 7.93
  classifications 7.91
  Close-Out Amounts 7.95
  Confirmation 7.92–7.93

Index

2006 ISDA definitions 7.91–7.240 *see also*
  2002 ISDA Equity Derivatives Definitions;
  2003 ISDA Credit Derivatives Definitions;
  2005 ISDA Commodity Definitions; 2006
  ISDA Fund Derivatives Definitions; 2006
  ISDA Rates Definitions *(cont)*:
  delivery obligations 7.94
  disclaimers 7.94
  exercise of rights 7.94
  extraordinary events 7.94
  matters covered 7.94–7.96
  payment obligations 7.94
  rating agencies 7.95
  representations 7.94
  underlying 7.91, 7.94, 7.96
  usefulness of 7.92
  valuations 7.94
  warranties 7.95
2006 ISDA Definitions 7.175–7.203
  Business Day 7.177
  Business Day Convention 7.177
  currency derivative transactions 7.175
  general definitions 7.176
  interest rates 7.175, 7.180
  mark-to-mark currency swap 7.185–7.188
  Option Transactions 7.189–7.192
    Cash Settlement Amount 7.190–7.191
    exercise 7.190
    Fixed Rate Payer 7.190–7.191
    Floating Rate Payer 7.190
    Swap Transaction 7.189
    Swaption 7.189
  rounding 7.179
  swap transactions 7.180–7.188, 7.203
    Calculation Amount 7.181, 7.183
    Calculation Periods 7.181
    Confirmation 7.183
    Day Count Fraction 7.180
    Fixed Amounts 7.183
    Fixed Rate Payer 7.180, 7.184
    Floating Amount 7.183–7.184
    Floating Rate Payer 7.180
    interest rates 7.180–7.184
    negative interest rates 7.184
    Payment Date 7.182, 7.184
  Swaption Straddle 7.197–7.202
  swaptions 7.193–7.202
2006 ISDA Fund Derivatives
  Definitions 7.204–7.240
  2002 ISDA Equity Definitions 7.204–7.208
  adjustments 7.229–7.237
  agreements 7.239
  barrier transactions 7.207
  Calculation Agent 7.212
  Calculation Agent Adjustment 7.230, 7.233
  Cancellation Amount 7.235–7.237
  Cancellation and Payment 7.233
  Change in Law 7.235
  Cut-Off Period 7.228
  crystallization of risks 7.205
  Deemed Payout Method 7.208–7.219, 7.224
  Delayed Settlement 7.234
  Disrupted Days 7.227–7.228
  disruptions to valuation 7.227–7.228
  Dividend Amount 7.238
  dividends 7.238
  Extraordinary Events 7.231–7.235
  Final Observation Date 7.218
  Final Price 7.210
  Fund Disruption Event 7.227–7.228
  Fund Interest Units 7.209–7.212, 7.216–7.218,
    7.220, 7.222, 7.225–7.234
  Fund Interests 7.206–7.212, 7.216–7.222,
    7.225–7.232, 7.239
  Fund Option Transactions 7.207
  Fund Reporting Date 7.222–7.223
  Fund Valuation Date 7.221–7.223
  general definitions 7.206
  Hypothetical Investor concept 7.208–7.214,
    7.238
  Increased Cost of Hedging 7.234
  Initial Observation Date 7.218
  Knock-in Event 7.207
  Knock-out Event 7.207
  modifications 7.229–7.237
  Partial Cancellation and Payment 7.233
  Potential Adjustment Event 7.230
  Price Adjustment 7.234
  Redemption Notice Date 7.213–7.214, 7.216
  Redemption Proceeds 7.212
  Redemption Valuation Date 7.212–7.213, 7.221
  Reference Fund 7.206, 7.209, 7.211–7.216,
    7.221–7.223, 7.239
  Relevant Price 7.210
  Reported Fund Interest Value 7.222
  Reported Valuation Conventions 7.224–7.225
  Reported Valuation Date 7.224
  Reported Value Method 7.208–7.210,
    7.220–7.226
  representations 7.239
  Scheduled Fund Valuation Date 7.221, 7.223,
    7.225
  Scheduled Redemption Payment Date
    7.214–7.216
  Scheduled Redemption Valuation Date 7.215,
    7.224–7.225
  Valuation Date 7.227–7.228
  valuing fund interests 7.209–7.210

Index

ICE Futures 2.41–2.43
  electronic trading 2.43
  futures contracts 2.42
  IntercontinentalExchange (ICE) 2.43
  International Petroleum Exchange (IPE) 2.41–2.43
  oil prices 2.41
  open-outcry trading 2.42
ICVC *see* variable capital, investment companies with (ICVC)
ijma 4.159
ijtihad 4.159
Illegality 7.44
income or capital gains tax
  accounting 11.33
  allowances 11.23, 11.37
  avoidance 11.35–11.40
  capital allowances 11.37
  cash flows 11.23, 11.27–11.28
  chargeable profits 11.24
  complex series of transactions 11.34–11.40
  contracts 11.29–11.33
  corporation tax 11.25
    branches or agencies 11.25
    calculation 11.25
  derivative contracts rules 11.29–11.33
  exemptions 11.23
  Income and Corporations Taxes Act 1988 11.24
  profit, calculation of 11.26, 11.29
  Ramsay principle 11.35–11.37, 11.40
  reliefs 11.23
  statutory interpretation 11.35–11.37
  tax avoidance 11.35–11.40
  Taxation of Chargeable Gains Act 1992 11.24
Increased Cost of Hedging 7.120, 7.234
indemnities 7.113
indices
  2002 ISDA Equity Derivatives Definitions 7.97, 7.115
  constant proportion portfolio insurance (CPPI) 4.02, 4.132–4.137
  credit derivatives 4.193
  extraordinary events 7.117–7.118
  freight derivatives 4.205
  hedge funds 9.30–9.36
  Index Adjustment Event 7.118
  share indices, structures linked to 7.97
inducement
  financial promotion 5.37, 5.43–5.44, 5.47
  misrepresentation 8.130–8.131
Industrial Revolution 2.35
inflation 4.115, 4.119, 4.253
information *see also* disclosure
  conduct of business 5.23–5.24, 5.26, 5.29–5.30

  Financial Ombudsman Service (FOS) 8.170
  insider information 5.30
  Notice of Publicly Available Information 7.148
  Publicly Available Information 7.147
  redeem or sell-back, provision of information on right to 8.165
  retail offers 8.154, 8.165, 8.170
  updated information, duty to provide 8.154
insider information 5.30
insolvency
  accreting strike call options 4.156
  bankruptcy 7.41, 7.138
  cherry-picking transactions 7.21
  Companies Act 1989 6.10–6.27
  credit derivatives 4.164
  credit risk 4.164
  disclaimer of onerous property 7.24
  exchange members 6.01, 6.10–6.27
  extraordinary events 7.119
  financing tools, derivatives as 4.156
  Insolvency Rules 7.22
  ISDA 2002 Master Agreement 7.21–7.22, 7.24, 7.28–7.30, 7.41
  netting 7.28–7.30
  recharacterization of derivative contracts 8.33
  risk 6.01, 6.10–6.27
insurance *see* constant proportion portfolio insurance (CPPI); insurance contracts
insurance contracts
  authorized persons 8.43
  catastrophe swaps 8.46
  civil sanctions 8.43
  credit default swaps 8.37
  credit derivatives 8.37, 8.40, 8.42, 8.45
  drafting 8.42
  economic effect of contract 8.40
  enforcement 8.39, 8.44
  event of defaults under ISDA 2002 Master Agreement 8.44
  general prohibition, civil sanctions for breach of the 8.43
  hedging 8.37
  insurable interest 8.41
  insurance transformer transaction structures 8.42, 8.46
  intention 8.40–8.41
  International Swaps and Derivatives Association, Inc. (ISDA)
    2002 Master Agreement 8.44
    legal opinion 8.45
  local authority swap cases 8.39, 8.44
  mortality rates 8.46
  Part IV permission 8.37, 8.43

Index

insurance contracts (*cont*):
    purpose 8.41
    recharacterization of derivative
        contracts 8.37–8.46
    regulated activities under Financial Services and
        Markets Act 2000 8.38, 8.43
    special purpose vehicles (SPVs) 8.42
    swaps 8.39–8.41, 8.44, 8.46
IntercontinentalExchange (ICE) 2.43
interest *see also* **interest rates**
    Applicable Close-Out Rate 7.68
    Applicable Deferral Rate 7.67
    calculation of 7.66–7.68
    collateralized debt obligations (CDOs) 4.186
    compound interest, awards of 8.06, 8.59–8.62,
        8.66, 8.73, 8.93
    convertible and exchangeable debt, wrapper
        for 4.241
    Default Rate 7.67
    Financial Ombudsman Service (FOS) 8.170
    hedge funds 4.199–4.200
    ISDA 2002 Master Agreement 7.66–7.68
    Islamic compliant derivatives 4.160
    local authority interest rate swaps cases,
        ultra vires and
        compound interest, awards of 8.06, 8.59–8.62,
            8.66, 8.73, 8.93
    misrepresentation 8.136
    retail offers 8.170
    simple interest 8.59, 8.66, 8.92, 8.93
    withholding tax 11.41–11.42
interest rate cap 4.125–4.126
interest rate collar 4.129–4.131
interest rate floor 4.127–4.128
interest rate swaps *see also* ***ultra vires*, local**
    authority interest rate swaps cases and
    at-the money 4.78
    balance sheet 4.92
    bid and offer spread 4.91
    collar 4.130
    comparative advantage, theory of 4.82
    confidentiality 4.92
    contract, swaps analysed as 8.183,
        8.188–8.189
    costs, achieving cheaper funding 4.82–4.93
    credit rating 4.83, 4.85, 4.92
    crystallization of interest rates 4.76–4.78
    currency swaps 4.101
    dealer, role of 4.89–4.93
    Deutsche Bank 4.123
    duration 4.93
    exposure wave 4.80, 4.85
    financial engineering 4.259
    first interest rate swaps 4.123

    fixed rate 4.71, 4.73, 4.77–4.78, 4.81–4.90,
        4.94–4.97, 4.100, 4.123
    floating or variable rate 4.71–4.88, 4.94–4.97,
        4.100, 4.123
    forward rate agreements, decomposition of swaps
        into a series of 4.97
    hedging 4.70–4.81, 4.95, 4.97–4.98, 4.101
    intermediaries 4.89, 4.91–4.92
    in-the-money 4.77, 4.79–4.80, 4.97
    loans 1.26–1.27, 4.71–4.98
    modelling movements 4.99
    Monte-Carlo simulation 4.99
    mortgage lending 1.26–1.27
    netting 4.97
    operation 4.70–4.81
    out-of-the-money 4.77, 4.79–4.80, 4.97
    plain vanilla 4.99
    price 4.95–4.99
    schedule of payments 4.97
    swap wave 4.80, 4.85
    tax 4.71
    terminology 4.94
    types of swap 4.100
    underlying 4.72–4.75
interest rates *see also* **interest; interest rate swaps**
    2006 ISDA Definitions 7.175, 7.180
    cap 4.125–4.126
    collar 4.129–4.131
    embedded derivatives 4.240
    floors 4.127–4.128
    forward rate agreements (FRA) 4.63–4.67
    futures contracts 4.18
    loans 4.64–4.65
    mortgage lending 1.24–1.27
    negative interest rates 7.182, 7.184
    repurchase and reverse repurchase
        agreements 4.247
    risk 1.26–1.27
    underlying 4.63
International Accounting Standards 11.12,
    11.08–11.10, 11.15–11.18
International Air Transport Association
    (IATA) 2.45
International Financial Reporting Board
    (IFRB) 11.12, 11.15–11.16
International Financial Reporting Standards
    (IFRS) 11.12, 11.15–11.17
International Monetary Fund (IMF), establishment
    of 4.114
International Petroleum Exchange
    (IPE) 2.41–2.43
International Swaps and Derivatives Association,
    Inc. (ISDA) 4.111, 4.124, 7.11–7.18 *see also*
    2006 ISDA definitions; ISDA 2002 Master

Index

Agreement and its Schedule; ISDA Credit
   Support Documents
activities 7.14
carbon trading 4.227
committees 7.14
Confirmation 7.88–7.90
formation 7.12
insurance contracts, legal opinion on 8.44
master agreements 7.15–7.18
Novation Agreement 2002 7.156
objectives 7.13
over-the-counter (OTC) market 7.15–7.17
restructuring 8.202–8.204
standard forms 7.11, 7.14–7.15
surveys 7.14
Swaps Code for US dollar interest rate swaps 7.15
Swaption Straddle 7.202
interpretation
construction of terms of derivative
   contract 8.28–8.32
income or capital gains tax 11.35–11.37
statutory interpretation 11.35–11.37
in-the-money
commodity swaps 4.105, 4.108–4.109
interest rate swaps 4.77, 4.79–4.80, 4.97
option contracts 4.44, 4.48
swaptions 7.194–7.195
**investment activities and commercial activities,
   differentiation between** 5.74–5.76
investment management industry 9.01–9.24
agreements 9.01
alternative investment industries 9.02
boilerplates 9.01
classification of investment vehicles 9.01
collective investment undertakings 9.03–9.07,
   9.12–9.15
hedge funds 4.202–4.203, 9.02
investment vehicles
   classification 9.01
   structure 9.01
liberalization 9.23–9.24
open-ended investment companies
   (OEICs) 9.08–9.11
performance 9.01
pooled investment management 9.01, 9.02
portfolio management 9.01
professional managers 9.02
regulated activities 5.71
regulation 9.01
remuneration 9.01
standards 9.01
termination of appointment of management 9.01
UCITS 9.03, 9.11–9.13, 9.15–9.24
unauthorized and unregulated funds 9.14

unit trust schemes 9.11–9.13
variable capital, investment companies with
   (ICVC) 9.09–9.11
Investment Services Directive 5.97–5.98
invitations or inducements 5.37, 5.43–5.44, 5.47
ISDA *see* International Swaps and Derivatives
   Association, Inc. (ISDA)
ISDA Confirmation 7.88–7.90
ISDA Credit Support Documents 7.69–7.87
2001 ISDA Margin Provisions 7.87
application of credit support 7.70–7.71
close-out netting provisions of 1992 Master
   Agreement 7.86
counterparty risk, reduction of 7.70–7.71, 7.82
Credit Support Annex (Bilateral
   Form—Transfer) 7.72–7.74, 7.78, 7.81
charges, creation of 7.73
close-out netting of 1992 Master
   Agreement 7.86
collateral, transfer of title to 7.72, 7.78
Credit Support Deed (Bilateral Form—Security
   Interest) 7.83–7.85
Eligible Credit Support 7.78–7.79, 7.83–7.84
equilibrium, deviation from the 7.83
Equivalent Credit Support 7.83
flexibility 7.85
implementation 7.86–7.87
ISDA 2002 Master Agreement and its
   Schedule 7.72
security interests, non-creation of 7.73
Credit Support Deed (Bilateral Form—Security
   Interest) 7.72, 7.75–7.78, 7.81
book debts 7.76
close-out netting of 1992 Master
   Agreement 7.86
Collateral Regulations 7.77
Credit Support Annex (Bilateral
   Form—Security Interest) 7.72,
   7.75–7.78, 7.81
Eligible Credit Support 7.78–7.79
equilibrium, deviation from 7.84
Equivalent Credit Support 7.83–7.84
fixed charges 7.75–7.76
floating and fixed charges, registration of 7.76
implementation 7.86–7.87
Posted Collateral 7.75, 7.84
registration of charges 7.76–7.77
transfer of collateral 7.75–7.78
Early Termination Amount 7.86
Eligible Credit Support 7.78–7.79, 7.83–7.84
equilibrium
   deviation from 7.82–7.84
   frequency for determining whether there
      is an 7.82

Index

ISDA Credit Support Documents (*cont*):
  Equivalent Credit Support 7.83
  exposure to counterparty 7.70–7.71, 7.81
  governing law 7.72
  implementation 7.86–7.87
  ISDA 2002 Master Agreement 7.24–7.25,
    7.31, 7.48
  margining 7.87
  negative feedback loop 7.80
  over-the-counter (OTC) market 7.69–7.70
  Posted Collateral 7.75, 7.84
  sensitivity 7.82
  transfer of value under credit support
    document 7.78–7.82
  value 7.78–7.82
ISDA 2002 Master Agreement and its
    Schedule 7.17–7.68
  Additional Termination Event,
    definition of 7.49
  Affected Transactions 7.33
  architecture 7.19
  Automatic Early Termination 7.54
  Bankruptcy, definition of 7.41
  Breach of Agreement, definition of 7.36
  cherry-picking transactions 7.21
  close-out netting 7.25, 7.70–7.71, 8.191
  Collateral Regulations 7.25
  compensation for early termination, calculation
    of 7.66–7.67
  complexity 7.17, 7.19
  contract, swaps analysed as 8.191
  counterparty risk 7.29, 7.32
  Credit Default Support, definition of 7.37
  Credit Event Upon Merger, definition of 7.48
  Credit Support Document 7.24–7.25, 7.31, 7.48
  Cross-Default, definition of 7.40
  Default Under Specified Transaction, definition
    of 7.39
  duty of care 8.109, 8.112
  early termination 7.50–7.65
    Automatic Early Termination 7.54
    compensation, calculation of 7.66–7.67
    crystallization of obligations 7.51
    Early Termination Amount 7.57–7.62, 7.65
    Early Termination Date 7.52, 7.54–7.56, 7.68
    Events of Default 7.52–7.54, 7.57–7.62
    interest, calculation of 7.66–7.68
    Market Quotation and Loss 7.63
    penalty clauses 7.64
    set-off 7.65
    Tax Event 7.55
    Termination Event 7.50, 7.52–7.53, 7.55,
      7.57–7.62
  Early Termination Amount 7.57–7.62, 7.65

    Affected Parties, number of 7.58
    calculation 7.57–7.62
    Close-out Amount 7.58–7.62
    Events of Default 7.57–7.62
    Market Quotation and Loss 7.63
    payment measures 7.63
    payment methods 7.63
    Termination Currency Equivalents 7.59
    Termination Event 7.57–7.62
    Unpaid Amounts 7.58–7.62
  Events of Default 7.31–7.50, 7.52–7.54, 8.44
    Bankruptcy, definition of 7.41
    Breach of Agreement, definition of 7.36
    Credit Default Support, definition of 7.37
    Cross-Default, definition of 7.40
    Default Under Specified Transaction, definition
      of 7.39
    definitions 7.34–7.42
    early termination 7.52–7.54, 7.57–7.63
    Failure to Pay or Deliver, definition of 7.35
    interest, calculation of 7.67
    Merger Without Assumption, definition of 7.42
    Misrepresentation, definition of 7.38
    Repudiation of Agreement, definition of 7.36
    Specified Transaction, definition of 7.39
    Termination Events 7.31–7.52
  Failure to Pay or Deliver, definition of 7.35
  Force Majeure
    definition of 7.45
    early termination 7.55
  framework 7.17, 7.19
  governing law 7.19
  Illegality, definition of 7.44
  insolvency 7.21–7.22
    bankruptcy 7.41
    cherry-picking transactions 7.21
    disclaimer of onerous property 7.24
    Insolvency Rules 7.22
    netting 7.28–7.30
  insurance contracts 8.45
  interest
    Applicable Close-out Rate 7.68
    Applicable Deferral Rate 7.67
    calculation of 7.66–7.68
    Default Rate 7.67
  local authority interest rate swaps cases, *ultra vires*
    and 8.85
  Market Quotation and Loss 7.63
  Merger Without Assumption 7.42, 7.46
  misrepresentation 8.136
  Multiple Transaction Payment Netting 7.27
  netting 7.25, 7.27–7.30, 8.191
  novation 7.28
  obligations of parties 7.26

origins 7.16–7.17
over-the-counter (OTC) market 7.17, 7.24, 7.29, 7.39
penalty clauses 7.64
representations by parties 7.31
Repudiation of Agreement, definition of 7.36
risk control 7.29
set-off 7.65
single agreement approach 7.21–7.23
Specified Transaction, definition of 7.39
swaps 7.60
Tax Event 7.46, 7.55
Tax Event upon Merger, definition of 7.47
Terminated Transactions 7.51, 7.60
Termination Currency Equivalents 7.59
Termination Events 7.31–7.53
   Additional Termination Event, definition of 7.49
   Credit Event Upon Merger, definition of 7.48
   definition 7.43–7.50
   early termination 7.50, 7.52–7.53, 7.55, 7.57–7.63
   Force Majeure Events 7.45
   Illegality, definition of 7.44
   notice 7.55
   Tax Event, definition of 7.46
   Tax Event upon Merger, definition of 7.47
withholding tax 11.43–11.44

Islamic compliant derivatives 4.04, 4.158–4.163
bei al-arboun (option contract) 4.162
contractual uncertainty, prohibition on 4.160
fatwas 4.159, 4.163
ijma 4.159
ijtihad 4.159
interest 4.160
investment return, prohibition on 4.160
legal opinions (fatwas) 4.159, 4.163
mudaraba (partnership financing) 4.161
murabaha (added cost financing) 4.161
musharaka (equity financing) 4.161
qiyas 4.159
Quran 4.159
Shari'a 4.158–4.163
sukuks (debt securities) 4.161
Sunna 4.159

key concept 3.01–3.18
bid and offer spread 3.03
'long' and 'short' 3.01–3.02
margin 3.05–3.18
tick and basis point 3.04
Knock-in Event 7.98, 7.160, 7.162, 7.207
Knock-out Event 7.98, 7.160, 7.162, 7.207

know your customer (KYC) 12.26

Japan 4.115–4.118
Joint Implementation (JI) 4.221
Jones, Alfred Winslow 9.27–9.28

Kyoto Protocol
carbon trading 4.220–4.222, 4.226
Joint Implementation (JI) 4.221

Lamfalussy Committee 5.94
LCH.Clearnet 2.46–2.48
agricultural produce 2.46
Beetroot Sugar Association 2.46
clearing 2.46–2.48
Clearnet SA 2.48
exchanges 2.46–2.48
International Petroleum Exchange (IPE) 2.47
LIFFE 2.47
London Metal Exchange 2.39, 2.47
London Produce Clearing House 2.46
over-the-counter (OTC) market 2.47
legal framework 5.01–5.102
EC law 5.87–5.102
Financial Services and Markets Act 2000 5.02–5.08
financial services legislation 5.01–5.08
general prohibition 5.48–5.55
legal market structures 5.78–5.86
regulated activities 5.56–5.77
regulation 5.01, 5.09–5.47, 5.56–5.86
legal issues 8.01–8.206
capacity 8.03
complex products 8.08
construction of contracts 8.04, 8.28–8.32
contracts 8.01–8.05, 8.07–8.09, 8.28–8.48, 8.182–8.191
credit derivative documentation, development of 8.10, 8.192–8.206
documentation 8.09–8.10, 8.192–8.206
duty of care 8.07, 8.94–8.141
exchanges 8.01
misrepresentations 8.03, 8.07
over-the-counter (OTC) market 8.01–8.02, 8.07
private customers 8.08, 8.142–8.181
recharacterization risk 8.05, 8.33–8.48
records 8.04
rectification of contracts 8.04
regulation 8.01, 8.08, 8.11–8.27
retail offers 8.08, 8.142–8.181
terms of contract 8.02, 8.07–8.08
ultra vires 8.49–8.51
   compound interest, awards of 8.06
   equitable trusts 8.06

Index

legal issues (*cont*):
   local authority swaps cases 8.06, 8.52–8.93
   over-the-counter (OTC) market 8.06
   restitution 8.06
  written terms, misrepresentation and 8.07
legal market structures 5.78–5.86
  Bank of England 5.83
  clearing 5.78
  conduct of business rules 5.79
  Conduct of Business Sourcebook 5.79, 5.85
  counterparties 5.78, 5.83
  exchange-based markets 5.78
  Financial Services Act 1986 5.83–5.84
  Financial Services and Markets Act 2000 5.84
  Financial Services Authority (FSA) 5.79–5.80, 5.83, 5.86
  FSA Handbook 5.83, 5.86
  Gilt Repo Code of Best Practice 5.83
  Grey Paper 5.83
  historical perspective 5.82–5.86
  listed money market institutions (LMMI) 5.83
  London Code of Conduct 5.83–5.84
  Market Conduct sourcebook (MAR) 5.79–5.81, 5.84–5.86
  Market in Financial Instruments Directive (MiFiD) 5.79, 5.85
  market service providers 5.78
  multilateral trading facilities 5.79–5.80
  over-the-counter (OTC) market 5.78, 5.83–5.84
  regulation 5.82–5.85
  settlement 5.78
  systematic internalizer 5.81
  transparency 5.80
  wholesale markets 5.83
legal risk 12.20–12.22
  accounting-driven transactions 12.22
  circular cash flows 12.22
  contracts, enforcement of 12.20
  delivery, process of 12.21
  enforcement 12.20
  inappropriate uses 12.22
  local authority interest rate swaps cases, *ultra vires* and 8.76
  misrepresentation 12.21
  product types 12.21
liberalization 9.23–9.24
liens 6.27
LIFFE 2.28–2.32, 2.47, 6.09
Limitation Acts 8.78
limitation of liability 8.94
liquidity
  contracts 2.20

  exchanges 2.14
  hedge funds 4.201
  market-makers 2.06
  open-ended investment companies (OEICs) 9.08
  over-the-counter (OTC) market 2.20, 7.02
  prime brokerage 9.42
  repurchase and reverse repurchase agreements 4.253
  retail offers, warnings and 8.165
  risk 12.18
  standard forms 7.08
  tick and basis point 3.04
  traders, role of 2.02
listed money market institutions (LMMI) 5.83
loans
  accounts 8.47
  accreting strike call options 8.47
  economic effect 8.47
  forward rate agreements (FRA) 4.64–4.65
  hedging 4.64–4.65
  interest rate swaps 4.71–4.98
  interest rates 4.64–4.65, 4.125–4.126, 4.129–4.131
  Islington case, discounted swap in the 8.47
  local authority interest rate swaps cases, *ultra vires* and 8.56
  mortgages 1.24–1.27
  recharacterization of derivative contracts 8.47–8.48
  records 8.47
local authorities *see ultra vires*, local authority interest rate swaps cases and
London Clearing House 6.09
London Code of Conduct 5.83–5.84
London Commodities Exchange 2.29
London Metal Exchange 2.33–2.40
  clearing 2.39
  coffee shops 2.34, 2.37
  contracts 2.39
  copper 2.36
  cost-of-carry concept 2.36
  electronic trading 2.39
  forward contracts 2.36
  futures contracts 2.39
  imports 2.36
  increasing demand for metal 2.35
  Industrial Revolution 2.35
  LCH.Clearnet system 2.39
  London Metals and Mining Company 2.38
  matching 2.39
  open-outcry trading 2.39
  physical metal, trading 2.40
  plastics 2.39
  price 2.36–2.39

Index

ring 2.37, 2.39
Royal Exchange 2.33–2.34
standard quantities and qualities 2.37
SWORD electronic database of warrants of
    ownership 2.40
telephone-based market 2.39
tin 2.36
London Produce Clearing House 2.46
London Stock Exchange 2.28–2.29
London Traded Options Market 2.29
'long' and 'short' positions 3.01–3.02
lookback options 4.34

margin
  accounts 3.06, 3.14–3.16
  clearing 2.08, 2.16, 3.05–3.18, 6.11
  collateral 2.08, 2.16, 3.07–3.08
  counterparties 3.07
  definition 3.05
  exchanges 2.08, 2.16, 3.05–3.07
  flow of payments in exchange-based markets 3.07
  futures contracts 3.12–3.18, 4.26
  initial margin 3.08, 3.13
  ISDA Credit Support Documents 7.87
  marking to market 3.09–3.10
  over-the-counter (OTC)
      market 2.21, 7.01
  prime brokerage 9.43
  purpose 3.11
  settlement price, calculation of 3.09, 3.14–3.15
  tick and margin, example of 3.12–3.18
  trading profit 3.17–3.18
  variation margin 3.09–3.11, 3.14–3.15
market abuse 5.30
Market Conduct sourcebook (MAR) 5.79–5.81, 5.84–5.86
market discipline 10.29
market disruption
  2005 ISDA Commodity
      Definitions 7.169–7.170
  Additional Disruption Events 7.120, 7.169
  Disrupted Days 7.112, 7.227–7.228
  Disruption Fallback 7.170
  Market Disruption Event 7.112
  valuations 7.112
market-makers
  exchanges 2.09
  hedging 2.03
  liquidity 2.06
  market or price risk 12.07
  market service providers 2.23
  participants 2.03
  sell-side 2.03
market or price risk 12.07–12.17

aggregate exposure, determination of 12.17
Basel 2 12.16
Basel Committee 10.22
calculation 10.14, 12.16
capital 10.11–10.12, 10.14, 12.16
commodity swaps 4.106
correlation risk 12.17
crystallization 12.07
data population 12.09–12.12
definition 12.07
extreme value theory 12.15
hedging 1.05, 12.07
market making 12.07
monitoring 12.08
out-of-the-money moves 12.08
proprietary models 12.16
purpose of derivatives 1.05, 1.07
standard deviation tool 12.10–12.12
statistical analysis 12.09–12.16
stress-testing 12.17
underlying, volatility of the 12.14
Value-at-Risk (VaR) 12.09–12.15
Market Quotation and Loss 7.63
market service providers 2.22–2.26
  counterparties 2.23, 2.25
  electronic trading 2.22
  exchange-based market 2.22, 2.25–2.26
  market-making 2.23
  order matching systems 2.24–2.25
  over-the-counter (OTC) market 2.22, 2.25
  regulation 2.26
  risk of counterparty default 2.25
**Market in Financial Instruments Directive
    (MiFiD)** 5.79, 5.85, 5.97–5.102
  ancillary services 5.100
  commodities, business relating to 5.98
  conduct of business 5.24
  definition of investment business 5.98
  duty of care 8.113
  European Economic Area (EEA) 5.98
  financial instruments, safekeeping and
      administration of 5.100–5.101
  Financial Services Authority (FSA) 5.98
  FSA Handbook 5.97
  investment firms 5.97–5.102
  Investment Services Directive 5.97–5.98
  list of services and activities 5.99
  passport 5.97–5.98
  permission 5.17–5.18
  professional client, definition of 5.102
  regulated activities 5.59–5.60
  standards 5.98
  suitability 8.137
  UCITS I Directive 5.97

Index

marketing *see* financial promotion
marking-to-market 3.09–3.10
mark-to-mark currency swap, 2006 ISDA
    Definitions and 7.185–7.188
  Calculation Amount 7.185
  Calculation Period 7.185, 7.188
  Constant Currency 7.185–7.186
  Constant Currency Payer 7.186
  exchange rates, exposure to 7.185–7.188
  ISDA MTM Matrix 7.186
  MTM Amount 7.187
  Payment Date 7.185
  Variable Currency 7.185–7.188
  Variable Currency Payer 7.186, 7.188
Marrakesh Accords 4.221
master agreements *see also* ISDA 2002 Master
    Agreement and its Schedule
  confirmations 7.04, 7.05
  contents 7.04
  examples 7.07
  International Swap and Derivatives
    Association 7.15–7.18
  languages 7.07
  over-the-counter (OTC) market
    documentation 7.03–7.07
mathematics
  ancient world 1.20
  liquidity risk 12.18
  multi-asset derivatives 4.197
  option contracts 4.45, 4.57, 4.59
  pricing 1.12–1.14, 4.45, 4.57, 4.59
  products 4.197
mergers
  Credit Event Upon Merger 7.46
  extraordinary events 7.119
  ISDA 2002 Master Agreement 7.42, 7.46
  Merger Event 7.119
  Merger Without Assumption 7.42, 7.46
  NYSE Euronext LIFFE 2.29, 2.32
misrepresentation 8.03, 8.07
  affirmation 8.131
  categories 8.131
  common law 8.130
  communications 8.129
  damages 8.130, 8.131–8.133
  deceit 8.130
  definition 8.131
  disclosure 8.129
  documentation 8.129
  duty of care 8.100, 8.106–8.107, 8.117–8.136
  economic loss 8.132
  equity 8.130
  fiduciary duties 8.136

forecasts 8.135
foreseeability 8.132
fraud 8.130, 8.131–8.133
hedging 8.136
inducement 8.130–8.131
innocent misrepresentation 8.131
interest 8.136
ISDA 2002 Master Agreement 8.136
legal risk 12.21
Misrepresentation Act 1967 8.133
negligent misrepresentation 8.131,
    8.132–8.134
opinions 8.131, 8.135
pre-contractual statements 8.130–8.131
reliance 8.131, 8.135
remedies 8.131–8.133, 8.136
repayment of money 8.136
rescission 8.130, 8.131, 8.136
retail offers 8.120, 8.160
sales practice 8.135
sophisticated and experienced investors 8.07
Springwell case 8.121–8.128, 8.129
written terms 8.07
misselling 8.120, 8.137
mistake
  fact, mistake of 8.78–8.79
  law, mistake of 8.78–8.79, 8.84
  local authority interest rate swaps cases,
    ultra vires and 8.78–8.81, 8.84, 8.93
  recovery of money 8.79–8.81, 8.84, 8.93
  restitution 8.78–8.79
modifications *see* adjustments and modifications
money laundering 5.12
Monte-Carlo simulation 4.99
mortgage lending
  fixed rate loans 1.24–1.27
  interest rate risk 1.26–1.27
  interest rates 1.24–1.26
  swaps 1.26–1.27
  variable (floating) rate loans 1.24, 1.26
mudaraba (partnership financing) 4.161
multi-asset derivatives 4.195–4.196
multilateral trading facilities (MTFs) 5.79–5.80
Multiple Transaction Payment Netting 7.27
murabaha (added cost financing) 4.161
musharaka (equity financing) 4.161

National Grid 4.209, 4.212, 4.214–4.215
National Power plc, demerger of 8.196
Nationalization 7.119
negligence
  misrepresentation 8.131, 8.132–8.134
  negligent misstatements 8.121, 8.126, 8.150

Index

operational risk 12.24
professional negligence 8.148, 8.150–8.152
retail offers 8.148, 8.150–8.152
netting
　capital 10.16
　close-out netting 7.25, 7.70–7.71, 8.181
　commodity swaps 4.102, 4.105
　contract, swaps analysed as 8.183–8.184, 8.188, 8.191
　equity swaps 4.110
　insolvency 7.28–7.30
　interest rate swaps 4.97
　ISDA 2002 Master Agreement 7.25, 7.27–7.30
　novation 7.28
　prime brokerage 9.43, 9.50
　UCITS 9.19
New York Stock Exchange (NYSE) 2.32
notes 4.183–4.185, 4.187, 4.189
novation
　2002 ISDA Novation Agreement 7.156
　2003 ISDA Credit Derivatives Definitions 7.156
　clearing 2.13–2.16
　contract 7.156
　definition 2.13, 2.15
　exchanges 2.13, 2.15
　give-up agreements 6.32–6.33
　ISDA 2002 Master Agreement 7.28
　netting 7.28
NYSE Euronext LIFFE 2.28–2.32
　Baltic International Freight Futures Exchange (BIFFEX) 2.29
　commodity derivatives 2.29
　demutualization 2.31
　electronic trading 2.30–2.31
　Euronext 2.32
　FTSE 100 index 2.28, 4.31
　LIFFE (London International Financial Futures and Options Exchange) 2.28–2.32
　London Commodities Exchange 2.29
　London Stock Exchange 2.28–2.29
　London Traded Options Market 2.29
　mergers 2.29, 2.32
　New York Stock Exchange (NYSE) 2.32
　open-outcry trading 2.30–2.31
　structure, changes in 2.31

obligations
　2003 ISDA Credit Derivatives Definitions 7.134–7.136
　Obligation Acceleration 7.137, 7.139–7.140
　credit risk 8.194, 8.197–8.198
　Default Requirement 7.137, 7.140

definition of a derivative 1.02
ISDA 2002 Master Agreement 7.26
Obligation Default 7.137, 7.140
restructuring 8.197–8.204
Variable Obligations 7.103
OEICs *see* **open-ended investment companies (OEICs)**
off-balance sheet instruments 11.04, 11.47
off-exchange contracts 2.11
oil prices 2.41
olive presses, options for 4.54
ombudsman *see* Financial Ombudsman Service (FOS)
onerous property, disclaimers of 6.19
on-exchange contracts 2.11
open-ended investment companies (OEICs) 9.04, 9.06–9.11
　authorization 9.11, 9.14
　collective investment scheme, as 9.04, 9.06–9.08
　Financial Services and Markets Act 2000 9.08
　hedge funds 9.25
　investment condition 9.08
　investment management 9.08–9.11
　liquidity 9.08
　property condition 9.08
　regulation 9.14
　variable capital, investment companies with (ICVC) 9.09–9.10
open-outcry trading 2.18, 2.30–2.31, 2.39, 2.42
operational risk
　advanced measurement approach 10.15, 12.25
　Basel 2 12.25
　Basel Committee 10.22
　calculation 10.15
　capital 10.11–10.12, 10.15
　conduct 12.24, 12.25
　criminal activities of employees 12.24
　definition 12.24
　external risk 12.25
　measurement and control 12.25
　mitigation 10.15
　negligence of employees 12.24
opinions
　local authority interest rate swaps cases, *ultra vires* and 8.88
　misrepresentation 8.131, 8.135
　over-the-counter (OTC) market, legal opinion letters and 7.01
option contracts 4.32–4.59 *see also* **call options; put options**
　2005 ISDA Commodity Definitions 7.172–7.174

473

Index

option contracts (*cont*):
American-style option 4.33
Asian (average rate) option 4.34
autocall (barrier) options 4.34, 4.52
automatic exercise 4.52
barrier options 4.34, 4.52
bei al-arboun (option contract) 4.162
Bermudan option 4.34
Black Scholes equation 4.53, 4.57, 4.59
bond options 4.59
Chiang and Okunev model 4.59
cliquet (ratchet) option 4.34
computers 4.58
Cox, Ingersoll and Ross model 4.59
credit spread 4.172, 4.178–4.182
definition 5.60
development of technique 4.54–4.59
digital option 4.34
European-style option 4.33
exchanges 4.35, 4.55
exercise of option by holder 4.32, 4.42, 4.52
exercise price 4.36–4.39, 4.41–4.44
exotic options 4.34
expiry 4.33, 4.34, 4.39, 4.41, 4.43, 4.52
extraordinary events 7.121–7.125
floor options 4.128, 4.257, 7.103
foreign exchange options 4.59
Garman and Kohlhagen model 4.59
general prohibition, civil sanctions for breach of 8.20
Grabbe model 4.59
Greek traders 4.54
Heath, Jarrow and Morton model 4.59
hedging 4.46
in-the-money, at-the-money and out-of-the money 4.44, 4.48
long call position, analysis of 4.37–4.38
long put position, analysis of 4.41
lookback option 4.34
mathematical pricing 4.45, 4.57, 4.59
open option positions, monitoring performance of 4.50
origins of option technique 4.54–4.59
over-the-counter (OTC) market 4.34–4.35
performance, monitoring 4.50
Phoenician traders 4.54
premiums 4.32, 4.36, 4.39, 4.41–4.42
price 4.44–4.51
    Asian (average rate) option 4.34
    barrier option 4.34
    Black Scholes equation 4.53, 4.57, 4.59
    bond options 4.59
    Chiang and Okunev model 4.59
    cliquet (ratchet) option 4.34
    complexity 4.45
    Cox, Ingersoll and Ross model 4.59
    digital option 4.34
    exercise of option 4.44
    foreign exchange options 4.59
    Garman and Kohlhagen model 4.59
    Grabbe model 4.59
    Heath, Jarrow and Morton model 4.59
    lookback option 4.34
    mathematical pricing 4.45, 4.57, 4.59
    models 4.49, 4.53, 4.56–4.57, 4.59
    probability theory 4.49
    profit 4.44
    rainbow option 4.34
    volatility 4.45–4.49
probability theory 4.49
profit and loss 4.37–4.44, 4.54
rainbow option 4.34
regulated activities 5.59–5.60
Roman traders 4.54
short call position, analysis of 4.39–4.40
short put position, analysing a 4.42
standard contracts 4.35
Swaption Straddle 7.197–7.200
underlying price 4.33, 4.36–4.49
vanilla options 4.33–4.34
volatility 4.45–4.49
warrants 4.60–4.61
Option Transaction
2002 ISDA Equity Derivatives Definitions 7.97, 7.99–7.100
2006 ISDA Definitions 7.189–7.192
American Option 7.99–7.100
Automatic Exercise 7.100
Bermuda Option 7.99–7.100
calls 7.99
Cash Settlement 7.99, 7.190–7.191
European Option 7.99
Exercise Date 7.100
Exercise Period 7.100
Expiration Date 7.100
exercise of options 7.99–7.100
Fixed Rate Payer 7.190–7.191
Floating Rate Payer 7.190
Physical Settlement 7.99
puts 7.99
Swap Transaction 7.189
Swaption 7.189
time for exercise of right 7.99
OTC market *see* **over-the-counter (OTC) market**
out-of-the-money
commodity swaps 4.108–4.109

Index

interest rate swaps 4.77, 4.79–4.80, 4.97
market or price risk 12.08
option contracts 4.44, 4.48
over-the-counter (OTC) market 2.19–2.21 *see also* over-the-counter (OTC) market documentation
  basis point 3.04
  benchmark 4.181–4.182
  brokers 2.20
  capacity risk 8.51
  carbon trading 4.226–4.227
  clearing houses 1.23
  collateral 2.21
  commodity swaps 4.103
  contracts 8.01–8.02
    complexity of 2.19–2.20
    interpretation 8.28–8.32
    liquidity 2.20
  counterparties 1.23, 2.20–2.21, 5.78, 7.01
  credit default swaps 4.172–4.174
  credit derivatives 4.172–4.182
  credit event 4.173, 4.177, 4.182
  credit risk 4.175–4.177
  credit spread option contracts 4.172, 4.178–4.182
  debt securities 4.178–4.182
  definition 2.19, 4.173–4.175, 4.178
  due diligence 7.01
  duty of care 8.07, 8.95, 8.97, 8.108, 8.112
  electricity and power trading 4.210
  exchanges 2.08, 6.01
  exotic options 4.34
  freight derivatives 4.205–4.206
  hedge funds 4.204, 9.31
  infrastructure of exchange market introduced in 1.23
  interpretation of contracts 8.28–8.32
  ISDA 2002 Master Agreement 7.17, 7.24, 7.29, 7.39
  LCH.Clearnet 2.47
  legal market structures 5.78, 5.83–5.84
  legislation 7.01
  liquidity 2.20
  local authority interest rate swaps cases, *ultra vires* and 8.06, 8.52, 8.90
  margining 2.21, 7.01
  market service providers 2.22, 2.25
  option contracts 4.34–4.35
  prime brokerage 9.43, 9.45, 9.48–9.50
  products 4.228–4.229
  risk control policies and processes 2.21, 7.01
  securitization 4.230, 4.239
  standard contracts 1.15
  tick and basis point 3.04
  total return swap contracts 4.172, 4.175–4.177
  UCITS 9.16–9.17
  ultra vires 8.51
over-the-counter (OTC) market documentation 7.01–7.10
  basic architecture 7.03–7.04
  confirmations 7.04, 7.05
  credit enhancement or credit support arrangements 7.06
  definitions 7.06
  generic blueprint 7.04
  International Swaps and Derivatives Association, Inc. (ISDA) 7.15–7.17
  ISDA Credit Support Documents 7.69–7.70
  legal opinion letters 7.01
  liquidity 7.02
  local authority interest rate swaps cases, *ultra vires* and 8.90
  master agreements 7.03–7.07
  risk control 7.01–7.02
  standard definitions 7.06
  standard form documentation, advantages and disadvantages of 7.08–7.10

Part IV permission 5.17–5.21, 8.37, 8.43, 10.03
participants in markets 2.01–2.06
  buy side 2.05
  liquidity 2.06
  market-makers 2.03
  regulation 2.05
  sell side 2.03, 2.04
  spread, definition of 2.06
  traders, role of 2.02, 2.06
parties
  2005 ISDA Commodity Definitions 7.161
  definition of a derivative 1.02
  rights and obligations 1.02
passport 5.94–5.95, 5.97–5.98
payment dates 4.102, 4.105–4.107, 4.110, 7.182, 7.184, 7.195
penalty clauses 7.64
permission
  capital 10.03
  close links 5.18
  Financial Services and Markets Act 2000 5.17–5.19
  groups, membership of 5.18
  guidance 5.19
  insurance contracts 8.37, 8.43

permission (*cont*):
   Market in Financial Instruments Directive
      (MiFiD) 5.17–5.18
   Part IV permission 5.17–5.21, 8.37, 8.43, 10.03
   regulated activities 5.17–5.20
   regulation 5.17–5.21
   resources 5.21
   standards 5.17
   threshold conditions 5.17, 5.21
   United Kingdom, carrying on business
      in the 5.18
Phoenician traders 4.54
Physical Delivery 8.205
physical settlement
   2003 ISDA Credit Derivatives Definitions 7.129,
      7.153–7.155
   contracts 1.08
   credit derivatives 4.167, 8.199–8.200
   Deliverable Obligations 7.153–7.155
   forward transactions 7.101, 7.104
   Option Transaction 7.99
   Physical Settlement Amount 7.153
   restructuring 8.199–8.200, 8.203, 8.205
   Restructuring Credit Event 7.154
   Swaption Straddle 7.201
   swaptions 7.196, 7.201
Plain English Campaign, Crystal Mark
      of 8.167, 8.180
plain vanilla swaps 4.99
plastics 2.30
pooled investment management 9.01, 9.02
portfolio management 9.01
power trading *see* **electricity and power trading**
premiums 1.03, 1.07, 4.32, 4.36, 4.39, 4.41–4.42
price *see also* **market or price risk; price, option
      contracts and; spot price**
   2002 ISDA Equity Derivatives
      Definitions 7.105–7.106, 7.109–7.110
   2005 ISDA Commodity
      Definitions 7.164–7.169
   2006 ISDA Fund Derivatives Definitions 7.234
   adjustments 7.234
   Asian (average rate) option 4.34
   barrier options 4.34
   bid and offer spread 3.03
   brokers 2.10
   cliquet (ratchet) option 4.34
   commodity swaps 4.102–4.108
   complexity 1.21
   contract
      certainty 1.21
      swaps analysed as 8.187
   convertible and exchangeable debt, wrapper
      for 4.241, 4.244

   credit derivatives 4.171
   digital options 4.34
   electricity and power trading 4.214–4.216
   end-users 2.10
   equity swaps 4.110
   exchanges 2.08, 2.10, 2.44
   exercise price 4.36–4.39, 4.41–4.44
   forward contracts 4.10–4.16
   forward transactions 7.101–7.103
   freight 4.103
   future price, quantification of 1.07
   futures contracts 4.20–4.31
   gearing 1.10
   hedge funds 4.200
   hedging 2.44
   interest rate swaps 4.95–4.99
   liquidity 2.06
   liquidity risk 12.18
   London Metal Exchange 2.36–2.37, 2.39
   lookback option 4.34
   magnitude of movements, 1.12
   mathematics 1.12–1.14
   oil prices 2.41
   prime brokerage 9.41
   purpose of derivatives 1.03, 1.07
   put options 4.44
   shares 4.200
   underlying 1.09, 1.11, 1.13, 4.102–4.108
price, option contracts and 4.44–4.51
   Asian (average rate) options 4.34
   barrier options 4.34
   Black Scholes equation 4.53, 4.57, 4.59
   bond options 4.59
   Chiang and Okunev model 4.59
   cliquet (ratchet) options 4.34
   complexity 4.45
   Cox, Ingersoll and Ross model 4.59
   digital options 4.34
   exercise of options 4.44
   foreign exchange options 4.59
   Garman and Kohlhagen model 4.59
   Grabbe model 4.59
   Heath, Jarrow and Morton model 4.59
   lookback options 4.34
   mathematical pricing 4.45, 4.57, 4.59
   models 4.49, 4.53, 4.56–4.57, 4.59
   probability theory 4.49
   profit 4.44
   rainbow options 4.34
   volatility 4.45–4.49
   warrants 4.60
prime brokerage 9.40–9.51
   administrative services 9.51
   balance sheet, lending of 9.41

Index

benefits 9.40–9.47
clearing 9.43, 9.45
collateral management 9.50
confirmations 9.50
credit risk 9.41
custody services 9.44
debt securities 9.44
definition 9.40
documentation 9.46, 9.48
equity securities 9.44
exchanges 9.43, 9.45
general support 9.47
give-up agreements 9.46, 9.48–9.49
hedge funds 9.40–9.44, 9.47, 9.49–9.50
introductions 9.47
liquidity 9.42
margining system 9.43
models 9.40
netting 9.43, 9.50
ongoing financing 9.42
over-the-counter (OTC) market 9.43, 9.45, 9.48–9.50
prices 9.41
purpose 9.40
rates 9.41
settlement 9.45
swaps 9.41
principal-protected structures 8.159–8.160, 8.162
Principles for Businesses (FSA) 5.14–5.15, 10.03
private customers *see* retail offers of derivatives
producer swaps 4.104, 4.109
products 4.01–4.259
  acquisition financing in derivative format 4.02
  carbon trading 4.197, 4.219–4.227
  computed data 4.207–4.208
  constant proportion portfolio insurance (CPPI) 4.02, 4.132–4.147
  convertible and exchangeable debt, wrapper for 4.241–4.244
  credit derivatives 4.03, 4.164–4.194, 4.228
  derivative cash flows, different wrappers of 4.229–4.244
  design 8.141, 8.162
  electricity trading 4.197, 4.209–4.218
  embedded derivatives, wrappers for 4.240
  financial engineering 4.08, 4.254–4.259
  financing tools 4.148–4.157
  formats or wrappers in which derivative exposure is delivered 4.07, 4.229–4.244
  forward cash flow 4.09
  forward contracts 4.10–4.16
  forward rate agreements 4.63–4.68
  freight derivatives 4.205–4.206
  futures contracts 4.17–4.31
  hedge funds 4.197, 4.199–4.204
  interest rate caps 4.125–4.126
  interest rate collar 4.129–4.131
  interest rate floor 4.127–4.128
  Islamic compliant derivatives 4.04, 4.158–4.163
  legal risk 12.21
  mathematical properties 4.197
  multi-asset derivatives 4.195–4.196
  option cash flow 4.09
  option contracts 4.32–4.59
  over-the-counter (OTC) market 4.228–4.229
  power trading 4.197, 4.209–4.218
  repurchase and reverse repurchase agreements 4.245–4.253
  securitization of derivative cash flows 4.07, 4.230–4.239
  silos 4.195
  swaps 4.69–4.124
  underlying price 4.197–4.229
    complexities 4.228
    future price 4.09
    new classes of 4.05, 4.197–4.227, 4.228
    valuation 4.06, 4.09, 4.228–4.229
  valuation of underlying, disruptions and adjustments 4.06, 4.228–4.229
  warrants 4.60–4.62
  wrappers of derivative cash flows, different 4.229–4.244
professional negligence 8.148, 8.150–8.152
promotion *see* financial promotion
Prospectus Directive 9.05
providers, responsibility of 8.145–8.157
proximity 8.103, 8.124, 8.151–8.152
Prudential Sourcebook (FSA) 10.05
prudential supervision 8.142
public offers of shares 9.05, 9.11
purpose of derivatives 1.04–1.07
  credit risk, transfer of 1.05
  exposure to underlying 1.04–1.06
  future price, quantification of 1.07
  future value of the underlying, quantification of 1.07
  hedging 1.05
  price or premium 1.03, 1.07
  price risk or market risk, transfer of 1.05, 1.07
  risk management tool, derivatives as 1.04
  value of the underlying 1.07
put options
  call options 4.43
  definition 4.33
  development 4.55, 4.57
  embedded derivatives 4.240
  exercise price 4.44
  financial engineering 4.257

put options (*cont*):
    long put position, analysis of 4.41
    Option Transaction 7.99
    rainbow option 4.34
    short put position, analysing a 4.42
    strategies 4.43
    Swaption Straddle 7.197
    underlying 4.33, 4.43, 4.44
    warrants 4.62

qiyas 4.159
Quran 4.159

Railway Clearing House 2.45
rainbow options 4.34
recharacterization of derivative contracts
    certainty 8.34
    gaming contracts 8.36
    insolvency 8.33
    insurance contracts 8.37–8.46
    loans 8.47–8.48
    risk 8.33–8.48
    shams 8.34–8.35
    tax 8.33
recognized investment exchanges (RIEs) and recognized clearing houses (RCHs) 6.02, 6.09
    consumer protection 6.05
    disclaimer of onerous property 6.19
    exchange contracts 6.09
    exemptions 6.05
    fiduciary duty, breach of 6.25
    Financial Services and Markets Act 2000 6.02–6.08
    Financial Services Authority (FSA) 6.05–6.08
    general prohibition 6.03–6.04
    Handbook of Recognised Investment Exchanges and Recognised Clearing Houses (REC) 6.08
    insolvency risk 6.11, 6.13–6.20
    LIFFE 6.09
    London Clearing House 6.09
    market charges 6.20
    market contracts 6.13–6.16, 6.19
    market property 6.25
    net sums 6.17–6.18
    overseas clearing houses 6.07
    overseas RIEs 6.13
    recognition and the effects of recognition 6.02–6.05
    recognition orders, obtaining 6.06–6.08
    regulated activities 5.63, 6.03
    standards 6.08
recommendations 5.27–5.28

records 8.04, 8.47
recovery of money
    general prohibition, civil sanctions for breach of 8.12
    Kleinwort Benson principle 8.93
    local authority interest rate swaps cases, *ultra vires* and 8.79–8.81, 8.84, 8.93
    misrepresentation 8.136
    mistake, paid under a 8.79–8.81, 8.84, 8.93
    ultra vires 8.50
rectification 8.04, 8.32
redeem or sell-back, provision of information on right to 8.165
Reference Entity
    2003 ISDA Credit Derivatives Definitions 7.129–7.136, 7.157
    credit events 7.137–7.144
    credit risk 8.194–8.198
    Successors of Reference Entities 7.131–7.132
Reference Obligations 8.199
regulated activities 5.56–5.77
    advice on investments 5.72
    arranging deals in investments 5.70
    authorization 5.08
    cash flows 5.58
    civil sanctions 8.12–8.27
    commercial activities and investment activities, differentiation between 5.74–5.76
    commercial purposes, contracts made for 5.64
    computer-based systems for investment instructions, using 5.73
    conduct of business 5.24
    controlled activities 5.77
    controlled investments 5.77
    dealing in investments 5.69–5.70
    definition 5.77
    differences, contracts for 5.65–5.66, 5.74–5.76
    EC law 5.97
    financial promotion 5.32, 5.77
    Financial Services and Markets Act 2000 5.07–5.08, 5.56–5.59, 5.62, 5.65, 5.67–5.77, 8.12–8.27
    Financial Services Authority (FSA) 5.13
    futures 5.61–5.64
    general prohibition 5.48–5.55, 5.68, 5.77, 8.12–8.27
    insurance contracts 8.38, 8.43
    investment exchanges 5.64
    investments 5.56–5.64, 5.69–5.76
    managing investments 5.71
    Market in Financial Instruments Directive (MiFiD) 5.59–5.60
    options 5.59–5.60
    permission 5.17–5.20

Index

recognised clearing houses (RCHs) 6.03
recognised investment exchanges
    (RIEs) 5.63, 6.03
  specified kind, activities of a 5.67–5.68
  specified kind, investments of a 5.58
  swaps 5.74–5.75
  terminology 5.77
  way of business test 5.56–5.57, 5.68
regulation 5.01, 5.09–5.86, 8.01, 8.08, 8.11–8.27
  see also **regulated activities**
  arbitrage 10.25
  Basel 2 10.25
  buy-side 2.05
  capital 10.01–10.08
  civil sanctions 8.12–8.27
  collective investment undertakings 9.14–9.15
  conduct of business 5.22–5.30
  financial promotion 5.32–5.36
  Financial Services and Markets Act 2000
    8.11–8.27
  Financial Services Authority (FSA) 5.10–5.47
  general prohibition, civil sanctions for breach
    of 5.48–5.55, 8.12–8.27
  hedge funds 4.203–4.204, 9.25
  investment management 9.01
  legal market structures 5.82–5.85
  market service providers 2.26
  open-ended investment companies (OEICs) 9.14
  participants in markets 2.05
  perimeter, definition of 8.11
  permission 5.17–5.21
  principles-based regulation 5.10–5.11, 5.16
  private customers 8.08
  retail customers 8.01, 8.08, 8.11–8.27, 8.142–
    8.144, 8.149, 8.156–8.157, 8.169–8.171
  sources of regulation 10.03–10.08
  systemic risk 6.11, 6.18, 9.28, 9.31–9.32
  standards 8.08
  UCITS 9.11, 9.15, 9.23
  unit trusts 9.11
  unregulated forwards 8.11–8.27
reliance
  duty of care 8.110–8.111, 8.122, 8.154
  misrepresentation 8.131, 8.135
  retail offers 8.154
repudiation
  ISDA 2002 Master Agreement 7.36
  Repudiation/Moratorium 7.137, 7.142–7.143,
    7.147
  Repudiation of Agreement, definition of 7.36
repurchase and reverse repurchase
    agreements 4.245–4.253
  basic or classic repo 4.246
  forward contracts 4.245–4.246

  fungibles 4.246, 4.251–4.252
  inflation 4.253
  initial sale 4.246, 4.249
  interest rate 4.247
  liquidity 4.253
  origins of market 4.253
  reverse repos 4.250
  subsequent repurchase 4.246
  tax 4.249
  underlying debt securities 4.245–4.253
  United States 4.252–4.253
reputation risk 12.26
rescission 6.19, 8.73, 8.130, 8.131, 8.136
research analysts 12.03
restitution
  classical principles 8.73
  compound interest 8.93
  conditions 8.64
  Limitation Acts 8.78
  local authority interest rate swaps cases, *ultra vires*
    and 8.06, 8.52, 8.56, 8.63–8.65, 8.77–8.80,
    8.84, 8.89, 8.93
  mistake of fact 8.78–8.79
  mistake of law 8.78–8.79
  rescission 8.73
  resulting trusts 8.72, 8.74
  unjust enrichment 8.64, 8.89, 8.93
restructuring, credit derivatives documentation and
  Cash Settlement 8.200
  credit event 7.137, 7.144–7.145, 7.154, 8.200
  Default Requirement 7.144
  definition 8.201
  Deliverable Obligations 8.200, 8.203–8.204
  ISDA Restructuring Supplement 8.202–8.204
  Modified Maturity Limitation 8.205
  modified restructuring 7.145
  Multiple Holder Obligation 8.202
  Obligations 8.197–8.204
  Physical Delivery 8.205
  Physical Settlement 8.199–8.200, 8.203, 8.205
  Reference Obligations 8.199
  Restructuring Credit Event 7.154
  Restructuring Maturity Limitation
    8.203–8.204
  Scheduled Termination Date 8.204
resulting trusts
  local authority interest rate swaps cases, *ultra vires*
    and 8.61–8.67, 8.70–8.74, 8.76
  presumed purpose 8.70–8.71
  restitution 8.72, 8.74
  trustees, role of 8.74
retail offers of derivatives 8.08, 8.142–8.181
  appropriateness 8.157, 8.158–8.161
  assumption of responsibility 8.152–8.153

Index

retail offers of derivatives (*cont*):
  capable and confident customers, promoting the development of 8.142
  commission, disclosure of 8.166
  compensation 8.170
  complaints 8.169–8.170
  complexity of products 8.158–8.159, 8.162
  conduct of business 5.25, 8.142
  consumer protection 8.143
  damages 8.155, 8.170
  debt securities 8.145
  decisions, customers taking responsibility for 8.143–8.144
  disclosure 8.163–8.168
  discounts, disclosure of 8.166
  distributors, responsibility of 8.145–8.157
  documentation 8.142, 8.162–8.168, 8.170
  duty of care 8.08, 8.120, 8.142–8.181
  economic loss 8.152
  education 8.142
  due diligence 8.157
  fair, just and reasonable test 8.151–8.152
  fair treatment concept 8.157, 8.162, 8.168, 8.181
  fees, disclosure of 8.166
  Financial Ombudsman Service (FOS) 8.169–8.171
    ancillary matters 8.171
    compensation 8.170
    interest 8.170
    production of information and disclosure 8.170
  financial promotion 8.142, 8.145, 8.160, 8.163
  Financial Services and Markets Act 2000 8.143–8.144, 8.169–8.171
  Financial Services Authority (FSA) 8.142–8.145, 8.157, 8.181
  foreseeability 8.151–8.152
  illiquidity, warnings of 8.165
  illustrations 8.162
  incremental approach 8.152
  innovation 8.143
  interest 8.170
  limited experience, customers with 8.140
  misrepresentation 8.120, 8.160
  negligent misstatements 8.150
  Ockwell case 8.146–8.157
  Plain English Campaign, Crystal Mark of 8.167
  principal-protected structures 8.159–8.160, 8.162
  product design 8.162
  production of information 8.170
  professional negligence 8.148, 8.150–8.152
  providers, responsibility of 8.145–8.157
  proximity 8.151–8.152
  prudential supervision 8.142
  redeem or sell-back, provision of information on right to 8.165
  regulation 8.08, 8.142–8.144, 8.149, 8.156–8.157, 8.169–8.171
  reliance 8.154
  special purpose vehicles (SPVs) 8.145
  standards 8.08
  suitability 8.139, 8.157, 8.159–8.160
  supply chain 8.157
  terms
    clarity and comprehensibility of 8.167
    unfair contract terms 8.172–8.180
  underlying, disclosure of attributes of 8.164
  unfair contract terms 8.172–8.180
  updated information, duty to provide 8.154
reverse repurchase agreements *see* **repurchase and reverse repurchase agreements**
risk *see also* **credit risk; market or price risk; operational risk**
  airlines 9.53
  audits 12.06
  back office of banks 12.05
  Basel 2 10.23, 10.25, 10.27–10.29
  basis risk 7.08
  buy-side 2.05
  capacity risk
    counterparties 12.19
    local authority interest rate swaps cases, *ultra vires* and 8.52–8.54, 8.69, 8.88–8.89
    over-the-counter (OTC) market 8.52–8.54, 8.69, 8.88–8.89
    ultra vires 8.51
  capital 10.02
  clearing 2.12, 2.14, 2.16
  committees of risk managers 12.27
  communications failure, risk of 2.44
  conduct of business 5.26
  constant proportion portfolio insurance (CPPI) 4.133–4.146
  corporate treasuries 9.52–9.54
  counterparty risk 2.12, 2.14, 6.01, 7.01, 7.29, 7.32, 7.70–7.71, 7.82, 10.16, 12.19, 12.26
  crystallization 12.01
  defining the risk map 12.01–12.28
  disclosure 8.113, 8.117
  documentation role of banks 12.05
  due diligence 8.88
  duty of care 8.113, 8.117
  end-users 2.12
  exchanges 2.12, 2.14, 2.16, 2.44
  framework of risk control 12.02–12.06
  hedge funds 4.201–4.204
  hedging 12.01, 12.03

Index

internal audits 12.06
investment banks 12.02–12.06, 12.27
ISDA 2002 Master Agreement 7.29
legal risk 8.76, 12.20–12.22
liquidity risk 12.18
local authority interest rate swaps cases, *ultra vires*
    and 8.52–8.54, 8.69, 8.85–8.90
management
    Basel 2 10.23, 10.25, 10.27–10.29
    purpose of derivatives 1.04
    tool, derivatives as 1.10
    UCITS 9.18, 9.21
market risk 12.07–12.17
middle office of banks 12.04, 12.06
monitoring 12.06
operational risk 12.24–12.25
over-the-counter (OTC) market 2.21, 7.01–7.02
recharacterization of derivative
    contracts 8.33–8.48
reputation risk 12.26
research analysts 12.03
risk committee of senior management of
    banks 12.06
risk controllers of banks 12.27
sales and marketing desks 12.03
sell-side 12.02
settlement risk 12.13, 12.23
solicitation of business 12.03
standard contracts 7.08
systemic risk 6.11, 6.18
taxonomy 12.07–12.26
UCITS 9.18, 9.21
valuation of trading business 12.04
warnings 5.26, 8.117
Roman Empire 1.18
Royal Exchange 2.33–2.34

sales and marketing desks 12.03
sales practice 8.135
Samuelson, Paul, *Brownian Motion in the Stock
    Market* 4.57
Scheduled Termination Date 8.204
Scheduling Trading Day 7.112
securitization of derivative cash flows 4.07,
    4.230–4.239
    capital gain, delivery of 4.238
    corporate trustees 4.230
    credit default swaps 4.183, 4.230
    debt securities 4.230–4.236, 4.239
    enforcement 4.230
    equity securities, issues of 4.233, 4.237, 4.239
    fixed charges 4.230
    floating charges 4.230
    hedging 4.239

income, delivery of 4.238
over-the-counter (OTC) market 4.230, 4.239
payouts 4.231
purpose 4.230
shares 4.236–4.237
tax 4.230, 4.238
underlying 4.235, 4.239
value 4.232, 4.235–4.237
wrappers 4.230–4.239
self-regulating organizations (SROs) 5.05
**sell-back, provision of information on right
    to** 8.165
sell-side 2.03 2.04
set-off 6.10, 7.65
settlement *see also* **cash settlement; physical
    settlement; settlement, 2003 ISDA Credit
    Derivatives Definitions and**
2002 ISDA Equity Derivatives Definitions 7.113
2003 ISDA Credit Derivatives
    Definitions 7.148–7.155, 7.157
contract, swaps analysed as 8.183
credit derivatives 4.166–4.167, 8.199–8.200,
    8.203, 8.205
credit event 4.167
credit risk 4.166–4.167
Delayed Settlement 7.234
electricity and power trading 4.211, 4.218
exchanges 2.44
forward transactions 7.101
futures contracts 3.09, 3.14–3.15
insolvency risk 6.16
legal market structures 5.78
margining 3.09, 3.14–3.15
prime brokerage 9.45
risk 12.23
Swaption Straddle 7.201–7.202
swaptions 7.194
UCITS 9.19
**settlement, 2003 ISDA Credit Derivatives
    Definitions and**
cash settlement 7.149–7.152
    Calculation Agent 7.151
    Cash Settlement Amount 7.149–7.150
    Cash Settlement Date 7.149
    Final Price 7.149, 7.151
    Partial Cash Settlement Terms 7.155
    Reference Obligation 7.149–7.152
    Reference Price 7.149
    Valuation Date 7.152
Conditions to Settlement 7.148
Credit Event 7.148, 7.150, 7.152, 7.154
Credit Event Notice 7.148
Notice of Physical Settlement 7.148
Notice of Publicly Available Information 7.148

Index

settlement, 2003 ISDA Credit Derivatives Definitions and (*cont*):
    Partial Cash Settlement Terms 7.155
    physical settlement 7.153–7.155
    Reference Entity 7.150
    Restructuring Credit Event 7.154
settlement, 2002 ISDA Equity Derivatives Definitions and
    dematerialized shares in clearing 7.113
    Fractional Share Amount 7.113
    indemnities 7.113
    Number of Baskets to be Delivered 7.113
    Number of Shares to be Delivered 7.113
shares
    2002 ISDA Equity Derivatives Definitions 7.97, 7.116
    adjustments and modifications affecting shares 7.116
    dematerialized shares in clearing 7.113
    equity swaps 4.110
    extraordinary events 7.117
    financing tools, derivatives as 4.149–4.156
    Fractional Share Amount 7.113
    hedge funds 4.200
    Number of Shares to be Delivered 7.113
    price 4.200
    public offers 9.11
    securitization 4.236–4.237
    Share Basket Transaction 7.97
    share indices, structures linked to 7.97
    Share Transaction 7.97
Shari'a 4.158–4.163
silos 4.195
single market 5.87–5.88
skill and care 8.94, 8.104
Smithsonian Agreement 4.119
solicitation of business 12.03
sophisticated investors
    duty of care 8.125–8.126
    Financial Services Authority (FSA) 5.12
    misrepresentation 8.07
special purpose vehicles (SPVs) 4.184, 8.42, 8.145
Specified Transaction, definition of 7.39
speculation 1.10, 1.13, 8.36
spread, definition of 2.06
spreadsheets 4.58
standard contracts
    adaptations 7.10
    basis risk 7.08
    boilerplates 9.01
    carbon trading 4.224, 4.227
    certainty 7.08
    credit derivatives 4.193
    credit exposures, reduction in 7.09
    credit risk 7.10
    exchanges 1.15, 2.07–2.08, 4.18
    forward contracts 4.18
    futures contracts 4.18
    give-up agreements 6.29
    International Swaps and Derivatives Association, Inc. (ISDA) 7.11, 7.14–7.15
    International Uniform Give-Up Agreement of the Futures and Options Association (FOA) 6.29
    liquidity 7.08
    option contracts 4.35
    over-the-counter (OTC) 1.15, 7.08–7.10
    swaps 7.08
    unfair contract terms 8.173, 8.175, 8.178–8.179
    XML message formats 7.08
standards
    accounting 11.03–11.05, 11.07–11.11
        Accounting Standards Board (ASB) 11.05, 11.07, 11.10, 11.12, 11.47
        Financial Accounting Standards Board (FASB) (United States) 11.13, 11.17
        financial accounting statements (FAS) (United States) 11.13–11.14, 11.17
        Financial Reporting Standards 11.05–11.10, 11.47–11.49
        International Accounting Standards 11.08–11.10, 11.12, 11.15–11.18
        International Financial Reporting Board (IFRB) 11.12, 11.15–11.16
        International Financial Reporting Standards (IFRS) 11.12, 11.15–11.17
    documentation 8.09
    duty of care 8.113
    Financial Accounting Standards Board (FASB) (United States) 11.13, 11.17
    financial accounting statements (FAS) (United States) 11.13–11.14, 11.17
    Financial Reporting Standards 11.05–11.10, 11.47–11.49
    Financial Services Authority (FSA) 5.14
    International Accounting Standards 11.08–11.10, 11.12, 11.15–11.18
    International Financial Reporting Board (IFRB) 11.12, 11.15–11.16
    International Financial Reporting Standards (IFRS) 11.12, 11.15–11.17
    investment management 9.01
    Market in Financial Instruments Directive (MiFiD) 5.98
    permission 5.17

Index

recognised investment exchanges (RIEs) and recognised clearing houses (RCHs) 6.08
regulation 8.08
retail offers 8.08
strike call options 4.149–4.156
Subordination 7.136
successors
  2003 ISDA Credit Derivatives Definitions 7.131–7.132
  credit derivatives documentation 8.193–8.198
  credit risk 8.193–8.198
  Successors of Reference Entities 7.131–7.132
suitability
  appropriateness 8.139, 8.157, 8.158–8.161
  conflicts of interest 8.140
  duty of care 8.137–8.140, 8.157, 8.159–8.161
  Financial Services Authority 8.137–8.138
    Handbook 8.137
    Principles for Business 8.137
  limited experience, customers with 8.140
  Market in Financial Instruments Directive (MiFiD) 8.137
  misselling 8.137
  retail 8.139, 8.157, 8.158–8.161
  UCITS 9.23
sukuks (debt securities) 4.161
Sunna 4.159
swaps 4.69–4.124 *see also* **commodity swaps; interest rate swaps**
  2006 ISDA Definitions 7.180–7.188, 7.203
  amount of payments 4.69
  Bank for International Settlements (BIS) 4.111
  Bretton Woods System 4.113–4.119
  Calculation Amount 7.181, 7.183
  Calculation Periods 7.181
  catastrophe swaps 8.46
  Confirmation 7.183
  contracts 4.69
  credit default swaps 8.28–8.32
  credit derivatives 4.124
  currency swaps 4.121–4.122
  Day Count Fraction 7.180
  debt capital market, first currency swap to complement a 4.121
  definition 4.69
  deutschmark
    debt capital market, first currency swap to complement a 4.121
    undervaluing of 4.115–4.118
  devaluation 4.119
  development of market 4.111–4.124
  duty of care 8.97–8.113
  economic policies, coordination of 4.115
  equity swaps 4.110
  first currency swap 4.120
  Fixed Amounts 7.183
  fixed currency exchange rates 4.113–4.120
  Fixed Rate Payer 7.180, 7.184
  Floating Amount 7.183–7.184
  Floating Rate Payer 7.180
  inflation 4.115, 4.119
  insurance contracts 8.39–8.41, 8.44, 8.46
  interest rates 1.26–1.27, 7.180–7.184
  International Monetary Fund (IMF), establishment of 4.114
  International Swaps and Derivatives Association, Inc. (ISDA) 4.111, 4.124
  ISDA 2002 Master Agreement 7.60
  mortgage lending 1.26–1.27
  negative interest rates 7.184
  origins of market 4.111–4.124
  Payment Date 7.182, 7.184
  prime brokerage 9.41
  producer swaps 4.104, 4.109
  regulated activities 5.74–5.75
  reserve currencies, designation of 4.114
  Second World War 4.112–4.113, 4.120
  single executory contract, swap as 8.186, 8.188, 8.190
  Smithsonian Agreement 4.119
  standard forms 7.08
  standardized transaction structures 4.124
  sterling as reserve currency 4.114
  timetable 4.69
  total return swap contracts 4.172, 4.175–4.177
  transaction implementation techniques 4.124
  underlying 4.69
  United States, inflation in 4.115
  US dollar
    devaluation 4.119
    fixed currency exchange rates 4.113–4.119
    gold, fixed to price of 4.114, 4.119
    inflation 4.115, 4.119
    reserve currency 4.114
    sterling 4.114
    Swaps Code for US dollar interest rate swaps 7.15
    World Bank and IBM, currency swap between 4.122
  World Bank and IBM, currency swap between 4.122
  yen, undervaluing of 4.115–4.118
Swaption Straddle, 2006 ISDA Definitions and 7.197–7.202
  American-style Straddle 7.200
  Bermuda-style Straddle 7.200
  Buyer of the Straddle 7.199–7.200

Index

Swaption Straddle, 2006 ISDA Definitions and (*cont*):
  calls 7.197
  cash settlement 7.201
  European-style Straddle 7.200
  exercise of Straddles 7.200–7.202
  Exercise Period 7.200
  Fixed Rate Payer 7.198–7.199
  Floating Rate Payer 7.199
  ISDA Settlement Matrix 7.202
  long straddle 7.197–7.199
  option contract, swaption straddle as 7.197–7.200
  physical settlement 7.201
  puts 7.197
  Seller of the Straddle 7.199
  settlement 7.201–7.202
  short straddle 7.197–7.199
  Underlying Payer Swap 7.198
  Underlying Receiver Swap 7.198
  Underlying Swap Transaction 7.197–7.199
swaptions, 2006 ISDA Definitions and 7.193–7.202
  Automatic Exercise 7.194
  cash settlement 7.195
  Confirmation 7.193
  Fixed Rate 7.194
  in-the-money 7.194–7.195
  option contract, swaption as 7.193–7.202
  Payment Date 7.195
  physical settlement 7.196
  Settlement Rate 7.194
  Underlying Swap Transaction 7.193–7.196
Switzerland 5.90
SWORD electronic database of warrants of ownership 2.40
synthetic collateralized debt obligations (CDOs)
  collateral 4.185
  credit default swaps 4.185–4.190
  credit derivatives 4.183–4.190, 4.192
  credit event 4.187
  credit risk 4.184, 4.187–4.188
  debt securities 4.183
  definition 4.183
  equity piece 4.189
  guaranteed investment contracts (GIC) 4.185–4.186
  interest 4.186
  managed synthetic CDOs 4.190
  notes 4.183–4.185, 4.187, 4.189
  purpose 4.183
  securitization of cash flow of credit default swap 4.183
  special purpose vehicles 4.184
  tranching 4.189
  wrapper 4.183
systemic risk 6.11, 6.18, 9.28, 9.31–9.32
systems and controls 10.18–10.19

taxation 11.19–11.45
  accounts 11.04, 11.11, 11.21
  accreting strike call options 4.156
  Affected Parties 7.55
  capital gains 11.23–11.40
  double tax treaties 11.45
  early termination 7.55
  hedging 11.19–11.23
  income 11.23–11.40
  interest rate swaps 4.71
  ISDA 2002 Master Agreement 7.46–7.47, 7.55
  recharacterization of derivative contracts 8.33
  repurchase and reverse repurchase agreements 4.249
  securitization 4.230, 4.238
  Tax Event 7.46, 7.55
  Tax Event upon Merger, definition of 7.47
  trading 11.19–11.23
  withholding tax 11.41–11.46
telephone-based market 2.39
Tender Offer 7.119
Terminated Transactions 7.51, 7.60
Termination Date 7.128, 7.162
Termination Events, ISDA 2002 Master Agreement and 7.31–7.53
  Additional Termination Event, definition of 7.49
  Credit Event Upon Merger, definition of 7.48
  definition 7.43–7.50
  early termination 7.50, 7.52–7.53, 7.55, 7.57–7.63
  Force Majeure Events 7.45
  Illegality, definition of 7.44
  notice 7.55
  Tax Event, definition of 7.46
  Tax Event upon Merger, definition of 7.47
terms
  clarity and comprehensibility of 8.167
  construction of terms of derivative contract 8.28–8.32
  duty of care 8.02, 8.07–8.08, 8.110
  retail offers 8.167, 8.172–8.180
  unfair contract terms 8.172–8.180
Thales 4.54
tick and basis point 3.04
tick and margin, example of 3.12–3.18
tin 2.36
title, dividing ownership between legal and equitable 8.67–8.69

484

Index

total return swap contracts 4.172, 4.175–4.177
traders, role of 2.02
tranching 4.189
treasuries 9.52–9.54
  airlines, risks and 9.53
  globalization 9.52
  hedging 9.54
  risk, exposure to 9.52–9.54
trusts
  collective investment undertakings 9.07
  constructive trusts 8.63, 8.66–8.69, 8.72
  corporate trustees 4.230
  equitable trusts 8.06, 8.65
  express trusts 8.67, 8.70
  implied trusts 8.67
  local authority interest rate swaps cases, *ultra vires* and 8.06, 8.56, 8.59, 8.61–8.71, 8.74
  resulting trusts 8.61–8.63, 8.65–8.67, 8.70–8.72, 8.84, 8.76

UCITS (undertakings for collective investment in transferable securities)
  approved terms 9.17
  authorization 9.11
  clearing 9.19
  COLL 9.13, 9.15, 9.23
  collateral arrangements 9.19
  concentrations of derivate exposure 9.16, 9.19–9.20
  credit risk 9.19
  EC law 5.95, 5.97
  exchanges 9.16–9.17, 9.19
  Financial Services and Markets Act 2000 9.11
  investment management 9.03, 9.11–9.13, 9.15–9.24
  investment methodology 9.13
  liberalization 9.23
  Market in Financial Instruments Directive (MiFiD) 5.97
  netting 9.19
  non-UCITS regulated scheme (NURS) 9.11
  objectives, divergence from investment 9.18
  over-the-counter (OTC) market 9.16–9.17
  passport 5.95
  public offers 9.11
  quantitative rules 9.19
  regulation 9.11, 9.15, 9.23
  risk management 9.18, 9.21
  settlement 9.19
  suitability 9.23
  UCITS I Directive 5.97
  UCITS 3 Directive 9.03, 9.11, 9.13, 9.20, 9.23

uncovered sales 9.18
underlying 9.17–9.18
use of derivatives 9.16–9.18
ultra vires 8.49–8.51 *see also* ***ultra vires***, local authority interest rate swaps cases and
  capacity risk 8.51
  clearing 8.51
  definition 8.49
  enforcement 8.50
  exchanges 8.51
  over-the-counter (OTC) market 8.51
  recovery of money 8.50
  unjust enrichment 8.50
  void, contract treated as 8.50
ultra vires, local authority interest rate swaps cases and 8.06, 8.52–8.93
  capacity risk 8.52–8.54, 8.69, 8.88–8.89
  certainty 1.21, 8.76
  commercial certainty 8.76
  common law remedies 8.60, 8.63, 8.93
  compound interest, awards of 8.06, 8.59–8.62, 8.66, 8.73, 8.93
  constructive trusts 8.63, 8.66–8.69, 8.72
  contract 1.21, 8.190–8.191
  credit risk 8.88
  damages 8.92
  discounted swaps 8.57–8.58
  documentation 8.90
  due diligence 8.88–8.89
  enforcement 8.55, 8.58
  equitable remedies 8.60, 8.63, 8.65–8.80, 8.83, 8.87, 8.89, 8.93
  equitable trusts 8.06, 8.65
  express trusts 8.67, 8.70
  fiduciary duties 8.59
  Financial Collateral Arrangements (No 2) Regulations 2003 8.90
  Hammersmith case 8.53–8.55, 8.69, 8.77, 8.80, 8.86
  hedging 8.53–8.54
  implied trusts 8.67
  insurance contracts 8.39, 8.44
  intention 8.76, 8.83
  interest
    compound interest, awards of 8.06, 8.59–8.62, 8.66, 8.73, 8.93
    simple interest 8.59, 8.66, 8.92, 8.93
  ISDA 2002 Master Agreement 8.85
  Islington case 8.47, 8.56–8.77, 8.84, 8.87, 8.90, 8.93
  Kleinwort Benson principle 8.93
  legal risk 8.76
  Limitation Acts 8.78

Index

ultra vires, local authority interest rate swaps cases and (*cont*):
　Lincoln case 8.77–8.82, 8.84, 8.93
　loans 8.56
　mistake
　　fact, of 8.78–8.79
　　law, of 8.78–8.79, 8.84
　　recovery of money 8.79–8.81, 8.84, 8.93
　opinion letters 8.88
　over-the-counter (OTC) market 8.06, 8.52, 8.90
　presumed purpose 8.70–8.71
　recovery of money 8.58, 8.79–8.81
　　Kleinwort Benson principle 8.93
　　mistake, under a 8.79–8.81, 8.84, 8.93
　remedies 8.06, 8.59–8.80, 8.83–8.84, 8.87–8.89, 8.92–8.93
　rescission 8.73
　restitution 8.06, 8.52, 8.56, 8.63–8.65, 8.77–8.80, 8.84
　　classical principles 8.73
　　compound interest 8.93
　　conditions 8.64
　　Limitation Acts 8.78
　　mistake of fact 8.78–8.79
　　mistake of law 8.78–8.79
　　rescission 8.73
　　resulting trusts 8.72, 8.74
　　unjust enrichment 8.64, 8.89, 8.93
　resulting trusts 8.61–8.63, 8.65–8.67, 8.76
　　presumed purpose 8.70–8.71
　　restitution 8.72, 8.74
　　trustees, role of 8.74
　risk
　　capacity 8.52–8.54, 8.69, 8.88–8.89
　　control 8.85–8.88
　　credit 8.88
　　documentation 8.90
　　due diligence 8.88
　simple interest 8.59, 8.66, 8.92, 8.93
　title, dividing ownership between legal and equitable 8.67–8.69
　trustees 8.59, 8.74
　trusts 8.06, 8.56, 8.61–8.71
　unjust enrichment 8.64
underlying
　2002 ISDA Equity Derivatives Definitions 7.107, 7.109–7.110
　2005 ISDA Commodity Definitions 7.159
　2006 ISDA definitions 7.91, 7.94, 7.96
　call options 4.33, 4.37, 4.43
　carbon trading 4.223, 4.226
　cash or spot market, 1.08
　commodity swaps 4.102–4.108
　computed data 4.207–4.208
　constant proportion portfolio insurance (CPPI) 4.02, 4.132–4.133
　contract, swaps analysed as 8.184, 8.189
　credit derivatives 4.03, 8.192
　definition of a derivative 1.01–1.02
　disproportionate control 1.10
　exposure 1.04–1.06
　financial engineering 4.257
　financing tools, derivatives as 4.148–4.156
　forward contracts 4.10
　forward rate agreements (FRA) 4.63
　futures contracts 4.17–4.30
　gearing 1.10
　hedge funds 4.199–4.201
　interest rate swaps 4.72–4.75
　interest rates 4.63
　market or price risk 12.14
　multi-asset derivatives 4.195
　new classes 4.05, 4.197–4.227, 4.228
　option contracts 4.36–4.47
　price 4.197–4.229
　　commodity swaps 4.102–4.108
　　exposure 1.09
　　future price 4.09
　　independence 1.11, 1.13
　　option contracts 4.36–4.47
　　risk 12.14
　put options 4.33, 4.43, 4.44
　repurchase and reverse repurchase agreements 4.245–4.253
　right to buy or sell 1.09
　securitization 4.235, 4.239
　swaps 4.69
　Swaption Straddle 7.197–7.199
　swaptions 7.193–7.199
　synthetic exposure to underlying 1.10
　UCITS 9.17–9.18
　Underlying Payer Swap 7.198
　Underlying Receiver Swap 7.198
　Underlying Swap Transaction 7.193–7.199
　valuation 1.07, 4.06, 4.09, 4.228–4.229
　warrants 4.60–4.61
unfair contract terms
　consumer
　　dealing as a 8.174–8.175, 8.178
　　definition 8.178
　course of a business 8.174
　directive 8.178, 8.180
　exclusions 8.174
　plain intelligible language, Crystal Mark for 8.180
　reasonableness 8.173, 8.175–8.177

Index

retail 8.172–8.180
standard form contracts 8.173, 8.175, 8.178–8.179
striking out terms 8.173, 8.179–8.180
unit trust schemes
  authorized unit trusts 9.07, 9.11
  collective investment undertakings 9.07
  investment management 9.11–9.13
  regulation 9.11
  trust deeds 9.07
United States
  accounts 11.13–11.14, 11.17
  devaluation 4.119
  Financial Accounting Standards Board (FASB) (United States) 11.13, 11.17
  financial accounting statements (FAS) (United States) 11.13–11.14, 11.17
  Financial Services Authority (FSA) 5.11
  fixed currency exchange rates 4.113–4.119
  fungibles 4.252
  gold, dollar fixed to price of 4.114, 4.119
  inflation 4.115, 4.119
  New York Stock Exchange (NYSE) 2.32
  NYSE Euronext LIFFE 2.28–2.32
  repurchase and reverse repurchase agreements 4.252–4.253
  reserve currency 4.114
  sterling 4.114
  swaps in US dollars
    devaluation 4.119
    fixed currency exchange rates 4.113–4.119
    gold, fixed to price of 4.114, 4.119
    inflation 4.115, 4.119
    reserve currency 4.114
    sterling 4.114
    Swaps Code for US dollar interest rate swaps 7.15
    World Bank and IBM, currency swap between 4.122
    World Bank and IBM, currency swap between 4.122
unjust enrichment 8.50, 8.64, 8.89, 8.93
unpaid vendors' liens 6.27
unusual or onerous clauses
  bringing party's attention to 8.127
  duty of care 8.127
updated information, duty to provide 8.154

valuations, 2002 ISDA Equity Derivatives Definitions and
  Averaging Date 7.112
  Disrupted Day 7.112
  Exchange-traded Contract 7.112
  Market Disruption Event 7.112
  Scheduling Trading Day 7.112
  Valuation Date 7.112
  Valuation Time 7.112
value
  2002 ISDA Equity Derivatives Definitions 7.112
  2006 ISDA definitions 7.94
  2006 ISDA Fund Derivatives Definitions 7.209–7.210, 7.227–7.228
  agents 4.200
  cash settlement 7.152
  constant proportion portfolio insurance (CPPI) 4.132–4.147
  financial engineering 4.259
  Fund Valuation Date 7.221–7.223
  future value of the underlying, quantification of, 1.07
  hedge funds 4.200, 9.28
  ISDA Credit Support Documents 7.78–7.82
  options 7.121–7.125
  securitization 4.232, 4.235–4.237
  trading business 12.04
  underlying 1.07, 4.06, 4.09, 4.228–4.229
  Value-at-Risk (VaR) 12.09–12.15
vanilla options 4.33–4.34
variable capital, investment companies with (ICVC) 9.09–9.11
  close-ended structure 9.10
  Financial Services and Markets Act 2000 9.09
  Financial Services Authority (FSA) 9.09
  investment management 9.09–9.11
  open-ended investment company, as 9.09–9.10
  open-ended structure 9.10
virtual exchanges 2.18, 2.27, 2.44

warrants 4.60–4.62
  call options 4.60
  call warrants 4.60–4.61
  options 4.60–4.61
  pay-off 4.60
  price 4.60
  put warrants 4.62
  stock exchanges 4.61
  underlying 4.60–4.61
way of business test 5.56–5.57, 5.68
weather derivatives
  definition 1.22
  freight derivatives 4.206
  Weather Index Derivative Transaction 7.167–7.168
wholesale markets 5.83
withholding tax 11.41–11.46
  banks, payment of interest to or from 11.42

Index

withholding tax (*cont*):
  definition 11.41
  double tax treaties
    definition 11.45
    jurisdiction 11.45
    treaties 11.45
  Indemnifiable Tax 11.44
  interest 11.41–11.42
  ISDA 2002 Master Agreement 11.43–11.44
  jurisdiction 11.45
  procedure 11.44
  United Kingdom, connection with 11.41–11.42
World Bank and IBM, currency swap between 4.122
wrappers
  collateralized debt obligations (CDOs) 4.183
  constant proportion portfolio insurance (CPPI) 4.132
  convertible and exchangeable debt, wrapper for 4.241–4.244
  delivery of derivative exposure 4.07, 4.229–4.244
  securitization 4.230–4.239

XML message formats 7.08

yen, undervaluing of 4.115–4.118

zero-coupon bonds 4.135